Harry Byrd
OF VIRGINIA

Harry Byrd

OF VIRGINIA

Ronald L. Heinemann

University Press of Virginia

Charlottesville and London

The University Press of Virginia
Copyright © 1996 by the Rector and Visitors
of the University of Virginia

First published 1996

Frontispiece: Governor Harry F. Byrd, 1927. (Dementi-Foster Studios)

♾The paper used in this publication meets the minimum requirements of the
American National Standard for Information Sciences—Permanence of Paper for
Printed Library Materials, ANSI Z39.48-1984.

Library of Congress Cataloging-in-Publication Data
Heinemann, Ronald L.
    Harry Byrd of Virginia / Ronald L. Heinemann.
        p.   cm.
    Includes bibliographical references and index.
    ISBN 0-8139-1642-9 (cloth : alk. paper)
    1. Byrd, Harry Flood, 1887–1966.   2. Legislators—United States—
Biography.   3. Governors—Virginia—Biography.   4. United States.
Congress. Senate—Biography.   5. Virginia—Politics and
government—20th century.   I. Title.
E748.B95H45   1996
975.504'092—dc20
[B]   95-38621
                                                                                    CIP

Printed in the United States of America

Contents

Contents

Illustrations

Photographs

Cartoons

Illustrations

Credits

Special Collections Department, University of Virginia Library: Prints file, photographs 1, 2, 5, 7, 9, 10; Harry F. Byrd, Sr., Papers, photographs 14, 16, cartoons, 1, 2, 3, 4, 6, 7, 8, 9, 10, 11, 12, 13; Fred Seibel Papers, cartoon 5

Dementi-Foster Studios: photographs 3, 4, 6, and frontispiece

Richmond Newspapers, Inc.: photographs 8, 11, 12, 13, 15, 17

Preface

WIELDING POWER CONCURRENTLY at the state and national levels for over three decades, Harry Byrd was a rarity in American politics. As governor of Virginia, United States senator, and longtime leader of the Virginia Democratic party, he dominated the politics of the Old Dominion for forty years. Through his selection of candidates for office, support of significant legislation, and imposition of conservative economic and social doctrines, he left an indelible mark on the state.

While he was less influential in the United States Senate, his thirty-two-year career in that body permitted him to touch every important event and political figure from the Great Depression to the Great Society. Best known for his advocacy of balanced budgets and his criticism of big government, he shaped national legislation through his chairmanship of the Senate Finance Committee, and he was a leader of the efforts to prevent desegregation of the South.

Because of the breadth of his career, I have used a "life and times" approach to analyze Byrd's political leadership, emphasizing his rise to power, his role as leader of the "Byrd Organization," and his achievements as governor and senator. Over the course of his public service, the world of Byrd's childhood changed dramatically, but his worldview did not. My purpose is both to illuminate the life of the most prominent Virginian of the twentieth century and to interpret the relationship between the times and the individual, between historical change and the human capacity to adapt to it.

I AM INDEBTED to many people for their assistance in this project. My greatest debt is to those scholars of twentieth-century Virginia history who have told Byrd's story in parts: the elections, the personalities, and the controversies. I have often merely summarized what they have discussed in far greater detail. Many of us worked under the direction of Dr. Edward Younger of the University of Virginia, who initiated the investigation of twentieth-century Virginia history and to whom all Virginians are beholden for opening this chapter in their past. I am particularly grateful to Robert Hawkes for his seminal dissertation on Byrd's governorship, James Sweeney for his many articles on Byrd's political contests, J. Harvie Wilkinson III for his study of the decline of Byrd's machine, and James Latimer, whose reportorial skills and political wit have enriched us all. (For an assessment of the literature in this field, see my bibliographic essay, "Virginia in the Twentieth Century: Recent Interpretations," *Virginia Magazine of History and Biography,* April 1986.)

To support my research, the Virginia Foundation for the Humanities awarded me a summer fellowship to review the Byrd papers at the University of Virginia. Hampden-Sydney College also provided me with several summer grants and a semester of release time for writing portions of the manuscript. Both the college and trustee Russell Newton generously provided funds for subvention of publication. I am grateful to Dean Scott Colley and the Faculty Professional Development Committee for their unfailing encouragement.

Hampden-Sydney students Randy Minter, Tim Riddell, Derek Brown, and Kip Woelper, former colleague S. Davis Bowman, neighbor Todd Waters, and my children, Erica and David, assisted my research by reading newspapers and locating materials at faraway libraries.

Good friends William Crawley, Stan Willis, and Brent Tarter read parts or all of the manuscript and offered helpful advice and criticism. And although he never read a line, William Harbaugh was always there with his exacting standards and encouraging voice.

The staffs of Eggleston Library at Hampden-Sydney, the University of Virginia Library, Swem Library at the College of William and Mary, the Library of Virginia in Richmond, the Virginia Historical Society, and the Richmond *Times-Dispatch* photographic library were invariably helpful and courteous and efficient, as were the staffs of many other libraries who searched and photographed materials. Florence Seamster, Gerry Randall, and Catherine Pollari at Eggleston Library were particularly accommodating. Stellar secretarial assistance was provided by Jane Mahne and Mary Buchanan.

I am grateful to the sons of Harry Byrd—Harry Jr., Beverley, and Richard—who generously provided invaluable information about their father. Political allies of the senator—Mills Godwin, Albertis Harrison, and Watkins Abbitt—were also unselfish with their time and comments.

And to my wife Sandra, thank you for your patience and love.

Harry Byrd
OF VIRGINIA

~ 1 ~

Legacies and Opportunities

HARRY BYRD'S HOMETOWN of Winchester, Virginia, had been in an unenviable location during the Civil War. Situated at the northern end of the Shenandoah Valley along invasion routes north and south, it had changed hands between the Yankees and rebels dozens of times, and several battles had been fought in the vicinity. Only days after Appomattox, the women of Winchester confronted the legacy of the war when a local farmer accidentally disinterred the bodies of two Confederate soldiers. What should be done with their remains? Spurred into action, the ladies began raising funds to purchase land for a cemetery in which to bury Southern soldiers who had been killed in the area during the "recent unpleasantness." Their success was immediate, and Stonewall Cemetery was dedicated on October 25, 1866; in individual graves or in common graves for the unknowns, over twenty-five hundred soldiers were eventually reinterred there. For years thereafter on Confederate Memorial Day, the citizens of Winchester, joined by hoary Confederate veterans, paraded through town before gathering at the cemetery to commemorate their war dead with speeches, prayers, and martial music. Cheers and tears accompanied the strains of "Dixie" as the participants renewed their loyalty to the Lost Cause.[1]

Although obsessed with their worship of the heroes of the Confederacy, the people of Winchester also were smitten by the spirit of a "New South" in the late nineteenth century. Prompted by the gifts of Pennsylvania philanthropist John Handley, they pursued a modest development program to enhance the town's traditional role as a depot for the commodities of the surrounding farms. The town boosters brought electricity and the telephone to Main Street, extolled the virtues of their private academies, and sought expanded rail facilities. Through the growth of the orchard industry and an improved road network, Winchester achieved commercial success, designating itself the apple capital of America with the inauguration of its Apple Blossom Festival in 1924. In this small Virginia town, with its fealty to the Lost Cause and its brash boosterism, Harry Flood Byrd was reared. Embodying these two passions of his native region, Byrd in many ways never left home.[2]

He was a direct descendant of the William Byrds who had been so influential in the development of the Virginia colony. The first William, son of a London goldsmith, arrived in America in 1669; a year later he inherited from his uncle 1,800 acres near the fall line on the James River, well upriver from the primary Virginia settlements. William parlayed his good fortune into a profitable trading business (which included dealing in slaves), a seat in the House of Burgesses, appointment to the Council of State, and expanded landholdings.

William II was born in Virginia in 1674 but was educated in England and admitted to the bar there in 1695. He returned to his birthplace a year later and was elected to the House of Burgesses, which sent him back to England as its legal representative. Upon his father's death in 1704, he took up permanent residence in Virginia, having inherited over 26,000 acres and 200 slaves. Although he remained active in the politics of the colony, serving on the Council like his father, William II was very much a Renaissance man. He built the beautiful colonial mansion at Westover, founded the city of Richmond, wrote poetry, surveyed the line between Virginia and North Carolina—an expedition described in his *History of the Dividing Line betwixt Virginia and North Carolina*—and kept one of the most informative, if not scandalous, diaries of the colonial period. When he died in 1744, he left an estate of almost 180,000 acres, which his son, the third William, squandered through bad investments and his love of gambling and fast horses. Having counseled moderation at the outbreak of the Revolution, William III was isolated from many of his old friends, and he committed suicide in 1777.[3]

Bereft of its resources and stigmatized by treason, the Byrd family retreated into relative obscurity for the next century and a half. Although Harry Byrd was certainly proud of the role his ancestors had played in the settling of the Virginia colony and was aware of the prominence of the family name in a state that venerated its colonial heritage, he did not traffic in his pedigree. He does not appear to have been motivated by any sense of lost status or by a desire to restore the family to its rightful place in society and government. His sons do not remember his ever mentioning the family line, and the only reference to the ancestral Byrds in his correspondence reflected a concern that the publication in 1941 and 1942 of the diaries of William II, a notorious Lothario, might tarnish his own reputation for puritanical respectability. However, if he inherited anything from the early generation of Byrds, it was not a libertine lifestyle but the will to succeed.[4]

The first Byrd to move into the Shenandoah Valley was a son of William III, Thomas Taylor Byrd, who, after serving his king, took up residence in Frederick County in 1786. His son, the first Richard Evelyn Byrd, represented Frederick and Winchester in the General Assembly for several terms between 1839 and 1851 and served in the Confederate army, as did his son William, who had moved to Texas before the war to establish a law practice. At war's end, after spending a year in a Northern prison, a weary William Byrd returned home to Winchester, moved into his father's house on Washington Street, and took up the law once again. He brought with him a Texas wife, Jennie Rivers Byrd, and a young son, Richard Evelyn, Harry's father.[5]

Like his ancestors, going all the way back to William II, the second Richard Byrd became a lawyer. Educated at the University of Virginia and the University of Maryland School of Law in Baltimore, he established a private practice in Winchester and served as commonwealth's attorney for Frederick County from 1884 to 1904. Thereafter he became active in state politics. His reputation as an attorney was legendary. His love of books and a photographic memory supported legal arguments that were "filled with persuasive oratory, power of presentation, clarity of judgment, a fluent diction, and a humor of wit unsurpassed. . . . His logic was so unerring, his exposition so lucid and his power to convince so strong," wrote the editor of the Richmond *Times-Dispatch*, "that he was able to lead others to the point of understanding he had already reached." Douglas Southall Freeman said of Dick Byrd to his son, "Your father had the most acute intellect possessed by any Virginian of my lifetime, and with it he had absolute, unhesitating courage and . . . the most complete candor in dealing with press and public that ever I had the privilege of observing."[6]

A stockily built man of average height, Richard Byrd had the high family forehead, a determined chin, and penetrating eyes; only the spectacles disguised an aggressive, short-tempered personality that made him a fearless and pugnacious competitor in the courtroom. He was known to throw apples and inkwells at opponents who verbally challenged him. Taking cases from rich and poor alike regardless of their ability to pay, "Mr. Dick," as he was known in Winchester, was a friend of the underdog and the children to whom he frequently dispensed candy on the streets. But he also had a strong affinity for the bottle which strained his marriage and may have prevented him from achieving greater prominence. Occasionally, he would retreat to a little cabin in the Blue Ridge Mountains named Byrd's Nest for periodic binges. One day prosecutor Byrd went for lunch during a court recess and did not return, whereupon the judge ordered the bailiff to search all the bars on Main Street until he found him. Escorted back to court, Byrd proceeded to argue the case for the defense. Informed of his mistake, he sputtered that he had just presented the best defense the defendant could get and now he would proceed to demolish it.[7]

On September 15, 1886, Richard Byrd married Eleanor Bolling Flood of Appomattox whose political lineage was the equal of her husband's. The Floods arrived from England in 1754, and the Bollings traced their lineage back to Pocahontas.[8] Eleanor's father, Major Joel Flood, served throughout the Civil War with Robert E. Lee. After the surrender at Appomattox Court House, he rode the few miles to his plantation, Eldon, where his wife served lunch to the major and a Union colonel. In the 1880s he was elected to the Virginia General Assembly. Eleanor's maternal grandfather, Charles James Faulkner, had been ambassador to France and also a member of the General Assembly; her uncle Charles James Faulkner, Jr., had been a United States senator from West Virginia; and her younger brother, Henry D. Flood, would soon be a United States congressman.

Born in 1863, "Miss Bolling" tired of the life of drudgery and isolation in rural central Virginia and moved to Winchester where she met Dick Byrd and married him two months later. They bought a big, rambling Victorian house on tree-lined Amherst Street on the west side of Winchester next to the railroad tracks. A three-story stucco house with a steep mansard roof and a large front porch, it became the boyhood home of two of America's most notable citizens. Out back were a garden and a stable for the boys' ponies. Mrs. Byrd, who lived there for nearly seventy years, used to wave to the engineers as the trains went by, unconcerned with the noise, which she thought was heavenly compared to the quiet of Appomattox. She loved to entertain. Guests would arrive at 7 o'clock and be served one drink; promptly at 7:30, dinner would be served, for she believed more than one drink "would ruin the conversation and the beef." Small in stature with a keen wit, she was a feisty woman who had a great influence on her sons, shaping their characters and motivating them to succeed through hard work and initiative.

The Byrds' marriage was not a perfect union. "Miss Bolling" was as tough and strong-willed as her husband. While she was not a teetotaler, she had no tolerance for excessive drinking, and he did not like her convivial gatherings. When his political career drew him to Richmond, they often lived apart, a separation that continued after his terms in the legislature when he established a private practice in the capital. They did not have much money. His service as commonwealth's attorney brought in only a pittance, and he was often paid in kind for his private work. They kept up a good front, with servants and horses and private schools for the boys, but there was not much left over. However, they did provide their sons with the love and discipline crucial to their future development. Theirs was a home of middle-class respectability in which the values of honesty, modesty, obedience to authority, self-discipline, and gentlemanliness were taught. Yet the Byrds were not strict disciplinarians; indeed, they were remarkably tolerant of their sons' exuberance and encouraged a strong independence that marked their careers. Mrs. Byrd said years later that there must have been something wrong with her because "the three boys were always plotting how they could best escape me." There may not have been great outward signs of affection within the Byrd family, but there was a stable environment in which both freedom and responsibility flourished.[9]

Richard and Eleanor had three children: Tom, Dick, and Harry in reverse order. Harry was born on June 10, 1887, not in Winchester, but in Martinsburg, West Virginia, where his mother had gone to be with family and be attended by an uncle who was a physician. Named for his uncle Henry Flood, Harry was the most studious and reserved of the three sons. Richard, a year younger, was named for his father and proved to be the most adventurous; his mother said of him: "Dick was always doing dangerous things. He was always on top of a house or tree. Danger was all that thrilled him." Tom, born in 1890, was the most convivial of the sons. In adulthood they all grew to medium height and stocky build, Tom being slightly larger than his brothers. They had the high Byrd forehead, large ears, high cheekbones, and ruddy complexions and retained a youthful countenance well into their older years. They had a happy childhood, complete with summer vacations with their mother's family at Eldon and the usual pranks and fights. On one occasion the Byrds' "Western Gang" got into a brawl with the rival "Potato Hill Gang," during which Harry was hit in the forehead by a rock. Dick was ready to kill the whole lot, but Harry, with blood dripping from his wound, pleaded with his brother to take him to the doctor, where he received stitches that left a scar for the remainder of his life. Reflecting their independent natures, they would often go riding and swimming miles from home.

While the brothers were close to one another, Harry was the favorite of his father, an affection the son reciprocated. He had a good relationship with both of his parents, but it was his father to whom he looked for guidance and approval, perhaps gaining from him his perceptive understanding of the personalities and ambitions of people. He loved to accompany him to his mountain retreat, where he developed his fondness for the out-of-doors and the majestic scenery of the Blue Ridge, but he did not look favorably on his father's drinking, which likely prompted his own code of abstinence. Furthermore, the failure of "Mr. Dick's" venture into the newspaper business probably activated in the son a compulsion for success. Byrd may have believed his father had fallen short of greatness because of these personal shortcomings, and he vowed not to make the same mistakes. Nevertheless, they remained very close, and when Harry moved into politics, the relationship deepened as they communicated frequently about career and policy decisions.[10]

Harry's early schooling was under the tutelage of Misses Jennie and Lizzie Sherrard just down the street from his home in a two-room schoolhouse with a dozen or so other children. The education was rudimentary, the boys remembering little more than stories about the Civil War. At age ten Harry went off to Shenandoah Valley Academy, up the street in the other direction. Encouraged by his parents "to love books," he became an avid reader, but formal education had little appeal for Byrd, so when his father announced that he was going to sell his nearly bankrupt newspaper, the fifteen-year-old boy jumped at the chance to leave school and assume its operation: "If you'll give the *Star* to me, Father, I'll see that it keeps on for a while anyway."[11]

Harry's request was not that unusual, for few Americans at the turn of the century graduated from high school and fewer still from college. The attraction of taking over a failing business and earning some money with it had a natural appeal to an already serious and ambitious young boy. Furthermore, brother Dick at the age of thirteen had withdrawn from school to take a yearlong solo trip to the Philippines. Leaving school was a decision Harry never regretted, but it likely stunted his intellectual development and shaped his own attitude toward higher education. Byrd had a quick and retentive mind, but his lack of education left it unrefined and provincial, wanting in tolerance, empathy, and detachment. He developed little appreciation for art, music, or literature, and his world was restricted to ledger sheets and election results. Although in later life he paid appropriate lip service to education and encouraged his own children to go to college, Byrd never was a strong supporter of higher education. His own experience told him that it was not necessary for success; hard work and individual initiative were more important.

Byrd left few accounts of his childhood, and fewer still of his schooling, perhaps embarrassed that he had not progressed very far. Years later, in response to an indirect criticism that his opponent was better educated than he, Byrd put out a public letter that stated, "Had I been born with a silver spoon in my mouth and had gone to college, perhaps I would be erudite enough to receive your support. I have worked hard ever since I was 15 and think I can classify myself as a self-made man, even though I may not have been educated up to your high standards."[12]

The business that Harry asked to manage was in serious trouble. Richard Byrd had purchased the Winchester *Evening Star,* a small daily newspaper, in 1902. He liked to write and was developing some political interests that he believed could be advanced through the editorial pages of the *Evening Star;* but he had very little business sense, and the paper was near bankruptcy when Harry made his offer. He thought his father, who had a high regard for education, would refuse him, but "Mr. Dick" saw little risk in the idea; it was an opportunity for his son to prove himself and perhaps save a potentially valuable political mouthpiece; if his son failed—and the confident father had no reason to believe he would—it would only delay the sale of the insolvent business.

Harry tackled the assignment with enthusiasm, determination, and a commitment to the pay-as-you-go financial policy that marked everything he did in life. The *Evening Star* had a $2,500 debt to the Antietam Paper Company, which now refused to ship any more newsprint on credit. To overcome this immediate problem, the teenager visited his Hagerstown, Maryland, supplier to request a COD arrangement on future daily shipments of paper; returning to Winchester, he collected the debts owed the *Evening Star* to pay for the first shipment and thereafter insisted that his advertisers pay on time. The arrangement continued for several months, with Byrd collecting in the morning, paying at noon, and putting out the paper in the late afternoon. Sometimes he spent a hectic morning looking for the last dollar to pay for the newsprint, but he never missed an edition, paid off the debt owed Antietam, and soon began turning a profit with increased circulation and advertising. Years later he recounted: "A good many days we were a little late in getting the paper out because I had to scour the town scraping up the six dollars to get the newsprint out of hock. When you have to hunt for them that way, you get to know how many cents there really are in a dollar."[13] If there was ever a man whose character and philosophy were shaped and reinforced by early personal experience, it was Harry Byrd.

For the youthful entrepreneur the newspaper was purely a business venture. "The Business Department," he wrote, "is the life blood of the paper." He was president and general manager, while his father, who remained editor, formulated policy on public questions and wrote the few editorials of any significance. The *Evening Star* was little more than a local gossip and commercial sheet, its front page carrying stories of community deaths, accidents, criminal proceedings, baseball games, and business activity, while three of its four pages were devoted almost exclusively to advertisements. It appeared six days a week—Monday through Saturday—and sold for one cent. But the budding businessman had more grandiose plans. Within a few years Byrd took over the Winchester *Times*, a weekly owned by his father and grandmother, and bought out the competing Winchester *News-Item*. Taking advantage of his monopoly in the town, he moved into new offices and purchased a brand new press that allowed him to expand to a six- or eight-page format, with increased news coverage and advertising space. In 1907, backed by money from the Faulkners and Floods, he started the Martinsburg *Journal*, a daily paper which he claimed would be like the *Evening Star*: "independent in thought and purpose, dealing with public questions with candor but without prejudice or partisanship."[14]

In time the *Evening Star* expanded its coverage of state and national politics, but in Harry Byrd's hands it remained primarily a small-town newspaper that reflected the interests of its publisher. It gave extensive play to Confederate Memorial Day ceremonies every June 6 and to Robert E. Lee's birthday on January 19 and praised the efforts of the local baseball teams, the competing volunteer fire companies, and noteworthy local citizens, including the Byrds, who were achieving fame beyond Winchester's borders. Harry was a notable booster of the town. On one occasion, at the risk of violating postal laws, he refused advertising from Washington, D.C., merchants who were trying to attract local shoppers at Christmastime with offers of free transportation to the nation's capital seventy miles away. Byrd prodded citizens to buy at home. He supported growth in his hometown, even if it involved going into debt, something an older Byrd would never approve. Urging construction of a city sewage system, he successfully lobbied his readers in one of his few signed editorials: "As a friend of progress and the advocate of every advance possible to Winchester, the *Evening Star* favors the issuance of $50,000 of sewer bonds and hopes the qualified voters of Winchester . . . will vote unanimously in favor of the sewer bonds."[15]

Once he had the newspaper on sound footing, Harry began seeking new opportunities to increase his income. In 1904, now sixteen, he became manager of the local Southern Bell Telephone Company exchange at a salary of $60 a month; he was likely assisted in acquiring the position through the good auspices of Uncle Hal Flood, who had substantial investments and connections in the telephone company. He supervised the Winchester exchange for three years before resigning in 1907 because he had not gotten a raise.[16]

A year later he was elected president of the Valley Turnpike Company, a position that would have long-term significance for his career. The job paid him $33 a month to travel this ninety-two-mile-long macadamized private toll road from Winchester to Staunton twice a month to inspect its condition, authorize necessary repairs, and handle complaints about its operation. As a champion of Winchester and a recent investor in some apple orchards, he supported the development of good roads to facilitate the growth of the area and the shipment of farm produce to market. Byrd was proud of the fact that the value of the road increased while toll costs were reduced during his ten-year tenure. His knowledge of the techniques and costs of road construction and maintenance gained through this experience made him a recognized expert in the field.[17]

In light of his fond memories of summers at Eldon, Byrd's venture into the apple business seems to have been motivated as much by his dreams of becoming a gentleman farmer as by his desire for money. With a penchant for perfection, he studied the opportunities around Winchester in that careful and systematic way of his and determined upon apple orcharding to satisfy his desire for an outdoor life that promised financial reward. In 1906, again with help from Uncle Hal, he began leasing some planted orchards. Six years later, with the profits from the sale of the Martinsburg *Journal* and in partnership with his Episcopalian minister, William D. Smith, Byrd bought 100 acres of what became the Rosemont Orchard in Clarke County near where his ancestor Thomas Byrd had settled in 1786. Within four years he was producing 6,000 barrels of apples, which ranked him among the middle producers in the northern Valley. He actively involved himself in all facets of the work from land purchases, tree plantings, and orchard upkeep to harvesting. It was the beginning of an empire that would make him one of the largest apple growers in the country and a millionaire.[18]

As a young businessman Byrd developed the traits that would mark his private and public life. He had an amazing eye for detail, especially numbers; production figures, profit lines, and schedules fascinated him, becoming so familiar to him that he could recite an entire balance sheet to convince his listeners of what had to be done. He did things with great purpose, knowing what he wanted to accomplish and charting his progress toward that end. In the process he was thorough and orderly to a fault, presiding over every aspect of the work until its completion. He was a "workaholic," running his own newspaper, supervising a telephone exchange, and harvesting orchards while still a teenager. Eighteen-hour days were not unusual, but they left him little time for continuing his education; beyond learning the details of his many jobs, he was not well traveled or widely read, partaking only of Civil War histories and trade journals.

Byrd moved in a man's world and did not develop the social graces that would allow him to be comfortable among women and in social gatherings. Although his twinkling blue eyes, reddish-blond hair, and infectious smile made him a desirable catch, he was shy around girls and dated infrequently. He would occasionally meet with his friends for talk or a soda, but he often arrived late after work and invariably was dressed more formally than they. He did not play games or sports. It was almost as if he had skipped his teen years to become an adult overnight. Years later, brother Tom's daughter, Margaret Byrd Stimpson, said of her father and Uncle Harry, "They did not know how to play; they were old when they were young."[19]

But Harry was content with his choice, and in the business environment in which he had proved himself at such a tender age, he was incredibly self-confident, believing fully in the capacity of the individual to chart his own destiny. Combining a quick and persevering, if somewhat limited, intellect with a powerful ambition to succeed, Byrd pursued the wealth and fame that had eluded his most recent ancestors. By 1915 he was earning the substantial income of $15,000. Yet money and renown were not ends in themselves; they were evidence of achievement. While Byrd certainly wanted to rise above the genteel poverty of his surroundings, he was not obsessed with the prospect of becoming rich. For all his success he was a man of simple needs and tastes, given to inexpensive clothes and cars because those things were so inconsequential compared to performance. He enjoyed the challenge of doing something well, doing it efficiently and economically in a way that would earn the adulation of his parents, his peers, and, later, the voters. As his father remarked to an associate, "Strode, I have a genius back home. My son Harry has recently taken charge

9

of the Winchester *Star* and is making money with it. He is making money with apples, too. He has a genius for business and for organization, and I am proud of him and expect great things of him."[20]

The final piece of the Byrd puzzle was politics. His associations with his father and his uncle, both of whom saw great promise in the successful entrepreneur, inexorably drew him first into local affairs and then into state politics. In later years Byrd always insisted that his entry into politics was happenstance, unpremeditated. In that self-effacing manner of the humble politician, he claimed that he had been asked to run for various offices. As he wrote Charles Elgin in 1957, "It just seemed to come about." But there is little doubt that ambition and self-interest were also behind his political service. He believed politics was an appropriate sphere for the businessman, whose experience would have prepared him for the efficient management of government. Before his first contest for public office in 1910, Byrd wrote, "We think that men of business ability and enterprise should be elected to the council, men who will do their duty without fear or favor, and men who will be willing to devote, time, energy and thought to giving the city a good, clean, healthy and efficient government." Time did not change that estimate. In an interview during his governorship, he explained: "Politics is not a separate branch of knowledge. It needs a very deep background of general experience. No man, in my opinion, is qualified to assume political power until he has served a long apprenticeship to private business and has learned its connections with public affairs."[21]

Byrd was attracted to politics by the relationship between public power and private interest. The responsibility of government, he believed, was to provide an environment in which individual opportunity might flourish and to facilitate the creation of wealth with minimal taxation and regulation. To ensure that government did not impose undesirable costs and restrictions on business, political authority was necessary. Byrd entered politics not primarily out of a sense of service to the larger community—although he always insisted that was his motive—but to preserve or advance that which was beneficial to himself and his interests. When rising newsprint prices in 1907 threatened the profit margin of the *Evening Star,* he organized the Valley publishers in protest and lobbied Washington for action against wood pulp tariffs and the "paper trust." This activism in defense of the free market was typical of his political career.[22]

The political world that Harry Byrd would be entering was a cauldron of competing issues and personalities. Virginia at the turn of the century was much like Winchester, inextricably bound to its Confederate past, mired in postwar depression, and searching for new opportunities. The Old Dominion was a tradition-oriented society whose political lineage originated in the colonial era when a breed of highly individualistic farmers-turned-planters assumed authority. By reason of blood, wealth, education, and social standing, their heirs led the Commonwealth through revolution and civil war, governing paternalistically but always intent on preserving their power, even as the world changed about them. Caretakers of the status quo and the public treasury, they were conservative to a fault, overseeing a Virginia that remained rural, racially divided, parsimonious in its services, suspicious of outsiders, and fiercely independent. Now the progressive currents sweeping the country in the early twentieth century challenged the stability of the old order once more.

Progressivism was a broad-based reform movement directed at the industrial/urban revolution that had devastated the landscape, changed the nature of work and human relationships, and made the United States into a world power. The reformers were upset with corrupt politicians, urban decay, social disarray, and powerful corporate monopolies that were destroying the competitive economic order. Across the land at every level of government, reforms were instituted to deal with these problems: railroad regulation, direct primaries, direct election of senators, prohibition, meat inspection, conservation of natural resources, child labor laws, and tariff and banking revisions. In the South more modest changes were introduced that regulated business, improved education, attacked the region's health problems, and reinvigorated politics. Similar advances occurred in the Old Dominion where insurgents challenged the political order dominated by the emerging machine of Senator Thomas Martin.[23]

Thomas Staples Martin was a modest, dignified lawyer from Scottsville who had an amazing facility for organization. More comfortable in boardrooms than on the stump, he was so unimposing a political figure that his enemies frequently misjudged him. After building up a successful legal practice in central Virginia, he became counsel for the Chesapeake and Ohio Railroad, whose money he dispensed to candidates who promised to support legislation beneficial to his client. At the same time he cozied up to Democratic leaders in the state and moved into the inner circles of power. When a United States Senate seat became available in 1893, Martin called upon his considerable resources—including railroad money—to curry favor among the state legislators and defeat former Governor Fitzhugh Lee for the position, thus establishing himself as the leader of the Democratic party in the Old Dominion.[24]

A key Martin operative in the Senate contest was Hal Flood. A young lawyer from Appomattox who had won a House of Delegates seat in 1887 and moved on to the state senate in 1891, Flood was attracted to Martin by his probusiness positions and his pragmatic politics. Relying on railroad money and control of the legislature, they constructed a political organization that would endure well into the twentieth century. But it was not an easy accomplishment. Over the next ten years, they confronted populists and progressives intent on destroying the machine by democratizing the election process and regulating the railroads. Leaders of the "Organization" (as the machine was known) were not always victorious, but their ability to unite and to compromise when their survival depended upon it ensured their longevity. In their favor was the absence of a strong Republican party in the state, which, except in the Valley and the southwest, could not overcome the legacy of Reconstruction. Virginia remained a Democratic stronghold well into the twentieth century.[25]

Aided by the growing reform impulse, especially the charges of vote buying against Martin, progressives elected independent Andrew Jackson Montague to the governorship in 1901 and won popular support for a constitutional convention to revamp state government. While Senator Martin objected to the convention, Hal Flood, joined by reformers and conservatives alike, favored it; he wanted to eliminate the black vote because he believed that its manipulation by politicians, himself included, created unwarranted corruption and unpredictability in the polling process.[26]

The constitutional convention, which met in Richmond from June 1901 to June 1902, disfranchised most black Virginians and about half of the white electorate as well—many of whom were Republicans—through the imposition of a poll tax and other constitutional restrictions. The poll tax was $1.50 per year for up to three years and had to be paid six months before the general election. The convention also restructured state and local government and created a State Corporation Commission to regulate public utilities. Ostensibly designed to liberalize politics and overthrow the machine, the new constitution, ironically, strengthened the Martin Organization. It eliminated voters who were more likely to vote against the machine; it undermined weaker parties and independent candidates by creating a smaller electorate that was more easily controlled by the group with the best organization and most money; and it placed a premium on control of patronage and election machinery.

Organization authority was further enhanced through the creation of a circuit court system. Appointed by the General Assembly, the new judges had the power to select county electoral boards and other local officials. They complemented the preexisting "ring" of local county or "courthouse" officials—commonwealth's attorney, treasurer, commissioner of revenue, clerk of the circuit court, and sheriff—who, along with their prescribed duties, were responsible for getting out the vote and dispensing patronage. An infamous fee system rewarded many of these local officials by allowing them to keep a portion of the fees they charged for their services; in time some of the fee officials were making more than the governor. The interlocking network of General Assembly members, circuit judges, "courthouse ring," and machine leaders, dependent upon one another for job security, salaries, and election support—and now undergirded by a constitution that kept the electorate small—became the key to the Organization's power for the next sixty years. In historian Raymond Pulley's view, progressivism in Virginia did more "to conserve and strengthen the Old Virginia order than to rid the state of political bosses and broaden the base of popular government." Virginia would change, but slowly, and certainly not at the expense of the ruling class, a lesson not unlearned by a young Harry Byrd.[27]

During the Montague governorship machine leadership fragmented, but with the election of Claude Swanson to the governorship and Martin's defeat of Montague in the Democratic senatorial primary in 1905, the Organization reunited and solidified its control of Virginia. Surprisingly, Swanson demonstrated his own brand of independence by expanding upon Montague's reform efforts in education and road building, which suggested that the difference between independent and machine Democrats was primarily one of power, not issues.[28]

Flushed with success, Hal Flood, who had been elected to Congress in 1900, encouraged his brother-in-law, Richard Byrd, to become more actively involved in public affairs. Having served several years on the Democratic state committee, Byrd won a seat in the House of Delegates in 1906. Shockingly for one with so little seniority, he was elected Speaker of the House two years later and held that position for six years, a tribute to his popularity and the power of the machine. His abilities and fairness as a legislative leader won him the admiration of his peers and the gratitude of the Organization leadership.[29]

The one irritant to the machine's hegemony was the liquor issue. Given new life during the Progressive Era, the temperance movement was strongest in the South, where Baptist and Methodist preachers, primarily through the Anti-Saloon League, fought to restrict the sale of liquor. By 1905 seventy of Virginia's one hundred counties and three independent cities were dry, but the antiliquor crusaders were not content with local option. Under the leadership of Methodist minister James Cannon, president of the Virginia Anti-Saloon League, they pursued statewide prohibition. Senator Martin, who had enjoyed the financial backing of the liquor interests, was loath to involve the Organization in such a volatile issue, but correctly reading the public temper, he began acceding to Cannon's wishes. The tacit alliance between the two men was revealed in 1908 when Richard Byrd, no teetotaler himself, sponsored legislation that restricted the liquor traffic in areas where there was no police protection. A year later Martin endorsed a noted prohibitionist, William Hodges Mann, for governor rather than risk a divisive primary fight on that issue. In return he and Flood convinced Cannon to moderate his campaign for statewide prohibition for the moment. Once again the machine chose pragmatism over principle.[30]

The election of Mann and the death in 1910 of aging Senator John Daniel forced another choice upon the machine that touched the lives of the Byrds. Both Hal Flood and Claude Swanson wanted the empty Senate seat. In return for Swanson's support in the 1909 gubernatorial election, Mann had promised to appoint him to the Senate should a vacancy occur, but the governor had also incurred obligations to Flood, with whom he was on much friendlier terms. Although young Harry Byrd emphatically argued that his uncle should not give way to Swanson, his father and Senator Martin prevailed upon Flood to concede, believing that his interim appointment would lead to a bitter party struggle between the two men in the 1911 senatorial primary that would encourage an independent candidacy and even risk Martin's reelection. Governor Mann agreed and selected Swanson. A year later, with the rift avoided, Martin and Swanson easily dispatched challenges to their Senate seats from independents William A. Jones and Carter Glass. The episode initiated a long feud between Claude Swanson and Harry Byrd, who always believed that Swanson had cost his uncle a treasured position in the United States Senate. Although they maintained a cordial relationship over the years, dictated largely by their common political interests, they grew more apart on issues, party leadership, and Organization candidates, and the association ended when Byrd went to the Senate in 1933.[31]

Another contest between the Organization and independents occurred during the presidential election of 1912. Virginia's native son Woodrow Wilson, now governor of New Jersey, had captured the hearts of progressives with his reform agenda. Fearing that a victorious Wilson would reward the anti-Organization faction in the Old Dominion, Senator Martin favored an uninstructed state delegation to the Democratic national convention. Disagreeing with Martin was Richard Byrd, whose party regularity stood second only to personal friendship. When Wilson, his old college chum, announced his candidacy, Byrd quickly rallied to his side, placing himself at odds with the machine. Faced with a divided state convention, both sides accepted a compromise that prevented the Virginia delegation from uniting behind any one candidate unless two-thirds of the delegates agreed. At the national convention in Baltimore—attended by *Evening Star* correspondent Harry Byrd—the split in the delegation was so substantial that the unit rule was not invoked until it became clear that Wilson would win the nomination. It was the pragmatic Tom Martin who recommended that Virginia unite behind him on the forty-third ballot. Three ballots later the Virginian was nominated, and his election followed in the fall.

Richard Byrd, who headed up Wilson's campaign in Virginia, was a key consultant to the new president on patronage for the Old Dominion. His continued allegiance to the machine ensured that it would be amply rewarded in spite of its early opposition to Wilson. Sure enough, Martin and Wilson mended fences, and the independents found themselves isolated once again. Byrd himself received an appointment as United States district attorney for the Western District of Virginia, a position he held from 1914 to 1920. He was then appointed special assistant to the attorney general of the United States for a six-month period at the end of Wilson's second term.[32]

The liquor question returned to haunt the Organization in 1912, as the national movement for total prohibition gathered speed. Pressing Senator Martin to support a statewide referendum on prohibition, the Reverend Mr. Cannon suggested that defeat of the enabling act could have political repercussions. When the Virginia Senate rejected the bill, Cannon indicated that his future endorsement of the machine was in question. By now Organization leaders were aware that another defeat of the act would have disastrous consequences for their political futures. Accordingly, the 1914 General Assembly passed a bill authorizing a public referendum on the question. The final senate tally was 20–19, with Lieutenant Governor J. Taylor Ellyson casting the key vote. On September 22, 1914, Virginians, by a three-to-two margin, converted the Old Dominion into a dry state, effective November 1, 1916. But the vote did not settle the issue, as prohibition remained a political hot potato for another nineteen years.[33]

Harry Byrd received his political education on this battlefield of machine politics, learning how to cope with power struggles, the reform impulse, and prohibition. His baptism in public service was a brief appointed term on the Winchester City Council in 1909–10.[34] Elected council members were usually local businessmen who met once a month to conduct the town's business, which included setting tax rates, maintaining the streets, and regulating the sale of giant firecrackers. A peer among friends despite his youth, Harry did little to upset this amiable gathering, but even friendship took a backseat to getting the town its money's worth. In the spring of 1910, Byrd shook up the council with his demand that the contractor who had installed the sewer system be required to restore the streets to their prior condition at his own expense. A compromise figure was reached, but not before Byrd orchestrated a public campaign in his newspaper to have the job done correctly; this occasioned one of the few examples of discord in the council's history and may have cost him his council seat. He was rudely awakened by political reality a year later when he ran last in a four-man contest for three seats on the council from his home ward. Having received one of the party nominations, he did no campaigning and lost to an independent incumbent. He later said that he would never again take an election so cavalierly. Rather than seek a return to the council, he contented himself with his duties as publisher of the *Evening Star* and with his expanding orchards, which were fast becoming his main preoccupation.[35]

In 1913 he took time out to get married. His bride was Anne Douglas Beverley, a childhood friend, who lived only a few blocks away. Born August 12, 1887, near Leesburg into another prominent Virginia family, she had come to Winchester in 1895 and later enrolled in the Episcopal Female Institute, which Harry's mother had also attended. A petite, attractive young woman with a lovely complexion, Anne, or "Sittie" as she was called by her younger brothers, was an accomplished dancer who had been Harry's steady for a number of years. They were married in Christ Episcopal Church in Winchester on October 7, 1913, but not without complications. A relative of Sittie's had died on the eve of the wedding, and her mother, a stickler for rules of mourning, decreed a very subdued celebration without reception or dancing. Following the evening ceremony, the couple left for a honeymoon at Atlantic City and then at Skyland in his father's cabin. During their early years of marriage, Harry and Sittie lived with her parents on Stewart Street. In 1916 Byrd built a large log cabin at the Rosemont Orchard in Berryville, not far from his future home, where they spent their summers. They had four children: Harry Jr., born in 1914; their only daughter, Westwood Beverley, in 1916; Bradshaw Beverley, in 1920; and Richard Evelyn, in 1923. Because of Byrd's extensive business and political interests, Sittie had the primary responsibility for rearing the children, but he was never far away, and he established a close, loving relationship with them.[36]

Byrd decided to run for the state senate in 1915. Maturing intellectually, the young publisher had begun to take a greater interest in public affairs, particularly in those areas which impinged directly on his own businesses: taxes, roads, and agriculture. Advancing the position advocated by his father, Byrd editorially endorsed tax segregation and equalization that would set apart certain taxes for the localities to collect and would provide for more equitable assessments. Showing unusual political courage for a future lawmaker, he chided Governor Henry Carter Stuart for not supporting more substantial tax segregation and expressed dissatisfaction with the compromise arranged by the General Assembly. A few weeks later, waving petitions signed by over a thousand voters, he announced his candidacy to "advance the interests of my constituents and of the state."[37]

Unopposed in the Democratic primary, Byrd faced Republican J. S. Haldeman, a Frederick County businessman, in the fall general election. He waged an aggressive campaign in which he used the pages of his newspaper to full advantage. Although he guaranteed Haldeman access to the columns of the *Evening Star*, Byrd monopolized the front page with his own testimonials from voters and endorsements from friendly editors. The issues were those on which Byrd would rest his political career: roads and governmental efficiency. On road building, Byrd wanted to give the localities more say in the distribution of money and in the types of roads to be built. Objecting to the emphasis on a permanent road system for tourists and city residents at the expense of farm-to-market roads, he claimed that farmers had to pay a "mud tax" on hauling produce to market because their roads were so bad. In another position paper he addressed the waste in Richmond, specifically the extended legislative sessions that he claimed cost the taxpayers $50,000. "I stand for strict economy in governmental affairs," he proclaimed. "The State of Virginia is similar to a great business corporation . . . and should be conducted with the same efficiency and economy as any private business."[38] In a fifty-year political career, no statement of Byrd's ever more succinctly spelled out his view of government.

On the education front Byrd announced his support for the popular election of school superintendents and for the less frequent purchase of new schoolbooks, but his discussion of education revealed another lifelong point of view. Criticizing the State Board of Education for teaching things of no practical benefit—like the distance to the moon and the builders of the pyramids—he declared: "Higher education is all right for those who desire it and can afford it, yet the foundation of all education is the attainment of knowledge which will be useful in the transaction of the duties of every day life. . . . It is a waste of time and money to prepare the school children of Virginia for University educations when 90% of them cannot afford or do not desire to go to a University." The man who had no education beyond the tenth grade did not seem to think that others needed it either.[39]

Remembering his sorry effort to win a council seat, Byrd adopted campaign tactics that he used in his business practices: organize thoroughly, pay attention to detail, and leave nothing to chance. Trying to evoke fear in the hearts of his followers, he pleaded with Samuel Kingree of Columbia Furnace: "The Republicans are making a desperate effort to carry this Senatorial District. It behooves every Democrat to actively support the Democratic ticket and to get out the full Democratic vote." He began a card index system which listed the name, address, and precinct of each voter in the Tenth Senatorial District; he then sent letters to them asking for their support and their views on the issues, enclosing a stamped, self-addressed envelope for replies, which, if favorable, were sometimes printed in the *Evening Star*. As he counseled a friend who was running for office two years later, "I would advise that nothing be taken for granted and that sufficient effort be made to assure your election. Now that you are in the fight you should leave nothing undone to assure success."[40]

As the campaign moved into its final stages, Byrd followed his own advice. An endorsement from Governor Stuart received prominent attention in several issues of the *Evening Star*; he appeared on the stump at several towns in the district with Congressman James Hay, who also endorsed the fledgling politician. In his standard speech Byrd reiterated his support for roads and schools and attacked his opponent for violating an obligation to the voters by running as a Republican after he had voted in the Democratic primary. Citing Halde-man's similar positions on the issues, Byrd claimed that if there were no differences between them, he could best serve the people because of the Democratic control of the legislature. On election eve fire badly damaged Byrd's residence—Harry Jr. escaped in the arms of his nurse—but the election proved less incendiary. Byrd received a substantial majority, winning both the city and county votes. Now it was on to Richmond and the beginning of a long, distinguished political career.[41]

~ 2 ~

The Apprenticeship

HARRY BYRD EMBARKED on his new career during a time of great turmoil. The issues of progressive reform and prohibition were redefining political loyalties in state and nation, while abroad the European powers were slaughtering men and sinking ships in a way that threatened to drag America into the conflict. In Virginia the Martin machine had come to an accommodation with the Reverend Mr. Cannon and his prohibition forces, but the subsequent debates over enforcement legislation, woman suffrage, better roads, and more efficient government splintered Organization unity. Wartime diversions further weakened Senator Martin's leadership, and with his death at the end of the decade, a struggle ensued for control of the Old Dominion's future.

Byrd did not join the ranks of assemblymen as a political unknown. The son of a former speaker of the House of Delegates and the nephew of one of the Organization's chief spokesmen, Harry was immediately recognized as a potential legislative leader. He obtained assignments on the important committees on roads and internal navigation, privileges and elections, and public institutions and education. He already knew many of the delegates and senators personally, and he cultivated additional friendships that would serve his political ambitions. Nevertheless, he was not a very visible legislator, writing little legislation and participating almost not at all in debate during his nearly ten years in the Virginia Senate. Years later he attributed his silence to a habit of learning by listening; furthermore, his defenders claimed that he was an effective behind-the-scenes legislator rather than a theatrical, headline-seeking politician. In actuality, except when the issue was the future of Virginia's roads, Byrd was not an influential lawmaker. In a forum dominated by attorneys familiar with constitutional questions and legal language, the untutored Winchester newspaperman deferred to those more experienced than he. Moreover, their skill at public debate intimidated him. Not blessed with a good speaking voice and lacking confidence in speaking extemporaneously, he deliberately chose not to participate in argumentation. It was a practice he adhered to throughout his career. When Harry Byrd spoke, it was usually through a written statement or prepared speech. Finally, there were many issues in which Byrd was not interested. He offered a few bills that addressed the needs of his constituents—requests that he received as soon as he was elected—but little significant legislation bore his signature. Roads and finances were his primary concerns.[1]

The advent of the automobile had created a growing demand for an improved road network in the state. The first State Highway Commission had been established in 1906, but it controlled no roads and had few funds to disburse. Most of the road building was done by counties and cities, which paid for it with bond issues. The result was a truncated system of roads that were poorly constructed and maintained except in places such as the Valley, which had invested in a private turnpike. Tourists were bypassing the Old Dominion to avoid the muddy roads, which in some areas were worsened by local inhabitants who created mudholes so their towing services would be used.[2]

Before he took the oath of office in January 1916, Byrd outlined a proposal to reorganize the highway department and improve the construction of roads; it was the first bill he offered as a freshman senator. An acknowledged authority on road building because of his eight-year management of the Valley Turnpike Company, Byrd cited the "impractical laws" that were costing the state money: the absence of provisions for road maintenance, excessive administrative costs, failure to use native materials, and restrictions on local control of road building. Over the years he would modify his preferences for farm-to-market roads and local control, but he never deviated from his insistence on good highways as a basis for a sound state economy.

Byrd presented his views to the fifth annual convention of the Virginia Road Builders Association, where critics, including Highway Commissioner George Coleman, condemned his idea of giving counties more authority in selecting routes. The cool reception and public criticism angered Byrd, whose relationship with Coleman thenceforth deteriorated. He immediately introduced a resolution asking the highway commissioner to furnish the senate more information on construction. His first statement on the senate floor, it suggested a tactic of his that would become habitual: when criticized, retaliate at once. Although his idea to decentralize state authority was sidetracked, the General Assembly did authorize money for highway maintenance and created a commission to prepare a state road plan as Byrd had requested. An additional bonus was his appointment to that commission along with senators A. Willis Robertson and C. O'Conor Goolrick and four members of the House of Delegates.[3]

The General Assembly session of 1916 was known as the "Great Moral Reform Session." It passed a prohibition bill, approved antigambling and anti–white slave laws, and attacked houses of ill repute. Believing that the bill indicting owners of property used for immoral purposes might work a hardship on innocent property owners, Byrd cast the only vote against it in the senate. When asked whether he would like to reconsider his vote, he replied: "No. In the first place, I don't know how to change my vote. In the second place, once I've made up my mind and voted, I don't think I should change." When he ran for governor in 1925, he might have wished he had accepted the offer, for his vote proved embarrassing.[4]

As he would throughout his career, Byrd supported prohibition legislation for personal and political reasons. He was a "dry" largely in reaction to his father's drinking, but he also knew it would be political suicide to oppose prohibition in a state overflowing with Methodist and Baptist preachers.[5] However, he was never a loud partisan on the issue, fearing that the continued acrimony between dispossessed drinkers and zealous prohibitionists would adversely affect politics in the state. In this concern he was correct, for the issue would haunt his career until repeal in 1933.[6]

Prohibition resurfaced in 1917 to undermine the carefully laid plans of the Organization to promote Lieutenant Governor J. Taylor Ellyson. The predicted contest with the antimachine forces, who were supporting Attorney General John Garland Pollard, was disrupted by the entry of Westmoreland Davis, a gentleman farmer from Loudoun County who had made his fortune through marriage and a lucrative New York legal practice. With both Ellyson and Pollard endorsing prohibition, Davis, who preferred local option, won the primary by a narrow plurality when his opponents split the "dry" vote. His victory over the Republicans in November proved a formality. Davis's advocacy of economy and efficiency augured well for his governorship, but his independence of the machine precluded any chance for a harmonious term. His aristocratic bearing, his support of state-owned fertilizer plants, and his efforts to build his own machine did not endear Davis to Harry Byrd, who had supported Ellyson in the governor's race. Contesting for power and recognition, they became bitter enemies, battling one another over the years through the editorial columns of Davis's *Southern Planter* and Byrd's *Evening Star*. Ironically, both men were passionate in their desire to modernize government in the Commonwealth.[7]

But in November 1917 Byrd had little time to worry about the new governor. Following America's declaration of war against Germany the previous spring, skyrocketing fuel demands forced President Wilson to create a federal Fuel Administration to ensure that production—particularly of coal—was increased and that fuel was properly allocated and distributed between defense plants, businesses, and consumers. On the verge of following his two brothers into the service, Byrd instead was appointed fuel administrator for Virginia, probably at the request of his father and uncle, both of whom had considerable influence with the Wilson administration. The father of two children, Byrd had good reason to avoid the trench warfare that was consuming the youth of Europe. The appointment provided a permanent deferment, and he accepted it reluctantly out of a sense of duty in the crisis, but for the remainder of his life he was nagged by conscience for his failure to enlist.[8]

Receiving no compensation even for living expenses, Byrd opened up a state office in Richmond and enthusiastically threw himself into his new assignment. Relying on his contacts with Uncle Hal, the "courthouse crowd," and friends in the business community, he appointed the local fuel commissioners and then surveyed them to ascertain fuel supplies, prices, and future requirements. Responsible for fuel conservation, distribution of coal, and elimination of hoarding, Byrd was an active administrator, issuing numerous bulletins and directives to the commissioners that outlined their duties and explained the rules of the national and state offices that they would be enforcing. He relied upon their reports and those of the coal retailers to determine equitable distribution levels and reasonable prices and profits. Employing the patriotic fervor that the war generated, Byrd urged Virginians to replace coal with wood in their furnaces and stoves, reduce the consumption of electricity, and meet in joint church services on Sundays. To avert a coal shortage in the state, he placed limits on the amount of coal that could be purchased and the supply that could be kept on hand.[9]

The winter of 1917–18 was colder than usual, complicating Byrd's job. Confronting national shortages due primarily to a breakdown in the railroad system, federal Fuel Administrator Harry Garfield shut down the nation's factories and businesses for five consecutive days in January and several Mondays thereafter. Because of Virginia's proximity to the coalfields, Byrd asked Garfield for an exemption to the "drastic regulations," but his request was denied. Nationwide exemptions did permit some businesses to remain open: laundries, barbershops, food processors, and those factories producing defense items such as the Du Pont powder plant in Hopewell and the Newport News Shipbuilding Company. The five-day shutdown produced a hectic few days in Byrd's Richmond office as he interpreted the orders for distressed businessmen and supervised their enforcement. Accustomed to the "meatless" and "wheatless" days that had already been dictated to conserve food supplies, Virginians cooperated fully with the "heatless" days of that winter. The few violations that occurred were due largely to honest misunderstandings of the orders.[10]

The end of winter and improvements in rail transportation alleviated the crisis, but Byrd did not relax his efforts to cultivate a conservation ethic in the Old Dominion. He exhorted the local commissioners in May: "This is not a time for State or Local pride. It is not a time for the selfish demand of the fullest measure of our rights. If we can help win the war by reducing our coal consumption, even at inconvenience by the substitution of other fuel, it is our duty to do it."[11] Fearing a future shortfall in production and another cold season ahead, he encouraged Virginians to conserve on fuel consumption and to lay in an early supply of coal while prices were down and railroad congestion was reduced. Having the power to control coal shipments, Byrd received many requests for increased allocations. Although he was fair in his assignments, his friends across the state, particularly in the Winchester area, received preferential treatment. He also lobbied Garfield to get Virginia firms on the preferred list for shipments.[12]

Byrd resigned as fuel administrator in September 1918, ostensibly to enter the military but more likely to tend to the apple harvest. He tried to obtain an officer's commission through the offices of Governor Stuart, but on Armistice Day, November 11, 1918, he withdrew his application. Work with the Fuel Administration proved a major bonus for Byrd's career. In an atmosphere of crisis, he refined his administrative skills for organization, decision making, and personal relations. He established important contacts with local officials and businessmen in dozens of communities across the state, people who appreciated the attention he gave their concerns and respected leaders such as William T. Reed of Larus and Brother Tobacco Company and Congressman Carter Glass, who saw promise in this young administrator.[13]

Byrd's work as fuel administrator interrupted the 1918 General Assembly session for him. During the first half of the session he was noticeably absent, but with the winter crisis abating, he became more involved in late February and March, missing very few votes. Once more he refrained from active debate, choosing to focus on the recommendations of the legislative highway commission on which he had served. He and senators Robertson and Goolrick proposed legislation that would establish a state highway system, provide state money for the improvement of roads, and facilitate use of newly appropriated federal funds for state roads. They visualized a $20 million, 3,500-mile road network to advance trade and tourism. Faced with the question of whether Virginia should finance this construction with taxes or with bonds, the assembly decided to use both sources, raising the property tax by four cents and voting to amend the constitution to permit the issuance of bonds. Byrd favored the tax increase, but he did not vote on the resolution proposing the bond amendment. Privately, he had doubts about the state going into long-term debt to pay for services. Referring to an appropriation for Virginia Polytechnic Institute that authorized construction bonds, he warned, "I am afraid if this institution is permitted to issue bonds that this is a most dangerous precedent and the result will be that every institution in Virginia will attempt to do the same."[14]

With the creation of a state road system, Byrd proposed that Virginia take over operation of the Valley Turnpike. The turnpike under his management was a well-maintained road that continued to break even in its operation, but it made sense for the state to assume control now that adequate maintenance funds had been appropriated. He knew the state was bound to build its own road and put the private turnpike out of business sooner or later. Initially, he wanted the state to make a specific appropriation to maintain the road adequately, but Governor Davis forced deletion of this provision. Davis also preferred that all turnpike funds be turned over to the state, but Byrd prevailed upon the legislators to allow a small payment to go to the stockholders. The conflict with the governor over one of Byrd's prized possessions may have triggered his break with Davis, who was attempting to impose his own views on economy in state government.[15]

In his initial message to the 1918 General Assembly, Governor Davis had challenged the lawmakers to modernize Virginia's government. Adhering to his campaign promises and the recommendations of the latest commission on economy and efficiency in government, Davis proposed enactment of the executive budget, centralization of state finances, a workmen's compensation law, and improvements in the school system. The budget bill, which transferred budget-making responsibility from the legislature to the executive and brought some rationality to the process, passed easily, as did the highway bill, the workmen's compensation bill, a compulsory education bill, and ratification of the national prohibition amendment, all of which Byrd supported even if he did not vote on them. He opposed the bill to admit women to the graduate programs at the University of Virginia (which was defeated) and the bill authorizing coeducation at the College of William and Mary (which was approved). On more personal matters, he got the Virginia Crop Pest Commission to prohibit shipments into the state of plants infected with insects—a boon to his apple business—and won authorization for Winchester citizens to vote on bonds for water improvements.[16]

On education issues Byrd backed the modest increases in state support, but he did not become a crusader for better schools. He sympathized with his constituents' requests for additional funds for schools, but that was the extent of his commitment. When his good friend Russell Cather wrote from army camp of the low educational levels of the draft registrants and urged Byrd to support increased taxes for education, Byrd responded that he would "assist in any way . . . to remedy the situation that you have so clearly set forth."[17] However, only a month later, despite acknowledging the "crying need" for improvements in the system, he argued that present financial conditions would not permit additional appropriations. During a special assembly session in August 1919, when new monies were raised for the highway system, Byrd advanced a similar argument, even though some localities were operating their schools only five to six months a year and teachers throughout the state were paid an average of $25 a month. Concluding that the roads were now well taken care of, Byrd promised, "The next session can be made a 'Good Schools Session' and there will be ample time to deal intelligently and adequately with the pressing needs of the Public School System." That pledge was never fulfilled during Byrd's lifetime; roads came first, and schools could always "wait 'til next year."[18]

All in all, the 1918 General Assembly enjoyed a productive session, but Governor Davis was not impressed. Carrying through on his commitment to economy, Davis called the legislators back to Richmond to reduce the appropriation for the prohibition department, rewrite the workmen's compensation bill to increase savings, and correct a million-dollar error in the appropriations bill. Charging dictatorial tactics, the delegates bristled at this effort by an outsider to humiliate them. With Harry Byrd among the leading dissenters, the assembly overrode Davis's veto of the compensation bill, refused to change the appropriation for liquor control, and only grudgingly accepted a compromise on the general appropriations bill that cut government salaries and monies for schools and roads. The battle between the governor and the Organization had been joined.[19]

Organization leaders correctly surmised that Davis was preparing to challenge their hegemony. Richard Byrd warned Senator Martin that Davis was "pulling every wire to build up a personal following and to control the next General Assembly" and was using the *Southern Planter* as a "political pamphlet devoted to his own interests and to the abuse of public men who are not his supporters." He urged Martin, Flood, and Swanson to get up some counterorganization "to protect ourselves."[20] The struggle for dominance in Virginia politics intensified the personal clash that was brewing between Harry Byrd and Westmoreland Davis, who now saw each other as competitors for future state leadership. Late in 1918 Byrd labeled Davis a demagogue who was "untrustworthy in all of his political transactions." Echoing his father's charge that Davis was using the *Planter* as a political organ, he claimed that the governor was violating the postage laws in distributing copies of the *Planter* and asked his congressman, T. W. Harrison, to initiate an investigation. Through the editorial pages of the *Evening Star,* he accused Davis of opposing the war policies of the Wilson administration at a meeting of the state Democratic Committee in September 1917, an accusation Davis vehemently denied.[21]

The feud continued during the 1920 legislative session when Byrd gleefully helped to defeat Davis's proposal for construction of another lime-grinding plant by the state. In 1922 the turnpike issue resurfaced when it was revealed that an oversight by attorney R. Gray Williams, Byrd's good friend and counsel for the turnpike, had delayed transfer of the turnpike deed to the state. Davis blamed Byrd for improprieties in the transaction, and an outraged Byrd responded with an extensive defense of his long stewardship of the road; he praised the bargain the state received and criticized the governor for his negligence and "dishonest vindictiveness." Davis replied: "As Governor I had not been advised you did not comply with the law. Your condemnation of me will always be accepted by me as a tribute to my efficiency and achievement." Like two alley cats fighting to expand their turf, they continued attacking one another until Davis's death in 1942. During his long political career, it is likely that Harry Byrd despised no one more than Westmoreland Davis.[22]

The hiatus between assembly sessions and the end of the war in Europe enabled Byrd to focus on his apple business, which had been disrupted by wartime dislocations. Having constructed an apple cold storage refrigeration facility in Winchester, he was presiding over its operation and financing. Brother Tom had returned from service to join him in the orchards, which they expanded with two new purchases. With so much of his time consumed by business, Byrd considered retiring from active politics for the moment. He was not involved in the decision making of the Organization and was out of favor with the governor. Furthermore, a serious bout with the influenza sweeping the country sapped his energy. In March 1919 he wrote E. D. Newman of Woodstock, "My business interests have recently so greatly extended that it would be a very great sacrifice for me to be a candidate again." But when the prospect arose for a special session of the assembly to match a large federal grant for highway construction, Byrd answered the call and ran unopposed in the Democratic primary.[23]

Initially, Byrd was opposed to the special session because he feared that the money appropriated would be spent on the main roads, not the county roads. But when the public clamor for road improvements grew, Byrd joined in, particularly when Governor Davis seemed to oppose expansion of the highway network. The General Assembly then called itself into session over the governor's objections. A giant auto parade, organized by good roads advocates who called for an end to "miry, rock-strewn, tortuous highways," greeted the legislators as they began their August deliberations. While chastising the delegates for their irregular action, Davis came out in favor of increased taxes on property and automobile licenses to fund new highway construction. Byrd was a co-patron of much of this legislation but again did not take an active role in the debates. The session restructured the Highway Commission, approved the tax increases, and much to Byrd's delight, appropriated $800,000 for county roads. Ironically, the bill matching federal highway money did not pass until the 1920 assembly.[24]

Governor Davis's success in turning the work of the session to his advantage, combined with Senator Martin's death in November, increased the anxiety of Organization leaders and ensured an acrimonious regular session in 1920 that opened with a heated debate over woman suffrage. Opposition to the newly enacted Nineteenth Amendment rested upon tradition and politics. Ear-

lier votes against equal education for women and equal access to the professions clearly indicated a male bias in the legislature against upsetting time-
honored gender distinctions; doubling the electorate risked control of the political order. As if these hurdles were not substantial enough, the opponents of
woman suffrage, playing upon racist fears, claimed that it would open the
doors to voting by black women, an argument used by Byrd in explaining his
reservations about the suffrage amendment.[25] He revealed his sentiments in a
letter to Mrs. E. Virginia Smith of Winchester:

> I agree that it would be impossible for the negroes to permanently dom-
> inate Virginia, yet in counties in southern Virginia, where the negro pre-
> dominates in number, it would certainly be a most dangerous thing to
> permit them to vote without restrictions—either the male or the fe-
> male. . . . I endeavored to make my position clear when I met your commit-
> tee; viz, that until the same restrictions in voting can be imposed upon the
> negro female as now are imposed upon the negro male, I would be opposed
> to the ratification of the Federal Suffrage Amendment by the State of Vir-
> ginia. When that objection has been removed, while I am frank to say that I
> have strong personal prejudice against women voting, yet if any substantial
> number of women desire to vote I can see no logical reason to deny to them
> this privilege.[26]

Byrd's votes on women's issues clearly placed him among the traditionalists. Throughout his life he treated women in a gentlemanly but condescending
manner. He tolerated them in public life, but he preferred them in their customary roles as wives, mothers, and homemakers. Women were not included
among his political friends and advisers and were even excluded from his dinner table when the talk concerned politics. He voted against the suffrage
amendment when the assembly rejected it in 1920, but ever the political prag-
matist, he moved quickly to incorporate women into the ranks of the Organization once it was clear that the Nineteenth Amendment would be ratified by
other states. He cosponsored a bill granting the vote to women in Virginia
upon payment of their poll taxes, a requirement satisfying his and Uncle Hal's
objections to black voting. Byrd also wrote bills to allow women to give bond
and to act as deputy clerks in county courts. In a follow-up letter to Mrs. Smith,
he concluded, "As you say, I was opposed to woman suffrage yet at the same
time, I think that now every woman should register and vote and I am inclined
to think that the influence of women in politics will tend to greatly improve
conditions providing that the better class of women take an active interest."[27]

Byrd was more absorbed with highway matters than with women's issues
during the 1920 session. He suggested several changes to the new highway department and supported a bill permitting new miles to be added to the system
without the recommendation of the commission. Over his objections the as-

sembly approved the use of bonds for highway construction (the electorate overwhelmingly ratified a constitutional amendment to this effect in the fall) and passed the Robertson Act that permitted localities to borrow money for building roads that would be included in the state system. The ease with which these latter bills sailed through gave no indication that financing roads would become the major controversy in state politics in the next two years.[28]

With the legislative session over, the Davis and Organization forces began jockeying for position in the governor's race in 1921 and the contest for Senator Swanson's seat in 1922. At the moment Westmoreland Davis appeared to hold a commanding lead. He had replaced many state officials with men loyal to his cause. Defiantly, he had maneuvered much of his legislative program through an obstinate assembly, winning public praise for his executive budget process that had worked so effectively for the first time in the 1920 session. And he had filled Senator Martin's vacated seat with Carter Glass, a longtime opponent of the machine, whom Davis believed would now become his ally in the battle with the Organization.[29]

Martin's unexpected death had left the already disarrayed Organization leaderless. As Richard Byrd observed, "The reins of leadership are lying on the ground."[30] Preoccupation with the prohibition issue had caused the Organization to ignore demands for improved state services, while wartime exigencies had forced Martin and Flood to attend to their congressional responsibilities and neglect important fence-mending tasks. The result was the election of an independent governor in 1917 and a General Assembly that divided on most of the major issues presented to it between 1916 and 1920. Yet the machine still commanded the loyalties of the courthouse people and the state Democratic Committee, and it had a talented group of battle-tested leaders who would not concede easily. The triumvirate of Flood, Swanson, and Rorer James now moved to restore authority. As a first step James agreed to remain as state party chairman, in spite of his upcoming race for Congress. They then sought to woo Carter Glass from the independent camp.

Carter Glass had been a thorn in the Organization's side for two decades. The diminutive Lynchburg newspaperman possessed a strong individualistic ethic that condemned any interference with a free political and economic order, whether by government or political machine. He led the fight at the 1901–2 constitutional convention to disfranchise African-Americans because he believed "negro domination" was responsible for the corruption of Virginia politics. He supported the Montague candidacies against the Martin machine and was elected to Congress himself in 1902. For the next fifteen years he was the most prominent opponent of the Organization, running an unsuccessful Senate campaign against Swanson in 1911 and supporting Wilson for the presidency in 1912. For his efforts in helping to create the new federal banking system—

for which he was known as the "Father of the Federal Reserve System"—he was appointed secretary of the treasury in 1918. One of the most popular men in the Commonwealth, the acerbic Glass could make Davis into a formidable opponent, but he had begun to tire of his constant struggles against Martin and Swanson. Although he had hailed Davis's victory in 1917 as a "rebuke to the ministerial machine and tyranny," he had accepted an early olive branch from the Organization in 1916 when Martin had made him Virginia's Democratic national committeeman.

The deliberate effort to convert Glass to the Organization standard began at the 1920 Democratic state convention, where party leaders permitted him to write the platform and then nominated him for president. Glass had no opposition from the Organization when he ran for the remainder of Martin's term that fall. Swanson, who faced a tough race against Davis in 1922, secured important Senate committee assignments for Glass and initiated a correspondence that sought to put to rest the enmity between them. Glass accepted the peace offerings and entered into a mutually supportive relationship with the Organization that lasted until his death in 1946. While Glass never became an Organization intimate, he was constantly lauded by party leaders, and he in turn generously supported their candidates and policies. Tired of fighting the machine, he now chose to join it. It was a simple matter of deciding which of the competing factions could best secure his political future.[31]

With Glass effectively neutralized, attention turned to the 1921 gubernatorial race. Supported by Governor Davis, Henry St. George Tucker of Lexington, another longtime independent, announced his candidacy. Tucker had crisscrossed the political landscape many times over, making and unmaking friends and enemies as he flitted from issue to issue with no recognizable consistency. With no other prospects from the Organization on the horizon, Hal Flood, with his nephew's enthusiastic support, considered making the run himself. After years of playing the good soldier, Flood hungered for one of the prestigious state positions to cap off his long career, but his wartime exertions had taken their toll, and he was not up to what promised to be a vigorous campaign. Furthermore, he was reluctant to give up his safe congressional seat and was being strongly urged by Democratic colleagues to stay in the House.[32]

In December 1920 Flood made up his mind not to run, and almost immediately E. Lee Trinkle, a state senator from Wytheville, announced his candidacy. Trinkle was a little-known forty-four-year-old attorney with only four years' experience in the legislature, but he had paid his dues in the rough-and-tumble world of the Ninth District where he had made a creditable race against Republican congressman Bascom Slemp in 1916. More importantly, Trinkle offered a progressive record with which to combat the elusive Tucker; he was "dry" where Tucker was "wet," and he had voted for woman suffrage and

Tucker against, a not insignificant fact in this first gubernatorial race in which women would vote. Organization forces quickly fell in behind Trinkle, including Harry Byrd, who promised his help if he could be relieved of a family pledge that had indirectly committed him to Tucker. "There is no man in the state that I would rather support than you," he wrote. Byrd himself was approached about running for lieutenant governor, but upon the recommendations of his uncle and his father, who thought it would be the "height of unwisdom" to enter that race, he declined.[33]

Within days of Trinkle's victory over Tucker in the August primary, party chairman Rorer James died. To solidify his position as party leader and perhaps to prepare the way for a gubernatorial campaign in 1925, Hal Flood sought the chairmanship. His primary contender was his nephew, who had considerable support from his father, Senator Glass, and younger faces in the party such as state senators Julien Gunn and Willis Robertson. Robertson wrote to Byrd, "It would give you an opportunity to make new friends, to bring your name to the attention of the voters of the state, and an opportunity to display your executive ability which should be very helpful to you when you run for Governor." State committeeman William Carson also urged Flood to consider Byrd: "He has executive and organization ability and would breathe life into and draw to the party organization young men who have been neglected for a decade." However, Flood feared that Harry might not have enough support to win and counseled his protégé to wait his turn, offering to pass the crown to him in due time. After their meeting Byrd wrote his uncle, "I doubt the wisdom of transferring the Chairmanship to me later on but we can discuss this at the time. . . . I am delighted that the unanimity of sentiment is in favor of your selection as State Chairman." The final vote at the committee meeting in late August was a mere formality.[34]

Hal Flood could not have known how quickly he would be transferring the chairmanship to his nephew. Having promised Trinkle to lead a vigorous campaign against the Republicans, he exhausted himself in the effort and died on December 8, 1921. There was little doubt as to whom his successor would be. Committee secretary Jake Brenaman advised Byrd: "I do not think it is necessary for you to be a candidate. All that is necessary for you to do, if you are approached on the question, is to state that you are not a candidate but that if the Committee thinks you are the man for the place you will not decline. Everybody that I have seen is for you and there will be no question about your election." Encouraged by his father to take the position, Byrd modestly responded to Brenaman, "It would be most distressing for me to be State Chairman after Uncle Hal, having the great love for him that I have, yet at the same time, if you and others think it necessary I will not decline the honor if it is offered me." Senator Swanson, in poor health and in the midst of his Senate campaign, surveyed his advisers and gave his blessing. On January 31, 1922, Harry Byrd was unanimously elected chairman of the Virginia Democratic Central Committee. After extolling his uncle, he pledged support for better roads and schools and advocated economy and efficiency in state government. It was a forecast of a campaign address three years later.[35]

~ 3 ~

Roads to Richmond

THE PIVOTAL YEAR in Harry Byrd's career was 1922. As the new party chairman he bore the primary responsibility for achieving victory in the crucial congressional races in the Seventh and Ninth districts and in Swanson's contest with former governor Davis. Even more importantly, in the General Assembly he emerged as the leading opponent of using bonds for the construction of Virginia's roads and so initiated the battle over the state's financial future that would be resolved in public referendum the following year. There were great risks for him in all of these endeavors, but his decisiveness, organizational skills, and energy secured his objectives and propelled him on to the governor's mansion in 1926.

Byrd had not always been such a strong foe of public indebtedness. Certainly his early experience with the newspaper convinced him of the soundness of a pay-as-you-go policy, but his own apple business was financed by personal debt, and he had supported the use of bonds to construct Winchester's water and sewer systems. To a neighbor in Clarke County in 1921 he admitted that he would favor a local bond issue for road building if the money could be returned in three years. At the state level he had acceded, if somewhat unenthusiastically, to building roads with borrowed money before 1920.[1] At this point several factors, all undergirded by his visceral objection to debt and the waste of interest payments, combined to turn him into a vigorous foe of state borrowing.

Much like Governor Davis, Harry Byrd believed in economy in government. Public indebtedness, he feared, would cultivate a spendthrift mentality, affecting not only road building but all other state services. Higher taxes and wasteful spending would result. He particularly disliked the long-term nature of bonds, which, like Virginia's nineteenth-century debt, could remain a burden for generations to come and hinder the state's development. Referring to that antebellum debt in 1962, Byrd said, "That's the reason I have always been so opposed to bond issues."[2]

Byrd also did not like the way the highway department was being operated. He opposed the emphasis on trunk lines at the expense of county roads. That preference would be even more exaggerated if the department had access to the large sums a bond act might bring in. In relaying his opposition to bonds to senate colleague Sam Ferguson, Byrd said, "I have come to the conclusion that the present highway department is very inefficient, and I say this reluctantly as I am very fond of Coleman."[3]

Finally, Byrd was influenced by his Valley constituents, who already enjoyed a good main road network and were strongly opposed to construction elsewhere in the state at their expense. He judged other rural voters to have the same reservations and so bet his political future on winning and maintaining their support for his views. In the 1920 bond vote, Byrd did not take an active public role in opposing it, but he urged his Valley friends such as Joe Bauserman to "do all you can to oppose the amendment for bond issue for roads. It is proposed to bond the state for untold millions so as to construct roads on the Eastern shore or elsewhere under the costly management of the State Highway Department." In frequent correspondence with Highway Commissioner Coleman about roads in his district, Byrd accentuated his opposition to bonds and his preference for tributary roads rather than main roads. During the 1921 gubernatorial campaign he strongly advised Lee Trinkle to soft-pedal the bond idea, and he began lining up his supporters for the next fight against the bond advocates, who included Coleman, C. O'Conor Goolrick, and the Virginia Good Roads Association. This contest came to a head in the General Assembly session of 1922.[4]

Byrd's deliberations on road building revealed the competing forces that were a part of his early career: a conservative preference for traditional practices, especially when it came to spending money, versus a zest for progress, for growth, for the utilization of resources in the most efficient and productive manner possible. Roads were necessary for development, but one had to be careful not to overextend in financing them. This personal dichotomy reflected the current mood of cautious progressivism in Virginia. The world war had been a mixed blessing for the Old Dominion. Thanks to increased foreign demand, farmers had enjoyed high prices for their crops. Norfolk and the Hampton Roads area were awash in shipbuilding contracts, and exports jumped from $9.5 million in 1914 to $138 million in 1926. Creation of army camps and defense plants and expansion of tobacco and textile production brought new prosperity to the state. But the war also ushered in changes that were less desirable, such as social unrest, strikes, racial violence, a Red Scare, and changes whose consequences were yet to be determined, especially prohibition and woman suffrage. Ambivalently, Virginians reveled in their good times but were uncertain of the future. The predictable postwar recession did little to reduce their anxiety as the state retreated to "normalcy." This was particularly true of farmers, who entered a deep trough that would last for two decades. Between 1919 and 1921 Virginia gross farm income declined by 55 percent and prices of produce by

65 percent; farmers' enthusiasm for more progress waned, and retrenchment became the order of the day. While urban residents and manufacturers—whose businesses continued to expand in the twenties—supported bond plans to underwrite good roads, rural residents, who made up two-thirds of the population, cautioned against debt that they feared would lead to higher property taxes. The onset of this farm recession may explain why state voters overwhelmingly voted for bonds in 1920 and rejected them by a similar margin three years later. And it may have accelerated, as well, the transformation of Harry Byrd, whose political career was dependent on satisfying rural voters.[5]

Byrd's first priority in the 1922 session was not bonds but the reorganization of the highway department. George Coleman, the department's commissioner since 1913, had enormous power to determine the types of roads to build, their location, and the materials to be used, issues over which he and Harry Byrd had already differed. His support for bonds with which to complete the primary road system further antagonized the senator from Winchester, who now decided that the department needed "a complete housekeeping." With the backing of governor-elect Trinkle, Byrd proposed abolishing the office of commissioner and replacing it with a state highway commission of five members, plus a chief engineer who would handle technical responsibilities. Senator Goolrick countered with a proposal that would also reorganize the commission but retain some powers for the commissioner.[6]

The debate over reorganization between Byrd and Goolrick—who also differed on the use of bonds—was exacerbated by a joint house-senate investigation of the Highway Commission initiated by Byrd. Although he denied it, Byrd wanted to discredit Coleman's administration in order to improve chances of passing his reorganization bill and to undermine Coleman's advocacy of bonds. The hearing dragged on for several weeks, producing acrimonious exchanges between Byrd, who chaired the joint committee, and Goolrick, who accused him of badgering witnesses and bringing them long distances for meaningless testimony. The majority report approved by Byrd and three other members found no graft in the department but criticized it for "unintelligible bookkeeping" and excessive costs in engineering and letting contracts.[7] Goolrick's minority report, supported by two other legislators, concluded that the department was "honestly, efficiently and economically administered." Neither man won accolades for his performance, but the hearings may have contributed to a compromise on the reorganization that established the five-member commission favored by Byrd but retained the office of highway commissioner for engineering functions for a four-year term. Retention of the title was a face-saving gesture for George Coleman, whom everyone knew would be appointed to the position.[8]

With the reorganization issue settled, the assembly turned to financing future road building. Goolrick and Senator C. C. Vaughn, backed by the Good Roads Association, introduced a $12 million highway bond bill that the Winchester *Evening Star* immediately condemned. But to Byrd's consternation, Governor Trinkle departed from his previous position and endorsed the use of bonds, claiming that department reorganization, improved economic conditions, and lower material costs had changed his mind on the efficacy of bonds. Although the bitterness of the debate over highways had upset his hopes for a peaceful resolution of the issue, the governor plunged ahead, encouraged by bond spokesmen in Bristol and Norfolk.[9]

Trinkle's conversion may have stimulated the bond forces to greater effort, for bills supporting a bond issue passed both houses. Even so, the differences in the two bills were never reconciled, thanks to Harry Byrd. The Goolrick-Vaughn bill cleared the Finance Committee by two votes and won approval in the full senate by a similar margin; Byrd voted no both times. The vote reflected clear differences between urban and mountain representatives, who favored the bill, and rural and Valley legislators, who opposed it. The house then amended the bill to call for a public referendum on the bonds, which the senate rejected. Led by the parliamentary maneuverings of Rockingham County's George Keezell, a close associate of Byrd's, the house refused to enter into a joint conference and the bills died. Outraged by the action of the lower chamber, Goolrick labeled it an "ignorant body of leaderless, irresponsible, incompetent reactionaries who would wreck any constructive plan."[10]

However, many rural delegates suggested that the real villain was Governor Trinkle, whose change of mind had violated campaign promises not to pursue bonds. Writing to the governor shortly after the session, an indignant Byrd reminded him of his statement against bonds in the 1921 campaign. When Trinkle testily complained that the Valley people did not appreciate the need for roads elsewhere, Byrd reiterated his reason for opposing bonds: "I wish you and others would disabuse your minds of the fact that the Valley is opposed to good roads because we opposed the bond issue. We favor good roads as strongly as any other part of the State. . . . It is simply a question of means to reach the end; because I am firmly convinced that this is simply an entering wedge, as Goolrick admitted on the floor of the senate, and that it is the purpose of the Good Roads Association to ultimately force a measure for $50,000,000 on bonds which I think would be disastrous to the State." Byrd did not want to offend the governor and precipitate an undesirable open break, but it was clear that their differences over bonds were leading to a less cordial relationship.[11]

To this point E. Lee Trinkle had retained a slim chance of contesting Harry Byrd for the future leadership of the Organization, but the defeat of the bond issue shifted momentum to Byrd and the pay-as-you-go crowd. To demands that a special session be called to pass the bond legislation, Trinkle weakly responded that he would do so only if support for it was overwhelming. Byrd, on the other hand, seized the initiative and lobbied hard with the governor and others against any special session.[12] He warned Senator Swanson of the danger that such a session and referendum might have on his upcoming election campaign, causing that anxious candidate to back off an earlier endorsement. Byrd also forcefully pressed the governor to appoint two close friends, Wade Massie of the town of Washington and Hugh Sproul of Staunton, to the Highway Commission. Trinkle acceded, and Byrd thereafter had ready influence on future highway policy and road selection, particularly in his own district. A tough new leader was acquiring the reins of power.[13]

A man of enormous energy with many activities, Byrd organized his personal life just as he pursued the restructuring of Virginia government: economically and efficiently. Not a moment could be wasted. He was involved in the disposition of Hal Flood's estate, having been made executor of the estate and guardian of his uncle's two young children. It was a complicated affair because Flood had many financial holdings in real estate and other businesses and a number of outstanding loans to the Democratic National Congressional Committee and the state Democratic Committee. Byrd did not relinquish this burden until 1936. He was also chairman of the building committee of the Handley Schools Board of Trustees in Winchester, which had just authorized construction of a new high school. Byrd made a financial contribution to this work and personally supervised the selection of materials to be used. Never an outwardly gregarious man, he nonetheless joined the fraternal associations of the Moose and the Odd Fellows for the political contacts. Similarly, he became a member of the Winchester Golf Club even though he did not golf. Most of his spare moments were given over to the apple orchards and to the expansion of the cold storage facilities. In fact, he had so little time for himself that he often had to ask for extensions for filing his income tax.[14]

Byrd still devoted considerable attention to publishing the *Evening Star*. He affiliated with the Associated Press and purchased a new press to expand his operation. In 1923 he and associates Shirley Carter and Gray Williams purchased the Harrisonburg *Daily News-Record* from George Keezell for approximately $140,000. Hiring John Crown to run the *News-Record*, Byrd frequently communicated with him about articles and editorials that should appear. Occasionally, he would write an editorial, but the newspapers were primarily a business enterprise, and only rarely did he use them to advance a political position or candidacy. His correspondence regarding the papers reveals his preoccupation with income and expenses. Indeed, when he ran for governor in 1925, he advised Crown, "I think it is all right to publish a reprint editorial from time to time, endorsing some of my policies, but do not publish anything of any nature that will appear too partisan."[15]

What consumed most of Byrd's time once the 1922 assembly adjourned were the problems he faced as the new state party chairman. It was an imposing task. The Organization of which he assumed command was in difficulty. It had captured an old adversary in Carter Glass and beaten back the independent challenge of Henry St. George Tucker, but it confronted additional contests in 1922 that could diminish its authority if lost. Former governor Davis, still intent on creating a political machine of his own, hoped to snare Senator Swanson's seat; and in the Seventh and Ninth District congressional races, Organization candidates were trying to retrieve seats from incumbent Republicans. Leadership for this effort remained in doubt. Martin and Flood were gone, and Swanson was in poor health and preoccupied with his own campaign. Young Byrd was an untested commodity in state races, and Governor Trinkle had lost momentum with the bond defeat. Furthermore, the machine had no money. For years the state committee had operated out of a shoe box, with Flood asking Secretary Jake Brenaman for money to pay bills or occasionally throwing in some of his own cash. Many bills were in arrears, and the committee was strapped with a $5,500 deficit from the 1921 gubernatorial campaign at a time when funds were needed for the elections of 1922. Whoever could provide the organizational skills and savvy decision making in a victorious election effort would be in a position to replace Martin as the acknowledged leader of the Organization.

It was an opportunity that Harry Byrd did not let pass. At once he displayed the political pragmatism for which his uncle had been so well known. Laying aside his personal preference for senate colleague Willis Robertson, Byrd conceded Flood's congressional seat to Henry Tucker, thus appeasing and silencing another old independent. Relying upon the "courthouse crowd" and the friendships he had made as state fuel administrator, Byrd used the organizational techniques he had developed for his own elections to the state senate: precinct organization, poll tax paying, voter registration, voter lists, and letter writing. Special efforts were made to qualify women voters. To raise money, he recommended that party leaders contribute $250 each; his was the first donation. Instead of using the money to pay the old bills, he channeled it to the local chairmen to pay the poll taxes of "reliable Democrats." From James Hayes, his personal choice as the new secretary of the state committee, he requested lists of state and local officeholders and "those that you think should contribute campaign funds."[16]

In the Seventh District, Byrd and Tom Harrison faced Republican incumbent John Paul, who had taken Harrison's seat from him in 1920 when election

irregularities were found. That campaign, the first in which women participated, had been a hotly contested race that Harrison won by 500 votes. Paul
challenged the results in the House of Representatives, claiming that he was
the victim of improper registration procedures and illegal assistance in ballot
marking at the polls, charges that Byrd labeled "technicalities." After lengthy
hearings the Republican-controlled House awarded the election to Paul with
back salary. Byrd and Harrison set about to reverse that decision at the polls,
taking great pains to ensure that the irregularities were not repeated. The Seventh had always had a sizable Republican contingent, but it was also Harry
Byrd's home district where his organizational practices were honed to a fine
edge. He lined up Swanson and Glass to come into the district on Harrison's
behalf, sent out thousands of circulars entitled "Thou Shalt Not Steal"—an
attack on the seating of Paul—distributed sample ballots, and arranged many
local meetings of Democrats in the district. In a less than subtle appeal to racism, the *Evening Star* printed lists of white women whose registrations had
been questioned by Republicans and a list of black women who had not been
challenged. The result was a comfortable Harrison victory.[17]

The fight to redeem the "Fighting Ninth" may have been the most crucial
for Byrd's subsequent rise to power. Republicans Campbell Slemp and his son
C. Bascom Slemp had controlled the district for twenty years, perfecting an
organization that was the equal of the Democrats in qualifying voters and distributing patronage. However, the untiring efforts of new district chairman
George Peery had enabled Trinkle to carry the Ninth in 1921, and Democrats
looked forward to defeating Bascom Slemp the following year. As a reward for
his efforts, Peery was nominated to run against the Republican. Everett Randolph ("Ebbie") Combs, clerk of Russell County, replaced Peery and assumed
control of his campaign. Byrd's relationship with Combs, begun on the hilly,
winding roads of southwest Virginia, deepened into a friendship and political
association that lasted thirty-five years.[18]

Because of the bitter competition between the parties in the Ninth District,
its politics were the dirtiest in the Old Dominion. Voting irregularities were
common, particularly abuses of absentee voting and block payment of poll
taxes, which voters had come to expect despite its illegality. "Qualifying" voters
meant ensuring that their poll taxes were paid six months before the general
election in the fall and then registering them. Money was essential for this practice. Combs appealed to R. W. Ervin, "Of course you understand that we must
have this [i.e., money] not later than May 6th in order that we may look after
their poll tax. Please be sure that you have the name of every man and woman
who will vote for Peery this fall at your precinct." A cozy relationship between
Democratic registrars and party officials guaranteed that reliable voters were
registered. Combs was so successful in this endeavor that he wrote Byrd a

month before the election, "We have qualified between two thousand and twenty-five hundred more new voters than they will. Things look mighty good."[19]

These practices, which occurred in every congressional district, persisted with the full knowledge and compliance of state leaders, who were also raising money for the effort. Sending $1,000 to the Ninth, Byrd commended A. K. Morison of Bristol, "I am delighted to hear you have made such good progress in the paying up of the poll taxes." Soliciting contributions from state employees, he directed state committee secretary Hayes "to write each of the more important employees a circular letter requesting a contribution to the Ninth District campaign." But he cautioned, "Use the utmost care not to send letters to any Republican as a copy of the letter might be published."[20] Estimating that the Democrats had spent $20,000 to $25,000 in their poll tax campaign, Slemp withdrew from the race in favor of John Hassinger, state senator from Abingdon.

Byrd made a personal appearance in the district in June—when he met Combs for the first time—and returned in August and October, making new friends and impressing all with his energy and advice. As in the Seventh District, he lined up speakers for the Ninth, distributed ten thousand cards presenting information on the candidate and the issues, welcomed the support of organized labor, and sent personal letters to local officials urging them to get out the vote. Assisted by the nationwide "Republican recession," Peery won a decisive victory over Hassinger, ending Republican hegemony in the Ninth; a solid Democratic congressional delegation was sent to Washington in 1923 for the first time in memory, along with the reelected Senator Swanson, who had easily turned aside Westmoreland Davis.[21]

Not content with the victory of the moment, Byrd corresponded with local officials after the election, commending them for their efforts and preparing them for the next series of local elections. Prophetically, he congratulated Peery: "I predict for you a wonderful career in Congress, and political honors in the future much greater than that of being a Congressman. I want you to know that if I can ever serve you in any way it will give me the greatest pleasure." To E. R. Combs, whom Byrd called the "best campaign manager in Virginia," went the ultimate praise: "The success is entirely due to the organization that you and other members of the committee effected." It was the Byrd "treatment" of profusely complimenting his subordinates and modestly offering to be of future service. Their gratitude to him for his efforts on their behalf was the solid foundation of a new machine. Acclaimed for his work in restoring Organization authority, Harry Byrd now turned back to the road question to consolidate his emerging status as the heir to Tom Martin.[22]

In actuality, the issue of bonds had never been far from his mind during the summer and fall campaigns. While Governor Trinkle had agreed to Byrd's request not to have a special assembly session before the election, he continued to endorse the use of bonds as the fastest means to build the roads required for industrial development. To this end his new highway chairman, Henry Shirley, proposed a bond plan for highway construction that required a two cents per gallon gasoline tax to pay off the debt in twenty-one years and complete the roads in eight to ten years. Anticipating the move, Byrd, Tom Ozlin of Lunenburg, and Louis Epes of Nottoway offered a three cents per gallon alternative that would build the highways in almost the same time but without bonded indebtedness. This threesome, who would lead the pay-as-you-go forces in the upcoming legislative struggle, reflected the important linkage between the Valley and the rural Southside, whose citizens wanted no higher property taxes but assurances that they would get their fair share of the roads. Byrd told Ozlin that he hoped at least 20 percent of the gas tax would go to the counties for farm-to-market roads.

With the congressional elections completed, Byrd and his friends conceded the inevitability of a special session and worked assiduously to sign up the uncommitted assembly delegates behind their plan.[23] As soon as Governor Trinkle summoned the legislature to convene on February 28, 1923, Byrd began arranging for antibond men to be placed on the road and finance committees. He and Epes lined up another rural legislator, Sam Ferguson of Appomattox, to head the powerful Democratic caucus, whose chairman made committee assignments. The post was deemed so important that Byrd asked Senator Swanson and other Virginia congressmen to support Ferguson, whose victory paid immediate dividends: Byrd was made chairman of the Roads Committee.[24]

In his opening address to the special session, Governor Trinkle dispassionately reviewed the case for both bonds and pay-as-you-go funding for the highways, and then, to the shock of many listeners, he voiced a preference for the latter, suggesting that revenues from the gas tax alone would be enough to complete the highway system within seven years. Applauding the governor's reconversion, Byrd also stressed that the gas tax would fund the same number of miles of roads as bonds in only two years' more time at a savings of millions of dollars in interest payments. Bond spokesmen retorted that highway building would be faster and more predictable and state development more rapid under their plan. The debate between the competing plans—the three-cent gas tax versus a $50 million bond issue—raged on for the duration of the monthlong session, each side challenging the figures of the other, each side looking for the votes to sustain its position.

Byrd was more involved in the legislative maneuvering and debate than he had been in any previous session of his senate career. By midsession it was clear that the antibond forces dominated the more rural house, which passed the gas tax and approved a referendum that would permit a vote for either bonds or pay-as-you-go financing by legislative districts, a suggestion of Harry Byrd's that favored the more numerous counties at the expense of the more heavily populated urban areas. Bond people wanted a statewide vote on bonds alone. In the senate the issue was much more in doubt. The gas tax plan emerged from Byrd's committee by the narrow margin of 9–7, causing the *Times-Dispatch* to predict a "titanic struggle" on the floor over the road bills. After a very bitter contest, the senate passed the three-cent gas tax bill, 24-15, giving the counties one cent for their roads. In a spirit of compromise, the upper chamber then passed a referendum bill that allowed a statewide vote on a $50 million bond issue in November. It was a risk that Byrd and the pay-as-you-go advocates were now willing to take. When the house concurred, bond people celebrated their modest victory, but Byrd's ally, Senator Henry Wickham, correctly concluded, "We have you whipped."[25]

Without pausing for a breath, Byrd turned his attention to preparations for the November vote. Having staked so much of his reputation on the superiority of a pay-as-you-go road-building plan, he knew that his political future depended upon defeating the bond issue. Understanding that present road conditions would influence a voter's decision about whether to spend more money on new construction, Byrd wrote Trinkle on March 27 that "much depends on efficient maintenance of roads for the next six months, as well as expediting the construction." He urged the governor, who readily complied, to take the matter up with Highway Chairman Shirley. On April 4 a circular went out from Byrd's office reminding Organization leaders of the importance of paying poll taxes before May 5 and urging them to establish a network of county and precinct chairmen to recruit enthusiastic workers for the fall campaign. Efforts were made to register new voters, especially women. It was as if Byrd himself were running for office.[26]

The seven-month-long debate replayed the discussions of the special session, usually with the same players involved. Coleman, now heading the Virginia Good Roads Association, and Goolrick, along with the Virginia Bankers Association and the Richmond *News Leader,* were the ever-present proponents of bonds. Their most effective argument was that the deadline for the completion of the road system and the amount of money required through the pay-as-you-go plan were grossly underestimated. Relying just on gasoline taxes was more likely to take twelve years, not seven. They also charged that the Byrd forces were not sincere in their support of good roads but only wanted to prevent state indebtedness.

To counter the arguments of the bond people, Byrd and his friends organized the Pay-As-You-Go Roads Association, with former governor Stuart as president, Epes as secretary-treasurer, Ozlin as chairman of the speakers com-

mittee, and Byrd in charge of publicity. Relentlessly, he pursued favorable newspaper coverage of their position, sending out articles every week to every
newspaper in the state. He did not hesitate to use state employees to mobilize
antibond sentiment across the Commonwealth. Enlisting E. R. Combs's organizational talents, he urged him to recruit antibond Republicans in the Ninth
District on this "non-political question." It would not be the last time in his
career that Byrd would turn to Republicans to assist him in winning an election. Looking ahead to the next legislative session when the referendum's results would be implemented, Byrd focused on securing some key assembly seats
in the August primary and won a notable victory in the twenty-eighth senatorial district where Goolrick was defeated by an all-out Organization effort
against him.[27]

Although wet weather on election eve turned roads into quagmires, damp-
ening the spirits of the antibond people, they need not have worried. Their
victory was substantial: 127,187 to 81,220. As predicted, only in the cities and in
some mountain counties did the bond issue do well. The rural sections of the
Valley and Southside, where taxes and debt were anathema, overwhelmingly
rejected the proposal. Byrd put it best to Trinkle: the vote against bonds was a
vote against increased taxes and for economy and efficiency in state government. The only consolation for the bond people was the fulfillment of their
prediction that the roads would not be built on time. Seven years later, the
gasoline tax was up to five cents per gallon and the system was still not complete. However, the 1923 bond referendum had a significance far beyond that
of the speed with which roads would be built in Virginia. Everyone recognized
Harry Byrd as the driving force behind the victory, as a man of rare organizational ability and indefatigable energy. This effort confirmed his leadership of
the Organization and launched his campaign for the governorship in 1925.
Years later Byrd said his political career would have died had he lost this election. The vote also solidified a pay-as-you-go mentality in the Old Dominion
that would be the ideological basis for the state's fiscal policy for the next several decades.[28]

Talk of a Byrd gubernatorial candidacy surfaced as soon as the referendum
was concluded. His friends had discussed such a possibility privately for some
time, but on each occasion he modestly declined the overture, sometimes with
near Shermanesque finality. Early in 1923 he told J. B. Beverley: "I appreciate
more than I can express your reference to my candidacy for Governor. I have
absolutely no intention in the world of announcing myself at this time or in
fact at any other time. I deeply appreciate the requests that have come to me
from several sections, especially the 9th District, that I consider the advisability
of being a candidate, but I do not feel that I am qualified for the position, and
furthermore my business is of such a nature that I could not possibly leave it

for the time necessary to make a canvass and then if elected to serve four years." He also worried that talk of running for governor would adversely affect the vote on the bond issue.[29]

Byrd raised another objection in his reply to Tom Ozlin's demand that he be a candidate: "While I appreciate your insisting on my candidacy for Governor, yet the more consideration I give this matter the more it appears to me that I could not be a candidate by reason of conditions here. My wife is tremendously opposed to it." Indeed, Sittie's health was deteriorating. The birth of their last child, Richard, in April 1923 had been more difficult than usual, weakening her already delicate constitution. However, although her physical condition would be a factor in his decisions to run for office throughout his career, it never proved an insurmountable obstacle. Byrd's disclaimers owed more to personal modesty and a political sense that politicians were better off if they were perceived as noble public servants responding to a call rather than ambitious office seekers. If the conditions were right, he would run. He had publicly disavowed such intentions right after the referendum, but when quizzed about his candidacy at the opening of the 1924 General Assembly, he admitted his desire to be governor; still, he refused to make any commitments at that time since the election was "a long way off."[30]

Consideration of the governorship, therefore, was deferred as Byrd, not resting on his laurels, immediately began planning for the upcoming assembly session. As he wrote to Trinkle, they would have to control the senate and the house to make their victory in the referendum effective. Louis Epes was even more emphatic in his supplication to Byrd: "I don't believe in declaring an armistice. We have defeated them today. Carry the fight to its conclusion, and make it an utter rout. If we stop now they are going to come back, and we may find ourselves less advantageously situated than at present. . . . If we fail to press home our advantage this time, the tables may be turned on us in 1924."[31] Once again, Byrd helped to organize the Democratic leadership. To caucus chairman Sam Ferguson, he suggested committee assignments that would reward loyal friends and deny those who had been against him in the bond fight. In the contest for the speakership of the house, Byrd revealed just how Machiavellian he had become. His ally in the road fight, Tom Ozlin, sought to unseat incumbent Richard Brewer, ostensibly to protect the gains of the recent vote. Byrd gave Ozlin assurances that he would do "everything possible for you," but after careful consideration he decided to back Brewer on the condition that the Speaker would endorse pay-as-you-go and give antibond legislators good committee assignments. He enlisted his father, who still had considerable influence in Richmond, to help out in this effort, encouraging the elder Byrd to get Ozlin to think "we have done all for him we could." Brewer was reelected, and Ozlin delayed his aspirations for two years.[32]

Louis Epes's admonition not to take any prisoners undoubtedly drove Byrd to an extreme defense of the pay-as-you-go policy and opened up an irreparable break with Governor Trinkle. Byrd would condone no challenge to his leadership or to the sanctity of balanced budgets. At the end of 1923, Trinkle announced an unexpected budget deficit of $1.8 million, blaming it on the nationwide recession, but he anticipated that revenues over the next two years would cover the deficit and leave a small reserve of $50,000. Byrd saw this as a gross violation of the principles they had been fighting for over the past two years; he likely believed it was also an example of Trinkle's negligence. In public exchanges with the governor in committee meetings and through the newspapers, Byrd criticized the deficit, the reserve, and future estimates of revenue and demanded a $2 million budget reduction. "Deficits cannot be safely ignored," he said. Repeated shortfalls could leave Virginia with a large debt, perhaps even force a new bond issue to pay for it. The oracle had spoken; pay-as-you-go would extend to all expenditures, not just roads.[33]

The 1924 General Assembly, graced for the first time by the presence of two women legislators—Sarah Lee Fain of Norfolk and Helen T. Henderson of Buchanan County—followed the advice of Harry Byrd, cutting appropriations and raising taxes to reduce the projected deficit.[34] Although the result was a compromise, Byrd clearly emerged the victor in the struggle. The legislature also made permanent the mill and gas taxes for highway construction and rejected the creation of a central tax board that had been recommended by the Commission on Simplification and Economy in Government but opposed by Byrd. As always, roads were never far from his mind. He was in constant communication with Henry Shirley about roadwork, fearing a new surge for bonds if highways were not taken care of. Little escaped him if it affected Organization policy or his political future.[35]

The rift between Byrd and Trinkle widened when stories surfaced of improprieties aboard Game and Inland Fisheries boats involving Commissioner W. McDonald Lee. After an investigating committee exonerated Lee, Trinkle allowed him to keep his post. For Harry Byrd, whose sense of propriety tolerated not even the whiff of scandal when it came to public officials, particularly when it might jeopardize his own career, Trinkle's decision was unacceptable. On the eve of his announcement for the governorship, he confided to Senator Swanson, "I certainly hope that something will be done about the McDonald Lee matter, as it is having a very bad effect all over the state." He maintained his silence during the affair, but his decision not to reappoint Lee when he became governor revealed his sentiments.[36]

In the two years since he had taken the helm of the state committee, Harry Byrd had assumed total command of the Organization. This had been no fluke; he had worked diligently to restore life to the machine and impose his leadership on it. Tough election contests saw Byrd diverting money and outside speakers to the appropriate districts and offering his own organizational advice. He continued to rely on the "lists": the rolls of loyal Democratic workers and voters in every county down to the precinct level that revealed the full extent of the machine's authority. Byrd often sent each of these people three separate letters over the course of a campaign, requesting their assistance, emphasizing the need to get out the vote, and thanking them for their efforts. As party chairman he was frequently asked to clarify primary election rules and voting eligibility; invariably his rulings were restrictive, excluding Republicans and blacks from participating in Democratic primaries. Emphasizing the importance of party loyalty, Byrd made it clear in the 1924 presidential election that Democrats voting for Progressive candidate Robert La Follette or Republican incumbent Calvin Coolidge would not be allowed to vote in subsequent Democratic primaries. "No man or woman," he proclaimed, "has a right to retain the prestige of being designated as a Democrat and participate in Democratic primaries who votes against the nominees of his or her national convention" (Years later, to suit his political fortunes, Byrd's definition of party loyalty would change). In matters of finance Byrd proved adept at raising funds from businessmen and party leaders; by the end of 1923, he had reduced the state committee's debt to $1,174. There were few political activities in the state that he did not direct or influence.[37]

His long apprenticeship in the Martin machine made Byrd remarkably well prepared to assume its command. Tutored by his father and uncle, he had mastered the arts of politics: tenacity, compromise, loyalty, and teamwork. Having watched Flood subordinate his personal ambitions for the good of the organization, curry favor with people in high places, and deftly carve up his opponents, Harry Byrd became just as adept in playing the game. He, too, would be a tough, ruthless machine politician. But Byrd also shared some of the softer qualities of his predecessor, Senator Martin, whom he greatly admired, calling him "a natural born leader." Both projected the image of a selfless public servant who did not run for office but was sought by the office, who did not dictate policies but consulted experts and suggested solutions. Theirs was a quiet, noncharismatic leadership, devoid of public demagoguery and display, reflecting personal integrity both in private and public life. They attracted people by force of character, by example, by commitment, and by pragmatic decision making. They were both capable of disciplining wayward members but tolerated some dissent as long as it did not undermine their guiding conservative principles of limited spending and low taxes. Distrustful of the masses, neither was committed to a freewheeling democratic political order but preferred the comfort of a controlled electorate whose will they could read with uncanny skill.[38]

The most significant difference between the Martin machine and the new Byrd machine was the close personal supervision that Byrd exercised over his forces. Control of the courthouse, the assembly, and the network of patronage and fees that sustained the loyalty between commanders and lieutenants remained the key to power, while constitutional limitations restricted the electorate, keeping it small and controllable. The Organization remained a group of like-minded men who agreed upon economic policy and paternalistic politics, but Byrd broadened its circle of supporters and established himself as first among equals. What Byrd brought to a revived Organization was an intimate approach. Whereas Martin had left much of the routine operation to Hal Flood and Claude Swanson, preferring to hobnob with railroad executives rather than clerks of the court, Byrd comfortably mingled with the local officeholders, relishing their Brunswick stews and talk of weather and farm prices. He maintained direct contact with them through his many letters and energetic campaigning at election time, and they reciprocated. In addition to the officeholders and farmers, Byrd cultivated friends in the business and banking communities and among journalists to whom he catered with his news releases. His way of leading was not to coerce but to reward with praise, jobs, roads, and legislation. His hands-on leadership generated a firm bond of loyalty that permitted Byrd great freedom to select his candidates for state office and implement the policies he desired. When he moved to the United States Senate in 1933 and had to reduce his participation in local affairs, he relied much more on Ebbie Combs, Frank Wysor, and others to run the state, but he never lost the personal touch. His letters, his attendance at county fairs, his spoken affection for Virginia and its people continued unabated. What he created was a political organization that ran smoothly, efficiently, powerfully, and was beholden to one man for its direction for forty years, an oligarchy far more dominant than the one Thomas Martin had ruled over.[39]

Yet Byrd's power never extended beyond the borders of the Old Dominion. He took his first swim in the waters of national politics in the 1924 presidential campaign. At their state convention Virginia Democrats once again pledged unequivocal support for favorite son Carter Glass as long as he permitted his name to remain in nomination. Reelected state chairman, Byrd assumed control of the Glass campaign at the national convention in New York, which became interminably divided between William Gibbs McAdoo, Wilson's secretary of the treasury from California, and Al Smith, governor of New York. Byrd had expressed "unalterable opposition" to McAdoo's candidacy and refused to let the Virginia delegation vote its mind, which may have cost Glass his only chance at the nomination.[40]

Glass and John W. Davis of West Virginia were the dark-horse candidates, waiting for the expected rush of delegates once the convention tired of the

McAdoo-Smith impasse, but a break appeared impossible as the exhausted delegates struggled through nine days of voting in the longest balloting in presidential convention history. Throughout the steamy Madison Square Garden sessions, Byrd remained confident of Glass's chances. At one point after the seventy-seventh ballot, he and representatives of the other candidates met at a "harmony conference" in Cordell Hull's suite at the Waldorf-Astoria to resolve the stalemate, but they reached no agreement.[41] Glass hoped that a shift of Virginia delegates to McAdoo would be reciprocated by the Californian once it was clear the deadlock could not be broken, but Byrd's insistence on keeping Virginia's vote for Glass throughout the weeklong balloting likely alienated the McAdoo forces, who, when finally released on the one hundredth ballot, looked elsewhere for a candidate.[42] At the end of the one hundred and second ballot, Davis had become the front-runner, but Senator Oscar Underwood of Alabama, known for his opposition to prohibition and the Ku Klux Klan, was making a strong bid. Fearful that Underwood might snatch victory from them, many "dry" delegates rushed to Davis on the next vote, and the suave, articulate corporation attorney was nominated. Glass was certain that on the next ballot he would have received a massive vote from the delegations of New York, New Jersey, Ohio, and Illinois.[43]

Supporters of Glass and McAdoo were furious with Byrd, believing that his mishandling of the Virginia delegation had cost their candidate the nomination. Norman Hamilton, editor of the Portsmouth *Star,* claimed that had Senator Swanson been head of the delegation, Glass would have been nominated. Glass accepted that assessment, telling Byrd personally that he disagreed with his convention strategy, but he did not hold any grudges toward his young friend and commended him for his loyalty, admitting that Byrd's ploy might have worked had one more ballot had been taken. That certainly was Byrd's analysis when he wrote Glass three weeks later that leaders of the New York and Illinois delegations had been ready to commit to him, but "the fear of Underwood . . . stampeded the convention to Davis." Byrd would not miss a Democratic presidential nominating convention for the next thirty-two years, but like this one, few turned out to be happy experiences. Indeed, he never backed a winner.[44]

Byrd gave little attention to the presidential campaign, concentrating instead on protecting Democratic hegemony in Virginia preparatory to his own run for the governorship in 1925. Great effort went into maintaining control of the redeemed Ninth: fund-raising for poll taxes, personal visits, and private correspondence. The major problem, as always, was money. Some help came from the state committee, whose coffers would be replenished by contributions from officeholders in the State Corporation Commission (SCC) and the Bureau of Labor and Industry. Later in the year Byrd wrote Berkley Adams, an

SCC commissioner: "My information is that the funds are not being collected as we expected in Richmond. I hope that your department will come up to your expectations, namely, a minimum of $2,000. The need for funds is much more urgent than ever."[45]

There was considerable Ku Klux Klan activity in the Ninth. Thanks to anti-foreign hysteria generated by the war, the "Invisible Empire" was making a comeback across America in the 1920s. It had little influence in the Old Dominion, but in the Ninth, where party competition forced politicians to latch on to any advantage, the Klan found fertile ground. It seemed to favor the Republicans, but politicians of both parties joined the organization out of political necessity, if only to keep tabs on the opposition. Ebbie Combs deemed it necessary to involve himself in local Klan politics as he was assisting Harry Byrd to become governor a year later. Only months after telling Byrd that he had helped break up a Klan meeting in Bristol that was urging people to vote Republican, Combs was petitioning George Bowden of the Industrial Commission of Virginia for a charter for a provisional Klan chapter in the nearby town of Lebanon. Later he enlisted Bowden and Congressman George Peery in a successful effort to prevent the selection of Republican C. E. Burchfield of Bristol—the personal choice of national leader Hiram Evans—as Grand Dragon for the state of Virginia. Whether Byrd, who never had any use for the Klan, knew of this activity is unknown.[46]

As state chairman Byrd had some difficulty in appeasing the new women voters who wanted equal representation on the state and local Democratic committees. He entreated Swanson: "In view of the great jealousy among the different women of the State, I think it would be probably better not to suggest the appointment of a woman as vice-chairman of the committee. In order to give the women recognition I would like you to think of the question of appointing an executive committee composed of women, one from each congressional district.... I have never seen such jealousy and friction among the women as exists throughout the State." Under Byrd the newly created executive committee did little more than organize women voters, but his successor, J. Murray Hooker, appointed a woman to serve as vice-chairman. Despite such diversions Byrd directed the party to another clean sweep in the 1924 elections. Although he had not used his position directly to advance his upcoming gubernatorial campaign, his frequent communications to the newspapers, public statements, and massive correspondence to party officials provided him with constant publicity and valuable contacts. The Organization that he had restored was stronger than it had ever been, ready now to support his own quest for the governorship.[47]

The Byrd bandwagon had begun as soon as victory in the bond referendum had been achieved, but the party chairman had modestly put off any formal declaration. Years later Byrd claimed that he had not intended to run in 1925 because of his business obligations, but an incident at the Democratic national convention changed his mind. He had been told by prohibition leader Cannon that he was "a promising young man but could not be elected next time because his [Cannon's] organization was supporting Walter Mapp." When Richard Byrd heard this remark, he reportedly told his son, "You have got to run now whether you want to or not."[48] The conversations probably occurred, contributing to the legend that Byrd was a reluctant office seeker, but it is not likely that they changed his mind on the question. He had been discussing the possibility with close advisers, including his father, for some time.[49] Besides, there was no other Organization leader of his stature who could so ably defend the policies he had put in place in the last two years. G. Walter Mapp of Accomac, best known for his authorship of Virginia's prohibition laws, was an Organization independent beholden to the Cannon forces. Congressman R. Walton Moore and former state senator Goolrick were also considered to be mavericks beyond Organization control, while Lieutenant Governor Junius West and state auditor C. Lee Moore had little popular support. The timing for Byrd was perfect; he had youthful energy and extensive support in all areas of the state and was coming off several successful political campaigns. After privately revealing his decision to close friends, Byrd announced for the governorship on November 22, 1924. A noteworthy supporter was Richmond businessman William T. Reed, who wrote his future protégé, "The next politics I expect to play in is to put you in for Governor, and which I feel sure will result in our having four years of business administration, which will materially strengthen our Party in the State."[50]

Byrd's business orientation was apparent in the statement announcing his candidacy, in which he pledged to give Virginia a "progressive, efficient, business-like administration." His biographical sketch, released at the same time, emphasized his experience with his newspaper, the apple orchards, and the Valley Turnpike. He also promised economy in government, early completion of the road system through a fair gas tax, and a reorganization of state government based on simplification, but he gave no details. Perfunctorily supporting public education and public health work, he hoped his ten-year record in the state senate would make further specifics unnecessary.[51]

Formally resigning his position as party chairman, Byrd began organizing immediately. To all his friends he urged an energetic early campaign, telling them to give the impression that victory was assured, a tactic he always found helpful in putting down his competitors. Indeed, early in March, before the race was under way, Byrd announced that he had "no doubt of my nomination or election." Many state officials, desirous of retaining their positions, quickly endorsed him. To manage his campaign he turned to a close friend of his father's, William E. Carson, president of Riverton Lime Company. Carson was an Irish immigrant who had come to America in 1885, taken over his father's lime plant at Riverton, and turned it into a lucrative business. He and his brother Kit developed a fast friendship with neighbor Richard Byrd, and each brother developed a friend-and-mentor relationship with a much-younger son of Byrd, Will with Harry and Kit with Dick. (It was Kit Carson who had invited young Richard to visit him in the Philippines.) The friendships moved Will Carson into Democratic party politics where he served thirty years on the state central committee. His opposition to the state-owned lime-grinding plants favored by Governor Westmoreland Davis cemented the relationship with Byrd, who had come to despise anything Davis supported.[52]

Several of Byrd's potential opponents soon eliminated themselves, leaving only C. Lee Moore and Walter Mapp, both of whom had declared their candidacies much earlier. Shortly after Byrd announced, he ran into Moore and jokingly shouted, "How is the next governor of Virginia?" How much of a jest it was became clear when Moore, whose platform was similar to Byrd's, could not generate any enthusiasm and withdrew from the race in June, not knowing that Byrd had helped to orchestrate "a movement to have [him] retire from the field."[53] All along, Byrd believed Mapp would be his principal rival. A prominent legislator from the Eastern Shore who was best known as the leader of the moral reform element in the state senate, Mapp counted on the vigorous backing of James Cannon and the "drys," but because of their long affiliation with the Organization and Byrd's strong prohibition record, the Anti-Saloon League and Cannon took no public stance in the race. Among Mapp's prominent supporters were bond advocates Goolrick, Coleman, and Vaughn and former governor Westmoreland Davis, who predictably conducted a diatribe against Byrd on the editorial pages of his *Southern Planter*.[54]

The Richmond newspapers also were wary of Byrd's Organization connections and took no partisan position during the campaign. Such impartiality irritated Byrd who did not look favorably on any unkind remarks or adverse publicity. Critical columns about his tenure with the Valley Turnpike led him to write to John Stewart Bryan, publisher of the *News Leader:* "It is obvious that this article was written to do injury to me. Barrett [R. L. C. Barrett, the reporter] has never lost an opportunity to use your columns to place me in an unfavorable light on all public questions." Defending his reporter, Bryan replied that he found nothing "deliberately hostile to you"; he upbraided Byrd for his sensitivity, reminding him, "As a publisher yourself you know by long experience that cost what it may a newspaper's first duty is to give the news, and this involves not only the bare statement of acts, but the current of opinion, and I hope and believe that the *News Leader*, throughout this coming campaign, will not only be a newspaper, but will be an absolutely unbiased, unpartisan, courageous newspaper."[55]

It is ironic that Byrd, who spent a lifetime in the newspaper business and in politics, never fully understood the role of the press in a free society, particularly the adversarial relationship between the press and politicians. He relished praise from the newspapers but became incensed when they "misrepresented" him. He used them constantly to his advantage but could not discern why they were not always so helpful. The fact that he considered Bryan; Louis Jaffe, editor of the Norfolk *Virginian-Pilot;* and Douglas Southall Freeman, editor of the Richmond *News Leader,* to be personal friends made their criticism all the more incomprehensible to him, and he was always trying to influence Bryan and his editors, usually through third parties, to tone down, if not to end, their negative comments. He even looked into the possibility of buying the *Times-Dispatch* during his governorship to counter their "misstatements." Perhaps because he perceived his own newspapers primarily as business enterprises and only occasionally as political soapboxes, he never appreciated the nature of independent investigative journalism. Perhaps it was, as Bryan suggested, a matter of thin skin. Until the fifties Byrd had a peculiar love-hate relationship with the Richmond newspapers whose independence he could not control.[56]

As the campaign opened, Mapp advanced a progressive platform and called upon Byrd to address the issues more specifically. He asked for strict enforcement of the liquor laws, simplified voter registration, revisions to the fee system, simplification in government, and tax equalization through a state tax board. Byrd initially referred voters to his senate record and refused to tie himself down regarding future conditions no one could foresee, but constant questioning from Mapp forced him to particularize. At an address to the Good Roads Association in April—after a *Times-Dispatch* straw poll showed him leading Mapp by a slight margin—Byrd called for a one-cent increase in the gas tax to facilitate road building. Stressing his long record of support for improving the highway system, he repeated his adherence to pay-as-you-go and his opposition to the sectionalism in Virginia that the bond fight had stimulated. Progress, he said, was necessary, but it should be related to the state's ability to pay. Two weeks later Byrd advanced his platform on tax equalization. Declaring that the state board favored by Mapp would be too costly, Byrd preferred local equalization and statewide tax segregation that would leave the taxation of real estate and personal property in the hands of the localities.[57]

In mid-May, Mapp officially began his campaign with a declaration of independence from machine politics. Although he did not repudiate the Organization, he clearly drew the major issue of the campaign. He also rejected the increase in the gas tax as inadequate for future road needs. In addition, the two candidates disagreed on the question of tax equalization and the calling of a constitutional convention through which to implement changes in the government. Mapp wanted a convention but Byrd labeled that process too costly and preferred making changes through the General Assembly. These longtime senate colleagues had a grudging admiration for one another, but in the heat of combat such affection quickly disappeared. Both sides traded accusations that the other was using the offices of the state government to advance his campaign. During their only formal debate—a four-hour marathon in Palmyra on June 22—Mapp claimed that Byrd had asked state employees for contributions when he was Democratic chairman. Since the charge was true, Byrd could not deny it. With about fifty women in the audience, Mapp reminded them that he had supported the suffrage amendment while Byrd had opposed it. Byrd's only defense was that he had voted as his constituents had wanted. These embarrassing moments contributed to Byrd's decision not to enter into another debate. He preferred meeting people rather than making formal speeches, and when he did speak, he wanted assurances that a friendly crowd would be on hand. The candidates made two additional appearances on the same platform in Richmond in late July, but there was no debate format. Their Palmyra confrontation also revealed that in their years in the assembly Byrd had offered only 7 bills and Mapp, 174, most of which Byrd had supported.[58]

The debate also produced the most controversial, if not humorous, issue of the contest. In recounting Byrd's voting record, Mapp offhandedly told his listeners that Byrd had voted against the bill attacking prostitution in the 1916 assembly. Two weeks later a circular appeared in Richmond accusing Byrd of supporting "commercialized sin" in his votes on prostitution and against the reading of the Bible in schools. It would be difficult to imagine a more ludicrous charge, but it was no laughing matter to the candidate. Stung by this attack—which had been attributed to the Anti-Saloon League but which he now blamed on Walter Mapp—Byrd turned the issue into one of his personal integrity. At a press conference, speaking "coolly and calmly," he defended himself against the "vile and malicious attacks." He explained his vote on the vice bill as an "honest and conscientious belief" against taking the property of innocent owners accused of running houses of ill repute. Regarding his vote against the Bible bill, he stated that he had voted only against taking it up out of order in the senate; he favored the reading of the Bible and made a practice of printing verses in his newspaper. He promised to sign such a bill as governor if it was passed by the legislature. Playing the role of the aggrieved victim, Byrd urged Virginians to go to his hometown and ask people about his character. A sheepish Mapp said he had nothing but the highest regard for Byrd's character and claimed that the "moral issue" was a fabrication that distracted attention from the real problems facing Virginia. The "moral issue," however, proved a

powerful plus for Byrd, who now asserted that his moral fitness was the dominant issue of the campaign.[59]

While Byrd did not miss an opportunity to assert his fitness for office, he
continued to avoid specifics on future legislation, preferring to hammer away
at the need for economy, efficiency, and simplicity in government; he likened
the state to a big corporation with the governor as president and the people as
stockholders, who had rights to health, education, and good roads. He could
afford to ignore many of Mapp's questions because of his organizational superiority. The machine that Byrd had put in place was operating flawlessly, while
its consummate director maintained his voluminous correspondence with his
"agents" in the field and toured the state pressing the flesh and speaking the
word. Byrd used all the tricks of modern technology—radio addresses, automobile stickers, slides in the movie houses, and the more traditional picture
cards and buttons—to advertise his candidacy.[60]

A network of people reported to him what Mapp was saying, which issues
concerned voters, how the campaign was going in their area, and what he
should do and to whom he should write. Ebbie Combs seemed to be everywhere in the Ninth District, organizing Byrd's visit, sending out letters, dispensing funds, and preparing the polls. Friends in the courthouses, state
departments, and the General Assembly were very active on his behalf. When
C. Lee Moore withdrew, Byrd quickly enlisted the aid of the auditor's friends,
graciously acknowledging their loyalty to Moore. One of the new converts was
Billy Prieur of Norfolk, who in time would become Byrd's key lieutenant in the
port city.[61] Richard Byrd was particularly helpful in determining strategy and
enlisting former associates to join in his son's crusade. He also served as a personal bodyguard. Before a rally in Purcellville, he heard that someone had
threatened to shoot Harry. A crack shot, "Mr. Dick" said he was going to sit in
the back, and if there was any shooting done, "I'm going to shoot first." The
family did not sit on the stage that night.[62]

The younger Byrd also involved businessmen, school superintendents, lawyers, and bankers in his cause, an indication that economy and efficiency had
replaced prohibition as the important issues in Virginia politics. As A. B. Rawlett of Norfolk reported to Byrd, "The class of people that I look to for support
of your cause in this section are the business men, professional men, men of the
shipping interest and the class of self respecting working men who are qualified
voters. The rabble is not worth a bean hill to any one."

Except for some "radical labor elements," Byrd captured the backing of
organized labor in Virginia. Secretary of Labor and Industry John Hopkins
Hall informed him that the convention of the Virginia Federation of Labor
(VFL) was overwhelmingly for him. Byrd affirmed his interest in the working-
man in his letter to P. W. Miller of the Norfolk Brotherhood of Locomotive

Engineers: "I will in all cases appoint only such men as will be entirely fair to labor and who will protect the rights of the citizens of Virginia. I would not consider any man qualified to hold such an office where the interests of labor are concerned who would not be fair to the laboring men. I have always endeavored, as I am sure an examination of my record will show, to safeguard the proper and legitimate interest of labor, and I have consistently supported legislation looking to that end." When it was discovered that Byrd's auto stickers had been printed in Baltimore without the use of Virginia labor, he quickly corrected the oversight. He would not always be so sensitive to the ranks of labor.[63]

Byrd made a strong effort to involve women in his campaign, despite his very weak record on their behalf. He thanked Mrs. G. T. W. Kern for the support of women, decrying the "slanderous charge" of the *Southern Planter* that he was "unfair" to women: "I have been brought up with a profound admiration for the splendid women of Virginia. . . . I pledge myself to do everything in my power for the women and children of Virginia." Richmond suffragette Mary Cooke Branch Munford promised her support but chided him: "Many of the good women of this City are suggesting that you are but little interested in women as factors in the political life of Virginia. . . . When I give my support it is done heartily and in perfect frankness. Please do not make it so hard in the light of my own experience for me to answer satisfactorily the questions of the women concerning your real interest in them." Adele Clark, president of the Virginia League of Women Voters, was less impressed and supported Mapp. Regarding the female vote in Norfolk, G. W. Lineweaver wrote to Byrd: "Don't let these fool women worry you. I doubt if there will be more than 1500 women votes if that many and we are bound to get at least half of them no matter whether the claquers who are claiming influence stand pat or not." Lineweaver also said they would be working on the Catholic vote in Norfolk but quietly so as not "to affect the anti-Catholic vote. . . . This is being done independently of your organization here for obvious reasons as if it should get out, it might affect the good work being done by leaders of the Ku Klux Klan, who all appear to be for you. . . . It might help if we were to do a little donating to some of Father Brosnan's charitable work in the poorer section of the city."[64]

The ease of Byrd's victory—a 40,000-vote margin—mocked the intensity of the campaign. Mapp ran a hard-fought race, offered some specific proposals, courageously challenged the fee system, and forced Harry Byrd to run an equally energetic campaign. He won what remained of the independent or antimachine vote (including such notables as Henry St. George Tucker and John Garland Pollard), bond supporters, his many friends on the Eastern Shore and in tidewater Virginia, and a few McAdoo people still smoldering from

Byrd's treatment of them at the national convention. But he could not over-come the advantages of the Organization, especially as Byrd had restructured it. The Democratic nominee now commanded a loyal cadre of officeholders from Wise County to Richmond and on to Norfolk who, out of awe for his amazing organizational skills, gratitude for jobs and money he directed their way, and appreciation for his personal interest in them, committed their futures to him. His preaching and practice of economy and efficiency, which he saw as the mandate of the election, attracted a friendly business community willing to underwrite such policies. It was no surprise that Byrd outspent Mapp two to one. The elements of the new machine were in place.

The general election in the fall against the Republicans would be a sleeper compared to the primary. Indeed, the *Times-Dispatch* proclaimed Byrd to be Virginia's next governor three months before the election. Confident of that victory, he resigned his seat in the state senate.[65] For the moment Byrd ap-peared to want "to do as little as possible on account of attending to my large apple crop," but behind the scenes he was preoccupied with matters of person-nel and programs. He worked hard during the fall to line up support for Tom Ozlin as Speaker of the House of Delegates, a key position for advancing his policies. He sounded out many people, particularly businessmen, on his tax segregation plan. Consulting experts in the tax commissioner's office, he care-fully reviewed the figures on real estate and personal property values all the way down to towns and magisterial districts. With C. H. Morrissett of the Leg-islative Reference Bureau, Byrd reviewed data on tax collections and the costs of all government departments. Clearly, some movement was afoot to consoli-date the commissions and departments.[66]

Facing a fait accompli, Republicans had trouble finding candidates. They selected Henry W. Anderson, their best-known spokesman, who had run against Trinkle four years earlier, but he declined the nomination. John Paul, the nominee for attorney general, also withdrew. The Republican state com-mittee then chose S. Harris Hoge of Roanoke, a federal assistant district attor-ney, who reluctantly accepted the nomination to maintain the facade of a two-party system. Democratic chairman Hooker described Hoge as "a very nice fellow, a good lawyer, [who] is well known in this end of the State." He had served a term in the legislature as a Democrat.[67]

Forecasting little difficulty with the Republicans, Byrd proposed to concen-trate on letter writing rather than speechmaking, but he told Combs, "We should take nothing . . . for granted." He instructed Chairman Hooker: "I sent a book of my organization to Vic Hanger, Richmond. Included in this book are about four thousand precinct chairmen and workers and I suggest that you prepare a letter as state chairman of the party and send it to Vic so that he can send it out to this list, urging them to get actively behind the full ticket and asking them to communicate with you in their section. . . . So far as I can see there is no difficulty except to get out the vote." On October 19 Byrd opened his campaign for the governorship with a speech in Harrisonburg that reiterated the themes and promises of the primary.[68]

Only days later Byrd's formal campaign came to an abrupt halt with the death of his father on October 23. Although Richard Byrd had been hospitalized since late September with undiagnosed problems, his death was a complete shock to the family. It was particularly tough on Harry who had relied so heavily on his father for advice and assistance from the beginning of his political career. As he told Billy Reed, "I loved him so dearly that I feel his loss very deeply. No father and son were closer or loved each other more." Gray Williams described the relationship as "so intimate, warm, and affectionate that they were more like two brothers." The elder Byrd had had a distinguished public career and a notable private legal practice. Even after he left the General Assembly to resume his law practice and serve as a United States district attorney, he continued to influence legislators and the law, serving on several commissions, drafting legislation, and advising party leaders, including his son.[69]

Byrd did not resume active campaigning after his father's death, relying on the traditional Democratic vote and the work of his friends, including Walter Mapp, to carry him to victory. Republicans Hoge and Anderson sniped at the Democrats but could do no damage. Byrd won by a 70,000-vote margin, but totals were down considerably from those of four years before. Nevertheless, the moment could be savored as expressions of congratulation poured in and letters of thanks went out. One proud well-wisher recounted an event on polling day that must have warmed his heart. A handicapped voter was making out her ballot in her car when a bird alighted on the hood to the amazement of all present; "this is certainly prophetic and a sign of approval," she wrote. Byrd's joy was tempered by the realization that his father was not there to share it. "I am very sad that Pop is not here to talk over my victory," he telegrammed his mother.[70]

Byrd's preparations for assuming power continued, disrupted only by the incessant pleas for jobs, recommendations for appointments, and requests for the governor-elect to speak and to donate money. He gave further attention to Ozlin's candidacy for the speakership, decided on appointments for state offices, and formalized the tax segregation plan, which was presented to the public just before Christmas 1925. He was particularly interested in the future decisions of the State Corporation Commission, an independent regulatory commission supposedly free from political influence. The SCC chairman, Berkley Adams, assured Byrd that the commission would do "everything in our power" to serve his administration. To demonstrate his frugality Byrd told

Martin Hutchinson that he would sign notary commissions "H. F. Byrd" as they had been mistakenly printed rather than have new ones printed with his name "Harry F. Byrd" as he preferred. Such economy and attention to detail would mark his governorship.[71]

~ 4 ~

Chief Executive

F EW PEOPLE have been as well prepared by temperament and experience
for executive leadership as Harry Byrd. And fewer still have achieved the
success and acclaim he enjoyed while governor. Byrd triumphed because
he knew exactly what he wanted to accomplish, and the strength of his personality and political support enabled him to implement that agenda. His own
success story, grounded on seizing opportunity and working hard, shaped his
view of the world. He desired for himself and for Virginia an environment with
maximum opportunity and minimal limitations for the individual. Government's role in creating this environment was to be helpful and unobtrusive, a
government that was "lean and mean," economical and efficient, with low
taxes, few regulations, and competent services. Byrd's model for success was
the corporation, whose survival was predicated on cutting costs, maximizing
profits, satisfying customers, and cultivating decisive executive leadership. He
was a businessman who wanted a businesslike government.

With some exceptions the previous ten years had witnessed nearly the opposite in the Old Dominion. Distracted by issues of prohibition and war, governors and legislators had allowed plans for modernizing state government to fall
victim to political infighting. The liquor issue had divided the electorate, and
the death of Senator Martin had led to a struggle for power within the Organization. Until Byrd assumed command, the state could not decide how it was
going to build its highways; proposals for governmental simplification led to
proposals to restudy the question; and no agreement could be reached on a
fairer tax structure. The environment for state growth was unstable. Out of a
concern for the future of the Old Dominion, Byrd sought to end this chaos.

Aside from his proposals for a gasoline tax increase and an expressed preference for tax segregation over tax centralization, Byrd had not revealed his
plans during the primary campaign. His almost perfunctory call for a progressive, businesslike government that would require some reorganization did not
inspire hope that he would escape the tradition of Organization orthodoxy. Yet
many clung to the belief that this fresh young face with the name that recalled
past glories would offer new challenges. Richmond *News Leader* editor Douglas

Southall Freeman, who invariably criticized machine politics, said Byrd had two choices. He could adhere to the prevailing conservative philosophy, or he could initiate a forward-looking reform program that would move Virginia into the modern era. Byrd would not disappoint him.[1]

In the interim between election and inauguration, Byrd carefully prepared his tax and reorganization plans, sounding out friends and political advisers.[2] Revealing his superb grasp of the importance of timing and publicity in all things political—a talent he always employed—Byrd counseled in private and then with much fanfare presented his ideas, not only to garner popular support but to generate suggestions that would improve them. As a newspaperman he knew the value of advertising, and throughout his administration he constantly utilized the media, both print and airwaves, to publicize his views. Careful cultivation of publishers and editors was always a high priority with him.

Byrd also made sure that friends were in key leadership positions. For months he had been working to get antibond spokesman Tom Ozlin elected Speaker of the House of Delegates. Ozlin succinctly put the case to him: Keezell "thinks my election is of far more importance to you than it is to me, for he feels that it would be disastrous for there to be a Speaker who is not your friend, and the important committees controlled by people who are not your real friends, but only pretended friends." He gave Byrd the names of legislators he could lobby. Senator Sam Ferguson thought Ozlin's defeat would be seen as a failure for Byrd. "We have simply got to win," he concluded. As a result of this effort, Ozlin eked out a narrow victory over Richmonder Jim Price in the January vote. The stage was now set for the governor-elect's entry.[3]

Preinaugural signs did not bode well for Byrd. A Christmas tree fire had ravaged the executive mansion, causing extensive damage to structure and contents. Mrs. Trinkle and her son, whose sparkler had ignited the tree, narrowly escaped the blaze. The Byrds would be forced to take up quarters in the Hotel Jefferson until the mansion could be repaired.[4] Just days before the inauguration, Sittie's father slipped on ice and suffered a heart attack, and she curtailed her participation in the festivities.[5] Driving himself and his children from Winchester to the city founded by his ancestor, the governor-elect confronted a chilly, drizzly capital that challenged his ever-optimistic disposition.

But the occasional sun that broke through the overcast on that damp first day of February 1926, was more prophetic of the future, as were the saluting cannon whose thunder broke downtown windows. Topped out in a businessman's derby—he had promised a Valley farmer that he would never wear the high silk hat of the patrician—thirty-eight-year-old Harry Byrd became Virginia's youngest governor since Thomas Jefferson.[6] Further befitting his bourgeois inclinations, the apple grower from Winchester rejected private invitations and bade all citizens welcome to the inauguration and the evening reception. Fifteen thousand Virginians braved the elements to accept his generosity and hear his address over loudspeakers, and other less hardy souls listened over the radio; both were firsts for a Virginia governor.[7]

Delivered in his flat, high-pitched voice, the address was vintage Byrd, specific in its points and without rhetorical flourish. After repeating his campaign pledges to reform the fee and tax systems and to promote education and industrial development, he announced his plans for reorganizing state government and increasing the authority of the governor. Evoking images of the Civil War, Byrd credited the heroism of that time for the foundations of today's progress, but he clearly urged Virginians to move beyond the past: "I construe my election as a mandate to me as a businessman to institute the best methods of efficiency and economy in State affairs, so that the people may obtain in the public service a dollar's value for every dollar spent. Useless offices must be abolished, duplicated services must be consolidated, and the manifold activities of the State systematized and directed with the efficiency of a great business corporation." As if to reinforce his intentions, his first official act within hours of his address was to order an eight-hour working day for state employees that would allow for staff reductions. Business had begun.[8]

The inaugural speech and prior publicity of his plans precluded any surprises when he twice addressed the General Assembly in the next two days, but the vigor with which he moved generated a wave of optimism and acclaim. Byrd's first message reiterated his already announced tax plan that had been submitted to the General Assembly the week before. Its primary feature was tax segregation—the separation of tax sources for state and localities—allocating real estate and tangible personal property to the local governments and leaving most of the remaining sources, such as personal income, to the state. This would remove the state from the land assessment business, costing it $3.5 million in revenues but eliminating 841 assessors. Byrd believed his system would provide some equity in local tax rates, thus quelling public dissatisfaction among farmers and landowners, without creating the central tax board preferred by advocates of statewide equalization. To guarantee the permanence of his proposal, he urged its incorporation in the constitution.

To make up for lost revenue, the governor asked for increases in the auto license tax—now to be based on automobile weight rather than horsepower—in the tax on public utilities income, and in taxes on rolling railroad stock. A one-cent increase in the gasoline tax, to be set aside for the counties, would compensate for termination of the $700,000 state appropriation for county road construction. Hoping to encourage new investment and promote industrial development, Byrd proposed cuts in the taxes on industrial capital and on stocks and bonds, but he called for a 1 percent increase in the tax on incomes over $5,000 to ensure there would be no deficit. Byrd's goals were fairness, simplicity, economy, and growth that in turn would reduce tax complaints, cut waste, and attract new residents. An added political bonus was keeping the boys in the courthouses happy by giving them exclusive control over property taxes.[9]

A day later he delivered his second message on governmental reorganization, the major achievement of his governorship. With proposals that one legislator called "revolutionary but sound," Byrd recommended the consolidation of nearly a hundred bureaus into eight departments, abolition of seven boards, commissions, and departments, and reduction of elected state officials from eight to three—the governor, lieutenant governor, and attorney general—creating the "short ballot." As an example of consolidation, the commissions on water power, geology, forestry, and the Hampton Roads Port would be merged into a new commission on conservation and development. Financial accountability would be improved by establishing a uniform accounting system and paying all general-fund collections into the treasury rather than the current arrangement of sixteen separate agencies carrying on fiscal functions.[10] The beneficiary of these changes would be the governor, whose authority to run the state would be vastly enhanced with greater appointive power over positions currently elected by the people or the legislature. To calm fears that he was seeking dictatorial powers, Byrd suggested that any changes in the governor's authority be made effective only after he left office. Future governors, he reminded, would be checked by the one-term rule and the power of the senate to confirm appointments.[11]

Most of the proposals were not new. Byrd himself pointed out that several states had already adopted similar measures. For years Old Dominion governors, notably Claude Swanson and Westmoreland Davis, and legislative commissions had recommended changes in the bureaucracy without success. Many of Byrd's suggestions came directly from the largely ignored 1924 report of the Commission on Simplification and Economy of State and Local Government, which had pointed out the duplication of work and absence of administrative control in its call for consolidation. In reversing this sequence of failures, Byrd relied upon a public now receptive to constructive change, his familiarity with the operations of state government, his personal control of the Organization, and his great attention to procedure and publicity.[12]

Even with a compliant and friendly legislature, Byrd actively lobbied legislators and public to win expeditious ratification of his recommendations. Subject to approval by the voters, the assembly limited statewide elections to the governor, lieutenant governor, and attorney general, with the formerly elected superintendent of public instruction, commissioner of agriculture and immigration, and state treasurer to be appointed by the governor and confirmed by the legislature. Additional appointive powers, such as nominating members of the important State Corporation Commission, were given to the governor. The legislators approved Byrd's request to hire a firm to survey government organization in Virginia at a cost of $25,000, awarded the newly created Conservation and Development Commission $50,000 for a campaign to advertise the assets of the Old Dominion, and placed a lower cap on the compensation of fee officers; to pacify local officials, who were in Richmond to lobby for an acceptable bill, they did not replace the fee system with a salary scale. Byrd's request for an amendment to reduce the lame-duck period of the outgoing governor was also approved, as was his preference to have all state law enforcement officers wear standard uniforms.[13]

The assembly likewise endorsed Byrd's fiscal proposals. Tax segregation passed almost unanimously. A uniform accounting system was adopted, and the number of commissioners of revenue was reduced to one per county. Budget appropriations exceeded projected revenues by $15,000, but Byrd anticipated that economies produced by simplification measures would more than match this, ignoring his earlier criticism of Trinkle, who had defended a similar situation in 1924. His one-cent gasoline tax increase was raised to one and one-half cents to further compensate the counties for their lost highway money, and the auto license tax was made dependent on auto weight. Byrd had taken the first steps in his thorough reorganization of Virginia government. Effusive in its praise of the governor for his masterful direction, the *Times-Dispatch* noted a new spirit of cooperation and harmony in the assembly that replaced the "trimming and trading" of politics as usual.[14]

In spite of its noteworthy accomplishments, the 1926 General Assembly was not marked by liberality. It rejected the federal child labor amendment (which Byrd opposed), killed a compulsory education bill that would have raised the required school age from twelve to fourteen, and, at the governor's request, cut in half a special appropriation for matching gifts to the University of Virginia.[15] More notable was its passage of the Public Assemblage Act that necessitated separate seating of the races at public gatherings. A small but influential group of Virginians, led by internationally known pianist-composer John Powell and Walter Scott Copeland, editor and publisher of the Newport News *Daily Press,* had lobbied for several years with some success to enact a more rigid color line in the Commonwealth. Disturbed by recent assemblies at Hampton Institute, where people had been seated without regard to race, they desired to segregate the races in public meetings. Despite vigorous lobbying by racial moderates and leaders of Hampton Institute, the public assembly segregation law won easy passage. Governor Byrd, who had been urged privately to veto the bill, allowed it to become law without his signature, making Virginia the first and only state to require racial segregation in all places of public entertainment or assemblage.[16]

While personally favoring racial separation, Byrd would have preferred not to have it injected into political debate. Like the liquor question, it was an emotional issue that threatened political stability and economic progress. Indeed, he publicly applauded defeat of a revised racial integrity bill that would have more strictly defined race by ancestry, and privately he told James E. Gregg, principal of Hampton Institute, that the public assemblage bill was "extremely regrettable"; he said he would not have voted for it had he been a member of the assembly but did not feel he could overturn legislation that had been so overwhelmingly approved.[17] His support for antilynching legislation two years later, which won the praise of several black leaders, was similarly motivated by a desire to quell public unrest and preserve a law-and-order image for the Old Dominion that was conducive to outside investment. He had also joined the Commission on Interracial Cooperation, which aimed at improving race relations in the South. But on the question of black voting, Byrd was less sensitive. He desired the retention of a "safeguard against the negro vote" because blacks could hold the balance of power if white apathy produced low voter turnouts. He attributed his gubernatorial victory to an entirely white vote. Writing Robert B. Tunstall on the necessity of keeping the poll tax, Byrd concluded, "I think we should exclude the negro population, as one-third of our population is negro."[18]

Such political self-interest was never far from Byrd's mind, always influencing the extent of his progressivism. The modest revisions to the fee system and the choice of tax segregation over tax centralization were dictated in part by the necessity of maintaining the allegiance of local political officials. Almost as important as the "courthouse crowd" to the perpetuation of his program and power was the creation of a loyal state bureaucracy, now made more responsive to the governor by the reorganization. Here, too, a degree of inefficiency could be tolerated if it served the machine. He advocated no civil service system and no uniform procedure for promotions or salary increases. Key administrative positions in state government were staffed by friends and political allies whose appointive power created a costly, ponderous patronage system where jobs were exchanged for votes and contributions. Virginia would soon have one of the largest state workforces per capita in the country. Harry Byrd's governorship—and succeeding administrations—was the ultimate in "old boy" networks; it included the likes of E. R. Combs, William Carson, Willis Robertson, E. G. Dodson, Hugh Sproul, Beverley Stras, Henry Barbee, and Robert Ailworth, his closest friends, correspondents, and political backers. In addition, already proven bureaucrats and loyalists like John Hopkins Hall, Henry Shirley, C. H. Morrissett, and James Hayes were rewarded with what seemed like lifetime sinecures. Although he often denied having any influence in procuring jobs and proclaimed his intention not to interfere in such matters, Byrd frequently referred supplicants to the appropriate department heads, often with entreaties of his own appended to their letters, especially if they were friends of close friends.[19]

The appointment of acquaintances to high positions gave Byrd not only considerable patronage power but also insights into and influence over the operation of government. Commissioners Louis Epes, Berkley Adams, and William Meade Fletcher were sources of information on the work of the State Corporation Commission, whose decisions impinged on business activity, including Byrd's own apple business. Reflecting his intense interest in road building, Byrd maintained a close relationship with Virginia's highway commissioner, Henry G. Shirley, who, having established a national reputation as director of Maryland's roads, had come to Virginia in 1922 to take over the emerging highway system. Initially, Byrd thought Governor Trinkle had made a mistake in appointing Shirley to be commissioner because he was an engineer and not a businessman, but he quickly changed his opinion. Shirley was now preoccupied with building a superior arterial network for the Old Dominion, but he could not avoid the enormous political pressures for jobs and roads. And Byrd was among the most demanding, lobbying his highway director or the regional commissioners to get roads completed, notably in the Winchester area. Shirley, whom Byrd now flattered as "the best highway head in the country," would dutifully reply with lengthy explanations on why he could or could not do the work.[20]

Byrd's interest in highways produced his first controversy as governor. The issue was the new gasoline tax. Ever since the highway bond issue was rejected in 1923, Byrd had had to walk a tightrope between advocates of faster road construction and defenders of low taxes. Increased construction costs necessitated the one-and-a-half-cent increase in the gas tax, but its unpopularity threatened to undermine pay-as-you-go road financing. When gasoline retailers added another half cent to the increase, Byrd turned on them in a fury, diverting consumer anger from himself to the oil companies. Deploring their action, he promised to publish prices in an effort to prove discrimination against Virginians. Carrying out his own private investigation of the price hikes, Byrd concluded that there was no justification for the increases and called for federal action on this interstate commodity over which states had limited regulatory power. An investigation by the Federal Trade Commission revealed no evidence of discrimination or collusion, but Governor Byrd won praise for his defense of consumer interests.[21]

Summer brought Byrd another chance to demonstrate his newfound consumer advocacy. The Chesapeake and Potomac Telephone Company had requested a $750,000 per year rate increase from the State Corporation Commission. A 1918 law, which Byrd as a state senator had voted for, allowed the company to put its new rates into effect during appeal of an adverse SCC opinion. If the company lost its appeal, it would have to repay the excessive charges, but not the interest earned or the principal to subscribers who had moved—an injustice in the eyes of the governor. On July 31 the SCC approved an increase of only $200,000, and Chesapeake and Potomac prepared to apply its higher rates as it readied an appeal. Probably through Commissioner Louis Epes, Byrd was informed of the adverse ruling before it came down, and rumors abounded that he was prepared to call the General Assembly into special session to change the law. Such intimidation worked. Meeting with company president A. E. Berry, Byrd arranged a "gentleman's agreement" by which Chesapeake and Potomac agreed to postpone application of the unapproved rates until the appeal procedure was completed, at which time it could collect any additional awards retroactively. The company lost its appeal, and Byrd won repeal of the law in the next General Assembly. Although criticized for his insider's knowledge of the SCC's decision (he had written Commissioner Adams about the financial affairs of Chesapeake and Potomac), Byrd was hailed as a champion of the people.[22]

These two examples of corporate selfishness pushed Byrd as far down the progressive road as he would ever go. For a time he continued to criticize the excesses of monopoly, even broaching the possibility of government ownership of utilities. He opposed such a step, but if great combinations of wealth led to unfair prices and reduced competition, he believed government might have to intervene. Corporations should make money, he said, but not at the expense of the people. This "radicalism" from such an arch defender of the free enterprise system may have reflected a brief flirtation with populism brought on by the responsibilities of the office, a feeling that he was the "tribune of the people." Or it may have been an example of the administrative syndrome, the compelling need of executive leaders to act, to meet problems head-on, to find solutions. More likely it represented Byrd's own standard of personal responsibility: corporate leaders, like politicians, should demonstrate a sense of public obligation. Addressing the Virginia Manufacturers Association in Staunton in October, he reiterated his concern about Virginians' lack of interest in public affairs and urged upon his listeners a respect for law and order. What he demanded of himself he was demanding of others.[23]

Riding a crest of public approval, Byrd used the momentum of the recently concluded legislative session to launch his reorganization effort. He wrote every governor to ask for the names and accomplishments of firms that had done efficiency studies in their states. On a trip to New York in early April to bid his brother bon voyage on an expedition to fly over the North Pole, Byrd interviewed several firms, one of which was the New York Bureau of Municipal Research, a branch of the National Institute of Public Administration, whose purpose was the promotion of efficient management of state and local government. Offering the job to Luther Gulick, director of the bureau, Byrd said, "We have a great opportunity to make Virginia one of the models for State government." He foresaw the consolidation of large departments, but he believed the greatest economies would come through small savings, including the elimination of positions. Gulick enthusiastically accepted, indicating that his people could do the work for $16,000—well within the $25,000 appropriation—and be done with a detailed study of the costs and staffing of both state and county administration by the end of the year.[24]

On June 11 Byrd announced formation of a citizens panel that would review the conclusions of the bureau and recommend changes appropriate for the Commonwealth. Composed of thirty-eight prominent Virginians, who served without compensation, the Citizens Committee on Consolidation and Simplification in State and County Governments ostensibly would add its knowledge of the local situation in order to avoid unworkable suggestions from outsiders unfamiliar with the idiosyncrasies of Virginia affairs. In reality, the Reed committee, chaired by William T. Reed, would be a control group to ensure that Byrd's own reorganization agenda was approved while politically undesirable changes were avoided. The group represented a cross section of interests, but most were close to Byrd; they included Organization stalwarts George Keezell, Thomas Burch, Ben Gunter, and Herbert Hutcheson; industrialists Homer Ferguson of Newport News Shipbuilding and Drydock Company and Luke Bradley, president of Virginia Electric Power; representatives of farmers' organizations; several newspapermen; and five women. The blue-ribbon quality of the Citizens Committee improved the chances that the legislature and the public would accept its recommendations.[25]

Two weeks later Byrd rounded out his reorganization team by appointing a constitutional commission to consider amendments to the state constitution required by the reorganization proposals; he preferred a cheaper and more controllable appointed group to an unpredictable constitutional convention. Chaired by Judge Robert Prentis of the Virginia Supreme Court, the commission was also a collection of Byrd associates that included R. Gray Williams (the governor's personal lawyer), William Meade Fletcher, Joseph Chitwood, and former governor Henry Carter Stuart. Byrd clearly knew what he wanted, and he created the requisite mechanisms to achieve it. The efficiency experts, respected Virginia citizens, and the political power and popularity of the governor were in place.[26]

First violin in this ensemble was Billy Reed, with whom Byrd had developed a close personal relationship. Twenty-three years Harry's senior, William T. Reed, Jr., was a wealthy Richmond businessman who became a benefactor of the Democratic Organization. He had worked his way up through his uncle's tobacco company to become president of Larus and Brother Tobacco Company in 1908. His success propelled him onto the boards of several major Virginia companies and to the chairmanships of civic and educational organizations. Five feet ten inches tall and heavyset, the amiable tobacco-chewing Reed entered Byrd's life through their joint service on the Democratic Central Committee and at the 1924 Democratic convention in New York. The death of Richard Byrd, who had been a friend of Reed's, encouraged Harry's reliance on the older man whose life and philosophy so closely paralleled his own. He wrote to Reed, "I expect to lean on you a great deal." And he did. Over the next decade he constantly depended upon Billy Reed for political and business advice, corresponding with him almost daily. Reed was more conservative than Byrd and likely influenced him in that direction as the relationship flourished. Confiding to Gray Williams, Byrd said of Reed: "He is a splendid fellow and one of the best friends I have. . . . He has more influence in public matters than any other man in Richmond."[27]

During the summer and fall of 1926, as the Bureau of Municipal Research investigated the condition of government in the Old Dominion, Byrd outlined his objectives and strategy to Reed. He did not want to push for anything that would not pass; therefore, he insisted that "Gulick, you, and I should not settle on any changes until we can all talk." Reed was in frequent contact with Gulick regarding Byrd's wishes. He confided to the New Yorker that he and Byrd would select men from the Citizens Committee for the subcommittees that would do the important review work and meet with the governor before anything went to the whole committee. The Richmonder was always aware of the political ramifications of the survey. When Gulick itemized valet charges on his expense account, Reed advised him to list such costs under "Laundry and Miscellaneous" in the future. "Some cheap politician could make an hour speech about the expense of the survey and the use of a valet," he warned.[28]

While the reorganization effort was Byrd's highest priority, he did not neglect the more ceremonial functions of his office: opening roads, receiving visiting dignitaries, accepting speaking invitations, and touting the glories of Virginia from Hampton Roads to Wytheville. Indeed, he used these opportunities to argue for his progressive changes that would move the Old Dominion into the front ranks of the states. Celebrating the industrial development of southwest Virginia in a speech at Wytheville in April, he proclaimed a "New Era in Virginia." A month later he was on a weeklong, thousand-mile goodwill tour of the state which took him through fifty-six towns. Conceived by Joseph Smith, head of the Virginia Chamber of Commerce, the entourage of politicians and businessmen rolled by bus through the Southside to Roanoke and the southwest and back to Richmond. At each stop the governor spoke of the need to end sectionalism in the state and to develop industry and tourism, pressing the point that his reorganization changes, especially the short ballot, would speed up that development. Marred only by a fire in a bus seat cushion, the trip, which played to large crowds, left Byrd enthusiastic about Virginia's future.[29]

In his promotional efforts he was careful to pay homage to Virginia's past. Speaking in Baltimore to the Southern Maryland Society, he noted the enormous sacrifices Virginians had made in overcoming the devastation of the Civil War, citing the "heroism [that] laid the foundation for recent progress." At a Fourth of July commemoration at Monticello, the governor lauded the spirit of Jefferson on the hundredth anniversary of his death. He attended the sesquicentennial of the Virginia Resolutions of 1776 with President Coolidge in Williamsburg, where they both spoke and received honorary degrees of law from the College of William and Mary, and he was in Philadelphia for the nation's sesquicentennial where he hailed Virginia's past and future glories. Byrd also instituted the highway signs that marked places of historical importance in the state. The Old Dominion's history would not be obscured in the quest for the "New Era."[30]

Byrd's stamina was remarkable, even for a governor so young. He seemed everywhere at once, pursuing a nonstop regimen that would have exhausted most people. And his finger was into every pie imaginable. He attended to pensions for Confederate veterans and established a special commission to consider battlefield markers on European battlefields where Virginians had fought. Concerned with the beautification of Capitol Square, he prohibited parking in most places and built up a squirrel population that had been depleted by inbreeding.[31] Even his vacations were work. Although he had placed his apple business in the competent hands of brother Tom and Lester Arnold, the governor kept a close eye on weather conditions in the frost-threatening early spring and spent his two-week fall vacation looking after the harvest. During his four years as governor, he never missed an Apple Blossom Festival and twice crowned the queen. It was a pleasant combination of promoting Virginia and his own interests at the same time.[32]

There was scant time for family. Sittie's poor health, now a chronic problem, and her preference for the private life over public ceremony often kept her at home while he was on the road. Because she was not much of a disciplinarian, the children became very independent and it was difficult for Byrd to rein them in as they grew up. Once when ten-year-old Westwood was informed that her father was in conference and could not see her, she grumbled, "Oh shucks. He makes me sick." He was closest to Harry Jr., who frequently went with his father to various activities decked out in the uniform of the governor's military staff given him by Adjutant General William Sale. Even though he had a chauffeur, Byrd preferred to drive himself. In December 1926, racing to Leesburg for a funeral, he skidded off the road and overturned his vehicle. Bruised but unhurt, he returned to Richmond in the same car.[33]

Family matters of another nature distracted Byrd in the spring of 1926. Brother Richard had succeeded in his heroic flight over the North Pole. The event produced a popular delirium that was repeated many times in this zany decade. Technological innovation, the political emancipation of women, greater sexual freedom, and postwar disillusionment forced Americans into an escapist mode during the 1920s. While the darker side of this behavior produced a Red Scare and the revival of the Ku Klux Klan, Americans in their frothier moments turned to sports, movies, and alcohol for their entertainment. Out of their anxiety and the materialistic pleasures of the day, they created bogus heroes and heroines to satisfy their inner needs: Rudolph Valentino, Harry Houdini, Jack Dempsey, Babe Ruth, and Clara Bow. A screw was temporarily loose in the American psyche. Dick Byrd knew this better than most. "Success," he wrote a colleague, "depends on more than hard work—fame will help you to success." This "hero business," as he called it, had to be exploited if his polar missions were to be adequately financed. The focus had to be on a brave, resourceful individual who could generate public acclaim and private funds.[34]

Unlike his more conservative and cautious brothers, Richard Byrd was a fearless adventurer in whom a quest for fame burned bright. His around-the-world tour as a thirteen-year-old had only whetted his enthusiasm for exploration. He graduated from the Naval Academy in 1912, but a football injury made him unfit for sea duty and forced his retirement as an ensign. However, the world war revived his military career, and he opted for flight training as a way to overcome the fleet restrictions. He also began thinking of the future of long-distance flying, but his active duty/retired status denied him significant service opportunities in this field. Duty in Washington, D.C., introduced him to many prominent people, among them Assistant Secretary of the Navy Franklin D. Roosevelt, whom he brought to Virginia for some hunting with his brother.[35]

By the mid-twenties, convinced of the scientific and commercial advances to be made in aviation and the prospects for improved international understanding to be gained through long-distance flying, Dick began to focus his attention on polar exploration. The "hero business" in such an endeavor was also obvious. Thwarted once more by the navy, he determined upon a private expedition, supported by Rockefeller and Ford money.[36] On May 9, 1926, Byrd and Floyd Bennett, flying out of Spitsbergen, Norway, flew over the North Pole, beating an expedition headed by Roald Amundsen of South Pole fame by three days.[37] They returned to America six weeks later to a ticker-tape parade in New York, a reception in Washington where Byrd was toasted by President Coolidge, and a more modest but still enthusiastic parade in Richmond. Congress followed with the Congressional Medal of Honor. Governor Byrd, his mother, and Harry Jr. hurried to New York to participate in the festivities where a photographer captured the aviator and his mother fondly embracing. A new American hero had been born. Harry was very proud of his brother and never begrudged him his notoriety. Their correspondence over the years reveals a close, mutually supportive relationship and sincere interest in each other's work. Indeed, it is likely that Harry believed Dick's stature enhanced his own, for he included him in Virginia affairs whenever possible.[38]

The summer of 1926 also brought with it the first unpleasantness for the new governor. On three consecutive nights in late July, moonshiners killed a state prohibition agent, a machine-gun battle occurred in the midst of a jail breakout in Nelson County, and Maryland crabbers battled officers of the Virginia Fisheries Commission over the seizure of undersized crabs from Virginia waters. Three weeks later a black prisoner accused of criminal assault was taken from the Wytheville jail by a masked mob and killed. His beaten, bullet-riddled body was then dragged behind a car for several miles. When local authorities were unable to determine who the lynchers were, the governor offered a $1,000 reward for their arrest and conviction, but they were never identified. Shortly thereafter Ku Klux Klan activity in the state increased. A Catholic priest was kidnapped in Norfolk, and a masked mob flogged two women in Bristol. In a more public ceremony attended by five thousand Klansmen, Hiram Evans, Imperial Wizard of the national Klan, presented an American flag and flagpole to the College of William and Mary. Although President J. A. C. Chandler received the gift in the spirit of tolerance and law and order—certainly a jibe at Klan activity—the mere acknowledgment of the Klan by a state institution was remarkable. These events may have stimulated the concern about citizen apathy and lawlessness that Byrd expressed to Virginia businessmen only two weeks later.[39]

Another problem for the governor arose in September when the Richmond *Times-Dispatch* published reports of inhumane treatment of veterans at the Davis Clinic adjacent to Southwestern State Hospital at Marion. Dr. E. H. Henderson, superintendent of the hospital and clinic, used the governor's stationery to ask for an investigation, making it likely that Byrd pressured him into the request. Carrying out a quick inquiry, the investigating committee appointed by Byrd concluded that most of the charges were unfounded, but it made several recommendations concerning food quality and support facilities. The governor insisted that Henderson comply with all the suggestions and indicated that he would submit stronger proposals to the General Assembly, but he merely reported compliance when the legislature met.[40]

Faced with such embarrassments, Byrd looked forward to the beginning of a new year and submission of the reorganization report.When the Bureau of Municipal Research delivered its recommendations to him on January 6, 1927, he turned them over to the Reed committee without revealing their substance. Playing the role of the cost-conscious public servant, Byrd did not commit himself to convening the legislature, but there is no doubt that he had decided to call a special session. Any constitutional changes necessitated by the reorganization required approval by two different assemblies—the second of which had to be a regular session—and by the voters. Any delay would push final implementation later into Byrd's term, perhaps even after his departure. He would then be functioning without the efficient restructuring he desired, and he might have to share credit for the changes with others. Besides, he knew exactly what he wanted and estimated that the extent of the economies would easily exceed the cost of a short session. On January 24 he called the special session for March 16, assuring the legislators that the reports of the Reed Citizens Committee and the Prentis Constitutional Commission on constitutional changes would be made public thirty days before this date.[41]

The charade of conscientious deliberation also characterized the committee discussions. Although it did not release its report to the public until February 12, the Reed committee submitted its preliminary recommendations to the governor on January 20, only a few days after receiving the Bureau's handiwork. Much of its work had been done in subcommittee by Reed and politicos George Keezell, Thomas Burch, and David Barger, with Byrd close at hand. At this point the full committee had not seen the complete Bureau survey and some members had not seen any of it.[42]

The committee's major recommendations approximated the proposals already set down by Byrd and those of the 1924 Commission on Simplification and Economy in Government: consolidation into eleven major departments, a uniform accounting system, and the short ballot. However, they were not so comprehensive as the still unpublished bureau report in streamlining structure and eliminating positions, efficiency that Byrd deemed politically unwise or, in the words of the committee, "not appealing to our sound judgment as being practical under conditions existing in Virginia." Bureau suggestions for eliminating the positions of lieutenant governor, state treasurer, and secretary of the Commonwealth were junked in accordance with Byrd's preferences.

Even the agreed-upon consolidation had its limits. Except for those matters in the hands of the governor, Byrd and Reed ensured power would remain decentralized. The new Finance Department, created to bring some unified control over revenues and expenditures in the state, would have no single powerful director, which left it a collection of separate agencies. Although many smaller agencies were abolished, others were retained to reward special interests and preserve patronage sources. Left untouched were the Prison Board and the

Board of Western State Hospital, whose chairmen were Winchester natives who had held their offices for many years. Only thirty offices were lost, not the anticipated eighty. Not all of the agencies dealing with fisheries and wildlife were placed under the new Commission on Conservation and Development as the bureau had recommended, which caused analyst Leslie Lipson to conclude, "The political necessity of conciliating these interests produced the administrative absurdity of a 'department' headed by three independent commissioners." Not surprisingly then, whereas the bureau had estimated its reforms would save $1,366,180, the Reed Committee's estimated savings from the acceptable changes totaled $500,000. Nevertheless, the Reed report, with its stated purpose of making state government more like a business enterprise in order to control the cost of government and lessen the burden of taxation, proposed a major reorganization of state government and was well received by the Virginia press.[43] Byrd was concerned about the differences between the two reports but admitted to Reed that both had to be published. The bureau's summary on county government reorganization, however, was a political bombshell, and Byrd and Reed concluded that that section should be withheld from consideration at this time lest it complicate passage of the state program.[44]

Similar speed and oversight control characterized the work of the Prentis commission. In early January the commission notified the governor that it would complete its work in ninety days, but Byrd urged its members to expedite their consideration, informing them of the amendments he wanted approved. He told Judge Prentis on February 14 that he wished him to speak publicly on the proposed constitutional changes three days later, even though the commission had not yet reported.[45] On February 15 the governor announced a conference on the seventeenth for all newspaper editors in the state to hear Reed and Prentis discuss their respective committees' proposals. Praising the patriotism and progressivism of the press, he stated, "Being a newspaper man myself, I well know the desire of the newspapers in Virginia to render service looking towards the advancement of the Commonwealth." He also knew the value of snaring favorable publicity for his handiwork.[46]

The final Prentis commission report proposed over eighty changes to the constitution, most of them minor, and recommended that they be submitted as a whole to the electorate, not separately. It endorsed the pending amendments on the short ballot and tax segregation. Among its more significant proposals were reduction of the residence requirement for voting from two years to one; reduction of the period for poll tax payments from three years to two; authorization for counties to adopt optional forms of government; election of school superintendents by local school boards; amendments to change the inauguration date of the governor and remove the $5,000 limit on his salary; and a limitation on future bond issues by the state of 1 percent of the assessed value of all land in the state (an estimated limit at that time of $12 million), with any bond issue to be approved by the people.[47]

With the committee reports in hand, Governor Byrd orchestrated a state-wide publicity campaign to win support for the proposals. He flooded the state with personal letters and press releases, mailed copies of the two reports to every member of the General Assembly, and communicated with Virginia's congressmen, asking their views on the amendments and soliciting their approval. Although Byrd knew his own mind and usually had it made up early, he did not make decisions in a vacuum but sought the opinions of friends and political associates. On the eve of the special session, which some called the most important gathering since the 1901–2 constitutional convention, columnist Earle Lutz of the *Times-Dispatch* reported much enthusiasm across the state for the Byrd program. The confident governor spent the preceding weekend in Winchester inspecting his orchards.[48]

On a warm March day that steamed the crowded House chamber, Governor Byrd delivered a thirty-five-minute address in which he reviewed the progress made in his first year and outlined and endorsed the recommendations of the Reed and Prentis committees. Subtly shifting pressure to the delegates, Byrd told them that adoption of the recommendations would fulfill the pledges he had made to the electorate. He proudly referred to the $5,000 cost of the Prentis commission, a figure far below the estimated cost of $500,000 for a constitutional convention. He also noted the increased tax assessments and a treasury surplus of $350,000 that, in his view, confirmed "progress without bonds." The *Times-Dispatch* called it a "business-like" address, without "florid" oratory, that was seriously received by its listeners—just what the head of a corporation would say to his board of directors.

The degree of unanimity in the General Assembly was remarkable. The reorganization bill passed both houses without dissent. The constitutional revisions were approved by the House of Delegates 76–6, and by the senate, 35–1. One reason for this accord was that two of the more controversial elements in the plan—the short ballot and tax segregation—were withdrawn from consideration. Having been approved at the 1926 session, they could not be debated until the next regular session, so to avoid any confusion and to "greatly relieve some of our friends," the governor sent a message to the assembly to eliminate them from discussion.[49]

A few changes to the recommendations, however, were agreed upon. Warned of the specter of "negro domination" if the three-year period for poll tax payments was reduced, the Committee on Privileges and Elections quietly reversed itself on lowering the requirement. The assembly also turned down the proposals for biennial automobile licenses, a reduction in the license fees, and another half-cent gas tax increase. The two houses divided on these issues and could not resolve their differences, in spite of the governor's intervention. Reed and Gulick, the architects of the reorganization, were disappointed that not everything was approved, but both were pleased that such a large portion of their handiwork had passed.[50]

On April 18 Byrd signed the reorganization bill, implementing those features that did not require a constitutional amendment. For the second time in little more than a year, he had masterfully directed his program for change through the legislature with hardly a murmur of opposition. Over that time he had determined what would be done, how it would be done, and who would do it. In the view of some, he was nothing short of being a magician. But Byrd was quick to share the credit with Billy Reed, who had paid the expenses of the Citizens Committee out of his own pocket. "The reforms in government have been due more to you than to any one else," the governor wrote. "Without your counsel and assistance I could have accomplished little."[51]

What remained to complete his program was another session of the General Assembly and a public referendum on the constitutional changes, both set for 1928. In the interim the governor continued to be Virginia's number one booster. Highways and tourism were his primary pursuits. He advocated building roads to state shrines such as Jamestown and Monticello and called for historical markers along roadways, the first of which appeared in Fredericksburg in November. He held regional meetings to bring about closer cooperation between state and county road officials, prophesying that the road system could be completed within ten years through such cooperation. Although he insisted that he had no intention of interfering with the administration of local roads, Byrd was moving toward a total integration of both systems. A tour of the highway system convinced him of the progress being made in extending the arterial network. Indeed, over 2,000 miles would be added to the system during Byrd's governorship, 1,787 of these miles in 1928. Road building was one way to keep the voters happy and prove the efficacy of pay-as-you-go, but the debate between the advocates of bonds and pay-as-you-go continued. North Carolina, which had opted for bonds, was the comparison state. While its citizens enjoyed traveling roads already built, Virginians, relying on the gas tax, inched forward with their road network. However, at the end of twenty years the newer Old Dominion roads were superior. Costs were approximately the same, the interest on bonds being balanced by increased construction costs incurred by waiting. The Tarheel advantage was faster economic development produced in part by earlier construction of its highways.[52]

But highway travel seemed a bit mundane compared to the excitement of the air, and in the spring and summer of 1927, the Lindbergh phenomenon captured the imagination of the world. Once again Harry Byrd was drawn into these events by the activities of his brother, who, casting about for new challenges, entered the competition for the $25,000 Orteig Prize for a flight from New York to Paris. However, when Dick's plane nosed over in a test flight, damaging the plane and injuring Dick and his pilot, the door was opened to a tall, slim stunt pilot from Minnesota named Charles Lindbergh. As four different teams readied their planes, Lindbergh took off from Roosevelt Field, Long Island, on the misty morning of May 20. Thirty-three hours later he landed at Le Bourget Field outside Paris and became an instant celebrity, perhaps the most heroic figure of the twentieth century. When he returned to this country, everyone clamored for a piece of the "Lone Eagle," including the governor of Virginia, who wanted him to stop off in Norfolk to receive the acclaim of Virginians before going on to Washington to meet the president. That could not be arranged, but through the cordial rivalry that had developed between Lindbergh and Dick Byrd, Harry Byrd eventually got to meet America's hero and they became fast friends.[53]

The Lindbergh flight was undoubtedly a spur to air travel, but not always for the good. It became the rage to be the first person to fly from the United States to Hawaii or Rio de Janeiro or Hong Kong. Air races received extensive press coverage, including details on pilots who did not make it; over that summer, twenty fliers were reported missing in various races. Capitalizing on the obsession with flying, Harry Byrd promoted its development in the Old Dominion, appointing a commission to recommend a plan for setting up a statewide network of airfields. When the United States Department of Commerce announced plans to coordinate efforts to paint roof markers for planes, Byrd agreed to join the effort. He also popularized flying by using blimps to travel from Richmond to ceremonial functions around the state, but he stopped the practice after 1929 "when one went out to sea and sunk."[54]

Aviation was just part of Byrd's overall plan to attract industry to the Old Dominion. Through articles, speeches, letters to potential newcomers, trips to New York, and favorable tax policies, he actively recruited new businesses and cultivated good relations with old ones. As he wrote to Pierre S. Du Pont, "If any of your industrial operations in Virginia have any difficulties that can be aided by the State administration, I would be very grateful if you would have your officials call the same to my attention." The first national advertisement extolling Virginia as a location for business appeared in the New York *Times* in September 1927, part of the $50,000 appropriation by the General Assembly to publicize the state. Coincidentally, just days later Du Pont announced construction of a rayon plant at Ampthill outside Richmond, and Allied Chemical Corporation indicated it would construct a nitrate plant at Hopewell. The International Rayon Corporation had earlier committed to a new plant in Covington after vigorous wooing by the governor.[55]

Along with the aviation craze and Gene Tunney's second victory over Jack

Dempsey in the famous "long count," Byrd could not be blamed if he thought he was reliving the events of the previous year. Gas prices came back for a second round of sparring with the governor. Once more Byrd complained that Virginians were paying too much for gas and accused Standard Oil of New Jersey of price fixing. He also protested high freight rates on coal coming from the Virginia fields, claiming that the Interstate Commerce Commission was not protecting consumers but northern mineowners who enjoyed lower rates. As with the gas prices, Byrd lacked authority to do anything, but his reputation as a defender of the public interest was enhanced. Another conflict with Virginia watermen, who had raided private oyster beds in the York River in violation of state lease arrangements, forced Byrd to arrange a truce that provided for a resurvey of the disputed area. And another lynching occurred, this one near the border between Kentucky and Virginia. Although the sheriff of Wise County reported that the lynching involved no Virginians and actually had occurred in Kentucky, Byrd was quick to condemn the crime as a "cowardly act" and offered the services of the state to apprehend the perpetrators.[56]

As Byrd prepared for his next and last General Assembly session, he generated controversy by appointing Ebbie Combs to be the state comptroller in the Division of Accounts and Control in the newly created Department of Finance. Combs was an Organization warhorse who had come up through the ranks of Ninth District politics and was now an influential member of the governor's inner circle of advisers. However, he lacked training in fiscal administration, and the appointment raised charges of cronyism from the press, especially the *News Leader*. Recognizing the essential contradiction between pursuing efficiency and distributing spoils, Byrd knew criticism would be forthcoming and so delayed the announcement for several months, but he desired a trusted friend in this position and wished to reward Combs for his loyal service.[57]

In December, Byrd convened a gathering of journalists to announce his "Program of Progress" for Virginia over the next two years. Highlighted by a $1 million tax cut to attract new industries and residents, the plan called for considerable money to be spent on state hospitals and the new Shenandoah National Park. Moreover, the governor boasted that the deficit had been turned into a $2.6 million surplus which justified the tax cuts and new expenditures. The *Times-Dispatch* complimented Byrd for not resting on his laurels but investing in Virginia's future.[58]

Ever the master publicist, Byrd distributed copies of his "Program of Progress" across the state to businessmen and members of the legislature. Predictably, support was nearly unanimous. Senator Glass's son Powell said that Byrd was "the only public man he had ever known who could raise the taxes of the people and make them like it and then reduce the taxes of the people in such as way as to make them forget you have ever raised them." Delegate Bill Tuck

wrote him: "The members of the General Assembly and the leaders are unafraid to follow you because they know that you will stick up and fight for what you believe to be right and for the policies of your administration. I believe you are popular because you seem to be unafraid of unpopularity."[59]

Tuck had accurately assessed the governor's support, but he exaggerated his willingness to do the unpopular thing. Byrd did not lack political backbone, but he usually carefully tested the political waters before embarking upon a course of action. This kept public controversy to a minimum, did not expend political capital, and maintained the image of the forceful but flexible leader who always seemed to do the right thing. Furthermore, Byrd knew that most of what he was pursuing already had the backing of Virginia's small electorate. And he knew the leaders of the Organization were committed to him as well. The risks of leadership in the Old Dominion were not very great.

Byrd's opening address to the General Assembly on January 11, 1928, aptly entitled "Virginia's Business Government," reviewed the successes of the past two years: the economic development, the implementation of the reorganization plan with its accompanying savings, the ending of sectionalism in the state, and the fiscal solvency of the Commonwealth. His second message five days later looked forward. Encompassing his "Program of Progress," it was divided into two sections, one on taxation and one on education. The governor wanted to repeal a variety of taxes on stocks and bonds, reduce the tax on capital in business, and make charitable contributions and some taxes deductible from income taxes. Increased revenues produced by prosperity and government economies would make up for the $1.2 million in tax cuts. Byrd requested an additional half-cent increase in the gasoline tax to add 1,500 miles to the highway system and to relieve the counties of road expenses. The nearly $38 million budget included a surplus of $317,000. Once more the editor of the *Times-Dispatch* praised the messages for their businesslike quality and the lack of "high flown phrases."[60]

In his education message the governor was following up on the recent findings of the Educational Survey Commission that he had created. Despite the rushed nature of the survey, the commission produced a very forthright document that analyzed the abysmal situation of education in the Old Dominion, now ranked forty-third in the nation in a federal Bureau of Education report. Surprisingly, the oversight citizens committee, chaired by James Barton, a Richmond attorney, concurred in most of the commission's recommendations. The report called for improvements in teachers' salaries and retirement systems, updated teaching methods, better supervision of teachers, better textbook adoption procedures, stronger compulsory attendance laws and a 160-day-minimum school year, free high schools, money for libraries, a uniform accounting system for all school systems, school consolidation, and more state aid to the weak rural schools. It urged that school boards be elected instead of being appointed and recommended that the local boards rather than the State Board of Education be allowed to appoint division superintendents, two very democratic suggestions that threatened machine power and patronage. In higher education the commission recommended that state aid be terminated for Virginia Military Institute because of duplication of programs elsewhere and time-consuming military training. It requested creation of a chancellor of higher education who would coordinate course and degree programs at state colleges in order to avoid duplication.[61]

Byrd's response was cautious. He called for an increase in the school appropriation of $1.25 million, but rejected the concept of a powerful university chancellor and opposed the end of state aid to VMI, a move he deemed "not acceptable to the people of the state" and objectionable to him personally. Byrd was very fond of VMI and hoped that all his sons might attend college there because of its reputation for building manliness and instilling discipline. On the issue of local school boards, he asked for their elimination rather than their popular election, with their work to be done by the boards of supervisors. Combs had convinced Byrd that more local elections would give the political opposition more opportunities to gain power. Other specifics of the report were ignored.[62]

The General Assembly took its lead from the governor, enacting a uniform accounting system for the schools and, in place of a state chancellor, establishing a council of state college presidents to reduce overlap. It did not abolish local school boards as Byrd had recommended, but neither did it allow for their election. The question of a coordinate women's liberal arts college at the University of Virginia, under consideration for over a decade, was referred to another commission to study, the assembly's usual tactic. Responding to concerns about improvements in black education, legislators defeated a compulsory education bill but passed a new school code that set a minimum school term of 140 days. There would be no revolution in Virginia education. On this occasion tradition, economy, and politics were more than a match for efficiency and competency.[63]

Byrd's concern for education was perfunctory. He was proud of the increased spending for schools during his administration—notably in capital outlays at Virginia's colleges—but this did not begin to meet the need. There was little effort to equalize expenditures between cities and counties and between white and black schools. Furthermore, his activity on behalf of education was modest. By law the governor was a member of the State Board of Education, but Byrd attended meetings infrequently, had minimal correspondence with State Superintendent Harris Hart, and offered no suggestions of his own in this area. He believed economies in present performance, not bond issues, would provide the capital for expansion without increasing taxes. That was Byrd's prescription for progress: do it better with what you have. For the moment that sufficed, but as times changed, it proved to be a prescription for backwardness. A student of education expenditures in Virginia concluded, "Unquestionably the failure on the part of the state to meet its obligations in the adequate support of education is due more to political attitude than to the inability to pay."[64]

The governor recommended two other items in his message of January 16. He requested authorization to solicit and collect private contributions for the raising of a statue of Robert E. Lee, to be placed inside the Capitol where Lee had accepted command of Virginia's troops. Byrd had long desired to initiate this effort to memorialize the greatest of all his heroes. The goal was $25,000 with no contribution to be more than $250.[65]

His other request was for a state antilynching law that would make such a crime a state offense and require localities where the lynchings occurred to pay $2,500 to the estates of the victims. Byrd had been angered by the recent mob actions in the state and sought legislation that would prevent their reoccurrence. He had also been influenced by the courageous editorials of Louis Jaffe of the Norfolk *Virginian-Pilot* and the possibility of a federal antilynching law, which he perceived to be an unwarranted intrusion into the rights of states.

Jaffe first broached the subject of a state antilynching law to Byrd after the Wytheville incident. When a potential lynching loomed in Isle of Wight County, Jaffe urged the governor to intervene, but Byrd demurred, believing publicity from his office would worsen the situation. After the second lynching occurred on the Kentucky border, Jaffe reminded Byrd of the need for state legislation and offered his own draft bill. He was quick to applaud the governor for proposing this law and wrote a series of hard-hitting editorials in its support. The final bill was stripped of its penalty provision, but what remained was one of the strongest antilynching laws in the country. Byrd proudly referred to the law for years thereafter, claiming that no lynchings had occurred in Virginia since its passage (it is likely that one did take place in Fauquier County in 1932). Jaffe, too, was amply rewarded for his efforts, receiving a 1929 Pulitzer Prize for his crusade against lynching.[66]

In addition to these requests, the governor submitted to the legislature the report of the New York Bureau of Municipal Research on county government in Virginia, a full year after its completion. Byrd and Reed had worked hard to prevent its publication until after the public referendum on the reorganization amendments was held. Copies of the report proved hard to come by; in fact, the governor, who never seemed to have one available, told Luther Gulick that the Virginia constitution prevented consideration of the report. Embarrassed by the subject, Byrd admitted to Professor Wilson Gee of the University of Virginia that he did not want his name mentioned in any debate on county government.[67]

The reason for his concern was apparent in the report's call for a total overhaul of local government in the state. The bureau concluded that county government had a "scattered, disjointed, and irresponsible type of organization" and was "grossly political, careless, wasteful and thoroughly inefficient." It believed a modest reform would save $1.5 million. It recommended a county manager or administrator system, administrative consolidation of counties that were too poor to operate effectively, elimination of the fee system, which was a haven of nepotism and corruption, and establishment of better accounting systems, including placing county funds into interest-paying accounts. It also suggested the elimination of several less significant county officers and an increase in the legislative authority of the boards of supervisors, which would give them power to do what the General Assembly now did for them.

Since the report threatened the local power base of the Organization, Byrd merely "commended" it to the assembly for its consideration, recommending only a few specific money savers like the interest-bearing accounts. He rationalized that under the new constitution counties would be able to reform themselves, but little was done. The failure to reform county government demonstrated once again the priority of politics over economy and efficiency; Byrd could not afford to alienate the local officials who were such an important cog in his machine by reducing their autonomy, regardless of their incompetence. As Reed remarked to Byrd two years later when another commission on county government was proposed, "I shudder to think of the trouble and ill feeling that is going to result from . . . any [proposal] that attempts to dictate to the clerks, treasurers, and county officials."[68]

Disregarding the bureau's report on county government, the 1928 General Assembly assented to the rest of the governor's agenda. The short ballot amendment passed easily, albeit with some opposition, including that of Delegate Jim Price of Richmond, a future adversary of Byrd. All but one of the other amendments was also approved. Organization leaders decided that the amendments—three on the short ballot, one on tax segregation, and one blanket amendment for all other changes—would each be listed separately on the ballot and would be presented to the people in a June referendum, thus avoiding conflicts with the upcoming primary and general elections. In fiscal matters the legislature approved the tax reductions, the gas tax increase, an additional advertising stipend for the Conservation and Development Commission, and a $1 million appropriation for the Shenandoah National Park. Based on his earlier experience, Byrd requested and won the right to obtain disclosure of gas prices from distributors. In what the *Times-Dispatch* called an "epochal" session, the legislature approved six hundred bills. Douglas Freeman described the proceedings for his vacationing boss, John Stewart Bryan: "The legislature has gone ahead on its program with very little interruption to the smooth and silk-like ease of Byrd's control. He has not lost a single measure of any consequence this year. . . . He is more persuasive with the General Assembly than ever."[69]

At a testimonial dinner for the governor on the eve of adjournment, Byrd cited the achievements of the assembly, which he believed put Virginia in the van of progressive states, particularly in its ability to attract new business. It was a joyous affair, with the delegates poking fun at the governor by "passing" a bill that required all apple growers to disclose their prices. The praise showered upon him by speaker after speaker only confirmed the enormous respect they had for his leadership. Days later editorial pages hailed him as one of Virginia's greatest chief executives.[70]

Byrd's success in the Old Dominion had also attracted national recognition. In the past year he had addressed the Georgia legislature on the subject of Virginia's reorganization and had convened the first session of the Institute of Public Affairs at the University of Virginia with a speech on the same topic. Praised by Governor Angus McLean of North Carolina as one of the nation's most effective governors, Byrd was being mentioned as a possible vice-presidential candidate in the upcoming election. He wrote and was the subject of magazine articles about his work, the titles and contents of which clearly revealed his concept of state government. "It is on the broad basis of sound business economics that the business of the state should be conducted," he stated. In a general letter to local officials, he declared, "Every Virginian is a stockholder in two great business corporations; first, the county or city in which he lives, and second, the State."[71] William Reed accurately described his friend's mind-set when, writing to George Allen of New York, he said, "We have a real business Governor, and his one idea is to put the old state on a sane, sound business basis, and with assurance to our citizens that their property will not be confiscated by taxation, and that the policy of the state will be to get near as possible a hundred percent out of every dollar now collected."[72]

For the moment Byrd deferred consideration of higher office, preoccupied as he was with the referendum on the constitutional amendments three months hence. A question had arisen over whether people would be able to vote in the June 19 election if they had not paid their $1.50 poll tax six months earlier. Byrd obtained a ruling from Attorney General John Saunders that those qualifying to vote in the November election by paying their poll tax by the May 5 deadline could vote in the forthcoming referendum. Another timing problem concerned the reporting of poll tax payers. The law allowed local officials so much time to post lists of paid-up voters that the referendum would be over before the lists were prepared. Byrd wrote every county and city treasurer requesting them to post the lists as soon as possible after the May 5 deadline, and with only one exception, all complied, another example of the esteem in which he was held.[73]

With the campaign under way, Byrd traveled to the courthouses to speak on the amendments, often driving himself to the talks; one day in Norfolk he made four separate speeches. He prepared position papers on the amendments and set up an organization much like that for regular elections with headquarters in Richmond and a speakers list of those who would carry the message to whoever would listen, all of this financed by private donations. The governor directed most of his effort toward defending the short ballot. The opposition claimed this mechanism was undemocratic and unduly increased the appointive power of the governor to dictatorial levels. Byrd responded by pointing out the many safeguards against the abuse of power. More positively, he argued that the change only affected three administrative positions and would allow the governor to build a more effective, efficient administration.[74]

Two very different organizations, the Virginia Education Association (VEA) and the Ku Klux Klan, provided the most vigorous dissent. The teachers' group believed that tax segregation might adversely affect the funding of education by denying the state needed revenue in times of depression; it also preferred the election of the state superintendent, fearing the position would become politicized if open to appointment. Resenting the governor's rejection of the Barton commission recommendations, VEA's president, J. J. Kelly, Jr., urged his sixteen thousand members to defeat the amendments. Accusing Kelly of advancing his own personal interests at the expense of state progress, Byrd defended his record of doing his "utmost to promote education in Virginia."[75]

The Klan, never strong in Virginia, was likely flexing its political muscle in preparation for a campaign against Al Smith in November. It may also have been upset with Byrd's antilynching efforts. In Covington the Klansmen distributed pamphlets opposing the amendments and burned crosses and exploded firecrackers near where the governor was speaking. Shortly afterward Byrd received an anonymous letter threatening him with a flogging and warning, "We will show you what power is when we finish with you." Although signed "KKK," it was disavowed by the Grand Dragon of Virginia. Byrd had no use for the Klan, and this episode confirmed his low estimate of the night riders.[76]

As the election drew to a close, Byrd seemed to be everywhere—tidewater, the southwest, the Valley—praising the amendments, emphasizing their importance for continuing Virginia's progress, and condemning his critics as naysayers. He warned that the nation would judge it a backward step for Virginia if the amendments were defeated. Although all the proposals passed, the final votes were well under the predicted victory margins of 20,000 to 30,000 votes. Tax segregation won by the largest margin, 15,560, but the three short ballot amendments squeaked through by margins of less than 4,000 votes each out of 135,000 to 145,000 votes cast. Many cities voted against the proposals, as did five of the nine congressional districts. Only solid majorities in the Valley and the southwest saved the day. As Byrd had feared, voter apathy, overconfidence, and a preoccupation with the national political scene kept the turnout low and almost cost him his victory.[77] Nevertheless, the success of the vote, however close, was the capstone to Byrd's reorganization efforts, a reward for his courage and perseverance and a confirmation of his leadership of state and party. As Henry Shirley wrote him, "If you had not thrown your whole energy and influence into the campaign the whole revision would have gone down in an avalanche of defeat." Summarizing his achievements in his own words a month later, Byrd said that he was saving the state $800,000 a year through a much more efficient bureaucracy, particularly the new accounting system which provided him at three o'clock every afternoon a detailed statement of disbursements, receipts, and balance for the day. Could anything be more beautiful to a chief executive officer?[78]

~ 5 ~

"Rum, Romanism, and Rebellion"

U
NTIL 1970, WHEN ANNUAL legislative sessions were adopted, Virginia's governor, limited to a single term, usually faced a lame-duck period
after the second General Assembly session. Talk immediately turned
to a possible successor, and the governor's last year was dominated by that
upcoming election. The incumbent had no additional legislative responsibilities other than to prepare a budget for the next assembly that would likely be
modified by the successor. Of course, new issues could arise and special sessions
could be called, but for the most part the productive years were over.

This was true for Harry Byrd as well, with the lame-duck period shortened
only by the additional three-month campaign to win public approval of his
reorganization scheme. The mountaintop had been reached. His remaining
eighteen months in office would be dominated by the presidential election in
1928 and the gubernatorial election in 1929, both very important to Byrd and
the future of Virginia politics but having little impact on his role as governor.
Much of his time would be spent fulfilling the ceremonial obligations of the
office, playing booster, activating the changes in government, and tying down
loose ends. However, the spirit with which Byrd pursued these more mundane
activities reinforced his image as a dynamic chief executive. Even though he
was a lame duck, he did not fly like one.

One problem which consumed his attention for the remainder of his term,
but for which he never found an adequate solution, was the "oyster war" in
Mobjack Bay. The issue pitted the individualistic watermen of the Chesapeake
Bay, who plied their trade on the "public rocks" of Virginia's tidal estuaries—
the natural oyster beds that were open to all—against the holders of "leased
rocks," who had exclusive rights to plant, cultivate, and harvest their leased
areas. In an effort to develop the oyster business, the state had entered into
these lease arrangements years before, conducting surveys to distinguish the
public rocks from the artificially planted areas. Disputes periodically arose over
the survey lines and the extent of these leases. The law supposedly restricted
them to 250 acres per individual, but two commissioners of fisheries, including
Byrd's appointee, Harry R. Houston, had liberally interpreted this as a limit on

a specific assignment, not the total number of acres one person could hold. As a result, Frank Darling of Hampton held 4,000 acres under eighteen different leases, each in a different name. The oystermen, facing depleted stocks and competition with the planters, a problem they had been experiencing for years, sought new surveys and interpretations and threatened to take sterner action if their demands were not met.[1]

The "tongers" (known by the tongs with which they picked the rocks) had already made one raid on Darling's planting beds in October 1927, and Governor Byrd intervened to arrange a truce by promising a new survey. Late in the year they invaded the leased grounds again, and Fisheries Commission boats drove them off. Darling asked for and won an injunction against the tongers for interfering with his business and violating the earlier agreement reached in Governor Byrd's office. The governor, adhering to his law and order precept, ordered Houston to prevent any trespassing, but shortly thereafter, he held a conference with Darling and Houston and reached a tentative compromise whereby Darling agreed to give up all but approximately forty acres in the area.[2]

Days later, as the 1928 General Assembly was convening, the war broke out in full. In the dead of night, the oystermen invaded Mobjack Bay, fired upon a state patrol boat, and proceeded to harvest Darling's beds. At the request of Houston and the commonwealth's attorney of Gloucester County, Byrd activated three state national guard units from Norfolk, Richmond, and Petersburg (145 men) and dispatched them to the war zone on January 13 to uphold the law, over the protests of the Gloucester sheriff, who believed the situation could be handled by local authorities. The peaceful community that the guardsmen found confirmed the sheriff's opinion, and the troops were withdrawn four days later. Assigned by the governor to investigate, Colonel Willard Newbill, assistant adjutant general of the Virginia National Guard, got Darling and the tongers to try their compromise again. Darling would give up 2,400 acres after dredging forty of them but could keep 1,600 acres on the Mathews County side of the bay. The tongers agreed to drop civil action against Darling for lease violations.[3]

For the next two years, an uneasy truce was maintained between tongers and planters while the issues between them proceeded through administrative and legal channels. In early 1929 the antagonists confronted one another on whether planters could clear their stock from resurveyed beds found to be public or had to turn over the beds to the public domain immediately. Fifty thousand bushels of oysters were at stake. Asked by Commissioner Houston for a ruling, Attorney General John Saunders decided that planters could scrape their beds before returning them to public use if their plantings had been based on an erroneous old survey. The Fisheries Commission would judge the validity of the claims. Believing the commission to be partial to planters, tongers announced that they would seize the grounds in defiance of the ruling. The oyster war threatened to erupt into violence once more.

On February 5, Houston's armed patrol boats and the Gloucester sheriff arrested sixty-two tongers for picking oysters from the disputed grounds. The governor, who had been told by Houston that troops would not be necessary, approved the action against the "illegal trespass," but he presided over yet another conference, which resulted in an agreement to let an impartial judge decide the matter with all arrest charges dropped. In appreciation, the tongers sent Byrd a barrel of oysters. Less than two weeks later, Judge Floyd Roberts from Bristol ruled in favor of the tongers and ordered an immediate abandonment of the beds, but his decision was reversed by the state supreme court seven months later, which gave the planters two years to remove oysters before returning the beds to the public. When rumors arose that the oystermen were going into the private beds before they could be dredged, an outraged governor ordered the Fisheries Commission to purchase 200 rounds of army ammunition. The law would be upheld. Ill will remained between the two groups, and Byrd was glad to pass the problem on to his successor and another fisheries study.[4]

Byrd's responses to the oyster war reflected his commitment to law and order but also a flexibility on negotiation and solution that was apparent in other legal disputes as well. Toughness was often tempered by considerations of economy, politics, and compassion. To save money as well as to decrease crime, he approved the use of jail prisoners on public roads. Tolerating no clemency for drunken drivers, he vigorously enforced the prohibition statutes, with the result that criminal convictions went up and prisons were overfilling. In 1928–29, 3,185 Virginians were arrested for violating the drinking laws and 35,655 gallons of liquor were seized. Rejecting the establishment of a parole program to alleviate jail crowding, he authorized another commission to investigate the problem.[5] Usually he granted no pardons before the prisoners served at least one-half their term, but he was open to clemency appeals and gained wide renown for pardoning Sidna Allen and Wesley Edwards, convicted accomplices of the Allen gang that had shot up the Carroll County courthouse in 1912. He also showed leniency to several county treasurers who were in arrears with their accounts, allowing them to retire gracefully and pay back the shortages without penalty.[6]

Another issue that consumed much of Byrd's time as governor was the creation of the Shenandoah National Park. Harry Byrd's concern for conservation was driven primarily by its connection to state development; he favored conserving resources to attract outside industry and tourists. His establishment of the aptly named Commission on Conservation and Development attests to this. Revealing of Byrd's sentiments was his advice to A. Willis Robertson, his

Game and Inland Fisheries commissioner, who claimed Virginia was one of the most backward states in the nation on pollution matters. When Robertson questioned the impact on fish of the effluent from the new rayon plant to be located in Covington, Byrd told him not to raise the issue lest he discourage the industry from coming.[7]

But Byrd also had a genuine love for the land that extended back to his childhood days on his grandfather's farm in Appomattox and was strengthened by his lifelong involvement in apple orcharding. He loved to hike and to hunt, especially in the Blue Ridge Mountains and the Shenandoah Valley. Harry had sold his father's cabin at the Skyland resort near Luray in 1921, but his fondness for the place certainly made him an enthusiastic backer of a national park in the area.[8]

George Freeman Pollock, the owner of Skyland, believed in the preservation of natural scenic wonders. Informed by a friend in 1924 of the search for a national park site in the southern Appalachians, Pollock leaped at the opportunity to save his treasured Skyland for posterity. He was joined by L. Ferdinand Zerkel, a Luray real estate salesman, who represented a local business group interested in developing the area's commercial opportunities. Pollock and Zerkel formed the Northern Virginia National Park Association to lobby a committee of conservationists set up by the Department of Interior for the Skyland site. They won the committee's recommendation for creation of a park in the northern Blue Ridge of Virginia, but competing proposals from other states threatened the selection. To secure their interests, five hundred Virginians traveled to Washington in late January 1925 to lobby congressmen and President Coolidge. Among their numbers were Governor Trinkle and Harry Byrd—only recently announced for the governorship—who was elected chairman of the steering committee. Byrd was likely drawn into this work by the overtures of Zerkel and John Crown, editor of Byrd's Harrisonburg newspaper. Since no federal funds were to be expended for the purchase of land for the park, Virginians launched a major fund-raising effort to demonstrate their commitment. The initial goal was $2.5 million, the amount estimated to purchase 400,000 acres between Front Royal and Waynesboro.[9]

From the day of his inauguration to the opening of Shenandoah National Park ten years later, Harry Byrd was actively involved in its establishment. When fund-raising slowed, he assumed the chairmanship of a statewide effort that raised a reduced $1.25 million objective within a month's time. In April 1926 the park commission recommended creation of the Shenandoah and Great Smoky national parks, and President Coolidge signed the implementing legislation on May 22, 1926.[10]

But all was not smooth sailing. Collection of pledges lagged and questions arose over the propriety of the fund-raising effort. Following the examples of

North Carolina and Tennessee, which were already using state funds to acquire land for the Great Smoky Park, Byrd directed Will Carson, chairman of the Commission on Conservation and Development, to assume the tasks of pledge collection and land acquisition. Seeing an opportunity to dramatize the work of the Commission, Carson energetically carried out his new charge. By spring 1927 he had collected about half of the pledges, but he also discovered that land prices far exceeded earlier estimates: the cost of the land would be $6 million, not $2 million. When the new estimate was announced, one commissioner recalled that it was like "a bomb had been exploded in the room."[11] Carson immediately urged Byrd to cut the size of the park in half by eliminating some of the higher-priced land. The governor, who had feared this predicament, lobbied with Department of Interior officials and won a reduction. He also asked the 1928 General Assembly for a $1 million appropriation for the park to supplement private contributions. Completion of the park, which was eventually reduced in size to 160,000 acres—a "shoestring" four miles wide and seventy-seven miles long—awaited the administration of Franklin Roosevelt, but its existence owed much to the vision and diligence of men like George Pollock, Will Carson, and Harry Byrd.[12]

The creation of Shenandoah National Park for both scenic and commercial purposes exemplified the schizophrenic nature of the Conservation and Development Commission, a split also apparent in the minds of its two creators, Harry Byrd and Will Carson. Both believed the commission could play a very constructive role in state development, but whereas Byrd emphasized the need to attract industry, Carson preferred to develop Virginia's natural resources and history to lure tourists and businessmen. The difference was one of style, a question of ballyhoo and boosterism versus a more subtle advertising effort. In tradition-bound Virginia, Carson found a ready audience for his approach, even within the business community. Byrd, who came to see the value of the tourist trade, met frequently with his new commission and offered many suggestions, but the driving force in its work was Will Carson.[13]

Carson eventually ran afoul of Harry Byrd, and their friendship withered because of Carson's ambition for higher office and his efforts to keep the commission out of politics. He was mentioned as a possible successor to Byrd but withdrew his name from consideration for the governorship in 1929 in the interests of party unity. Shortly thereafter he had a run-in with the departing governor over the restructuring of his agency. Tom Ozlin, retiring Speaker of the House, wanted a new position in the state bureaucracy; he had his eye on the post of executive secretary to the commission, then held by Elmer O. Fippin. Ozlin supported a bill in the 1930 General Assembly that would have vested most of the commission's powers in the executive secretary with the commissioners as advisers, a bill Carson found totally offensive. Intimidated, Fippin resigned, and Byrd urged Carson to replace him with Ozlin, who was lobbying Byrd for the position.[14] An angry Carson wrote Byrd, "The avowed purpose of the bill as disclosed by its supporters was to make Ozlin Secretary, and it further developed that he was behind the bill pushing it vigorously." The bill was defeated, but the affair and ensuing correspondence between the three gentlemen embittered their relationship. Byrd was on the fence between two old friends, trying to mediate and console before disgustedly washing his hands of it, but he may have felt more animosity toward Carson, who had rebuffed his efforts to find a job for a friend. When Carson's name resurfaced as a possible candidate for governor in 1933, Byrd remained silent before giving the nod to George Peery. By then, lingering problems over the Shenandoah Park had driven them far apart, and there was almost no correspondence between these former comrades-in-arms after 1932. When the commission was reorganized in 1934, Carson was not offered the paid position of chairman.[15]

His relationship with Carson reveals one of Harry Byrd's less admirable qualities. Challenges to his authority and reputation could lead to grudges, even when the challenger was a friend. Byrd valued loyalty over every other personal quality, and he gave as much as he demanded. His friendships across the Old Dominion were legion and long-lasting, but he had difficulty tolerating criticism and opposing points of view. Politics naturally generates enemies, and Byrd had legitimate reasons for retaliating against those who had unfairly maligned him. Bishop Cannon and Westmoreland Davis were appropriate targets. Even Carson was not beyond reproach in this affair, for he, too, had come to believe that he knew better than others what was good for Virginia. Nevertheless, he did not deserve to be cast away after years of generous service. He would not be the last to feel the sting of retribution.

Byrd's political headaches did not wait for the end of his governorship. The presidential election of 1928 and the gubernatorial election of 1929 challenged his leadership of the state and threatened his "Program of Progress." The injection of religion and prohibition into these campaigns made the elections uncontrollable and unpredictable, the very things that Byrd dreaded. The culprits were the alien spirits of nativism and modernism that afflicted the 1920s. Made insecure by the fast-paced cultural and technological changes of the day, many Americans took out their frustrations on the weak, the different, and the new: blacks, Catholics, Jews, and immigrants. One means of controlling undesirable behavior by these "outsiders" was prohibition, which had been turned into national dogma by the Eighteenth Amendment and the Volstead Act. Although observed more in principle than in practice during the unbridled Jazz Age, prohibition represented an attempt by the middle class to preserve the values of abstinence, discipline, and law and order that seemed so lacking at this time. Although not restricted to the South, these fears and desires made that rural,

Protestant region particularly vulnerable to political demagoguery. The nomination of New York governor Al Smith, a Catholic who opposed prohibition, caused Virginia's leaders to worry about their political future.

The important assembly session in 1928 and the referendum on the reorganization amendments that spring had put off all thought of national politics by Organization leaders. Then within a week's time, only days after the vote, they confronted the issues and the candidates at both the state Democratic convention in Roanoke and the national convention in Houston, where Senator Glass wrote a watered-down prohibition plank that merely pledged the party and nominee to uphold the law. In his acceptance telegram Al Smith agreed to the language of the platform, but he urged a review of national prohibition to permit some sort of local option. With that statement, Virginia Democrats knew they were in for a fight in November. James Cannon, now a Methodist bishop, attended the convention and immediately called for a party revolt and the election of a "dry" Democrat. No longer as influential in state politics since the election of Harry Byrd, Cannon was searching for issues and candidates that would restore his prominence.[16]

In the face of President Coolidge's decision not to run again, Republicans nominated his secretary of commerce, Herbert Hoover, a wealthy mining engineer who had garnered an international reputation for his relief work during the war. Most importantly, Hoover was personally "dry" and would be running on a prohibition platform. Although state Democratic leaders publicly expressed optimism about carrying the Old Dominion for Smith, privately they had reservations. Party chairman J. Murray Hooker, who would run the campaign in Virginia, told the newspapers that he saw "no reason for apprehension," but to vice-presidential nominee Joseph Robinson he wrote: "Many are in open revolt and actively and openly opposing Governor Smith's election. This is particularly true of the dry people and the church people." He believed the Democrats were in danger of losing Virginia's electoral vote, but he pledged a full effort by the leadership to avoid this.[17] Only days later Governor Byrd, who had just been appointed one of five vice-chairmen of the Democratic National Committee, announced that he would support the party nominees "to the utmost of my ability." Other congressional and assembly leaders followed suit, but Senator Glass confided to his friends that Smith's telegram had nullified the platform and the selection of John Raskob, another "wet" Catholic, as party chairman would now require "the interposition of God and the entire heavenly host to win the ensuing election."[18]

Both Byrd and Glass appealed to Smith to moderate his prohibition position. In an August 10 letter to the New York governor, Byrd warned him that persistence in pursuing modification of the Eighteenth Amendment would cost him Virginia's vote. Smith thanked him for the advice but insisted on following his own convictions. Glass traveled to Albany to deliver personally a similar caution, but he received the same response. "I had as well have talked against the storm which recently swept the Atlantic coast," he wrote Byrd upon his return. Smith believed that the South would remain loyal to the party regardless of his stands, but Glass, who thought Smith to be a very good candidate on all but this one issue, said he was "confusing courage with recklessness."[19]

Focusing on the prohibition issue, Byrd and Glass at first overlooked the ominous religious factor. They should not have. In 1925, John Purcell, a Catholic, had been elected state treasurer by a much smaller margin than the rest of the ticket won. He had confronted a whispering campaign about his religion despite being a loyal member of the Democratic Organization. Three years later the religious opposition became more outspoken. Bishop Cannon and Baptist minister Arthur J. Barton convened a conference of anti-Smith Democrats in Asheville, North Carolina, on July 18. Their "Declaration of Principles and Purposes" stressed the prohibition issue, but it was reported that most of the delegates opposed Smith because of his religion. Although the Protestant leaders always denied that Smith's religion was an issue, they never failed to raise it. As Virginius Dabney has written in his biography of Cannon, "On the farms and in the small towns, where Catholics were regarded as strange beings from some remote planet, the possibilities for a campaign addressed to the prejudices of the mob were practically unlimited." As the campaign progressed, references to the power of "Romanism" became more frequent. For Harry Byrd the stakes in the election had become a little higher.[20]

In spite of Smith's liabilities, Virginia's political leaders resolved to back the nominee, fearing that a Republican victory would threaten their control of the party and state politics. Their dander was also up because of the possibility that Virginia might be turned into a pigsty of religious bigotry. In his endorsement Byrd unequivocally supported Smith, stressing his ability, the need for religious tolerance, and the importance of keeping Virginia Democratic. No Democrat, he said, had a "valid excuse" to desert the party. Smith, he claimed, was a great state administrator who had pledged to uphold the law, and since there was no chance for repeal of prohibition, Smith's position on the issue should be seen as a forthright statement about which people could honestly disagree. Deploring religious prejudice, he recalled Thomas Jefferson's firm support of religious freedom. The attacks on Smith, he said, were "violent" and "sinister" and had no place in the Old Dominion. It was a noble statement but for one flaw. In warning against the prospects of a Republican victory, he revived the memory of Black Reconstruction and appealed to racial prejudice in order to combat religious bigotry. "Virginia owes white supremacy to the Democratic Party," he reminded voters. Similar endorsements of Smith by Glass and Swanson suggested the Organization strategy: avoid prohibition, challenge the enemy on religious bias, and emphasize party loyalty. But Richmond columnist Allen Cleaton believed the election in Virginia was a totally unpredictable affair "beyond the control of the political leaders."[21]

The fall campaign in Virginia was marked by demagoguery, acrimony, and vituperation not witnessed in a presidential contest in the Old Dominion in years. Republican ranks were swelled by Klansmen, Anti-Saloon League advocates, and rabble-rousing preachers, all challenging the "rum and Romanism" of the Democrats. That very charge was made by Mrs. Willie Caldwell of Roanoke, Virginia's Republican national committeewoman, who warned Republican women in a circular letter, "We must save the United States from being Romanized and rum-ridden." Although candidate Hoover repudiated the letter, it was not an isolated expression. The Patriotic Sons of America distributed a pamphlet in the state claiming a Smith victory would result in the teaching of the Catholic religion in the public schools. Additional propaganda predicted papal rule, Spanish inquisition, and wars against Protestants, causing Senator Glass later to say that he could not recall a campaign of such "cheap depravity." The Klan, continuing its activity of the previous spring, was reported to be very aggressive in Roanoke, and the Virginia Anti-Saloon League even brought the well-known evangelist Billy Sunday to the state to berate Al Smith. Byrd wrote to Billy Reed, "We have a terrific fight on hand and we must exert every possible effort."[22]

The leaders of the Organization responded forcefully. A well-organized speakers bureau scattered its orators across the Old Dominion in what was called the "hottest and most intensive speaking campaign in Virginia's political history." Senator Glass, well known for his caustic tongue, was among the most passionate spokesman for Smith, likely reflecting the contempt that he held for Cannon. John Garland Pollard, a recognized "dry," was very active in eastern Virginia on behalf of the party. Approached by Republicans and anti-Smith Democrats with an offer of support for the next governorship if he deserted Smith, Pollard affirmed his support for Harry Byrd, which, ironically, may have secured him the gubernatorial nomination. Senator Swanson, who was running for reelection, also campaigned for Smith, but not fervently enough to please Byrd, which further weakened their already shaky relationship.

Governor Byrd was in the forefront of the effort to elect Smith. Stressing the importance of continuing Democratic control of Virginia, he warned that a Cannon-Republican victory jeopardized the state's prosperity. He continued to play upon his listeners' racial fears by raising the specter of Reconstruction when blacks sat side by side with whites in the General Assembly: this was what Southerners could expect if the Democrats lost. Because Byrd so rarely used the race issue in his long political career, his several references to it in 1928 indicate the desperation of the cause. After graciously welcoming Governor

Smith to Virginia on his brief stopover in Richmond, Byrd embarked upon a seventeen-speech tour of southwest Virginia and the Valley, pounding away on the theme of progress and decrying the negative campaign against Smith's religion. Perhaps convinced by the large crowds that turned out for his talks and Smith's visit to Richmond, Byrd expressed optimism about the ballot. So did party chairman Hooker, who predicted a victory margin of 30,000 votes. He was close, but he picked the wrong winner.[23]

The impact of emotional issues like prohibition and religion and the booming prosperity of the 1920s that many attributed to Republican policies made Hoover's nationwide landslide predictable, but the results in the Old Dominion could not have been more astonishing. In the biggest turnout for a presidential election since 1888, Republicans carried Virginia for the first time since Reconstruction. Hoover won all but one congressional district in the Old Dominion and carried the urban vote in his majority of nearly 25,000 votes. He even won Harry Byrd's hometown. The most devastating losses for the Organization were three congressional seats, the Second, Seventh, and Ninth, the latter two where Byrd had made a major effort.[24]

Postmortems were immediately forthcoming. The Organization was accused of running too negative a campaign, of starting too late, and of not being more committed to Smith's candidacy. The charges all had some currency but do not explain the defeat. Confronted with a mean whispering campaign, Byrd and Glass felt compelled to fight back with some questionable demagoguery of their own, but much of their retort was an advocacy of religious tolerance. Editor Louis Jaffe later praised the governor for championing "the cause of intellectual and religious liberty."[25] Their effort was late in taking off, but that was due in part to Smith's own delay in initiating the campaign and their own misjudgment of the enemy's strength and tactics. Their attempts to conceal or defuse the prohibition issue were ineffectual since the New Yorker's well-known position was a real liability in Virginia and he refused to modify it. Certainly Byrd and Glass were not enamored with Smith, knowing his candidacy would create problems with the state's "dry" electorate; but once he was in the race, their enthusiasm and loyalty were beyond question. As Byrd said some years later, "So far as I am personally concerned, I exercised every possible influence I possessed in behalf of Governor Smith. I personally contributed heavily to his campaign and were it necessary to refight the 1928 campaign, I do not know what I could have done effectively that was not done." Glass, who blamed the loss on "political parsons and innate religious prejudices," echoed these sentiments. The conclusion is clear. Smith lost despite massive and vigorous support from a united party leadership. His Virginia disaster is ample testimony to the power of prejudice and fear in politics.[26]

Byrd emerged from the race scarred but not broken. Almost immediately he began thinking about the gubernatorial contest only months away, believing that the future of the Organization rested on its outcome. He predicted "that the Democratic Party in Virginia will rise from the ashes in vigor and strength."[27] Anticipating that the Cannon forces would want to muscle in on the selection of the candidate in 1929, he told Glass, "I want you to know I am in favor of no compromise with Cannon, Hepburn and the combination that tried to destroy the Democratic Party." He was supported in this decision by Glass, Swanson, Pollard, and Assemblyman Bill Tuck of Halifax, who advised him: "I hope you will not allow the Democratic party to make friends with the political preachers. We must whip them." Most importantly, Byrd understood the necessity of reuniting the party, wanting no obstacles raised that would prevent Democrats who had voted for Hoover from returning to the fold. Virginius Dabney has claimed that the Democratic leaders in Virginia were "paralyzed" by Smith's defeat, but that was not true of Harry Byrd.[28]

After the election, with no General Assembly session to look forward to, the governor continued his ceremonial and promotional duties. In early January he hosted the entire Arkansas state legislature and the governor who were in the Old Dominion to discover the secrets of state reorganization. If they were looking for answers to the agricultural problems that had gripped the nation for most of the decade, they would not find them in Virginia. Governor Byrd saw this as the "only cloud in the sky" in Virginia's success story, but he did not give the problems of Old Dominion farmers much attention. Two-thirds of the state's population still lived in rural areas, and farm income in 1929 was only three-fourths of what it had been in 1919. Over a quarter of the Commonwealth's farmers eked out subsistence livings on submarginal land and required little or no cash income to sustain their meager existence. Two-fifths of the farmers made less than $600, and one-quarter of them were tenants. This segment of the population was definitely not sharing in the business prosperity of the times. Byrd may have assumed that his tax and road policies were "trickling down," but they had not been designed for that purpose. The tax reductions on bonds and capital did not affect small farmers, and tax segregation merely changed the name of the collector; it did not guarantee tax cuts. The increased road building emphasized the arterial network, not the farm-to-market roads of the county system. Being a farmer himself, Byrd may have believed that this group of rugged individualists could survive on its own, but in the more complex world of increased mechanization and international competition, the small, self-sufficient yeoman was becoming extinct. Yet despite his inattention, the rural areas of the Commonwealth gave the governor and his programs the largest margins of support at the ballot box.[29]

To his credit, Byrd in August 1928 appointed a Commission to Study the Conditions of the Farmers of Virginia. Addressing the new commission in January, he offered it some general objectives: promote a "stay on the land" campaign, seek cooperation with the federal government on a relief program, improve transportation facilities, and press for rural electrification, inspections of farm produce, and tax reductions. Never missing an opportunity for publicity, Byrd had five thousand copies of his remarks sent to farmers in the state. Just before he left office, the farm commission finished its report, but it offered only another long list of self-help suggestions. Given more commissions and recommendations but no action, Virginia farmers would have to wait for Franklin Roosevelt's New Deal for more decisive efforts.[30]

As 1929 progressed, attention turned to the race for governor. At a meeting of the state Democratic Central Committee, Byrd stressed the need for harmony, urging that anti-Smith Democrats not be excluded from the party. The one obstacle was Virginia's electoral law, which stipulated that a vote against the party in the election preceding the primary prevented voting in the primary. The committee requested and received a ruling from Attorney General Saunders that a national election where voters cast ballots for presidential electors was not a party vote because the electors were not nominees of the state party; thus, Democrats who had voted Republican in 1928 were eligible to vote in the 1929 Democratic primary. Critics argued that this was a violation of the spirit if not the letter of the laws and rules which Byrd himself had advanced in the 1924 election, but political necessity proved stronger than the law. Although Byrd was merely trying to get people back into the Democratic ranks, in time this ruling came to serve entirely different purposes.[31]

The immediate impact of the ruling was a contest for the allegiance of the Hoover Democrats. Republican chairman Robert Angell was welcoming these people to his party, while anti-Smith leaders, at the behest of Bishop Cannon, were encouraging them to refrain from voting in the Democratic primary. Both of these groups were looking toward an alliance against the Democrats. That only hardened Byrd's resolve not to share power with the preachers as some in the Organization were advising.[32] He decided that the surest way to retrieve the rebellious rank and file was to give them a candidate they could like but one who was committed to his reorganization. That person had to be "dry," a man of some independence, and preferably from the tidewater area to attract voters from that heavily populated region that had not had a governor since Andrew Jackson Montague. Lieutenant Governor West was the only announced candidate in the field, but his fifteen-month candidacy had not generated much enthusiasm, and his close relationship with the Organization was deemed a liability. Other names surfaced, but no one matched the desired profile except John Garland Pollard, dean of the School of Government and Citizenship at the College of William and Mary.

Pollard was an unusual choice, for he had spent most of his adult life fighting the Organization. The son of a Baptist preacher, he grew up in Richmond where he went to college and began his law practice. He was a delegate to the 1901–2 constitutional convention before joining the ranks of the progressives opposing the Martin machine. Elected attorney general in 1913, he lost his bid for the governorship in the three-way race of 1917. With his political ambitions thwarted, Pollard retreated to the less hectic life of college teaching, looking very much the part as a stout, balding, bespectacled, good-humored professor. But his commitment to public service had not abated, and he served on Governor Trinkle's Committee on Simplification and Economy in Government and on William Reed's reorganization committee where his knowledge of government and tax law was put to good use. Pollard had supported Mapp in 1925, and his political independence disturbed Byrd; but the professor's active campaigning for the reorganization amendments and Al Smith's candidacy demonstrated both his support of the Byrd program and his feistiness against Bishop Cannon. His prominence as a Baptist layman would also put the religious issue to rest. Ever concerned about the future of his policies, Byrd sent Combs to Williamsburg to sound Pollard out. At a subsequent visit with the governor in Richmond, Pollard pledged his personal allegiance and won Byrd's endorsement; he announced his candidacy on March 2, 1929.[33]

Byrd's old foe G. Walter Mapp entered the race and won endorsements from former governors Davis and Trinkle and Lieutenant Governor West, who withdrew on doctor's advice to become Mapp's campaign manager. Hailing from the Eastern Shore with impeccable "dry" credentials, Mapp seemed to meet Byrd's criteria for success, but his opposition to the governor's programs and his association with Bishop Cannon precluded his consideration. Senator Swanson likely preferred Mapp or longtime ally Patrick Henry Drewry, but after carefully assessing the situation, he accepted the Organization's choice, another indication of his slipping leadership position. The field was rounded out a few weeks later with the entry of long shot Rosewell Page, a delegate from Hanover County.[34]

Mapp's hopes were dealt a damaging blow on May 31 when Bishop Cannon urged the anti-Smith people to stay on the sidelines. He could support none of the candidates, all of whom had voted for Smith. He also bitterly denounced state Democratic leaders for their failure to repudiate the Smith-Raskob national leadership. Cannon's decision to break completely with the Virginia Democratic party indicated his desire for a new political organization that he alone could command; Harry Byrd could not be bargained with. Thus, both the primary and general elections would become contests about the future leadership and direction of the Old Dominion. Since Byrd had won only a narrow victory in the referendum and then suffered a reverse in the Smith fiasco, the results were not assured.[35]

As in 1925, Mapp ran an aggressive campaign, putting forward a progressive platform that included improvements in education, tax reductions, and abolition of the fee system. He attacked the short ballot and centralization of power under the governor, challenging Pollard to debate the issues with him. Confident of success, Pollard relied on a defense of Byrd's record and refused to debate. He did eventually urge tax cuts and equalization of educational opportunities, but he sidestepped the short ballot question, maintaining that it was a matter for future consideration by the assembly no matter who the governor. Pollard's overwhelming victory was a smashing vote of confidence for the Byrd program.[36]

During the Democratic primary race, the anti-Smith forces entered into the anticipated coalition with the Republicans. The small but enthusiastic band of renegades gathered in Roanoke to nominate Dr. William Moseley Brown, professor of psychology and education at Washington and Lee University, who as a "dry" Democrat had voted for Hoover. They adopted a platform that denounced the short ballot and current election laws and praised the sanctity of the Eighteenth Amendment. Urging voters to "Smash the Machine," they left the position of lieutenant governor open as a generous invitation to Republicans to join them. Although the Grand Old Party seemed to have been co-opted, in reality Republican leader Henry Anderson had been privy to Brown's selection, and the party faithful willingly assented to his nomination and the platform a week later.[37]

Over the summer coalition forces were staggered by the revelations that their acknowledged leader, Bishop Cannon, had been involved in shady practices: stock market gambling, flour hoarding during the world war, and misappropriation of church funds. Some of the charges were traced to Senator Glass, who had been feuding with Cannon for two decades. The embarrassed churchman withdrew from the campaign, and in mid-October he sailed for Brazil to oversee his episcopal conferences. Not only was the bishop discredited as a moral leader, but his departure signaled the defeat of William Moseley Brown.[38]

Virginia's gubernatorial election in 1929 drew national attention as politicians and pundits wondered whether the issues of 1928 still carried weight and the Republican breakthrough in the South had substance. The results suggested neither was true. Brown and the Republicans made a determined effort but could not overcome their own foibles and the successful record of the opposition. The Cannon people wanted to emphasize the national issue of prohibition and the Organization's association with Smith-Raskobism, while Republicans preferred the target to be "bossism" in Virginia and local issues of taxes and schools. Brown initially split the difference between the two sides, but with the departure of Cannon, he shifted the emphasis to state issues, and the campaign fell apart. Pollard was too pure. Charges of machine politics or "wet" politics did not stick to him. When Brown harped on the short ballot, Byrd publicly asked him how he had voted on the constitutional amendments; after some evasion the candidate admitted that he had supported all of them, rationalizing that he now perceived the short ballot to be an "example of Tammany methods."[39]

For their own part the Democrats were united, organized, better funded, and enjoyed media support. Pollard matched Brown's rhetoric and stamina and avoided any references to national party figures while defending the Byrd program. The governor himself was very active in the campaign, particularly in the last month, challenging any "erroneous" statement about his administration, ridiculing Brown's figures on taxes and road expenditures, and accusing him of "indulging in hysterical denunciations of the Democratic Party as a branch of Tammany Hall." From Goochland to Norfolk, from Warrenton to Abingdon, Byrd roamed the state bashing Republicans and defending his administration. Glass, Goolrick, Shirley, Morrissett, and others followed in his footsteps with a similar refrain.[40]

Pollard's landslide triumph on November 5 laid to rest hopes of a two-party system in Virginia for another twenty-four years. In running up a margin of 70,000, he carried every congressional district and 97 of 100 counties. Losing only eight of seventy-six contests for the House of Delegates to anti-Smith men, the Organization retained its dominance of the legislature as well. Cannonism had been repudiated. Political power in Virginia once more rested firmly in the hands of a united Democratic party. The result was an enormous vote of confidence for Harry Byrd, his program, and his party, but even as he enjoyed his victory, the governor looked to solidify his power, inviting those independents and Republicans who had rejected Brown's "program of destruction" to join his crusade. All were welcome in the house of Byrd.[41]

Byrd's last year as governor was busier than usual, for he continued his active schedule while overseeing the gubernatorial election. His reputation as a reorganization wizard garnered many invitations from political and business groups to speak about his magic; he addressed the Vermont legislature, the Tennessee Chamber of Commerce, the Downtown Association of New York, the Governor's Conference at New London, Connecticut, and the Taxpayers' Research League in Wilmington, Delaware.[42]

Byrd also renewed his acquaintance with Franklin Roosevelt, recently elected governor of New York. These two active politicians, both highly visible in the Democratic party, seemed destined for higher service, and for the moment they shared an admiration for each other's work. Roosevelt had written a mutual friend in 1927: "Harry Byrd will make the greatest record of any recent Governor of Virginia if he can get this reorganization through. When you see him give him my warm regards and congratulations." Upon hearing this, Byrd commented, "Franklin is a splendid fellow." After Roosevelt's narrow victory in the midst of the Smith defeat, Byrd wrote to him: "You have no friend in this whole country whose wishes for your success are more sincere than mine. It seems to me you are the hope of the Democratic party and everything you do must be considered from that standpoint."[43]

The development of air travel continued to influence the governor. As soon as Pollard's victory was secured, Byrd was off on a three-day, sixteen-plane tour of the state to promote airport construction and the use of roof markers to aid aerial navigation. He tried to get aviation promoters Harry Guggenheim and Charles Lindbergh to go along, but fortunately for their reputations they were unavailable. Shirley had warned him about the bad weather of late November, but the unflappable, ever-optimistic Harry and his entourage of businessmen and politicians took off anyway. At their first stop in Emporia, the trimotored plane got stuck in the mud and almost nosed over. After it was pulled out by a tractor, they flew on to Martinsville where a snowstorm grounded the tour. They drove to Roanoke, hoping for a break in the weather, but the continuing clouds forced cancellation of the adventure. Back in the safety of Richmond, the governor announced that he would request $50,000 for airport development from the next assembly. His ambitious program included emergency landing fields at ten-mile intervals across the state.[44]

In his final days as governor, Byrd concerned himself with budget preparations and appointments. The recent stock market crash raised nary an eyebrow. He heartily concurred with President Hoover's request to maintain prosperity by increasing road building and other construction. In his New Year's Day message, he commented: "The close of the year 1929 sees Virginia facing a bright future. Never, probably, in the long history of the Old Dominion has she faced a destiny more filled with promise." In that same message Byrd thanked Virginians for the honor they had bestowed upon him and for the progress they had made together. Anxious about the continuity between the two administrations, he filled key posts with loyal operatives. Louis Epes was elevated to the state supreme court and replaced on the Corporation Commission by George Peery. The governor also lobbied with the next Speaker of the House, Sinclair Brown, about committee assignments for friends. But Byrd need not have worried about his continuing influence in Virginia government, for Governor Pollard reappointed most of the state officials who had served with Byrd and pledged to continue and expand on the work begun.[45]

In his last address to the General Assembly, Governor Byrd reviewed the past record one more time: the industrial progress, a $4 million treasury surplus, tax segregation, the reorganization of the executive branch, over 2,000 miles of new highways, and the Shenandoah Park. He thanked the members for their support but urged them to continue the work of reform, particularly

The Song Is Ended, But The Melody Lingers On!

— RICHMOND TIMES DISPATCH , JANUARY 12, 1930

in the agricultural sector. His last budget included an increase of $3.3 million in appropriations with new capital outlays of $5.2 million, mostly for education. On January 15, 1930, wearing a high silk hat in deference to Pollard's wishes, Byrd watched his successor inaugurated in a driving rainstorm. His last piece of advice for the new governor (at least on that day) was to buy a new desk chair. With that, he headed for Winchester to get there "in time for supper," driving himself just as he had four years before.[46]

Few men have left office with the universal adulation that was showered upon Harry Byrd. He was honored by the assembly and lauded by his successor.

Commenting on his "incomparable administration of state affairs," Senator Glass wrote him, "The fact that my own judgment of your character and capabilities has been fully justified is a source of pride and satisfaction." The editor of the *Times-Dispatch,* referring to Byrd as a "genius of political leadership," eulogized: "In all the history of Virginia no brief period has been more fruitful in the advancement of governmental ideals than that covered by this administration. . . . The State has been re-born." Similar assessments poured in from across the state.[47]

Such praise had begun very early in Byrd's administration. Less than a year into his term, journalist French Strother was writing "the story of how a young governor and a group of young men with a new viewpoint have put new life and spirit into an old state." Overcoming the inertia of the past, these "liberals" were looking to put Virginia back into the first rank of states in wealth and power.[48] "New life" to Strother meant tax reform, highway construction, and governmental efficiency, the essence of Byrd's program, or what historian George Tindall later called "business progressivism." For Tindall, this was a new progressivism that emphasized efficiency and expanded governmental services for purposes of economic development, as opposed to an older, more moralistic brand of progressivism that accentuated democracy, corporate regulation, and social justice.

Virginia was not alone in experiencing this reincarnation of a New South in the 1920s, as North Carolina, Alabama, and Tennessee pursued similar programs. Consumed by the "Atlanta Spirit," many southern leaders believed that the way out of backwardness was through industrial growth. Breaking from a laissez-faire tradition, they adopted the progressive impulse of using the power of government as "an agent for industrial prosperity." Thus, state government expenditures for highway construction and schools rose significantly in the twenties. In Virginia this was accompanied by sizable increases in the number of businesses, capital invested, value of production, and manufacturing employment. However, "business progressivism" did not run very deep. Little attention was paid to the problems of agriculture, poverty, labor relations, or child labor, not to mention race relations. Social control, not social uplift, was the objective, and, therefore, its legacy was severely restricted.[49]

Any assessment of Byrd's governorship must start from the perspective of the twenties. Certainly the prosperity of the Jazz Age, especially during the years of Byrd's governorship, provided the revenues and a liberality of spirit necessary for expanded programs. Had Byrd governed during a depression, as was the lot of Governor Pollard, he would have received messages of sympathy, not applause for success. Nor was Byrd an innovator. Earlier commissions on simplification and economy in government had recommended reorganizations of the bureaucracy. His "Program of Progress" was a replica of the Virginia

Chamber of Commerce program for economic revitalization put forth in 1923: development of Hampton Roads, equitable taxation, development of water-power resources for industrial growth, simplicity and economy in government, and agricultural advances. And other southern governors charted a course for Virginia to follow, notably Governor Austin Peay of Tennessee (1923–27), who consolidated sixty-four agencies into eight departments, overhauled the state tax system, and expanded the road network. But Byrd succeeded where his predecessors had failed by winning legislative and public approval of these ideas. Building on the excitement of the times, the initiatives of others, and his own vision for the Old Dominion, Harry Byrd deserves much credit for generating some specific programs and providing the enthusiasm necessary for their implementation. Within the narrow parameters of "business progressivism," Harry Byrd was a successful governor.[50]

His success was primarily attributable to the power of his personality. Strother defined his positive qualities perfectly: "sound business judgment, energy, force of character, practical imagination, attractive personality, a great power of conciliating people, and great political skill." Under any definition he was a leader. He had a vision, constricted though it was, of what he wanted to accomplish. He knew the mechanisms and the people of the system through which change was to be realized. Indeed, he had helped create that organization of state and local officials whose votes, money, and participation were so crucial to success. Working for them, winning their confidence, and rewarding them for services rendered, he enjoyed remarkable support from the assembly and the "courthouse crowd." During his governorship Byrd returned forty-two bills to the legislature, and all were amended as he desired; he vetoed only three bills, none of which was overridden.[51] It was not due to charisma; he lacked flair for the dramatic, he was not a particularly handsome man, and his oratorical powers were modest at best. Instead, Byrd led by example. He was indefatigable; no one outdid him in his commitment to a new Virginia. He aroused enthusiasm with appropriate deference to the past while proclaiming glories of the future. And he willingly shared the acclaim with fellow politicians and Virginians. He deserved their adulation.[52]

One reason Byrd received so much applause at the time was that his contemporaries thought the way he did. They, too, were imbued with the spirit of southern progressivism that sought to reconcile progress with tradition, believed economic growth remedied all problems, relished the application of efficiency, and equated action with substance. They were the "young men" referred to by French Strother who were making a difference in a state that once seemed in perpetual slumber.

From a more distant perspective, however, a different picture of Byrd's governorship emerges. While he moved Virginia forward, he did not move it very far. For all the bright lights—and unquestionably the excitement of the times contributed to a sense of forward motion—Virginia changed very little in the twenties. Its industrial growth was impressive, but the Commonwealth continued to languish at the bottom of the states in school and public welfare appropriations, state hospital care, and correctional facilities. Even in highway construction, despite all the hoopla, the Old Dominion was lagging behind North Carolina, and it was costing more than predicted. The reforms that were adopted had a superficial quality to them, a musical chairs arrangement that shifted agencies around but left them without central direction, notably in finance, public welfare, and conservation. While the improvements in fiscal accountability produced real savings through centralized accounting procedures, the attention to patronage did not shrink the bureaucracy. Calling some of the reorganization "nomenclature only," analyst Arthur Buck accepted Budget Director Bradford's estimate that the reorganization saved little more than half of the $800,000 claimed by Byrd.[53]

In fiscal matters, tax segregation may have made tax collection more efficient and somewhat fairer to the local observer, but it did not address questions of appropriate tax rates and tax purposes. Pay-as-you-go forced state institutions to pay higher interest on bonds because the credit of the state was not behind them. Most of Byrd's tax cuts were for businesses and the well-to-do, ostensibly to get them to settle in Virginia, but lower taxes also let the rich get richer. Byrd left Virginia's finances in good order for the depression—low tax rates and low indebtedness were desirable attributes for bad economic times—but the absence of a broader social conscience and an unwillingness to spend restricted the Commonwealth's ability to assist its citizens in that time of need. Economy became another word for stinginess. Public administration analyst Leslie Lipson has concluded, "Virginia reorganization was decidedly that of a governor who placed questions of cost before those of service." It was a "child of vested interests," in which economy and efficiency were little more than disguises for reducing taxes for landowners and manufacturers. Lipson also claimed that Byrd used reorganization as a political vehicle for consolidating his control over Virginia.[54]

Byrd could never divorce himself from the need to strengthen his power base. Almost every action (or inaction) reflected his concern for the impact it would have on the Organization, now and in the future. He left the fee system intact and the grossly incompetent and inefficient county government untouched. People of questionable ability but unquestioned loyalty to Byrd were given positions in government, and pressing issues were ignored or passed on to another commission. At a time when Byrd was proclaiming the beauties of centralization, he was decentralizing the tax system to retain the support of rural elements who wanted local tax control. It was not political courage Byrd lacked but the larger social vision of what was truly good for Virginia and all its citizens, rather than what was good for the business community, or the Organization, or Harry Byrd. As historian Raymond Pulley has written about Virginia, "During the late 1920's the traditionalist ruling class of the Old Dominion simply lost interest in creating better social services for the people."[55]

That attitude endured, and its legacy was even more negative than its immediate results. The constitutional amendments, especially the restrictions on borrowing and tax segregation, straitjacketed the state, costing it flexibility as economic conditions changed. The overwhelming authority of the Organization, self-perpetuated by a bloated bureaucracy and obsequious local officials, obstructed the development of a political opposition that might have constructively challenged outdated policies. It allowed Byrd to prevent any tampering with his monument of reorganization and the philosophy of pay-as-you-go. These factors kept Virginia locked into a 1920s mode for another generation, a backward state with untapped potential.

Nevertheless, the judgment of the long-range perspective may be too harsh. If Byrd's "Program of Progress" had its limitations, so, too, did the other examples of progressive reform in the country. The 1920s were better known for political retrenchment and business dominance than for manifesting a social conscience. At the very least, Byrd's "business progressivism" was moving the Old Dominion off the treadmill. And even had he wanted to, it is doubtful whether he could have done more, for no leader can stray far from his followers. The social and political cultures of the Old Dominion were deeply rooted. It was not a reform-oriented society; its leaders always had been content to wait and see, their outstanding characteristic being, in the words of Jean Gottmann, a "resistance to change." Race and class lines were not easily crossed. Political structures were constitutionally fixed, and the resulting one-party tradition inhibited competition. Byrd's conservative views on politics and social issues were in keeping with those of a majority of his constituents. Virginians liked their native son. Harry Byrd was not brilliant, but he was solid, and he came close to being a political genius. The record of achievements that he recounted in his final speech to the legislature was substantial and significant. He was a good governor for the times.[56]

1. A young Harry Byrd with his uncle Hal Flood

2. The three Byrd brothers: Tom, Harry, and Dick

3. Four generations of Byrds—Mrs. Jennie Rivers Byrd, Harry Sr., Harry Jr., and Richard Evelyn Byrd—seated on the porch of the Rosemont cabin, 1925

4. Governor Byrd and his family at the executive mansion, 1926; from left, Beverley, Harry Jr., Sittie, Richard, and Westwood

5. Governor Byrd and Mrs. Byrd flanked by some of his predecessors, 1926: from left, Henry C. Stuart, E. Lee Trinkle, Claude A. Swanson, and Andrew J. Montague

6. The three Byrd brothers—Dick, Tom, and Harry—with their mother, 1927

7. Off on a hunting trip, 1928: *from left,* Harry Guggenheim, Charles Lindbergh, Governor Byrd, Henry Shirley, and Nelson Page

8. In 1934 newly inaugurated Governor George Peery, *center,* is congratulated by his predecessor, John Garland Pollard. Lieutenant Governor James Price looks on at the left.

9. Senator Carter Glass welcomes Harry Byrd to the Senate.

~ 6 ~

"Retirement"

IT WAS NOT A SOMBER RIDE home from Richmond. Byrd and his family eagerly looked forward to moving into their new home, Rosemont, on the outskirts of Berryville—especially Sittie, who had not relished the public clamor around the executive mansion. Constructed in the early nineteenth century and renovated in the antebellum period with the addition of a huge portico with Doric columns, Rosemont had been purchased by Byrd in 1929 from J. Low Harriman, its owner since 1902. Harriman had made some unimpressive additions to the house and had allowed the grounds to fall into disarray, but that did not concern the governor, who had long eyed this imposing structure that was almost completely surrounded by his orchards. It would be the first and only year-round home he and Sittie would ever own. From the front porch and upstairs bedrooms, he could view his beloved Blue Ridge Mountains and acres of orchards, a truly magnificent sight in the spring when the apple trees were flowering. The one significant improvement he made to Rosemont was the extensive landscaping of the grounds with azaleas, rhododendrons, willows, and maples, all adding to the seasonal profusion of colors.[1]

Byrd loved Rosemont and its environs so much that he spent most of his free time there over the next thirty-six years, running the apple business, walking the orchards, and enjoying his family. Visitors were always welcome, and he would frequently escort them around the grounds. Barry Goldwater recalled that his first meeting with his future colleague occurred during his student days at Staunton Military Academy when he lost his way one day and responded to the "Visitors Welcome" sign on the Rosemont front gate. Such hospitality, however, had its drawbacks. Early one morning Byrd and his grandson Harry III were skinny-dipping in the pool when they were surprised by a couple whose protracted conversation forced the two swimmers to cling to the side of the pool for what seemed like hours.[2]

The early thirties were the only years in Byrd's half-century political career that he was out of public office or not running for office, but his apple business and his obsession with Virginia politics kept him so busy that he had little time for retirement. Nevertheless, there was more opportunity to be with his family than there had been in Richmond. Byrd was a devoted and caring father, but his political life and a stern no-nonsense attitude inhibited him from developing intimate relationships with his children. He was home on weekends, but even then there was not much time for play. While the family might vacation in Atlantic City for a week in the summer, Byrd seldom took time off himself, except when they all went up to Skyland for a weekend. He did not play cards or board games or participate in sports, listened to the radio very little, and only later went to the movies with his grandchildren, where he soon would fall asleep. His interests were two: politics and business.

With his own rigorous activity Byrd communicated his work ethic to his children. "You work for what you get in this life," he told them. To his young ward Bolling Flood, he wrote, "All of us must remember, Bolling, that in this world we have to do a lot of things we do not want to do and that the doing of these things makes better people of us." He taught largely by example, assuming that the children were intelligent enough to absorb what he was driving at; his strong personality converted them to his philosophy. He expected them to stick to their allowances and to pay back any advances. Although not a stern disciplinarian, he could get testy with them regarding their intemperance with money and liquor.[3]

Byrd had no favorites among his children, but he developed the closest relationship with Harry Jr., who as a young teenager began accompanying his father on trips during the governorship. It was apparent that the eldest son was being groomed for a future in Virginia politics as the father introduced him to all his political friends in the farthest reaches of the state. Harry Jr. remembered, "He would talk to me as if I were grown-up—a politician; he was thinking out loud; I didn't know what he was talking about, but gradually it caused me to take an interest in politics; I was in every county and city in the state by the time I was thirteen years old."[4] At his father's insistence, the younger Byrd reluctantly enrolled at Virginia Military Institute in the fall of 1931. Two years at VMI were followed by two years at the University of Virginia, but not being an enthusiastic student, Harry Jr. left in 1935 without a degree when he saw an opportunity to take over the Winchester *Evening Star*, much as his dad had done thirty-two years before him. The paper had been languishing without an active editor since Byrd left for the United States Senate in 1933. The senator encouraged the move but warned his son, "If you make too many mistakes, you're gone." Within a year Harry Jr. was editor and publisher, although his father retained financial control and continued to send him advice on editorials. For a while he worked under the tutelage of John Crown at the Harrisonburg *Daily News-Record*, but when Crown died in 1939, Harry Jr. took over that newspaper as well. Thereafter, the senator had little to do with the newspapers except to forward his son material for editorial comment. Their relationship deepened as young Harry became his closest political confidant.[5]

The other children were sent away to boarding school in the thirties, leaving Byrd the task of parenting from a distance. Westwood went to Gunston Hall Girls School in Washington, D.C., and Beverley and Dick to Episcopal High School in Alexandria. Byrd's letters reveal the typical fatherly interest in grades, spending money, and poor behavior. When Westwood lost a key, he told her he would not stop her allowance but would withhold the cost of the key. "Westy" was a vivacious, attractive young woman who had her father's enormous energy. "She would have been great as a man," said her sister-in-law Helen Byrd. Queen of a number of festivals, she entered into an unhappy early marriage that ended in divorce and came back to Rosemont during the Second World War at her father's request to help look after her mother.

To Beverley, who initially disliked his new school, Byrd wrote that his mother's health would be harmed if he did not stick it out: "I have confidence in your character; this is a real test; you cannot leave without my consent." Byrd later warned him that if he deliberately misbehaved to get expelled he would not let him have a car until he was eighteen. Beverley straightened out, graduated from Episcopal, and went on to study agriculture at VPI and Cornell before returning to work in the orchards.

Dick was the least studious and most rebellious of the children, sometimes referring to his parents as "Sit" and "Governor" in his letters to them. His father enrolled him at Culver Military Academy in Indiana in 1939 to prepare him for VMI. "Keep him under firm control," he wrote to the commandant. Culver was not a success, and Dick transferred to St. Christopher's in Richmond to complete high school.[6]

Byrd's relationship with his wife was very loving, marred only by her poor health. Sittie had developed a heart condition, perhaps brought on by the influenza epidemic of 1918, that led to angina and several serious heart attacks over the years and frequently left her bedridden. Byrd's correspondence with friends is replete with references to her condition. In early 1933 on a trip to visit the Harry Guggenheims in Cuba, she had a very severe attack. Byrd reported to their host, "We had a difficult trip home with her." Billy Reed, who had accompanied them, did not think she would survive. In 1934 she was in bed for six months with "the worst attack she has ever had"; she was in and out of hospitals thereafter until 1956 when she suffered two debilitating strokes that left her an invalid until her death eight years later.[7] In Sittie's remarkable struggle against illness, Byrd was an attentive husband, often administering her medicine and telephoning her every night when he was traveling. When her condition forced her to move into a downstairs bedroom, he moved as well to a small adjacent bedroom. Years later, on Saturday evenings he would watch "The Lawrence Welk Show" with her, the only concession he ever made to watching television.[8]

Until her 1933 heart attack, Sittie was a good political soldier for her husband, performing the ceremonial functions even though she did not like the crowds on the campaign trail or at the state dinners, preferring instead more intimate dinner parties with close friends such as the Reeds, Fergusons, and Dodsons. Although they included the Guggenheims and Charles Lindbergh among their friends, the Byrds were not high-society people. Sittie was a very fastidious woman who dressed very stylishly and wanted her home kept in immaculate condition and filled with flowers, whether it be Rosemont or their Shoreham Hotel apartment in Washington. Never as outwardly warm as the governor, she was remembered by her close friends as a very caring person who was a lovely hostess and a pleasant conversationalist who enjoyed a good bridge game. Although her poor health may have restricted her spouse's political exposure, her illnesses often gave him the perfect excuse to refuse requests for speaking and social engagements.[9]

Their relationship was formal and traditional. She looked after the house and the children, while he took care of politics and apples. She deferred to his judgment on almost everything and granted him enormous freedom to come and go as he pleased. Byrd never violated this trust and was usually with her at the end of the workday, but their appearances in public together were very rare, and on weekends he was off to Skyland to relax or to Winchester for business. During the last ten years of their marriage, when she was often bedridden, he took his vacations, usually to national parks, with his close friend E. Blackburn ("Blackie") Moore. Her illness most certainly was a great burden to him, and he desperately needed some time away.

There was no elemental passion between them, probably reflecting the Victorian code under which both of them had been reared that demanded emotions be controlled. Indeed, self-control was a primary feature of Byrd's public and private life. He did not smoke, rarely swore, and was not a womanizer. Displays of temper were also rare with Byrd, usually being reserved for liberal opponents and columnists who had challenged his integrity, the most important part of his persona. In reaction to his father's excessive drinking, Sittie's preferences, and the enforced habits of prohibition, he was a near teetotaler, even banning alcoholic beverages from his daughter's wedding in 1936. During his governorship, when Winston Churchill visited the executive mansion, Byrd had to obtain Churchill's daily quota of brandy from John Stewart Bryan. Mrs. Byrd called the Englishman "the worst house guest I ever had." Later in life Byrd would drink a beer or two after walking the orchards, sometimes have a cocktail before a public dinner, and finally consented to serve liquor at his

Rosemont luncheons. Watkins Abbitt remembered that Byrd's inexperience with liquor left him no judgment when serving others, which often caused him to pour a full glass of straight whiskey. One evening even the hard-drinking Bill Tuck exploded, "Good God Senator, do you have some water?"[10]

Byrd occupied a man's world in work and play. He had no women friends, consulted no female politicians (although a few wrote to him), and invariably voted against legislation that advanced women's interests from suffrage to equal rights, but he was always a gentleman in their company. His primary diversions were hunting and hiking. Before World War II, Byrd hunted all over the state with a coterie of friends both political and personal, many of whom were quite wealthy: Billy Reed, Wat Ellerson, president of Albemarle Paper Manufacturing Company, Spencer Carter of Virginia-Carolina Chemical Corporation, Harry Guggenheim, Bernard Baruch, Willis Robertson, H. B. Sproul of the Highway Commission, and Tom Gathright of the Game Commission. Around Berryville his favorite hunting companion was Ralph Dorsey, a fellow apple grower. Using a twelve-gauge shotgun, Byrd usually targeted birds and was a good shot. The hunting relaxed him, got him into the outdoors he loved, and gave him much-needed exercise. When he went into southwest Virginia to hunt with Frank Wysor, political discussions intruded on the recreation.[11]

Byrd had a vast number of friends across the state who were devoted to him, and he to them, from courthouse politicians such as Emory Elmore in Brunswick, Sam Carter in Bristol, and Harry Green in Arlington to General Assembly cronies Sam Ferguson and Louis Epes. Many of them had been friends of his father. In the Valley his oldest political supporters included Joe Bauserman and Charlie Louderback. Bauserman, a Woodstock lawyer, was always sending Byrd information about Valley politics, but his loyalty was balanced by an avalanche of job requests for himself, family, and friends.[12] Finally there were associates in the business world from the apple industry, chambers of commerce, banking, and other major industries. All of them were sources of information about elections and markets, and Byrd returned the favor through patronage, support for legislation, and a box of apples at Christmas time. He sent so many apples to his friends it was a wonder he had any left for the supermarkets. While these relationships were politically useful, there was nothing counterfeit about them. Byrd frequently used the word love in expressing affection for his friends. He wrote to John Williams of Blacksburg in 1943, "I love you very dearly, as you know, and your friendship has been one of the greatest gratifications in my life." That affection was reciprocated. Henry Wickham of Ashland wrote the senator in 1940: "As you know, I am your devoted friend. I think you are one of the wisest and greatest leaders Virginia has ever had. May you ever be right, but right or wrong I will follow to the death."[13]

Undoubtedly, the two great friendships of his life were those with Ebbie

Combs and Billy Reed. Reared in a politically active family, Combs won election as clerk of Russell County in 1911 and quickly developed the organizational skills that would lead to future prominence. After contributing to party victories in 1921 and 1922, he tied his future to Byrd in the great road fight of 1923, always putting Byrd's political fortunes ahead of his own. Byrd was well aware of Combs's talents and loyalty. Following his gubernatorial primary victory over Mapp in 1925, he wrote: "My Dear Ebby, There is no man in the State that I feel under more obligations to than I do to you. . . . I am looking forward to a much closer association with you in the future."[14]

Over the next three decades Combs became Byrd's alter ego, a political confidant of incredible influence. Their minds ran along the same path, being fully committed to Organization success and fully prepared for all elections. Invariably requested and freely given, Combs's advice to Byrd on the fee system and on prospective state and local candidates was unparalleled in its wisdom. Serving sixteen years as a county clerk, Ebbie Combs knew the "courthouse ring" better than anyone else. In former governor Stuart's view, Combs was "a man who has had contact with and who understands the people he is to deal with. . . . [He has] keenness of judgment and perception in dealing with men of all kinds including his subordinates, . . . a man of acknowledged ability in dealing successfully with large and complicated affairs." Stuart's assessment of this big, unpretentious "mountain man" proved uncannily accurate, as Byrd discovered. Except for two brief periods in the thirties, Combs retained key positions in the state government for thirty years, from which he oversaw the operation of the Organization. Befittingly called "The Chief," he was an impressive-looking man, standing slightly taller than Byrd, with square jaw and square shoulders and a full head of snow-white hair. Grandfatherly looking and soft-spoken, Combs could play hardball with the best of them. His rule of operation was simple: "To get along you go along."[15]

Byrd's friendship with Reed was of an entirely different nature; though just as deep, it was more personal. Whereas Combs was a brother-in-arms, preparing for the next day's battle, Reed was the elder mentor, dispensing advice on a wider spectrum of issues, including national politics and political philosophy. Byrd employed Reed on the most significant venture of his governorship, the reorganization, and when he left Richmond, he continued to use Reed as a lobbyist and informant to advance his interests in state politics, particularly with the Richmond newspapers, which Byrd thought were unfairly hostile. They hunted together, their families socialized together, and they shared business information. Reed was a heavy contributor to Byrd's campaigns, and on one occasion he quietly covered a $5,000 note of Byrd's due on the Timberville orchard. When Harry left the governorship, Reed wrote to him: "Whenever you come to Richmond I want you to make my house your home.

You and Sittie in the four years have become a part of Richmond, and are held in the highest esteem by all of its citizens, and Mrs. Reed and I regard you as part of our family. None of us can figure what the future has in store for us, but I want you to know that you can depend on my sympathetic cooperation in your future endeavors in such channels as may seem worthy to you." And Reed did have higher aspirations for his young friend, who credited his accomplishments as governor to Reed's "assistance and inspiration."[16]

Another friendship that Byrd solidified in these years was with Senator Carter Glass. From the 1924 Democratic convention, through Byrd's election to the governorship, to the bitter state campaigns of 1928 and 1929 against Bishop Cannon, they had grown closer. Generous in his contributions to congressional campaigns in Virginia and in his support of Organization candidates, Glass was receptive to Byrd's requests for assistance on legislation and patronage. Byrd reciprocated by brutally snuffing out E. Lee Trinkle's aspiration to seek Glass's Senate seat in 1930. Trinkle went to Winchester to see Harry, who told him that he could not win and would get no support. Trinkle immediately decided not to enter the race. Given the disparity in their ages and backgrounds, the relationship between Glass and Byrd rested on mutual admiration rather than deep affection. Responding to one of Byrd's expressions of respect, Glass wrote, "Needless to say I deeply appreciate and cherish the warm personal expressions of your letter and reciprocate them in full degree." It was a relationship that would flourish when Byrd arrived in the Senate in 1933.[17]

This network of friends may have been Byrd's greatest asset during his years as the leader of the Organization. They were the political operatives who knew the system inside and out and who were totally dedicated to advancing the career of Harry Byrd, knowing that he returned their favors in kind. In the early thirties Byrd lost a number of these close friends who had been with him at the beginning: Captain D. H. Barger died in 1931; George Keezell in 1932; Henry Carter Stuart in 1933; Bauserman, Ferguson, and Herbert Hutcheson in 1934; and then Billy Reed and Louis Epes in 1935. But Byrd's career was so long that it cut across several generations of Old Dominion politicians, and as old friends died, he cultivated new ones who were as loyal and supportive as their predecessors.

His return to private life hardly produced the quiet he had hoped for. Dozens of organizations clamored for the former governor's time, hoping his public luster would rub off on their cause. He was inundated with requests to serve on boards, to join societies, and to speak at commencements and county fairs, even to straighten out tickets for reckless drivers, most of which he declined. As he told Edwin Alderman, "The fact is I have neglected my business here and must give it all my attention for the next few years."[18] But he could not always refuse. He was appointed to the Board of Visitors at VPI and was immediately asked to contact his wealthy friend Harry Guggenheim for support in developing an aeronautical engineering program at the school. His long and continuing interest in the Commission on Interracial Cooperation led to his appointment to the Board of Trustees of the Anna T. Jeanes Foundation, which supported black education in the South. He served on the Potomac River Commission, the George Washington Potomac Parkway Board, the Thomas Jefferson Memorial Foundation, and the Board of Directors of the United States Chamber of Commerce.[19]

Byrd had a long-standing association with the University of Virginia dating from his governorship that led to his consideration for its presidency in 1931 after Edwin Alderman died. His good friend Frederic Scott of Scott and Stringfellow was on the Board of Visitors and was likely responsible for the offer, which Byrd, a man without a high school degree, graciously declined, saying that he was "not qualified by training or temperament" for the position. Byrd's self-assessment proved correct. Responding to a report in 1932 that Virginia had the highest salary scale and lowest teaching load among southern universities, Byrd told his personal attorney, Gray Williams, who also was on the board, "Perhaps we went a little too fast in increasing salaries at the University." Williams had to explain to him that the article was a compliment to the university, not a criticism.[20] Scott, who had asked Byrd to give the dedication speech for the stadium he had donated to the university, then urged him to use his influence with John W. Davis to accept the presidency. Byrd made the effort, but to no avail. Scott turned next to Professor John Newcomb for the position and pressured the reluctant Byrd to lobby for his nominee with other board members, notably Williams. Newcomb was subsequently selected. A few years later Byrd successfully lobbied for Williams to be made rector of the university.[21]

Over the years Byrd was actively involved in promoting the Institute of Public Affairs at the university, which held a yearly public forum on major issues. The former governor was instrumental in getting Governor Roosevelt of New York and Admiral Byrd to attend the forum. The appointment of his friend and political protégé Colgate Darden to the presidency of the university in 1947 increased Byrd's participation in its affairs. He was made treasurer of the university's Development Fund, whose directors included Admiral William Halsey and former secretary of state Edward Stettinius. Byrd, who gave $2,500 to the fund, had little to do in the job but sign a few checks. Darden also sought Byrd's help, this time without success, in encouraging John D. Rockefeller, Jr., to contribute to a fund-raising effort for a graduate school of business, a program Byrd enthusiastically supported.[22]

Byrd's gift to the university was a particularly large one for him. Generally his philanthropy was more modest, albeit extensive: many small donations to

churches or organizations doing benefits, apples for schools, and the expected
political contributions to the state Democratic party and its candidates. He
later established scholarships for students at VPI's College of Agriculture. Byrd
believed in charitable giving, but not of an unqualified sort. As he stated in a
1939 article worthy of Andrew Carnegie, "Of all the Christian virtues, none is
more to be emulated, I believe, than generosity. It is the expression of many
fine qualities all in one—kindness and sympathy, unselfishness and humility,
and even thrift and industry, because he alone can give who has earned something to give. But giving may be a vice, too, if it is not attended by wisdom and
foresight, as well as kindness and sympathy."[23] His generosity grew as his personal wealth increased, but he never relinquished his penchant for saving a
dollar, especially during the depression years. This was exemplified in his directions to Lester Arnold to discontinue phone service at Rosement for three
months, saving himself $6, and to discontinue Mrs. Bessie Massie's free sub-
scription to the *Evening Star*.[24]

The depression also affected Byrd's newspaper operations. Circulation of
the *Evening Star* and *News-Record* had reached 5,000 and 9,000, respectively,
but it declined during the economic crisis, forcing Byrd to cut salaries and slash
dividends. He was constantly advising his editors and business managers to
institute greater economies, being much more concerned with costs than with
editorial policy. Faced with competition from E. E. Keister's *Northern Virginia
Daily* in Strasburg, Byrd tried to put him out of business. He wrote Gray Williams: "In my judgment, he is not solvent and has not been paying his bills. I
thought perhaps you could mention this matter also to the Farmers and Merchants [bank] without of course mentioning my name." He told directors of
the Associated Press, to whom Keister was applying for membership, that he
was "doomed to failure." But these efforts miscarried, and Byrd reconciled himself to the competition.[25]

Harry's involvement in the business affairs of his brother Richard continued to consume much of his time. Never having the organizational or business
sense of his older brother, the admiral functioned in a chaotic world. Returning
from his flight over the South Pole in 1929, he was confronted with speaking
engagements, award ceremonies, investment opportunities, and book contracts. At one point in late 1930 Harry was promoting the admiral's lectures
and supervising the financial arrangements of the tour of his supply ship, *City
of New York*. As compensation, Dick's contacts with influential people proved
helpful in advancing Harry's political career.[26]

Although that career was on temporary hold, Byrd did not lack political
involvement in the early thirties. He became the Democratic national committeeman from Virginia but turned down requests to run for Congress from his
home district, accepting the advice of Reed, who at this point was thinking of

him for the Senate or the presidency.[27] Byrd used this period to consolidate his control of the Organization and to preserve the reforms he had introduced into state government. With the assistance of Combs, with whom he worked very closely in these matters, Byrd involved himself in local election campaigns across the state, sending letters to precinct chairmen to encourage them to qualify the vote, contributing funds where most needed, advising candidates of appropriate campaign tactics, and then campaigning for them in the fall general elections.[28]

Almost as soon as he arrived home in Berryville, he was writing his friends in Richmond about legislation, executive appointments, and even salary increases. His advice was very much in demand. Combs, who was sending Byrd almost daily reports of legislative progress, requested his help with assemblymen in getting specific legislation passed, and Sam Ferguson wailed: "You are now and have been since your campaign for Governor, the dominant leader of the majority party in this State. . . . We miss your generalship."[29]

Byrd reserved much of his counsel for his successor, John Garland Pollard. An able individual, Pollard was more adept at teaching a government class at William and Mary than he was at running the state government. Overwhelmed at first by the stifling authority of the Organization and then by the impact of the Great Depression—both of which limited his freedom of action—he resigned himself to following the lead of his predecessor. "It is indeed comforting," he told Byrd, "to feel that I have so strong an arm to lean upon." His admiration for Byrd's ability was so great that he felt no obsequiousness in the act. "As I have often said to you," he admitted, "I distrust my own political judgment, especially as against your own which has proven so wise in the past. I am so sincerely devoted to you and have such great confidence in your statesmanship that I would do all things in my power to add to your already great prestige." Pollard's ready wit softened the inevitable comparisons between the two. As he said on more than one occasion, patting his protruding belly, "I got that by swallowing the Byrd machine."[30]

Byrd came to have great respect for Pollard as he struggled with the terrible economic conditions that arose during his term. He wrote the governor in March, 1931: "I have been more than delighted to be of what little service I could to you. . . . You, however, had made all of the decisions and have yourself met the difficult problems confronting you in a manner that has created great admiration not only in Virginia but wherever I go."[31] He always treated Pollard cordially and respectfully, but there was no question that Byrd was the real teacher. The two vacationed together in Florida before the inauguration, and Byrd gave Pollard a quick course in Organization politics. Once the new governor took office, the lessons continued. Byrd suggested amendments to legislation and urged reappointment of his appointees or dismissal of disloyalists. He advised the governor not to veto a bill unless "a matter of principle was involved." Pollard frequently asked how to deal with specific problems, even to the point of wondering what working hours he should set for state employees. Byrd's suggestions were based on his experience as governor but also on his desire to protect his programs and his leadership of the Organization. Pollard had hopes of moving beyond the Byrd reorganization to tackle the ignored issues of education, agriculture, and local government, but he was only marginally successful. The inevitable commissions were established to study the questions, and some improvements were made in the oyster industry and the workmen's compensation law, but at the end of the 1930 session, Senator Ferguson reported to Byrd, "There were few matters of great importance for our consideration and legislation, but so far as I know your every wish was done."[32]

In the summer of 1930, the country experienced a widespread drought, one of the most severe in the nation's history. Virginia's rainfall for the year was 60 percent of normal, with July and August especially dry. Heavy losses were expected in corn, peanuts, and apples. Orchardist Byrd wrote Reed: "I have been in the apple business twenty-five years but conditions look to me to be more unsettled and more difficult than I have ever experienced. . . . Unless some relief occurs in the next few days not only will a large part of our crop be destroyed but many trees will die." It was so bad that he drained the swimming pool at Rosemont. Byrd later estimated his losses due to the drought to be $100,000.[33]

Moving quickly to combat the emergency, Governor Pollard, in accordance with President Hoover's drought relief proposals, created a state Drought Relief Committee and asked Byrd to chair it. Initially reluctant to accept, Byrd was caught between his desire to help and his fear of making farmers the victims of charity. After sounding out Billy Reed, who urged caution, he took the post, convinced of the growing need for action and feeling some obligation to help the governor. He favored giving immediate federal loans to farmers who needed credit for fertilizer, seed, and spring planting materials. Although the job interfered with the apple harvest, Byrd managed to spend one day a week in Richmond during the fall of 1930 without compensation.[34]

Much like his work with the Fuel Administration, Byrd organized drought relief by counties, each county having a chairman who was to report on local conditions and coordinate loan transactions. On the committee with Byrd was John Hutcheson, director of the Extension Service at VPI, who had contact with the farmers through his county extension agents and seed loan committees, and Robert Angell, head of the Roanoke Red Cross, who had worked with Byrd on the fuel conservation effort. Henry Shirley's highway department complemented their endeavors by putting farmers to work on the roads with advances on future federal highway allocations and matching short-term loans from the state, an idea first suggested by Governor Pollard. Railroads contributed by reducing rates 50 percent on shipments of hay, feed, and livestock. Reflecting his preference for private aid, Byrd urged his hunting partner Wat Ellerson of the Albemarle Paper Company to encourage all pulpwood users to increase the amount of wood they purchased from destitute farmers.[35]

Despite these efforts the relief program fizzled as conditions worsened, particularly in the tobacco counties of the Southside, where Reed reported the crop to be "the worst that ever came out of the ground." Rural banks were closing their doors. According to Tom Ozlin, relief chairman in Lunenburg, "Thousands of our people are facing absolute want and inability to rehabilitate themselves." Byrd complained that the $200,000 in federal loans was "an absurdity" compared to the need. He recommended a comprehensive relief program that continued the railroad rate reductions, extended credit for farmers, and expanded the road program with fewer restrictions on who could participate. Although at one point he suggested the formation of a Virginia credit corporation to finance relief, he shied away from more vigorous state action, rejecting a special General Assembly session to consider tax reductions or issuance of bonds as recommended by Lieutenant Governor James Price. Nevertheless, in a position of administrative responsibility, Byrd seemed more open to federal and state intervention than at any other time in his public life. Having approved Governor Pollard's short-term borrowing for road building, he declared in October: "We of course know in Virginia that self-help is always the best help. The individual must do mainly for himself, but in disasters of this kind our coordinated governmental agencies may render the task of the individual less severe."[36]

Byrd was particularly incensed by the failure of President Hoover and Secretary of Agriculture Arthur Hyde to press for a larger federal loan program. He wrote to Congressman R. Walton Moore, "I have the utmost contempt for Hyde, but if possible, I want to avoid any more friction than we have already had as it lies in his power to punish Virginia by making the regulations so severe that we will get very little benefit from the loans." However, like the president, Byrd feared the beginning of a dole system, and so he agreed with Hoover that the loans should not be used to provide food for the farmers, a task that he thought should be left to the Red Cross. Their future opposition to the New Deal of Franklin Roosevelt was in the making.[37]

In November, Byrd met with the other state relief chairmen in Washington, D.C., to share information and draw up new proposals. He discovered that Virginia, along with West Virginia, Arkansas, and Kentucky, was among the states hardest hit by the drought. He was appointed to a steering committee that recommended enactment of $60 million in federal loans for farmers' planting needs, $50 million in federal loans for road improvements in the twenty hardest-hit states—to be repaid over ten years—and full compensation for farm agents by the federal government.[38] After the meeting he urged Senator Glass to do all he could to get the $60 million measure through Congress. At the same time he asked Glass and Congressman James Aswell of Louisiana to ensure that the language of the loan bill included loans for activities such as spraying fruits and vegetables. Although Aswell turned him down, this provision was written into the final bill that authorized $45 million in loans. However, as Glass later proclaimed, "In the farce of drought relief, we were led up the hill, with flags flying and trumpets blowing, and then right back down again."[39]

Winter precipitation alleviated drought conditions and put the relief program out of business, but not before charges of political partisanship in the makeup of the local committees caused Byrd and Hutcheson to devise a more representative means of selection. Local committees and county agents continued to distribute loan money for spring planting, while the Red Cross provided for those in more desperate shape. Byrd was inclined to attribute reports of suffering to the larger economic crisis in the nation rather than the drought. He wrote Reed: "I am sorry about the newspapers publishing the articles in regard to the alleged suffering. So far as I know there is no suffering anywhere in the state and we are keeping closely in touch with the matter. It is true that the Red Cross is looking after a number of families but this is being done with local funds."[40]

In his final report to the governor, Byrd commended the work of local charities and the Red Cross, the cooperation of the railroads whose rate reductions saved farmers $1 million in shipping costs, the paper mills that purchased pulpwood, and the farmers who took care of themselves in half the counties. Since federal loans to 14,500 Virginia farmers totaled only $2 million, a negligible sum compared to the estimated $100 million in losses they had suffered, the Drought Relief Committee had emphasized a spirit of self-help. Byrd proudly concluded that the work of the committee had cost the state only $1,186. Demonstrating an attitude prominent at the national level, Virginia's leaders were reluctant to institute expensive relief measures, believing that budget balancing would have a more vital impact on business confidence. When the depression replaced the drought as the primary crisis, the precedent for inaction had been established.[41]

Byrd was both right and wrong in his assessment of economic conditions in Virginia in the first half of 1931. Much of the difficulty was, indeed, caused by the encroaching depression, not the drought, but suffering was increasing rapidly. Governor Pollard admitted as much when he asked Byrd to continue on as chairman of a new Committee on Unemployment, so named at Byrd's suggestion rather than the Unemployment Relief Committee. Byrd declined the offer, excusing himself on grounds of business demands—another harvest required his presence—but he recommended Reed for the post, and that public servant accepted. Little did they know of the crisis at hand.[42]

The Great Depression of the thirties was one of the watershed events of twentieth-century America, shattering the people's optimistic faith in a utopian future, challenging their belief in rugged individualism, and leading to a revolution in the role of government in their lives. Virginia had a delayed reaction to the financial catastrophe. The nature of its economy—the balance between agriculture, industry, and commerce, subsistence-level farming, and the support of federal money in the Washington and Norfolk areas—immunized the state from the immediate effects of the crash. These buffers eventually broke down, but they did minimize the total effect of the depression in Virginia and contributed to its more rapid recovery by 1935. The conservative nature of the Old Dominion and the strength of traditionalism also helped to insulate the state from the worst shocks of the crash. Virginia was, in a sense, not only resistant to progressive innovation but impervious to regressive change as well. Ledger books in the black, a reluctance to borrow, a stoical outlook, and a strong self-help ethic had a very stabilizing effect when times turned bad. One Red Cross official remarked during the 1930 drought, "Virginians are prouder and less willing to seek outside help than citizens of the other states in the drought areas."[43]

Nevertheless, the depression delivered a major blow to the state's economy. Although it was late arriving, its impact was strongly felt by early 1931. Unemployed Danville strikers, unsuccessful in their four-month effort to restore wage cuts at Dan River Mills, were on the verge of starvation;[44] soup kitchens were feeding hungry schoolchildren in the mountain regions, and school terms were ending early in several counties; cities were making major budget cuts; farm prices, notably for tobacco, continued downward; and the unthinkable occurred: Governor Pollard announced a possible budget deficit. C. D. Bryant, director of a Danville tobacco warehouse, wrote his congressman: "The farmers are wrought up at a high pitch, a great many declaring vengeance due to the deplorable condition of their families suffering for want of clothing, medicine and other absolute necessities. . . . We find men on our warehouse floor actually weeping after they have had to sell their tobacco at prices that will mean nothing less than complete disaster."[45]

Reed and Byrd saw little of this. Trying to preserve an illusion of prosperity in order to protect Byrd's gubernatorial reforms and to maintain his image as a master administrator, they emphasized the favorable signs rather than the reality of depression. As Byrd told Reed before Pollard's announcement, "A deficit would create a very serious situation for us. . . . If Virginia can stand as the only state in the Union without a deficit and without the need of increasing taxes we will impress the business world with our conservative method of financing."[46]

Having taken the unemployment post "to keep the state out of trouble," Reed relied on the structure and personnel of the Drought Relief Committee to conduct his survey of economic conditions in the state, meeting as infrequently with them as possible to avoid disturbing the members' schedules. He optimistically concluded, "I believe Virginia is in better shape in this respect than any state in the Union, . . . even better than she was a year ago." Grossly underestimating the number out of work at less than twenty thousand, probably only a third of the real figure, the Committee on Unemployment called on businesses to shorten the workweek to five days and to initiate new building projects. Opposed to expensive work relief programs, it suggested no state relief effort, preferring, instead, reliance on Community Chest and Red Cross funds. Reed told committee member Robert Angell to avoid association with the Welfare Department and its employees lest that encourage the counties to seek help from the state. The committee's job, he said, was to suggest how work could be provided to the unemployed. He believed that if businesses would employ three workers where there were now two, there would be no unemployment problem. A compassionate, generous man, Reed could not visualize suffering on a large scale, fearing that public efforts to deal with it would undermine individual character and the "Virginia Way." He advised Byrd, "We must keep Virginia like she is without any changes."[47]

Byrd's vision and fears were the same. In his view, times were not so bad that people could not find work, and if they were in need, private charity would assist them. Government assistance was to be avoided because it was costly and obtrusive. Commenting on his experience with his apple pickers in the 1931 harvest season, he observed,

> I have never seen the general run of men and women more anxious to work than they are now. It is really pathetic to see the desire of whole families to pick in apple orchards. They are certainly doing all they can to meet conditions but, of course, if there is no work to be given them they will have to get some aid from some source. I would strongly advise that any relief work be handled by the Red Cross. I was greatly impressed with the work they did in Virginia last year and with the fact that they only gave relief when it was needed and warranted and they avoided in every possible way to pauperize people.[48]

On the question of assisting people in need, Byrd confronted an intellectual hurdle imposed by his life experiences. He had worked hard to achieve success, taking advantage of opportunities that were available, like the newspaper and apple growing. The newspaper had been a gift from his father, the gift of a challenge: "To succeed, I had to sit up night thumping my skull over editorial copy. I had to walk my legs off all day long to make ends meet. The more I worked, the more I discovered I didn't know. To win, I had to learn, and as I learned, I grew. I think that gift made a man of me." Unquestionably, Byrd had benefited from that experience, but he never appreciated the fact that such opportunities were not available to all. To him, public aid, while well intended, was a misguided gift; it did not challenge but instead it bankrupted character "by removing incentive and limiting opportunity." Yet Byrd never explained why private charity was less bankrupting, and he had no answers for what to do when the Red Cross ran out of money. He never understood that it was the loss of opportunity that forced people to turn to government as a last resort in the face of catastrophe. It was a blind spot in his already narrow social conscience.[49]

The depression also complicated Byrd's efforts to maintain a balanced state budget. As he told Frederic Scott in June, "The chief desire that I have in public affairs is to see Virginia maintain her present position of freedom from bonded indebtedness, freedom of deficit and without the need of increasing taxes." To this end Byrd essentially took over the budget process in 1931 from Governor Pollard, who, not surprisingly, had expressed a desire for consultations on the issue.[50] Worried that deficits would lead to attacks on his tax segregation system, he advised Pollard to reduce appropriations, especially for criminal expenses. Urging Reed to lobby the governor likewise, he cautioned: "Do not mention this as I do not want the Governor to think I am taking any part in his duties. . . . I believe that if the policies that . . . both of us have advocated go through the next General Assembly they will be permanent in Virginia for many, many years, and will place Virginia in a very advantageous position." Byrd also asked Highway Commissioner Shirley to maintain road construction at present levels, concerned that a decline would raise questions about pay-as-you-go roads and the tax segregation system financing them.[51] So obsessed was he by the specter of debt that Byrd considered disguising the deficit; he rationalized to Combs: "The people of the state are so blue that I believe it a mistake to add still further to their depression." Already facing the evaporation of his $4 million surplus, he feared that Pollard's continued short-term borrowing for highway construction to relieve unemployment would produce a deficit by the end of the fiscal year, so privately he and Reed prevailed upon bankers not to extend loans for the extra road building.[52]

In a lengthy October letter to the governor on the budget, Byrd recommended that Pollard stay within current revenues, approve no tax increases, cut appropriations uniformly, but maintain appropriations for schools and roads to avoid burdening localities and increasing unemployment. "I am only recommending to you what I would do myself were I in your position, and . . .

whatever decision you make will have my loyal and cordial support." He pointedly rejected the plans of Junius West and Tom Ozlin for higher taxes and relief plans, telling Pollard not to let Ozlin appear before the budget commission because he had become too emotional about the distressing conditions in his tobacco-producing section.[53]

When the budget commission met in the fall of 1931, Byrd was in close communication with commission member Sam Ferguson, who briefed him about its deliberations. On the last evening of the hearing, when Pollard asked each member for his recommendations to meet the emergency, Ferguson summarized Byrd's views, which were "practically agreed to by each member of the commission." Byrd's power could not have been more complete had he been in the room himself. Only days later Byrd put the final touches on his budget by recommending to Pollard and Ferguson an additional $1.4 million savings to be gained by an across-the-board 10 percent cut in state salaries from governor to office boys. Almost without exception his proposals to maintain a balanced budget were presented to the 1932 General Assembly by Governor Pollard and enacted into law.[54]

Byrd's phobia over deficits was deeply rooted in his experience and personal philosophy of government. One friendly biographer labeled it a "pathological abhorrence for borrowing."[55] This was likely reinforced by matters of ego and power, for Byrd feared that any policy failure—such as a deficit—might be attributed to him personally and might undermine Organization authority. He once stated to Reed: "All of us of course recognize that the worst thing that could happen to us now would be to have a deficit. It has been heralded over the country that we do not have a deficit, and if we have one it will result in very bad advertising for the State, and our enemies will attack us on all sides, especially the Richmond newspapers."[56] Nor could he tolerate any talk of revising Virginia's segregated tax system, the reorganized executive branch, or the short ballot, all of which had been major innovations of his governorship.

His hostility toward the Richmond newspapers remained strong. Earlier in 1931 the *News Leader* had given ample coverage to Westmoreland Davis's charge that Comptroller Combs had cost the state $100,000 by not taking advantage of discounts in the quick payment of bills. An audit of Combs's work revealed a loss of $45,000 but acquitted him any wrongdoing. A relieved Byrd wrote his friend: "I am proud of the way in which you have emerged from this controversy. I always think of your appointment as one of the most useful acts of my administration. . . . You must always remember that Douglas Freeman will never lose an opportunity to discredit you. . . . If he had a proper sense of fairness, he would now write an editorial commending you and acknowledging that he was wrong." Although the Organization had avoided a potentially damaging scandal, no one emerged from the affair untainted. Byrd cried to Reed that Bryan "has permitted his newspaper to consistently misrepresent everything we have done, and this is still continuing. What I would like to know is whether he is conducting a campaign to discredit me, and, if so, I think we should know it and take proper steps to protect ourselves." Such sensitivity denied legitimate criticism, and Byrd was not a forgiving adversary.[57]

Byrd's success in budget control was only a preliminary to his major achievement in the 1932 legislative session, the Byrd Road Act. Worsening economic conditions were creating new demands for state action, and the ever-cautious Byrd and Reed were apprehensive about the possibility of a revolt in the General Assembly. There was little opposition to the spending cuts that would keep Virginia's finances sound, but there was a growing clamor over maintaining highway department expenditures at the expense of other services. Spending on roads became the volatile issue, entangled in political infighting because of its association with the Byrd tax and road programs. Delegates from the Norfolk area, where most of the road building had been completed, proposed a $5 million diversion of auto license taxes from roads to schools. The Richmond *Times-Dispatch* agreed: "It is ethical and practical for Virginia to use part of its road revenue for schools to relieve the burden of local taxation in these hard times." That burden was increasing as the depression squeezed Virginia's taxpayers, who began forming associations to pressure local officials to cut taxes. Farmers claimed that the earnings from their crops were hardly enough to pay the taxes on their land. It was a message the legislators in Richmond could hear.

But Byrd and Pollard resisted the calls for diversion and relief. The governor argued that this would reduce the amount of highway work available for the unemployed. Byrd agreed, but mostly because of the effect diversion would have on highway development and tax segregation; it would "kill the Goose that laid the golden egg" and "tear down everything that has been done." He told Louis Epes it was their "patriotic duty" to oppose diversion because it would violate the long-standing pledge to Virginians that user taxes on licenses and gasoline were to pay for roads. If road building stopped, motorists would want the gas tax reduced. With the present and former governors opposing it, the diversion bill died in committee.[58]

However, to placate those demanding tax relief and to avert further criticism of tax segregation, Byrd proposed a road plan under which the state would take over the county road system, saving the counties $3.4 million in road expenditures and adding 36,000 miles to the state system. It had the added benefit of increasing the patronage available to the Organization. Rural interests applauded the plan, but urban representatives balked at the absence of relief for their constituents. The Norfolk *Virginian-Pilot* caustically editorialized,

"Highwayolotry as a State Religion." Claiming that Byrd had distorted the importance of highways to the state economy, the newspaper asserted that education, hospitals, asylums, and public health in Virginia were being shortchanged. When Byrd broached the idea to Senator Ferguson, the chairman of the Roads Committee exploded: "Harry, you have gone crazy. Absolutely crazy. We have spent a whole week here discussing whether we will put 800 miles in the state system, and now you come and want to put forty-some thousand miles in addition to what we already have. It can't be done." In spite of this opposition, the road bill, slightly amended, passed the rural-dominated assembly overwhelmingly, leaving no doubt about Byrd's strength in state politics. As soon as the road bill was enacted, Byrd urged county taxpayers to pressure their supervisors to pass the savings of the road plan directly on to them.[59]

Byrd's influence did not stop with highways. Legislation giving the governor authority to cut appropriations in the face of revenue shortfalls also sailed through, and the effort to overturn the short ballot was defeated in committee at Byrd's request. On those items important to him, he completed a clean sweep. He commended Pollard for his leadership, but in reality Byrd had been the consummate director. Late in the session a big blizzard hit the Valley, keeping Byrd out of Richmond for a few days. He joked to Reed, "As I was being mixed up in everything that came up in the legislature, . . . I thought it wise to stay away." Editor Freeman wrote his publisher that Byrd's "prestige is as great as it was when he was in office."[60] In many respects the 1932 General Assembly session was the culmination of Harry Byrd's career in Virginia politics. He would, of course, remain the dominant leader of the Organization for another three decades, but never again would he wield power so directly and effectively over the governor, legislature, and machine, a remarkable achievement for one out of elective office.

~ 7 ~

The Apple King

JOHN GARLAND POLLARD once remarked: "I go to some men's houses and they offer me a drink; to other houses and they offer me a cigar. But when I go to Harry Byrd's . . . he offers me an apple."[1]

Byrd's primary occupation in his midlife "retirement" was apples, the business he never left and to which he always returned. It was his avocation, his relaxation, his source of wealth; indeed, his experience in the apple business reinforced everything he ever knew about the free enterprise system and its relationship with government. And he was eminently successful at it. In 1933 his orchards were producing half-a-million bushels of apples from over 150,000 trees. He was president of the Winchester Cold Storage Company, the largest cold storage facility for apples in the world with a capacity of 1.5 million bushels, and he was a leader in the industry with a net worth of $1 million. He was "the 'Apple King' of America."[2]

Byrd began his other career in 1906 by leasing orchards near Winchester. Six years later he copurchased with his minister the Rosemont Orchard, and in 1918, this time with friend and fellow grower Shirley Carter, he bought the Green Orchard on Apple Pie Ridge eight miles northwest of Winchester, one of the largest orchards in the Valley. A year later he joined with brother Tom to buy the Kelley Orchard near Timberville. Usually sharing initial capital expenses with a partner, Byrd then bought out that partner as his own financial position improved, except for his brother with whom he remained partners in the Timberville orchard until the mid-fifties.[3]

Although he could not have foreseen how large his holdings would become, Byrd embarked upon this business with every intention of making it a long-term career. Sounding out Department of Agriculture experts on soil qualities, studying market possibilities, and pressing for improved storage and shipping facilities, he dedicated himself to becoming the biggest and best apple grower in the region. Wanting to be up-to-date on the latest scientific information, equipment, and farming methods, he read every pamphlet he could get his hands on to learn about growing apples. A quick learner, he investigated the use of heaters to protect the crop from early spring freezes and he was among the first to use tractors in the orchards. Throughout his career, in a mutually beneficial arrangement, he allowed Virginia experiment station personnel to conduct tests in his orchards with fertilizers and sprays, and he exchanged information with the Department of Agriculture on new varieties of apples. Ranging across his fields on foot, horseback, and motorcycle, he involved himself in every phase of the operation from purchasing land to planting trees—whose quality he was very particular about—to harvesting and selling the fruit.[4]

Byrd became a leader in all areas of the industry, known for the quality of his product and the integrity of his operation. When fruit wholesalers complained to him about the quality, size, or deteriorating condition of fruit sent to them, he made good on the shipment if he could trace the problem to his responsibility. Once when he was forced to cover a $3 per barrel loss on one shipment that he claimed had deteriorated in storage, Byrd ruminated, "This will be a lesson to me, as I do not expect in the future to ever store any apples unless paid for in full."[5] Inferior storage facilities, hot weather, and delayed shipments hurt the sale of apples, so he vigorously advocated the construction of larger and better cold storage facilities that slow the ripening of the fruit up to six months and allow the growers greater flexibility in their marketing strategies. (Later a controlled atmosphere cold storage plant, in which the oxygen is withdrawn, was developed, permitting a yearlong season because the fruit actually stops ripening.)[6]

Byrd had begun making inquiries into constructing a cold storage plant when he was leasing his first orchards. After considering purchase of an older plant, he decided to invest in a larger, more economical new facility. The Winchester Cold Storage Company, of which he was the founder, first president, and primary stockholder, was not the first in the area, but in time it became the world's largest. He spent an enormous amount of time on its planning, corresponding with construction firms and refrigeration and insulation experts, selecting the site, and arranging for the construction of railroad lines adjacent to the building. Since the plant's cost was beyond his own financial resources, he recruited other stockholders and users by advertising the advantages of the facility. Investors would have first option on space.[7] Financed through the sale of common stock and bonds and some borrowed money, the $225,000 plant, with a capacity of 120,000 barrels, was constructed in 1917 in spite of competition with wartime demands. Having promised partial completion to many users, Byrd was thrown into a panic when the motors for the refrigeration equipment were delayed in delivery, but they eventually arrived and the plant opened for business on September 22 with two rooms operative. Three years later, with his orchard holdings expanding rapidly, Byrd constructed another storage facility costing $350,000 with a capacity of 175,000 barrels.[8]

Increasing competition with apples from Washington State compelled Byrd and other Virginia growers to pay greater attention to the quality of the apples and their shipment. They had been in the habit of packing the apples in barrels of three bushels each with little regard to size or grade or protection; consistency in quality was marginal. Byrd needed little encouragement to turn to smaller barrels and boxes with corrugated pads to protect the fruit and then to advocate state inspection to ensure advertised quality. As he told Frederick County fruit growers in 1919, the apple industry was no longer a local institution; because of climate, soil, and adjacent markets, he believed they could be the greatest apple producers in the world, but they had to pay more attention to scientific farming, improved shipping methods, better advertising, and better organization of labor to compete with the boxed apples of the West. Organization of the growers, just as in politics, was essential to success.[9]

But Byrd's energy and interest could not control weather and war. Spring freezes are the worst enemy of the orchardist. Extended warm weather causes the trees to bud and flower; if a heavy freeze occurs at this time, most of the summer's fruit can be lost. Byrd searched for orchards with good elevation with few low places where the frost is most killing. He invested in heating equipment—smudge pots—to reduce the losses, but they were only marginally effective. Although severe losses in 1921 and 1922, when he harvested about 30 percent of the usual crop, may have encouraged him to take a greater interest in a political career, Byrd took his failure stoically. "The apple business," he told his brother, "is simply a business of averages and we should be satisfied if the average return over a period of 10 years is satisfactory and this has been the case in the past and I am certain it will be in the future." He was right. Beverley Byrd remembered three huge freezes in 1945 that produced apples the size of marbles. A recurrence in 1947 forced his father to buy 25,000 smudge pots, but they saw limited use over the next eight years because the freezes were modest and the crops enormous.[10]

Hail is another natural disaster, bruising the fruit and knocking it from the trees before it matures. Byrd took out some insurance, but this, too, was a hit-or-miss proposition. In June 1930 he bought $4,000 worth of hail insurance on 40 acres at Timberville, and three weeks later the icy pellets fell. One year he had insurance on half of a 1,000-acre orchard divided by a railroad track; the hail hit the side he had no insurance on, and he received checks for only $15 from four insurance companies. A severe storm at the Timberville orchard in August 1934 destroyed three-fourths of the crop, and insurance covered only half the estimated losses. Mother Nature, whether in the guise of frost, hail, locusts, or mice, was a formidable opponent.[11]

The world war disrupted Byrd's expanding empire, and he used all of his personal contacts to limit that damage. Having decided to build the cold storage plant only days after Congress declared war against Germany on April 6,

1917, he immediately asked his congressman and good friend, T. W. Harrison, to help ensure that enough railroad cars were available for the construction needs of the plant. Urging Harrison to use his influence with the National Council of Defense, Byrd claimed that his new facility would aid in the conservation of food. Harrison contacted Congressman Flood, Senator Martin, and Secretary of War Newton Baker, who approved preferential treatment for the project.[12]

Another wartime problem for Byrd was the chaotic situation on the nation's railroads, which complicated the shipment of apples and threatened loss of fruit due to longer trips and an absence of refrigeration cars. The cold storage company was shipping 700 cars of apples annually, and the trips were taking twice as long. Byrd found the government-controlled railroads so inefficient that at war's end he urged the immediate return of the roads to private hands.[13] The war also created labor problems by pulling away workers and driving up costs. In two years' time wages in the orchards went from $1.50 a day plus board to $2.50. Byrd tried to get a deferment for his barrel maker, Hugh Racer, arguing that he was more valuable to a 500-acre farm than being drafted, but he was unsuccessful.[14]

If Byrd ever had any conflict of interest with his apple business, it came during his tenure as state senator. His initiation and support of legislation that would benefit the apple growers was significant. He introduced bills to increase the authority of the Crop Pest Commission, to control the level of arsenic in the lead arsenic used for spraying, and to increase the quality of fruit inspection.[15] To combat cedar rust—a fungus that travels from cedar trees to apple trees, spotting their leaves and inhibiting their productivity—Byrd introduced legislation to prevent the planting of cedars within two miles of orchards and to allow counties to assess the growers $1 per orchard acre for removing cedars. Arrangements for the cutting would be made between the orchardist and the cedar tree owner. In the face of demands from apple growers for compulsory cutting, Byrd defended this cooperative provision that protected property rights, but such neighborliness did not always work; some people who did not want their cedar trees cut down were shocked to find them "accidentally" destroyed.[16]

To promote his apple interests, Byrd also lobbied the highway department to improve Winchester's road network, cut cedars along roadsides, enforce apple inspection laws, and approve a right-of-way for the extension of electric lines to supply the cold storage plant with additional power. Once the lines were approved, Byrd then pressured the Northern Virginia Power Company to maintain low rates, threatening on one occasion to petition the State Corporation Commission about rate increases. He prodded his father to use his influence with the SCC to keep the rates low.[17]

Because of his traditional laissez-faire attitude, Byrd had reservations about state inspections and grading of the fruit, but in time he became an advocate of strong standards that protected his place in the market. The costs of inspections and cedar cuttings were borne by the growers, but they ensured a better-quality product. For Byrd such costs were negligible; whether he appreciated their burden on small orchardists is unknown. The grading laws, for example, gave him a competitive edge over growers who were less able to afford the costs of the spraying and culling necessary for apples to pass inspection. On the other hand, Byrd opposed legislation that limited the size of trucks on the roads because it would raise the cost of hauling apples; moreover, he wanted no government regulation of the cold storage plants. He tolerated regulation that benefited him but not that which was costly and seemed to have larger social implications.[18]

Byrd's legislative and lobbying efforts should not obscure his commitment to an ethic of self-help and voluntarism in the apple business. He urged growers to cooperate in sharing information and pursuing joint action that advanced their interests, but always as a matter of choice. He simply believed that organization would lead to a better product, improved sales, and lower costs. To this end, he promoted fruit growers' associations and encouraged frequent communications between growers and horticulturists. Beginning in 1923 he held an August picnic at his Rosemont Orchard to bring apple men together to exchange ideas and good talk. Within a decade the annual affair was attracting fifteen hundred guests.[19]

What Byrd really loved about the apple business was its association with nature and its seasonal diversity, which challenged his talents while giving him time for other interests. The highlight of the year came in the physically taxing harvest months of September and October with picking, washing, packing, and cleanup. From harvest through the following May, he concentrated on sales and orchard maintenance—discing, poisoning mice to protect the tree roots, fertilizing, and major pruning. Byrd took care of the sales, and his managers, under his supervision, did the maintenance. In April, following the bloom, bees were introduced into the orchard for two weeks of pollination, and then spraying began that continued on a periodic basis until September. From June through August the trees were thinned to allow sunlight in and to reduce the weight of the limbs. It was an operation which Byrd came to know almost instinctively, reacting beforehand to every change in weather or market, always searching for a better way to survive.[20]

By the end of 1920, Byrd listed assets of $370,000, including $47,000 worth of stock in the cold storage plant, and debts of $153,000. He owned 700 acres of the expanded Rosemont Orchard, now worth $210,000; one-third of the Lupton Orchard, which he had purchased in 1919 with Fred Robinson; one-half of the Timberville orchard, shared with Tom Byrd; and one-half of the Green Orchard, valued at $200,000, on which he owed $65,000; within the year he would own all of the Green Orchard after exercising his option to buy out Shirley Carter. By 1924 he owned 75,000 apple trees that were producing close to 40,000 barrels of apples. Everything was not reinvested in the orchards; he began buying blue-chip stocks that in time became a major source of his income.[21]

Byrd's rapid rise to prominence in the field elevated him from student to teacher. His orchards were known for their size, uniformity, healthy look, and lack of overgrowth. Elected president of the Frederick County Fruit Growers Association in 1920, he became a much-sought-after speaker at association meetings, first at the local level and then at state and national gatherings. Invitations to write articles in professional journals, in which he disseminated his knowledge and apple-growing techniques, soon followed. In time, as his political stature rose, he became the subject of such articles rather than their author.[22]

Byrd's speech to the Virginia Horticultural Society in January 1925, just as he was kicking off his campaign for governor, was typical of his efforts. Entitled "The Future of Apple Growing in Virginia," it combined his assessment of the current state of affairs in the business with his highly technical discussion of the process. As he saw things, Virginia, with over a third of its trees less than twelve years old, was in an enviable position to increase its share of the market. Despite rising costs and an increasingly complex operation, Virginia growers could take advantage of their location and good transportation facilities to compete favorably with westerners for the home and foreign markets. In a highly detailed description of his own techniques, Byrd laid out the solution: (1) standardize and inspect produce on a voluntary basis with the costs borne by the growers; (2) grow a better-quality apple; (3) improve pollination; (4) spray, spray, spray, morning, noon, and night; (5) fertilize the soil; (6) pick 'em, pack 'em, and ship 'em with great care. Here Byrd was truly leading the way, for he was trying to convince these old-fashioned farmers, who believed that apples sold because they were a healthy food, that they had to adopt new marketing techniques such as protective packaging and advertising in order to survive; he encouraged them to share advertising costs by contributing to a central fund to be used to hire marketing agents and pay for ads.[23]

The early efforts to promote Virginia's apples culminated in 1924 with the celebration of the Shenandoah Apple Blossom Festival. Initially conceived to publicize the beauty and productivity of the Valley, the festival was turned into a booster operation by Winchester's mayor, William Glass, and supported by the town's businessmen and the area's apple growers, including Harry Byrd. On the first governing board were Tom Byrd and Harry's close friends H. B.

McCormac and R. Gray Williams. In time the extravaganza witnessed the introduction of pageants, parades, and the crowning of queen and court amid the springtime splendor of a land blanketed with white apple blossoms. Byrd was never at a loss to promote the affair, encouraging famous friends to attend and flying to Winchester in a blimp in 1928 to crown the queen himself. Byrd used his own apples as a self-promotional tool, giving hundreds of boxes to personal and political friends—including presidents, senators, and assemblymen—as gestures of generosity and apple-polishing.[24]

Byrd's election to the governorship restricted some of his time for the orchards, but never at harvest time. Indeed, throughout his political life, when September came, he was in Winchester and Berryville overseeing the picking. Sessions of Congress, special sessions of the General Assembly, even his gubernatorial campaign did not intrude. While governor, he took his vacations in the fall and went home to the orchards, even missing the State Fair one year on Governor's Day.[25]

Nevertheless, during his governorship much more responsibility for the daily management of the orchards fell on the shoulders of Tom Byrd. Tom, "the other brother," was a round-faced, jovial soul who never envied his illustrious siblings the fame they had captured. To him, "they were damn fools; [I] wouldn't have done what either of them did."[26] Slightly larger than his older brothers and with a personality as relaxed as theirs was competitive, he enjoyed being the very good farmer that he was. Their father good-naturedly claimed that he had no choice but to name his third son Tom, following Harry and Dick, but, in fact, Thomas was a family name. He spent two years at the University of Virginia, took a law degree at the University of Richmond, and entered law practice with his father in the capital. At the outbreak of war in 1917, he enlisted, won a commission, and compiled a distinguished service record, being so loved by the men who served under him that they frequently reunited with him after the war. When he returned from Europe, he entered into a partnership with Harry through the purchase of the Timberville orchard, which they later expanded with acquisitions in the Mount Jackson area. Tom worked these orchards during the week and came to Berryville on weekends to check on his brother's trees when Harry was in Richmond or Washington. Recognized in the apple community for his own abilities, he was elected president of the state horticultural society and was consulted by orchardists around the country. Harry said of his brother, "Tom is one of the best practical orchardists to be found anywhere." Unquestionably, he was of great help in building the orchards.[27]

Another individual who assumed prominence in managing the Byrd orchards during the gubernatorial years was Lester Arnold. Having served as personal secretary to Hal Flood and Byrd, he shifted into the apple business when

Byrd became governor. A thin, long-faced, but jolly individual of medium height, Arnold for most of his forty years with Byrd was the bookkeeper who arranged sales and paid the bills, but in addition to his apple work, he was Byrd's general business manager, tax consultant, stockbroker, research assistant, and sometime editor of the Winchester *Evening Star.* Much like his boss, Arnold was known as a straight shooter whose word was his bond. Popular among the fruit brokers and his Winchester friends, he had a quick wit, a great memory, and a perceptive eye for the market, qualities which Byrd truly admired. When Byrd was in the Senate, he would meet with Lester almost every weekend in the *Evening Star* office to go over the books.[28]

The final links in the hierarchy were Byrd's orchard managers, many of whom worked for him for thirty and forty years. John Livengood, who managed Rosemont no. 1, started with Byrd in 1918; William Neurdenburg, in 1926; and Clarence Singhass, a year later. They were all still managing in 1956. Byrd communicated with them frequently about operations, costs, and schedules. At harvest time they worked side by side. The managers were assisted by a small permanent workforce that cultivated, pruned, sprayed, and made barrels in the off-season. In the fall the labor force increased tenfold for the picking and packing. Labor costs were the largest operating costs, followed closely by barrels and spraying.[29]

Although never very far away from the actual operation during his years in Richmond, Byrd returned to the business in 1930 with renewed passion, purchasing new orchards, visiting foreign export markets, and taking over leadership of the Winchester Cold Storage Company once again. He had expanded into West Virginia and would soon pick up a big orchard in Mount Jackson and increase the acreage around Rosemont. Succeeding his brother as president of the Virginia Horticultural Society in 1931, he resumed his activities in the professional societies, giving talks, writing articles on different aspects of orcharding, and sending advice to growers across the country. Continuing his interest in the scientific side of the business, he experimented with new spraying techniques and the use of bees in pollination.[30]

With the onset of the depression, Byrd concentrated on lowering costs, improving his pack, and enhancing his reputation. He tried out a new pack on Billy Reed, sending him a dozen apples in a tightly fastened box with a small window for viewing the product. "I believe something like this is coming in order to increase the consumption of apples," he wrote. He also announced the selection of a brand name: the "Byrd Tin Plate Brand."[31] Placing the Byrd name on these apples was of considerable importance to him. He instructed his managers: "We have built up a reputation for apples packed with the Byrd Brand and tin tag as shown above on this letter head. This is to request that you do not put the tinplate brand on any fruit of inferior quality. Whenever in doubt please consult either Tom or myself. This is very important as one shipment of inferior apples bearing the tin tag will injure our reputation greatly, especially where the apples are for export to England." Arnold commented on Byrd's concern with quality: "His motto in packing his own apples is to make the fruit in each barrel or basket better than the grade marked on the outside. Much of his fruit could be marked Fancy, but he chooses the next lower grade of U.S. No. 1, so that the buyer will obtain a better grade than his package indicates."[32]

But reputation could not overcome the magnitude of the depression crisis. The difficulty was not with the home market, where apples continued to sell very well on urban street corners, but with the foreign market. A decade earlier Byrd had aggressively entered the export field in Europe and Latin America, perhaps to avoid competition with the better-packaged western apples or to take advantage of the lower shipping costs from the East Coast. By 1930 he was exporting 75 percent of his apples to Britain, Germany, Argentina, and Cuba, personally visiting London and Havana to arrange transactions. Deteriorating world economic conditions understandably heightened Byrd's concern for his business. He predicted to Sam Ferguson that the collapse of the pound sterling in England would cost him his profit in 1931.[33]

Out of the foundering global economy came a tide of economic nationalism that excluded foreign commodities in order to protect home markets and jobs. Justifications for such action often took the guise of consumer protection: diseased apples, toxic apples, and lower-grade apples must be kept out. In July 1930 Argentina embargoed shipments of barreled apples, claiming the widespread existence of decay; Britain followed suit, arguing prevalence of the fruit fly in shipments; six months later Poland held up shipments of American apples because of spray residue; and Germany barred all apples because of apple maggot and other pests. The International Apple Association blamed "bootleggers," but that was small comfort to Byrd, who had labored to raise those standards which he invariably exceeded. His apples did not have the maggot; they were carefully packed, albeit in barrels; and there was no rationale for requiring high color content in apples that were to be used for cooking purposes. Nonetheless, his apples were being barred, too. Bitterly he told Will Carson that Argentina's new rules would require every apple to be individually wrapped in oil paper and that Poland's arsenic tolerance level was so low that all apples would have to be washed individually.[34]

Part of the problem could be traced to the United States' own pursuit of economic nationalism. In the spring of 1930, Congress passed and the president signed the Hawley-Smoot tariff which raised average duties on many foreign goods to a new high of 50 percent. Because of his philosophical commitment to open markets and his concern for the impact this would have on his business, Byrd had urged a presidential veto. He blamed the higher tariff for restricting the sale of apples abroad and for raising the prices of foreign goods he purchased, such as arsenic. Responding to Byrd's suggestion for a national meeting of apple growers to discuss foreign trade, J. W. Herbert, a Washington grower replied: "I would say that what we need first of all is a strong Democratic administration. Or else that we create one more Cabinet officer similar to the Lord High Executioner . . . whom we might designate as the Lord High Fool Killer whose job it would be to kill off every man in Congress who proposed another fool tariff measure."[35]

Byrd's response was more in keeping with his traditional behavior: do the job better and lobby hard to reverse the restrictions. He improved his pack by wrapping apples and trying the smaller pony barrel, baskets, and boxes to meet Argentine requirements. He and Tom installed a washing and brushing machine at the Turkey Knob packinghouse for cleaning the apples and removing the spray. He corresponded with senators Glass and Swanson, Ambassador Walter Edge in France, and his European and New York buyers, asking them to lobby for reduced quotas and duties. He continued this effort when he became a United States senator in 1933, writing to Secretary of State Cordell Hull, President Roosevelt, and Commerce Secretary Daniel Roper. The experience confirmed in Byrd's mind the necessity of keeping government out of the marketplace. Thereafter, he invariably voted for reciprocal trade treaties that kept tariffs low and against governmental efforts to regulate agricultural commodities.[36]

In combating the depressed foreign market, Byrd pursued one other option he had long recommended: improved marketing facilities abroad. He urged the Virginia Horticultural Society to levy a three cents per barrel assessment on all Virginia apples shipped for export (which he estimated would raise $45,000 to $60,000) to advertise Virginia apples at home and in foreign markets and to employ a representative in those markets as the society's agent. It passed overwhelmingly. Byrd also got the society to endorse a uniform spray residue of 1 percent per pound of fruit in order to meet world tolerances and reduce foreign barriers.[37]

Despite his constant appeals for participation, the number of subscribers to the marketing campaign fell short of expectations. Nevertheless, as the biggest grower in the Valley and, thus, the largest contributor to the campaign, Byrd was able to turn this group effort to his personal advantage. The Virginia apple growers' representative abroad, G. S. Ralston, a former state extension horticulturist, with whom Byrd had frequently corresponded, reported his findings directly to the society's president, so that Byrd in effect had his own agent in the field. Ralston's long, almost weekly reports mixed praise and criticism of Byrd and the Virginia growers. "Your own pack is so superior, " he wrote, that it "commands a premium over the other fruit," but "it suffers . . .

from a Virginia pack which is infinitely inferior to your own." Confirming weak market conditions brought on by the depression, Ralston recommended improving standardization and packing procedures before spending more money on advertising.[38] He also advised Byrd to give greater consideration to the color of apples: "I rather feel that you have been opposed to stronger color requirements. I think you would be convinced otherwise if you could spend a couple of weeks with us in Europe. It is the most important factor of all." Byrd was already shifting in this direction when he moved back to Rosemont. His purchase of 6,000 trees of the Starking, Rome Beauty, and Delicious varieties in 1930 with an option to take 15,000 more later in the year indicated that he was searching for a redder apple. Color sport varieties would be his future.[39]

If anything, it was the depression that delayed this conversion, squeezing his resources and his ability to expand. Like any large farmer, Byrd had great assets but many debts occasioned by orchard expansion and increasing overhead costs: packinghouses, equipment, and acquisition of new trees, which usually took seven to ten years to mature before paying a return.[40] These long-term investments required heavy borrowing. Furthermore, Byrd was always taking out short-term loans to finance that year's maintenance costs and the harvest. An example of the magnitude of his operation was his request of John Miller, president of First and Merchants National Bank of Richmond, his biggest creditor, for an advance of $200,000 for harvesting in 1933. In these loan requests Byrd always carefully assessed current conditions in the apple market and summarized his present and future prospects. His 1931 report emphasized the cost-effectiveness of his operation. Producing apples at the lowest cost since 1914 ($1.50 a barrel), he claimed that his large holdings were permitting him to produce 25 to 50 cents per barrel cheaper than smaller competitors. His expected return, in spite of a large crop and poor European conditions, was $2 to $2.50 a barrel on 200,000 barrels. Sixteen months later Miller warned him against having too high a debt, and Byrd replied, "Of course, I fully realize that I went into debt too heavily [in 1932], but I regard my condition as being considerably better than it was last year."[41]

Byrd had a comfortable relationship with the financial community. He relied on his success as a businessman and a politician to win approval of his loan requests. This was particularly true among the smaller bankers of the Valley who were his friends and fellow politicians, such as Charlie Louderback, a key Byrd political operative in Page County, or "Uncle Doug" Fuller of the Farmers and Merchants National Bank of Winchester, which helped finance the cold storage plant. On one occasion in 1923 when Byrd was rather desperate for money to pay off the note on the Kelley Orchard, he was granted a note for $32,500 from the Shenandoah Valley Joint Stock Land Bank, whose president, H. B. Sproul, had been appointed to the State Highway Commission with

Byrd's endorsement. For banker George Michie, to whom he owed $25,000, Byrd agreed to help Michie's relative get a job. Byrd was also a director of First and Merchants Bank in Richmond and Farmers and Merchants Bank in Winchester, to both of which he was heavily indebted. There was never a hint of impropriety in these arrangements, but there is little doubt that Byrd was taking advantage of his position.[42]

However, the primary reason bankers liked Byrd was that he was good for their money. He was a prosperous businessman who paid his debts on time. They also knew that he was careful with a nickel, as he had been from the beginning of his business career. Byrd was frugal to a fault; "Waste Not, Want Not" was his abiding motto. Helen Byrd remembers her father-in-law once berating her for picking an apple off the tree to eat rather then taking one off the ground; he explained that the ones still on the tree were not yet ripe. Once when he was leaving Berryville for a few months, he discontinued telephone service at the bungalow, admonishing the telephone company not to charge him a reinstallation fee. And in a particularly ungenerous act, he told an Alexandria school principal, who wanted permission to gather unpicked apples after the harvest to feed schoolchildren, to go to the apple dealers in Winchester.[43]

Since the apple business involved tremendous debt and high risks, it was not the most appealing prospect for one who was so parsimonious and unlikely to take chances. But as he told his brother-in-law Grey Beverley, who kidded him about gambling on the stock market, "I'm not gambling at all; I'm investing." Similarly, he viewed the borrowing to finance his orchards as an investment that would produce additional capital. This kind of private debt contrasted starkly with a public debt, which, he believed, was an unproductive use of the taxpayers' money that was absorbed by the recipients without being invested or returned.

His public stand on this issue sometimes produced cries of hypocrisy from his political enemies. Byrd accepted loans from the Federal Land Bank and the Reconstruction Finance Corporation to finance his orchards, but he likely reasoned that these were debts that would be repaid to the federal treasury. However, after he went to the Senate, he firmly refused any federal subsidies for surplus apples, for utilizing soil conservation practices, and for rebuilding his burned-down cannery that was already covered by insurance. He told Lester Arnold, "I should dislike very much to see any apples in which I have any interest whatever sold to the government." Later in his career he acknowledged that he could have earned upwards of $200,000 in conservation payments, but he did not think he deserved money for practices he was already performing. He even refused to sell apples to countries where shipments were financed with Economic Cooperation Administration funds. As a United States senator he did not think he should benefit directly from legislation that he was responsible for passing. Although on rare occasions he deviated from this rule, few public servants have ever been as scrupulously observant of it.[44]

Byrd's cost-conscious efforts had their most negative effect on wages and labor relations, particularly during the depression. Starting in 1930 when wages at the Green Orchard were cut to $2 a day, they bottomed out at ten cents an hour for a ten-hour day in early 1933. He wrote to foremen John Livengood and William Neurdenburg, whose salaries had been cut by as much as one-third, that they must watch "the expenditure of every single dollar." He anticipated selling apples out of storage for less than the cost of production. Paying some of his men in kind, he wrote to Livengood, "I will fatten two hogs and furnish feed and pasture for one cow and provide two tons of coal and rest of fuel in wood and fruit." Byrd tried to comply with local wage scales, usually paying a little more at the orchards in the Winchester area than at those in West Virginia and Shenandoah County.[45]

Years later, reports surfaced about the low wages in Byrd's orchards. When told that Byrd was complaining about federal relief payments siphoning off workers from private labor, Franklin Roosevelt reportedly said to Rexford Tugwell: "I know what's the matter with Harry Byrd. He's afraid you'll force him to pay more than ten cents an hour for his apple pickers." Columnist Drew Pearson picked up this story and repeated it several times over the years; on each occasion, Byrd felt obliged to explain that he was paying more than prevailing rates for labor in his area, but his strong opposition to unions and labor legislation guaranteed that the issue would not die. While he seemed to get along quite well with his workers, particularly those who stayed with him a long time, he was less sympathetic to the needs of the harvest laborers, many of whom were mountain people, who, Byrd declared, could make enough in two months to hold them for the year.[46]

During World War II, conscription and industrial demands for labor severely reduced the available number of apple pickers. Byrd put in long hours at harvest time in these years, even when the Senate was in session. On occasion he used Boy Scouts and German prisoners of war as pickers. He wrote to Douglas Southall Freeman in October 1944: "I have never had such difficulties in the harvesting of an apple crop, due both to weather conditions and to the shortage of labor. You will be interested to know that the only able-bodied labor we have had of any consequence are some White Russian prisoners, who were captured while fighting with the Germans, although they now profess great hatred for the Germans. I have only 35 of these, but they are willing to do the heavy work, which the local labor does not want to do; neither will the Bahamans and Jamaicans, who have been imported here, undertake it."[47]

The expansion of his orchards and the postwar economic revolution that changed the nature of American labor forced Byrd to turn more to migrant laborers. Housing and payroll costs rose; the migrants were less dependable and more likely to cause trouble among the locals than were native pickers. By 1955 he had constructed five camp houses to accommodate 500 transient workers; at times he had 1,800 men, women, and children in the orchards with a daily payroll of $20,000. They worked in teams of eight to ten, going over each tree three times with ten days between each pick; an average worker could pick eighty bushels a day. Picking apples at the right moment was an art as well as a physically demanding chore that required handling heavy ladders and carrying a fifty-five-pound sack of apples around one's neck. The widespread use of migrant labor led to federal regulation, which Byrd worked to limit. In 1961 he opposed legislation to pay Mexican farm laborers 90 percent of the average farm wages in the state of employment.[48]

Despite the difficulties with labor and new federal regulations, Byrd remained committed to orcharding. Not only did it still absorb him, but he had embarked upon a major expansion of his business in the late thirties that propelled him to new levels of production and wealth. The problems with the foreign markets, his interest in the new color sport varieties, and his own pioneering spirit led him to buy five farms that totaled one thousand acres south of Charles Town, West Virginia, in 1937. His old Berryville friend Ralph Dorsey, whom he had talked into going into the apple business in 1929 and who was dabbling in real estate in West Virginia, sold him the land for what came to be known as the Jefferson Orchard, the largest single orchard in the world at that time.[49]

As always, Byrd prepared well for this venture, analyzing market conditions, studying every phase of the operation as it would relate to the new varieties, consolidating his debts, and selling off some of the smaller, older orchards. The depression and rising trade barriers had crippled the export trade, which had become the heart of his operation. Switching from the foreign to the domestic market required a change in the kinds of apples produced to meet the preferences of American consumers for a less blemished, more colorful apple.[50] In the fall of 1937, 35,000 new trees arrived at the Jefferson farm for planting, the first large-scale planting of the color sports in the East. In some areas the rows of alternating varieties ran two miles long. As the trees matured over seven to ten years, Byrd added a cold storage plant and a packinghouse in 1945 with a capacity for washing, waxing, and wrapping 10,000 to 12,000 bushels a day. This operation became his pride and joy.[51]

In the postwar period the senator refined and diversified the business with the assistance of his sons. To reduce waste and to maximize profit, Byrd turned to producing apple by-products with the culls, the lower-quality fruit. A cannery was constructed next to the railroad tracks in Berryville in 1948 with Dick in charge; it started producing jellies and apple butter and later moved to apple-sauce, sliced apples, and apple cider. Although Byrd was proud of the final product, he was a "fresh apple man" with little interest in the cannery other than its profit. Even so, when the cannery burned down in April 1962, he had no reservations about rebuilding it.[52]

Although he now left much of the marketing phase to Harry Jr. and Lester Arnold, he continued to be on top of the business, which had changed remark-ably over the fifty years of his involvement. Everything was now more scientific and automated: apples were sprayed fourteen times a year with milder, more disease-specific sprays, and the sprayers were more mechanized; fertilizers were better balanced; and handling and packaging were more sophisticated. Yet Byrd was still telling his managers and sons how to prune and spray the trees and to watch out for fire.[53]

Rarely missing weekend trips to the orchards, he would arrive at Rosemont from Washington every Friday evening. The next morning he rose at 6 A.M. and was in the shop or orchards talking with his managers until 9 A.M., when he returned to the house for a big breakfast before driving to Winchester to go over records with Arnold at the *Evening Star* office. He would mix in visits to the packinghouses or cannery when they were in operation, relishing the conversation with the people working for him. On one Saturday morning, dressed in his baggy khaki trousers and collarless shirt, he was outside the can-nery when a man advised him, "Buddy, no use going in there, they're not hiring anybody." On Sunday he would walk for several hours in the orchards, in-specting the crop and enjoying his Blue Ridge Mountains, before returning to Washington in the evening, ready to take on the forces of liberalism on Mon-day morning.[54]

By the mid-fifties, H. F. Byrd, Inc., had become a modest little empire in the northern Shenandoah Valley. Employing 1,800 workers at the height of the season with sales in excess of $5 million, Byrd, Inc., owned 200,000 trees in eleven orchards on 5,000 acres, five packinghouses, one cannery, three cold storage units, five camp houses, sixty two-ton trucks, twenty-two buses, fifty-three high-pressure sprayers, 400,000 picking boxes, and 25,000 smudge pots. Production peaked in 1958 at over two million bushels, 2 percent of the national crop. Byrd's was the largest individually owned orchard business in the world. A balance sheet for December 31, 1963 showed his physical assets at $4.5 million and an almost equal amount in stocks such as Armstrong Cork, Eastman Ko-dak, Safeway, Royal Dutch Petroleum, and, of course, H. F. Byrd, Inc., now worth $1.5 million, all of which were paying him $80,000 a year in addition to his apple profits. His income after taxes of $80,561 was $180,000, and his chari-table contributions totaled $53,000. The poor newspaper boy had prospered.[55]

All his sons and grandson agree that Byrd was more of a businessman than he was an orchardist. Although he loved the country and could be near-euphoric about the natural beauty surrounding Rosemont, he was not a gentleman farmer. Acclaimed by the agricultural experts for his knowledge, he was a progressive, scientific farmer who turned a small leasing operation into a commercial empire for the purpose of making money. He was successful because of his administrative skills, energy, innovation, and foresight. Only in his final years did he seem to lose his zest for the competition. Although he was still planting new trees to replace old ones, he had stopped buying orchards, and the declining productivity of the older ones after forty years of peak production did not enable him to sustain growth. Rising costs of labor and equipment and government regulations inhibited further expansion. Perhaps he had finally grown tired of competing with frosts and uncooperative bees, ready to retire like his older trees. After his death his sons continued to run the company, but they sold the cannery and the Jefferson Orchard in 1970, and the remaining orchards were divided among the heirs in 1979. Nevertheless, fields of Byrd apple trees still bloom in the shadow of Rosemont.[56]

～ 8 ～

A Presidential Campaign

FOR MUCH OF 1932 Harry Byrd had more important things than apples on his mind. He began the year running for the presidency and ended it pursuing a seat in the United States Senate. Despite the well-publicized success of his governorship, he was initially reluctant to press his candidacy for the nation's highest elective office, concerned as he was with his apple business, his wife's health, and maintaining control of affairs in Virginia. Nor did he have an appetite for the rough-and-tumble nature of national politics, where southern conservatives had little chance of winning the prize. His patrician style was more suited to Virginia where politics was tightly controlled by the Organization. Personally gregarious on his own territory, he was not a naturally outgoing individual or a polished speaker. As he wrote Billy Reed in the fall of 1930, "I think the time has come for me to make a definite statement that I do not desire to be considered in connection with the presidential nomination. I think this is wise, first, because I have no chance; second, because I do not want to be bothered with invitations to speak and to have people come to see me; and thirdly, because I want to attend to my own business and have more time to see my family and friends." Reed was sympathetic to Byrd's personal feelings, but he replied, "I don't think you are going to be able to get out of it."[1]

From the moment his young friend began to receive critical acclaim for his state reorganization efforts, Reed projected him for higher office, broaching the subject to Byrd as soon as he left the executive mansion. Others were similarly impressed. From his fellow governor O. Max Gardner, Byrd heard that his chances for nomination and election were "growing brighter every day." Gardner, who was following Byrd's lead in reorganizing state government in North Carolina, assigned a young aide, Tyre Taylor, a leader of the Young Democrats in North Carolina, to this presidential project. Perhaps even more than Reed, Taylor was driven by the prospect of a Byrd presidency, but he advised that they needed to move quickly or "the Roosevelt boom will have flattened us out before we get started."[2]

Throughout 1931 Byrd remained ambivalent. His work on the Democratic National Committee and his frequent contacts with front-runners Franklin

Roosevelt and Al Smith strengthened Byrd's position as a compromise candidate. At this time an alliance with Roosevelt appeared more likely. The two had begun a long-distance association in 1919 when brother Dick brought then Assistant Secretary of the Navy Roosevelt to Virginia for a hunting trip. The friendship deepened through their shared gubernatorial responsibilities and the close ties between Roosevelt and Admiral Byrd, who had a high regard for the New Yorker. Enthusiastic about his brother's candidacy, Dick served as a conduit for political information between the two candidates, urging them to see more of each other. Harry remained skeptical, but he never closed the door, telling his brother to keep him advised about what he heard.[3]

Another factor driving Byrd toward Roosevelt was the strong antiprohibition position of Smith, his campaign manager Jouett Shouse, and Democratic national chairman John J. Raskob, all "wet" Catholics who had frightened so many Virginia voters in the 1928 campaign. Byrd and Roosevelt succeeded in blocking Raskob's effort to write a repeal plank for the party at a March 1931 meeting of the Democratic National Committee. The Virginian feared that a dogmatic antiprohibition platform would cost the Democrats the state once again and destroy the organization that he had reinvigorated after the 1928 fiasco. That threat motivated his efforts to find a compromise position and stimulated his interest in the nomination.[4]

His interest was also piqued by his brother's encouragement and that of a growing number of supporters both within and outside Virginia. Senator Josiah Bailey confirmed North Carolina's support, while soon-to-be lieutenant governor A. B. ("Happy") Chandler of Kentucky declared, "It seems high time that the Democrats should turn to the Old South and to you for its nominee." James Thomson, publisher of the New Orleans *Item-Tribune*, encouraged him to make contacts among southern newspapermen.[5] Back home, Governor Pollard offered to call a conference of southern leaders who might support a Byrd candidacy. He wrote: "Modesty is your outstanding fault and that fault is so beautiful that I sometimes find myself counting it a virtue. I shall consider it a great compliment to your confidence in me as a friend if you will use me in every possible way to advance your leadership which I consider exceedingly important, especially in this crisis." Louis Epes had already polled several Virginia congressmen about a Byrd presidential bid; he found Clifton Woodrum and Pat Drewry enthusiastic, Glass supportive but doubtful of success, and Swanson noncommittal. "The more I think about this thing," said Epes, "the more convinced I am that an early effort ought to be made to put you forward."[6]

By this time Reed was encouraging Byrd to become independent of Roosevelt, whom he accused of "playing every political trick from the ward politician down to the court house gang . . . to get the nomination." Roosevelt's liberalism was driving Reed and his New York business acquaintances into a desperate search for an alternative to the governor. Reporting on a recent visit to New York, Reed told Byrd: "Our friend Page . . . with the A.T.&T. Co . . . stated in the presence of several people that there was no question in his mind, from the names so far mentioned, as your being head and shoulders above them all. . . . Dr. Grosvenor . . . stated that between you and Roosevelt, you were decidedly his preference." Reed became so disenchanted with Roosevelt that he preferred Hoover's reelection to victory by the New Yorker.[7]

It was becoming clear, as well, that Roosevelt was using Byrd to counter Smith. He asked Byrd to take the chairmanship of the party, which would have isolated the Smith-Raskob forces and removed Byrd as an opponent; the Virginian declined. Later that summer, after attending the Institute of Public Affairs in Charlottesville, Franklin stopped to see Harry at Rosemont, inspiring rumors that Byrd had been offered second place on the ticket. Having determined with Reed that second fiddle was unacceptable, Byrd quickly squelched these stories. Furthermore, lengthy correspondence and meetings with Raskob, with whom he was to develop a strong friendship, were pushing Byrd to greater neutrality, even though it was apparent that Raskob was playing the same game as Roosevelt by encouraging favorite-son candidates to become stalking-horses for Smith until he became an active candidate.

Byrd wavered on pursuing the top prize, telling Reed on June 27 that it would be "best to abandon all thought of me being a candidate for any office." And yet two days later he invited Henry Carter Stuart to send letters about his candidacy to southern editors. To other Virginia friends he cautioned delay, but in July he went to New York with Reed to meet with interested parties. For once in Byrd's life, this indecisiveness was to undermine his ambition for higher office. Additionally, two other intrusions—Sittie's illness and the budget crisis in the state—forced him to cancel speaking engagements in order to spend more time with her and with the governor. As he told Reed, "I am more interested in maintaining what we have done in Virginia than anything else in a political way."[8]

The growing division between Roosevelt and Smith and the addition to the Byrd campaign of Henry Breckinridge, a wealthy New York attorney and former assistant secretary of war under Wilson, reignited Byrd's interest. Nurtured by Reed, Breckinridge easily became the most rabid "Byrd for President" advocate in the country, flattering the man and extolling his chances. "By reason of your vigor, experience, personality and character," he enthused, "you seem to be the best among the outstanding personalities of the Democratic Party." He saw real interest around the country in Byrd's candidacy. Indirectly referring to Roosevelt's crippled condition, Breckinridge wrote, "We need a man who has the moral, mental and physical power to fulfill the exacting duties of the President." While Byrd believed Breckinridge to be "an idealist" with little "real influence," he did nothing to discourage his efforts.[9]

Breckinridge began plotting strategy in the fall of 1931. Virginia had to be unified behind Byrd, additional support in the South had to be cultivated, and his friends were to circulate Byrd's record and personality throughout the country. But it was imperative, Breckinridge counseled, that Byrd decide on the course to follow: "Every day that passes without launching an effort in your behalf will carry politicians by default into the camp of Roosevelt. The decision for you is a ticklish one. Of course, what immediately occurs to one's mind is whether it is better to do nothing and trust to the gradual evolution and growth of your prestige and influence or to act. This is the decision that you alone can make. My judgment is for action." As he put it, to lose an election would be politically unhealthy, but to go for the nomination and lose would be less damaging. Byrd's congenital political pessimism and his determination not to weaken his leadership in Virginia produced an entirely different assessment. Any loss would have negative consequences. He explained to Reed, "I have enemies of great political importance in Washington who would never lose an opportunity to discredit me and embarrass me in every possible way."[10]

Predictably then, Byrd opted for a low-key campaign, letting his friends emphasize his availability and record, waiting for the primary dust to settle, and then, in the eventuality of a stalemate, emerging as the candidate who could best unify the party. This was consistent with Byrd's lifetime approach to seeking political office: Do not overplay your hand, leave all the doors open, and appear to be the unassuming candidate who is sought by the office. While Byrd's chances for the nomination were always slim, this conservative strategy ensured that they would get no better. This was nowhere more apparent than in the South. A respected former governor with strong conservative credentials, Byrd should have been a regional favorite son. As George Milton counseled him, "I still feel that it should be possible for the substantial block of Southern votes to be arranged behind a proper Southern candidate such as yourself, if a vigorous effort to do so could be made." Reed, too, was certain they could secure most of the southern states, but Byrd's apparent public indifference toward the nomination forced southerners who feared Smith and the prohibition issue to flock to Roosevelt, leaving Byrd no regional support except for a few prominent politicians.[11]

Nevertheless, Byrd's candidacy, however modest, created problems for Roosevelt. If the favorite sons and the Smith supporters could produce a deadlock at the convention, they might derail the Roosevelt bandwagon. To avoid this prospect Roosevelt's political aides, Louis McHenry Howe and Jim Farley, assiduously courted the favorite sons, including Byrd, enticing them with vice-presidential bids or putting out rumors to this effect in order to divert attention from their presidential efforts. They used Admiral Byrd to this end. He wrote his brother in early November: "I had a long talk with Franklin Roosevelt and Louis Howe.... As long as you have any chances Franklin, of course, wants you to stand firm for yourself, but he would like to feel that, at any time, should you feel there is no chance for you, you will turn your influence and votes over to him.... I believe they would be in favor of you for the vice presidency. At least that is what Howe, who is a great friend of mine, said Franklin felt about it.... Of course he is smart as the devil and completely attached to Franklin so it is well to remember that."[12]

Byrd continued to play a mediating role between Roosevelt and Smith, both to maintain party harmony and to sustain his own candidacy by preventing either New Yorker from sewing up an early victory. Reluctantly he accepted Roosevelt's offer to block Raskob's last effort to get a prohibition vote at the National Committee meeting in January 1932. While the press praised him for his diplomacy, it was the shrewd Raskob who backed away from a vote and offered a local option plan, hoping his conciliation would encourage an anti-Roosevelt coalition that would eventually give the nomination to Smith. Byrd saw this movement as his only chance for the nomination and so tilted toward the Smith-Raskob forces. Years later Jim Farley recalled that at first Byrd "participated in most of the strategy meetings called by the Roosevelt side and he was looked upon as an inner member of the council," but when it appeared that a deadlocked convention might result, Byrd "was tempted by the hope that the nomination would come his way."[13]

Byrd earlier had quietly thrown his hat into the ring. Local groups throughout Virginia began to endorse him for the nomination. On January 13, 1932, the General Assembly enthusiastically backed Byrd for the presidency, and a few weeks later the state's congressional delegation added its endorsement. A Virginia Byrd Committee was formed, chaired by Governor Pollard, managed by *News Leader* columnist Roy Flannagan, and financed by Billy Reed. Over the next few months right up to the convention, the committee mailed out thousands of biographical sketches of Byrd, reprints of favorable editorial comments, and the General Assembly and congressional endorsements. Ever the modest public servant, Byrd expressed his appreciation for this support but noted that the good of the party and the nation was more important than personal advancement. Nevertheless, he had succumbed to presidential ambition. "While I do not think it would be wise for you to make any great effort at this moment," he wrote Reed, "yet the endorsement of West Virginia would be very helpful." He encouraged Charles Harkrader, editor of the Bristol *Herald-Courier*, to advance his nomination: "I wish you could write all the

Our Favorite Son

newspaper men you know. The field is undoubtedly wide open as you say." Byrd personally asked R. Gray Williams to write the General Assembly resolution endorsing him for president.[14]

Despite advising Flannagan to make clear that this was a movement being conducted by his friends, Byrd began to increase his public exposure. As Reed told Breckinridge, it was time to "get out of the lunch club stage." On a trip to New York in early February, he paid courtesy calls to the Smith and Roosevelt headquarters, where he had to put out the predictable disclaimers that he was not out to stop anyone and that he was not going to be Roosevelt's running mate. Byrd had been approached by Jouett Shouse to let his name be used in "dry" sections of Pennsylvania against Roosevelt in that state's primary, but he declined, knowing that this would mark him as an anti-Roosevelt man and cost him FDR's supporters.[15] A week later Byrd addressed the Kentucky General Assembly, where Lieutenant Governor Chandler claimed that he was "well worthy to make the ninth president Virginia has furnished this nation." Outside the state a half-dozen newspapers endorsed him, and politicians began to comment seriously about his candidacy. Byrd's star was clearly on the rise. "There is no doubt about Harry being a serious contender," Reed wrote to Willis Robertson. Even the candidate euphorically saw a deadlock developing and predicted the choice would be between Newton Baker and himself. "I feel more encouraged every day," he told Reed.[16]

Yet the Byrd campaign was still infected with the candidate's own self-doubts and personal idiosyncrasies. Byrd was meeting more regularly now with the Smith forces even as his brother kept communications open to Roosevelt, and after a thoughtful analysis of the delegate count with Shouse, he told Reed that there were very few votes out there for himself. His innate modesty compelled him to tell Flannagan to tone down the flattering press releases about him. As always, his parsimonious nature led him to emphasize the need to control expenses. "Don't spend too much," he repeatedly implored Reed. "I am very anxious that the expenses be held down. Don't forget that I am to pay one-half of what you contribute as this has always been our custom in such matters." Up until the last moment, he opposed hiring a band for convention demonstrations.[17]

Other factors beyond his control were also working against him. A major blow to the campaign was the kidnapping of the Lindbergh baby on March 2, which not only caused Byrd personal distress over this tragedy to his friend but also prompted Breckinridge, a very close friend of the colonel's, to leave the campaign in order to help find the child. The loss of this enthusiastic supporter was crucial. Sittie's illness continued to intervene, preventing Byrd on more than one occasion from addressing Democrats in faraway states. More critically, Smith's declaration of candidacy on February 8 had stimulated a predictable rush to Roosevelt, especially in the South. Even Gardner and Chandler could not hold North Carolina and Kentucky for Byrd, despite his favorably reported speech to the Kentucky legislature. He was appalled at the ineptitude of the anti-Roosevelt effort, but in actuality it was the planning and work of Roosevelt's managers that produced significant primary victories and numerous endorsements and contributed to the belief that FDR would capture the nomination before the convention met, exactly what Howe and Farley hoped would happen.[18]

At a planning session in April for the national convention, Byrd found himself once more caught up in the Smith-Roosevelt rivalry. Raskob wanted Shouse made temporary chairman in order to influence the seating of contested delegates; Farley preferred Senator Alben Barkley of Kentucky. After extensive debate Byrd suggested that Barkley deliver the keynote address and be made temporary chairman, while Shouse be elected permanent chairman to preside over platform deliberations and the actual nomination. Both parties agreed, although the language adopted at Roosevelt's behest to "commend" rather than "recommend" Shouse would later create controversy. Byrd's involvement suggested to the Roosevelt people that he was definitely allied with Smith and Raskob.[19]

Byrd stumbled as well on the prohibition issue. Being a lifetime teetotaler but no fanatic on the question, he hoped to defuse the issue by proposing a complex plan that combined constitutional amendment and national referendum. "We must realize," he stated, "that no law is stronger than the public sentiment to support it." Byrd may also have believed the plan would improve his own chances for the nomination, for it was, in the view of Franklin Waltman of the Baltimore *Sun*, a real concession from a real "dry." However, after some initial enthusiasm for the proposal, his attempt to walk a tightrope on the issue of prohibition cost him national support. Prohibitionists feared that a popular vote would lead to repeal of the Eighteenth Amendment, and his suggestion fell short of the outright repeal favored by the "wet" forces who now dominated Democratic party ranks.[20]

Even though these events dampened Byrd's optimism, Roosevelt's defeats in the Massachusetts and California primaries revived his hopes. "Things have been shaping up a little better," he wrote to Breckinridge on May 13, "but, of course, it may be that my name will receive no consideration in Chicago. If it does receive consideration I am inclined to think that my chances will be fairly good." His confidence was buoyed by a successful trip to Philadelphia in mid-May and by assurances that delegates and governors from four states would support him if the convention deadlocked. A report from Oklahoma indicated interest in Byrd, especially after the state convention instructed for Governor "Alfalfa Bill" Murray. An Associated Press story tapped Byrd as the choice of the anti-Roosevelt forces if Smith dropped out of the race, and political columnist Mark Sullivan wrote, "Put your money on Dark Horse Harry Byrd." Byrd even considered liberalizing his political position to accommodate those to his left, perhaps the most telling evidence that he had caught the presidential bug, but Reed, who thought that progressivism was only a few steps removed from socialism, counseled that his gubernatorial record would show him to be progressive enough to win wider support within the party.[21] Daily correspondence with Flannagan, who saw things "looking brighter every day," also lifted his spirits and increased his involvement in the campaign.[22]

Meanwhile, Byrd prepared carefully for the state convention in Richmond. Although endorsed by the General Assembly, the leading state newspapers, and the Virginia Federation of Labor, he turned to his Organization "to write letters . . . to all parts of the state urging that the county conventions endorse me. Of course, do not say that I have asked you to do this. . . . Simply say that you think it would be a nice compliment if the county conventions would endorse me when they meet." Seeking a unanimous front, he advised no action where there was any opposition. Meeting on June 9, the convention overwhelmingly selected Byrd as its favorite-son nominee, giving him full control of the delegation under the unit rule. The party gathering also endorsed Byrd's prohibition referendum, although many in the hall favored outright repeal. It had "turned out just about as well as any of us could expect," he concluded.[23]

With this endorsement Byrd moved to the center stage at Chicago. He realized that his chances for victory were slim, but Roosevelt's primary defeats indicated that he could be stopped. Byrd's hopes were buoyed by statements, particularly from Raskob, that Byrd was high on the list of possible nominees if the convention deadlocked. He continued to state that he was not part of any "stop Roosevelt" movement, but that was only technically true. If not in league with Smith and Raskob, he was working the same street. As Richard Crane, a Roosevelt supporter from Virginia, wrote to his candidate, "The situation in Virginia is not as favorable as it was because Harry Byrd's backers think he has a good chance and consequently are working against you as the leading candidate. Harry, himself, I am convinced, is engaged only in promoting his own candidacy and would not be a party to any general movement to block your candidacy or that of anyone else." That prophecy would be tested at the convention.[24]

When Byrd arrived in Chicago on June 21, the "Byrd for President" badges and buttons were ready, Breckinridge had paid for a band, doorkeepers were assigned to "get some of our people in if necessary," and the candidate was quietly optimistic. "Conditions here appear fairly satisfactory," he wired Reed the following day. A discouraging note was the loss of the North Carolina delegation, which pledged to support Roosevelt. As the remaining Democrats converged on the Windy City, including Virginia's delegation of sixty-six delegates and sixty alternates, they were hard-pressed to contain their enthusiasm and feistiness, certain as they were of victory in November. Roosevelt controlled a majority of the delegates but was about one hundred votes short of the two-thirds majority then necessary for nomination. The resulting contest, rife with rumors and horse trading, was one of the more tumultuous and significant conventions in American political history.[25]

Byrd's headquarters in the Congress Hotel was a popular meeting place; delegates and Chicagoans were attracted by the presence of General Billy

Mitchell and Admiral Richard E. Byrd in the Byrd entourage. When Will Rogers arrived on the scene, he and the admiral attracted such a crowd of women that for a moment Byrd appeared to be a sure winner. Rogers wrote in his newspaper column, "Talked with Governor Byrd of Virginia, a very high class man, which is practically his only handicap."[26]

Blustering Huey Long, governor of Louisiana, was also housed in the Congress Hotel, and upon his arrival he threatened to "kill" Governor Byrd because of a disagreement over competing delegations from Louisiana. When he asked Byrd to come to his suite two floors above, both the admiral and Harry Jr. opposed it; Dick exclaimed: "Hell you're not going; that guy's crazy. He threatened to kill you two days ago." Byrd insisted on going, and after a three-hour meeting, during which his brother and son were beside themselves with worry, he returned to say that Long wanted to support him for vice-president.[27] Since Long was committed to Roosevelt, it may have been another backdoor effort to shake loose Virginia's twenty-four votes for Roosevelt.

When the convention opened on Monday, June 27, it was clear that the Albany crowd had enough votes to control procedural questions. Although the traditionalists forced Roosevelt to abandon his plan to change the two-thirds rule, his backers won the delegate challenges and elected Senator Thomas J. Walsh of Montana as permanent chairman over Jouett Shouse in a close vote. The "stop-Roosevelt" people felt betrayed, believing the New York governor had reneged on a promise to back Shouse at the April arrangements meeting. Farley's reminder that they had "commended," not recommended, Shouse did little to calm them and probably strengthened their resistance. Casting Virginia's votes each time against the Roosevelt positions, Byrd could only hope that the coalition would hold together long enough to stop the Roosevelt momentum. On the controversial prohibition issue, the "wets" overwhelmed the "drys," unequivocally committing the party to repeal of the Eighteenth Amendment. If Byrd was displeased with that result, he could not have been happier with the platform's endorsement of economy in government, a commitment that he would remind party leaders of long afterwards.[28]

The nominating process began on Thursday afternoon and endured into the evening hours when Carter Glass nominated Byrd, Virginia's "best loved governor in three-quarters of a century.... What Byrd did for Virginia, he would do for the country." Seconding speeches were given by Gray Williams and Colonel Breckinridge, who labeled Byrd "your man of destiny, the organizer of success and victory." A modest ovation and a twenty-minute demonstration, led by the Richmond Light Infantry Blues Band, followed the nomination. It was, the New York *Times* reported, "the restrained sort of demonstration fit for a gentleman from Virginia." With the admiral carrying a Byrd banner, other delegates from Georgia, New Jersey, Texas, and Oklahoma joined the festivities, some hoping forlornly to prolong the session so that balloting could be put off until the next day, thus slowing the Roosevelt bandwagon.[29]

The balloting for the nine nominated candidates plus Newton Baker began at 4:30 A.M. and dragged on through three ballots until 9 A.M., when the exhausted delegates stumbled out of the hall, suffering from too much stale air and oratory. Byrd received 25 votes on the first ballot, one from Indiana and all the rest from Virginia. On the second ballot he lost the vote from Indiana, but on the third he picked up 96/100ths of a vote from North Carolina, likely a mathematical record for convention vote splitting. Roosevelt, meanwhile, inched forward from his first ballot figure of 666, but after the third ballot he was still 87 votes shy of the two-thirds majority, and there were reports that a few of his pledged delegations were weakening.

Chagrined by the failure of any of the favorite sons to start a stampede to Roosevelt, his managers nervously moved among the delegations the following day seeking additional support. As he had been all along, Byrd was a natural target. Many accounts have been related about the deals that the Virginian turned down—the vice-presidency, a cabinet seat, or a cabinet seat for Glass or Swanson so that Byrd could gain the vacated Senate seat—but the most authoritative report comes from the diary of Robert Jackson, a close adviser to the future president. Jackson asked Roosevelt over the phone if he could offer Byrd the secretaryship of the navy in return for releasing his Virginia delegates. FDR reportedly said, "Go ahead, and if he doesn't want it, tell him his brother Dick can have it." Jackson went to Byrd, who declined, saying: "One must have his own code. Maybe mine is too rigid, but it is the only one I have and I must live by it."[30] Clearly, the Roosevelt people were in a panic, looking for some commitment to save his candidacy, offering anything to anybody to break the logjam. Although Byrd was not a party to any deals, he and his advisers were also searching for delegates. Reed and Breckinridge met with Raskob, hoping he could convince Smith to withdraw, but Raskob now had swung his support to Newton Baker and had little influence left with Smith, who had no inclination to leave the race.[31]

In near desperation the Roosevelt forces decided to concentrate their efforts on John Nance Garner of Texas, promising him the vice-presidency in exchange for the release of the Texas and California delegates who had been pledged to vote for him. With enormous satisfaction William McAdoo, who had been denied the party's nomination by Smith in 1924, announced the switch of California to Roosevelt. As the hall erupted in a mass demonstration, the standard of the Old Dominion momentarily remained motionless until Harry Byrd released the Virginia delegates to join the parade. When the balloting resumed, Texas put Roosevelt over the top, and Virginia's twenty-four votes were only a perfunctory addition. Byrd quickly and magnanimously announced his support for Roosevelt and served on the committee that escorted him to the platform for his acceptance speech that promised a "new deal" for the American people. The following day Byrd and his brother visited Roosevelt and Farley to receive assurances that they harbored no grudges for the Virginian's participation in the "stop-Roosevelt" effort.[32]

As the delegates left Chicago, analysts pondered what might have happened had Roosevelt been stopped. Some thought that Byrd would have picked up significant strength on the fourth ballot from North Carolina, Indiana, and Oklahoma.[33] This, combined with the crumbling of Roosevelt's support, they believed, would have triggered a surge to Byrd, a man recognized by all within the party for his abilities as an administrator and a conciliator. Much of this speculation, however, had little foundation. Newspaper reports of the convention confirm the general admiration for Byrd but suggest that he had little national influence and only a slim chance at the nomination. Had Roosevelt been defeated because of the two-thirds rule, Newton Baker probably would have been the strongest compromise candidate. Byrd himself believed that Baker was better presidential timber than Roosevelt and might have served as Baker's running mate had the Ohioan been nominated.[34]

This may account for why Byrd held out so long against Roosevelt's nomination. After the convention Byrd said that he "would not have permitted the Virginia delegation to be a part of the deadlock for the sole purpose of defeating Roosevelt. . . . I felt that four ballots would decide it."[35] This assertion may have been designed to assuage pro-Roosevelt voices in the Old Dominion who were upset with his actions, but it does not explain why he helped to create a deadlock in the first place. It was not due to a dislike of FDR. While he did not agree with many of Roosevelt's policies and statements—a disagreement that henceforth would grow rapidly—there was not enough of a philosophical difference between them at this time to account for his opposition to an individual with whom he was personally friendly. A second possibility was a commitment to the Smith forces. Although he always denied that he had made any deals, Byrd may have given assurances to Raskob that he would hold his delegation through several ballots, and, being a man of honor he felt obligated to fulfill that promise. In a letter to Reed, he referred to the "combination we made with Smith and Raskob," but that was surely a tacit agreement to advance the ends of each candidate, not a personal commitment to support Smith.[36]

A more likely explanation for Byrd's obstructionism is his ambition for higher office. Throughout the campaign he had remained realistic about his chances, but that did not diminish his hopes, which were constantly nurtured by adoring but less objective friends. The list of prominent politicians who told him he was their second choice was long. As he wrote to Happy Chandler,

"There was a chance for me in the event Roosevelt had not been nominated." And if that fourth ballot did not produce a tidal wave for Byrd, perhaps it would have for Baker, a man whose political philosophy was acceptable to Byrd. As Baker said to Carter Glass at the end of the summer, "I am frank to admit to you that a ticket of Baker and Byrd would not have been a bad combination from my point of view." Glass agreed, and that may have been why Byrd stayed in the running so long, and why McAdoo, who feared Baker, broke the deadlock.[37]

Harry Byrd wanted the presidency in 1932. His persistent support up to the eleventh hour of the stop-Roosevelt effort was driven by his own ambition, not by fears of a Roosevelt presidency. However, his southern background, the hesitant nature of his campaign, his niggardliness on spending money, and his reluctance to move early and forcefully toward the goal diminished his prospects.[38] He did not have Roosevelt's lust for the office, the New Yorker's popular image as a depression-fighting governor, or the high-powered campaign organization that accounted for Roosevelt's eventual success. His brother, who saw the Roosevelt operation firsthand, complained about the amateurism of the Richmond committee. And while Byrd personally projected an image of competence, which was the emphasis of his public relations effort, his candidacy never caught fire. His platform, calling for reduced government spending, reciprocal trade agreements, a referendum on prohibition, and more income tax exemptions, was not likely to arouse popular acclaim among a depression-ridden people. Nevertheless, had Roosevelt faltered, as seemed possible on the morning of July 1, Harry Byrd was ready and willing to seize the prize.[39]

Since his chance of capturing the nomination had been remote, Byrd's disappointment was mild. He thanked his many friends for their support and said that he had "no regrets" about the convention. Trying to console Billy Reed, who was blaming himself for a poorly organized effort, Byrd said there was "nothing Virginia could have done to change the result in any way." Virginia, he declared, could have switched to Roosevelt earlier, but he had wanted no deals. He was, he said, "happy that I did not get on the ticket as I am certain Sittie could not have stood it."[40]

Henry Breckinridge, however, refused to give up the fight for the presidency. He urged Byrd to expand his acquaintances and to keep himself in the public eye by running either for governor again or for a seat in the United States Senate. Breckinridge was so persistent with his advice that Byrd finally asked Reed: "Don't you think that you could in some way induce Henry to abandon the idea of continuing to push me for the presidential nomination? I would much prefer that he cease any activities along this line, as I think the case is hopeless."[41] Indeed it would be. The future success and popularity of

Roosevelt's New Deal stamped his policies on the Democratic party for years to come, forcing Byrd into the role of an outsider. Never again would he have a genuine opportunity to run for the White House.

After the Chicago convention Byrd was concerned that his Virginia opponents, in order to gain control of patronage from a Roosevelt administration, would accuse him of having consorted with the Smith faction. Alarmed, he wrote to Reed, "I think the great crisis of our wing of the organization will come during the gubernatorial election. Every enemy we have will concentrate against us, aided and abetted by Swanson, if they think they can beat us. . . . I have the feeling, which is instinct more than anything else as I have nothing concrete to base it on, that our wing of the organization is not as strong as it was. . . . If the National patronage is used against us we will be placed in quite a serious position."[42]

Despite Reed's assurances that he was as strong as ever, Byrd began mending fences, preparing for congressional elections in the fall, and overseeing implementation of his road program. He lobbied hard with Shirley to speed up road construction in order to keep counties from withdrawing from the plan. The specter of a $1 million state deficit also drew his immediate attention, largely because of the adverse publicity he believed it would create. By delaying payment of an appropriation for the Shenandoah National Park, relying on federal money to maintain roadwork, and pursuing some bookkeeping legerdemain, he and Combs hoped to disguise it for another year.[43]

As much as he would have liked, Byrd could not give full attention to events in the Old Dominion, for Roosevelt had invited him to play an active role in his campaign for the presidency. Almost as soon as the convention was over, the two recent adversaries exchanged felicitations, and Roosevelt invited him to Hyde Park where, on August 9, he offered Byrd the chairmanship of the campaign finance committee. Byrd declined because of the workload, but he accepted the less demanding chairmanship of the executive finance committee. He also joined a group called Minute Men of the Democratic National Committee," high-ranking party officials who pledged to work for the party and raise money for it. It proved a more difficult task than he had imagined. The depression hindered all fund-raising efforts, leaving the more impoverished Democrats in desperate straits. He personally contributed $500 to the national campaign and another $500 to the Virginia campaign, some of which was to pay for local Democratic races, but he complained about the duplication in soliciting funds at the state and national levels. He also was appalled at the final campaign deficit of $700,000 to $800,000 caused primarily by advertising.[44]

Byrd had little to do with the substance of the Roosevelt campaign, but as it progressed, it became clear to him that he and Roosevelt did not agree philosophically. After the New Yorker spoke in Detroit about old-age pensions,

Byrd wrote to Reed, who was already convinced of Roosevelt's extremism: "I think old age pensions are just as bad as pensions to the nondisabled servicemen. The children are supposed to look after their parents, and it would be a great misfortune for this country if we adopted a universal old age pension system, therefore relieving their children of this responsibility." Nevertheless, when Roosevelt stopped briefly in Richmond, Harry Byrd led the cheers, praising the candidate as an "apostle of Thomas Jefferson." Election Day brought the expected Roosevelt landslide, and Byrd wired his congratulations. Roosevelt responded appreciatively, "Certainly Virginia made Democratic history, and I feel that congratulations are due you for the splendid part you played in bringing about the final result both in the state and in the nation."[45]

The Democratic victory opened the door for Byrd's appointment to the United States Senate. His prominence in the party and the campaign created speculation about his reward; a cabinet position was most frequently mentioned, either Agriculture, Commerce, or Navy. Byrd ruled himself out of these jobs, suspicious as he was of Roosevelt's direction. Having heard about a domestic allotment farm program, which he termed an "autocratic and costly bureau," he disclosed to Reed: "I am more convinced than ever that I should not go into the Cabinet, and I have asked Frank Walker to convey this information to Roosevelt, that I do not desire to be in the cabinet even though he has such an offer in mind. In view of the attitude of the Democratic leaders toward economy, I am very fearful as to what is going to happen to the Party." Furthermore, Byrd backed away from the cabinet because he had finally decided to pursue the Senate seat. He put it frankly to his brother on December 13: "I would like very much to see Swanson offered the position as Secretary of the Navy so I could succeed him in the Senate."[46]

The complication, of course, was Swanson. The ambivalent relationship between Byrd and the senior senator, both of whom had contested for leadership of the Organization in Virginia, had finally deteriorated into a nasty rupture, produced primarily by Byrd's ambition for higher office and his suspicion that Swanson was obstructing him. Swanson, for his part, had not enjoyed being superseded by Byrd as the dominant politician in the Old Dominion and worried about being peremptorily retired by the younger man before he was ready. The final breach had begun during Byrd's governorship when Swanson had objected to some minor reform proposals and only lukewarmly supported the candidacies of Al Smith in 1928 and John Garland Pollard in 1929.

When the 1932 presidential sweepstakes opened, Swanson spoke favorably of Franklin Roosevelt and talked of Byrd as a vice-presidential candidate, at least until protocol dictated that he join his Virginia colleagues in endorsing Byrd. Reed and Byrd thought Swanson was trying to ease Byrd out of the Virginia picture in order to eliminate him as a potential rival in the 1934 Senate race. At each point Swanson swore support for Byrd, but his pledges were unconvincing. Reed also thought the talk of the vice-presidency was doing untold harm to Byrd's presidential efforts.[47] Reports that Swanson was purposefully aggravating relations between Byrd and John Raskob did nothing to calm the controversy. After the convention, when Swanson apparently told Governor Pollard that Byrd could have a place in the cabinet if he wanted it, Byrd correctly assumed that he was "trying to buy off any possibility of opposition to him."[48]

It was also clear that Swanson was aligned with political friends who were less than enthusiastic supporters of Harry Byrd: Patrick Henry Drewry, J. Murray Hooker, Joseph Deal, and Norman Hamilton. He reportedly preferred a 1933 Virginia election ticket of Drewry for governor and Goolrick for attorney general, a team that would have denied Byrd continued control of the Organization. Control of patronage was one of Byrd's biggest concerns, and it produced a major row with Swanson over whom Roosevelt would appoint as collector of customs in Norfolk. Swanson supported Norman Hamilton, editor of the Portsmouth *Star,* and Byrd and Glass backed I. Walke Truxton, the Norfolk city manager. This bitter contest lasted a year before Byrd prevailed upon Roosevelt to appoint Truxton. As Byrd had said, Swanson was "aiding and abetting" the enemy.[49]

Roosevelt's election success forced both men to consider their future options, and this produced an unusual meanness in Byrd, who believed Swanson was out to "discredit" him. When told by William Battle that Swanson was "in a terrible state of mind and actually cried," Byrd callously refused to relieve the old man's pain by explaining his own intentions. Instead, he made it clear to Reed that he would throw his weight against Swanson's reelection in 1934: "I do not know that I will run myself, but the more I think of the way he has acted the less inclined I am to support him." He advised Ebbie Combs that "no committals should be made by any of our friends for the 1934 senatorial campaign." One report actually had Byrd telling Swanson that he was going to the Senate regardless of what the incumbent did.[50]

Carter Glass was being considered for a cabinet position as well. Although Byrd preferred that Swanson be the one selected, his strategy was to lobby with Roosevelt through his brother to have one of the Virginians appointed. Indeed, he told both Dick and Billy Reed that he was writing to Bob Jackson to advise Roosevelt to offer a cabinet position first to Glass, and if he declined, to Swanson. He made the same request of Frank Walker on a trip to New York in mid-December, intimating to him that "it would be very agreeable to me that in the event Glass refused . . . to offer a Cabinet position to Swanson." Shortly after the election, Glass told Byrd that he would not go into the cabinet and that Swanson was likely to get the secretaryship of the navy, but when Roosevelt turned up the heat on the "father of the Federal Reserve" to become secretary of the treasury, the three Virginians jockeyed for advantage.[51]

Roosevelt's intentions are not clear. He may have wanted Glass out of the Senate where he could do damage to his New Deal programs, but more positively, he could also use the Virginian's conservative reputation in the Treasury Department to calm the frayed nerves of the banking community. He may have wanted Swanson out to avoid his becoming chairman of the Foreign Relations Committee.[52] Ironically as it turns out, he likely desired Byrd in the Senate, since he believed the Virginian's campaign effort would transfer into support for his programs. There were reports that Roosevelt wanted Byrd to lead his "New Deal" through the Senate, but Byrd denied them.[53]

Poor Swanson, too, was in a dilemma. A Senate race against Byrd would likely end his long distinguished career in a humiliating defeat, so he pursued the goal of arranging a cabinet post for either Byrd, Glass, or himself. Through Willis Robertson he indicated that he would do anything for Byrd if Harry would help him stay in the Senate, but at the same time he gained the backing of Louis Howe for the secretaryship of the navy. In January he went to New York to see Roosevelt, intent on saving his career.[54]

Byrd's impatience with this irresolution grew. In December he told his brother that he would be "entirely content if I can go to the Senate within a reasonable time." But a month later he was pressing Dick to use his influence with Franklin Roosevelt, Eleanor Roosevelt, and Louis Howe to get Glass or Swanson in the cabinet. The admiral did as he was told and in a few days reported that one or the other would be appointed, a report that was confirmed by Glass.[55] Byrd wrote to Henry Breckinridge that Glass

> said that Roosevelt is urging him strongly to be in the Cabinet, but he is undecided, mainly, I gather, because he fears that the President-elect favors some method of inflation by changing the gold content of the dollar, and he is opposed to this. He then said that he asked Roosevelt whether in the event he was compelled to refuse the appointment any other Virginian is being considered. Roosevelt replied and said that Howe had made a committal to Swanson prior to the election to appoint him Secretary of the Navy in the event Glass declined the Treasuryship. This is another evidence of Swanson's deceit, as the day after the election he sent me a copy of a letter he had written Roosevelt urging my appointment to the Cabinet, although he had a committal. Glass then asked me yesterday whether I was certain Pollard would appoint me. The matter will be decided shortly.[56]

In early February, Glass finally gave the president-elect his answer, bowing out ostensibly for health reasons. He immediately communicated his decision to Byrd, along with the news that Swanson would get the navy post; the "Senate will be open to you," he said.[57] Still, Byrd could not be sure, and he urged his brother to check with Howe on the Swanson appointment, which was publicly announced on February 21, 1933. A week later Byrd was appointed to the Senate vacancy by Governor Pollard. But Swanson would have the last laugh. Irked at Byrd's callous treatment of him, he declined to resign his Senate seat early so that Byrd might enjoy seniority over fourteen other newly elected senators. Byrd talked personally with Swanson and asked Farley to intervene with the senator on his behalf, but the old man was unforgiving. Harry would start his Senate career at the bottom.[58]

9

New Deals

H ARRY BYRD was sworn in as a United States senator on March 4, 1933, in the midst of national despair. As it turned out, the winter of 1932–33 was the nadir of the depression. For millions of Americans, the necessities of life had become luxuries; itinerants, soup kitchens, and "Hoovervilles" were common features on the urban landscape; steel production had fallen to 12 percent of capacity, and industrial construction was less than 8 percent of what it had been in 1929; more than a quarter of the workforce was unemployed. In the countryside farmers struggled to prevent foreclosures on their farms, declared farm holidays, and destroyed farm produce rather than sell it at ridiculously low prices. At the moment of Franklin Roosevelt's inauguration, the nation's banking system was on the verge of collapse.

In Byrd's Virginia the situation was slightly better. Unemployment averaged 100,000 workers during 1932. Industrial wages had declined 35 percent, and manufacturing output had fallen to $575 million, 64 percent of the 1929 figure; farm income had been cut in half. Faced with falling revenues, city, county, and state governments reduced salaries, staffs, and services, leaving a depleted private relief sector to cope with growing relief rolls. Hunger marches occurred in the Capital of the Confederacy. Virginia avoided the worst aspects of the crash, but suffering in the Commonwealth differed from hardships elsewhere only by a matter of degree.[1]

Confronting such a crisis, President Roosevelt, in an inspiring but candid and somber inaugural address, called on Americans for new resolve and asked for "broad executive power to wage a war against the emergency, as great as the power that would be given to me if we were in fact invaded by a foreign foe." Sworn in only moments before on that cold, blustery March morning, Senator Byrd, who would be given assignments on the finance, naval affairs, and rules committees, responded enthusiastically to the president's call, supporting limited debate on his program in order not to impede its progress. The Richmond *Times-Dispatch* commented: "In short Senator Byrd stands ready to grant the President dictatorial powers during the period of the emergency. And we believe the people of Virginia would back him on that issue."[2]

The ensuing congressional session of 1933—the Hundred Days—produced more significant legislation than that of any previous American Congress, and Harry Byrd was a notable advocate. Within a week the president closed the banks, stampeded Congress into passing emergency banking legislation, delivered the first of his comforting fireside chats, and reopened the banks, all leading to a restoration of public confidence in the government and its new leader. Carried along by the bold initiatives of Roosevelt's New Deal, most Virginians greeted the legislation of the Hundred Days warmly. Even such radical departures from traditional governmental practices as the Tennessee Valley Authority (TVA), the Agricultural Adjustment Administration (AAA), and the Civilian Conservation Corps (CCC) drew general praise from the state's congressional delegation and press.[3]

Only Senator Glass among leading Virginians criticized the measures adopted by the New Dealers, warning: "Roosevelt is driving this country to destruction faster than it has ever moved before. Congress is giving this inexperienced man greater power than that possessed by Mussolini and Stalin, put together."[4] But Glass's votes against most of the important pieces of legislation put him in the minority. Except for the beer bill and a vote on the National Industrial Recovery Act (NIRA), Harry Byrd did not join his senior colleague in protest of the New Deal. Although he favored the repeal of prohibition, he opposed the authorized sale of intoxicating beverages proposed by Roosevelt. It was a matter of conscience and Virginia politics, although given the dissatisfaction with prohibition even in the Old Dominion, his vote against beer may have been an act of courage. Harry Jr. says his father "caught more hell" on the beer bill than "almost anything he'd ever voted on."[5] Byrd also disliked the licensing feature of the Recovery Act, which he thought created too much bureaucratic power in Washington, but he supported the final conference report. Having been attacked by the *Southern Planter* for opposing the president, Byrd vigorously defended his 90 percent agreement with Roosevelt over the course of the session. Privately he was less lyrical, writing Billy Reed, "Many things have been done here that I think will have a very bad effect."[6]

The optimism of the Hundred Days carried over into the summer, propelled primarily by the "Blue Eagle" campaign of the National Recovery Administration (NRA) that was designed to stimulate economic recovery. Overnight the country was transformed into a mass parade demonstrating support for the NRA. A blue eagle emblem, displayed to indicate an employer's adoption of the new wage and hour standards, found its way onto the windows and mastheads of two million businesses, including Harry Byrd's Winchester *Evening Star*. In a nationwide radio address, Byrd enlisted in the effort, proclaiming, "We are at war; at war against the terrifying forces of an economic depression" that justified the concentration of power in Washington. He praised Roosevelt as a leader who had "subdued the panic" and restored confidence. Reassuring his listeners that the hand of government would be taken from business when the "war" was won, he urged them to sign the reemployment agreements.[7]

Given his later condemnation of the New Deal, Byrd's early support demands explanation.[8] The severity of the depression, party loyalty, and political reality dictated a careful response. Recognizing the extreme emergency of the situation, the Virginian may have been willing to forgo personal preferences to allow the president freedom to pursue his policies, just as Byrd had been given a free hand as governor to reorganize the state executive department. His affinity for administrative action had been exemplified in his governorship and the chairmanships of the Fuel Administration and the Drought Relief Committee.

Furthermore, with his own election coming up in the fall, the freshman senator may have been unwilling to challenge a popular president. Such an insurgency might have jeopardized his own election chances and encouraged an intraparty struggle in Virginia. Bill Tuck of Halifax had forewarned him of this:

> The plain people are wrought up, and are very critical of your vote on
> Beer. . . . Approximately ninety percent of the people of Southside Virginia
> are broke. . . . They are willing to follow anybody, right or wrong, who will
> bring about a change. They are in the frame of mind that Roosevelt will
> save us. . . . I am of the opinion that it is very unsafe politically for you to
> vote against any more of Roosevelt's measures. I have discussed this with
> our leading people in Halifax County, many of whom love you, and all of
> those with whom I have discussed this question are of the opinion that if
> you oppose the Roosevelt farm measure, in spite of your popularity here
> and everything that could be done, we will be annihilated politically in
> Halifax.[9]

Byrd appreciated the advice. Only weeks before his election, he publicly approved the course of the New Deal: "March 4 last, in my opinion, was the most critical day in American history. . . . No man since March 4 has labored . . . more . . . to alleviate the needs of the people and to restore something like normal conditions than Mr. Roosevelt. . . . He has done many things which seem like experiments. But these extraordinary times need extraordinary measures."[10] Once the crisis moderated, Byrd became more independent, more doctrinaire, and more negative in his actions—a senatorial gadfly free to criticize and vote with only a glance to see how it played at home—but not just yet.

Another explanation for Byrd's early endorsement of the New Deal was his preoccupation with patronage demands and the upcoming gubernatorial campaign in Virginia. Coming after twelve years of Republican presidents, Roosevelt's victory inundated Washington with Democratic job seekers. One Virginia congressman cynically said that no more than 75 percent of Virginians were seeking federal jobs. Faced with a continuing battle at home with the friends of Swanson and Westmoreland Davis, Byrd knew that control of federal patronage was vital to the Organization's ascendancy. He could not afford to antagonize Roosevelt into rewarding his enemies. Referring to rumors that Swanson's allies had final approval of appointees, Byrd warned Glass that they "must carefully watch patronage matters." It was also necessary to reward the faithful lest they get restless. Demanding that the Ninth District be compensated for its support of the Organization, Ellis Hargis appealed to Byrd: "You have always stood by us when we really needed to be stood by, and now we come to you again, with the plea that we be recognized in the distribution of Federal offices in accordance with our showing at the polls. . . . we, as the organization, must be able to bring home the bacon, when bacon is to be brought home, otherwise we cannot control our vote." Byrd assured him that he would continue to stand "for a square deal for the 9th District."[11]

With his appointment to the Senate, Byrd got more control over patronage than he had anticipated. The independent Glass had little zest for rewarding party loyalists and so deferred to his junior colleague on most job requests. This left Harry as the major dispenser of spoils, free to reward some of his friends but obliged to reject others as well, for there were more applicants than jobs. Indeed, thousands of requests to be district attorneys, judges, marshals, postmasters, and tax collectors flowed into his new quarters in the Senate Office Building. He was aware of the political implications of his actions: his enemies would accuse him of spoilsmanship, and those not receiving positions would be angry. Exasperated, Byrd wrote to Billy Reed: "This Senate job is the worst I have ever tackled and the sooner I can get out of it the better. . . . I am simply being harassed to death by job seekers, and I do not know which way to turn."[12] He finally devised a patronage plan, agreeable to Glass, that equitably distributed federal jobs among the counties and cities by relying on loyal bureaucrats such as Nat Early in the Richmond Internal Revenue Office to dole out subordinate positions.[13]

Of even greater concern to Byrd was the impending election to choose a successor to John Garland Pollard, another crucial contest that risked Byrd's leadership in Virginia. The selection of an unfriendly candidate or a weak showing by an anointed candidate might jeopardize that hegemony and Byrd's own Senate election as well. As T. McCall Frazier, director of the Division of Motor Vehicles, pointed out to Senator Glass, "The most compelling reason underlying our desire to fully qualify our vote and to perfect an organization that will assure us a tremendous majority is to prevent next year any trouble that may be . . . in store for Senator Byrd."[14]

George Campbell Peery was Byrd's choice to avert "any trouble." A tall, distinguished-looking lawyer from Tazewell, Peery had impeccable Organization credentials. He had redeemed the "Fighting Ninth" from the Republicans in 1922—solidifying Byrd's leadership of the party—and he had served three unnotable terms in Congress. Loyally, he had withdrawn from the 1929 gubernatorial race in favor of Pollard and had been rewarded with a seat on the State Corporation Commission, which led several newspapers to conclude that he would receive the next nod. By the summer of 1932, Byrd and Reed had concluded that Peery would carry the Organization banner in the next election.[15]

Even before he opened his campaign on April 6, 1933, with an endorsement of the Byrd reforms and a balanced budget, Peery was embroiled in a controversy that required Byrd's intervention. Charges had been made that the State Corporation Commission, while Peery was chairman, had sanctioned an investigation of utility rates that was to be partially funded by the power companies. Aware of the seriousness of the issue when the newspapers seized on its political ramifications—"dynamite" he called it—Byrd advised Peery to remain silent and urged Governor Pollard to provide state funds for the investigation even though the General Assembly had made no appropriation for it. Divorcing the power companies from the review killed the issue.[16]

An even more inflammable issue was prohibition. Personally "dry" but favoring repeal of the Eighteenth Amendment, Byrd and Peery equivocated on what course Virginia should follow. Given Byrd's unpopular vote against the beer bill and the "wet" position of Peery's two opponents, Joseph T. Deal of Norfolk and W. Worth Smith of Louisa County, the issue threatened to undermine their well-planned campaign. With Richmond restaurants openly selling beer and opponents calling for an end to prohibition in order to create a new source of revenue in liquor taxes, the senator conceded, revealing his strong pragmatic streak that would not allow principle to get in the way of political success. As he rationalized to prohibitionist George Conrad, law enforcement had broken down with respect to beer and there was a need to control its legal sale.[17]

Meeting secretly with Peery and Combs at Billy Reed's home in late June, Byrd devised the plan of retreat. On June 27 he and Peery announced their support for a special session of the legislature to legalize the sale of beer and to establish procedures for repealing state and national prohibition laws. To overcome a "drier" Governor Pollard, who opposed a special session for repeal, Byrd delegated Bill Tuck to telegraph and telephone all assembly members to petition the governor to call such a session. As Tuck recounted to Byrd, "It could not have been put over without you and Mr. Combs. As soon as I would tell the members that you were in hearty sympathy with the movement, favorable replies came in promptly. . . . You are by far the strongest and most popular man in the state."[18] Pollard quickly capitulated and called an August session that legalized beer, taxed it, and set up an October referendum on the Twenty-first Amendment that overwhelmingly ended the "noble experiment" in Virginia. Before the vote, Byrd announced his support for repeal while remaining committed to "true temperance." Not wanting the referendum to interfere with his own election, Byrd had advised Pollard to hold a separate poll on repeal at an estimated cost to the state of $20,000, suggesting once again that Byrd's economizing had its limits when it conflicted with political objectives.[19]

The Peery bandwagon rolled on to predicted victory, with Byrd the masterful director. Informed by Sixth District congressman Clifton Woodrum that a Peery defeat would be "heralded as a repudiation of you," Byrd left nothing to chance. He worked to eliminate potentially strong opponents such as Jim Price and O'Conor Goolrick; he advised Peery where to go and whom to see; and he sent out letters to the Organization faithful that cautioned against overconfidence. It all paid off with a handsome victory for Peery, as he captured 62 percent of the primary vote in the three-man contest and went on to defeat Republican Fred McWane in November.[20]

Nor would Byrd overlook the details in his first election foray as a senator, concerned as he was that his handling of patronage might backfire on him. He had no primary opposition in 1933, but he confronted a feisty Republican, Henry Wise from the Eastern Shore, in the general election. A veteran of the world war, Wise tried to use his service record against Byrd, accusing the senator of building a machine during the war with which to plunder Virginia. Although one veterans' group, the Military Order of '76, demanded that Byrd be retired because of his votes against legislation benefiting veterans, Wise's ploy had little effect. Fearing that his opponent would attack him on the wages he paid in his orchards, Byrd gathered information on what Wise paid his farm laborers as well as whether Wise had paid his poll tax and registered to vote. Such shadowboxing was meaningless as Byrd handily defeated the Republican with 73 percent of the vote.[21]

Almost immediately, he turned his attention to the 1934 legislative session in Richmond, disregarding for the moment the looming battles with New Deal adversaries in Washington. As with Pollard four years before, Byrd advised Peery on legislation and appointments, even though he had said that he would not intervene in the latter area. The recommendations were the same: no diversion of gas and license taxes; no cuts in road spending; no sales tax. "In the final analysis," he said, "the Virginia people are conservative in thought. They are opposed to bond issues and high taxes, and want every possible economy in government." Confident that he had insured a smooth transition, Byrd predicted to Reed that Peery "is in line with all our ideas and will do everything in his power to carry them out."[22]

Peery proved slightly more independent of Byrd than his predecessor. Although he paid homage to economy in government and did not overturn any of Byrd's reforms, he did request tax increases to maintain an eight-month school term. Surprisingly, in the face of considerable clamor against the increases, Byrd intervened on the side of the governor, editorializing in his newspapers and lobbying with his friends and legislators on behalf of Peery. Having been advised by Combs that a small increase in the school appropriation would avert conflict with the school lobby, Byrd once again proved his political pragmatism.

On the liquor control issue—with Byrd's approval—Peery insisted on tight state control rather than liquor-by-the-drink and private licensing. The result was the creation of a three-man Alcoholic Beverage Control Board (ABC) to supervise operation of state liquor stores. Even at that, Byrd was concerned with the possibility of bribery and graft that could wreck the Organization's scandal-free record. He claimed that six liquor companies had already asked him to recommend someone to represent them in Virginia. "I refused to have anything to do with it," he wrote John Stewart Bryan. "They even went so far as to offer my secretary, [H. E.] Dameron, $10,000 a year, which he refused. We must keep this business clean." Over time, with careful appointments, the ABC Board remained free of reproach and funneled millions of dollars in liquor taxes into state coffers. With the governorship in friendly hands, the legislature doing as it was told, and his reforms preserved for another term, Byrd could now turn to national issues with gusto, certain in the knowledge that his political base was secure.[23]

With the ink hardly dry on the handiwork of the assembly, Byrd made his first major disavowal of the New Deal over agricultural policy. This was rather surprising because he had endorsed the first farm act in 1933 that had offered farmers money in return for reducing acreage planted, and he had worked vigorously in early 1934 to have peanuts included in the basic commodity program. But he did not like the coercive and bureaucratic features of the legislation, and when a new farm bill was introduced which extended the licensing power of the secretary of agriculture and permitted stricter production controls, Byrd rebelled. In Congress on May 22 and in a widely broadcast radio address on May 28, he condemned the bill for giving the secretary the power to determine what and how much was to be produced, power "inconsistent with the ideals of the Democratic Party [that] will . . . menace, if not destroy, the broad program of economic recovery sponsored by the President." "We do not want," he declared, "a Hitler of American agriculture." At the same time he charged that the Bankhead Cotton Act, which had imposed hefty taxes on excess production, was confiscating property without due process, claiming that it made "criminals of those who plant in excess." In the face of New Deal arguments to the contrary, the senator led the fight against many of the amendments to the AAA. His tactics were also responsible for the inclusion in the Kerr-Smith Tobacco Control Act of a provision stipulating that two-thirds of the farmers had to approve the program before it became operative. He exulted to Frederic Scott, "This is the first set-back in the general scheme to regiment the people of this country."[24]

Part of Byrd's dissatisfaction with the farm programs originated in his suspicion of the men Roosevelt had selected to oversee them. He had never liked Secretary of Agriculture Henry Wallace, calling him even before his confirmation a "radical inflationist, [who] will do all he can if appointed to further absurd schemes which will result in miserable failure." Byrd never deviated from that estimate, and the two of them had numerous face-offs over the years that ended with Byrd playing a leading role in Wallace's rejection in 1944 for a second term as vice-president. Similarly, Byrd opposed the nomination of brain truster Rexford Tugwell as undersecretary of agriculture on the ground that "he had no proper conception of the principles of this government." Tugwell, however, was confirmed over Byrd's objections.[25]

Many Virginians did not agree with the senator on the farm legislation. Representative John Flannagan declared: "I am not in sympathy with those who seem to think the Agriculture Department is trying to Hitlerize the farmers. The farm program with one exception is a voluntary program. It hasn't been imposed upon the farmers, it has been worked out in cooperation with the farmers. I do not know of any farmers who think they are being Hitlerized." Another Virginian wrote to Tugwell, "I do criticize him [Byrd] for masquerading under false colors. He belongs in the old line Republican ranks whose program includes no money experiments, the balanced budget, no direct relief, no public works, in fact the program followed between 1920 and 1932."[26] A survey of the Southside tobacco region gave Byrd mixed reviews. A Nottoway farmer said: "Byrd is about right. Wallace is a good man but I don't like the idea of him having complete say over what I must do on my farm." Commented an Amelia merchant, "Byrd hit the nail on the head when he said we'd be like Russia if more power is given Wallace." However, a Southside assemblyman represented the majority opinion when he accused Byrd of "obstructing farm recovery. . . . I hope he cannot stop the passage of the amendment to the AAA." The best indication of the popularity of the farm program was the overwhelming approval farmers gave it in their votes to remain under its controls. In 1934, 99 percent of flue-cured tobacco farmers in Virginia voted to join the program. A year later, by a vote of 19,229 to 293, they endorsed continued participation in acreage control, crediting the AAA with higher prices and incomes. Such support could not be ignored.[27]

Nevertheless, Byrd leveled another blast at the growing Washington bureaucracy in an essay for the July 4 *Herald Tribune Magazine* and associated papers across the country entitled "Is Regimentation Robbing Us of Freedom and Independence?" Renewing a practice of his governorship of writing for national and state publications, he began an important secondary career as a spokesman for conservative principles in the country. The articles, which he wrote with the assistance of Lester Arnold, were often condensations of his speeches that called for economical, efficient, and limited government. Having a negative view of government—"that government is best that governs least"—he feared that its power, cost, and wasteful bureaucracy threatened individual liberty. Regrettably, his obsession with debt prevented him from adequately supporting governmental services that even he acknowledged were fundamental: education, care of the unfortunate, and preservation of health.[28]

Relieved at the early July congressional adjournment and the departure of the New Dealers from Washington—which he called "a very good thing for the country"—Byrd turned his attention to his reelection for a full six-year term, concerned that his votes against New Deal legislation, particularly his attack of the agriculture bill, would reduce the size of his November victory. The Washington *Post* had identified him, along with senators Glass, Millard Tydings of Maryland, and Josiah Bailey of North Carolina, as leaders of an anti–New Deal coalition.[29]

Byrd's opposition to Roosevelt was further magnified by a series of critical editorials in the Bristol *Herald-Courier* that received widespread publicity across the state. Even more shocking was their source: editor Charles Harkrader, a longtime supporter of Byrd and the Organization. Seeking an explanation while at the same time asserting his support of the administration, an angry Byrd wrote Harkrader, "Very frankly Charlie, I do not see any great reason why this editorial should have been written. . . . I feel certain you knew nothing about [it]." Harkrader confessed that he had written the piece, justifying it as representative of public sentiment favoring Roosevelt's programs. "There is a feeling in high circles in Washington," he explained, "that you are secretly not in entire sympathy with the Administration. . . . I have no personal quarrel with you for voting your convictions. I am only sorry that Roosevelt sentiment in Virginia is not more articulate and more effectively expressed. Roosevelt is in my judgment the best friend capitalism has." The editorials and letters continued over the summer, with both parties trying to reassure the other of their continued affection for one another but not retreating from their stated positions. Finally, Byrd concluded that they could agree to disagree, declaring that he did not mind criticism but disliked misrepresentation. Greatly upset at these editorials, he had friends distribute long defenses of his record to the newspapers. Coming as it did in an election campaign, the Harkrader controversy not only eroded a friendship but stimulated a growing conflict within the Organization, as a small minority of the faithful—the "antis" as they would be called—began to challenge Byrd's domination of the party.[30]

The implication that Harkrader was misrepresenting his views was disingenuous. Byrd was technically correct when he said that he had backed all but three major Roosevelt measures in the 1934 session—the St. Lawrence Waterway Treaty, which was detrimental to Virginia shipping interests, the AAA amendments, and the Tugwell nomination—but it is clear that he had little sympathy for the New Deal programs. His public references to "Hitler" and "regimentation" suggest a hostility that was simmering below the surface, just now restrained in this election year. Privately, his disdain for the New Dealers had already boiled over. Referring to Representative Woodrum's characterization of March 4—Roosevelt's inauguration day—as another July 4, Byrd commented to Glass, "I assume that he means by that that our freedom was given us on July 4 and taken away on March 4."[31]

To counter Harkrader's charges that he was opposed to Roosevelt, Byrd released a form letter from Jim Farley thanking him for his support of the administration's programs. He also contacted many friends in the tobacco belt in an attempt to distinguish his opposition to the AAA amendments from his support for tobacco legislation. He reminded several correspondents of his mother's ownership of a tobacco farm outside Lynchburg. To neutralize talk of his break with Roosevelt, he attended the October dedication of the Veterans Hospital in Roanoke with the president. Byrd's concern, however, was unfounded, for he rolled up an even greater margin of victory (80 percent) than the year before, this time over Lawrence Page of Norfolk. This triumph further secured his independence as a spokesman for those principles he held dear.[32]

Another manifestation of the widespread perception of Byrd's hostility to the New Deal was the invitation to him and Glass to join the American Liberty League. The league, formed in August, 1934 to combat the "leftist" tendencies of the "Brains Trust" and to return the nation to sound constitutional principles, was the creation of conservative elements of American society who were fearful of losing their wealth and influence. While sympathetic, Glass quickly declined the overture, but Byrd seemed mildly interested in the establishment of an organization "to preserve the liberties of the people." Henry Breckinridge, then running for the Senate on the conservative Constitutional party ticket in New York, reported to Byrd that John Raskob wanted "you, Al Smith, Lindbergh and a few others to head up an executive committee. His plan is to get sixty men to give $25,000 apiece and then set forth to save the country." Byrd concluded, however, that it would not be "wise for either me or Glass or anyone

else to be a party to any bloc which the public thinks is acting as an obstruction." To the newspapers he released a statement that he would do nothing "to
obstruct or embarrass President Roosevelt in his efforts to end the deplorable
conditions which resulted from twelve years of Republican misrule." Loyalty to
the party as well as political reality in an election year determined Byrd's decision, but his increasingly active opposition to the New Deal continued to warm
conservative hearts. Within the year Reed, Breckinridge, and Tyre Taylor were
discussing the possibility of another Byrd campaign for the presidency in
1940.[33]

Another point of contention with Roosevelt was emerging over Virginia's
response to the New Deal relief programs. Long-term high unemployment levels had exhausted the capacities of private charities and local and state relief
agencies to deal with the problem, leading to the creation of a federal program
operated by the Federal Emergency Relief Administration. FERA proposed to
furnish food, clothing, and shelter for the destitute and to provide work relief
for employables where possible. State agencies would supervise the program
and submit plans for federal approval, while local relief units would direct individual projects. This division of responsibilities limited federal control and led
to frequent debates between Washington and state capitals over policy and
funding. The conflicts prevented the achievement of uniform minimum standards, but suffering was greatly relieved because FERA usually followed the
more generous policy of giving funds where the needs were greatest, often disregarding the failure of many states to match the grants.

Virginia was one of those states which never authorized funds for direct
relief until after FERA was terminated. From the inception of the program,
state leaders claimed that money spent providing work for the unemployed on
the highways was the equivalent of direct relief appropriations. Federal relief
officials, notably Director Harry Hopkins, retorted that Virginia was sacrificing
not at all since other states were spending for both roads and relief. The argument lasted for the life of FERA, and although Hopkins threatened to end allot-
ments to Virginia, he never carried out his ultimatum, a decision which
allowed the Old Dominion to follow a more independent course of action.[34]

Senator Byrd dictated the state's position. In early 1934, Hopkins wrote to
his assistant, Aubrey Williams: "I think Virginia should be made to defray a
share of the cost of relief. You will recall that the Governor was agreeable to
this, but the matter was held up due to the attitude of Senator Byrd." When
FERA field representative Alan Johnstone tried to pressure the General Assembly into appropriating $2 million for relief at the risk of losing federal money,
Byrd indignantly labeled this an unauthorized ultimatum, and the legislature
adjourned without making the appropriation. Johnstone attributed the action
to the "machine" and the "able and astute Senator Byrd."[35]

Central to this dispute was the propriety of Virginia's response to the depression. The conflict with Washington was a result of different social and economic philosophies. Hopkins believed that immediate aid to those in need should be the primary mission of the government, no matter what the means or costs. The leaders of the Organization, although not entirely unsympathetic to the needs of Virginians, were more concerned about the preservation of individual character and fiscal integrity. They believed their highway relief program satisfied these objectives while federal handouts would destroy individualism and encroach on state authority. Committed to a balanced budget, they shied away from the higher taxes they believed necessary to finance relief appropriations, in spite of the fact that Virginia had one of the lowest tax rates in the nation. Byrd claimed not to be insensitive to the problem. "I would empty the treasury to keep Americans from being hungry or cold," he said, "but by the same token, no one undeserving of relief should be permitted to sap funds appropriated for the needy." Calling for local administration of relief funds, he was upset that any talk of cuts brought forth "charges of inhumanity" from the "sob sisters." He complained that Virginia was getting no credit for holding down expenditures while those states that wasted money continued to receive it.[36]

Although Hopkins once stated that Old Dominion leaders "made a pretty good case" on behalf of their highway relief program, it is likely that the real reasons he did not cut off federal relief funds were his desire not to withhold aid from Virginia's needy and his unwillingness to antagonize Glass and Byrd. The senators were not unusual among public officials in their reluctance to use local money for relief, but Virginia was better able than most states to pay its share, particularly since its relief load did not compare to that of other states, being only half the national average for 1934–35. Faced with such obstruction, the federal government wound up paying 92 percent of Virginia's relief bill ($26 million), with the localities putting up about 8 percent and the state contributing a paltry $34,000. The *Times-Dispatch* criticized the selfishness of state officials: "They are determined not to spend any of the State's money for the State's neediest unemployed. They are great advocates of state rights when such advocacy meets their convenience, but when it doesn't they believe in letting Uncle Sam hold the bag."[37]

In his increasingly hostile attitude toward the New Deal, Byrd remained blind to the continuing effects of the depression. Nothing in his correspondence suggests that he was aware of or sympathetic to the personal suffering it caused. He spoke of bad business conditions and bad times for farmers in terms of the market, but not in terms of people being hurt. He agreed with Billy Reed's estimate of the poor that they had become lazy and were now "expecting to be supported by the community." Furthermore, Byrd's later behavior reveals an ignorance of the larger significance of the depression as a symptom of a changing economic order and as a harbinger of new economic and political realities. Many of the problems of American society—the decline of the family farm, environmental pollution, long-term unemployment, an aging population—could no longer be solved with a self-help ethic. They were national in scope, requiring resources that only government could provide. Byrd's failure to appreciate and adapt to these changes consigned him to the footnotes of history. His days as a constructive leader were largely over.[38]

The advent of a new relief program in 1935, the Works Progress Administration (WPA), which emphasized work rather than the dole, did not convert Byrd, who lobbied to reduce the size of this $4 billion relief bill, the largest peacetime appropriation in United States history to that point. With words that would echo through the halls of Congress for another thirty years, he called for an end to the "spending orgy at Washington," declaring that he was "opposed to mortgaging the future welfare of our children, grandchildren, and even generations to come." For him, the government needed to restore business confidence by rejecting tax increases and excessive spending. Crisis legislation must now yield to sound principles. A final Byrd amendment to pare the appropriation to $1.9 billion failed, and the relief act passed the Senate, 68–16, with both Virginia senators joining four other Democrats in opposition. Still aware of the liability of opposing a popular president, Byrd had letters prepared in his office, to be signed and sent to the newspapers by friends, defending his position.[39]

Since the WPA was a federally directed program that required no matching state funds, Organization leaders could do little to obstruct its work other than to admonish Washington for its extravagances. Although it was susceptible to "goldbricking" and "leaf-raking," the WPA performed splendidly in the state during its eight-year life, employing an estimated 95,000 Virginians who earned $66 million. It built schools, roads, and airports, provided school lunches, produced clothes in its sewing rooms, employed jobless white-collar workers in art, library, and music projects, and improved public health through its clinics and construction of privies. While unimpressed with such beneficence, Byrd did try to get as much WPA money for Virginia as he could, particularly for projects that he found worthwhile, such as farm-to-market roads. Aubrey Williams called Byrd one of the "worst" in trying to arrange appointments to WPA positions; but knowing of his influence, Williams appeased him by approving his pet projects. Since the WPA was free of excessive waste and scandal in Virginia, Byrd had few criticisms of it, but he did grumble about the relief work siphoning off his apple pickers.[40]

The WPA was part of a new legislative program put forth in 1935 (called by some historians a second New Deal) to address the more deeply rooted social and economic ills affecting American life. Other major components included social security legislation, the Wagner Labor Act, and new farm legislation. Roosevelt was likely spurred into action by the radical voices of Huey Long, Francis Townsend, and Father Charles Coughlin, who were demanding a major redistribution of wealth in the country. Furthermore, the failure of the president's first efforts to solve the depression, highlighted by the Supreme Court's adverse ruling on the NRA, required additional action. Invariably, Harry Byrd, who had predicted such a leftward turn to Senator Josiah Bailey the previous October, cast a negative vote on most of these proposals.[41]

The introduction of a national social security program was dictated by the inadequacy of private and state support for the aged, the disabled, and the unemployed. At the time Virginia's welfare commitment was judged among the worst in the country, the product of a blind devotion to fiscal conservatism and a faith in the power of self-help. Recoiling from the potential expense and permanence of the new security plan, Byrd threw down the gauntlet by attacking its funding. Taking exception to his cost estimates and fears of federal control, the *Times-Dispatch* believed better standards could be ensured through supervision in Washington. Editor Virginius Dabney scolded the senator: "The most disturbing aspect of Senator Byrd's statement is to be found in the fact that nowhere in it does he indicate that he regards social security legislation as either necessary or desirable. . . . There is the apparent lack of interest on Senator Byrd's part in these humanitarian measures. The United States is the only major nation in the world except India and China which has no social security laws. Does Mr. Byrd wish this country to continue to trail along with the backward nations of Asia instead of going in the van with the socially enlightened nations of Europe?"[42]

Publicly wounded, the senator immediately responded that he was not "opposed to any reasonable plan of economic security for the individual citizen which contemplates joint contributions," but that he would continue to oppose disastrous fiscal policies even if it made him unpopular. Despite his rebuttal, criticism mounted. Federal and state officials swiftly refuted his cost estimates, finding them far exaggerated. The Old Age Pension League of Virginia contended that Byrd was "more concerned with public expenditures than he is with private suffering; [he] thinks more of property rights than he does of human rights." And a seventy-six-year-old constituent wrote to him, "How are the old people to survive? . . . small farmers who have no labor of their own are doomed to the loss of what they have and the 'almshouse' for their home and old age protection, when a small annual Federal allowance would give great relief to those who are now suffering from the infirmities of age." Nevertheless, Byrd remained unconvinced, and he and Glass were paired against the measure approved by the Senate in June, 76–6. Even in defeat, however, Byrd was not without some influence. Fearing federal control over Virginia's contributions to the security programs, he obtained an amendment that allowed states to determine the aid levels commensurate with their financial means. This led to inadequate funding in many states.[43]

So powerful were the senator, the self-help ethic, and Virginia's parsimonious tradition that the Old Dominion became the last state to join the security program. Fearing that passage of social security legislation and a sales tax to pay for it would adversely affect the next gubernatorial election, Byrd urged Combs to talk the issues over with the governor. Predicting that the idea would "last throughout the future of our country," he suggested deferring "action on the old age pensions until 1939 by appointing a commission and ascertaining how the plan works out in other states." Two weeks later he wrote directly to Governor Peery to ask for a delay for up to two years, now advising that the plan would destroy Virginia's tax system. Citing the need for balanced budgets and additional study, the compliant Peery put off recommending approval even though his own study showed the costs to be well below Byrd's estimates. In 1938 the General Assembly consented to have Virginia join the other forty-seven states in the social security program but on a more limited basis than that recommended by the Virginia Commission on Old Age Assistance. Virginians began receiving benefits three years after Congress had enacted the plan into law.[44]

Byrd's record on labor had also taken a decidedly negative cast, culminating with his vote against the Wagner Labor Relations Act in May 1935. The Wagner Act placed the power of government behind the rights of workers to organize and bargain collectively. Byrd was one of only four Democratic senators to vote against the bill, a vote he would speak of with pride years later. It precipitated bad blood between the senator and unions in the Old Dominion, which up to this time had praised his support for working men and women. Only days after passage of the Wagner Act, the Virginia Federation of Labor assailed Byrd and Glass for "the unfairness and unreasonableness of their attitude on New Deal legislation." R. T. Bowden, past VFL president, saw them as "absolutely worthless to the labor movement. Both are anti-anything." Although he thought the VFL attacks against him unwarranted, Byrd became one of the most virulent antilabor voices in the Senate, condemning the 1937 "sit-down" strikes and opposing passage of the 1938 Fair Labor Standards Act that established a minimum wage.[45]

Byrd never fully understood the unlevel playing field that working people had to endure. Individualizing economic relationships, he found union bargaining distasteful, government mediation unfair, and the collective power of unions threatening both to public order and business profits. It was not the way one dealt with apple pickers. Much to his dismay, the labor-management-government relationship was being revolutionized in the depression years. The

Wagner Act allowed unions to win some spectacular victories in the late thirties, and membership more than doubled. Byrd's antilabor votes, which were votes for an older relationship, naturally angered union representatives, who threw their political support to his opponents. Because their voices were inconsequential in the Old Dominion, he could easily dismiss them; but rankled by their attacks on him, he would use the labor issue to his advantage in subsequent campaigns.

Byrd also fought changes to the 1935 farm bill that gave more power to Wallace, especially over commodities not then under contract, such as fruits and vegetables. As an apple grower he was not entirely disinterested. Sarcastically he prophesied, "Only the person who eats the food will escape this Federal dictatorship." He won amendments to the bill that exempted fruits prepared for canning from control, deleted a rayon-processing tax, and required 75 percent of the producers of a commodity to approve controls before they became effective. Byrd was assisted by Senator Glass on one occasion when, in reference to a proposed marketing arrangement for honey, the venerable statesman claimed that he did not want to go to jail because he could not "control the activities of my queen bee." The amendment was laughed down. With many of the objectionable sections removed, Byrd supported the final bill. Proving the value of an opposition voice, his performance strengthened the act and won him a place on the cover of *Time*.[46]

In one field of New Deal work, conservation, Byrd proved more agreeable. Reflecting his love of the out-of-doors and his own farming practices, Byrd approved the creation and extension of the Civilian Conservation Corps and the Soil Conservation and Domestic Allotment Act, which replaced the defunct AAA allotment program that the Supreme Court invalidated in 1936. Continuing efforts begun during his governorship to complete the Shenandoah National Park, he encouraged the building of Skyline Drive in the park. Many problems delayed the opening of the drive, including a dispute over the relocation of park inhabitants that Byrd unsuccessfully opposed.Constant bickering between Public Works Administrator Harold Ickes and senators Byrd and Glass occurred over funding of the road. Ickes tried to silence the senators' criticism of New Deal relief by halting work on the road, ostensibly for lack of funds, but when Byrd asked for a probe of PWA monies to determine how much was left, Ickes backed down and work was resumed. President Roosevelt formally dedicated the road and park on July 3, 1936. Only a few months before, construction had begun to extend the drive southward to the Great Smoky National Park. Three years earlier Byrd had suggested to Roosevelt the possibility of connecting the two parks, and the Blue Ridge Parkway was born. Motivated by the need for depression jobs and the prospects for increased tourism, the senator, who Ickes credited with the "vision" for the parkway, helped obtain federal funds for the project.[47]

Throughout 1935, as he developed into one of the New Deal's harshest critics, Byrd delivered a series of speeches that articulated his opposition to the growth of government and refined the economic and legal arguments that he would use in all subsequent debates. Relying on the facts and figures he always found so compelling, he called for tax and fiscal policies that would restore business confidence. Addressing graduates at the College of William and Mary, he waxed more philosophical, warning his listeners that the "economic law of what you spend, you must pay" still existed. He urged them to "deny your appetites and strengthen your spirits and discipline your powers until you are in the pink of condition to make good. If you do this, you should win, for remember that America is still a land of opportunity. No one can justify failure here with the excuse that success is based on 'pull' and that only the privileged can succeed." Using a favorite passage from George Mason, one of the Founding Fathers he was fond of quoting, he spoke of the need to preserve "fundamental principles": representative democracy, states' rights, and the checks and balances of the constitutional system, particularly the independence of the Supreme Court. In the Court, Byrd believed he had located his "bulwark against confiscation of the property or liberty of the individual," an opinion that would be severely tested as that body became more liberal over the next two decades.[48]

In October, Byrd delivered a radio talk which summarized his view of the depression in Virginia and confirmed once and for all the policies that the state would henceforth follow. According to Byrd, the failure of the depression to bring great hardship to the state was attributable in large measure to the frugal policies of reduced expenditures and balanced budgets that the leadership had enforced. Taking pride in the fact that Virginia was the only state not to increase taxes during the depression, he declared: "I confidently predict an era of prosperity for Virginia which may not come immediately, but it is certain to come in strong measure if we adhere to the general policies that have stood so successfully the acid test of the most serious financial emergency ever experienced by the American people. . . . Let us continue to keep our budget in balance and to live within our income. . . . Let other states go the way they prefer, but we in Virginia can continue the less spectacular paths of industry and thrift; paying as we go and then pay just as little in taxes as necessary for our essential functions of government."[49]

Juxtaposed against the New Deal's more liberal bent and its willingness to use the resources of government to serve those in need, this laissez-faire philosophy explains Byrd's opposition to almost every facet of Roosevelt's program. Advocating strict economy for the state, he could not honestly vote for large federal expenditures that created deficits. Believing in self-help, he could not endorse government handouts. And his adherence to states' rights also forced him to reject legislation that he feared would lead to widespread federal interference in the affairs of Virginia, a fear rooted in the South's Civil War and Reconstruction experience. Ironically, his failure to respond to depression conditions only encouraged greater federal intervention.

There was some validity to Byrd's thinking. Balanced budgets and reduced expenditures had preserved the financial integrity of the Old Dominion, contributing to a faster recovery; but these measures had not prevented adversity from gripping the state, nor had they alleviated the more deep-seated problems affecting the state. Yet Byrd and his lieutenants became captives of their own propaganda about how well-off Virginia was and refused to recognize and correct existing conditions. Hardened into dogma, pay-as-you-go became the icon before which all future Virginia leaders had to bow. Saddling the state with the balanced budgets and minimal expenditures that were presumed to be its salvation in the thirties actually condemned Virginia to social backwardness for the next generation. The traditionalism that permitted Virginians to endure the bad times of the crash gracefully became a barrier obstructing the road to progress. This was the sterile legacy which the depression and Harry Byrd bequeathed Virginia.[50]

Byrd's forceful dissent against New Deal policies raised questions about his position in the upcoming presidential sweepstakes in 1936. Retreating to his orchards after the long and disappointing 1935 congressional session, he could not escape reports that he and his senior colleague were about to bolt the party. He quickly denied these stories, as well as a suggestion from William Randolph Hearst that he run on a Liberty League ticket with Al Smith. To stop all rumors of a party split, Byrd had Harry Jr. write an editorial predicting that Roosevelt would have the unequivocal support of Virginia for renomination. But his professions of loyalty did not prevent further entreaties from conservatives to defect to the Republicans or lead the fight against Roosevelt.[51]

Convinced that their leaders would remain loyal to the Democratic party, Virginians joined the Roosevelt bandwagon in 1936. Calling Roosevelt a "great Democrat, a courageous, humanitarian President," Governor Peery, along with Lieutenant Governor Price and former governors Davis and Trinkle, enthusiastically took to the campaign trail to support the New Deal. Earlier, Representative Woodrum, who had become one of the president's legislative leaders in Congress, confided to Martin Hutchinson, "I am thoroughly convinced that the people of Virginia are with the Administration."[52] Even Harry Byrd campaigned modestly for the ticket, praising Roosevelt for steps taken that "won the unqualified approval and praise of men and women of all parties." But at the same time he defended his independent record. "It is my duty as a Senator from Virginia," he declared, "to examine carefully the bills presented to the Senate and to vote my honest convictions. This I have done to the best of my ability. . . . I have voted for the recommendations of the administration when I believed the proposals wise; I have voted against them when I thought they were wrong. . . . I have no apologies to make for my votes in the Senate either for or against the administration. My record I could not change if I would and I would not if I could." Carter Glass, however, remained totally "unreconstructed." Writing to Byrd on the eve of the election, he remarked, "I hate the New Deal just as much as I ever did and have not the remotest idea of making any speeches for it."[53]

Certain of Roosevelt's victory in the Old Dominion, Byrd devoted his attention to minimizing a pro-Roosevelt rebellion within the state party. At the Ninth District convention, Byrd, Glass, and Peery secured an embarrassingly narrow vote of confidence; one of Combs's operatives from Dickenson County reported that he had never heard so much talk against Harry Byrd as he did before the meeting. At the state Democratic convention in June—switched from Roanoke to Norfolk at Byrd's request to reduce the influence of the mutinous southwest—damage was contained as the delegates gave ringing endorsements to Roosevelt, Byrd, and Glass. But in a major upset in the August primary in the Second District, Norman Hamilton defeated the incumbent congressman, Colgate Darden, whose opposition to much of the New Deal was well known.[54]

The 1936 results belie the intensity with which the presidential campaign was waged and mock the validity of pollsters' predictions. Until the last few weeks of the campaign, the Gallup poll envisioned a very close race, perhaps the closest since 1916, while the hapless *Literary Digest* forecast a Republican success. Roosevelt's overwhelming victory was the high-water mark of the New Deal nationally and in Virginia, where he won 70 percent of the ballots cast; in some rural counties he won over 90 percent of the vote, which gave credence to Bill Tuck's warning that votes against the farm program jeopardized future Organization success in his area. But in reality it was only a personal victory for the president. The New Deal had not disturbed the hierarchical nature of Virginia society or located a political voice in the state as liberal as that in Washington. The president had done little to cultivate opposition to the machine by directing patronage away from the Byrd-Glass faction because the senators were deemed too powerful and their Virginia adversaries too few and ineffectual.[55]

Roosevelt's 1936 mandate apparently convinced him that he could pursue a more authoritative course of action with his new Congress. The major obstacle to his legislative programs had been the Supreme Court, whose conservative majority repeatedly had found New Deal legislation unconstitutional. Consequently, in February 1937 he presented to Congress a federal judiciary bill which included a provision for increasing the size of the Court by up to six new justices. Designed to liberalize the high tribunal, the proposal triggered a debate that had marked consequences for the Court and the New Deal.

Public criticism of this plan in Virginia was immediate and sharp. The Lynchburg *News* called it "immoral," a "scheme ... to destroy the judicial branch," a "conspiracy against democracy." Even normally pro–New Deal newspapers labeled it a deception because it had not been presented during the 1936 campaign. After some weeks of silence, Senator Glass, in a nationwide radio address, vehemently and sarcastically attacked the plan as an attempt "to make a political plaything of the Court." He predicted that the present judges would be replaced with "judicial marionettes to speak the ventriloquisms of the White House." Senator Byrd, on the other hand, remained silent, reflecting an apprehension created by the 1936 landslide. He asked Bill Tuck to sound out public sentiment on the plan, and Tuck responded with an enthusiastic endorsement, estimating that 90 percent of his people supported the Court proposal. Although Byrd's mail was running overwhelmingly against the plan, he chose the path of caution, referring obliquely to the need to preserve the independence of the Court and publicizing his position only at the end when he joined Glass in voting to return the bill to committee, thus killing it.[56]

In actuality, Byrd and Glass had been part of a conservative effort to rally votes to defeat the plan from the beginning. Selecting Montana's old Progressive, Burton K. Wheeler, as their front man, the group, which included senators Kenneth McKellar of Tennessee, Royal Copeland of New York, and Edward Burke of Nebraska, met secretly in the Capitol to determine strategy. They appointed a steering committee and began lobbying other senators. Wheeler recalled Byrd saying, "We can't lick it but we'll fight it. . . . It's wrong in principle." While their numbers grew over the course of the debate, it was the Court itself, by altering its position on several key New Deal measures, that forestalled the liberals' effort to change its size.[57]

Although Roosevelt's ill-conceived and poorly handled plan may have pressured the Court into retreating, the political price of the victory was high. It undoubtedly cost him the sympathy and allegiance of many voters in Congress and in the country at large, who felt the president was trying to usurp the power of the other two branches in a dictatorial fashion. The issue forged a conservative coalition in Congress that consisted of longtime opponents of the New Deal, such as Byrd, Glass, and Bailey, and other men of conservative leaning who had supported the president through the emergency but now had an excuse to return to their philosophical home. After several meetings of these New Deal critics late in 1937, Senator Bailey, with help from Byrd and others, drafted a statement of principles for the group entitled "An Address to the

People of the United States." A mild anti–New Deal piece that called for cuts in federal spending and taxes, its authorship made it seem more hostile than it really was. Because of Roosevelt's continued popularity, many feared to sign it, but the alliance was revealed when the New York *Times* printed a copy of the "conservative manifesto" and identified the participants. The opposition to the president was now out in the open. Strengthened by other examples of Rooseveltian imperiousness, such as the executive reorganization bill and the 1938 "purge" attempts, this coalition would delay, sidetrack, and finally halt the New Deal legislative train.[58]

Government reorganization was a much-debated issue over the next two sessions of Congress. The explosion of the federal bureaucracy to deal with problems created by the depression raised questions about cost, waste, and duplication of effort, particularly as the economic crisis seemed to ease. No one was more obsessed with the need to reduce the size of government than Harry Byrd. At the beginning of the 1936 congressional session, he had dedicated his senatorial career to "drastic reorganization and simplification of the Federal Government through abolition of useless agencies and consolidation of overlapping bureaus until there is relief." Offering a plan to cut spending by 25 percent through the elimination of unnecessary bureaus, he called for the creation of a Senate committee to investigate the activities of the executive branch. The Senate concurred, establishing a Select Committee to Investigate Executive Agencies of the Government to be chaired by Byrd. For the remainder of his public life, in service on this and its successor committees, his consuming passion was discovering waste in government. He became the acknowledged master of the cost and size of governmental operations.[59]

On January 11, 1937, Byrd delivered a radio talk on the need for government reorganization, the theme of so many of his addresses thereafter. He spoke of "constructive reorganization" to save tax money and restore simplicity, but the speech was primarily a statement of facts designed to shock his listeners. The federal government had 34 agencies concerned with the acquisition of land and 9 dealing with credit and finance; there were 46 personnel offices and 126 libraries; the Resettlement Administration (RA) had 13 separate Washington addresses; there were twice as many federal employees as there had been in 1927 and almost twice as many telephones. While he acknowledged the need to increase services in difficult times, there was no reason for that growth to be uneconomical and inefficient.[60]

A day later, upstaging the senator, President Roosevelt submitted his own reorganization plan, which proposed the addition of two new federal departments and six presidential assistants and the replacement of the comptroller general with an auditor general without authority to pass on the legality of expenditures. Byrd later said that Roosevelt asked him to introduce the bill,

"Fine Feathers No'er Make Fine Birds"

FRED O. SEIBEL

— RICHMOND TIMES-DISPATCH — JANUARY 12, 1936

but not knowing its contents, he hesitated. FDR shot back, "Harry, take it or leave it." Byrd replied, "Mr. President, I will have to leave it."[61] Publicly responding to the new bill, Byrd objected to what he called "mere regrouping" as well as the loss of the comptroller's watchdog function. He also predicted that the creation of new departments of social welfare and public works would be the route to perpetual relief spending. Byrd might have supported the president's plan had it been accompanied by substantial economies, but Roosevelt, who was more interested in the efficient management of government than its costs, said he could not promise any savings. Aware of the senator's obstructionism, Roosevelt sidestepped Byrd and his committee by forcing creation of a new Joint Committee on Government Reorganization to be chaired by Senator James Byrnes of South Carolina. The president initially fought Byrd's appointment to the new committee, but at the insistence of Vice-President Garner, Secretary of Interior Ickes, and Jim Farley, he finally relented.[62]

Meanwhile, the Virginian's own select committee plodded along, releasing several findings that pointed to the need for consolidation. His temper rising as a result of the president's slight, Byrd struck out at the bureaucratic "Frankensteins—the contrivances of ingenious idealistic theorists—that may grow so powerful as to destroy the right of citizens to life, liberty and happiness." Citing the government as "the most wasteful and bureaucratic form of government that has been known in our history," he demanded a federal pay-as-you-go approach to spending.[63] In June he retaliated with a reorganization plan of his own that advocated abolition and consolidation of several agencies and establishment of a more independent budget bureau.

In the face of numerous congressional committees and competing personalities and plans, efforts to reorganize the government fell short of expectations. Roosevelt's handling of the reorganization bill, particularly his failure to consult Byrd, the acknowledged authority on waste in government, may have triggered a final personal break with the Virginian and contributed to the eventual defeat of the reorganization bill in 1938. Coming on the heels of his abortive Court fight, this was a devastating blow to Roosevelt's legislative leadership. Byrd applauded the result and called for a renewed effort to achieve reorganization with economy.[64]

The animosity generated by the reorganization struggle likely contributed to Byrd's renewed sparring with Henry Wallace, this time over the work of the Resettlement Administration and the new Farm Security Administration (FSA). Created in 1935 when FERA was terminated, the RA continued its efforts in rural rehabilitation by attempting to turn farmers on relief into self-sufficient producers. One of its most visionary programs was the subsistence homesteads project designed to resettle in small communities people who had little hope of escaping their impoverished environments. Subject to charges of waste and communism, the program had a rather tortured existence, made so in part by the unrelenting opposition of the junior senator from Virginia. Two of these settlements were in Virginia: Aberdeen Gardens in Newport News, the first black subsistence homestead community in the country, and Shenandoah Homesteads, created to take care of the farmers forced off their land in the Shenandoah National Park. The latter was the object of Senator Byrd's attack. Believing that simple mountain folk could do without modern conveniences such as electricity and indoor privies, he charged the RA with erecting "a permanent monument to waste and extravagance such as has never been known in a civilized country." Irate at the discovery of a cooperative farm at one community site, he demanded that Secretary Wallace end the expensive project. Cost figures seemed to support Byrd, who felt vindicated when the RA was abolished and replaced by the FSA. But the new agency, which oversaw a loan program that encouraged tenant farmers to buy the farms they worked, also knew no respite from the senator's paring knife. Until it died at his hands during the war, he fought its every appropriation.[65]

Byrd's independent political course in the face of Roosevelt's popularity in the Old Dominion defied all logic, yet Virginians, in a surprising display of impartiality, divided their loyalties between the New Deal and the Organization in the mid-1930s. Other than the political leadership and the business community, few groups in the state were openly hostile to the national program; most Virginians endorsed the energetic actions of an administration that had pulled the nation out of the despair of 1932. Roosevelt was particularly beloved as "a God-sent man," a man whose "personality and promise gave most people new hope." Yet these same people also returned to office Organization men whose philosophies were diametrically opposed to those of the New Dealers. Senator Byrd and his pay-as-you-go program were equally well liked. Indeed, loyalty to the Byrd name bordered on idolatry; he was the "greatest statesman Virginia ever produced," a man who was "honest, frugal, and very wise—an honest to goodness real American."

The structure of Old Dominion politics permitted the coexistence of the New Deal and the Organization. The state's off-year election arrangement kept state elections from being influenced by the heat of a national contest. The electorate remained small and controllable. Provided with jobs in a period of great scarcity, the "courthouse crowd" remained intensely loyal to the leadership. The people who received most of the New Deal money and who might have opposed the Organization had no political voice. Likewise, urban interests, which tended to favor increased spending for educational and welfare facilities, were grossly underrepresented in the legislature and, thus, powerless. Finally, there was rarely an alternative to vote for. Virginia was a Democratic stronghold, and party loyalty demanded that both state and national leaders be endorsed. Republicans were hard to find, and the avid New Dealers were pitifully weak.

Coexistence, however, did have its limitations. FDR's popularity waned in the late thirties as Senator Byrd's economy drive received greater support. Most Virginians still liked Roosevelt, but his spending policies and political maneuverings made it unlikely that they would depose their favorite son, who was trying to protect them from the high taxes and federal interference that had always been anathema to them. As one writer told the senator, "Many Roosevelt voters are for you, as they now believe that your criticisms are constructive."[66] Once better times returned to the Commonwealth, voters were more receptive to traditional politics. They would not turn their backs on the federal largesse, but neither would they reject the time-honored clichés of states' rights, rugged individualism, and economy and efficiency. Such an attitude permitted Byrd to follow his independent course of attacking the New Deal while maintaining his personal hegemony over the Old Dominion.[67]

~ 10 ~

Rebellion in Richmond

B YRD'S PLATE WAS FULL in 1937. Not only was he waging critical battles with the New Dealers, but he also confronted a serious challenge to his leadership of Virginia: Jim Price's election to the governorship. Price's candidacy was not unexpected, but its timing and its strength caught Byrd unprepared. His elevation to the Senate had imposed new constraints on the time he could give to Virginia affairs. Patronage proved particularly burdensome, as did the lengthening congressional sessions and the bitter debates over new programs. His growing national stature as an anti–New Deal spokesman increased his correspondence and invitations to speak. To compensate, he reduced his letters to his own constituents and turned to the telephone as his primary means of communication. Although friends were dutifully reporting to him about election prospects and results, Byrd's attention was elsewhere.

The loss of Billy Reed in September 1935 was a tremendous blow to him. For ten years they had worked on state reorganization, plotted campaigns and hunted together, and exchanged family and business news on an almost daily basis. Here was a private counselor who could not be replaced. Reed had urgently requested Byrd's presence at dinner in his Richmond home; as they were dining, he collapsed and died. Grief-stricken, Byrd said of the loss: "I have lost my dearest friend and Virginia one of her greatest and most beloved sons. Without hope or desire for reward no man in many years has contributed so much to the welfare and progress of Virginia. Only his intimate friends know the extent of the unselfish service he has rendered."[1] A few weeks later in a letter to Reed's brother, Pleasant, Byrd dedicated himself "to carry out those things that Billy Reed accomplished for Virginia . . . namely continue the present sound policies that make Virginia such an outstanding contrast to the waste and extravagance of the Federal Government as well as virtually every other State in the Union"—as Reed had counseled, "to keep Virginia like she is without any changes."[2]

There were also distractions in his personal life. He had minor surgery to remove a kidney stone in the fall of 1936. All the children were out of the nest, but Bev and Dick were still in boarding school, testing Byrd's patience with

184

their erratic progress, while Harry Jr. had taken over operation of the *Evening Star* and required some supervision from afar as he completed his apprenticeship. In 1936 Byrd oversaw the final disposition of Uncle Hal Flood's estate, of which he had been the administrator and guardian of the children for fifteen years. In that same year he reshuffled his office staff. Marvin James ("Peachy") Menefee, a hero of the world war and former commissioner of revenue from Page County, moved over from Representative Robertson's office and replaced H. E. Dameron as Byrd's administrative assistant; a heavyset, jovial sort, Menefee remained with him for thirty years. They would be joined shortly by J. Heywood Bell, a newspaper reporter for the Associated Press and Richmond *News Leader,* who would become Byrd's major speechwriter and staff investigator. At the same time the senator was tackling a major expansion of his orchards with the planting of the color sport varieties at the new Jefferson Orchard. Celebrating his fiftieth birthday in 1937, Byrd could be excused if he had become inattentive to what was happening in Virginia politics. As he wrote William Battle, "Sometimes I get so tired of it that I feel like giving it up and perhaps I will."[3]

Byrd may have been lulled into a false sense of security by Peery's easy victory in 1933 and his own electoral successes. He had even sanctioned Ebbie Combs's departure from Richmond in December 1933 for a better-paying job with the Reconstruction Finance Corporation. While Combs was helpful in getting RFC money for Virginia, he was needed more in Richmond, so Reed and Byrd worked with Governor Peery to get Combs two jobs in the capital equal in pay to his RFC salary: his old position as comptroller and the chairmanship of the new Compensation Board authorized to fix the salaries and expenses of local officials now that the discredited fee system had been reformed. Changes to that system had been obstructed for years by the fee officers, but shortages in several counties pressured Byrd into supporting the revisions. While the Compensation Board, which consisted of the chairman, state tax commissioner, and state treasurer, was an improvement, it gave whoever controlled it vast power over the "courthouse crowd." Frank Wysor, treasurer of Pulaski County, put it succinctly to Byrd: "I think now we have the best law of this kind that has ever been passed. . . . With a man like Combs in touch with these city and county officers we should be able to put across worthy things. However, should the opposition get in, Heaven help us." Years later, an investigation of the Compensation Board found no pattern of political motivation in its activities, but James J. Kilpatrick of the *News Leader* concluded that "Mr. Combs has walked softy, but has carried a mighty big stick."[4]

The opposition Wysor referred to seemed insignificant in 1934, but three years later it was a menace to the Organization. There had always been a difference of opinion between moderate reformers and conservatives within the machine dating back to the Martin years, but Byrd's rise to power and the progressive nature of his governorship had unified the two wings of the party, leaving only a few renegades and discontented office seekers such as Westmoreland Davis and G. Walter Mapp on the outside. However, the scarcity of political jobs at the state level, the lengthening lines of candidates for the few top positions, and a difference of opinion over ways to combat the depression produced a growing number of dissatisfied followers who were soon to be labeled anti-Organization or "antis," enemies of the machine. Complaining about the obstructive tactics of Byrd and Glass, Robert Whitehead of Lovingston, who would become an articulate opponent of the Organization in the years ahead, said, "As one long identified with the so called 'organization,' and who supported both Senators, I feel that the time has come for us to take inventory of the situation, and ask ourselves: Are we being represented or misrepresented in the Senate of the U.S.?"[5]

The "antis" eventually included former governors Davis and E. Lee Trinkle, Lieutenant Governor James Price, Congressman John Flannagan, party secretary Martin Hutchinson, and editors Norman Hamilton and Charles Harkrader. Although they remained loyal Democrats, their political ambitions and personal philosophies were incompatible with Organization objectives. While a few of them had liberal backgrounds, most were fiscal conservatives who simply believed that more money should be made available for services other than highways. The allegiance Byrd demanded precluded their kind of independence, and while many of them remained on the fringes of the Organization because there was no alternative, they chafed at their forced subservience. Worth Smith, who had defeated Byrd's bond nemesis, O'Conor Goolrick, in 1923 but who had lost to Peery in 1934, characterized their frustration: "Personally, I tried to be loyal to Senator Byrd, but after a few years I found out that in order to be loyal to him I'd have to become a bullfrog and jump every time he said jump, regardless of my personal views on any subject." For the "antis," the New Deal offered hope of political emancipation.[6]

Byrd and his allies were not unaware of this discontent. The senator's concern about his gubernatorial reforms, control of patronage, and selection of state leaders, although at times a bit paranoid, proved the existence of others who wanted to share power.[7] And he was not always in a position to deny them. Federal jobs had been so numerous that with the exception of the most visible and powerful positions, he had been forced to dispense them among both wings of the party. Nor was he always able to impose his will on Old Dominion politics. With some frequency Organization candidates lost elections because of local issues or because two of them ran for the same post. In retaining the loyalty of the county leaders, Byrd sometimes alienated urban politicians, which caused Richmond, Norfolk, and Roanoke to be much more independent of his rule. And southwest Virginia was always a battleground with the Republicans.

Recognizing the limitations of his power, Byrd was very pragmatic in choosing when to fight and when to retreat. Permitting a degree of internal strife, he accepted persons who, while not wholly in accord with every one of his votes, supported balanced budgets and low taxes. On the other hand, if members demonstrated too much independence and threatened his power, they faced political oblivion: ostracism from the inner circle, defeat at the polls, or loss of appointment.[8] An example of Byrd's political artistry was his treatment of Jim Price. Rather than risk losing to the extremely popular lieutenant governor in the 1937 gubernatorial race, Byrd gave him a tepid endorsement, believing that in one term as governor he could be controlled by a hostile assembly. But when Price challenged Byrd's domination, the Organization smashed him.

The specter of Jim Price had been in the minds of Organization leaders for years. Handsome, gregarious, and active in several fraternal organizations, he had represented Richmond in the House of Delegates for seven terms before the machine selected him to be Pollard's running mate in the crucial 1929 race against the Cannonites. While his popularity had made him acceptable to the leadership, he did not move into the inner circle primarily because he had taken positions at variance with those of the Organization, expressing reservations about the short ballot, advocating a state work relief program in 1931, and supporting the New Deal. Worried that Price might run for the governorship in 1933, Byrd and Reed pressed the candidacy of George Peery earlier than usual and prevailed upon Price to run again for lieutenant governor, which he did, outpolling every candidate on the ballot, including Harry Byrd.

Desiring to be governor more for the honor than the power but aware that Byrd's disfavor might deny him that reward, Price disrupted the normal selection procedure by announcing in July 1935 that he would be a candidate for governor in 1937. The silence with which the Organization received his declaration revealed Byrd's surprise and dismay. Cognizant of Price's ambition, he was floating a few trial balloons of his own, none of which had yet found a wind. Congressman Thomas Burch of Martinsville had been receiving the most attention, but he had attracted little support outside his Fifth District. Byrd's initial reaction to Price's announcement was to write friends across the state to ask them not to commit on the gubernatorial election. Combs, meanwhile, was emphasizing the need to back whomever Byrd decided to support. Anything else, he said, would be the "grossest kind of ingratitude and disloyalty to a real friend." At the same time they did nothing to disparage Price, perhaps realizing that they might have to support him down the line. To one correspondent Byrd denied that he had any influence in the selection process, claiming that his only interest would be the election of a governor who would continue conservative spending policies in Virginia.[9]

Byrd's cautious response caused consternation among members of the Organization, who were caught between loyalty to Byrd and the beginning of a bandwagon for Price. "If Price is elected," one of them said, the "antis" would "empty the officebuilding of present office holders."[10] An irate W. Y. Hosier in Norfolk analyzed the Organization's problems for Byrd:

> It is a noticeable fact, that in the past two years, nearly all of the appointments to these good federal jobs have gone to men who in many instances don't even know the number of the precinct in which they vote. . . . If we are to go ahead politically in Virginia, if Virginia is to carry on, as she has, since you became a power politically, then we must build up. We must reward those who go out and bear the brunt of battle. . . . It's time to rebuild the old machine in every precinct in the state, and it's up to us to do it now. . . . From now on, regardless of how small a job, that it be known publicly that he is a Byrd machine man or he can't get the job. You can't tame a rattlesnake.[11]

But the rattlesnakes were on the loose. Encouraged by the Harkrader editorials of the year before and Roosevelt's growing popularity, the "antis" rushed to climb aboard the Price bandwagon. Martin Hutchinson and E. Lee Trinkle were urging their friends to commit to the lieutenant governor. For his own part Price traveled across the state, winning the backing of many county clerks and state legislators. As one state senator said, "We will string along with Harry Byrd in anything he wants, but we'd like to see him accept Jim Price as the organization's candidate." The "antis" were also making more serious contact with friends in the Roosevelt administration, notably R. Walton Moore, former Virginia congressman and now assistant secretary of state, in order to obtain jobs.[12]

In the fall of 1935, Byrd sought to turn the Burch balloon into a live candidacy. Advising the congressman to become more active, he consulted his friends about Burch's chances. The reports varied, but the negative ones carried more authority: the phlegmatic Burch could not beat the effervescent Price. Abe Schewel of Lynchburg counseled Byrd that it "would be a mistake and a tragedy to 'sidetrack' Price again in favor of Burch, or anyone else. If ever there was a sure winner for the governorship, it is Price." When Burch endorsed a tax increase to pay for higher teacher salaries, his support at the courthouse waned. Sadly, Byrd wrote William Battle, "We are having some difficult complications with respect to the gubernatorial situation."[13]

Hearing pleas from local officeholders for a signal and receiving advice from others that the longer he waited to pick an opponent the stronger Price would become, Byrd frantically turned in early 1936 from Burch to Sinclair Brown, Speaker of the House of Delegates from Salem, to save the Organization. Brown's name had surfaced in earlier discussions, but he had displayed no desire to get involved. Finally, Byrd asked the Speaker to meet him in Washington for an eleventh-hour arm-twisting. It was such a last-minute effort that the senator left Winchester without shaving. He later told his son: "I spent hours and hours with Sinclair Brown. I thought I had him where he would agree to run, but told him that as a candidate he would have to put up some of his own money, but that we would help him raise funds. By the end of the conversation I had the feeling he would not run. So if he doesn't run, I'm going to forget about it. Price will be elected and we'll just have to see what happens." Byrd rationalized his failure to Lou Jaffe: "My duties at Washington are so engrossing that I am not able to give much attention to the Virginia political situation and as time goes on I expect to give much less, as I believe in the matters of purely State politics that the people of Virginia should themselves decide what is best." For the only time in his forty-year reign as head of the Organization, he would not personally influence the selection of the governor.[14]

Despite the urging of some Organization leaders to fight Price, Byrd stuck to his decision, adhering to the principle that entering a race and losing was worse than not entering at all. Faced with some dissension across the state because of his criticism of the New Deal, he did not want to further undermine his popularity and control of the Organization with a futile contest against Price. Although the election was a year and a half away and Price might still stumble, Byrd would not obstruct him. Instead, he concentrated on securing his leadership of a fragmenting Organization.[15]

The final act was played out over Christmas dinner, 1936. Roosevelt's overwhelming triumph nationally and in the Old Dominion strengthened Price's hand immeasurably. On December 22 the lieutenant governor seized the opportunity Byrd had offered months before and committed himself to a "sound and conservative fiscal policy" and "efficiency in State government." With that, practically every Organization officeholder quickly announced his support for Price's candidacy. Without making any commitment, Byrd praised Price personally, declaring that he had "no desire whatsoever to exert a personal influence over political affairs in Virginia except to lend my support as a citizen to a more efficient and progressive government in the State." As Hutchinson said to Lee Trinkle, Byrd had discovered that "the boys back home did not want a hopeless fight." The senator had suffered a reverse, but not a mortal one.[16]

While the Organization conceded Price's victory, the Richmonder's unwillingness to endorse candidates for lieutenant governor and attorney general left Byrd and Combs free to contest those positions, and they did so with abandon.

They selected state senator Saxon Holt of Newport News and incumbent Abram P. Staples of Roanoke as their two candidates. Lined up against them were the choices of the "antis," Robert Daniel and John Galleher. Daniel, who clearly had higher office in mind, was especially obnoxious to Byrd for having demonstrated his independence of the machine at the 1932 national convention. Byrd believed that John Flannagan was grooming Daniel for the governorship four years hence. Since Price was friendly to both Holt and Daniel, he endorsed both of them, greatly disappointing the latter, who continued to foster the impression that he was Price's running mate. It was the first sign to the independents that Jim Price might not have the "fire in the belly" to take on the Organization. He just wanted to be governor.[17]

Knowing that they were in a real fight, Byrd and Combs ran the Holt campaign as if it were for the governorship. The letters went out to local officeholders, editorial support was arranged, and the leadership took to the campaign trail. A Holt victory took on new urgency when rumors arose—substantiated by meetings that Price and Charles Harkrader had with President Roosevelt—that the new governor would have control of federal patronage in Virginia. Byrd remarked to Glass, "Roosevelt is actively supporting all the forces hostile to us." Nevertheless, the senator's active involvement in the campaign paid off with relatively easy victories for Holt and Staples in the August primary. In gratitude, Holt wrote to him: "I feel that it was a great victory, not only for me but for you. I thoroughly realize that I could not have won this fight except for your aid." Reassured that the Organization was still in control in the Old Dominion, Byrd graciously wired his congratulations to Price, who won just as handily against Republican J. Powell Royal in November. But as Bill Tuck warned the senator, "Our immediate past trouble demonstrates clearly the absolute necessity for eternal vigilance and 'Keeping our hand upon the throttle and our eye upon the rail.'"[18]

Price's first session with the General Assembly in 1938 proved to be the pinnacle of his success against the machine. Much of his legislative program was passed over minimal opposition: social security, a forty-eight-hour workweek for women, and increased aid to schools. The major controversy came when he fired Ebbie Combs from his two positions as comptroller and chairman of the Compensation Board. Coming as it did just a day before another meeting between Price and Roosevelt, the firing reignited the struggle for supremacy between the Organization and the "antis." Although the governor also replaced the heads of several other departments, his action against Combs, Harry Byrd's longtime friend, was deemed most offensive and threatening, especially because of the crucial patronage power held by the Compensation Board.

Aware of the desire of the "antis" to have him removed, Combs had orchestrated a major endorsement effort by his friends to protect his positions. He urged Byrd to come to Richmond for the Jackson Day dinner in January as a sign of cooperation with Price but also as a show of strength. Without mentioning Combs, Byrd wrote to Price, commending the tone of his inaugural message, but if he intended to influence the governor indirectly, he failed, for less than two weeks into his term Price asked Combs to step down. Upset at this action, Byrd urged his lieutenant "to get out of the files all of your personal letters."[19]

Price's biographer, Alvin Hall, believed that the governor was not out to make war against the machine; otherwise he would have replaced all of the Byrd men in the state government instead of retaining most of them as he did. The idea of governing through competent professionals rather than political appointees appealed to him. Hall has said that Price yielded to the demands of the "antis" for Combs's head and his own "impulse to retaliate" against the Organization for originally opposing him. Perhaps, too, he remembered Combs's work in denying him the speakership of the House of Delegates back in 1926, or he may have worried that Combs's influence with the legislature would limit his programs. But the governor was not entirely innocent in his actions. His subsequent appointment in 1939 of Martin Hutchinson, by then considered one of the most notorious of the "antis," to the chairmanship of the Compensation Board was hardly above politics. Price remained in close communication with the Roosevelt administration, primarily through R. Walton Moore, with whom he exchanged ideas on how Roosevelt's use of patronage could strengthen Price's position. He was forthright in asking that the men he had just fired not be given federal jobs in Virginia with which they could help the Organization and embarrass him. He entreated Moore, "If the Federal administration will back us up in the individual cases, it would be a tremendous help." Price may not have been out to get Byrd, but his preferences surely lay with the "antis" and the New Dealers.[20]

If, as Hall has said, Price "had no temperament to carry the battle beyond this point," that was not the way Organization people perceived it. Tom Ozlin bellowed to Byrd, "The gage of battle has been thrown down and . . . it is incumbent upon us to prepare to take it up, and meet it at every opportunity." Without Byrd's direct involvement, but certainly with his knowledge and likely with his approval, several legislators introduced an amendment to curtail the governor's power by denying him the right to appoint the chairman of the Compensation Board. This would keep patronage power in the hands of the Organization and deny it to Price. The Coleman amendment passed the House of Delegates, 60–37, and Combs and Tuck both urged Byrd to help them line up support for it in the state senate. "It is the most important roll call in my opinion . . . since I have been a member of the Senate," Tuck fretted.[21] But they did not have the votes to defeat Price. Asked by an anguished Senator Aubrey Weaver if they should proceed with the ballot, Byrd inquired whether he would vote for the amendment. Weaver replied that he would. "Well," said Byrd, "if you've got one vote, my advice is to call the roll." He did not think they could let down their friends in the House of Delegates who had supported it. Price, who insisted on retaining "the prerogative exercised by my predecessors," rallied public support against this rebuke to the governor and won a sizable victory when the state senate voted 23–15 for the budget bill without the disruptive amendment. The lower house then concurred by the narrow margin of 49–44.

The "antis" rejoiced at what they believed was the dawning of a new day in Commonwealth politics, but they overlooked the fact that Price had been sustained by many Organization members who did not want to embarrass a newly inaugurated governor with whom they would have to work for the next four years. Changing the rules in midstream would be a bad precedent for the future and would generate much sympathy for Price. It would be better to let the issue die. Byrd may have agreed, for he certainly had the political muscle to call on longtime friends for support. It was another example of his choosing his fights carefully. Nevertheless, Organization leaders had their guard up, concerned about renewed reports out of Washington that the administration was out to challenge Byrd's rule in Virginia. With the *Times-Dispatch* predicting a real fight between the Organization and Price, Bill Tuck warned Byrd, "I doubt not that they plan to oppose you in 1940."[22]

Events in the spring of 1938 confirmed in Byrd's mind that he and Glass were the objects of an administration attack on their power. The president, emboldened by his election success and bitter over the Court defeat, set out to remove some of his prominent congressional critics from office by endorsing their more liberal opposition. It was only natural that the home state of two of the most vociferous antagonists of the New Deal would receive attention. Although the only Virginian targeted by the administration in the ill-fated purges of 1938 was Howard Smith in the Eighth District—an attempt he easily beat back—Price's victory encouraged Roosevelt to try to break the Byrd machine. Thinking ahead to the 1940 national convention, he may have wanted Price to replace Byrd as the head of a Virginia delegation more favorably disposed toward him or his choice of a successor; if so, he should have listened to John Garner, who told him: "There is no sense playing with the Governor down there because he won't control the delegation in 1940. It will be controlled by the Glass-Byrd crowd."[23]

The senators were not taken by surprise. Glass, in particular, was always sensitive to the slightest challenge to his authority and prerogative, ferreting out any rumor to this effect and demanding an explanation. When Charles

Harkrader in March 1938 proclaimed that Jim Price had been given "veto power on all appointments of any consequence in Virginia," Glass went straight to Roosevelt. The president gingerly explained that the senator's recommendations would continue to be given every consideration but that he would not be bound by them. Later that summer Glass relayed Cliff Woodrum's warning to Byrd "that Price and his miserable gang, abetted by the White House, were surely after you." While Byrd undoubtedly agreed with this estimate, he was forced by his upcoming reelection campaign to assume a lower profile on patronage issues, still unsure of the power of the Roosevelt/Price coalition.[24]

The confrontation broke in July 1938 with Roosevelt's recess appointment of Judge Floyd Roberts of Bristol to a newly created federal judgeship in the Western District of Virginia. Carter Glass termed Roberts's nomination, endorsed by Flannagan, Westmoreland Davis, and Price, "personally offensive" and claimed the president had disregarded the two recommendations he and Byrd had submitted. The senior senator had already told Byrd that Roberts's appointment to a federal judgeship would be an "intentional affront" that they would have to oppose. He also warned Jim Farley that he and Byrd would do all they could to block Roberts's confirmation, but when Farley advised Roosevelt to heed this threat, the president reportedly said that he was "not going to let Glass or Byrd make any appointments in Virginia." This slap at two revered representatives undermined public support in the Old Dominion for both Roosevelt and Jim Price. Although he had not initiated the nomination of Roberts but had been drawn into it at the urging of Flannagan and Harkrader, Price paid a high price for his participation when the next assembly session convened.[25]

As the governor continued to replace a few more Organization people in the executive branch, Byrd sought to strengthen the machine prior to his 1940 race, meeting with some regularity with his closest advisers at Skyland for strategy sessions. Unable to tolerate another setback, he allowed Glass to carry the fight against Roberts but cautioned him about jeopardizing his reelection chances. By late fall, however, having witnessed Roosevelt's failure with the purges, the resurgence of the Republicans at the polls, and Colgate Darden's recapture of the congressional seat in the Second District, Byrd informed Glass that his reelection was of no concern in the fight against "this deliberate effort to insult us." But he appended, "I agree with you that our victory will be helpful to me."[26]

Anti-Organization forces actively supported Roberts, seeing this contest as another step on the road to defeating the Organization. R. Walton Moore told Roosevelt adviser Edwin ("Pa") Watson that the Roberts appointment would strengthen Price's hand in Virginia. However, they relied too heavily on the prestige of President Roosevelt and Governor Price, who proved no match

Holding the Fort

against the power of senatorial courtesy. Furthermore, the state press supported the senators' position, denying the "antis" a means of rallying public opinion.

As the confirmation hearings opened on January 31, 1939, Senator Glass, puffed up like a bantam rooster, launched into an exhaustive attack against the president and the governor for humiliating him and his colleague. He spoke of a conspiracy to deny the senators any say in the matter and to give the governor veto power over federal appointments in Virginia. For his part, Harry Byrd merely stated that the nomination was "personally offensive and obnoxious." The efforts of Governor Price to deny the charges of complicity and the character defenses of Roberts by former governors Davis and Trinkle fell on deaf ears. The Judiciary Committee rejected the nomination, and in a full Senate vote, much to the glee of Senator Glass, Roberts was denied his appointment by a vote of 72–9, reportedly the largest vote ever cast against a presidential nominee. It was an ignominious defeat for the president, the governor, and the "antis." Roosevelt immediately tried to limit the damage by commending his nominee and criticizing senatorial courtesy for obstructing the president's constitutional power to make appointments. Byrd responded with his lengthiest comment on the whole affair, defending the Senate's right to advise and consent and vigorously attacking the president for his politically motivated actions that were designed "to create a political issue in the Senatorial campaign in 1940." He was publicly accusing Roosevelt of trying to purge him.[27]

Abruptly, Roosevelt did an about-face and contributed to the perpetuation of the old order in Virginia politics. Having overestimated the potential of Price and the "antis" to construct a competing machine in the Old Dominion more favorable to his New Deal, FDR revealed that he, too, could be very pragmatic. Concerned over the possible outbreak of war in Europe and likely thinking about the 1940 presidential election, he carefully pulled back from his liaison with the "antis," reconciled with Carter Glass, and began deferring once again to Byrd and Glass on patronage matters. Jim Price's protests were unavailing. Even John Flannagan gave up the cause and made his peace with the Organization.[28]

The Roberts affair seemed to have been a significant chapter in the history of the Byrd Organization. The effort to undermine Byrd's rule in Virginia failed miserably, discrediting the "antis," tarnishing the governor, and strengthening the Organization among Virginia voters. From another perspective, however, the Roberts appointment was not so important a juncture in Harry Byrd's career. Not only did Roosevelt misjudge the likely success of challenging Byrd's authority, but so did the "antis" and the Organization. Although Byrd's natural pessimism heightened his concern, his fears were groundless. Price had neither the power nor the desire to take on Byrd. Without his leadership and with Roosevelt's popularity declining, the "antis" were a hollow shell. The rapidity with which Roosevelt backed off demonstrated Byrd's dominance in the Old Dominion.[29]

Byrd, of course, did not see it that way. His political success had depended upon not underestimating his enemies. Roosevelt's landslide victory in 1936, followed by Price's success a year later, concerned him, so much so that he had moderated his criticism of the president and allowed Price some leeway in the General Assembly session. He could not know what Price's intentions for 1940 were; the governor was always so ambivalent in word and deed regarding his objectives that Byrd could not risk doing nothing; to the senator, the Roberts affair was another contest that had to be won against those who sought to destroy the Organization. More critical struggles now lay ahead: the 1939 elections, which would determine control of the General Assembly, the 1940 legislative session, and his Senate race later that year.

A confrontation was brewing that neither Price nor Byrd wanted, stoked by every issue, every appointment, and many bitter words. Combs told Byrd that Price was sending his agents all over the state "with a view of bringing out candidates against members friendly to us in districts where he thinks he would have some prospects of victory." He was certain that Price would be running against Byrd the following year. The continued replacement of Organization people by the governor, who was very dilatory in completing his executive appointments, remained another sore point between them. The removal of J. H. Bradford, who had been budget director since 1924, was particularly distressful to Byrd.[30] When Tom Ozlin told him that his reelection was being threatened by the opposition's hardball tactics, Byrd replied, "The fight is on and there will be no compromise." To another correspondent who appealed for party harmony, Byrd retorted, "I have done my utmost from the beginning to avoid friction in the Party, but, at the same time, there are some things you simply cannot stand for." Every gauge of approval was measured; Bill Tuck reported to Byrd that "deafening applause" greeted the senator's telegram at the Jackson Day dinner while the governor was only "politely received."[31]

As the primary elections for the assembly approached, the Organization rose to the challenge. The indefatigable Combs was everywhere, but particularly in the Ninth District, making it safe once again with the assistance of former governor Peery. To tackle the independent delegate Berkley Adams in Charlotte County, Byrd courted millionaire David K. Bruce, who had only recently moved to the county and had voted for Republican Alf Landon in 1936. Elsewhere he and Combs considered supporting Republicans in the general election against Price candidates who were sure to win in the primary. As Charles Harkrader put it to Martin Hutchinson, "Harry the Hater" was out to get all of them.[32] Faced with the ever-present rumors that Price would run against him in 1940, Byrd piggybacked his own reelection efforts onto the assembly contests, campaigning in problem counties and getting commitments from the local officeholders and newspaper editors.[33]

The primary results were unclear, confused by local issues and the ambiguous loyalties of several of the candidates. Both sides claimed success. Of the twenty-one contests that Combs listed as demanding their "careful attention," there was an even split of 4–4 in the senate races and a victory of 8–5 in the house races. Byrd was "exceedingly satisfied" with the results. Burr Harrison's defeat of Russell Cather, Byrd's old friend who had defected to Price, and David Bruce's triumph over Berkley Adams were the Organization's most significant victories. The *Times-Dispatch* saw no major gains for either faction and expected no obstruction of the governor's program in the next session, but the Organization had retained large majorities in both houses of the legislature.[34]

Although both the governor and senator called for an end to the factionalism, Price's impolitic remarks following a meeting with President Roosevelt shortly after the primary intensified the division. Commenting that the president had expressed satisfaction with the results, Price indicated that his control over the legislature had been strengthened, a statement the *Evening Star* was quick to criticize. Proceeding on the assumption that Price would oppose him in 1940 for the Senate, Byrd began his petitions for the race earlier than usual, ordering Peachy Menefee to start the mailings to farmers and preachers at the end of the year. Aware that a successful legislative session could be a springboard for the governor's campaign, Byrd prepared to obstruct Price, telling Combs to find out all he could about the plans for the budget.[35]

The return of Ebbie Combs to political favor on the eve of the 1940 legislative session was an ominous sign for the governor. Combs was overwhelmingly elected to replace the deceased Vic Hanger as clerk of the senate, a position with few responsibilities and much time for politicking. Price had wanted to elevate Hanger's assistant, John Jeter, but the Organization's vigorous effort in Combs's behalf forced him to back down after he consulted many of the senators. He recovered nicely with a forceful opening address and budget message to the legislature that called for improvements in education and an executive reorganization grounded on a fiscally sound foundation. These were proposals that in another time might have won Harry Byrd's enthusiastic support, but since they challenged his own reform record and came from a potential opponent, he ignored them.[36]

At this point a weird incident occurred that undermined Price's credibility with the assembly. In December reporter Joseph Leib had approached Senator Glass about a rumor that Price intended to keep Glass off the Virginia delegation to the 1940 national convention. A few days later he asked Price about the reports. Without denying the story, the governor referred Leib to Hutchinson, who indicated his annoyance with Byrd and Glass and a willingness to talk with Leib. When Leib said he could not meet with him, Hutchinson, asking for confidentiality, wrote that he knew of no movement to keep any individual from going to the convention; furthermore, he said, it would be unwise to block Byrd and Glass from going. Leib sent Glass all the correspondence and added to the intrigue by implicating Hutchinson and Tommy Corcoran, a Roosevelt adviser, in a plot to let Price control a Virginia delegation instructed for Roosevelt. He then turned all the letters over to David Lawrence of the

United States News, who published them in early February. Price immediately denied involvement and termed the story "asinine," indicating that he planned to support Byrd and Glass as delegates. Nevertheless, Byrd thought "there [was] a great deal of truth" in the story and stepped up his effort to secure control of the state convention. The affair was largely a fabrication by Leib, who was little more than a provocateur, but unfortunately for Jim Price, Leib's machinations confirmed the suspicions of Organization leaders about the governor's intentions.[37]

Only a few days before the correspondence was published, Price gave the leadership a vehicle for acting on their suspicions. He finally specified the extent of his reorganization plans: a thorough consolidation of departments, notably in conservation and welfare, with the duties of the Division of Motor Vehicles to be taken over by the Department of Taxation; he estimated savings of $350,000. It was a masterful proposal, but the threat to patronage in the lucrative conservation agencies and the Division of Motor Vehicles was obvious. William Meade Fletcher estimated to Byrd that the plan would guarantee Price 50,000 votes, and Tom Ozlin urged the senator to contact his friends in the legislature with a recommendation of caution. Two weeks later, led by E. Blackburn Moore and G. Alvin Massenburg, the House of Delegates killed the governor's plan. A bitter Price blamed his loss on "thinly disguised political activity."[38]

Both in public and private utterances, Byrd denied any responsibility for what had happened. He wrote Douglas Freeman, "I have done nothing directly or indirectly to obstruct a single reform advocated by Governor Price. To the contrary, I have done what I could to prevent factionalism, which has been increasing in Virginia for the past several years." Freeman replied somewhat skeptically, "There is no denying the fact that many of the 'old boys' got together with amazing speed when any law that seemed to impair their organization was before the Assembly."[39] While Byrd told most people that duties in Washington kept him from taking part in the assembly's deliberations, some of his letters indicate not only an interest in getting involved but discussions "with some of our friends." Certainly Price's people thought he had interfered, and even a few Byrd leaders were reported as saying that the reorganization bill was defeated as the result of a phone call from Washington.

It is difficult to believe, after years of heated conflict with Price and the "antis" and with his own reelection on the line, that Byrd was merely an interested spectator. If he was not giving the marching orders, the work of the obstructionists certainly had his blessing. As John Hart had predicted to Martin Hutchinson the year before, "The Byrd crowd has decided to embarrass him [Price] in every way possible at the coming session of the Legislature. They are bent on crucifying him, at which they are expert. . . . They will so discount what he does as to make him unpopular." The script was carried out perfectly. The Organization once again reigned supreme in Virginia, and Price was so discredited that Harry Byrd was reelected to the Senate in 1940 without any opposition. While it is true that Organization leaders sometimes did things without consulting Byrd—which left him very frustrated—his correspondence confirms his continued involvement in state politics. Furthermore, leadership, particularly of the autocratic kind, carries with it responsibility for what lieutenants do in the leader's name.[40]

∼ 11 ∽

A National Reputation

ARRY BYRD'S INFLUENCE and authority were enhanced not only by
his success in turning back Jim Price's challenge but also by his growing prominence as the nation's leading spokesman for reduced federal
spending and against waste in government. As a freshman senator from Virginia, he had had limited national exposure and little influence in an institution
that venerated seniority, but his opposition to court packing, his support of
the "conservative manifesto," and his advocacy of reorganization had increased
his stature. During this time he had also published a series of articles on government spending in a variety of publications that advanced his reputation
as the nation's leading economizer: "Lumping Debts on Uncle Sam," "The
Cost of Our Government," "Pump Priming a Failure While Deficits Mount,"
"Uncle Sam's Cash Register," "Government Reorganization," and "Waste and
Its Effect."[1]

The event, however, that propelled Byrd into the spotlight was his debate in
the newspapers with Marriner Eccles, chairman of the Federal Reserve Board. It
highlighted the widening chasm between conservatives and liberals over the
proper role of government in American life, a division that dramatized American politics for the next fifty years. For half of that time, Harry Byrd was the
best-known political advocate for unregulated markets, balanced budgets, and
reduced government spending. The debate was initiated by Byrd's speech to
the Massachusetts Federation of Taxpayers Association on December 10, 1938,
in which he called for an end to "nine years of fiscal insanity" in Washington.
Labeling the New Deal spending program a "tragic failure," he castigated the
idea of Chairman Eccles and other brain trusters that recovery from the depression could be achieved through borrowing: the theory of British economist
John Maynard Keynes that government spending or "pump priming" could
compensate for reduced consumer spending and business investment to restore
the market to health. For Byrd this view indicated "to what depths of false
reasoning we have sunk in the crackpot legislative ideas of those holding important public positions." His solution for the depression was to reorganize
the government, reduce its activity to a minimum, and cancel the borrowing
authority of thirty federal agencies. The speech was standard pay-as-you-go

fare, which normally would have created few ripples, but Byrd's attack on Eccles elicited a response from the chairman that focused attention on the continuing discussion of how best to escape the clutches of depression.[2]

Franklin Roosevelt's New Deal had imaginatively attacked the economic collapse with a vast array of alphabet agencies designed to provide relief and recovery. While its programs had mitigated the worst aspects of the crisis, it had not solved the underlying problems of unemployment, low business confidence, and sputtering productivity. Nevertheless, its early successes and declining joblessness caused the president and his advisers to cut back on government spending after his reelection landslide in 1936; but a sharp recession, induced by the reduced expenditures and aggravated by the Federal Reserve Board's tight money policy, hit the following year and renewed the debate over economic policy. Budget balancers like Treasury Secretary Henry Morgenthau preferred reliance on private initiatives to revive the economy, while "pump primers" such as Harry Hopkins called for renewed federal spending. Marriner Eccles, appointed chairman of the Federal Reserve Board in 1934, also favored more spending. Although he denied knowledge of the ideas of Keynes, Eccles was a believer. "The Government," he later wrote, "must be the compensatory agent in this economy; it must unbalance its budget during deflation and create surpluses in periods of great business activity." Throughout the winter of 1937–38, Roosevelt hesitated to renew spending, but as conditions worsened, he moved to the side of the spenders, and in April he asked Congress for $4.5 billion for relief, public works, flood control, housing, and highways. Over Senator Byrd's opposition, the request, with a slightly reduced price tag, easily passed. Byrd explained his view to Clarence Marshall, managing editor of the *United States News:* "I do not think that government pump priming is economically sound because at best activity created is temporary, the prosperity created is synthetic, and it becomes increasingly dangerous in proportion to the extent borrowed money is used." His continued frustration with this spending, even though it did not approach the amounts suggested by Keynes, generated his vitriolic attack on Eccles late in the year.[3]

Two weeks after Byrd's Massachusetts talk, Eccles addressed a public letter to the senator that challenged his economic thinking and advanced the New Deal philosophy of government:

> You stated that you are concerned about "the character of the individual citizen and the dignity and the rights of the individual." So am I. I believe, however, that the most basic right of all is the right to live and next to that, the right to work. I do not think empty stomachs build character, nor do I think the substitution of idleness and a dole for useful work relief will improve either the dignity or the character of the people affected. . . . Further than the right to eat and the right to a position, I think the individual, whether rich or poor, has a right to a decent place to live. I think he has a

right to security in old age and to protection against temporary unemployment. I think he has a right to adequate medical attention and to equal educational opportunities with the rest of his countrymen. The Government expenditures which you condemn have in large part been the means of translating these basic rights into realities. . . . I am convinced that your program is not only a defeatist one, a program of retrogression and not of progress, but that it would jeopardize the salvation of our democracy, which I know you are as sincerely desirous of preserving as I am.

Eccles went on to ridicule Byrd's "misunderstanding" of the nature of capitalism and the role of debt in that system. The new thinking was that public debt, which Byrd condemned, could be just as productive as private debt, which Byrd applauded. "Can it be said," wrote Eccles, "that the creation of debt, either public or private, that utilizes productively otherwise unused human and material resources, that creates real wealth, that adds both to existing real wealth and to national income, is an evil?" Finally he pointed to the economic improvement since 1933 when government expenditures increased compared to the stagnation between 1929 and 1932 when there was minimal federal involvement and no recovery.[4]

Byrd's lengthy reply came in mid-January 1939 and was quoted at length in newspapers across the country. Full of figures about higher debts and higher taxes, his letter rejected the "doctrine and dogma of that erratic English economist, Dr. J. M. Keynes." For economic wisdom he relied instead upon Will Rogers, Thomas Jefferson, and Andrew Jackson, all of whom had criticized public indebtedness. For Byrd there was an enormous difference between public and private debt:

The ends are different and the ways and means of payment are different. As respects a private debt, the person who makes the debt expects, and is expected, to pay the debt. In respect to a public debt, the government makes the promise, and the people, or the taxpayers, perform the promise. A private debtor enters into the promise voluntarily, upon his own motion, and for his own interest. The government creates the public debt, and those who must pay are compelled to pay whether they would have entered into that promise or not. The obligations of a private debt rest upon those who made it and may, or may not be, secured. A public debt is a universal mortgage. It is a first lien on every acre of land, on every house and home, on every piece of property, on every service that is rendered, on every transaction that is made.

Byrd's response virtually ignored the question raised by Eccles of government's responsibility for the needy, and it revealed a simplistic grasp of economics. He argued that the current debt would be calamitous in the likelihood of another world war. In actuality, the government spending of Keynesian proportions during World War II ended the depression and moved America into an era of unparalleled prosperity. To the end of his life Byrd remained an economic Cassandra forecasting doom, unable to admit the achievements of the postwar American economy that was fueled in part by a growing but productive public debt. He never accepted the Keynesian revolution. He could not escape the limitations of his own experience with debt or his outdated faith in the unregulated free market. Nevertheless, in spite of his unsophisticated analysis, Byrd raised some appropriate warning flags about long-term public debt, its affect on business confidence, and the difficulty of turning off the spigot of federal spending at some future date. Clairvoyantly he sounded the alarm: "These vast sums are spent by gigantic government bureaus reaching into every nook and corner and manned by politicians of influence." The shadow of the welfare state and its costs were unsettling to him.[5]

Byrd's popularity soared after this exchange with Eccles, indicating that he was not alone in his economic assessment of public policy. Clinging to the archaic laissez-faire theories disgraced by the depression, the business community provided Byrd with a platform for his critique of government spending and bureaucracy. Although recent studies suggest that segments of the private sector, as well as New Deal economists, had adopted Keynesian ideas even before the war, businessmen generally were loath to give up their reputations as independent entrepreneurs, and they continued to pay lip service to the old icons of rugged individualism and unregulated free enterprise. Their courting of Harry Byrd was one way to reaffirm these traditional loyalties.[6]

The day after his reply to Eccles was printed, Byrd delivered a national radio address on government spending. Thereafter, his speeches to conservative groups nationwide increased in number; his correspondence with like-minded people grew to considerable proportions; and his magazine articles found a larger audience. A friend from Tennessee extolled him: "I along with millions of people am deeply grateful to you as a sort of pioneer with simple common sense in a chaotic spending orgy who stoutly stood always for economy and the preservation of our form of government." The Atlanta *Georgian* produced a full-page spread on Byrd and mentioned him as a presidential candidate. Thinking along similar lines, New Yorker J. Hampton Baumgartner wrote to Byrd, "With that in mind, . . . I have been active for a long while building up a strong sentiment among friends throughout the country, including many who are influential in public affairs and in business in support of your attitude and position as a statesman." Harry Byrd had become a national figure with a national following.[7]

The conservative resurgence in Congress gave Byrd hope that the New Deal could be curtailed if not terminated. Roosevelt's failures with court packing and reorganization along with the misguided effort to purge selected conservatives in the 1938 elections set the stage for a spirited battle between New Dealers and the reinvigorated Republicans and their conservative Democratic allies in the 1939 session. The contest came to a head with the presentation of a new reorganization bill that was stripped of its most controversial features but retained presidential authority to transfer, consolidate, or abolish federal agencies unless the proposal was rejected by Congress within sixty days. The debate over the bill was heated because Congress feared losing control of the bureaucracy to the White House and because Harry Byrd, using the findings of his select investigating committee, was insisting on economy and efficiency over rearrangement. As Senator Carl Hayden of Arizona said, everyone favored reorganization in principle but was against it in some particulars.

Renewing his attack on Marriner Eccles as a propaganda agent for waste in government, Byrd offered an amendment that would require reductions in spending. Citing the largest peacetime expenditure and the highest national debt in American history, he argued, "We cannot operate for too long, without disaster, a government costing more than the ability of people to pay. . . . As sensible people, we know that the extravagances of today must be paid by the greater taxation of tomorrow."[8] Encouraged by Senator James Byrnes, chairman of the Joint Committee on Government Reorganization, who led the fight for the president's bill, Byrd modified his amendment to make such reductions "desirable."

The debate moved to a dramatic conclusion on March 21 in votes on Senator Wheeler's amendment stipulating that both houses of Congress would have to approve any reorganization plans before their implementation rather than merely reject plans already executed. The first vote produced a 46–43 victory for the Wheeler amendment, but on a subsequent maneuvering measure, it lost on a tie vote, 44–44. Byrd commented, "We made the best fight we could . . . and would have won in the Senate excepting that Senator Borah declined to vote." The following day, after much lobbying and vote trading, the Senate finally defeated the amendment, 46–44, and passed the reorganization bill, 63–23, with Byrd shifting to the majority. "The bill is so greatly modified," he concluded, "that most of the objections have been removed." His economy amendment had been incorporated in the legislation and an indirect congressional veto power sustained. Roosevelt signed the bill in early April, and initiated a reorganization that created the Federal Security and Federal Works agencies and reshuffled other departments.[9]

For the remainder of the session, Byrd was a thorn in the side of the Roosevelt-Eccles forces. Perhaps looking ahead to his 1940 reelection bid, the senator did not want to appear too obstructionist and so on occasion supported the president, even lauding the administration's trade policies, banking legislation, and conservation programs. He backed passage of a significant transportation act that broadened the powers of the Interstate Commerce Commission over rail, motor, and water carriers, and he voted for the record-breaking $1.2 billion farm bill. But those votes of confidence were rare. Byrd was lumped with ten other Democratic senators, half of them southerners, who usually voted with Republicans against the administration. Now the acknowledged leader of the "economy bloc," the Old Dominion senator continued to denounce New Deal spending and lending policies.[10] When the administration unveiled a $2.5 billion lending program for roads, public works, reclamation projects, and farm tenancy, Byrd labeled it "a spending scheme masquerading as a lending scheme." Heading up the bipartisan coalition fighting the bill, he was successful in excising $850 million for toll roads and railroad equipment. "Jubilant" at this "first major victory" for economy since the New Deal began, he claimed that the "day of toll roads is over." He could not have been happier when the House, with Virginians Woodrum and Robertson leading the way, killed the entire bill.[11]

He was less successful, however, in stopping additional appropriations for the more popular social security program. Fighting an amendment proposed by Texas senator Tom Connally to increase the federal government's contribution to the state old-age pension plans, Byrd charged that the expenditures were greater than the eventual 9 percent payroll tax could carry. He accurately predicted, "Sooner or later, this nine percent payroll tax has got to be twelve or fifteen percent if this thing goes on. We might better frankly go to the Townsend Plan than unfrankly to proceed to make appropriations when we haven't the slightest idea how we are going to pay for them." Despite his appeal, the amendment passed in a more liberal form than originally proposed; he then voted for the amended final bill.[12]

The 1939 session was an important milestone in Harry Byrd's Senate career. The New Deal legislative initiatives came to an end, hindered by conservative political victories, the president's own missteps, competition with threatening foreign events, and the natural evolution of a reform wave that reaches a peak of activity and then subsides. As a philosophy of government—that government's responsibility is to provide for the social and economic well-being of the nation—the New Deal endured into the 1970s, but as a legislative program it was reduced to fighting a rearguard action to preserve what it had wrought, losing most of its relief programs to the demands of war. Byrd took advantage of the shift in political winds to articulate a more traditional view of government and step up his criticism of federal programs and expenditures. Senator Josiah Bailey wrote to him, "You came a long way to your own in the recent session, and you are destined to go much farther; you are the real leader of our group—in the Senate and in the country. This will be realized more and more. You have all the qualities and when the country comes to itself, as it will, all will turn to you. I expect you to be President." [13]

On September 1, 1939, Adolf Hitler marched into Poland and changed Harry Byrd's world forever. More than the depression and New Deal, World War II transformed the country into a modern welfare state with new international responsibilities. No region experienced greater change than the South, with its one-party politics, sleepy rural existence, one-crop agriculture, and racial segregation all on the verge of extinction. And although the changes were not quite so dramatic in Virginia, it, too, would undergo a transformation. [14]

Perhaps Byrd knew better than most what war would mean for the United States, particularly its impact on the economy and government spending. Therefore, on the question of America's involvement in foreign events, he was a reluctant interventionist, a position that most Americans adhered to at some time during the interwar years. The World War I experience had disillusioned them about the desirability of American intervention in world affairs. The world had not been saved for democracy; the specter of communism raised by the war had contributed to a Red Scare at home; and a chauvinistic Senate had rejected participation in the new international order. Subsequently, the onset of depression and the rise of militarism in Germany, Italy, and Japan caused Congress to enact neutrality legislation in the thirties that was designed to keep the country out of foreign wars. However, acts of aggression in Europe and the Pacific nudged most Americans to a position of reluctant intervention, a willingness to part with some of their treasure to defeat aggression but a desire to avoid a full commitment.

Harry Byrd's attitude on war followed a similar metamorphosis. Unlike some of his Senate colleagues, he never was an isolationist who preferred a withdrawal from the affairs of the world. Being a major apple exporter, he was a committed free trader who supported Secretary of State Cordell Hull's reciprocal trade agreements reducing the tariffs that Byrd blamed for the decline in agricultural exports. He constantly lobbied with Hull to ensure that apples and tobacco—major Virginia exports—were included among the approved commodities or were removed from any list of embargoed goods. [15] Senator Byrd supported Roosevelt's Good Neighbor policy for the same reasons; it promised improved trade with Latin America, including Cuba and Argentina where he had a thriving apple trade. Byrd's devotion to a peaceful world order was further strengthened by his English roots, the Anglophilia of the Old Dominion, and the internationalist legacy of native Virginian Woodrow Wilson, his father's old friend. He supported America's entry into the World Court in 1935 and opposed the Johnson amendment in 1934 that prevented loans to countries defaulting on their war debts. The senator also approved the president's requests for increases in defense spending as the foreign situation worsened.[16]

Yet like most Americans of that time, Byrd abhorred the thought of another war. His wartime experience with the Fuel Administration proved to him how disruptive war could be for individuals and businesses whose well-being was complicated by the intrusions of government regulation and red tape, the very interference he had been denouncing throughout the thirties. He feared another such experience could lead to greater regimentation of American life and a debt that, when added to New Deal indebtedness, would prove insurmountable for future generations. Thus, Byrd had no reservations about endorsing the neutrality legislation that embargoed arms sales to belligerents, restricted loans to nations at war, and prohibited travel on their vessels. Byrd was absent for many of the final votes on this legislation, but his votes on amendments and his announced sentiments indicated his support. He was not a participant in the debates, reflecting both the apathy and ignorance about the bills of many of his fellow senators.[17]

Not widely read or traveled, the provincial Byrd had little knowledge of what was happening abroad outside the apple business. Indeed, he seemed rather infatuated with the Italian dictator, Benito Mussolini. During his governorship he had praised the fascist; and just four months before the invasion of Ethiopia in October 1935 he called Mussolini "a great ruler of extraordinary courage and capacity. All of us applaud his poise and the power of his leadership through the last five years of economic difficulty and distress, but no true American would be satisfied for a day to be denied the right to criticize governmental action or to join a party in opposition to the government's policies and acts."[18] As Japan invaded China in 1937 and Hitler marched into Austria and then seized part of Czechoslovakia through the Munich agreement in 1938, Senator Byrd had no public comment to make. Certainly he disapproved of this aggression, but he did not think it warranted a response from the United States. He was preoccupied with reorganization, federal spending, the challenge from Jim Price, and his new orchards. Early in 1939 when a European war seemed imminent, Byrd explained that he was "opposed to foreign entanglements"; he believed that the sale of planes to France was permissible only if it was done within the neutrality laws. However, most of this speech to the Virginia Retail Hardware Association was a recitation of waste in government and the failure of pump priming.[19]

Part of Byrd's reluctance to support greater aid for the democracies of Europe may have been his association with two friends who had strong reservations about further involvement. Douglas Southall Freeman, editor of the Richmond *News Leader* and biographer of Robert E. Lee, was a member of the Richmond Peace Council, Virginia's strongest antiwar group. Founded in 1933, the organization had supported the Senate investigations of the World War I munitions trade, held peace rallies in the state capital, and lobbied Virginia's congressmen on the neutrality legislation. While a confirmed internationalist, Freeman strongly believed that America's interests would be best served by remaining neutral; thus, his editorials supported the neutrality legislation and urged American noninvolvement in the major crises of the late thirties. Only months before Pearl Harbor did Freeman finally give up on neutrality. Byrd's own slow transformation to an interventionist position mirrored that of the Richmond editor whose opinions about foreign affairs he highly respected.[20]

Another more ardent noninterventionist was Charles Lindbergh, whom Byrd met on several occasions between May 1939 and April 1941 as the debate raged over America's entry into war. They discussed neutrality legislation, their mutual distrust of Roosevelt, and the 1940 election. In a September 5, 1940, diary entry, Lindbergh wrote: "Byrd is definitely opposed to our entering the war. He told me that the way he now feels, he would rather resign his seat in the Senate than vote for war." Lindbergh, who had warned Byrd of the repercussions of a European war for America, likely influenced the senator's thinking on intervention, but their paths would diverge as America's hero became more strident in opposing involvement and Byrd came to see the need for aiding the democracies. Lindbergh's anti-Semitic remarks and his seemingly profascist sentiments, both exaggerated by the press, would prove an embarrassment to the senator, but he did not repudiate their friendship.[21]

In August 1939, on the eve of conflict, Senator Byrd addressed Virginia's American Legion convention, aware now of what was forthcoming but still praying "that the dark clouds of war will be swept away by the sunlight of peace." He pledged support for the administration's foreign policies and an "adequate national defense." Repeating some of the themes he had advanced at a Memorial Day talk at Gettysburg, he urged national unity in meeting the European crisis. Americans, he said, must put aside class, race, and religious prejudices and emphasize the "old-time virtues of thrift, frugality, self-reliance, and industry" while preserving the freedom of the individual. The ideals Byrd enunciated that day would carry the nation through the years ahead.[22]

President Roosevelt, moving more quickly than the American people to support the European democracies, invoked the neutrality proclamation only days after Hitler's invasion of Poland, but he set out to change the provisions of the law, telling his countrymen that he could not expect them to remain neutral in thought. Calling Congress into special session, he asked it to repeal the arms embargo to allow the United States to arm the victims of aggression, a request that congressional leaders had turned down earlier in the year. The appeal initiated a two-year debate between isolationists, who favored noninvolvement, and "internationalists," who advocated aid to the foes of fascism as the best way to avoid future participation. The latter group, however, was not united; the majority, which included Harry Byrd, emphasized the priority of staying out of war, while a minority preferred a stronger commitment against aggression. Byrd wrote to Josiah Bailey: "I think we should avoid opposition to the President in his foreign policies so long as these policies are designed and will in actuality keep us out of war. At the same time I think we should fight more strongly than ever for economy and retrenchment."[23] It would be Roosevelt's task to maintain and strengthen this coalition while moving the majority to accept new international responsibilities.

Byrd responded favorably to the president's September 21 call to end the arms embargo. He favored the "strictest sort of cash and carry neutrality vigorously enforced" as "America's best safeguard for peace." Cash and carry, a provision of the 1937 neutrality act, permitted other nations to obtain crucial commodities if they paid for them up front and transported them on their own vessels. It had been allowed to lapse in May but now was revived as a means of assisting Britain and France. Only days later, Byrd asked Lindbergh and a group of other senators to join him for lunch to discuss the embargo question. Having already spoken out against American involvement in the European war, Lindbergh supported continuation of the embargo, arguing (correctly as it turned out) that any assistance would eventually drag the country into the war. Byrd disagreed, and in his first major statement on neutrality legislation, he asserted: "I am convinced that the existing law is much more likely to involve us in war than the proposed legislation now pending before Congress. I have differed with the President on important domestic policies but I wholeheartedly give him my support in the essentials of his present foreign policies." However, he stressed that his goal was to remain out of war and that this could be done only with a careful construction of cash and carry rules which did not permit any credit advances. After four weeks of heated oratory, Congress, with Byrd joining the majority, amended the neutrality laws by abolishing the embargo, reinstituting the cash and carry provision, and establishing North Atlantic combat zones in which American ships could not travel. The defeat of the arms embargo was a major turning point on the road to war.[24]

During the months of the "Phony War" between the fall of Poland and Hitler's spring offensive in April 1940, Byrd advocated neutrality and preparedness as the best ways to avoid foreign wars. He opposed transfer of United States ships to Panamanian registry, calling it a subterfuge to sidestep Congress's creation of the war zones. At a February keel laying of the battleship *Alabama,* Byrd declared, "America, I pray God, will never again enter a foreign war, yet we must not forget that in this day of ruthless dictators and uncurbed ambitions the best insurance for peace is national preparedness." Undersecretary of State R. Walton Moore believed that Byrd was stressing his support for preparedness in order to shore up political fences in Virginia before his reelection campaign. There was likely some truth to this since Byrd was still unsure of what Jim Price was going to do. It was only after the senator's allies in the General Assembly had sabotaged Price's legislative program that Byrd felt secure enough to strike out on his own, using preparedness as a vehicle for his attacks on waste in government.[25]

As German armies hurtled into France and the Low Countries, Byrd cited the need to put the nation's financial house in order so as to facilitate defense preparations. "It is the compelling duty of Congress," he said, "to eliminate every extravagance, to abolish every unnecessary expenditure, to devote our resources to the vital necessity of preparing ourselves to meet any contingency and any crisis that may occur. . . . Financial preparedness is just as important as military preparedness. . . . The surest way to avoid war is to be ready for it." In the face of President Roosevelt's request for $1.2 billion for defense—notably to build 50,000 airplanes a year—Byrd advanced his own readiness plan in a May 28 Senate speech, which at the time he called one of the "vital utterances" of his career. He advocated a 10 percent tax increase to raise revenue for increased defense spending and a 10 percent cut in all nondefense expenditures to maintain a balanced budget. He also recommended creation of a nonpartisan commission of congressmen and businessmen to study the financing of defense, the elimination of nonessential spending, and a revision of the tax system. The talk echoed previous themes and forecast his wartime activity.[26]

Senator Byrd's reluctance to support greater involvement weakened following the collapse of France in June. Letters from his constituents, running in favor of greater intervention, were pushing him in that direction. After he delivered a warning against war hysteria, one irate Virginian challenged his delay in assisting the allies: "It very much appears that those who were alert and anxious to help the allies when war broke probably had much more vision than the ones who sat idly by and did nothing. . . . If Hitler wins, and establishes National Socialism, do you think your dollars and your orchards, and your stocks and bonds in five years will be worth as much as they are today?" Almost defensively, Byrd responded by pointing out that for seven years he had supported military preparedness.[27] In a June 1 speech, he favored "every possible aid to France and England short of war"; and only days later at the Democratic state convention, he promised to "do all in my power short of war to send material aid to the democratic nations France and Great Britain in their mighty struggle to preserve their very existence." The convention responded with a call for full economic aid for Hitler's enemies. Byrd was following the trail blazed earlier by Carter Glass, who had become one of the country's most vociferous critics of Hitler and an ardent advocate of aid for the allies. In fact, Glass—only recently married again at the age of eighty-two with Harry Byrd serving as best man—favored a declaration of war against Germany in the summer of 1940.[28]

Byrd's and Glass's support for the president did not extend to FDR's renomination for the presidency. The worsening foreign scene and the failure of any other New Deal Democrat to emerge as a viable candidate suggested the likelihood of a third term. Upset with the court-packing scheme and the attempted purges, party conservatives, including Byrd, Glass, party chairman Farley, and Vice-President Garner, lauded the two-term tradition in their arguments against another term for Roosevelt. The president was saying nothing about his own candidacy, but as an absentee candidate in the spring primaries, he had easily defeated Garner and seemed poised to run again. Byrd judged that Roosevelt's decision would be determined by European conditions.[29]

In addition to having philosophical reservations about Roosevelt, Byrd had more personal reasons for wanting FDR to step down. His growing stature among conservative businessmen had produced some modest support for a Byrd nomination. Henry Breckinridge, his most enthusiastic backer in 1932, was once again promoting the senator, who privately denied he had any aspirations for the office. David Bruce, whom Byrd had recruited to run for a General Assembly seat, advised delay but concluded, "You are the only Presidential candidate who could be nominated by the Democrats who would be sure to defeat any Republican candidate, and I am convinced you are the best qualified man for the office in either party, without any shadow of a doubt." Byrd realistically summed up his chances for Bruce: "I think it would be extremely inadvisable to have my name considered for the Presidency. I have no inclination whatever to be a candidate, and, secondly, in view of the situation existing in the Democratic Party I can see no possibility of success. I have opposed so many of the major New Deal policies that my nomination would be, in fact, a repudiation of quite a substantial part of what the Democratic Party has claimed as worthwhile achievements under the New Deal."[30]

Facing such prospects, Byrd concentrated on maintaining his ascendancy in Virginia politics and securing his reelection. He worked assiduously with Ebbie Combs to ensure a favorable delegation at the state convention in June, calling prospective delegates and plotting strategy. A potential difficulty was removed when the May deadline for candidates to file for office passed with no one offering to challenge him. At the Roanoke gathering Organization forces defeated a resolution to instruct for Roosevelt and sent an uninstructed delegation to the national convention, leaving Byrd free to attack the president and his policies without fear of political repercussions at home.[31]

At the Chicago convention Byrd, as a member of the Resolutions Committee, favored a resolution against a third term, but the president's control of the proceedings precluded such an effort. Conservatives vented their frustration by nominating several candidates, but that, too, was superfluous as Roosevelt, who had belatedly decided to accept the nomination, won an overwhelming victory on the first ballot. The Virginia delegation, released from the unit rule upon the motion of Senator Byrd, split its vote between Garner, Roosevelt, Hull, and Farley. Byrd voted for Garner, while Governor Price supported the president. It was reported that Byrd would not let the Virginia standard march in celebration for Roosevelt because of the booing of Senator Glass after he had nominated Jim Farley; Ashton Dovell remembered that Governor Price had to go outside the hall to buy a banner so Virginia could be represented in the demonstration.[32] The affair then turned bitter when Roosevelt selected Henry Wallace, an avowed New Dealer, to replace Garner on the ticket, a choice particularly galling to the conservatives. Senator Byrd angrily stomped off the convention floor when Wallace's name was presented. Combs, who was succeeding Byrd as Virginia's national committeeman, described the ensuing scene to him as an "open revolt" and an "embarrassment."

In spite of their reservations, Virginia's senators pledged their support for the party. Byrd reportedly told a gathering of Young Democrats in Alexandria that he would support "our great leader Franklin D. Roosevelt and the whole Democratic ticket." Privately he denied such enthusiasm but admitted that he would back the full ticket. Approached by several Republicans to throw his support to their candidate, Wendell Willkie, Byrd expressed admiration for the Indianan but indicated that his signed pledge to support all nominees of the party would require allegiance to Roosevelt. Nevertheless, hoping for a Republican upset, he said very little during the campaign. His own reelection campaign was so effortless that he had no expenses and did not even attend party rallies, perhaps to avoid any association with the national ticket. Although he faced only Socialist and Communist opposition, he was pleased that he outpolled the president in Virginia, winning 95 percent of the vote.[33]

When Congress reconvened after the Democratic convention, Byrd opened his attack on the inadequacies of the administration's preparedness program, citing production figures provided to the Naval Affairs Committee. With German bombers blitzing London, Byrd struck hard at Roosevelt's failure to advance the defense effort:

> I am disturbed and astonished to find that in more than 100 days after this assurance [that the United States would build 50,000 planes a year] was given, only 343 combat planes have been ordered . . . and of these none will be delivered in this calendar year and some will not be delivered until 1942. . . . If red tape is to blame, the country should know it. If the blame is due to inefficient bureaucratic administration, it should be known. If it is due to the refusal of business enterprise to accept contracts from the government, we should know it. . . . I am not an alarmist, but no sensible person

He Needs Wings Now

ONLY 343 WAR
PLANES ORDERED
BY THE ARMY, NAVY
AND MARINE CORPS
IN MORE THAN
100 DAYS!

U.S.
NATIONAL
DEFENSE
PROGRAM

SENATOR
BYRD

FRED O. SEIBEL

8-27-40

To Senator Byrd
- with my compliments
Fred O. Seibel

– RICHMOND TIMES- DISPATCH - AUGUST 27, 1940

can view the world situation without the conviction that in this day of brutal force only the strong will survive. If America remains a weak military nation, as we are today, we may go the tragic way of those nations conquered by superior force whose manhood and freedom and the right to live their own lives have been ruthlessly destroyed by brutal dictators.

Byrd reiterated his reluctance to criticize but said that it was time to explain why there were fewer than 2,000 planes in military service.[34]

Involved in negotiations to transfer American destroyers to the British and facing a vigorous election opponent in Willkie, President Roosevelt personally responded to Byrd's charges. Acknowledging that Byrd's figures were technically accurate, he rejected the implications of the criticism as "dead wrong." Over 10,000 planes were in the works, he said, with contracts placed for 6,361 and an additional 3,654 being manufactured under letters of intent pending new appropriations. Claiming that additional orders could not be made until Congress passed his most recent request for another $5 billion, he encouraged any investigation of delays that might speed up delivery.

Dissatisfied with the administration's explanations, Senator Byrd retaliated with a resolution calling for a Senate investigation of the delays in the defense program. "What 'in the works' means, I do not know," he declared. "What people of America today are concerned about is definite and constructive steps toward the early and quick preparation of our military defenses. I am concerned that these preparations are lagging to the extent that our national security is seriously menaced. They want airplanes not 'on order' for delivery a year or so hence but for delivery with promptness." He urged the Senate to stay in session day and night to complete work on legislation establishing the first peacetime draft in American history. The Senate passed that bill on August 28 with both Byrd and Glass in favor. The House followed suit a few days later.[35]

Byrd's criticism of the administration's defense effort, which continued up to and after Pearl Harbor, was justified. Bureaucratic logjams and Roosevelt's own vacillation hampered military production well into 1942. Competing interests of the military, labor, business, and consumers inhibited the imposition of the strict government controls that would have forged a more efficient war machine, but the president, ever the politician who preferred cooperation to dictation, handled the conflict between public and private interests indecisively. He feared a more vigorous preparedness effort would be interpreted as a decision to intervene in the war; this would not only threaten his reelection, but would also undermine his efforts to convert Americans to interventionism. A Gallup poll in mid-October showed that 83 percent of Americans wanted to stay out of the war. Therefore, Roosevelt pursued a more gradual transition to a wartime economy. Although many of the constraints evaporated when America entered the war, the tangled mess of prewar preparedness deserved the attention Harry Byrd brought to it.[36]

Nevertheless, the timing of his August assault was peculiar, coming when delicate Anglo-American negotiations were taking place and a presidential election campaign was getting underway. The low production figures were undesirable, but Byrd was not very tolerant of the understandable delays between appropriations and assembly-line results. Having long been suspicious of New Deal bookkeeping, he may have been more upset with unspent appropriated dollars than with planes not yet produced. Moreover, his late-blooming interventionism raises doubts about his preparedness credentials. In 1939 he had voted against an amendment to increase the number of army air corps planes from 5,500 to 6,000. While he had usually supported military appropriations, he had not strongly advocated aiding the allies and remained very cool to the prospects of getting into the war. In December 1940 he wrote his colleague Peter Gerry that he was glad that Walter George had been made chairman of the Senate Foreign Relations Committee, for "he will do his best to keep us out of the war."[37]

Piqued by Roosevelt's devious reelection plans, Byrd may have created an issue that would assist Wendell Willkie, the man he secretly wanted to win. Clearly the administration was embarrassed by his inferences of incompetence or, worse, a lack of patriotism. Unlike that of Senator Glass, who had reconciled with Roosevelt, Byrd's relationship with the president continued to deteriorate. With his own political career secure, the senator no longer felt constrained to withhold his hardest punches at a longtime enemy. As one disaffected constituent wrote him, "Your only value is your 'nuisance value' as an 'obstructionist.'. . . It begins to seem to us that you live for nothing except your hatred and spite of Mr. Roosevelt, and that too is a mighty poor thing."[38] Byrd was sincere in his criticism of the defense effort—and rightly so for the nation's sake—but political considerations likely exaggerated his concern. That was clear once the nation was at war, for Byrd became almost oblivious to the continuing problems of wartime production while he continued to hammer away at New Deal labor and spending policies.

Byrd resumed his attack on the administration four months later. Threatening to reveal military secrets so that the people would know the extent of the dilemma, he renewed his request for a Senate inquiry into the defense program. Privately, Byrd asked Douglas Freeman if he should release the information that showed a "desperate situation in the preparedness program." Something extraordinary had to be done, he said, to offset the "misleading propaganda" that suggested the country was actually prepared. Recommending discretion, the biographer of Robert E. Lee reminded the senator of the Congressional Committee on the Conduct of the War Between the States which was created with good intentions but did more harm than good. Peachy Menefee was more direct in telling his boss to accede to Secretary of War Henry Stimson's request not to divulge the material. A few months later he warned the senator not to contribute to disunity at a time of national crisis. Do not let your influence be interpreted as being with "those people who would not fight for the liberties they howl about," he advised."[39]

The Senate finally agreed to Byrd's request to create a committee to investigate the defense effort, but he was not included among its members. Senator Harry Truman of Missouri had taken a monthlong tour of the nation's military bases in January 1941 and returned with tales of waste and mismanagement. Recommending establishment of an investigating committee, he was rewarded with its chairmanship. Like Freeman, Truman was aware of the damage done by congressional inquiries during the Civil War and promised that there would be no head-hunting or administration bashing, only a conscientious effort to expose waste that was impeding the preparedness program. Under his leadership the Special Committee to Investigate the National Defense Program ably served the country during the war, looking into problems of production, collusion, labor hoarding, and waste in procurement. One estimate credited the committee with saving $15 billion; it also served as a springboard to the presidency for Truman.[40]

In January 1941, President Roosevelt, who had handily won reelection, presented Congress his "Lend-Lease" proposal—the loaning of equipment to nations whose defense was deemed vital to America's defense. "We must be the great arsenal of democracy," he had stated in a December fireside chat. Isolationists denounced the bill as a step toward war, but after heated debate Lend-Lease passed by a comfortable margin, indicating the conversion of Americans to a more interventionist position. The president then asked for and received from Congress $7 billion in Lend-Lease aid.

Senator Byrd, who voted for the final bill, was noticeably reluctant to spend large sums of taxpayers' dollars on the British war effort. For a long time he was listed as one of the uncommitted senators on Lend-Lease, and he may have needed some pushing from constituents before deciding to back it. In keeping with his spending concerns, he offered an amendment requiring congressional authorization for future diversions of defense materials to foreign nations. "I do not believe," he argued, "that the Congress . . . should enact any law which would give the President, or anyone else, authority to transfer without limit the defense articles provided for in future appropriations." A similar though less restrictive amendment was added to the bill. Despite his vote for Lend-Lease, Byrd remained a skeptic, constantly harassing its administrator, Harry Hopkins, about delays in implementing the aid program. In August he asked Hopkins for a more detailed accounting of expenditures. "I am wholeheartedly for 'all out' aid to Britain and her allies in the fight to preserve democracy," he asserted, "but I want Congress and the country to know how and to whom the money under the lend-lease program is being committed." His criticisms of Lend-Lease reinforced his continued attacks on the preparedness program.[41]

By this time, however, Byrd had found another issue with which to assail the administration: strikes of defense plants by organized labor. In the face of renewed prosperity that was directly related to defense spending, workers pursued their fair share of the profits gained through these contracts. Opposition from management led to an increasing number of strikes early in 1941 that threatened America's ability to aid the allies and prepare its own defenses. To settle these disputes President Roosevelt established the National Defense Mediation Board in March 1941, but the board's decisions were not binding and many strikes were not prevented. Harry Byrd was quick to sound the alarm. In the face of twenty-five strikes affecting War Department contracts and an equal number slowing down the navy, Byrd insisted that such strikes be concluded in order to avoid interruptions in the preparedness program. He ridiculed the mediation board as a powerless entity and called for an end to the forty-hour workweek, which he believed was unconscionable in a time of crisis. In early April he demanded that the government force the reopening of the Allis Chalmers plant in Milwaukee which had $45 million in defense orders and had been closed for seventy-five days. He charged Secretary of Labor Frances Perkins with being "derelict" in delaying certification of the strike to the mediation board as required by the executive order that had set up the arbitration procedure. Once notified, the board intervened and settled the strike within days.[42]

Two weeks later Byrd renewed his attack on Secretary Perkins, wanting to know why she had not certified the strike in the southern coalfields where miners wanted an end to the wage differential with northern mines. "Your public statement clearly indicates that your efforts to mediate have failed," he telegrammed. "Why do you delay in certifying this strike to the National Mediation Board for immediate action? The longer you delay the more critical will become the condition and more difficult the task to accomplish mediation to immediately reopen the mines." Defense officials predicted that continuation of the strike would curtail production in nineteen major arms plants. When Perkins finally certified the strike twenty-three days after it began, Byrd called for her resignation and the appointment of a "two-fisted man" with the "intestinal fortitude to say to labor as well as to capital that no interruptions in the defense program by unnecessary strikes will be tolerated." He accused her of "bungling and lack of courage. . . . Her inefficiency and lack of decision and firmness in dealing with this responsibility, has made herself one of the most serious bottlenecks in our national preparedness efforts. . . . As a strike settler, she has proved to be a complete wash-out." He suggested that her performance was due to her desire not to offend John L. Lewis, president of the United Mine Workers (UMW). "Is John L. Lewis bigger than the Secretary of Labor? He may be, but he is not bigger than the Government of the United States in this hour of national peril."[43]

It was an uncharacteristic performance by this southern gentleman. Rarely in Byrd's career did he belabor a public official with the language he used to criticize Frances Perkins, the first woman cabinet member in American history. Clearly, Perkins sympathized with the union effort and may have been somewhat dilatory in certifying strikes, but her task was made difficult by the novelty and complexity of the settlement mechanism and her desire, along with that of the president, to arrange settlements before resorting to semicoercive arbitration that might prove fruitless. There were many strikes going on at the time, and even as Byrd spoke, she was referring them to the board. Her actions did not warrant her resignation or the attack on her competence. The intensity of Byrd's verbal assault can only be explained by his concern for preparedness, his gut reaction against strikers, and a male chauvinism that permitted such a put-down of a woman.

In the spring of 1941, Harry Byrd was taking on the Roosevelt Administration everywhere, blaming it for the delays in military production and in facilitating Lend-Lease and the failure to prevent strikes in vital defense plants. With the exception of his unfair attack on Secretary Perkins, his criticism was appropriate and had a positive effect on correcting these situations. But he and other more politically motivated critics were not very understanding of the problems Roosevelt faced in constructing a war machine and converting Americans to interventionism, for the polls still showed that the people opposed entry.[44]

Later that summer Byrd resumed his attack on the preparedness program in a dramatic Senate speech on August 19 in which he claimed that aid to the allies—who now included the Russians—was "appallingly ineffective." He accused the administration of not coordinating industrial production, cutting nondefense spending, and ending strikes that had cost the defense industry five million man-days of labor. It was a well-organized address supported with specific production figures and suggestions for improvement. In the last two years, he said, the United States had spent $10 billion on defense but had sent no antiaircraft guns or tanks to England; navy and merchant ship production was slow; and plane production was falling further behind schedule. What was needed, Byrd demanded, was a unified command for the defense program—what Bernard Baruch, the czar of the War Industries Board in World War I and a close friend of Byrd's, was advising Roosevelt to do.[45]

At his press conference a day later the president took issue with Byrd's figures. Somebody, he said, had "sold Senator Byrd down the river on his figures." Several hundred tanks had been given the British, and production of antiaircraft guns, mortars, and antitank guns was considerably higher than the figures Byrd provided. He acknowledged that the senator's numbers on planes were correct but claimed that production was not behind schedule when the number of training planes was added to combat planes. It was a weak defense, and Roosevelt knew it. So did Byrd, for within hours he responded, presenting letters from military commanders that confirmed his figures on ships and explained the discrepancies between the two sets of figures on guns and tanks. More significantly, Byrd pointed out that the differences were inconsequential. "Whether the guns produced are a few more or a few less alters the picture but little," he said. "Taking the President's statement from the best standpoint, we are not preparing our defense quickly; we are not giving the aid we should to England." He concluded: "My only desire is to be constructive in our defense program and in giving aid to England. I have supported this program in its entirety and, with many other Americans, I believe the production has lagged dangerously and that the people should be told the truth." Within days the president created a Supplies Priorities and Allocation Board to establish priorities between military and civilian needs and properly allocate resources.[46]

Byrd's next major contribution came in amendments to the new tax bill that proposed increasing taxes by $3.5 billion to underwrite the defense program. Requesting the Bureau of the Budget to furnish estimates on savings up to $2 billion on nondefense items, he recommended the creation of a joint congressional committee to include the secretary of the treasury and the director of the budget to locate additional ways of eliminating or reducing "all such expenditures deemed by the committee to be non-essential." It was "outrageous," Byrd said, to impose new taxes without looking for ways to cut expenditures. The Revenue Act of 1941 passed as amended, and Byrd finally had the committee that he had long sought to investigate the excesses of the New Deal. The Joint Committee on Reduction of Non-essential Federal Expenditures was formed in late September; Byrd, who had lobbied hard for membership, was elected chairman, a position he would not relinquish for over twenty years, reportedly the longest unbroken term of a committee chairman in congressional history.[47] Composed of six senators, six representatives, and the two executive branch members, the joint committee was stacked in favor of economy and against liberal programs. It included such staunch conservatives as Carter Glass, Kenneth McKellar, Walter George, Gerald Nye, Robert Doughton, and John Taber.

Byrd zealously plunged into his new assignment. Within two months he had the committee's first report ready for publication, a speed that suggested a prearranged agenda to dismantle the New Deal. It recommended cessation of new public works programs during the war, abolition of the Civilian Conservation Corps and the National Youth Administration, phasing out of the Works Progress Administration, abolition of the Farm Security Administration and the farm tenant program, deferral of rural electrification expansion and highway appropriations, and the return to the treasury of any funds not yet expended. It projected savings of $1.3 billion plus whatever funds might be returned. Since the recommendations cut into many local programs, there was no unanimity on the report. Even conservatives wanted to protect specific projects. Senator Robert La Follette, Jr., of Wisconsin, the committee's most liberal member, presented a minority report that criticized the "hasty and unwarranted" proposals based on brief hearings and scattered testimony. He said the conclusions were grounded on what was easiest to cut rather than the merit or fairness of the programs, many of which were crucial to people in lower income levels. Because the full report was released three weeks after the attack on Pearl Harbor it attracted little attention.[48]

In time the joint committee on nonessential spending became known as the Byrd committee. The budget director and treasury secretary were little more than ex officio members, and the committee was transformed into a tool of the economy bloc for attacking social programs and waste in government. Although the war was primarily responsible for killing the relief agencies such as the CCC and WPA, Byrd claimed credit for their deaths. Compiling a mass of figures and producing reports that kept his name in the public's eye, Byrd relished the committee's work, but in reality it became a liability for him since it solidified the negativism that became the hallmark of his Senate career. Thereafter, he had very little to say or do that was constructive, preoccupied as he was with "nickel and dimeing" the government. His recent criticism of the preparedness effort, which had drawn so much praise and had contributed directly to improvements, came to a halt; his focus now was on excessive spending in the nondefense sector. He almost seemed to forget there was a war going on. After a morning meeting with the Byrd committee on the eve of Pearl Harbor, Harold Smith, director of the budget, lamented, "Here we are, possibly days from a war with Japan, . . . and this group is concerned about . . . NYA's expenditures for automobiles, [and] the expense accounts of their officials."[49]

Francis Pickens Miller, an assemblyman from Fairfax County, had accurately analyzed Byrd's obsession months before in correspondence with Virginius Dabney about the senator's efforts to aid the British. Because Byrd rarely had said anything about the potential consequences of fascist aggression and had always qualified his support for the allies, Miller concluded that the senator's preparedness attacks were really inspired by his "hatred of this Democratic administration," not the threat to Western civilization. "He reminds me," said Miller, "of a man whose wife is undergoing a major operation, from which she may not recover. The man has secured the best surgeon available, but his principal preoccupation is with the costs of the operation. [During the operation] he is down in the hospital office complaining about the management of the hospital, and dickering for a reduction in rates."[50] So it was with the committee on nonessential spending, the senator's primary plaything, which looked at figures, not the needs behind them or ways to put them to better use. Its agenda was a hatchet job on big government, but because it had such a limited perspective, it had no influence on postwar policy, surviving only because no one wanted to tell its chairman that it had become nonessential. Commenting on such an "adding machine mentality," V. O. Key stated: "Attached to the fetish of a balanced budget, it takes a short-run view that almost invariably militates against the long-run interests of the state. Men with the minds of tradesmen do not become statesmen." The nonessential spending committee turned Harry Byrd into a bookkeeper.[51]

Thereafter, the emphasis of Byrd's writings was on government waste and deficits. His only solutions were cut, cut, and cut again, even as the greatest war in history required an explosion in spending, bureaucracy, and manpower with their predictable excesses. His speeches, usually delivered to taxpayers associations, bankers, manufacturers, or other business groups, also took on this shrill and petty tone in succeeding years. State socialism, regimentation, autocracy, and labor excesses became his standard themes, pleasant rhetoric to Republican and conservative audiences who liked to hear criticism of Democratic administrations. Such diatribes were good editorial fodder as well, for they were succinct, full of figures, and had a liberal villain. Byrd, of course, had always been against government growth and spending, so this was not a dramatic change in character or philosophy. The new level of negativism was more the result of frustration over what was happening to his way of life, to an older America. He could not understand, tolerate, or control the change. He did not fully comprehend the magnitude and majesty of the war, and he certainly never appreciated the revolutions that it unleashed. He was content to peck away at the periphery of activity, hoping that he could contain its influence, a Canute bidding the waves to recede.[52]

This may also explain his growing reluctance to see the United States go to war. While more and more Americans were shifting toward intervention, Byrd stiffened. He wrote to Mrs. Virgil Cox in July 1941, "I am opposed to becoming a voluntary participant in the present war and do not think we should become involved unless we are attacked." Yet the United States was on a collision course with Germany. Roosevelt's August meeting with British prime minister Winston Churchill off Newfoundland produced no commitment to intervene, but their agreement on the principles of the Atlantic Charter bound the two nations more closely together. The U-boat attack on the destroyer USS *Greer* led Roosevelt to authorize American convoys of Lend-Lease cargoes (as the isolationists had predicted) and to ask Congress for revisions to the neutrality act that would allow the arming of merchantmen and entry into the designated war zones. Byrd was listed among those "desiring more time to study" the issue, whereas Senator Glass wanted an immediate repeal of the entire act. Almost three-quarters of the people interviewed favored arming the ships, but only a bare majority approved permitting ships to travel into the combat zones. Amid news of more American destroyers being attacked and sunk and the Nazis driving within sixty miles of Moscow, Congress debated and approved the revisions by relatively narrow margins.[53]

Harry Byrd and Howard Smith were the only Virginia congressmen to vote against the revisions, ostensibly as a protest against the administration's failure to deal more severely with striking workers, particularly John L. Lewis's coal miners. Byrd served notice that he would not vote for any steps leading to war until all strikes were dealt with forcefully and the inefficiency in the defense program was corrected. Since Byrd's stipulations were too broad to have been met before the vote repealing the neutrality act, his ultimatum may have been partly a disguise for his reservations against this direct step toward war. During the height of the debate, he angrily wrote H. G. Kump: "The situation confronting us here at Washington, I think, is the most perilous we ever faced. We are being led straight into war, and the worst of it is that our leaders do not have the courage to meet the menaces at home. Up to date we have miserably failed to become prepared, and there is no prospect of any change on the part of the administration, so far as I can see. The same inefficiency exists, and the same subservience to labor leaders, such as John L. Lewis. Are we to follow the footsteps of France?" Two weeks later, in a letter to Mrs. William T. Reed, he was more specific: "I have done, and shall continue to do, everything in my power to prevent us from becoming a belligerent in the war, to a greater extent than we are already. I voted against the repeal of the Neutrality Act, because I was convinced this would mean a Naval warfare and that a Naval warfare would nearly certainly end in a land warfare."[54]

Harry Byrd's neutrality vote was an example of his shortsightedness on fascism. His brother, on the other hand, had spoken out forcefully for greater aid to the Allies throughout the months of debate over intervention. At an August 19, 1941, rally, with the passion and vision Harry lacked, the admiral proclaimed: "This is the age-old struggle between democracy and tyranny, between freedom and slavery, between good and evil. This is everybody's war."[55]

～ 12 ～

The War Years

ON DECEMBER 7, 1941, the Byrd family was sitting down to its Sunday midday meal at Rosemont when the senator was called to the phone in the pantry. Returning to the table, he announced that Pearl Harbor had been attacked. Someone asked where Pearl Harbor was, and he explained. Like many Americans, the Byrds were not well informed about events and places in the Pacific and so were shocked to learn that war had begun there rather than in Europe. Relations with the Japanese had been deteriorating for most of the previous decade and had worsened considerably in the last year, but negotiations were still going on, and few suspected an outright attack on the United States. The following day, with the family listening on the radio, the senator sat in the House chamber and applauded the president's request to recognize a state of war with Japan. Three days later Hitler declared war on the United States, action that was quickly reciprocated by Congress. The war that Byrd had hoped to avoid now received his firmest blessing.[1]

The attack on Pearl Harbor united the country behind Roosevelt as no other incident could have. "Dr. New Deal" had become "Dr. Win the War." Senator Byrd commended FDR's State of the Union address which called for vast new armaments. "Nothing must be permitted to interfere with that," he said. The next day Roosevelt submitted a $59 billion war budget that included authorization for a $9 billion tax increase and $35 billion in additional borrowing. To coordinate the defense effort, the president created a new federal bureaucracy, but the task of converting from peacetime to wartime production, of resolving competing interests and allocating resources, conflicted with a private enterprise ethic. Only the bountiful productivity of America's industrial capacity prevented the mobilization effort from degenerating into chaos. Finally, in October 1942 Roosevelt brought in Supreme Court Justice James Byrnes to head a new Office of Economic Stabilization; with near-dictatorial power, Byrnes began cutting through the bottlenecks. A vast war machine that included conscription and rationing had taken over the country, forcing all to adjust to a new condition.[2]

The engines of this transformation—federal power, bureaucracy, and spending—were the very things that Harry Byrd detested and had fought so hard to minimize throughout the thirties. Even more authority was now flowing to Washington, upsetting the relationships between the federal government and the states and between the executive and legislative branches. Presidential command of the war—which even Byrd admitted was necessary—pushed senators and congressmen to the sidelines, there to applaud, wring their hands, or pick small fights on the periphery that would not undermine the war effort or tarnish their patriotism. For Byrd, this meant carefully utilizing the nonessential spending committee to locate waste in the government's war machinery, taking on union leaders whose strike policies threatened the fight against fascism, and standing up for states' rights to prevent federal interference with voting laws.

After an appropriate period of senatorial deference, on February 12, 1942, Byrd established the ground rules of his campaign for winning the war. The problem, he claimed, was government:

> The first battle we have to win is the battle of Washington. The executive branch must end the fantastic and increasing confusion and strip the government of nonessentials so we can devote all our energies to winning the war. The need is here for universal sacrifice and self-denial. The people already are sacrificing; the government must. There must be an end of jealousies between departments and officials, for these are seriously hampering the war effort. Thousands of nonessential parasites in official agencies could be transferred to more useful activities. The government should set an example. We are asking citizens to conserve their resources and the government in Washington must do the same.[3]

As proof of his willingness to sacrifice, Byrd called on Congress to scrap its own pension plan, which it immediately did. He then announced that his committee would investigate the Office of Civilian Defense (OCD), now under Republican fire for some controversial appointments of left-wingers and the operation of a recreation program. His research turned up sixty-one coordinators of sports and recreation programs who were supervising Ping-Pong, horseshoes, marbles, and bowling—"nonessential activities" in a time of peril. When he was informed that this was a voluntary program involving no funds for such personnel, Byrd switched tack and charged OCD with plotting a "gigantic plan of regimentation for physical fitness" and hiring people who had conflicts of interest. He pointed to a bowling coordinator who was an advertising executive handling the account of the Brunswick Company, a bowling equipment firm. The war would be won only if such conflicts were eliminated.[4]

Byrd next took on Lowell Mellett, director of the Office of Government Reports. When the senator criticized the expenditure of $28 million for publicity work, Mellett retaliated by challenging him to find one nickel spent by his office on publicity. He said Byrd's kind of criticism was "not honest" and was in "willful disregard of the truth." Never one to allow a challenge to his veracity to pass, Byrd accused Mellett of using extravagant language and then labeled him an "arrogant and proud bureaucrat" who ruled over "the monstrosity commonly known as the Mellett Madhouse." Byrd said he did not want to split hairs over whether the Office of Government Reports put out information, publicity, or propaganda; what it did in any form was a waste of the taxpayer's dollar. The senator was comforted by columnist Frank Kent of the Baltimore *Sun*, who interpreted Mellett's outburst as an example of "the extreme bitterness among the more advanced New Dealers toward the Virginia Senator. It is no exaggeration to say that the higher Administration politicians hate this Democrat more than they do any other man in public life." Unquestionably, the feeling was mutual.[5]

The dispute, which faded away as quickly as it had come on, was an example of the senator's investigative tactics and explains why the committee on nonessential spending and its chairman never achieved the success and reputation of the Truman committee that was also investigating waste and corruption in the war effort. Byrd's style was to shoot from the hip against New Deal creations that were unpopular in the conservative community. A Byrd committee report was usually crammed full of figures that tried to persuade by their number and magnitude that waste was present. Had he truly wanted to get at the inefficiency, he might have been more specific with his charges and remedies. Specifics, however, entailed time-consuming, costly studies, hearing witnesses, and using committee staff to arrive at recommendations for action; but he did not want to spend money to save money, always being proud of how little money his committee spent. When Byrd was specific, the issue was frequently so petty and laughable that it registered only with conservatives who wanted a juicy story with which to bash the big spenders. During a debate over the appropriation for the Agriculture Department, Byrd claimed that the department was driving more automobiles than any other agency except the War Department. He then expanded the discussion to the use of vehicles by the federal government, pointing out the existence of 19,000 federal vehicles, which traveled 212 million miles at a cost of $4.8 million. He did not specify what percentage of this automobile use was frivolous. He also completely ignored the problems confronting American agriculture, such as crop subsidies, tenancy, and the decline of the family farm. Certainly Byrd and his committee found governmental waste and saved taxpayers some dollars, but the effort often lacked substance and paled in significance alongside larger issues.[6]

Byrd won his first major triumph in July 1942 when the House refused to go along with the Senate in funding the Civilian Conservation Corps. The committee on nonessential spending had claimed that $247 million could be saved by eliminating this agency. Created in the midst of depression to put young Americans to work on much-needed conservation projects, the CCC had been one of the unqualified success stories of the New Deal, one which Senator Byrd had enthusiastically voted for time after time. Now with prosperity returning and the military needing young men, there was no longer a need for it, other than providing military training for future draftees. Its death was predictable, but Byrd claimed it as a victory for his committee. Similarly, funds for another year of the WPA, the primary relief agency of the depression, were severely reduced as the number of unemployed diminished, but the senator cut another notch on his measuring stick of killed nonessentials. Although his attempt to terminate the Farm Security Administration was thwarted by southern conservatives, the *Times-Dispatch* called the Byrd committee the "spearhead of the economy drive." A year later its lances pierced the bodies of the already comatose WPA, its student appendage, the National Youth Administration, and the dreaded FSA.[7]

Byrd's support for the war and his spartan patriotism meant that he and the administration often agreed on the means with which to fight the enemy. Influenced by his brother's career and his own membership on the Naval Affairs Committee, the senator was an advocate of increased funds for the navy, particularly for the construction of aircraft carriers instead of battleships. "Experiences of this war have demonstrated the importance of air power," he said in May 1942, "and the only way to get naval planes within striking distance of the enemy at this time is by use of carriers." The floating runways could also be built more cheaply and quickly than the dreadnoughts. Confirmation of Byrd's arguments came three weeks later in the great battle of Midway, the decisive battle of the Pacific war. As soon as reports of that encounter were known, he urged a readjustment of war production to give priority to construction of a large carrier fleet. The senator also called for the rapid neutralization, if not the takeover, of the French island of Martinique so that American warships patrolling the waters of the Caribbean could be transferred to the Atlantic where German submarines were sinking numerous vessels, many within sight of Virginia Beach.[8]

Furthermore, Byrd was becoming a strong adherent of more stringent wage and price controls. He worried about the rising cost of inflation and the unfairness with which present controls were being applied, preferring rigid controls over "every single element of cost, both of labor, agricultural products, and all other elements entering into the cost of the finished article offered for sale." He also asked for nationwide gasoline rationing to compensate for shortages. The Office of Price Administration (OPA) had already instituted a number of rationing programs for gasoline, coffee, canned foods, and shoes, and statewide drives were being conducted to collect paper, metal, grease, and rubber. In the fall Congress gave the president greater power to institute strict wage and price controls, but the self-interested cries of labor, farmers, and businessmen deterred him from enforcing them until April 1943.[9]

Late in 1942 Byrd renewed his attack on nonessential spending. His committee may have been the first to delineate the enormous waste of filing federal regulatory reports—seven thousand reports required by forty-eight different agencies—a "quiz-mania" that "burdened business and individuals with needless and costly inquisitions." Byrd cited one manufacturer who claimed it cost him $500,000 a year to prepare reports required by the government. "It is," said the senator, "a bureaucracy gone mad."[10]

A new target was the exploding number of federal employees, now totaling three million. Calling for the dismissal of one-third of them as a way to aid the war effort, Byrd charged that the government was the "chief offender in the waste and hoarding of manpower." His committee investigators had located dozens of honest bureaucrats who testified to the "thumb-twiddling" that was going on in government offices. One worker for the War Production Board reported: "We have to manufacture jobs to make us look busy. We seem to do nothing but harass and needle the businessmen with our demands, suits and everlasting forms of the most complicated order. Most of our overpaid men are busy dodging the draft." Another woman who was in charge of thirty stenographers at the War Department said they sat around all day loafing. When the director of the Manpower Commission, Paul McNutt, echoed Byrd's complaints about the hoarding of federal workers, Roosevelt moved to end deferments for federal employees. Byrd's efforts once again proved beneficial to the war effort, but their partisan nature cannot be denied. It was hard to believe that the "men in Washington who wantonly waste money" were, in his words, "sabotaging our war efforts as much as the spy who puts a bomb under a bridge." Perhaps one columnist was correct when he wrote, "Economy in government looks like a good issue in 1944." The primary duty of Byrd's committee for the rest of its life was submitting almost monthly reports on the number of federal employees.[11]

Conservative columnists highlighted the senator's economy effort. Carl McCardle portrayed him as an amiable budget-cutter who was "scaring the daylights out of the drones and profligates on the Federal pay roll." Calling Byrd "the nation's foremost economizer," McCardle recounted the story of the young boy who had turned a bankrupt newspaper into a success and was now continuing to promote fiscal solvency in his confrontations with the spendthrift Roosevelt. Using the senator's figures, the author credited Byrd with saving taxpayers $2 billion by dismantling New Deal agencies, slashing federal aid to highways, paring down agricultural appropriations, and reducing public works expenditures.[12]

Byrd's own articles repeated the theme of waste in government: "Waste Goes On," "U.S. versus the Frankenstein Monster," and "Are We Losing Our Freedom?" In the latter essay, fearing that his constant criticism of the government might be misinterpreted, Byrd asserted his patriotism: "No man is a traitor who criticizes waste and bungling, who wants the war machine to function more effectively, who protests the obstinate and inept conduct of bureaucracy, and who wants to live again in a democracy when the war ends. He is actually a patriot." In the April 24, 1943, edition of the *Saturday Evening Post,* Byrd was poetically eulogized by Ethel Jacobson:

Sprung from illustrious progenitors;
One of the wilderness-crying senators
　Trying to spike
　The raging flood,
　His hand's in the dike
　And his name is mud.
　　He fights inefficiency,
Wars on waste,
And marks Dead Wood,
　　However high-placed.
Taxpayers too? him a grateful word,
But otherwise what does he get? The byrd.[13]

In 1943 the tide of war turned in favor of the Allies with the German defeat at Stalingrad and the American advances in the Pacific. Feeling freer to criticize the direction of the war without seeming to undermine its progress, the conservative coalition, strengthened by Republican victories in 1942, went after the New Deal. Anticipating the attack, Roosevelt quietly performed the funeral rites for the WPA in December 1942. The fight for the NYA was more heated, but the Senate defeated continuing legislation in July 1943. The Farm Security Administration, long condemned by Byrd for its "Communistic resettlement projects," illegal tenant loans, and high rate of loan defaults, had its budget cut to the bone, but its many defenders put off his efforts to abolish it altogether. Confronting complaints that he was against the small farmer, Byrd argued that the farmers could be better served by other lending agencies. Conservatives also terminated the National Resources Planning Board, accusing it of being a haven for collectivists. Byrd claimed that any postwar planning should be the responsibility of Congress. In a May 1943 speech to the New Jersey Bankers Association, he outlined what that might mean: liquidation of government-owned property, the removal of government from business, the dismantling of the federal bureaucracy, balancing the budget with no debt repudiation, and simplification of the tax system. He charged that the administration was using the war to pursue social reform, but, in fact, it was the conservatives who were using the war to overturn the reforms of the Thirties.[14]

The spring of 1943 also witnessed the reemergence of labor problems. Concerned with inflation and unsafe working conditions, many workers went out on strike, violating their no-strike pledge given at the start of the war. There were three times as many workers out as there had been in 1942. Although the strikes occurred in a number of key defense industries, the walkouts by John L. Lewis's coal miners drew the most attention. Demanding a $2-a-day wage increase and improvements in benefits, the cagey Lewis orchestrated a series of brief strikes designed to pressure the government into intervening without cutting off production altogether. In the process the miners lost the goodwill of the American people, who were infuriated at what they believed was a selfish act that threatened the war effort. Lewis became the most hated man in the country.

On March 1 Harry Byrd offered his own "work or fight" bill that would have subjected any striker between the ages of eighteen and sixty-five to the draft. He condemned the "weak and indecisive labor policies" of the last six years that, he claimed, encouraged this impasse. Criticizing Lewis for hurting troop morale and encouraging the enemy, Byrd declared, "No nation can win a bitter and terrible war if it permits any citizen . . . to place his own selfish interests and the interests of his followers ahead of the vital needs of his country." Warning that any appeasement of Lewis would encourage other acts of defiance and stimulate inflation, he renewed his support for legislation that would prevent strikes in the defense industries.[15]

The Smith-Connally War Labor Disputes Act was framed to accomplish this and more. Similar to the tough antilabor legislation that had been shelved after Pearl Harbor, it extended the president's power to seize struck defense plants, required a thirty-day cooling-off period before strikes, required a vote of the workers before calling a strike, and outlawed union contributions to political campaigns; the last provision had nothing to do with strikes but was part of the conservatives' effort to hurt FDR politically. Roosevelt wanted the additional power granted by the bill but was opposed to the features that antagonized organized labor—one of his primary supporters—so he vetoed the bill. Congress, however, was in no mood to compromise and quickly passed the bill over his veto, with Byrd in the majority.

Despite the union protests the War Labor Disputes Act had little impact on labor activity during the war. When the coal strike ended on terms favorable to the miners, Byrd was angered at the "coddling" of UMW leader Lewis, who, he thought, ought to be prosecuted under the Smith-Connally Act. It was ironic that one of the most publicized uses of the legislation was not against labor but against the chairman of Montgomery Ward, Sewell Avery, who was carried from his office by soldiers in April 1944 for violating a labor agreement. Outraged by this assault on a businessman when John L. Lewis had never had a hand laid on him, Senator Byrd demanded a full report from the War Labor Board of its action in the case and introduced a resolution calling for a Judiciary Committee inquiry into the seizure. He compared Attorney General "Generalissimo" Francis Biddle to Gestapo chief Heinrich Himmler, both of them "dragging men from their business by physical force."[16]

Congress took a much-needed recess in the summer of 1943—the first since the war began—but that did not stop the Virginia senator from continuing his investigations into anything that moved in government—the ever-bloated bureaucracy, unexpended funds, Lend-Lease spending, excessive use of automobiles, too many lawyers in the OPA, free-mailing privileges, telephone bills, and the use of telegrams when three-cent stamps were cheaper. There were few examples of government spending that the committee did not look at. "Government," said Byrd, "is wonderfully like an orchard. It, too, requires constant attention: regular prunings to keep it fruitful and frequent sprayings to defeat attacks of blight, analogous to the growth found on unwatched trees. Weeds and underbrush must be kept cleared from the orchard floor just as the excess should be stricken from the Federal pay roll." One story surfaced that no photographs should be taken of Roosevelt signing legislation with several pens and then distributing them to friends for fear that "Byrd might see the picture." When Undersecretary of War Robert Patterson appeared before Byrd's committee to boast of reductions in civilian personnel, the ever-dubious senator retorted, "Frankly, I don't think your figures mean a thing." To the New Dealers, Byrd was, in reporter Forrest Davis's words, "a horse-and-buggy reactionary, . . . a humorless, dusty Scrooge able to skin a flint and likely to hoist a civil servant into stir for joy-riding in a Government motor-car."[17]

Although he was concerned about government infringing upon individual opportunity, Byrd's personal commitment to democracy remained questionable. In the election years of 1942 and 1944, motivated by political as well as patriotic considerations, Democratic politicians attempted to facilitate the voting of servicemen and broaden the suffrage by eliminating the poll tax. Harry Byrd and his southern colleagues, relying on the defense of states' rights, obstructed all of these efforts. As Byrd wrote the ill Senator Glass, a federal anti–poll tax bill would be the first step toward federal control of state elections. It would "destroy the last vestige of States Rights and would give the New Deal, with its 3,000,000 civilian employees, the Negroes, and the labor unions control of the country." The southerners were joined by many Republicans, who, aware that servicemen usually vote for the party in power, preferred to limit that segment of the vote.[18]

Southern objections were heightened by wartime pressures that threatened to upset not only political equilibrium but traditional race relations as well. The war was presenting black Americans with new opportunities for advancement. Proposing a march on Washington in 1941 to protest segregation, A. Philip Randolph had pressured President Roosevelt into creating a Fair Employment Practices Commission (FEPC) to eliminate discrimination in the defense plants of the country. In the capital of the Confederacy, the *Times-Dispatch* called for an end to segregation on the city's buses and trolleys and asked for improvements in education, health, and employment for Richmond's black citizens. Even Senator Byrd seemed aware of the changes taking place when he wrote to a constituent: "In regard to the negroes, it is my understanding that plans are under way to use them to a greater degree in the Army. I agree with you they should have an equal opportunity in this." A war against fascism abroad could not sustain racism at home, but many southerners would try.[19]

Failing to prevent an amendment to the 1942 Soldier Voting Act that exempted members of the armed forces from paying poll taxes, southern senators ran up the battle flag against broader legislation that would ban the poll tax as a requirement for voting in federal elections. Byrd, who blamed Mrs. Roosevelt for instigating the bill, encouraged a filibuster that eventually killed it in November 1942. Late in 1943 a new Soldier Voting Act passed the Senate, 42–37, which recommended that the states make ballots available to servicemen rather than permit a federal absentee ballot as the administration had wanted. Senator James Eastland of Mississippi hailed it as a victory for states' rights that would leave states in control of registration, residence, and poll tax requirements. President Roosevelt labeled it a "fraud" perpetrated on America's fighting men.[20]

Days later Senator Joseph Guffey of Pennsylvania accused Byrd and other southern senators of being in an "unholy alliance" with the Republicans to deprive soldiers of the right to vote. Infuriated by what he considered an attack on his honor, the Virginian charged into the Senate chamber to defend his integrity and that of the other forty-one senators who had voted for the bill. "In all my experience in the affairs of the United States Senate," Byrd fumed, "I have never known a more deliberately offensive or a more untruthful charge to be made against a group of fellow senators than this charge made by Senator Guffey. . . . There is not one iota of truth in his charge." Accusing Guffey of not having the "courage and fairness" to make his assertions on the Senate floor, he demanded that he resign as chairman of the Democratic Senatorial Campaign

Committee, ridiculing the Pennsylvanian for "strutting around like a pouter pigeon in the reflected glory of an honor, in the administration of which he has shown very barren results." An even more indignant Senator Bailey unknowingly predicted a course of action that some southerners would soon be following: "If we cannot have a party in which we are respected; if we must be in a party in which we are scorned as Southern Democrats, we will find a party which honors us, not because we are Southerners and not because of politics, but because we love our country and believe in the Constitution from which it draws its life day by day."[21]

Guffey had little evidence that there was a conspiracy afoot between Republicans and southern Democrats, but he was right to imply that the 1943 Soldier Voting Act, which was modified early in 1944 to permit a federal ballot, but only with a state's approval, reflected a pinched spirit of democracy. As the *Times-Dispatch* concluded, the act would make it difficult for servicemen to vote. When Senator Byrd, to prove his good intentions, said he would encourage Governor Darden to initiate a movement to get uniform voting procedures in all the states, the editor said that this would not help in the states whose legislatures were not meeting in 1944. Byrd then said he would try to get all the states to call special sessions to expedite service voting. Having polled all the governors, he was confident that adequate soldier-voting legislation would be enacted.[22]

The unwieldiness of this process was revealed in the deliberations of Virginia's General Assembly. So, too, were Senator Byrd's undemocratic inclinations. A bill proposed by the American Legion approving the vote for servicemen in all elections passed the House of Delegates unanimously, but Byrd reportedly lobbied with legislators to reject the Legion's bill and substitute one that would give servicemen the vote only in national elections. The state senate passed such a bill that excused service personnel from paying their poll tax and created a fund that would pay it for them, even though the attorney general indicated that this provision might be unconstitutional. The house, after a stiff fight, reversed itself and approved the senate bill. Months later, after the 1944 election, the state supreme court threw out Virginia's War Voters Act because the fund paying for the poll tax was a circumvention of the state constitution. With the spotlight on Virginia because of Senator Byrd's earlier blusterings, Governor Darden was forced to call a special session of the legislature to arrange a constitutional convention to exempt soldiers from the poll tax. Despite the lobbying of the state's major newspapers and support from a few highly placed Organization people to repeal the poll tax for all voters, Byrd prevailed upon the assembly to limit consideration to the soldier vote. Denied broader authority, the convention completed its task four days before the war ended in Europe, another testament to the fact that democracy counted for very little when the power of the Organization was at stake.[23]

Although the war years were professionally rewarding for the senator, they were personally difficult.[24] Sittie's health did not improve; she suffered another heart attack in 1942 and was in and out of the hospital. His mother, still living alone in the old homeplace, fell and broke her hip in 1944. Westwood's youthful marriage had failed, and she alternated time between Rosemont and Washington where she was working for the Office of Strategic Services (OSS). Death once again took the lives of many of his close friends: John Stewart Bryan, Aubrey Weaver, who was killed in a fire in the Hotel Jefferson in Richmond, Joe Chitwood, Tom Ozlin, William Meade Fletcher, and Wade Massie.

The departure of his three boys for the front was particularly hard on Byrd, not only because he was concerned for their personal safety, but because it threw the full responsibility for the newspapers and the orchards back on his shoulders. The senator was extremely proud of his sons' service in the war. All three volunteered and went their separate ways. Harry Jr. served as a naval officer in the Central Pacific with a squadron of PB-2Ys. Byrd communicated with him frequently, relaying information about the family (especially Harry Jr.'s new son), the operation of the orchards and the newspapers, and his own political activities.[25] Beverley had been at Cornell for a year working on a process for controlled-atmosphere storage before returning to work in the orchards. He enlisted in the army in 1942 and joined the airborne troops, jumping in the D-Day invasion where he was shot in the arm and wrist. The senator heard nothing from him for several weeks and assumed the worst. He wrote Harry Jr., "Of course, we will not give up hope but I think he has gone, but do not write your mother anything about this." The family was much relieved to hear that he had been wounded and not killed, but the wound produced nerve damage in his left arm that never fully healed. While recuperating in France, he was visited by his father who was on an inspection tour of Europe with the Naval Affairs Committee after the war ended. In letters to Beverley and Dick, Byrd recounted his memories of the trip that included interviews with Churchill and Eisenhower, the devastation in Germany, Hitler's home at Berchtesgaden, the downcast American boys who were now on their way to the Pacific theater, and the "dirtiest people I ever saw" in the walled city of Casablanca.[26]

Youngest son Dick had been a special problem. He desperately wanted to enlist, but his father prevailed upon him to complete one year at Washington and Lee University first. At the end of the school year, he joined the army and was sent to Wisconsin for military police training. At his request the senator arranged for his transfer back into the infantry, and he was sent abroad with

Patton's forces after D-Day. Following the Battle of the Bulge in December 1944, Dick developed a case of trench foot and was returned to the states. Byrd's letters to Bev and Dick were as newsy as those to Harry, but, predictably for younger sons, they were more instructive. All the boys were home for a memorable Christmas in 1945. Byrd had missed them terribly, reporting how "lonesome" it had been without them.[27]

The senator's wartime problems were compounded by the absence of Senator Glass. Frail and infirm, Glass had not answered a Senate roll call since June 1942. Even before his reelection that year, Combs and Byrd were aware of his incapacitation, but they were reluctant to intercede, "hoping for the best." The Waynesboro *News-Virginian* later accused the Organization of letting Glass run to prevent Jim Price from taking his seat. After his reelection, private efforts to arrange his resignation proved fruitless. With his absence becoming an embarrassment to the state, a more public campaign was begun to get the inactive senator to resign, but it was ineffective due to a lingering awe for the little giant and the problem of appointing a successor. Congressmen Woodrum, Robertson, and Smith all coveted the seat. Byrd met with Glass on occasion but did not have the heart to ask his colleague to step down, concluding that it was "a decision that Senator Glass himself must make." Glass died in office, May 28, 1946. For four years the Old Dominion in effect had only one senator, which had placed a great burden on Senator Byrd's office to treat all of Virginia's constituents, a fact that was not lost on Byrd when the time came to consider his own retirement.[28]

As if Senator Byrd did not have enough to do during the war years, he ran for president again. Following Joe Guffey's accusations against southern Democrats during the fight over the Soldier Voting Act in December 1943, Senator "Cotton Ed" Smith of South Carolina "nominated" Harry Byrd for the presidency under the banner of a Southern Democratic party. Surprised and embarrassed, Byrd declined the offer, but in actuality a movement was already under way to promote a Byrd candidacy. Conservative businessmen, looking for an alternative to Franklin Roosevelt, and southern Democrats, searching for a new political home, settled on the junior senator from Virginia as an acceptable candidate.[29]

For much of his first two terms, Roosevelt had enjoyed considerable support from southern legislators, who, out of party loyalty, a populist tradition, and the depression crisis, enthusiastically voted for New Deal programs. Opposition from conservatives such as Byrd, Glass, and Bailey was primarily philosophical, not sectional. Although court packing and purges weakened the South's affection for the president, the war produced a reconciliation with southern congressmen, who were among FDR's strongest supporters on intervention and mobilization.

However, the further liberalization of the Democratic party and the social and economic changes brought on by the war began to upset this unity. The party was expanding to take in elements formerly underrepresented—women, blue-collar workers, and blacks—whose voices now had more influence in party deliberations and policy making. The Soldier Voting Acts, the anti–poll tax legislation, and the creation of the FEPC were seen by many southern politicians as efforts to undermine their political control by upsetting race relations in the region. They also believed that Roosevelt's favoritism toward organized labor, demonstrated in his handling of labor disputes and his veto of the Smith-Connally bill, would contribute to a political revolution in the low-wage, non-union South. Although the coalition of conservatives had turned back the tide of New Deal liberalism, southerners felt their influence in the party waning. As Shelby Myrick of the Savannah *Morning News* commented, the South did not like being the tail of the northern Democratic donkey, which was supporting centralized government, extravagant spending, Supreme Court packing, black voters, and abolition of the poll tax and the white primary.[30]

Confronting these changes, many southern politicians looked to the 1944 presidential election to demonstrate their dissatisfaction with the direction of the party. Various options for action included joining the Republicans in a coalition effort, creating a Southern Democratic party, or merely replacing Henry Wallace on the Democratic ticket. Running a candidate against Roosevelt was a long shot, given the president's continued popularity in the region, but these men were getting desperate. Jim Farley confided to former vice-president Garner, "I am convinced that both Byrd and Bailey are so strongly opposed to a fourth term that they would be willing to participate in an organization which would be called 'the Southern Democratic party,' . . . or do what in their judgment is best to prevent the re-election of President Roosevelt."[31]

Also reaching a high level of frustration were wealthy conservative businessmen whose financial support would be desirable if a rebel candidacy developed. This group had signed off on Roosevelt early in his administration, and the war had done nothing to change their minds about him. In fact, the more stringent wartime controls and tax policies had intensified their hatred of "that man in the White House," and they desperately searched for another candidate. Broker E. F. Hutton wrote to John Shephard, who had been in contact with Senator Byrd, "It is my candid opinion today that the straight Republican ticket, with no consideration for the sound Democrats of the country, has the possibilities of defeat. A coalition ticket eliminates that possibility. That's the idea but it has got to be sold to the Republican machine. . . . If we miss out this time so help me God I see nothing but ruination."[32]

Byrd was a likely choice for these groups if Roosevelt was to be directly challenged. Having acquired a national reputation for his criticism of the administration's handling of the preparedness program, labor disputes, and waste in government, Byrd had perfect credentials. Through 1941 and 1942 he received a trickle of letters from Virginians and others outside the state urging him to run for the presidency in 1944. His usual response included a thank-you, a denial of any ambition for the office, an assessment that he would have little chance, but no Shermanesque removal of his name from consideration.[33] The trickle became a torrent in 1943 and was not confined to the letterhead stationery of lawyers and businessmen but included many handwritten notes. Still denying any aspirations, Byrd was now linking his antiadministration efforts to "those principles for which our boys are fighting abroad." His article in *American Magazine* in August 1943 ("Are We Losing Our Freedom?") produced an outpouring of favorable comment. Magazine and newspaper editors began to tout him as a possible candidate in 1944, although polls that included him among the possibilities revealed scant public support for him.[34]

The sudden appearance of a large number of editorials discussing Byrd as a possible candidate was the result of a letter-writing campaign by James Thomson, the former New Orleans newspaperman who had actively supported Byrd in 1932.[35] Without Byrd's knowledge, Thomson, who was now living in Clarke County, had written his former newspaper associates to drum up support for a coalition ticket headed by the senator. Byrd received much publicity out of this, but not all of it was favorable. Many publishers were enthusiastic for him but saw too many obstacles: Roosevelt's popularity and wartime leadership, the historical weakness of third-party efforts, and the reluctance of Republicans to nominate a Democrat. E. P. Adler of the *Daily Times* of Davenport, Iowa, said Byrd was too much of an isolationist, while Ralph Coghlan, editor of the St. Louis *Post Dispatch,* stated that Byrd's "political philosophy is not abreast of the times." Support was strongest among southern newspapermen, but even that was not unanimous.[36]

Byrd was frequently mentioned as a possible candidate on a coalition ticket with Republicans, running with Wendell Willkie, General Douglas MacArthur, or Ohio senator John Bricker. To New Jersey banker Harvey Knight, who had suggested such a prospect, Byrd replied: "Very frankly, it is difficult to determine what can be done along the lines of your letter. I imagine the sentiment will crystallize regarding this after the Fall election, or certainly by next Spring." But others were more sanguine. E. F. Hutton wrote to Frank Gannett of the Gannett newspaper chain: "Now what's wrong with Senator Byrd as President? Nothing that I can see. He preaches and practices economy and efficiency."[37]

One of Byrd's most persistent supporters was Gleason Archer, president of Suffolk University in Boston, who told Byrd of the considerable interest in his candidacy among New York bankers, former Massachusetts governor Channing Cox, New York *Times* columnist Arthur Krock, and Frank Gannett. Archer suggested that Byrd meet with David Sarnoff of RCA and John D. Rockefeller, who, he said, had the "very highest regard for you." Byrd appreciated Archer's comments but said that he was "unable to reach the conclusion that I fit into the picture in such a way as to be formidable." He did indicate, however, that he was willing to discuss the matter further with Archer and urged him to contact Jim Farley, "who is very much interested in the same way you and I are." After his meeting with Farley, Archer wrote the senator: "I am happy to report that Mr. Farley and I see eye to eye on the political situation. He agrees that you are the logical man to make the contest for delegates both in the South and in the North. He believes moreover that you can win the nomination and become the Democratic standardbearer in 1944 with a very good prospect of winning the Presidency." Archer's strategy was to line up all the anti–New Deal Democrats in Congress and pursue a draft, "a nationwide uprising," with Farley as chairman of the effort.[38]

The alarm with which these gentlemen peered into the future is not difficult to comprehend. They feared a postwar world in which their freedom to increase their wealth and control their workers would be restricted. They hated Roosevelt, one of their own kind, because he had saved them from a disaster of their own making. They were men of the old order whom the world was passing by. As Byrd wrote to James McLemore, "We are certainly in a very critical condition. I fear very much for the post-war period, when we may see the final blow to our representative democracy, unless there is a great uprising on the part of the people. The war and the extravagance and radical tendencies of the New Deal have set the stage. I hope the people will see the dangers in time—before we go over the precipice." In actuality, these conservatives had little knowledge of "the people," who yearned for new opportunities that had been denied them: jobs, education, health care, and political participation. A different kind of "uprising" was already occurring, and Byrd and his friends could feel it. And this was not just a class phenomenon. The younger industrialists and financiers, who were working on government contracts, consulting with union leaders, and accommodating to changing times, saw a new world of government-management-labor cooperation before them. They were willing now to use the state to economic advantage and were not among the advocates of a Byrd candidacy.[39]

In October 1943, without consulting Byrd, a group of New Orleans businessmen under the leadership of John U. Barr, owner of a rope-manufacturing business and a vice-president of the Southern States Industrial Council, formed a Byrd for President Committee and began soliciting support from southern governors. Groups in Mississippi and Florida followed suit. Friends in Virginia were also enthusiastic, but Byrd counseled caution.

The formation of the committee and the appearance of a column in the

Olathe, Kansas, *Mirror* touting Byrd at the head of a Republican or coalition ticket generated another spate of editorial writing. Said the Boise, Idaho, *Statesman,* "Byrd hasn't a Jap's chance of getting the call." The Hickory, North Carolina, *Record* was frank: "His campaign may be a great success in the director's rooms and the caucuses of certain politicians but it will fall flat in the factory and down on the farm. Most of the folks there will give Byrd the bird, if you'll pardon our Brooklynese." Bill Cunningham of the Boston *Herald* correctly attributed the discontent behind Byrd's candidacy to the South's disaffection with the New Deal's labor policy, its racial liberalism, and Mrs. Roosevelt's "social dabblings." Although most commentators recognized Byrd's outstanding personal and conservative credentials, few believed that he could unseat Roosevelt or win the nomination of the opposition party.[40]

That, too, was Byrd's assessment. Corresponding with Henry Woodring, FDR's first secretary of war, who had suggested that Byrd carry the coalition banner, the senator said that his business and the illnesses of his wife and mother precluded such an effort. Yet he retained hopes of unseating Roosevelt. Referring Woodring to Farley, Byrd concluded, "I find a great many Democrats think as you and I do and if they could be welded together it would be very formidable and may discourage the present incumbent from being a candidate, although I say again that you or someone else of our lot would be much better to lead the fight."[41]

Byrd did not want to be president, but he was so consumed by his hatred of "New Dealism" that he thought some challenge to Roosevelt and his policies was worth making, no matter how sacrificial. "The New Deal party is not the Democratic Party and never has been," he told Robert Watts. "I think the consequences of a fourth term would be little short of disastrous, and I intend to say so at the proper time." As in 1932, the further the campaign progressed and the more praise he received as the savior of the country—saving it from the New Deal, a fourth term, and dictatorship—the more Byrd's appetite was whetted for something more than a candidacy of principle. As Woodring wrote him after a meeting of his American Democratic National Committee, "There is preponderant sentiment expressed for you for president."[42]

On February 28, 1944, Byrd met with John Barr in his Washington office to tell the New Orleans businessman that he was not a candidate for higher office, a statement he reaffirmed publicly. Nevertheless, Barr interpreted the senator's remarks as not rejecting a draft possibility and so announced expansion of his efforts to achieve that goal within the Democratic party. Rallies for a Byrd candidacy soon followed, but the results were not very promising. The first of these in Richmond on March 31 drew only twenty-six people; Remmie Arnold, a Petersburg pen manufacturer, was selected to head the local group. Notably absent were leaders of the Organization, with whom Byrd had met the night before to reiterate that he was not and would not be a candidate. Not wanting to embarrass him, they respected his request and did not support a Byrd for President movement in Virginia. Ebbie Combs maintained contact with the Arnold group but did nothing publicly to indicate that Byrd was interested. Yet Combs and Byrd were tantalized enough to prepare statements for subsequent rallies and distribute articles to the newspapers praising the senator. Meetings in Greensboro, North Carolina, and Atlanta, Georgia, in the next two weeks attracted only slightly more attention, despite Senator Bailey's call for a Byrd-Farley ticket.[43]

Farley, who had broken with Roosevelt in 1940 over the third-term issue, was an enigmatic figure in these proceedings. He and Byrd had met several times over the last year to discuss ways of defeating a fourth term for the president, either by constitutional amendment or direct opposition. They met again with Combs and Governor Darden in late April 1944. Farley, who knew of Roosevelt's poor health, was touting Byrd for the vice-presidency; but knowing that the Virginian was an unlikely choice, he may have been using Byrd as a stalking-horse for his own candidacy. The possibility of a Cordell Hull–Jim Farley ticket intrigued him.[44]

In spite of these efforts, Gallup polls continued to show the president to be the overwhelming choice in the South, with Byrd running second in Mississippi with 8 percent of those interviewed and third in South Carolina with 11 percent. The *Times-Dispatch* labeled the draft effort "the height of futility;" Barr, it said, had been unable to convince people that his efforts had a future. Even if Roosevelt did not run for reelection, the newspaper concluded that he would not let Byrd be nominated. Punning on Barr's business, the Norfolk *Virginian-Pilot* said that the rope manufacturer was offering Byrd "enough rope to hang himself with."[45]

But the optimistic Barr would not despair. He announced plans to expand his efforts into the North and East, citing the increasing momentum in the South. Byrd, he said, "is the only true Democrat who can save the party." Meetings in Memphis and Dallas revealed the growing animosity toward the New Deal in the Deep South where talk of bolting the party was building. Zach Lamar Cobb, a Los Angeles attorney from Texas, was as enthusiastic as Barr about the effort. Delivering the keynote address to the Dallas conference, Cobb shouted, "As the truth is brought home to them that Senator Byrd is fighting to defend the faith of our fathers, against those who would revolutionize our government, I can hear the loyal voice of Texans ring: Hold fast to the faith! Travis never surrendered the Alamo!" Cobb recommended that Byrd convene a mass meeting of southerners to state his case. In a two-part article on Byrd's candidacy in the *Saturday Evening Post* in mid-April 1944, Forrest Davis concluded that Byrd was not a "Don Quixote" sallying forth in a "mere token campaign;" his candidacy was a protest against the New Deal that could turn into something more substantial if Roosevelt chose not to run. But the journalist pessimistically noted that the Byrds had historically aligned themselves with lost causes: Charles I against Cromwell, Governor Dunmore in the American Revolution, and the Confederacy in the Civil War.[46]

As summer approached, reports from the South were favorable. Byrd won four out of eighteen delegates and 45 percent of the vote in the Florida Democratic primary; the Texas Democratic convention split wide open, and control was wrested from Roosevelt forces by the anti–New Deal regulars; and South Carolina and Mississippi were sending uninstructed delegations to the Chicago convention. There was talk now of an independent Byrd candidacy that would siphon off enough electoral votes to throw the election into the House of Representatives. Karl Crowley in Texas told Byrd that four southern states were pursuing the scheme of independent presidential electors. Unlike Texas and South Carolina, Virginia required the names of the nominees to be printed on the ballot with voters voting directly for the nominees, but Byrd said he would give "the fullest consideration to all angles of this matter." He commented to C. S. Carter, "I think the results in Texas, Mississippi, South Carolina and some of the other Southern states are very significant and may have powerful consequences."[47]

Even so, Byrd's optimism dimmed as the convention approached. To one of Billy Reed's sons, he wrote, "I think we should recognize the realities of the situation, and, in my judgment, there is no hope whatever of anyone successfully opposing Roosevelt in the Democratic Convention, in the event that he desires to be renominated." His inquiries about modifying the Virginia election laws proved fruitless because any changes required a session of the General Assembly.[48] There continued to be scattered expressions of support from Republicans, but the strong surge among the moderates of that party for Thomas Dewey, governor of New York, precluded any hopes for a coalition with the GOP, especially after General MacArthur rejected a draft. The senator received some overtures from backers of Senator Bricker, and there was a boomlet for the Virginian on the eve of the Republican convention, but the efforts seemed to be directed at winning support for the party in the South, not linking up with a Democrat. Byrd declined the vice-presidency on any ticket and concluded, "The time has not yet come when there can be an effective coalition between the two major parties."[49]

Whatever hopes Byrd had of winning the nomination died on July 11 when the president, who had the strong support of rank-and-file party faithful and who was bolstered by the success of the D-Day invasion, decided to be "a good soldier . . . and accept and serve." What remained for Byrd was to be the protest nominee of the southern delegates—a role he preferred to avoid—and also to try to block the renomination of Vice-President Wallace. As he had told one correspondent some weeks earlier, "There are certain fundamental principles for which we must fight, even though we may lose temporarily."[50]

Before the Chicago convention Byrd had to tend to a minirevolt at home and secure control of the Virginia delegation. In early June a group of "antis," joined by Rixey Smith, secretary to Senator Glass, and Representative Flannagan, announced formation of a Committee of 100 to support the reelection of President Roosevelt. The Roanoke *Times* judged it to be an effort to usurp the role of the central committee and serve as a wedge for a new Democratic organization in the state. Predictably, it proved to be an ineffectual group, unable to dent the Organization's control of the convention. On the eve of the state conclave, Byrd held several strategy meetings with Combs, Robertson, and Fred Switzer to consider bolting the party, but they decided to avoid controversy and concentrate on defeating Wallace. As planned, the Roanoke convention in early July did not endorse Roosevelt, although mention of his name brought great applause from the delegates, who instructed their representatives to the national convention to oppose Wallace. Byrd delivered a convention speech notable for its high praise of the wartime contributions of Virginians without once mentioning the commander-in-chief, the nation's leader and the party's leader. "Anti" Lloyd Robinette described the proceedings as "a Roman holiday for the organization and they strutted on and off the stage with great display of imperial authority." Byrd was pleased with the Roanoke results, but he did not look forward to going to Chicago. "It is a choice between two evils," he told Howard Smith. "If I did not go, I would be charged with not being present on some vital issues that may be presented there with respect to the attitude of the South and the Vice Presidency. I have never undertaken anything that I relish less than going."[51]

For a convention whose nominee was the overwhelming choice of the delegates, the 1944 Democratic gathering was not a happy occasion. Many southern delegates were seething with resentment over their perceived second-class citizenship and were ready to do battle on the platform and the vice-presidency. Acknowledging Roosevelt's insurmountable lead, they wanted to use Byrd's candidacy as a statement of their dissatisfaction. As John Barr said, they did not want to be "bossed and kicked around by some 400,000 New York Communists." At a caucus of seven southern states, Ebbie Combs told those present that Byrd did not want to be nominated, but he would not object to those wanting to vote for him. The caucus then gave Byrd its nonbinding endorsement. With some irony, Byrd was nominated by Mrs. Fred T. Nooney, Jr., one of his Florida delegates, who reportedly was the first woman ever to make a nominating speech for a presidential candidate at a major party's national convention. Following a short demonstration, Mississippi, Texas, and Virginia seconded the nomination. Byrd thanked the Virginia delegation for its support and freed the members to vote their own mind, which they did: unanimously for Byrd. The senator received 89 votes, second to Roosevelt's 1,086. He got all of the Virginia, Mississippi, and Louisiana votes, 12 from Texas, a scattering from Alabama, Florida, South Carolina, and West Virginia, and half a vote from Jim Farley in New York. He might have received a few more from Texas, but many of the anti–New Deal delegates walked out when both contesting delegations were seated. The South won a modest victory on the platform when a vague civil rights plank without specifics on the poll tax and antilynching law was adopted.[52]

Attention then focused on the choice for vice-president. Roosevelt preferred to retain Henry Wallace because of his strong New Deal credentials, but that was also the vice-president's major liability. Therefore, the president gave Wallace only a lukewarm endorsement and threw the choice open to the convention, with some direction. Apparently his second choice was Jimmy Byrnes, who claimed FDR had committed to him, but the president withdrew his blessing at the last moment when confronted with the objections of organized labor and black delegates. At this point Harry Truman emerged as a compromise candidate. Truman had been a supporter of the New Deal, but he had demonstrated his independence of the administration by chairing a fair investigation of waste in the defense program. Wallace led on the first ballot, but a number of states, including Virginia, which had supported Senator John Bankhead on the first vote, switched to Truman, and the Missouri senator was selected. Colgate Darden remembered Truman approaching Byrd and asking for his assistance. "Harry," he said, "I hope you can help me in this thing. I'm not going to talk to many people about it, but I do want to call on a few of my friends to see if they will help me out." Without making any promises, Byrd replied that he would see what he could do. It was not a difficult decision since he would have done anything to prevent Wallace from being renominated. *Life* columnist Gerald Johnson credited Byrd with being the "kingpin" of the southern revolt that split the Democratic convention, but the Wallace defeat was the only thing about the meeting that pleased him. Even his accommodations proved troublesome. A female reporter, given a room number similar to Byrd's, was bothered so frequently by reporters looking for the senator that on one occasion she opened the door while undressing and, when asked whether Byrd was there, said, "Yes, but he's asleep." The senator was happy to leave Chicago.[53]

Although southerners had won all that could have been expected, the extremists, who were largely political amateurs, indicated that this would not be the end of their quest for separation from a national party made up of "crackpots and bureaucrats [who] are . . . running as the communists and race inciters they really are." John Barr announced plans for a third-party effort, holding the Byrd for President organization intact as the vehicle for an effort to throw the election into the House of Representatives. Texas and Mississippi Democrats freed their electors to vote for any candidate, and folks in Louisiana and Alabama were working on it. Byrd's support for such an effort was critical to its success, and he received many requests, particularly from the Texans, to break with Roosevelt. But the senator had had enough. He wrote Zach Cobb, "It now appears that a third Southern party would be impractical at this time." He thanked Cobb for his efforts and promised to remain committed to the principles of sound government.[54]

Several factors determined Byrd's decision. He did not like losing, even in token protest efforts. One of his cardinal political principles was to avoid defeat because it suggested weakness and encouraged opposition. If one were to be involved in a campaign of protest that stood little chance of winning, one should disguise participation in it, deny it, and prepare for a quiet withdrawal. The convention proceedings had been an embarrassment to him. Through his frequent denials of candidacy he had tried to control the use of his name in the anti-Roosevelt effort, but the situation had gotten out of hand. He told friends that he had allowed his name to go forth "for the purposes of establishing the fact that a fourth term nomination was not unanimous," but he regretted his participation. His distaste for the whole affair was so strong that two years later, when approached by Karl Crowley about an effort to defeat Truman, Byrd was emphatic: "I never intend . . . to have my name brought up again as a candidate for any national office." Byrd was certain that the third-party effort was similarly doomed. Prophetically, he wrote his brother that "the South will not stand long after the war for the recent policies of New Dealism." But he concluded, "They have no place to go except to a third party, and this is not constructive, as I do not think a southern third party could ever win nationally."[55]

Perhaps more importantly, Byrd worried about what a defection to a third party would mean for the Virginia Organization. This had bothered him as talk mounted over the last year about a coalition ticket with Republicans. His entire political career had rested on the premise of party loyalty; he had preached it, and he had practiced it. Could he now renounce that principle? What would that do to the Organization? The "antis" had remained loyal to the Democratic party, and his defection now might precipitate a new challenge. In a rare expression of his feelings on this question, he had written to Frank Wysor before the convention:

> For thirty years I have been in public life, and I have fought for certain definite principles. Virginia owes me nothing, but I owe a great deal to Virginia. A fourth term nomination now confronts me with the question as to whether I must abandon these principles and vote a so-called Democratic ticket, which is, in fact, completely foreign to the true principles of democracy, or whether I should stand on the principles I have advocated all these

years. What I am more concerned about than anything else is conducting myself so that I will not injure those who are associated with me and the Democratic organization. As you know, all of my political life I have taken great pride in our Democratic organization in Virginia, so whatever course I may feel impelled to take, I want to do it in such a way that the least possible injury will be done to this organization, which I think has had a very wholesome and beneficial influence in Virginia for many years.[56]

The senator was not giving up his fight against "this gigantic bureaucracy . . . which has abandoned all of the principles of the Democratic party," but now was not the time to participate in lost causes and risk damaging the Organization.

Finally, Byrd did not want to chance losing the benefits of party loyalty in an effort that promised so little in return. That did not mean acquiescence to liberal leadership. Indeed, the acclaim he received in this campaign reinforced his negative conservatism and strengthened him in the Old Dominion. Preparing for future battles, he would use the lessons learned in the 1944 campaign—notably the Texas example of manipulating electoral machinery and the separation of the state party from the national party—to "protect ourselves and the principles we represent."[57] Therefore, Byrd remained silent on the third-party effort, but he did not repudiate it entirely. While he continued to say he was not a candidate, he did not disavow the independent electors who were pledged to vote for him if they won. Combs was in correspondence with the Texans, assisting them in orchestrating the electoral vote for Byrd.[58]

Byrd was also silent about supporting either major party candidate. It was the first of what was to become a sequence of "golden silences" in future presidential races. There was much speculation about what Byrd was going to do. Regulars demanded that he come out for Roosevelt, while the Virginia press argued that Byrd's prominence required some statement of commitment. "Is he a Democrat or isn't he?" questioned the *Times-Dispatch*. The "antis" were particularly incensed at his "hostile opposition" to the president when all other Virginia congressmen, including Senator Glass, were reported to have endorsed Roosevelt with varying degrees of enthusiasm. Although Frank Kent of the Baltimore *Sun* conjectured that Byrd's silence was "equivalent to saying he would not vote at all," it is likely that, out of moral obligation, he voted for Roosevelt, despite his "embarrassment . . . with regard to the national ticket." He informed John Q. Rhodes, "You, of course, know my democracy and how I intend to vote." And Harry Jr. stated categorically, "Father, of course, voted the full Democratic ticket." But if Byrd voted the party line, he still recognized the possibility of Democrats voting Republican; and recalling the opinions of past attorneys general, he surmised that a vote for Dewey would not disqualify one from participating in future Democratic primary elections.[59]

Roosevelt won his fourth term handily, although the gap with the Republicans narrowed. The electors pledged to Byrd picked up some support, but in no state did they come close to outpolling the president. The southern insurgency of 1944 was defeated because of its amateurish effort to remove a popular president during a popular war with issues that did not yet have meaning for most of the electorate. There was an oddball conspiratorial mentality driving these people who believed Communists and union leaders and racial liberals were joining forces to bring America down. Nevertheless, the movement did not die. The issues behind the Byrd candidacy—taxes, social welfare legislation, the federal ballot, race and labor policies, and communism—foreshadowed a deeper cleavage in the Democratic party and the development of a southern sectionalism that would transform national and regional politics. The end of the one-party South began in 1944. The Dixiecrats were only four years away.[60]

Roosevelt's reelection was a precursor to a successful termination of the war and preparation for a peaceful postwar world. At home it was politics as usual, although in one of the more bizarre political marriages of the war, Harry Byrd found himself chairing the Arrangements Committee for Franklin Roosevelt's fourth inauguration, which was held at the White House. When the president announced that he did not want a cent spent on the ceremony, the senator took him at his word, spending a miserly $526.12, most of it for invitations.[61]

The animosity between Byrd and Roosevelt increased with the president's appointment of Henry Wallace to be secretary of commerce and federal loan administrator. It was payment for Wallace's peaceful withdrawal from the vice-presidency and support for Roosevelt in the 1944 campaign. Leading irate southern conservatives in an effort to defeat the nomination, Byrd labeled Wallace a radical who was unsuited to take over management of the Reconstruction Finance Corporation, the major federal lending agency. In hopes of pacifying some critics, Roosevelt agreed to separate the two jobs, and after a well-considered delay, Wallace was confirmed as commerce secretary, but by the embarrassingly close margin of 56–32. The disappointed Byrd got a small measure of revenge by helping to defeat another New Dealer, Aubrey Williams, the former head of the NYA whom Roosevelt had appointed to direct the Rural Electrification Administration. Byrd called Williams "second only to Henry Wallace [in] obnoxiousness."[62]

Further acrimony came to a halt on April 12 when Franklin Roosevelt died of a cerebral hemorrhage and Harry Truman assumed the presidency under the most difficult of circumstances. Although Byrd privately called the president's death "tragic" and publicly paid Roosevelt a respectful tribute by calling for renewed dedication to carry out his plans for world peace, he could not have been more pleased with the assumption of power by Truman. As he wrote to Zach Cobb, "I have served in the Senate with him for ten years and have respect for his capacity and good intentions." The years ahead would severely test that relationship. They would also test Harry Byrd's adaptability to a new world order. The war in Europe would be over in a month, and the Pacific conflict would end in nuclear fire three months later. What was left was a war-torn globe, the looming presence of a more imposing totalitarianism, and a revived America on the brink of unprecedented prosperity, social transformation, and world leadership. Yet, instead of seeing the war as an agent of vast new opportunities, Harry Byrd chose to see it as a harbinger of decline, a falling away to tyranny and the "road to serfdom." The America he knew and loved was no more.[63]

~ 13 ~

An Unsettled World

ORLD WAR II had a profound effect on the United States. It ended the depression, restored economic vitality to the nation, and left a vastly altered world that demanded greater American involvement, at a cost to the country of $320 billion and over 400,000 lives. It uprooted Americans, forcing them into new occupations and places, accelerated urbanization and suburbanization, precipitated a rising birthrate, and empowered blacks and women with ideas and experiences that would lead to subsequent upheavals. Continuing a trend begun during the New Deal, power shifted to Washington—particularly through a strengthened presidency—to deal with the domestic and foreign problems produced by the war. Although many New Deal relief programs were terminated, the foreign conflict increased the role of government in American life through a greatly enlarged defense establishment, a wide array of programs for veterans, greater aid for education, health care, and public housing, and a new commitment to national economic planning. An older America of small farms and towns, stable family life, white over black, men over women, and worldly isolation was vanishing. In confronting these changes, the postwar political debate was carried on between those who, like Harry Byrd, wished to restore the old order and those who believed new problems demanded new solutions.

In the aftermath of Roosevelt's death and the subsequent euphoria of victory, Byrd seemed ready to support the creation of a new international community. He approved American participation in the International Monetary Fund and the international bank. As a member of the Senate Naval Affairs Committee, he traveled to San Francisco for the United Nations conference to participate in the discussions on the disposition of Japan's Pacific bases. Opposing a United Nations trusteeship for them, he preferred that they be retained by the United States for security purposes. Fearing a challenge to American interests, Byrd objected to the veto power of the Big Five; but as he told his brother, it was "impossible under present conditions to make any fight whatever against the veto," and he joined the majority of senators approving the United Nations charter. In reality, Byrd's "internationalism," rather than being modeled after that of Woodrow Wilson, was similar to the economic and political nationalism of Wilson's enemy, Henry Cabot Lodge, who had been distrustful of foreign intentions and protective of American interests.[1]

With the defeat of Germany, longtime suspicions and hostilities between the United States and the Soviet Union erupted to upset the Grand Alliance. An "iron curtain" gradually descended over Central Europe, dividing East from West and commencing the Cold War. Preoccupied with the economic chaos of postwar demobilization, most Americans were unaware of the depth of Soviet-American enmity until late 1946 when Russian intractability and expansionist objectives became more apparent. The confrontation emerged in a dispute between Secretary of State James Byrnes, who was becoming more bellicose toward the Soviets, and Commerce Secretary Wallace, who publicly challenged the administration's hardening line with Russia. Senator Byrd urged President Truman to repudiate Wallace's criticism, calling it "inexcusable and thoughtless." He wired Byrnes, then in Paris negotiating with the Russians, to assure him that he had the "overwhelming support and confidence of the American people." At the insistence of Byrnes, who believed the credibility of American foreign policy was at stake, Truman fired Wallace, thus solidifying the hawkish position the United States would take toward the Soviet Union for the next several decades.[2]

That hard line became more apparent the following spring when President Truman asked Congress for $400 million in military and economic aid to resist Soviet influence in Greece and Turkey. In enunciating his Truman Doctrine, the president drew a clear distinction between the free world and the Communist world and implied that America was prepared to oppose the expansion of communism anywhere in the world. "I believe," he stated, "that it must be the foreign policy of the United States to support free peoples who are resisting attempted subjugation by armed minorities or by outside pressures."[3]

To Harry Byrd, this open-ended invitation to protect the free world would entail exorbitant costs and be of questionable value. He had no doubts about the Soviet threat. His anti-Communist sentiments, reinforced by the experiences of his friends Bernard Baruch and Jimmy Byrnes in dealing with the Russians, easily converted him into a Cold War warrior, but unlike many southern politicians, he did not give unqualified support to flag and military in the postwar world. His fiscal preferences and provincial nationalism pushed him toward a Fortress America posture rather than advocacy of more vigorous global involvement. Having opposed sharing nuclear secrets with other nations, he believed America's best defense against communism was a strong national defense and economy. Therefore, he favored most defense appropriations—although not uncritically—and backed most of the alliance systems the country would enter into, but he rejected foreign aid programs and questioned committing troops into battle, inasmuch as both could adversely affect the budget. Some of Byrd's reservations about foreign involvement were valid, but his opposition to foreign aid on fiscal grounds was so categorical that his opinions lacked credibility. Having limited interest in foreign affairs, he did not analyze aid programs on their individual merits. In short, despite the changed nature of the world and America's new global role, Harry Byrd was still adhering to the qualified interventionism that had dictated his course of action before World War II.[4]

The senator's opposition to increased foreign aid had developed even before the Soviet threat became apparent. On a trip to Europe in late 1945, he found the relief efforts of the United Nations Relief and Rehabilitation Administration (UNRRA) "inefficient and wasteful," and he demanded a reorganization of the agency. He acknowledged America's responsibility to feed the hungry of Europe but declared that the country could not be a "Santa Claus" to the rest of the world—a description of foreign aid he would use frequently thereafter. Although he predicted that many European nations would become Communist, he still voted against the $3.75 billion loan for Great Britain for postwar reconstruction in May 1946, claiming that the loan would never be repaid and eventually would create bitterness between the two countries.[5]

The Greek-Turkish aid program of 1947 presented a different set of problems for Byrd. Terming the president's message as the "most important world event since V. J. Day" because it forecast a "drastic change" in American foreign policy, he questioned the appropriateness of bypassing the United Nations and predicted the imposition of new military and economic burdens on America. "In voting on military and economic aid to Greece and Turkey we are not voting for aid to these two nations," he prophesied, "but we are voting on a global policy enunciated by the President which will carry American dollars to many other foreign countries. It is certainly the part of prudence to survey our resources before we undertake new and gigantic financial obligations."[6]

In subsequent speeches Byrd elaborated on his objections to the proposal. A continuation of aid programs, he believed, would create large deficits and would propel the United States down the path blazed by England to financial ruin. To him the civil war in Greece was a "bandit" conflict that might best be dealt with through economic sanctions rather than direct aid, while the crisis in Turkey he labeled a "war of nerves" with the Russians. "I cannot escape the conclusion," he stated, "that the effort to dramatize this as an imminent crisis has been over-emphasized and exaggerated." Byrd predicted that unilateral action by the United States would be the beginning of many other interventions that would lead to the ultimate collapse of the United Nations.[7]

Despite his impassioned pleas the Senate passed the Truman Doctrine, 67–23. Labeling it a "tragic mistake," Byrd was one of only seven Democrats voting no, the first time, he said, that he had ever voted against a foreign policy initiative of the chief executive, forgetting his vote against terminating the neutrality legislation. His critique of foreign aid was prescient, for the Truman Doctrine moved beyond the specific case of Greece and Turkey to become an expensive, open-ended aid program that operated more on fear and ideology than on national security interests. It unduly alarmed both Americans and Soviets, thereby exacerbating the tensions of the Cold War.[8]

Less defensible is Byrd's opposition to the other major foreign aid initiative of the day, the Marshall Plan. Beset by staggering postwar economic woes, countries of Western Europe teetered on the brink of collapse and possible takeover by Communist parties. To preserve democracy and revive their economies, Secretary of State George Marshall in June 1947 offered American assistance to European nations willing to participate in a broad program of economic reconstruction. These countries—minus the Communist nations who declined to participate—submitted a $22 billion recovery plan to the United States, which President Truman pared to a first-year appropriation of $5.3 billion to make it more palatable to Congress. But the sum mattered little when a Communist coup in Czechoslovakia in February 1948 raised the stakes in the Cold War and assured its passage.[9]

Harry Byrd, however, was not persuaded. His initial response to the European aid package was that America could not afford "to finance a world WPA"; needy nations should be helped within reason, but "dollars alone cannot save them." He argued that the total costs of the program were unpredictable and that such excessive spending threatened to weaken America financially. Byrd had come to believe that the greatest danger to the country's security came not from military power but from fiscal insolvency; if the Russians were to beat the United States, it would be through a financial collapse. Moreover, he had little confidence that the Europeans could succeed, fearing that the factories rebuilt with American money would fall into the hands of the Russians.[10]

Over Byrd's objections the Senate passed the recovery plan, 69–17. Although the money spent multiplied several times over the initial appropriation as Byrd had predicted, the Marshall Plan proved the most brilliant of all of America's foreign aid programs. It saved Western Europe from economic catastrophe and possible takeover by communism, and by reviving those economies, it also benefited the American economy. The money could not have been better spent. In this case Byrd's obsession with spending caused him to overlook the necessity of helping the one area of the world most critical to American interests and to ignore the self-contained nature of the plan which European leaders themselves had helped to create. Although he did not change his mind about foreign aid, he later regretted his opposition to the Marshall Plan.[11]

Having always been an advocate of a strong military capability for defen-

An Unsettled World

sive purposes, Byrd continued his support for preparedness in the postwar years. He had approved the use of the atomic bomb against Japan, and he served on the special Senate committee that drafted legislation creating an Atomic Energy Commission to oversee America's nuclear development.[12] His service on the Armed Services Committee (successor to the military and naval affairs committees), along with the influence of his brother, his suspicions of Russian intentions, and the financial gains to Virginia through the emerging military-industrial complex, reinforced his inherent belief in military readiness. Although he would insist that even the generals and admirals be conscious of "economy and efficiency," spending on the defense establishment was the exception to his rule of cutting back federal expenditures. "Frankly," he told Hunsdon Cary, "I think this is vitally more important than spending our money all over the world in an effort to combat communism." But he was appalled at how much preparedness would cost. The menace of Russia, he predicted to Douglas Freeman, would continue until the Soviets disarmed or changed their form of government, and "neither, in my judgment, will occur. . . . I favor a strong military but, if wartime spending is to be made a part of our budget in peacetime, and continued for many years, our system simply will not stand it."[13]

Although the Cold War would become an increasingly ominous presence over the next decade, Americans were more concerned in the immediate postwar years with the conversion to a peacetime economy. They clamored for reducing troop strength from three million to 400,000 within a year and doing away overnight with all price controls. In President Truman's words, the country was not following a policy of "demobilization" but one of "disintegration." An apprehensive Senator Byrd wrote Bill Tuck, "The whole world is very unsettled."[14]

Byrd sympathized with the plight of the president and pledged his support. He was ecstatic when his former colleague called for a reorganization of the government to achieve greater efficiency, replaced Frances Perkins as secretary of labor, and approved a bill sponsored by Byrd and Senator Hugh Butler, a Nebraska Republican, that prohibited any government corporation from doing business without the approval of Congress. In a cordial letter to the president, Byrd urged an immediate reduction in federal employees and a cut in federal working hours from forty-eight to forty-four that he claimed would save $200 million. Two months into the Truman presidency, Byrd assessed his performance as "splendid."[15]

However, such congenial relations began to deteriorate when Truman presented a domestic agenda to Congress in September 1945 that gave new life to the New Deal: expansion of social security, an increase in the minimum wage, national health insurance, public housing, additional regional projects like the

251

TVA, a full employment bill, and continuation of economic controls. Byrd could not have been more disappointed, and along with other conservative congressmen, he began to obstruct much of the president's program.[16]

He was further alienated from his old Senate deskmate by Truman's handling of problems with organized labor. In the years after World War II, a vigorous debate occurred over the role of unions in American life. Wary of postwar inflation, unemployment, and a return to depression, union leaders sought to consolidate their recent gains by pressing for greater authority in the workplace. They confronted business leaders, who desired to reassert their control over labor, and conservative politicians, who wished to curb union power. A wave of strikes in the months after V-J Day—albeit predictable in a time of economic uncertainty—alarmed Americans and their political representatives. Although many strikes were settled amicably, the walkouts in the coal mines and on the railroads in the spring of 1946 caused an angry president to seize these properties and request authority to draft strikers into the army so that industries vital to the nation's security would not shut down. Truman was not unsympathetic to the demands of the workers and did not want to see the gains of the last decade evaporate, but he could not tolerate threats to the postwar recovery.[17]

Supporting the president's request, Senator Byrd argued that unions, like businesses, should be incorporated so that they could be sued for damages caused by violation of contracts and destruction of property. Insisting that he favored workers' rights to organize and bargain collectively, he offered legislation requiring unions to register with the Securities and Exchange Commission and to pay damages for broken contracts. He wrote to one constituent: "I do not know why the labor unions are opposed to my bill, as I think, in the long run, it will strengthen them. I have reached the conclusion that if unions are made responsible for their acts they would certainly not be damaged thereby. They have a great influence in the economic life of our country now and must take their share of the responsibility."[18]

Part of Byrd's proposal was included in the Case bill that was directed at the recent strikes. It provided for a sixty-day cooling-off period before walkouts in crucial industries could occur, outlawed secondary boycotts by unions, and allowed unions to be sued for breach of contract. Once again upset by the tactics of John L. Lewis, whom he accused of "holding up the country at the point of a gun," Byrd tried to prevent the mineworkers from collecting royalties that would be paid into their health and welfare funds. Predicting that other unions would adopt the same tactic, he proposed an amendment to the Case bill which would prevent employer payments to employee representatives or funds. When Senator Claude Pepper of Florida pointed out that this would prevent management from giving money to anything—including workers' baseball teams—Byrd amended his proposal to allow payment into funds that were administered by both employers and employees. Pepper then attacked Byrd personally, accusing him of advising coal operators to stall on any settlement with the unions until labor legislation had been passed. Acknowledging that some Virginia operators had contacted him, Byrd bitterly denounced the "false innuendo." When Pepper did not recant, Byrd remarked that Senator Glass once told him that "it never paid to get into a contest with a skunk." The Floridian retorted by contrasting Senator Byrd's lifestyle to the squalid living conditions of the miners whose welfare funds he was restricting. After the two senators exchanged further words, Pepper apologized for any unintended insult and said he hoped "to enjoy [Byrd's] personal friendship whether I ever get out of his skunk class or not." He never did. A day later when Senator Homer Ferguson suggested that Byrd apologize for his remark, the Virginian responded, "I'll apologize to the whole skunk family."[19] Pepper also lost the battle of amendments; the Senate rejected his proposal to allow union control of welfare funds and approved Byrd's amendment that provided for shared administration of the funds.[20]

The Senate passed the Case bill the same day that President Truman asked for additional authority to quell strikes, but the abrupt end of the coal and railroad walkouts rendered Truman's request moot and prompted rumors of a presidential veto of the bill. Senator Byrd urged Truman to sign it because he believed the bill corrected defects in the labor laws. Blaming the Wagner Act and the sit-down strikes for the present crisis, Byrd said that democracy must find a way to stop harmful work stoppages. His disposition was not improved when Truman vetoed the Case bill. Calling the veto "little short of a national tragedy," Byrd tried to arrange an "override" strategy with Senate and House colleagues, but he was unsuccessful as the House narrowly sustained the veto.[21]

Republican victories in the 1946 fall elections, coupled with continued strike activity, ensured that the Case legislation would be reintroduced. In a New York speech to a friendly audience of four thousand members of the National Association of Manufacturers, Byrd reiterated his call for a special session of Congress to "crush" Lewis and destroy "a Frankenstein that threatens to destroy us." Blaming the recent Democratic defeats on appeasement of a "labor dictatorship," he demanded tough new labor laws to terminate the privileged position granted unions by the Wagner Act.[22]

The Senate that Harry Byrd entered in 1947 was unlike any in recent memory. It would be controlled by Republicans, who had exploited postwar economic woes and public discontent with labor to recapture both houses of Congress for the first time since 1931. The conversion cost Byrd his chairmanship of the Rules Committee, but in a most unusual move, Republicans allowed him to retain control of the joint committee on government spending, proving the affection they had for a senator whose criticism of Democratic policies delighted them. Since a coalition of Republicans and southern Democrats had wielded great influence in Congress for the past four years, there was little perceptible change in the operation of the two chambers or in the deadlock that had been created between the executive and legislative branches, a crisis so barren of solution that Senator J. William Fulbright, an Arkansas Democrat, suggested that President Truman resign.[23]

The struggle reached its zenith in the debates over the major labor legislation of the postwar years, the Taft-Hartley Act of 1947, of which Harry Byrd was a leading architect. His earlier proposals to require incorporation of unions and joint administration of welfare funds, along with a new measure to outlaw the closed shop—an institution he had always deemed undemocratic—were included in the bill. Along with senators Joseph Ball of Minnesota and Walter George of Georgia, he attempted to toughen it even further, but their efforts to ban the union shop and to curb industrywide bargaining failed, 57–21 and 44–43, respectively. The final version included provisions of the previously vetoed Case bill, outlawed the closed shop, permitted state right-to-work laws, and required unions to register and file financial reports with the secretary of labor.[24]

Although not the "slave-labor law" President Truman called it, the Taft-Hartley Act restricted the activities of unions and made them more vulnerable to management. As a friend of labor and also as a recipient of labor's political support, Truman vetoed the bill, in spite of Harry Byrd's warning that vetoing it would brand the Democrats as the party of labor and lead to a Republican victory in 1948. Noting the terrific pressure to sustain the veto, Byrd suggested that such a result would be "calamitous" and a "green light to arrogant and willful labor leaders to strike in vital industries. . . . If we cannot manage John L. Lewis at home, how can we expect to protect ourselves against Joe Stalin abroad?" Much to his relief, both the House and the Senate overrode the veto, producing what one historian has called "the most important conservative triumph of the postwar era." The enactment of the Taft-Hartley Act climaxed Harry Byrd's long struggle to reverse what he believed were the negative consequences of the Wagner Act that had increased the power of workers and their unions.[25]

Just as Truman's defense of labor interests alienated the Virginian, so, too, did his failure to pursue appropriate retrenchment and budget-balancing policies. Joining Republican critics, Byrd lambasted Truman's 1947 and 1948 budgets for failing to reduce spending; he claimed the projected positive balances—the treasury had its first surplus in seventeen years in fiscal year 1947—were not large enough to compensate for potential recessions. Unaware of the future tolerance for deficits, Byrd predicted that their continuation "would shake the confidence of the American people to its very foundations." He made his first of many attempts to consolidate all federal appropriations into a single bill to facilitate cost reduction measures. He asserted that with eleven different bills to consider, Congress never knew how much money was available and how much was being spent. More and more the senator found himself allied with Republicans in trying to override presidential vetoes of spending and tax cut bills, earning Truman's derisive tag, "Mr. Demopublican."[26]

Undoubtedly, the upcoming presidential election dictated much of the posturing between president and Congress in 1948. Banking on public dissatisfaction with inflation and strikes, Republicans eagerly awaited a return to the White House they had not held since 1933. Their chances were improved immeasurably by the dissension within Democratic ranks. Displeased with Truman's hard line toward the Soviets and his failure to advance New Deal policies, progressives rallied around the independent candidacy of Henry Wallace. Other liberals, dissatisfied with Truman's leadership and convinced of his defeat, sought to replace him with General Dwight Eisenhower or Supreme Court justice William O. Douglas. Conservative southern Democrats, on the other hand, were increasingly disgruntled with the liberal tilt of the party—particularly by Truman's new civil rights initiatives—and threatened to bolt.

Harry Truman from the Jim Crow border state of Missouri was an unlikely candidate to become a civil rights advocate. His conversion resulted from several considerations: his basic decency toward people, an understanding of the international implications of America's discrimination against blacks, and a pinch of politics. At war's end he had endorsed making the Fair Employment Practices Commission permanent, but southerners had filibustered it to death. During his participation in the debates, Senator Byrd called it "the most dangerous proposal ever seriously considered by Congress during my thirteen years of service in the Senate of the United States." It was in his view the essence of "totalitarianism," an expansion of federal control into American lives that would force employers to hire certain people and deny them jury trials.[27]

Defeat of the FEPC, however, did not deter the president. A spate of racial violence in the South caused Truman to create a President's Committee on Civil Rights in December 1946 to investigate ways of protecting the civil rights of American citizens. A year later, in a stunning recommendation, the committee urged an immediate end to segregation in American life. Its report, *To Secure These Rights,* called for passage of a federal antilynching law, abolition of the poll tax, creation of a permanent fair employment practices commission, and stronger enforcement of civil rights. The president applauded the report and endorsed its recommendations in a special message to Congress on February 2, 1948. He also launched the desegregation of the armed forces, and his Commission on Higher Education proposed an end to segregated schools.

Most southerners were shocked by such developments. Even the moderate *Times-Dispatch,* which had cultivated improved race relations, condemned these suggestions as "radical . . . unwise and dangerous." Arkansas Democrats demanded creation of a Dixie party with Jimmy Byrnes or Harry Byrd as its presidential standard-bearer.

The political implications of his civil rights program were not unknown to Truman. Like his vetoes of antilabor legislation, Truman's stand on civil rights may have expressed a calculated choice to side with party liberals rather than the South. Obviously, if civil rights became part of the Democratic platform, it would split the party. Hoping that defections in the one-party South could be minimized, Truman courted northern liberals and blacks whose allegiance would be necessary if he was to win the Democratic nomination and the election against the Republicans, whose own civil rights platform was moderately progressive. That, at least, was Byrd's estimation of the situation. "Both political parties," he surmised, "are willing to mis-use the South in any way they see fit in order to try to gain a few voters in the Northern States. I think we have got to fight back in every way we can." Once again, Harry Byrd became the focus of regional disaffection within the party.[28]

The senator came out swinging at the Jefferson-Jackson Day dinner at the Hotel John Marshall in Richmond on February 19. Byrd was present to introduce the main speaker, Senator Clyde Hoey of North Carolina, but he turned his remarks into a tirade against a "mass invasion of states rights never before even suggested . . . by any previous President of any party affiliation in the nation's history." Itemizing Truman's proposals, he condemned the coercive nature of the FEPC, defended Virginia's antilynching record, and compared federal interference with election laws to the dictatorships of Hitler and Stalin. He forecast an invasion of the South by a host of federal officials who would strike down all segregation laws. Faced with possible loss of federal funds if the states did not remove such laws, Virginia, he said, should "lead the Southern States in renouncing for all time every dollar of Federal aid. We must not sell our right of self-government for a mess of Federal pottage." Having aroused his audience to resistance, Byrd then closed with a call for calm deliberation and a remarkable plea for racial progress:

> As Governor of Virginia, and as a Senator from Virginia, not one word has ever passed my lips which could be used to enflame any prejudice between the races. I deplore such action on the part of any public man! As Governor, and as Senator, my office door has always been open to every citizen of Virginia, regardless of race, creed or color. As a public official, I have never failed to do all within my power to advance the proper interests of the Negro citizens of Virginia. . . . I have seen, with gratification and approval, the steady improvement in the economic condition of the Negroes of Virginia

and throughout the South. I want to see this progress continue. . . . Our racial problems—and I admit there are many—must be worked out by constitutional methods and by the calm and considered action of the leaders of both races.[29]

Byrd did not recommend any immediate action by the South, but within days President Truman had Harry Byrd's answer. On February 26, amid an overflowing gallery in Virginia's House of Delegates, Governor William Tuck urged the General Assembly to pass legislation that would avoid placing the names of presidential candidates on the ballot; this would permit voters to vote only for presidential electors under the name of their party. The state party, either through its central committee or in convention, could instruct the electors to vote for a candidate other than the national party candidate if it so decided. Since this might permit the Virginia Democratic party to instruct for someone other than President Truman, the law became known as the "anti-Truman" bill. Furthermore, only those parties that had appeared on the ballot in 1944 or had received more than 10 percent of the vote in the last five years could be represented on the ballot, a tactic clearly aimed at eliminating Henry Wallace's Progressive party from consideration. Commending Tuck's "notable message," Harry Byrd viewed his suggestions as a mechanism designed to protect Virginia and states' rights. He inserted Tuck's message in the *Congressional Record* and had ten thousand copies of it reproduced.[30]

It is likely that the senator originated the idea and orchestrated its presentation, notwithstanding Bill Tuck's claim that the bill was his own handiwork.[31] Five days before Tuck's action, Byrd instructed Ebbie Combs that the legislation "should provide clearly that the names of the candidates are not to be printed on the ticket. . . . The main purpose is to get the names of the candidates off of the ballot." He had learned of the mechanism of instructed electors during the 1944 presidential campaign when that ploy had been pursued by his supporters in other states.[32] He and Tuck were in close communication on the matter before the announcement, and almost immediately after the message was read, identical bills implementing the proposals were introduced by Organization stalwart E. Blackburn Moore in the house and recently elected Harry Byrd, Jr., in the senate. Harry Jr. later remarked that this was the only time he ever signed a bill without reading it.[33] Clearly, Senator Byrd was intimately involved in attempting to blackmail the national party into rejecting President Truman's renomination or at least watering down the civil rights platform by threatening to withhold Virginia's support from the party. It constituted nothing less than a brazen attempt to deny Virginians an opportunity to cast their ballots for whomever they pleased.[34]

Although most of the Organization leaders in the General Assembly dutifully endorsed the proposal, opposition was immediate and vociferous, even among other party notables. State chairman Horace Edwards raised doubts about the legitimacy of the plan, and Second District representative Porter Hardy questioned its wisdom, noting the danger in giving a few party officials the right to cast Virginia's ballot. Reporting dissatisfaction in Norfolk, Billy Prieur remonstrated that the bill would do "irreparable harm . . . to the Democratic Party in Virginia and inestimable damage to the State organization." Newspapers across the Old Dominion likewise excoriated the idea; the *Times-Dispatch* called it "dangerous and undemocratic"; the Newport News *Times-Herald* said the bill did "violence" to democracy; and Douglas Southall Freeman in the *News Leader* concluded, "No more undemocratic proposal ever was advanced responsibly in the General Assembly of Virginia." Predictably, Virginia Republicans were quick to condemn it, while the "antis," rejuvenated by what they considered an outrageous act of despotism, began planning an independent state convention.[35]

Surprised by the extent and vehemence of the opposition, the leadership offered modifications the next day whereby parties on the ballot in at least ten other states could appear on the Virginia ballot, while only a reconvened state convention, not the state committee, could decide if the electors were to be instructed.[36] Still the clamor did not die down. When Martin Hutchinson threatened to send a rival delegation of "real Democrats" to the national convention, apprehensive Organization leaders met for a final strategy session at the governor's mansion on March 6. As Fred Switzer reported to Willis Robertson, Byrd went "to bat with the Governor on this bill and is backing him in every respect." Although the hierarchy did approve another amended version of the bill to permit candidates' names to appear on the ballot and to allow any party to get on the ballot by obtaining one thousand voters' signatures, it still gave the state convention the authority to instruct electors if it did so sixty days before the election. In a letter to Senator Fulbright, Byrd frankly explained that the bill "permits the State Convention of the Democratic Party to select its own Democratic candidate and, if Mr. Truman is a candidate, or someone else on the National ticket whom the State Convention of Virginia does not approve, then the electors of such a candidate can be placed on the ballot only by petition and will not be regarded as the candidate of the official Democratic Party of Virginia."[37]

Committed to the substitute election bill, the leadership pressured the assembly to approve it. In its final form the law tolerated a wide array of candidates, but it left open the possibility that Virginia voters might be denied a full expression of their choice by party leaders. As criticism of the bill continued, notably among members of the Organization, Byrd and Tuck conducted a "campaign of enlightenment" to combat the "deliberate misrepresentations" of the press. As part of this effort, the House of Delegates passed a resolution that called for an SCC investigation of the Richmond newspapers for their "iniquitous editorials." Nothing came of this, but such a blatant assault on a free press revealed a bumbling, antiquated machine relying on old-time political head-bashing to preserve its authority. The "anti-Truman" bill was the first of several missteps that the Organization made in the next decade that would lead to its eventual demise.[38]

As events proceeded in Richmond, Byrd moved quickly to carry his fight against Truman and his civil rights program to the national level. Copies of Tuck's speech and the resolution of the state committee condemning Truman's program were distributed nationwide. Southern senators, convening in Byrd's office on March 5, vowed to fight any civil rights legislation and asked the president to withdraw from the race. Undeterred, Truman announced his candidacy three days later.

From the beginning Byrd believed that Truman would drop out in the face of almost certain defeat. Representing Governor Tuck at a conference of Dixie governors, he spoke of a potential schism at the national convention, implying that Truman could not win without southern support. Enthusiastically, he encouraged friends in the region to pledge their opposition to the president. Gratified by evidence of widespread disaffection, he predicted to Tuck: "The action taken by the Alabama candidates for electors is conclusive in that it shows Mr. Truman cannot possibly be elected. In my opinion he will seek an opportunity to withdraw between now and the Convention." Proudly, he told Ebbie Combs that Virginia deserved much of the credit for this outcome. So sure was he of Truman's unpopularity that he did not think the president could carry Virginia with or without a third party, the likelihood of which now loomed larger. Dissident southern Democrats, meeting in Jackson, Mississippi, in May, took no action but left open the possibility of reconvening after the national convention if the platform or candidate proved unacceptable to them.[39]

Byrd, who was not at the Jackson meeting, was widely regarded as a possible nominee of any new southern party. He had maintained a correspondence with John Barr, his "campaign director" in 1944, who, along with others, was again urging him to run for the presidency. But Byrd had had enough of presidential politics. He wrote Bill Tuck: "I greatly appreciate the compliment you pay me with respect to being a candidate of the Southern States, but, frankly, under no conditions could I consider this. I have been approached by the leaders in three or four of the Southern States and told them this. . . . What you say gratifies me tremendously, as do the letters I am receiving from over the country." To Frank Wysor, Byrd indicated that he did not want his name presented at the national convention. He had no chance of winning and no desire to run; twice had been enough.[40]

Despite the objections of the southern renegades, it appeared that Truman would be nominated by default. No other Democrat had emerged to challenge him within the party, and he had begun traveling around the country preparing the ground for his eventual "give 'em hell" attack on the GOP. Aware that the "stop-Truman" effort had faltered, Byrd moved to consolidate Organization forces preparatory to the governor's race in 1949. Since a tough contest with the "antis" appeared likely, the risk of irreparably splitting state Democrats by bolting the national party was inadvisable. On June 4 at the governor's mansion, Tuck, Byrd, Combs, and Burch decided not to desert the party at the national convention or in the November election. They agreed that the state convention would instruct against Truman and empower the state committee to call it back into session if necessary—in accordance with the procedures outlined in the "anti-Truman" bill—but these were essentially face-saving measures.[41]

The state convention in Richmond in early July was a memorable event that reflected the decline of Organization fortunes brought on by the imprudent "anti-Truman" bill. The night before the meeting, in Byrd's hotel room, Bill Tuck and Willis Robertson hotly debated Tuck's proposal for a states' rights convention, an argument that the senior senator finally settled by rejecting the divisive resolution.[42] Even so, from the opening gavel, when state chairman Horace Edwards spoke against party dissension and keynoter W. Tayloe Murphy attacked the Truman administration, there was tension between the moderates, who sought compromise, and the zealous defenders of southern rights, who breathed defiance. Unaccustomed to such squabbling among his political lieutenants, Byrd was unsure of whom to recommend to the convention as the party's nominee. According to Harry Jr., he and his father circled the block outside the Mosque four or five times discussing the possibilities. When the senator suggested General Eisenhower, young Harry inquired whether he was a Republican or a Democrat. "I don't know what he is," said Byrd, "but he's a very popular man."[43]

As the convention drew to a close, Tuck presented the report of the resolutions committee that endorsed states' rights, condemned the civil rights program, instructed Virginia's delegates to the national convention to support Eisenhower, and allowed for the recall of the state convention by a two-thirds vote of the state committee if the proceedings of the national convention were unsatisfactory. G. Alvin Massenburg, permanent chairman of the convention and the new state chairman, asked for a voice vote on the resolutions. Receiving what appeared to observers to be an equally mixed number of ayes and nays, he ruled the adoption of the report and refused a demand for a roll call. Amid cheers, boos, and walkouts, the convention adjourned. Coming on the heels of the "anti-Truman" bill, the high-handed tactics of the convention reinforced the public perception of a machine running roughshod over its members and invigorated the efforts of the "antis" to challenge the Organization. The Richmond *News Leader* commented that the machine had not been in worse shape since Jim Price's candidacy. Even insider Billy Prieur said as much when he chided Byrd for having lost contact with the people whose support he needed. To make matters worse, General Eisenhower emphatically reiterated his decision not to accept a draft a few days later.[44]

The 1948 national convention in Philadelphia was not an enjoyable experience for Harry Byrd or for many Democrats. Having failed to find an alternative to Truman, they faced the bleak prospect of contesting a confident Republican party with an unpopular incumbent who presided over a divided party. James Latimer reported that the delegates looked like pallbearers at a funeral. After a bitter struggle over the civil rights plank that concluded with an endorsement of Truman's program by a vote of 651.5 to 582.5, delegates from Alabama and Mississippi walked out of the convention hall. Those remaining then proceeded to renominate the president. Byrd summed up the convention as "a terrible experience." Comparing it to the 1928 conclave that had selected Al Smith, he said that back then they could at least "make an honorable fight for Smith, because we believed in most of the things for which he stood." Governor Tuck concluded that they had been "soundly thrashed on every issue in the convention."[45]

Two days after the convention ended, southern dissidents, many of them holdovers from the 1944 revolt, met in Birmingham, Alabama, amid a bevy of Confederate flags to create a National States Rights party and nominate Governor Strom Thurmond of South Carolina for president. Angered at the loss of southern influence in the Democratic party and upset with federal intrusion into state affairs, the "Dixiecrats" hoped to unite the South behind Thurmond and throw the election into the House of Representatives where they might bargain with both parties on the choice of the next president and the elimination of civil rights legislation. Congressman Albert Gore of Tennessee referred to them as the "old Bourbon leaders of the South who believed that by 'hollering nigger' and waving the flag they could once more control the Southern states."[46]

The emergence of a southern party threw Organization leaders, who had chosen not to attend the Birmingham gathering, into a quandary. They desperately wanted to defeat Truman, but a public defection from the Democratic party posed substantial risks. It would threaten the fall campaigns of Senator Robertson and seven Old Dominion congressmen who had Republican opposition, but more importantly, it risked the race for governor the following year. The "antis" traditionally began each contest with a solid third of the electorate in their column; increasing political participation by blacks and labor would add to their numbers; moreover, loyal Democrats, already angered by the "anti-Truman" bill and the "cooked" resolutions at the state convention, might choose to join them if the national party was so cavalierly rejected for a third-party fling. On the other hand, support for Truman, no matter how grudging, would alienate states' rights advocates, possibly causing them to refrain from voting for Organization candidates. While Governor Tuck was inclined to join the Dixiecrats, Senator Byrd opted for a middle course which he hoped would defeat Truman and still leave the Organization forces intact: a "golden silence." By not committing to a candidate, he would put no pressure on his followers to support either Truman or Thurmond, but his silence would imply a rejection of the president and encourage those so inclined to vote for the Dixiecrats. With an inactive state committee, Democratic chances of carrying the state would be greatly diminished, and either Republican Tom Dewey or Thurmond could win Virginia, thus delivering a devastating blow to Truman. In addition to the political calculus involved, Byrd also had a personal reason for not switching parties. Having spent a lifetime as a Democrat, he could not leave the party of his father. He had spoken forcefully on earlier occasions of the need for party loyalty, and regardless of the findings of the attorneys general, the defection of the party's leader would be an obvious sign of disloyalty that might encourage others to rebel.

Byrd's predicament was reflected among his advisers. Tuck and Lieutenant Governor L. Preston Collins preferred to go with the southern ticket. Tuck even suggested switching the electors chosen at the state convention to the Dixiecrat ticket, which would leave Truman without any electors in Virginia, but Byrd rejected this maneuver which undoubtedly would have raised another firestorm in the newspapers. On the other hand, congressional candidates up for reelection, such as Robertson and Smith, felt compelled to back the president, believing that party unity was essential to their chances. Byrd was upset with the enthusiasm of their support, but he appreciated their dilemma. Facing such conflicting advice, he chose to follow his instincts as well as the suggestion of the reliable Ebbie Combs, who urged him and other leaders to "try to get through this campaign somewhat as we did in 1944," that is, by remaining publicly uncommitted.[47]

The passing of the sixty-day deadline for the recall of the state convention indicated the decision of the Organization hierarchy: Democratic electors were henceforth bound to Truman, and there would be no other Democratic ticket. At a brief meeting of the state committee in late September, the party pledged to get out a full Democratic vote but made no endorsement in the presidential race. Clearly the Virginia Democratic party was having nothing to do with the national party. In the absence of a Truman campaign in the state, it seemed possible that Virginia would go for Thurmond or Dewey.[48]

But Byrd had not counted on the "antis." Martin Hutchinson had predicted this "sit-down strike" by the Organization and urged his colleagues to organize for Truman if the regulars did not. Angered by the capricious and dictatorial methods of party leaders throughout the year and not unmindful that their loyalty might be rewarded with national support in the future, they organized a Straight Democratic Ticket Committee to back the president. Their leaders included Hutchinson, Francis Pickens Miller, and state senators Robert Whitehead and Lloyd Robinette. They were aided by a small group of Organization Democrats in Richmond whose speakers included Attorney General Lindsay Almond and Third District representative J. Vaughan Gary.[49]

Throughout the campaign Byrd maintained his silence. The only public display of his preference was Mrs. Byrd's attendance at a banquet for Strom Thurmond in Richmond. Governor Tuck declined to make a public pronouncement, but he gave Thurmond a rousing introduction when he appeared at the Richmond fairgrounds. A number of well-known Democrats publicly endorsed the Dixiecrat, while most of the Democrats running for office generally aligned themselves with Truman. Attorney General Almond offered a colorful defense for loyalty when he hyperbolized: "The only sane and constructive course to follow is to remain in the house of our fathers—even though the roof leaks and there may be bats in the belfry, rats in the pantry, a cockroach waltz in the kitchen, and skunks in the parlor. . . . We cannot take our inheritance and depart into a far country."[50]

Compared to what was going on nationally, the campaign in the Old Dominion was a tame affair. Shortly after the convention, President Truman had called Congress back into session and presented it with requests for civil rights legislation, price controls, public housing, and increases in social security and the minimum wage. Stonewalled at every turn, he undertook a 30,000-mile, 351-whistle-stop tour of the country, lambasting the Republicans and the "do-nothing" Eightieth Congress. Appealing to a variety of interest groups, he called for repeal of the Taft-Hartley Act, passage of his civil rights program, and an expansion of federal programs that included national health insurance, aid to education, higher price supports for farmers, and more social security benefits. It was enough to gag Harry Byrd. On the advice of the "antis," Truman did not venture into Virginia with his liberal crusade. Neither did Tom Dewey who, confident of victory, ran a very low-key campaign.

Despite all the polls predicting a GOP triumph—even in Virginia— Truman won a smashing upset: 303 to 189 in the electoral college and 49.6 percent to 45.1 percent in the popular vote. Peace, prosperity, and interest group politics won the day. Thurmond and Wallace ran far behind, although the Dixiecrat did win four Deep South states with 39 electoral votes, a result far short of his goal of a united South. There were rumors right after the election that states' rights Democrats, led by senators Byrd and George, were going to obstruct Truman's victory by having electors withhold their votes unless he capitulated on civil rights, but Byrd said that he would have no part of such a plan that violated "honor and good faith."

Surprisingly, Truman's margin of victory in Virginia was even greater: 48 percent to 41 percent for Dewey and 10 percent for Thurmond.[51] Senator Robertson and the other Democratic congressmen also won handily. Traditional party loyalty and the hard work of the Straight Ticket people were largely responsible for these results, but the "antis" exaggerated the extent of their victory over the Organization. Forecasting a new day in Virginia politics, Francis Pickens Miller predicted that leadership of the Democratic party in Virginia was within their grasp, but his hope that this would translate into patronage and financial support from the national party was never fulfilled.[52]

The election of 1948 in state and region and nation was highly significant. It further liberalized the Democratic party, opening doors long closed to black Americans; it began the realignment of politics in the South that would end the long run of one-party rule and restore the region's importance in presidential elections; and it initiated the era of "massive resistance" in which race came to dominate southern elections. In Virginia, Truman's success in the face of machine opposition was a major blow to Byrd's prestige and an encouragement to his opponents, but it did not mortally wound the Organization. It did, however, accelerate its shift away from the national party; more "golden silences" were in the offing. The senator claimed that he had no regrets, telling Tuck, "Everything we did was a choice of evils." Lulled into complacency by the easy gubernatorial victories of the early forties and the absence of any political competition, Organization leaders had arrogantly tried to impose their wishes on a changing electorate. Shocked into reality by the consequences of their own blunders, they prepared for upcoming contests with renewed vigor. It had been a bad year, but the Organization had recovered from such reverses before.[53]

~ 14 ~

A Changing Virginia

A S IN THE world and nation, World War II also produced significant economic and social changes in Virginia. Federal income payments in the Old Dominion rose from $122 million in 1939 to $902 million in 1945, a sum which constituted 30 percent of all the money Virginians were earning; as a result, per capita income rose almost 150 percent. The war proved to be a particular boon to shipbuilding and production of chemicals, clothing, furniture, and tobacco in the state. Population explosions occurred in the Norfolk and northern Virginia areas, leading to overcrowding, deterioration of roads, and inadequate public services. While organized labor and blacks improved their situations, their gains produced increased tensions that would play out in the postwar years. Now less rural, more crowded, and wealthier, the Old Dominion would have to adjust to these changes, but the conservatism of the state's political and social systems ensured a delayed response.[1]

During World War II, Senator Byrd had paid less attention to what was happening in Richmond than at any time since his election to the state senate in 1915. Wartime issues, lengthier congressional sessions, and national politics had absorbed his interest. His letters to Virginia friends about state affairs were briefer and less substantive. Fortunately, he could afford to be preoccupied elsewhere. Political opposition in the state had been effectively quieted by the defeat of Governor Price's legislative program in the 1940 General Assembly and the loss of New Deal patronage. With attention focused on events abroad, political debate, at least at the state level, was set aside for the sake of national unity. Even Byrd's attacks on federal spending did him no harm with his constituents; party chairman Horace Edwards told him his popularity was "at its highest peak since 1933."[2]

The Organization had secured ascendancy once again, but the selection of a new governor in 1941 was important in maintaining that control and minimizing factional squabbles. The process by which Harry Byrd selected governors—"giving the nod" as it was called—was complex but orderly. It was not dictatorial, impulsive, or isolated. Prospects with recognized records of service to the Commonwealth often visited the senator in Washington; their names, along with those of other possibilities, were floated before the "courthouse crowd," whose sentiments carried great weight because their enthusiasm for the nominee would be crucial in the primary. Information and advice were exchanged. Considerable attention was also given to the opinions of influential state legislators and close advisers such as Combs, Wysor, and Prieur. Demanding integrity, loyalty, and electability in his candidates, Byrd gave consideration to longevity of service and place of residence. Within the bounds of fiscal conservatism, he accepted persons who had demonstrated streaks of independence but were the men most likely to unite the party and win elections. "Success in politics," he reportedly said, "is the candidate—don't ever try to carry a dead horse."[3] Usually through this weeding-out process, one candidate emerged as the obvious choice. Though the final decision was likely made by consensus, Byrd's opinion counted more than all the others combined, despite his consistent denial that he exercised such power. Writing to Hunsdon Cary, who had inquired of his position on the candidates in 1940, the senator responded: "I have never desired to hand-pick a Governor. . . . The selection must be made by the people themselves. . . . I can assure you that I am not a party and will not be a party to any movement that will attempt to prevent those who desire to be a candidate for Governor from doing so." But Benjamin Muse was closer to the truth when he declared, with only slight exaggeration, that "Governors of Virginia are appointed by Harry Byrd, subject to confirmation by the electorate. . . . He ruled not with a command but with a nod." It was not without justification that the Organization was frequently labeled the Byrd machine.[4]

In 1940 the two leading contenders for Byrd's nod were Bill Tuck and Colgate Darden. Tuck was the front-runner because of his impeccable Organization credentials, his strong support from the Southside, and his friendship with Byrd. But the affable, earthy legislator had an unpolished manner about him that may have worried the more genteel Byrd. More importantly, Tuck's partisanship in the struggles against Price had alienated moderates and "antis" whom Byrd was trying to win back to the Organization. This favored the tall and handsome Darden, who had recaptured the Second District seat from Norman Hamilton in 1938 and had been uninvolved in assembly politics. His support of Ninth District renegade John Flannagan's reelection bid as well as Roosevelt's third-term effort won the praise of anti-Byrd elements. His wealth—he had married into the Du Pont family—his heroic World War I record, and his current service on a naval affairs subcommittee were attractive attributes for the times. Finally, his triumph over Hamilton, a bitter foe of Byrd's, deserved to be rewarded. As Ernest Smith, a local official from Grundy, put it to Combs, Darden was a "bigger man" than Tuck.[5]

The decision to support Darden apparently was made sometime during the fall. There was no formal anointment. Darden recalled that when Ebbie Combs started helping him, he "knew mighty well he wasn't helping me without Harry's approval."[6] Without any direct communication, Tuck knew that he had lost. After a meeting with Byrd in early November, he remembered that the senator seemed "cold as an iceberg. I could see that he preferred Darden." Lack of support from close friends also discouraged him, and he told Combs that he was retiring from the race. "The Chief" asked him to delay his announcement to preclude further challenges to Darden, but he also suggested that Tuck run for lieutenant governor, which would create a true Organization ticket. After some deliberation Tuck announced for lieutenant governor on December 14, and a week later Darden formally declared. Thereafter, Byrd's only problem was refuting the stories that he, as the leader of a powerful machine, had handpicked the candidates.[7]

Darden won a handsome primary victory on August 5, 1941 against two antimachine candidates. Although an appendectomy limited his campaigning, he repeated his success in the November election, handily defeating Republican Benjamin Muse, who was running only to preserve the semblance of a two-party system in Virginia. As they had done so often before, Byrd and Combs advised the governor-elect on several important appointments and attempted to manipulate some votes for important assembly positions to ensure that the governor's legislative efforts would prevail. Aided by the war and the weakness of the "antis," who lacked money, candidates, and issues, Byrd's control of Virginia politics would never be more secure than it was during Darden's governorship.[8]

It was this political security in Virginia that permitted Byrd to be the independent senator that he became over the next twenty years, free to speak his own mind, to make no deals, to challenge the president on any issue, and to flout his own party and its candidates. Texas congressman Sam Rayburn aptly analyzed Byrd's independence: "The only man up here that I know of that is in the unique position where he can be effective both on a state level and a national level is Harry Byrd of Virginia. He runs Virginia. He can do what he pleases here or there, but the rest of us have to look at our congressional district or our state as a base of operation in order to perform on a national level." Once when Harry vetoed a veterans pension bill, brother Richard inquired, "How in the name of heaven you can do so many unpopular things and still keep the people of Virginia with you I don't understand."[9]

What the admiral did not appreciate was Byrd's protected position in the Old Dominion. Single-party politics, a small and apathetic electorate, and a powerful machine that imposed its will on the state required no accountability from him. He was beholden only to his own conscience. This risk-free environment made Byrd a predictable commodity, a politician without grandiose ambitions, deceptive rhetoric, or secret machinations—a delightfully unique officeholder in many respects but one whose uncompromising attitude and limited vision curtailed his influence. And without competition he was not challenged to think anew, to be a problem solver. Furthermore, his indifference toward the legislative process—how bills are created, won, and lost—meant his name would never be associated with any significant legislation. But as a gadfly, provoking colleagues and executive branch officials alike, he had few peers.

Byrd was so indifferent to Washington politicking that he made no effort to enforce discipline among the Virginia congressional delegation. He wrote Douglas Freeman in 1947 that never in fourteen years had he asked members of the Virginia delegation to vote for or against legislation. Certainly their agreement with Byrd's philosophy and voting record made such requests unnecessary, but even when they did disagree, especially on foreign policy questions, he tolerated that dissent because he, too, was something of a maverick on many issues. These colleagues often sought Byrd's guidance in their early years in Congress, but in time they felt free to vote their preferences. Byrd was content to be the autonomous senator from Virginia, and Virginians were satisfied with that as well.[10]

Such independence was permissible when the state government was in friendly hands, as it was during the war years with Colgate Darden as governor. The crisis atmosphere enabled Darden to push through the General Assembly many of the things Jim Price had requested—a Board of Corrections and a Pardon and Parole Board to upgrade Virginia's penal system, a Department of Hygiene and Hospitals, abolition of the fee system for sheriffs, redistricting of the state, increased teachers' salaries, and expanded workmen's compensation. The *Times-Dispatch* called it the most productive legislative session since Byrd's governorship.

Darden proved to be an unusually capable person whose personal stature and bearing exuded confidence in a time of anxiety. The governor was a political moderate who could accommodate different factions while addressing pressing needs in education and penal reform. Byrd was comfortable with his selection of Darden. To a friend he wrote: "I shall be very glad at all times to give my advice but will not attempt to influence him in any acts that he might undertake. So far as I am concerned, believing so firmly, as I do, in the capacity of Colgate, I shall say frankly to you that any action he may take in this or any other matter will be acceptable to me and received without any complaint."[11] Nevertheless, Byrd did not hesitate to offer his advice on appointments and policies, particularly the protection of the $12 million surplus in the state treasury, much of it from taxes on liquor sales. "Don't let the spenders appropriate it for current expenditures," he wrote. "No one can tell in these perilous days what will happen." For Harry Byrd, the times were always perilous when it came to spending money. Obediently, Darden agreed to hold the surplus for future contingencies. Byrd applauded the governor's handling of his first legislative session, and although they met with some frequency thereafter, he made few suggestions.[12]

One of the reasons Byrd could feel so comfortable with Darden was knowing that Ebbie Combs was on the scene in Richmond. Restored to his position on the State Compensation Board, Combs boasted that no Price employee would be left after his term expired. Ever the affable, courteous southern gentleman, Combs did not present the image of a political gamesman, but he was an aggressive, iron-willed operative who was devoted to Byrd. The senator once wrote him, "The greatest thing in life is such a friendship as that which exists between you and me;" and Combs had responded that their "unfailing friendship" had meant more to him than anything else in his career.[13] Adviser, dispenser of patronage, and troubleshooter in his two positions as chairman of the Compensation Board and clerk of the state senate, Combs was the nerve center of the Organization, maintaining contacts with local officeholders, assembly members, and the leadership. In almost daily communication with the senator when the legislature was in session, Combs kept him apprised of what was happening in Richmond, especially when Byrd was needed for a conference or for some arm-twisting on a vote. Although the deferential Combs always recognized who the senior partner was, his influence in shaping Byrd's views and determining appointments was incalculable. He was, according to his biographer, the "indispensable" man for Byrd's continued dominance of the Organization.[14]

Another friend who was growing increasingly influential in the Byrd entourage was E. Blackburn ("Blackie") Moore, his neighbor and fellow apple grower from Berryville. A member of the House of Delegates since 1933, he had been largely responsible for disrupting Price's program in the 1940 assembly. As reporter James Latimer observed, "Moore and Byrd think alike politically and economically; if anything, Moore may be a little bit to the right of Byrd. . . . Almost invariably Moore reflects Byrd's views—though they are also Moore's—on state legislative issues." A reserved, good-looking man of medium height, Moore, who would become Speaker of the House in 1950, was described by Gi Stephens as "being able to walk through dried leaves up to his knees and never make a sound." His power was in his position, not his rhetoric.[15]

Two other close confidants who had joined the inner circle were Frank Wysor, treasurer of Pulaski County, and Billy Prieur, clerk of the corporation court in Norfolk. Wysor, who had replaced Combs as the voice of the Ninth District, was a modest, laconic hunting companion of the senator. They exchanged frequent letters about dogs and birds, poll taxes and candidates.

Prieur, coming from the more liberal Second District, was a brash, outspoken politician who could be counted on to give an independent assessment of conditions there.[16]

The machine that Byrd had assumed command of twenty years before and molded into his own fiefdom was running as flawlessly as ever. Not so close to the day-to-day operations as he once was, Byrd ruled from afar, relying on the telephone and advisers Combs and Menefee for passing on advice and information. He would meet periodically with members of the inner circle to discuss strategy and candidates for an upcoming election or an agenda for a legislative session. Listening carefully to the opinions of his colleagues, he did not impose his views on them, but there was never a doubt about who was in charge. Colgate Darden summed up the keys to Byrd's success as the leader of the Organization: "Nobody in the world ever loved politics like Harry loved politics. He just lived on it. He loved the organizing, loved working on it. . . . He'd work at it morning, noon, and night. Harry would talk to you about doing something in the middle of the day and he'd call you by supper and want to know if you'd gotten it done. He was indefatigable. . . . He was a tremendously able administrator. But he was one who took into account what the Organization as a whole wanted." It did not hurt that there was near unanimity among Organization leaders concerning what policies would be good for Virginia: low taxes, frugal and honest government, and local autonomy. Their power continued to rest on a controllable electorate, the loyalty of the "courthouse ring"—which functioned beautifully as an intelligence network and electoral machine—and the patronage that maintained that loyalty. With good reason the Organization was once labeled "The Great Virginia Officeholders Mutual Protection Agency."[17]

With things functioning so smoothly during Darden's administration, Byrd's next political "crisis" was the selection of a gubernatorial candidate for the 1945 election. Congressional sessions, the 1944 presidential election, and the poll tax issue had combined to put off consideration of candidates, and this time the delay and his own indecision presented him with a fait accompli, albeit an acceptable one. The two most likely contestants were Tom Stanley and Bill Tuck, both of whom were friendly with the senator but neither of whom had his complete confidence. Speaker of the House of Delegates, Stanley was a wealthy furniture manufacturer from Henry County who had money and a friendly disposition but lacked spark. Lieutenant Governor Tuck, on the other hand, did not want for a colorful personality. A rotund, Rabelaisian country boy from Halifax County, Tuck had a reputation for fast talk and hard drinking that offended Byrd's image of what a Virginia governor should be: quiet, courtly, and deferential. Both Stanley and Tuck persistently lobbied Byrd for the nod and both seemed to have strong support across the state, which made the decision difficult. As Byrd told Richard Stokes, it was hard to be the arbiter between two friends.

Worried that any delay would work to the advantage of his adversaries, Tuck chose to announce his candidacy informally in early February. In the midst of ascertaining the sentiments of Organization leaders, Byrd was upset that Tuck had preempted his decision with a "premature announcement" that threatened to split their ranks before the leadership had spoken. However, by this time Tuck commanded most of the Organization loyalists, including Governor Darden, who in a March conference convinced Byrd to give his reluctant blessing to the lieutenant governor. A longtime associate once said that Byrd "never bought a ticket before the train was ready to leave the station," but on this occasion he had to run to catch it. He later regretted having doubted Tuck's capacity for state leadership, for their friendship deepened in the years ahead as Tuck became the most outspoken front man for Byrd's policies.[18]

Tuck won an easy primary victory over "anti" Moss Plunkett, but the race for the lieutenant governorship produced a scandal that marred the Organization's self-proclaimed record of honest government in the Old Dominion. That record had never been as clean as the Organization wanted voters to believe. Dating all the way back to Tom Martin's payments to legislators, there had been numerous violations of electoral laws—notably the block payments of poll taxes and misuse of absentee ballots—along with many examples of minor official malfeasance, a shortage of funds in local treasuries being the most common. The Ninth District was particularly vulnerable to scandal due to intense competition between Democrats and Republicans. Ed Hargis once told Combs, "You couldn't elect a Democrat west of the Blue Ridge without the absent vote."[19]

In the 1945 primary contest for lieutenant governor, Byrd refrained from selecting a candidate among L. Preston Collins of Marion, Charles Fenwick of Arlington—both members of the Organization—and "anti" Leonard Muse of Roanoke. Byrd conferred with Collins and Fenwick, but neither one withdrew. Many friends pleaded with him to anoint one of the two to avoid splitting the Organization vote and giving the position to Muse, but Byrd refused to make public his decision, which forced members of the machine to make their own choice.[20] The result was a close primary won by Fenwick with some very unusual voting patterns. Wise County went for Fenwick, 3,307 to 122; Appomattox County backed Collins by an equally suspicious margin, 1,610 to 25. Collins challenged the vote in Wise, and when the county clerk announced that the polling books had been stolen, Richmond judge Julien Gunn threw out the Wise figures and declared Collins the victor. Fenwick accepted the decision without pursuing a broader inquiry into all returns.[21] Virginians were aghast at such chicanery, and all officials, including an indignant Harry Byrd, publicly clamored for a full-scale investigation of the fraud. The senator urged both Governor Darden and Ebbie Combs to use the full resources of the state to get to the bottom of the problem. However, he did caution Darden not to allow federal officials into the investigation. Although Byrd demanded punishment of the guilty (no indictments were ever handed down) and suggested a review of the election laws, election irregularities did not cease in the Old Dominion.[22]

The immediate concern was the extent to which Republicans could exploit the Wise scandal to their advantage against Tuck. They made every effort to implicate the Democratic nominee but were not successful since Tuck had nothing to do with what happened in Wise; besides, their own record in Southwest Virginia was not without irregularities. Worried that "a lie told often enough is usually believed," Byrd instructed Tuck to campaign aggressively against the charges by promising to strengthen and enforce the election laws to prevent future fraud. He need not have bothered, for not even the whiff of scandal could overcome the power of the Organization. Tuck won handily by a two-to-one margin and immediately received advice from his mentor on appointments and the need for frugality in government. Alarmed that current expenditures were two-and-a-half times those in his 1929 budget, Byrd warned Tuck to stay within his budget. "There is quite an evolution in progress in all public matters," he wrote. "People are restless and complaining and I think will continue to do so for sometime to come."[23]

A more significant impact of the scandal was the renewed interest in changing the election laws, specifically repealing the poll tax. Virginia was one of only eight states still using the poll tax as a weapon to restrict black voting and keep the electorate small. Despite a concerted effort by the "antis" and leading editorial opinion in the state, the Organization had been powerful enough to spurn these overtures on several occasions. Byrd and others insisted that the tax was a necessary source of income for schools that could not easily be replaced, but they could not adequately explain why it had to be tied to voting. Their intention was clear. The poll tax was an electoral mechanism that obstructed the mobilization of poor voters who would likely oppose Organization economic and social policies. Byrd cited the repeal movement as an effort to "New-Dealize our State Government." Only a "motley group of Republicans, Negroes, CIOs, Communists, ardent New dealers, and 'antis'" were for it, he sarcastically told Frank Wysor.[24]

But the desires of Byrd and the Organization to preserve a restricted electorate were running counter to the democratic spirit ignited by the war. Such a mood was invading even their own ranks. Favoring liberalization of the servicemen's vote and eventual action on the poll tax, state senator Ed Breeden of Norfolk wrote to Governor Darden: "The Democratic Organization could stand a little leavening of progressiveness. In my short experience in the legislature, I have seen all too many measures resisted only to be eventually accepted, though often with poor grace." Byrd was aware of the growing pressure on public officials to support repeal, but he refused to concede the poll tax unless it could be replaced with something equally restrictive.[25]

Such pressure increased with the revelations of fraud in Wise County and the publicity given the extremely low voter participation in Virginia. North Carolinian Jonathan Daniels ridiculed the Old Dominion as "the birthplace and grave of democracy." In an article entitled "Carry Me Back to Dear Ole Bulgaria," he scathingly indicted political bossism and the block payment of poll taxes. Virginia might be getting efficient government, he said, "but trains have run on time where democracy has died." Indeed, Virginia ranked forty-third in the nation in the percentage of its adult population voting in the 1940 election: 22 percent. From 1920 to 1946 an average of 12 percent of the eligible voters participated in Democratic gubernatorial primaries, the lowest percentage in the nation. Worse than that were the percentages voting for governor in the general elections: 1937, 9.5 percent; 1941, 7.8 percent; and 1945, 9.4 percent.[26]

Such criticism struck a raw nerve in the Organization, which was searching for some replacement for the poll tax without giving up a limited suffrage. Frank Wysor, Billy Prieur, and Governor Darden had already discussed the possibility of replacing it with a new suffrage plan that would enlarge the electorate but erect enough obstacles to prevent universal suffrage. Having been appointed to a new commission to study the question, Wysor warned of the consequences: "To liberalize further will . . . be about equal to 'Unconditional Surrender' to the forces which have opposed the democratic party and the democratic organization for forty years." Both Byrd and Darden worried about the effect that repeal would have on the black vote. Nevertheless, the commission recommended abolition of the tax as a requirement for voting, replacing it with an annual registration procedure and a literacy test. Wysor told Watt Abbitt, "The provisions . . . will cause the voters little inconvenience, especially to the type of people in whom we are most interested." The changes passed the General Assembly with strong backing from Organization leaders, but the Campbell amendments were so complicated and so patently undemocratic that voters overwhelmingly rejected them in a 1949 referendum. The poll tax survived.[27]

Another embarrassment to Byrd was the report by the *Times-Dispatch* that Virginia had more state employees (16,300 as of January 1942) than all but eight states and the greatest number proportionate to population of the nineteen most populous states. For the nation's foremost critic of bloated federal employment, this was a charge that could not go unanswered. Writing to Governor Tuck, Byrd griped, "I do not think Dabney should be permitted to get away with this and think some reply should be made to him." Using Byrd's defense that Virginia's operation of county roads and state liquor stores necessitated more employees, Tuck did as requested. The newspaper reiterated its findings, pointing out that other states performed services that Virginia did not. A few months later the Roanoke *World News* reported that Virginia had one of the costliest governments in the United States. Byrd's concern was real, for his old Senate adversary, Joe Guffey, quoted the newspaper figures and accused Byrd of not practicing in Virginia what he preached against in Washington.[28]

All of Byrd's troubles with state politics may have occasioned his spontaneous offer to Colgate Darden to hand over operation of the machine. He wanted to be rid of these noxious state details and their association with his name—the things "done in the name of the Byrd organization which I knew nothing about," he complained to Oscar Smith. Darden politely refused; he did not want it, and he knew that Byrd could not put it down. "You wouldn't be up in the orchards a week before you would be bitterly sorry that you had ever given any indication that you didn't want to run the Organization," he told Harry. "All your old cronies in Virginia would be phoning you and telling you what a mess everything was in, and imploring you to come back and straighten it out. Don't give a damn how well it was run, it wouldn't suit them and it wouldn't suit you."[29]

Even as it reached the pinnacle of its success, the Organization was growing complacent in its authority, being untested at the polls since 1937. The apathy of the electorate had carried over to the politicians, who were paying little attention to local issues such as the Wise County scandal. This complacency was occurring at a time when Virginia was undergoing significant economic and demographic changes. The growing electorate meant that older methods of campaigning would no longer be so effective. Issues were emerging, such as schools and poll taxes, that could no longer be ignored. There was growing criticism of the failure of state government to deliver. Although they offered little more than the Organization, the "antis" caught the scent of dissatisfaction and resurrected their challenge to the Byrd machine. For the first time in his Senate career, Harry Byrd faced opposition in the primary in 1946.[30]

The major issue in the campaign was organized labor. In November 1944, the Tidewater Council of the CIO, reacting to Byrd's criticism of labor activities during the war, had called for his defeat in 1946 for his failure to support the president and to represent the wishes of the voters. The state CIO endorsed this action a month later. The break was made permanent in January 1946 when the Political Action Committee (PAC) of the Virginia CIO compared Byrdism to nazism and fascism and unanimously voted to unseat the senator. Citing the short ballot and the manipulation of voting procedures, it accused the machine of threatening the democratic process in Virginia. In a burst of hyperbole, it claimed Byrd plotted to rule the Commonwealth as Hitler had plotted to rule the world: "The theory of Byrdism is substantially that found in 'Mein Kampf.'" Infuriated by such drivel, Byrd turned up his attack on unions, particularly the PACs, and used them as whipping boys in all his subsequent campaigns. Although their influence in the state was minimal, the public image of unions in the postwar period was so negative that they made a convenient target for Organization politicians, who thenceforth associated political opponents with labor and frightened voters with visions of a union takeover of Virginia.[31]

The portent of a labor takeover had a certain plausibility in the early months of 1946. Both the AFL and CIO undertook membership drives in the unorganized South. Steel, coal, and rail strikes threatened to bring the nation's economy to a halt, while in Virginia the proposed walkout by workers of the Virginia Electric and Power Company (VEPCO) raised the specter of power blackouts. Governor Tuck attempted to mediate the local crisis, but when union officials refused to participate, he warned of a possible seizure of VEPCO plants. "I'll be damned if they're going to cut the lights out in Virginia," he exclaimed. "It's just like sticking a gun in your back. And they'll not get away with it as long as I'm governor."[32] Two days before the strike deadline, Tuck declared a state emergency and used an obscure statute of questionable authority to draft the VEPCO employees into the service of the Commonwealth. The ploy worked; union officials called off the strike, resumed contract negotiations, and agreed to a settlement two weeks later. Despite some criticism, most Virginians, including Harry Byrd, believed it was a courageous act that protected the public interest against greedy, irresponsible union officials. Although Boyd Payton, president of the Virginia CIO Council, tried to associate Tuck's policy with the "high command of Byrdism," there is no evidence that Byrd had any input other than constantly giving the governor encouragement. However, there is little doubt that labor troubles in Virginia spurred the senator's efforts to rein in unions through tougher national legislation such as the Case bill and the Taft-Hartley Act.[33]

Coming as it did in this election year, the VEPCO incident clearly drew the line between the Organization and labor, much to Byrd's benefit. As Ebbie Combs said to him, "I am convinced that Tuck's courageous stand in this matter has helped us tremendously over the state." Prophetically, he added, "If you should have opposition in the primary this year, and your opponent should be so indiscreet as to undertake to make an issue of Tuck's action in this case, I believe it would help you tremendously."[34]

That opposition emerged on April 28 when Martin Hutchinson announced his candidacy for Byrd's Senate seat, setting the stage for Virginia's first senatorial primary since 1922. Active in Democratic party politics for twenty years, Hutchinson had been appointed secretary of the Commonwealth by Byrd in 1927 and had served as secretary of the state committee from 1925 to 1939, but he had grown dissatisfied with the inertia of the Organization. Hoping for a political awakening in the Old Dominion, he threw his support to Jim Price and was rewarded with Combs's position as chairman of the Compensation Board. In the aftermath of Price's defeat, he resigned and returned to his law practice. A member of the Committee of 100 to re-elect Roosevelt in 1944, Hutchinson was angered by the Organization's failure to support the president. Encouraged by recent signs of weakness, especially the Wise County scandal, he decided to challenge the incumbent, believing, despite the odds, that Virginians should be provided an alternative. In that spirit Virginius Dabney congratulated Hutchinson: "I think the State owes you a debt for putting on a contest this year, and I hope it will be a vigorous one. Virginia is dead from the neck up politically and your candidacy should do much to remedy the situation."[35]

Aware of the recent negative publicity and the changing nature of Virginia's electorate, the Byrd forces took Hutchinson's candidacy seriously. The senator wanted to know "what class of people" were paying their poll taxes. There were reports of heavy registration and payment of poll taxes among union members, returning servicemen, and blacks. A worried Byrd wrote Watt Abbitt, "I have an idea practically all of them will vote against me." It is important, he ordered, that "our friends be qualified." He expected malicious opposition from labor because "I refuse to take orders from the CIO and have voted my convictions on these questions."[36]

The labor unrest in the country and in Virginia worked to his advantage, and on May 10 the national CIO-PAC handed Byrd the rope with which to hang Hutchinson when it put the senator on its purge list. An indignant Byrd responded: "Yesterday in Atlantic City Sidney Hillman and his racketeer associates of the CIO-PAC officially placed me on their purge list. I regard this as a badge of honor and appreciate the compliment." Exhuming the earlier comparison with Hitler, he labeled the charges "intemperate, personally abusive, scurrilous, . . . direct lies and false insinuations." Virginians could hardly tolerate such a vicious attack on their beloved senator, especially when it came from outside the state. Tuck consoled him, "As long as we can keep the CIO fighting out in the open, I think you are all right." An angry Byrd later told O'Conor Goolrick, "I would not be a candidate now except that I was not willing to have the CIO take credit for running me out of public life." Although he had mentioned the possibility of retirement to a few close friends, Byrd took too much pleasure in his Senate work to step down at this stage in his career, but undoubtedly the labor challenge foreclosed even the temptation of retirement.[37]

Backed by his liberal friends and the ranks of organized labor, Hutchinson ran an aggressive campaign against the machine and Byrd's record of voting with the Republicans, offering a platform that favored federal housing, fair labor practices, continued price controls, support for the United Nations, and an American loan to Great Britain. W. M. Kemper applauded him: "The complete domination of government by Harry and his henchmen is bitterly resented; and this domination should be vigorously asserted. In fact, I hope you will forget that you are a gentleman and wade into the whole outfit mercilessly—give them hell." But Hutchinson could never overcome the charge that he was labor's handpicked candidate. As Lloyd Robinette observed, the CIO blast at Byrd gave the Organization an opening and "they grasped this straw with alacrity; . . . now they brand every man who does not approve Byrd in Virginia as being a CIO, a PAC, and a communist."[38]

The better organized and financed Byrd forces won a relatively easy victory in the August primary, 141,923 to 81,605, winning all congressional districts, but it was a respectable showing for Hutchinson and the "antis," especially in the cities, where they took almost 45 percent of the vote. An indication of urban dissatisfaction with the machine was Porter Hardy's defeat of incumbent Ralph Daughton in the Second District. Consoling themselves with the thought that thousands of Republicans had voted for Byrd, the "antis" looked forward to the next contest, but they were never able to obtain more than 37 percent of the vote in any election against the machine. The senator's victory over the Republicans in the fall was effortless. But the primary had not been a pleasant campaign, and he reportedly told Willis Robertson that he would not go through another one like it "for anything in the world." At his orchard picnic a year later, he indicated his intention not to run for another term.[39]

Early in the campaign Carter Glass had died, thereby removing an issue that had become an embarrassment to the Organization. He had not cast a single vote on the Senate floor since his reelection in 1942. Governor Tuck appointed Tom Burch to succeed him, but since the Fifth District congressman was seventy-six years old, he was not expected to contend for Glass's seat at the state convention that would nominate the candidate. Knowing that several close friends were interested in running, Byrd declared his neutrality in the race, dictating only that the convention be delayed until after his own primary contest. Byrd and many Organization leaders preferred Colgate Darden to succeed Glass, but the former governor declined a draft, not wanting to return to the patronage hassles of Washington. The other front-runners were congressmen Willis Robertson and Howard Smith, two longtime loyalists whom Byrd did not want to offend by picking a favorite.

A. Willis Robertson was a loquacious country boy from Lexington who had been friends with Harry since they had entered the state senate together in 1916. A lanky, good-looking man with an unflagging tongue and pen, he had served as Game and Inland Fisheries commissioner during Byrd's governorship and was elected to Congress from the Seventh District in 1932. In search of advice, or perhaps a commendation, Robertson often wrote voluminous letters to Byrd explaining his votes or views on various legislation. Byrd once told Darden that Robertson had given a speech about the history of carillons at the dedication of the bell tower at Luray. "I'm sure you learned all about them," said Darden. "No," replied Harry. "Willis had only reached the time of the birth of Christ when night fell, and we had to shut down." Although they remained friends and hunting companions, their relationship had begun to cool as Robertson manifested a growing independence from the Organization.[40]

Smith, who was as taciturn as Robertson was garrulous, was an attorney and judge who had risen through the ranks of Alexandria politics to be elected to Congress from the Eighth District in 1930. Winning a position on the House Rules Committee, he later turned it into his own political fiefdom, obstructing legislation undesirable to him, notably in civil rights. Speaker of the House Carl Albert said Smith was "the smartest man and the most able legislator" he ever saw in Congress. "Reaction was his religion." A slightly built man with large ears and bushy eyebrows, Smith was an independent sort, but he invariably voted an Organization line and was one of Byrd's most trusted advisers. Byrd may have preferred Smith (after Darden) since they were so much in agreement, particularly on labor issues, but he feared losing Smith's seniority on the Rules Committee if he moved to the Senate; even more, he worried that Smith's antilabor record would prove harmful to the Organization in the Second and Ninth districts.[41]

Robertson's course to the nomination was bizarre. He enthusiastically prepared for the contest but then hastily withdrew in June when Byrd declared his neutrality. Privately, he began putting the pieces together again, only to withdraw once more in early August out of fear that he could not win. Mortified, twice-designated campaign manager Fred Switzer wrote his irresolute friend: "Of course, Willis, you have to run some risk in everything you do. Life is just that way; in your case I certainly think the risk is well worth the opportunity. . . . Keep calm!" At the September convention Darden led on the first ballot with Smith second and Robertson fourth, but after the former governor withdrew for the last time, many of his supporters shifted to the indecisive Robertson, who won following the third ballot. Byrd was pleased with the result, primarily because he had been perceived as "entirely neutral" in the procedure. Switzer wrote to him afterwards: "Sometime I want to see you so I can tell you the whole story about Willis and his campaign. It was really one of the most unusual experiences I have ever had."[42]

Election victories, however, did not alleviate the problems confronting Virginia. On January 6, 1947, Governor Tuck addressed another special session of the General Assembly to ask for more money to meet an "acute emergency" in the state's school system that had been documented in the 1944 Denny commission on education. In spite of modest advances made during the Darden Administration, Virginia still languished near the bottom of the states in its commitment to education and public health and welfare services. The obsession of Harry Byrd and the Organization with balanced budgets, treasury surpluses, and low taxes had created a crisis in the Old Dominion that was worsening with the postwar population growth. Virginia ranked forty-fourth in percentage of income spent on education, forty-fourth in percentage of persons receiving welfare assistance, and last in old age assistance. School building needs were estimated at $396 million over the next ten years; more than one thousand schools were deemed fire or health hazards and were labeled "unsuitable" for students. The problem was compounded by Virginia's maintenance of separate public schools for black and white children. Conditions were so unequal that even friendly judges were now ruling that the state would have to improve the black schools at considerable cost or risk integration. Virginia's leaders did not appreciate the growing demands on government in a changing society. Citizens who had been made less self-sufficient by industrialization and urbanization required more than one-room schoolhouses if they were to be productive; they needed better roads, hospitals, and housing if they were to share in the wealth of that society.[43]

While in agreement with Organization philosophy and cost-consciousness, Governor Tuck felt compelled to take some action, asking the special session for funds to increase teacher salaries. A year later he requested additional expenditures for schools and welfare services and took the revolutionary step of proposing increases in corporate and personal income taxes to pay for them. Sitting in Washington, removed from the direct responsibility of dealing with Virginia's problems, an alarmed Harry Byrd cautioned Tuck to maintain surpluses and avoid deficits. He could not understand how the cost of government had gone up so fast since he had been governor, especially for education; things seemed to be getting out of hand. Fearing the political repercussions of raising taxes, he recommended squeezing the last drop of efficiency out of the schools and changing tax brackets instead of increasing taxes. He predicted rainy days ahead that would require large surpluses on hand, larger even than the current treasury surplus of $20 million. He wrote Combs and Wysor: "The rock upon which our democratic organization has stood since 1923 when we defeated the bond issue is fiscal conservatism in our state government. . . . We can't talk economy and fiscal conservatism for 25 years and then expect the people to change around with us in a short time."[44]

The debate over taxes and schools epitomized Byrd's dilemma. He had legitimate concerns about the rising costs of government and its potential waste, but balanced budgets and deficits had become fetishes for him, blinding him to human needs and new economic thinking on government fiscal policy.

Intellectually, he was locked into the world of 1923, unable to adjust to new ideas or new conditions. The result was a barren political career over the last twenty years of his life. In Washington he became an anachronism, powerless to deter the changes or obstruct the responses to them, but in Virginia his continuing influence would cost the state years of progress and a measure of dignity. The modest expenditure increases of the Darden and Tuck administrations only enabled the Commonwealth to hold its ground at the bottom of the rankings.

For Harry Byrd, there had always been a direct relationship between fiscal policies and political fortunes. Low taxes and nonobtrusive government attracted and retained the support of conservative voters and contributors. With another gubernatorial election approaching, it was understandable that he worried about Tuck's tax increases. To avoid repeating the last contentious selection process when Tuck had preempted the nod, Byrd and his advisers determined to select a successor well before the election to unify Organization forces and to forestall any opposition. Nevertheless, despite their well-laid plans, political conditions in Virginia and events elsewhere produced a multicandidate race that threatened to defeat the machine.

The man chosen to lead the Organization into the fray was John S. Battle, state senator from Charlottesville. Looking like the quintessential governor—tall, handsome, dignified, and mild-mannered—the fifty-nine-year-old Battle had impeccable credentials as a longtime supporter of the machine, but he also had a moderate legislative record that would attract independents. Having considered Battle for the job in 1945, Byrd assured his friend of his support in early 1947 and urged him to consult other party leaders about a possible candidacy. In June, Combs told Wysor to let their friends know that Battle would be their candidate for governor. The word was passed to key subordinates, who responded favorably, and the decision was confirmed at a meeting at Skyland in August. Battle formally announced his candidacy in June 1948, over a year before the primary.[45]

Within weeks it was a crowded field. Horace Edwards, the forty-six-year-old state party chairman, former state legislator, and mayor of Richmond, entered the race as a representative of younger Organization members who had grown impatient with a selection process that seemed to reward only seniority. The leadership was well aware that Edwards was preparing to run. Fearing the damage such a split would cause, both Byrd and Combs attempted to persuade him to wait his turn, but without success. "The bee was in my bonnet," Edwards said afterwards. He hoped to appeal to urban areas with a school program financed with a sales tax.[46]

Buoyed by the prospect of an Organization split, Francis Pickens Miller, a longtime opponent of the machine, entered the contest in late July. A man of scholarly bent, Miller had a distinguished Virginia background, had served in both world wars, and, as a devout Christian, had been involved with the ecumenical movement. He had served two terms in the General Assembly but had been defeated for reelection in 1941 by a smear campaign that misidentified his wife with a woman of the same name who was a Communist. The only incumbent Democrat to lose that year, Miller vowed "to destroy a system which could destroy men."

A fourth candidate joined the field in November: Remmie Arnold, a wealthy self-made businessman from Petersburg, who promised to bring business practices to the governor's mansion. He was a relative unknown, but his conservative rhetoric threatened to attract votes away from Battle. Very much aware of this, both Byrd and Combs told Arnold, who had asked for their support, that it would be a mistake for him to run, but as with Edwards, their pleas were ignored. Byrd warned Combs that Arnold should not be underrated: "He has colossal energy—something our man lacks." Thus, despite all his efforts, Byrd confronted a difficult four-man contest for the governorship in 1949 that raised the possibility of defeat for the Organization.[47]

Byrd threw himself into the campaign with an intensity not witnessed since John Garland Pollard's election in 1929. His major problem was Battle's easygoing nature and lack of competitive campaign experience. Byrd and Combs began advising the candidate almost at once about his correspondence, campaign management, issues, and publicity. They instructed him to secure a manager in every county and city, announce his platform, appoint a treasurer, answer his mail promptly, and place his picture and biography in the local newspapers. Worried by the possible consequences of an imperfect campaign organization, the master campaigner was teaching the novice the catechism of Organization politics.[48]

A new problem surfaced when it was reported that Congressman Tom Stanley, who twice had been rejected by Byrd for the governorship, was going to run on his own. To discourage him, Byrd urged Battle to become more active, but the candidate's efforts stirred no enthusiasm, and by the end of the year the threat from Stanley loomed large. Fred Switzer warned Byrd, "If Tom would refuse to stay out of the race, we could not possibly survive with both he and John dividing the Organization votes." Combs, who believed the removal of Stanley was of "transcendent importance," advised Byrd to "call his attention to the fact that he is now in position to render an outstanding service to the State and to the State organization, and that if he takes advantage of this opportunity the friends of the organization and of good government in Virginia will feel under many obligations to him." Byrd met with Stanley in Washington in January and likely offered his support for the governorship in 1953 in return for his withdrawal now. He wrote Combs: "I had a very satisfactory talk with Tom Stanley yesterday afternoon. He will announce immediately after the inauguration [of Truman] that he will not be a candidate." A few days later, Stanley endorsed Battle.[49]

In his first major campaign address on February 10, 1949, Miller set the tone with a stinging attack on the Organization, claiming it was responsible for shortcomings in education, a deteriorating seafood industry, and poor health conditions. Given Miller's religious background, "crusade" was not too strong a term to describe the effort of the anti-Organization Democrats. As the candidate proclaimed late in the campaign, "We are fighting . . . because we believe that God has better things in store for us and by our struggles we demonstrate the reality of our faith in Him."[50]

By this time Byrd was clearly concerned. With no provision for a runoff election, the prospect of Miller winning a plurality victory in the face of an Organization split was a distinct possibility. Personally committing himself to organizing the Seventh District, the senator lined up Sidney Kellam, the veteran Virginia Beach boss, to run Battle's campaign. Hearing that Battle, who had a moderate labor record, was considering a reexamination of the labor bills passed by the 1947 General Assembly, he cautioned the candidate not to have anything to do with organized labor, predicting that this might be the key issue in the campaign.

To jump-start the Battle campaign, Byrd called a meeting of top Organization leaders in Richmond the evening before the annual Jefferson-Jackson dinner. Combs, Wysor, Kellam, Battle, Stanley, Robertson, Harry Jr., and several others were present to discuss campaign strategy and issues. The following day Byrd met with other close friends at the Hotel John Marshall to encourage their active participation on behalf of Battle. In the weeks thereafter the senator continued to advise the lethargic Battle about such practical matters as answering his mail, making speeches, publicizing his record, and organizing women's clubs similar to those supporting Miller. This election, he warned, "was one of the most momentous we have ever had in Virginia."[51]

To blunt Miller's attacks on the machine, the Organization defended its honest and solvent record and portrayed Miller as a radical bent on upsetting this secure environment. In its defense Battle offered what came to be the standard description of the Organization: "It is nothing more nor less than a loosely knit group of Virginians . . . who usually think alike, who are interested in the welfare of the Commonwealth, who are supremely interested in giving Virginia good government and good public servants, and they usually act together." Byrd could not have said it better, and he frequently referred to this statement in future years when asked to explain his political machine in Virginia.[52]

Although Miller campaigned aggressively on the machine issue, it paled in significance to the charge that he was the pawn of organized labor. Correctly gauging the antiunion sentiment in the state after years of strikes and aggressive CIO-PAC lobbying, Byrd chose to inject life into the Battle campaign by utilizing the issue that had propelled him to victory over Hutchinson three years earlier. Breaking his pledge not to interfere in Democratic primaries, Byrd addressed a Harrisonburg rally in July and warned against giving the election to "a CIO-supported candidate." He ranted about "outside labor leaders" gaining control of Virginia and repealing the recently passed state right-to-work law. Without mentioning Miller by name, he accused him of using "weasel words" and "pussy-footing" on Virginia's labor laws. Fred Switzer believed Byrd's appearance had a "telling effect" on the campaign. The coup de grâce was the publication late in the race of a letter reputedly sent by James C. Petrillo, president of the American Federation of Musicians, to his several hundred union members in the state asking them to vote for Miller. Used by Battle, the letter reinforced the image of a "labor thug" attempting to dictate Virginia's politics. Although Miller labeled this the "worn-out trick of conjuring up ghosts" and vowed to enforce Virginia's labor laws, he could not recover from the impression that he was in labor's pocket.[53]

The Byrd-Battle forces employed two other tactics to ensure their victory. To undermine Edwards's candidacy, Organization leaders began insinuating that Edwards could not win, that a vote for him was essentially a vote for Miller. Byrd's son remembers driving his father to the Harrisonburg rally and reading his speech as the senator was putting the final touches to it. He noticed that there was no mention of Horace Edwards in it. Byrd Sr. replied: "That's the best way to kill Edwards—not to mention him. This is a battle between Battle and Miller. Exactly what we need to do is to get people feeling that Edwards is not in this thing." While Sidney Kellam orchestrated a telephone campaign against Edwards, Ebbie Combs exhorted local officeholders to switch to Battle. One of them wrote to an associate: "Mr. Combs, Chairman of the Compensation Board, who sets your salary and mine, . . . is interested in seeing John S. Battle elected our Governor. Since Mr. Combs is a good friend of ours, I think it would be to our interest to get every vote we can for Mr. Battle."[54] Aware of this activity and disheartened by the collapse of his campaign, Edwards lashed out at Combs, promising to remove him from his position if he were elected. He called Senator Byrd's direct entry into the campaign a "move of desperation" designed to derail his candidacy. It achieved just that.[55]

The final Organization ploy to win the election for Battle involved the encouragement of Republican voters to participate in the Democratic primary. Years before, Combs had shrewdly advised against separate party registration because Republicans had always been friendly to the Organization in Democratic primaries. The Republicans were having their own primary on the same day, but their races had elicited no enthusiasm. On July 13 Henry Wise, a prominent Republican from the Eastern Shore who had once run against Byrd, urged his fellow Republicans to enter the Democratic primary and vote for Battle in order to turn away this "invasion by aliens." An opinion of Attorney General Almond approved the crossover. Combs wrote to E. F. Hargis that Republicans could vote unless they were challenged, noting that "it is not up to the election officers to challenge anyone. I am sure you will know how to handle this at some of our precincts." The Miller forces charged that Byrd made a deal with Wise, but there is no evidence to substantiate the claim. Republicans agreed with Organization policies, and knowing that the Democratic nominee would be victorious in the fall election, they preferred Battle to Miller.[56]

The events of the final month of the campaign—Harry Byrd's public endorsement, the Petrillo letter, the deflation of Edwards, and the entry of the Republicans—turned the election in Battle's favor. In the largest primary turnout in Virginia history to that time, he won a sizable plurality, gaining 43 percent of the vote to Miller's 35 percent, Edward's 15 percent, and Arnold's 7 percent. Battle had broad support across the state, while Miller carried the urban vote and the Norfolk area and the southwest. Most commentators, including Miller and his supporters, believed the Republican vote turned the tide that had been running in favor of the "antis," an assessment confirmed by the large turnouts for Battle in heavily Republican areas. But even more important was the work of Harry Byrd, who quite correctly referred to "my election success in Virginia" when he described the victory to his brother. Had he chosen to remain uninvolved, Miller likely would have won. His advice, his active participation in the campaign (along with that of Ebbie Combs), his selection of the labor issue, and his possible influence with Republicans added up to another triumph for the Organization.[57]

Harry Byrd's political life was a succession of elections, each one crucial to the perpetuation of his machine and the legacy of his governorship. Convinced that the results of gubernatorial and presidential races, not to mention his own reelection bids, were a reflection of his authority and image in the Old Dominion, he was forever directing campaigns. Like cultivating apple trees, winning elections absorbed his complete attention. And Battle's victory over Miller proved to be a banner harvest.

~ 15 ~

"Too Many Byrds"

THROUGHOUT 1949, despite the distractions with the Virginia gubernatorial race, Byrd continued his sparring with the Truman administration, but he found the atmosphere even less congenial than it had been
over the last two years. Bolstered by the return of Congress to Democratic control—a restoration highlighted by one of the most brilliant freshman classes in
Senate history—progressives looked forward to the revival of New Deal activism under the leadership of a confident reelected president. Robert Kerr of
Oklahoma, Paul Douglas of Illinois, Estes Kefauver of Tennessee, Hubert Humphrey of Minnesota, Clinton Anderson of New Mexico, Lyndon Johnson of
Texas, and Russell Long of Louisiana would all make a significant legislative
contribution over the next fifteen years, usually over the objections of Harry
Byrd.

Much like the nation at large, the United States Senate was being transformed. For much of Byrd's first fifteen years there, the chamber had operated
as a dignified association of friends and colleagues who respected one another
and paid great allegiance to the traditions of the body. Seniority, formality in
language and dress, and civility were its totems. Once in heated debate with
Texan Tom Connally over social security legislation, Byrd paused to say that
Connally was "one of the most eloquent and graceful speakers on the floor of
the Senate. I would rather hear him speak than almost any other member of
the Senate, because even when he disagrees with me it is most enjoyable to hear
him." Violators of these genteel rules of behavior were ostracized. Because of
the exclusivity of the club, senators tended to have a heightened estimation
of their ability and power, which made their battles with similarly egocentric
presidents more heated.[1]

Without question, the majordomos of this body were the southerners. Assured the chairmanships of major committees through their longevity, they
wielded power disproportionate to their numbers. William S. White commented that the Senate was "the South's revenge for Gettysburg." Decked out
in their white linen suits, speaking a stilted tongue, protecting their rights, and
resenting any slurs on person or region, the southerners became the caricatures

of senators. Sectional pride produced a unity that enabled them to influence legislation and fend off outside attacks. They knew the rules of the Senate inside and out, and the filibuster was their sword and shield. Denied access to national leadership by their regional heritage, they made the Senate their home, their ultimate position in life; they were "Senate men," the "guardians of Senate tradition." Those who were most senior and who adhered most closely to the customs of the Senate constituted its inner club, of which Byrd was now a member. Aside from the squabbles over patronage, he enjoyed being in the Senate. Its intimate, tradition-oriented environment reflected his own personality as well as the mode of political operation in the Old Dominion with which he was most comfortable. However, the issues of race and social reform and new world responsibilities were creating greater divisiveness in the body, weakening party loyalty, elevating tempers, and isolating the southerners. The new senators were more oriented toward national rather than state or regional interests and were more open to rules changes. The upper house was becoming less collegial.[2]

Performing as he did in the Virginia Senate thirty years earlier, Byrd wrote very few bills; but as a member of the conservative coalition of southern Democrats and Republicans, he became very influential in stymieing executive initiatives. He was the foremost opponent of increased federal spending and the acknowledged expert on budgets and bureaucracy. In this regard Byrd was used by conservative politicians and businessmen to advance their own agendas, but it was a service he enjoyed rendering.

Out of such a mutual relationship, he developed a strong friendship with Robert Taft, the Republican leader in the Senate. Byrd was attracted by Taft's sincerity, sense of honor, and views on budgets and government. That shared philosophy was the reason Taft let Byrd keep his chairmanship of the joint committee on government spending when the Republicans took control of Congress in 1947, the only Democrat to be so rewarded. The balding, portly Ohioan recommended Byrd for an honorary degree from his own alma mater, Yale University, and urged President Eisenhower to appoint him secretary of the treasury in 1952. He once said that Byrd and he saw eye-to-eye nine times out of ten, and "that's about as high a degree of agreement as I have with any Republican Senator."[3] Taft and Byrd were primary mobilizers of the conservative coalition that sought to overturn the New Deal and obstruct Truman's Fair Deal. As Senator Douglas remembered, "Its members always showed up for roll calls, and its power was occasionally openly flaunted, as when Harry F. Byrd and Robert A. Taft sat together on the floor checking the list of Senators and sending out for the absent or the few recalcitrants." The two conservatives served together on the Finance Committee where Byrd also developed friendships with Republicans Eugene Millikin of Colorado and Hugh Butler of Nebraska. Among his Democratic colleagues, he became friendly with most of the southerners, particularly Richard Russell of Georgia, who had entered the Senate at the same time as he. He numbered no liberals among his close associates. But whatever their political persuasion, his colleagues held Byrd in high esteem, regarding him as a gracious gentleman who was direct but friendly and who rarely raised his voice in anger.[4]

The proximity of his Berryville estate to Washington made life in the capital less onerous for Byrd. He could easily escape the clamor and heat of Washington summers for the real work of the orchards on weekends and during extended recesses. Sometimes he would spend the weekend at Skyland in a cottage that the Skyline Corporation had built for him and kept reserved for him on a moment's notice. Influenced by Sittie's illness and his own innate modesty, Byrd was not a great socializer, having no use for the Washington social whirl; when the Byrds did entertain, they confined themselves to small dinner parties at Rosemont or at their apartment suite at the Shoreham Hotel in northwest Washington. The one exception was his annual spring luncheon at Rosemont—during the apple blossom season—to which he invited his Senate colleagues, cabinet officials, Virginia politicians, and neighbors. Each year from 1948 to 1964, over three successive Sundays, he entertained the elite of Washington, who seemed to enjoy thoroughly this brief respite from their official duties. Otherwise, Harry and Sittie preferred family gatherings. The senator loved to play with his grandchildren, especially when the entire clan was at Rosemont for Thanksgiving and Christmas dinners. Election nights were also exciting times for the family as they apprehensively awaited the returns, even though these were usually highly predictable.[5]

One social diversion he allowed himself was membership in the Alfalfa Club, a Washington political group like the Gridiron Club, which met once a year for good-humored toasts and testimonials. Byrd would often take his sons, a few close political and journalist friends, and his doctor, Howard Smith, to the festivities. Frequently the butt of many jokes about his budget-balancing activities, the senator served as president of the club in 1947 and had to deliver his own good-natured ribbing, a speech that son Dick found unusual for such a serious-minded fellow who could not tell jokes because he forgot the punch lines. Byrd was a convivial soul but was not known for his wit.[6]

In temperament, he shifted from being charming, gracious, and generous when on familiar ground to being cold and guarded on foreign terrain. He had a wide array of political friends in Virginia with whom he enjoyed plotting the next election or spinning a yarn about a past campaign. To them Harry was warm, affable, and unpretentious, a man who, despite his wealth, maintained a common touch, who relished the campaign trail and his associations with local officeholders. Yet he could also be a very private person, often isolating himself in the mountains or orchards, especially when he did not want to be found. He never became one of the Senate's gamesmen, disdaining their hand-grabbing, back-slapping, elbow-bending, arm-twisting politics. He was not one for small talk; his conversation and correspondence, while polite, were businesslike, direct and to the point. Quiet and dignified, he was a loner who did not frequently socialize with his colleagues, which limited his influence with them.[7]

This duality in character also reflected Byrd's obsession with his personal integrity. It was his coat of armor. Like the plantation owners of the antebellum South, Byrd lived the code of the gentleman, giving no offense but quick to take offense. Fearful of change that threatened his power and the comfortable life of the Virginia squirearchy, Byrd was suspicious of those proposing new courses of action or those who held a point of view different from his. Friendly at heart, he had little tolerance for criticism. Personal attacks were matters of honor that required immediate replies, which he clothed in the language of constitutionalism and indignance—a twentieth-century form of the code duello. As Forrest Davis wrote of him, "His boiling point is . . . low. The righteous anger of a Virginia gentleman proverbially glows into incandescence at the drop of a hat. Scratch Byrd's pride in his integrity, his state, or his section, and you get a hotblood as fierce as any of the cloak-and-dagger lads that ever brawled in the Raleigh tavern at Williamsburg."[8]

Predictably, the preeminent defender of the status quo in America was a creature of habit. Byrd rose at 6:30 every morning, dressed in old khakis and uncollared shirt, and took a long walk before breakfast. When in Washington, that stroll took him through Rock Creek Park and sometimes the national zoo, where he stopped to chat with the animals. On one occasion, looking disheveled and lacking identification, he was interrogated by a park policeman, who doubted his claim that he was a United States senator before letting him go on. Virginius Dabney found Byrd's clothes "so lacking in style as to be bizarre"; he recalled then Governor Byrd walking into his office in pants so tight and so short that they "had the appearance of having shrunk to those dimensions after a fall by the wearer into the nearby James."[9] Washington would improve his taste, but not by much. Some thought him the "least well-dressed" senator. Except for his traditional white summer suits, there was a certain sameness in his clothes; they were adequate but not flashy. That was also true of his taste in food. Whether in Washington or at Rosemont, he enjoyed a big breakfast, occasionally having salt roe herring or quail along with eggs, pancakes, and fried tomatoes; as he once told his son, "The work of the world is done by the breakfast eaters." He had a light lunch and finished the day with a solid meal of meat and potatoes and vegetables topped by a favorite dessert.

After his morning constitutional Byrd would typically take a cold shower, have breakfast, and drive himself across town to work, where his unwashed Chevrolet was easily detected in the Senate parking lot. At his cluttered Senate office, whose walls were covered with cartoons highlighting his political battles, he spent his mornings on the telephone, reading mail, and greeting approximately fifty to one hundred visitors each day. Two talents enabled him to accomplish these tasks: he could talk on the telephone and read his mail at the same time; and with an almost photographic memory, he could rapidly digest and retain large chunks of information, particularly quantifiable data. Such abilities were essential, for Byrd maintained a very small office staff for his entire career. Peachy Menefee remained his administrative assistant for almost thirty years, and Meda Dick was his office secretary for even longer. J. Heywood Bell was his longtime staff researcher and writer, the person most responsible for the many articles and speeches that Byrd presented. Four or five other secretaries rounded out the congenial group, whom Byrd called the most "efficient and loyal" staff on the Hill. He was proud of the fact that he returned money for office expenses to the treasury. He held committee meetings in early afternoon and ended the day with a workout and swim in the Senate gym. Home at the Shoreham by 7:15, he would read in the evenings after dinner and retire early, spending little time listening to the radio or watching television. His reading included Civil War history and conservative tracts such as John Flynn's *The Road Ahead* and Friedrich Hayek's *The Road to Serfdom*. He admitted to Lenoir Chambers: "My two heroes are Lee and Jackson. Maybe that is one of the reasons why I am so strong to defend the rights of the States." Certainly Lee's loyalty to his home state was not lost on Byrd.[10]

Relaxation for the senator came in his work and in his hunting and hiking with his dogs, who were always with him, even in his Senate office. He became an avid bird-watcher and loved to swim. He put on a little weight over the years and his hair thinned somewhat, but he retained his ruddy complexion and youthful vigor. Byrd was an advocate of physical fitness long before that activity was in vogue. He wrote in 1959: "In this age and time, it is essential that we be in good health, and possessed of fitness and stamina—both physical and mental. Throughout the years, I have found that daily swimming contributes much, and perhaps more than any other exercise, to these essentials." He preferred cold water and cool air. The heat was always down at Rosemont, and the radiators in his Senate office were off. But he did not like air-conditioning, on which he blamed the longer congressional sessions; legislators could now avoid the steamy summer heat of the nation's capital that used to drive them to early adjournments.[11]

Byrd was not an outwardly religious man. An Episcopalian by birth and membership, he attended church infrequently. However, he prayed regularly and had deep spiritual convictions. His friends remembered that no matter where he was, the senator would get down on his knees and say his prayers at the end of the day. He held no religious prejudice, numbering Jews and Catholics among his friends, and throughout his political life he spoke out against religious bigotry. He believed a person's relationship with his Maker was private and should be of no concern to the public or the state. Yet his religious convictions informed his political philosophy. For Byrd, Christianity undergirded American institutions. "Christianity is the fountain-head of civilization," he said in 1939. It was a religion of individual liberty which encouraged moral self-reliance and improved one's capacity for self-government. "Absolute rule and Christianity are inconsistent," he wrote some years later. "Absolute rule exalts the state and debases the individual. Christianity dignifies the individual as a child of God." The American constitutional system, he argued, was created by the Founding Fathers to enhance the liberty of the individual while checking the authority of the government. Therefore, the Christian in politics was obligated to adhere to these principles. In his effort to put his religion to political use, however, Byrd was more inclined to emphasize the rhetoric of "thou shalt not" over being "thy brother's keeper."[12]

While Byrd's routine changed very little over the years, the changes in the country and in the Senate began to make the job more contentious and frustrating. The depression and war had already shifted power from Capitol Hill down Pennsylvania Avenue to the White House, creating a battle line that, with the exception of the Eisenhower years, was increasingly antagonistic to Byrd. As the Cold War heated up, anti-Communist ideologues, seeking political advantage, turned Congress into a testing ground of patriotic loyalties; name-calling, back stabbing, and guilt by association disrupted the congenial nature of the institution. At the same time the civil rights issue fragmented the Senate into northern and southern camps, obstructing legislation and undermining party loyalty and much of the collegiality of the club. By the late fifties, the political pendulum was swinging back toward liberalism, and the conservative coalition was losing its veto power; the elections of 1958 and 1964 brought in new classes of liberal senators who began changing the rules by which the southerners had prevented tampering with their most sacred ground. Finally, congressional sessions were getting longer, lasting well into the fall, cutting into time for the orchards. Not surprisingly, Byrd began to think of retirement. It was not so much fun any more.

Nor was it much fun for Harry Truman, whose second term was a legislative stalemate and a political nightmare complete with war and Red Scare. Announced with great fanfare, his Fair Deal, despite the Democratic majorities, could not overcome conservative opposition and competition with Korean War spending. Congressman Richard Bolling remarked, "The conservatives in the Eighty-first Congress did not have the strength to undo the New Deal, but they could block Harry Truman's Fair Deal."[13] The president's own missteps, weak congressional leadership, and squabbling among Democrats contributed to the deadlock. Modest extensions were made to the minimum wage, social security, TVA, REA, and public housing, but new initiatives in civil rights, health care, aid to education, farm programs, and river valley development were defeated, as were attempts to repeal the Taft-Hartley Act. The president was able to maintain bipartisan support for his foreign policy of containment thanks in large measure to the work of Michigan Republican Senator Arthur Vandenberg; but with Vandenberg's death in 1951 and the stalemating of the war in Korea, that support also waned. Undoubtedly, Truman's unexpected victory in 1948 had intensified the animosity of his enemies toward him. Holding positions on two key committees—Finance and Armed Services—and continuing to chair the joint committee on federal spending, Harry Byrd persisted in his role of obstructionist, winning Truman's enmity and embittering their relationship.

The Virginia senator next butted heads with the president over his nomination of Mon Wallgren to head the National Security Resources Board. A former governor of Washington and senator, Wallgren was a close friend of Truman's who in Byrd's view (and that of many others) was "not qualified" for the position. Byrd was the only Democrat on the Armed Services Committee who sided with Republicans to defeat the nomination in committee by a vote of 7 to 6. Truman considered pressing the fight for Wallgren in the full Senate but dropped the idea upon the advice of aides. Late in the year he found a place for his crony on the Federal Power Commission (FPC); once again, Byrd was the only Democrat to vote against him.

The FPC opening had been created by the defeat of Leland Olds's reappointment. Olds's affiliation with the political left was damaging enough in the wake of a new Red Scare, but Truman's mishandling of the nomination killed whatever chances he might have had. Using the offices of the national party chairman, the president attempted to pressure senators into supporting Olds. Senator Byrd was indignant. Accusing Truman of "dictatorial government," he protested that in his sixteen years in Washington, he had "never seen a more deliberate effort to threaten and coerce the Senate." He gleefully joined the large majority defeating the nomination. There was a cost, however, for Byrd's obstructionism. His own recommendations for presidential appointments often went unfulfilled. So, too, did his brother's hope to arrange another expedition to Antarctica.[14]

Byrd frustrated the president on several other issues in 1949. Offering his first "Byrd's-eye" view of the government's fiscal situation, he predicted an $11 billion deficit over the next three years that would lead to regimentation equal to that in England, this despite the fact that Truman had presented Congress a balanced budget that was dependent upon a tax increase. Since he believed a tax increase would be recessionary, Byrd's solution was spending cuts. Attacking Truman's budget as wasteful and inefficient, he asked for cuts in public works and federal payrolls, more efficient unification of the armed services, and a reorganization of the executive branch. The farm plan was "horrible" and health insurance was a form of "socialized medicine." Labeling a $300 million federal aid to education bill a "Pandora's box of expense" that would lead to bureaucratic control of the schools, he argued that states could use their surpluses or raise taxes if they wanted to improve education, a somewhat hypocritical remark in light of his recommendations to Governor Tuck to do neither. There seemed to be nothing on which he and the president could agree.[15]

Angered by the delays to his legislative program, which he blamed on "Byrdites" and Republicans, President Truman struck back on May 9 with a call for the election of congressmen who would have a national rather than a local perspective on issues. Upset with members of his own party—particularly the Dixiecrats—who were not backing him, he threatened to withhold patronage from them. Reflecting his frustration but also his wit, he threw out the barb that there were "too many Byrds in Congress."[16] The senator did not take kindly to the remark. "If the President means he intends to purge me from the Senate because I will not accept his dictation in matters of legislation, then I'll be on hand when the purging starts," he cried. "I owe my allegiance to my constituency in Virginia. So long as I remain in the Senate, I will vote as my conscience dictates and to represent the wishes of my constituents." Although Democratic national chairman J. Howard McGrath denied that there were any purge plans, Byrd declared that he would put off any thoughts of retirement if a purge attempt was made. He reported receiving thousands of letters, only two of which were not complimentary, that demanded "more Byrds in Congress," not fewer. The president also heard from Byrd's defenders, one of whom, in reference to Truman's early career failure, remarked, "If Harry Byrd had been your business partner, your haberdashery might still be open for business."[17]

Thin-skinned, defensive, and pontifical, Byrd turned what might have been a humorous incident into Armageddon. It was vintage Byrd: the attack mode of a humorless politician who converted every issue into one of darkness or light, into one of chaos or sanity, into one involving his personal integrity. No one ever doubted that Harry Byrd voted his conscience or suggested that he should do any differently; there remained considerable question, however, about the depth of his social conscience. Earlier in his life he had said that government should be run with the efficiency of a corporation but a "corporation with a heart because, of course, the human affairs of people old and young, rich and poor, cannot be conceived in terms of dollars and cents alone." Sadly, dollars and cents now seemed to be the only thing that counted with him.[18] Whereas other members of the conservative bloc frequently compromised with

"Too Many Byrds"

the president, Byrd more and more could be found among a small group of reactionaries opposing any kind of social legislation. Several analyses of Senate roll-call votes from 1933 to 1965 reveal the Virginian to have been among the most conservative senators, one of the least supportive of significant legislation among Democrats, and the most Republican of all Democrats. George Reedy said of Byrd, "He was probably the most conservative member in either party of the Senate. He was as far to the right as a man could be and still remain in the bounds of sanity." His negativism had come to define his senatorial career.[19]

For the remainder of the 1949 session, Byrd sniped at Truman's aid requests and budget proposals and the supposed drift toward socialism. He criticized the Council of Economic Advisers as a "strange group of men" who seemed to be following some foreign ideology. He equated deficit spending with capitulation to the Russians and labeled the Brannan farm plan socialistic for its guaranteed income payments and modified price supports. Byrd and the president did finally agree on the Reorganization Act that implemented many of the recommendations of the Hoover Commission to save money and consolidate federal agencies, but even then Byrd added an amendment requiring the president to estimate the savings from each change he proposed. They also agreed on American participation in the North Atlantic Treaty Organization (NATO) alliance, but the senator vigorously, albeit unsuccessfully, fought the NATO appropriations bill, predicting that it would lead to a twenty-year arms program that would bankrupt the country. A strong America, he insisted, should cut down on foreign giveaways, strive for more efficiency in the military and more frugality in domestic programs, and shift government responsibilities back to the states. The approval of NATO, a new farm bill, more public housing, and a new trade bill marked a productive first year for the Eighty-first Congress, but it was a weary and disgruntled group of representatives who adjourned in late October, in no mood for the political reconciliation that events in 1950 would demand. The man from Winchester had voted more often with the opposition party than any other senator. Editor Benjamin Muse wittily remarked, "Byrd was born out of his time and into the wrong political party."[20]

If Byrd's message of economy found few listeners in Washington, it had considerable appeal elsewhere across the country. He delivered numerous speeches and wrote a multitude of magazine articles that described the dangers of socialism and the need for retrenchment. His rhetoric began to take on an irrational, hyperbolic, apocalyptic quality. The nation seemed to be forever on the verge of bankruptcy, socialism, and decay; every event, every election was crucial, the most important in the history of the Commonwealth or the Republic. Speaking to the Wholesale Druggists Association in October 1949, he noted the development of an "American brand of socialism" which forecast the death of the free enterprise system. To the Charleston, South Carolina, Chamber of Commerce, he lamented, "The last hope of freedom-loving people in the world hangs upon maintaining the integrity of American money." The articles were picked up by other journals and newspapers and condensed and reprinted, making Byrd one of the most widely read and oft-quoted Americans. There was a certain sameness to them—sometimes only the dollar figures would change from year to year when budgets were being discussed—but they had great appeal to many Americans, who, as they adjusted to the demands of modern life, longed for a simpler and more orderly society and world, especially in the face of a Communist conspiracy. Harry Byrd became revered as the archetype of the rugged individualist, the self-made businessman—now almost extinct—who had made America great. Like retired ballplayers whose names are called forth to prove the superiority of the old game, Byrd became the exemplar of an older way of doing things. His friend Bernard Baruch lauded him: "I think there is no man in Congress who compares either in integrity or patriotism or ability with you."[21]

Such acclaim was particularly strong when he was locked in combat with the liberals. In December 1949 at the annual meeting of the Academy of Political Science in New York, Byrd and Senator Paul Douglas of Illinois "debated" the subject of American democracy and the welfare state. The professorial Douglas, a noted economist, gave a scholarly discourse on the historical abuses of power in which he suggested that the welfare state had grown out of the necessity to combat injustice, economic monopoly, depression, and war. Byrd's address, culled from his speeches of the past year, was a recitation on socialism in government. Injecting stories about his voting record into his talk ("I don't follow Republicans; my name begins with 'B' and Republicans follow me"), he offered a patriotic defense of the free enterprise system that brought the pro-business crowd to its feet. He was pleased with his performance against the more erudite Douglas.[22]

Two months later freshman Senator Hubert Humphrey of Minnesota, perhaps spurred on by Senate liberals and administration strategists, took on Byrd and his joint committee on federal spending. On the Senate floor Humphrey called the Byrd economy committee a "publicity medium" and the "number one example of waste and extravagance" in the government. He asserted that it produced undocumented reports based on outdated information and duplicated the work of other committees. Offering a bill to abolish Byrd's committee, he pointed to waste in its expenditures, in the time spent by government agencies in compiling data asked for by the committee, and in the printing of its reports. Much of what Humphrey said about the economy committee was true, but he had attacked the wrong man and in the wrong way.[23]

Byrd, who had not been present for this speech, first retaliated in public, insisting that his "watchdogs of the Treasury" had saved the country millions of dollars and exposed the waste of millions more. "I am complimented," he boasted, "that the extravagant spenders in Congress want to kill our committee. It shows we are getting under their skins." Speaking on the Senate floor six days later, he orchestrated a masterful put-down of the Minnesotan, accusing Humphrey of making misstatements of record and distorting the work of the committee. No senator, he said, pursued publicity like "Mr. Humphrey," who was never known for "hiding his light under a bushel." Byrd offered to resign from the committee and have it abolished, but not as a result of misinformation. At this point fifteen of the Virginian's colleagues, each one recognized by Byrd, who held the floor, rose to praise their friend and his committee.[24] When Humphrey attempted to respond, Byrd and his cohorts walked out, leaving a near-empty chamber and a humiliated junior senator. Journalist Richard Cope called it "one of the most complete insults any Senator has delivered or received in a long time."

Although he always thought that "Byrd was a phony on this issue," Humphrey acknowledged that he had chosen the wrong target and had violated a Senate tradition by attacking a member when he was not on the floor. Shortly thereafter he ran into Byrd on the elevator and offered his hand and his apology. When his original sources offered him more material with which to attack the committee, Humphrey exclaimed: "I wouldn't care if what you have is a newly discovered chapter from the Bible. I'm not about ready to open up another attack on Senator Byrd. I've been walloped, beaten, worked over. . . . The trouble is that you've been giving me blanks, and they've got howitzers." Remembering this as "the most miserable period of my life," he had discovered where power was located in the Senate.[25]

Only days after Byrd's confrontation with Humphrey, President Truman, without consulting Virginia's senators, appointed Martin Hutchinson to a position on the Federal Trade Commission. The selection was clearly a rebuke to Harry Byrd, who angrily told a friend that "the President desired to slap me" by rewarding "my most conspicuous opponent in Virginia." No one missed the intent. Disappointed with the lack of patronage coming their way after their loyal support of Truman in the 1948 election, the "antis" were jubilant over the Hutchinson nomination. Moss Plunkett wrote the president: "You have dropped your first political atomic bomb on the followers of the Byrd machine in Virginia. No one realizes this better than the gentlemen of the press of the State." Truman had no misconceptions about the ability of the "antis" to depose Byrd; he merely wanted to demonstrate that loyalty was a two-way street; patronage at his disposal was not going to his enemies. And if, as in this case, he could deliver a broadside at one who had so often opposed his policies and his nominees, so much the better.[26]

Almost at once parallels were drawn between the Hutchinson nomination and the Roberts nomination in 1938 that Byrd and Glass had defeated through senatorial courtesy. However, since the FTC post was a Washington position that did not require consultation with senators, observers predicted that Byrd would not challenge the nomination. Nor did Truman believe Byrd would accept the discomfort of opposing Hutchinson on political grounds alone. They all underestimated the senator, for if the president's intention was primarily personal, Byrd saw its political ramifications for the Old Dominion. His own reelection—if he chose to run—would be the next major contest in the state, and he could not permit any encouragement of the recently revived "antis," no matter how modest. As Fred Switzer told him, this was an attempt to "humiliate and embarrass" him and to remove him from the Democratic party in Virginia. Unless it was fought to "the bitter end," it would lead to further purge efforts. Moreover, in the just-adjourned General Assembly, a group of young delegates—"Young Turks" they were called—had demonstrated dissatisfaction with Organization orthodoxy on expenditures for state services; their independence could not be emboldened by a sign of weakness.[27]

To kill Hutchinson's nomination, Byrd, joined by Senator Robertson, directed a 3,000-word letter to the Senate Commerce Committee in which he derided Hutchinson's training and competence for the position.[28] He saw the appointment as a personal affront that had a "definite political purpose," namely, "to unseat the senior senator from his position of power." Demonstrating the unwillingness of the club to offend one of its own, the committee reported the nomination unfavorably, and the full Senate rejected it two months later, 59–14, furnishing further evidence of Byrd's enduring authority and his ability to insulate his regime from outside interference. Consoling a disillusioned Hutchinson, Douglas Freeman told him that Byrd's opposition was due to "political spite . . . the same spirit that often deters able men from entering the public service."[29]

It would have been easy for Byrd to have capitalized on these liberal assaults by tying his rhetoric against socialist trends to the wave of anti-Communist hysteria that was gripping the country. Confrontation with the Soviets—exacerbated by Communist takeovers in Hungary and Czechoslovakia, the Berlin airlift, expensive military and economic aid programs, and the creation of NATO—had generated understandable concern about another war. Upon discovery of Soviet spy networks in America, highlighted by the cases against Alger Hiss and the Rosenbergs, this concern turned first into suspicion and then fear that the Communists had infiltrated America and might bring it down from within. Into this climate of fear and self-doubt strode the junior senator from Wisconsin, Joseph R. McCarthy, to create a new Red Scare. From February 1950, when he claimed to have the names of 205 Communists working for the State Department, until the Army-McCarthy hearings four years later, Joe McCarthy rode the crest of this hysteria, intimidating two administrations and the United States Senate, ruining reputations of ordinary citizens, and fouling the political climate with his vulgar and abusive tactics.

To his credit, Harry Byrd had little to do with Joe McCarthy; nor did he play the demagogue as did many of his Republican colleagues such as Taft, Richard Nixon, William Jenner, and Kenneth Wherry, all of whom relished the political benefits of McCarthy's attacks on the Truman administration. Like most Americans, Byrd loathed communism and worried about his nation's security, which led him to support the making of the H-bomb. On occasion he voted against Truman's nominees on the grounds that they were too far left, as when he opposed the appointment of David Lilienthal to head the Atomic Energy Commission; the nominee was, in Byrd's view, "as dangerous as if he were an avowed apostle of Communism." But he bravely defended fellow Virginian George Marshall when the Republican right condemned his appointment to be secretary of defense in September 1950.[30] He approved of investigations of Communists in government, but he made no claims about their presence there, likely because the self-ordained investigators found very few. For Byrd, the real threat was not unidentifiable subversives but the financial insolvency or socialist trends that would bring the government down. He did not approve of McCarthy's methods, especially when they involved false charges against Virginians, and he had little contact with the Wisconsin senator whom he called "mischievous."[31]

The American engagement in Korea fueled this anti-Communist crusade, but the war at least provided an issue on which Senator Byrd and President Truman could agree, however temporarily. On June 25, 1950, North Korea invaded South Korea, crossing another of the borders created by World War II and made permanent by the impasse between the United States and the Soviet Union. Truman immediately judged the conflict to be fomented by the Russians or the Chinese Communists and ordered American units stationed in Japan to respond, fearing that inaction would destabilize America's position in the Far East and encourage other acts of aggression.

Except for some grumbling by Senator Taft about "usurpation" of constitutional authority, Truman had considerable congressional backing as well as popular approval for his initial response, in spite of the nation's unpreparedness. Senator Byrd pledged his "full and unqualified support" to the president to drive the North Koreans out of South Korea. He especially commended the joint action with the United Nations, seeing this as an opportunity for that organization to prove itself. "This is the time for unity, for we must win," he declared. Byrd realized that the war would lead to a major long-range national defense program, so even in the midst of a crisis, he could not refrain from demanding cuts in nondefense spending if a full mobilization was implemented. Nor could he resist commenting on the "ineffectiveness" of foreign aid as demonstrated by the collapse of the South Koreans despite the millions spent for their arming and training. "We cannot carry the world on our shoulders abroad and the New Deal on our backs at home without destroying the foundation principles of our democracy," he warned.[32]

With the rest of the nation, Byrd savored General Douglas MacArthur's brilliant September victory at Inchon that turned the tide of war and initiated a triumphal march up the Korean peninsula. But the entry of the Chinese Communists in November, followed by the massive retreat southward, pushed Byrd into the camp of the defeatists who claimed that it had been a mistake to go to war in Korea and an even greater mistake to cross the thirty-eighth parallel. In his view it was only a "sideline war" that did not justify the effort to make "democrats out of people who do not want to be democrats." Byrd wailed, "We are outnumbered and defeated in Korea to the extent that death or capture is inevitable unless retreat and evacuation is possible." Disillusioned, he wrote to Frank Wysor, "Things are rapidly going from bad to worse here in Washington, and if we do not get our boys out of Korea they will either be captured or massacred."[33]

Joining Senator Taft and former president Hoover, Byrd called for a full examination of American foreign and domestic policies and enumerated his solutions for the crisis: an impregnable national defense (which included "compulsory military training, the largest supply of A-bombs, a 70-group air force, and a radar screen"), an end to foreign giveaways, cuts in nondefense spending, and acceptance of austerity for the foreseeable future. Part of his critique had merit, particularly his warnings about the limitations of America's power and the dangers of being drawn into future sideline wars against Russian surrogates, but his timing was unfortunate. With the nation's army in retreat, it was not the time for concession speeches and hindsight evaluations. Byrd badly erred in his recommendation to evacuate Korea. Even if the initial commitment had been questionable, a withdrawal at this point would have sent the wrong signal to the enemy. It was imperative to stabilize the front and preserve the integrity of South Korea.[34]

The crisis in Korea was brought to a head in the spring of 1951 when Truman fired MacArthur as commander of the United Nations forces for insubordination. Senator Byrd hewed a middle road between Republicans, who demanded the president's head, and Democrats, who defended Truman against a general who had challenged civilian control of the military. He first referred to the inept way in which MacArthur had been dismissed. A few days later, as the general returned to popular acclaim, Byrd praised MacArthur and suggested that he be made governor of Japan until the peace treaty formally ending World War II could be signed. Accusing Truman of personally slighting MacArthur and producing national disunity through his "tragedy of errors," he approved of an invitation to MacArthur to address Congress and confer with appropriate committees. Although Willis Robertson tried to convince him that the general had left Truman no choice but to dismiss him, Byrd did not comment on the substantive issues raised by the firing. As a member of the Armed Services Committee, he listened to the testimony of MacArthur and administration officials regarding American policy in the Far East, but he was not an active participant in the questioning. While the MacArthur controversy was politically damaging to Truman, the Senate hearings undermined the general's credibility and restored a degree of faith in the administration's Korean policy.[35]

The Korean War, especially in its first year, consumed much of Congress's time, but it did not distract Byrd from his primary interest, the budget. In 1950 Congress adopted the single appropriation bill that he had first recommended in 1947. He believed the consolidated bill would result in more orderly fiscal planning by enabling legislators to see total revenues, appropriations, and projected expenditures all at one time and so compare the relative merits of all programs. Having tried unsuccessfully to get the Hoover Commission on Organization of the Executive Branch of the Government to recommend this change in budgeting methods to Congress, Byrd persevered and, with help from Clarence Cannon, chairman of the House Appropriations Committee, won a trial run for the procedure in 1950.

Byrd claimed that the single appropriation method was responsible for cutting $2 billion from Truman's budget, but he could not get the House to continue the experiment. In opposing the idea, Representative John Taber argued that since the budget figures had not gone through the normal subcommittee review, they were too raw for a full Congress to analyze. He summarized the process: "The Bill came into the full [Appropriations] Committee. Instead of having a presentation of the whole picture in detail from the Chairman of each sub-committee, each Chairman was allowed ten to fifteen minutes and the Minority about the same. We got on the floor and I had to stay there for six solid weeks for five hours and sometimes more a day. That was the worst drilling I ever went through. . . . Frankly, I do not like that way of legislating." The omnibus budget bill of 1950 had, indeed, produced a chaotic situation that was complicated by the supplemental appropriations required by the Korean War. All regular appropriation bills had been dumped into one bill with no controls on annual obligations and no expenditure estimates. Byrd urged refinements to correct these deficiencies, but he was unable to convince his colleagues on the House side.[36]

This defeat, however, did not deter him from persisting in his efforts to reduce federal spending. The Korean War prompted a threefold increase in military spending that resulted in a $30 billion jump in the administration's budget for 1951. The president also asked for a large tax increase to put the defense effort on a pay-as-you-go basis. Raising another alarm, Senator Byrd, "in a spirit of cooperation and constructive suggestion," asked Truman to trim $7.6 billion in nondefense spending. He pleaded: "Your leadership is required. Without it, drastic budget reductions may be difficult, if not impossible." Although privately thanking Byrd for his suggestions, the president cavalierly told a press conference that Byrd did not know enough about the budget to criticize it, whereupon the senator responded that Truman did not comprehend the need to cut expenditures in the face of "financial chaos and ultimate disaster." When the budget finally appeared, Byrd said it represented the "height of fiscal irresponsibility."[37]

Try as he might, Byrd was unable to influence government spending to any significant degree in 1951. The demands of the Korean War and the Cold War, as well as the greater demand for more government services, triumphed over his objections. By harping on waste and sniping at excessive requests, he was able to achieve some savings, beneficial to be sure, but far short of his goals. To highlight government excesses, he cited publication of pamphlets on *Raccoons in North America* and *Can Elephants and Water Buffaloes Outwork Machinery?* He won amendments to cut funds for government press agents and White House staff and entertainment. In concert with Republicans, Byrd helped reduce foreign aid by $1 billion and military appropriations by $3 billion and keep the tax increase to half of what the president wanted. It was time, he said, to "put Santa Claus in a deep freeze." Reflecting on his work at the time of his sixty-fourth birthday, Byrd said it was an unpleasant task that needed to be done if the rising tide of state socialism and national insolvency was to be rolled back. As if to accentuate his differences with the architects of the New Deal and Fair Deal, he remarked that he had been to dinner at the White House only once in eighteen years. This was not likely to change in the near future. Nevertheless, in a poll of Washington newspaper and radio correspondents, Byrd was ranked as one of the ten best senators.[38]

It was no surprise when Senator Byrd kicked off the 1952 presidential sweepstakes with a bitter denunciation of the Truman administration in a speech to Georgia Democrats in June 1951. Repeating many of his previous indictments of socialistic legislation, civil rights programs, and waste in government, Byrd threatened a southern secession from the party. "The South," he warned, "is not impotent. The true principles of our constitutional democracy are immortal. These fundamentals cannot be dimmed by age or distorted by demagogues." Although he denied any threat, the message was clear. Truman would not be supported by southern Democrats in 1952.[39]

By distinguishing between Truman Democrats and "real" Democrats, Byrd was following the lead of the Dixiecrats of 1948, who were planning another bolt if Truman was nominated. Since he had a hundred thousand copies of his speech printed for distribution, some observers saw it as the opening of his own campaign for the presidency. Senator Karl Mundt of South Dakota called for a coalition of Jeffersonian Democrats and states' rights Republicans to support Byrd for president. A poll of newspaper editors ranked Byrd a close third behind Truman and Senator Douglas as the likely nominee of the Democratic party. But Byrd had no such ambition. His obsession now was the defeat of a man whose continuation in office he found philosophically reprehensible and personally offensive. Senator Robertson predicted that if Truman ran for re-election, "Byrd will not be a candidate for re-election to the Senate but will spend all of his time and energy in defeating Truman without accepting the nomination to head a splinter party." Appearing on the covers of *Pathfinder* and *U.S. News and World Report,* Byrd was portrayed as the leader of the southern effort to defeat Truman.[40]

Despite the illness of Mrs. Byrd, who had suffered two heart attacks in early October, Byrd, accompanied by former governor Tuck, traveled to Selma, Alabama, to deliver an even more powerful broadside against Truman to the Dallas County Farm Bureau on November 1. Wearing a gray tie with a Confederate battle flag embroidered on it, he addressed 2,800 of the faithful in a drizzling rain with a scathing indictment of the "Trumanites"—the Boyles, Pendergasts, and Humphreys—for attempting to take over the party with "an unholy alliance of tin-horn political incompetents and socialistic do-gooders." Before a sympathetic audience he lambasted the administration's civil rights program and, in the light of new disclosures of scandal, condemned the debauchery and moral weakness in Washington. It was the South's responsibility to save the party from this corrupt gang: "Democrats of the South will not permit the Trumanites to press down on the brow of America the undemocratic crown of waste, of socialism, and of dictation from Washington." Having no specific plan of action, Byrd urged his listeners to stand ready for "courageous action" that might necessitate reforming the national party. The *Times-Dispatch* called it a "pungent and provocative speech." Bill Tuck, who could well have written parts of the speech (along with William Jennings Bryan), was more reverential; he told Byrd that he was "the greatest living man in American public life."[41]

Few senators have ever spoken out so forcefully against the leader of their own party. Over the next month Byrd reiterated his message in a series of speeches across the country. Sounding more like a Republican than a Democrat, he labeled the Trumanites "a greater menace to this country than Russians." The drift to socialism, he said, was playing into the hands of the Kremlin, and the reelection of the administration would "push us over the precipice into a form of government that did not make America great." Appearing with Senator Taft before the Los Angeles convention of the American Medical Association, he attacked the socialist trends in government and indicated that the southern Democrats might vote Republican if Truman was the Democratic nominee. A former law partner of Senator Richard Nixon's commented on Byrd's performance: "Byrd almost stole the show. He was witty, clever, and had the audience in stitches. . . . There was a general surge of feeling throughout the meeting that Byrd and Taft should be nominated by the Republicans."[42]

The intensity of Byrd's hostility toward Truman cannot be explained merely as a difference of opinion over policy, although their disagreement on every major issue of the last two years was almost total. He wrote James J.

Kilpatrick, "If we re-elect this regime here in Washington I doubt whether we will ever get rid of it before we go into bankruptcy and a moral deterioration from which we will never recover." Byrd also feared federal intrusion in the civil rights field, but other factors turned a philosophical difference into a visceral antagonism. Having committed to a "golden silence" in 1948, Byrd, like the Republicans, was shocked by Truman's victory and spent four years plotting revenge. Truman had invited Byrd's further animosity with his comment that there were "too many Byrds in Congress" and with his appointment of Martin Hutchinson to the Federal Trade Commission. Finally, having decided to run for reelection, Byrd wanted to draw the clearest distinction between himself and the president in order to distinguish himself from any candidate the "antis" might run against him in 1952. Conservative T. Coleman Andrews encouraged Byrd to lead a movement for party realignment, but the senator refused. He never considered leaving the Democrats for the Republicans, because of both sentiment and the fear that his departure would destroy his political organization in Virginia.[43]

On February 28, 1952, Senator Russell announced his presidential candidacy and received the quick endorsement of his colleague from Virginia. There were rumors that Russell, Byrd, and Jimmy Byrnes had joined forces to stop Truman. Columnist Ray Tucker wrote that the three southerners had met after the Alfalfa Club dinner in mid-January to plot strategy—the "Alfalfa breakaway" Tucker called it. According to Tucker, Byrnes and Russell first suggested that Byrd run against the president, but the Virginian declined, arguing that as a foe of labor and a noted sectionalist with little appeal beyond the South he had no hope of victory. Dick Russell, on the other hand, was a Senate leader who had much broader appeal and had not been identified as an opponent of the New Deal or Truman. A superb parliamentarian with strong interests in defense and farm legislation, he was one of the smartest and shrewdest members of the club. Like Byrd, Russell also believed that he had little chance for the nomination because of his position on civil rights, but under pressure from his southern colleagues, who feared that liberal Tennessee senator Estes Kefauver might control southern state delegations, he decided to run in order to increase the South's influence in the party. Russell's candidacy moved from the token stage to a full-fledged effort when President Truman withdrew from the race in late March.[44]

The president obviously had had enough. Despite the opening of truce talks the previous summer, the Korean War was dragging on with no immediate prospects of an ending. A cloud of scandal hovered over his administration; within days of his withdrawal, he fired his attorney general for failure to pursue vigorously an investigation into charges of government corruption. Senator McCarthy's attacks on Communists in government continued to reverberate, implicating even the venerable George Marshall, now retired after a lifetime of service to his country. Although Truman had not announced his candidacy, his name was on the ballot in the New Hampshire primary, where he was trounced decisively by Senator Kefauver. Unpopular, discredited, and dispirited, Truman called it quits. Although the *Times-Dispatch* credited Byrd, Byrnes, and Russell for eliminating him, it was the issues of the forthcoming campaign—K_1C_2: Korea, communism, and corruption—that ended the political career of the man from Missouri.[45]

∽ 16 ∾

The Organization Totters

WITH TRUMAN removed from the arena, Byrd turned his attention in 1952 to state politics, specifically to another challenge to the Organization mounted by the "antis." Although John Battle's administration was addressing the problems of education and mental hospitals, there was growing dissatisfaction with the pace of progress and the wielding of authoritarian control. Francis Pickens Miller, preparing for a senate race against Byrd, emphasized this point by referring to the "dry rot" in the Virginia Democracy: the "anti-Truman" bill, the invitation to Republicans to vote in Democratic primaries, and the rejection of a popular vote on the poll tax. Faced with such charges, Byrd saw no machine candidate, with the possible exception of Bill Tuck, who could fend off the aggressive Miller. On April 10 he announced his intention to run for a fourth term, declaring that his preference not to run was overruled by his desire to preserve the fundamental principles of government. He stressed his independence and his votes of conscience. "I have worn no man's collar," he said, "and the only test on my voting was whether it was best for the United States."[1]

Within the week Miller declared his candidacy, vowing a "hot fight" against a record of "isolationism and indifference." Citing Byrd's votes against the Marshall Plan, the Truman Doctrine, and the loan to Great Britain, he accused Byrd of joining the Taft wing of the Republican party. As he had indicated earlier, the other issue of his campaign would be Organization control of Virginia politics. Although there had been some reservations in the "anti" camp about making a fruitless race against the popular incumbent, Miller could rely upon the avid support of that intrepid band led by Robert Whitehead, who was considering a run of his own for the governorship the following year. They had little money and had to rely upon their enthusiasm and an implacable hatred of the machine. As Vic Wilson of Hampton, who had defeated Organization stalwart G. Alvin Massenburg for a seat in the General Assembly, told Martin Hutchinson, "Let me live long enough to witness the complete annihilation of Harry Byrd and his stooges."[2]

Taking Miller's candidacy seriously, Byrd organized his campaign as diligently as any he had ever run. Anticipating the contest, he audaciously recommended that the date of the primary be moved from its traditional time in early August to July 15, a request to which the General Assembly graciously assented. The shift placed the election before both the state and national party conventions, enabling Byrd to avoid having to commit to the Democratic platform and presidential candidate during his own campaign. The senator also convinced Bill Tuck to assume chairmanship of the state party, and he persuaded Governor Battle to delay calling a special session of the legislature that was to consider reapportionment until after the primary. Albertis Harrison, state senator from Brunswick in the crucial Southside, assumed command of the campaign. He would be aided by the old guard of Frank Wysor in the southwest, Billy Prieur and Sidney Kellam in the Norfolk area, congressmen Watkins Abbitt and Howard Smith, Bill Tuck, and the ubiquitous Ebbie Combs. To his campaign managers Byrd wrote: "Take nothing for granted. . . . Effect a thorough organization to get our vote to the polls on election day. . . . Leave no stone unturned." The old network of local officeholders was revived, poll taxes of dependable voters were paid, and the channels of correspondence to precinct workers were reopened. He rejected Miller's offer to debate the issues, knowing his own weakness in such unpredictable forums. Byrd's commitment to his reelection campaign was so intense that his Senate chores suffered; he was on hand for only 60 percent of the roll calls, one of the lowest attendance figures in the Senate.[3]

Byrd needed no encouragement to crusade against the "Trumanites," but a personal tragedy increased his absorption in the campaign. In late March his daughter Westwood died of an overdose of sleeping pills; whether they were taken accidentally or intentionally was never fully determined. At the request of her father, she had stayed on at Rosemont after her divorce to take care of the estate and her mother, but being a very energetic person, she found those tasks left her too little to do. An avid horsewoman, Westy had been thrown from horses in 1946 and 1951 and broke her neck and back. Although not incapacitated, she lived with intense pain and required sedatives to sleep. Friends and relatives believe she was in good spirits at the time and could not possibly have taken her own life. Her death touched the Byrds deeply, and Harry Jr. was glad his father had the race against Miller to take his mind off it.[4]

Byrd's strategy in the campaign was obvious: tie Miller to the Truman administration and run against that record. Campaign manager Harrison said the choice was clear between the Truman philosophy of taxation, spending, and socialism and Byrd's advocacy of private initiative and free enterprise. Although Miller was aware of the liability of his association with Truman, he opened himself to attack when he offhandedly said, "On every one of the great issues which have confronted him, the President has made the right decision."

After that comment, he never succeeded in shaking the label of "Trumanite." Moreover, his statement about "dry rot" in Virginia politics was turned against him as a disparaging remark about Virginia itself, something a true native son would never say about the Old Dominion. Harry Byrd was "not ashamed of Virginia"; as he told his campaign managers, "Mr. Miller has never had a kind word to say about Virginia, but apparently approves of practically everything being done at Washington." Finally, Byrd used Miller's pro-labor record to good advantage, reminding his listeners of the efforts of organized labor to take over the state.

Truman's seizure of the nation's steel mills in early April played to Byrd's strength by highlighting the president's own heavy-handed methods as well as the threat to national security of strikes by selfish unions. Byrd condemned the seizure, calling it "the most autocratic, the most Caesar-like action taken in Washington since I have been in the Senate." Voting to deny Truman funds to carry out his plans, he applauded the Supreme Court's decision that found the president's action unconstitutional. Truman ignored Byrd's request to invoke the Taft-Hartley Act to end the strike, and it dragged on until late July when the steelworkers accepted a sizable pay increase. Miller doubtlessly regretted his statement of faith in the president.[5]

Motivated by Miller's aggressive campaign and his own personal tragedy, Byrd turned the Old Dominion into a "burned-over" district, delivering over three hundred speeches—sometimes as many as eight a day—in all corners of the state. Dressed in his double-breasted white suit, he spoke rapidly, occasionally gesturing or pounding the podium, his face reddening as he moved to the attack. Time after time he threw the "dry rot" statement in Miller's face with an impressive set of statistics showing the progress in the state and its secure financial position, asserting that Virginia was "like an oasis in a desert of corruption." "Dry rot" was "tommy-rot." To lay to rest the implication that he, too, might be over the hill, Byrd challenged Miller to a climb up Old Rag Mountain. It produced the only humorous note in an otherwise bitter campaign when Miller accepted contingent upon Byrd's debating him after they reached the top. Columnists began rating the candidates' mountain-climbing abilities and predicting the finish, but the hike was never held.[6]

As the campaign moved into its middle stage, it began to degenerate into a name-calling contest. Byrd labeled Miller a New Deal spendthrift and a CIO-sponsored candidate who associated with liberals and supported their civil rights legislation. When Robert Whitehead inappropriately referred to the increase in Byrd's wealth since his arrival in the Senate, the senator called it "a slimy and contemptible bit of political demagoguery." Retaliating with a bit of demagoguery himself, he suggested that Miller had studied at Oxford as a Rhodes Scholar because the University of Virginia was not good enough for him. Reminding voters that he had gone to Washington and Lee University before furthering his education abroad, Miller responded, "If Harry Byrd had ever studied in Europe or if he knew anything at first hand about the rest of the world he would have been spared some of his worst errors of judgment." Blaming both parties, the *Times-Dispatch* concluded that the campaign was getting "badly off base," leaving accuracy and good taste behind.[7]

Despite the adverse publicity neither side backed off, and the campaign disintegrated into a series of charges and countercharges that rehashed stale and specious issues. Claiming that he had never had so many charges and misrepresentations thrown at him, Byrd lamented that he was being blamed for everything that had happened in Virginia since 1775. Old Dominion voters felt otherwise. In a record vote for a Virginia primary, Byrd won 63 percent of the total, taking every district but the Ninth. The "antis" blamed "Trumanism" and the Republicans for their defeat, but in reality it was Harry Byrd who had defeated Miller. His record of economy and efficiency and his independence and incorruptibility still proved congenial to a majority of the voters.[8]

Perhaps the most significant result of the 1952 primary was the death of the "anti" movement in Virginia. Carrying on a twentieth-century tradition of opposition to the entrenched machine, the "antis" had emerged in the 1930s to challenge Harry Byrd's control of Virginia politics. Though occasionally creating consternation among Organization leaders, they achieved little, with the possible exception of Jim Price's victory in 1937, and that was more a personal triumph than a group success. Relatively liberal in a very conservative state, without adequate funds, and confronting a powerful machine that denied them access to all levers of power—the legislature, state bureaucracy, and local offices—they won no major election after 1937 and did not push the Organization to a more liberal position. Only the missteps of the Organization in the 1948 effort to defeat President Truman and the multicandidate gubernatorial election in 1949 offered them any real opportunity to succeed. But the passage of a runoff primary law in 1952 which prevented victory by plurality, the moderate record of Governor Battle, Harry Truman's unpopularity, and Harry Byrd's prestige rendered them impotent. The subsequent struggle over school desegregation in the Old Dominion overwhelmed liberal efforts to move Virginia forward. The only consolation for the "antis" was that in time the goals that they had been fighting for—abolition of the poll tax, more funding for education, and an end to machine rule—came to pass in the 1960s.[9]

Byrd had little time to savor his victory, for within the week—because of his own nefarious planning—he had to attend the state and national party conventions that would determine his and Virginia's course in the upcoming presidential election. Committed to Senator Russell, Byrd prepared to give him the endorsement of the Virginia convention, but at the last moment the Georgian seemed to waver on the question of repealing the Taft-Hartley Act, and the stunned delegates threw away their Russell buttons and voted for an unin- structed delegation. Byrd and Governor Battle were disappointed with Russell's politicking for the labor vote but reaffirmed their personal support for the Georgian. In a stirring keynote address to the Roanoke throng, former gover- nor Tuck, ever the picturesque phrasemaker, delivered a blistering attack on the "pompous and arrogant Lilliputian leadership" in Washington. Warning that Virginia would not "genuflect to Trumanism and Fair Dealism," Tuck, on behalf of the state committee, asked for and received authority under the "anti- Truman" bill to recall the state convention if the results of the national gather- ing were unacceptable. He made no mention of bolting the party, but his inten- tion was clear. Byrd and Tuck went to Chicago two days later prepared to battle for an acceptable candidate and against a strong civil rights plank, using a threatened walkout as their trump card. The Republicans' nomination of Gen- eral Eisenhower made that possibility all the more appealing.[10]

The 1952 Democratic national convention was one of the more tumultuous meetings in party history. Already regionally divided over nominees and plat- form, the Democrats almost came apart on the question of loyalty oaths. Northern Democrats were upset with southerners who enjoyed the benefits of party membership—seniority, campaign funds, and patronage—but who gave minimal support to party nominees and programs. Angered by the 1948 defec- tions, they determined to impose a modest pledge on all delegates to the effect that it would be the "honorable course of every delegate . . . to support the majority decisions of this convention here and hereafter." Senator Byrd consid- ered this an insult to his integrity. Terming the pledge "untenable" in light of the state convention's resolution for a possible recall that might reinstruct the delegates, Byrd vowed to fight the oath, declaring, "My votes in the Senate will not be controlled by some resolutions here in Chicago."[11]

Party liberals supporting the candidacies of New York's Averell Harriman and Tennessee's Estes Kefauver also were dissatisfied with the pledge, but for different reasons. Hoping to improve their chances of victory by diffusing southern power in the convention, they sought a more specific commitment that would require delegates to ensure that the nominees would be on the state ballot under the name of the Democratic party, a reasonable expectation of any national party, but one which Virginia Democrats had been trying to circum- vent for four years. Although the pledge did not require them to support the party's nominees, Byrd, Tuck, and Battle were incensed at the continuing effort to restrict their freedom of action. Governor Battle fumed, "The democracy of Virginia is not accustomed to being put on terms." The senator was more di- rect, castigating the pledge as "improper and absurd . . . the most asinine thing

I've ever heard of." Despite such protestations, the convention approved the substitute resolution offered by Michigan Senator Blair Moody.[12]

Opposed to signing any loyalty oath, Virginia delegates met in a Tuesday morning caucus on July 22 to consider their options. No one—at least publicly—was willing to sign the pledge, but a more moderate element, led by Lieutenant Governor Preston Collins and state senator Charles Fenwick, preferred to give the convention assurances that the names of party nominees would be on the ballot—in accordance with Virginia law—while reserving the right to withdraw from the convention if they could not honorably accept some action. The Old Guard, led by Byrd, Tuck, and Robertson, wanted no assurances proffered that might imply a concession on Virginia's part. After heated debate the caucus, at Senator Byrd's suggestion, appointed a six-man committee to draft Virginia's response. The statement conformed closely to Collins's position. Referring the convention to Virginia laws that made it mandatory that nominees be on the ballot under the party's name, it reserved freedom of action for the delegates from convention decisions as defined in the resolution of the state convention. In accordance with Byrd's desires, the statement would merely be published; it offered no concession and requested none. "Our strategy," he defiantly remarked, "is not to communicate with the Credentials Committee, but just remain in our seats and let them be the aggressors and let them read us out of the convention or throw us out bodily if they will." In passing the statement to the Credentials Committee, Governor Battle added the provision that under no circumstances would they sign the loyalty pledge.

While the Virginians caucused, leaders of the Harriman and Kefauver factions, fearful of widening a split that might harm the party in the fall elections, produced a compromise interpretation intended to meet southern objections. Delegates would not be bound by the pledge if such action contravened state law or the instructions of the governing body of the state party. The compromise won the approval of most southern delegations, but Virginia, joined by South Carolina and Louisiana, was not mollified. Its leaders argued that the oath implied acceptance of everything the convention might do. Seemingly oblivious to the permutations of the pledge, which was now so watered down as to be meaningless, Byrd continued to insist that his future votes in the Senate would not be bound by a convention loyalty oath. He blamed the pledge on New Dealers "who want all delegates to obey their commands."[13]

On Wednesday the crisis over the seating of the three recalcitrant delegations came to a head. Given the Credentials Committee report that they had not signed the pledge, temporary convention chairman Paul Dever ruled that they would not be allowed to vote on the seating of the contested delegations from Texas and Mississippi. An embittered Byrd said to Governor Byrnes of

South Carolina: "Well, that ends it. We'll use our seats as spectators. They'll have to throw us out." Searching for a solution, an anxious national party chairman Frank McKinney invited Senator Byrd, Governor Battle, Governor Byrnes, and Governor Robert Kennon of Louisiana to a conference where he offered to seat the three delegations by declaring that party leaders had ruled that they were in substantial compliance with the pledge. Byrd and Battle rejected his interpretation as a subterfuge that implied a concession on Virginia's part. They demanded the rescission of the Moody resolution or an opportunity to state publicly that Virginia had not backed down. They wanted their seats without reservations. McKinney was not prepared to go this far, and the forty-five-minute session ended with Byrd blustering: "We are not going to yield one damn inch. . . . They are trying to maneuver around now to get us to vote but we are not going to sign anything." Back in caucus where Virginians rousingly endorsed his actions, Byrd haughtily declared, "Virginia has not budged one iota—has not dotted an 'i' or crossed a 't'—from its original position."[14]

For three days, while party leaders dithered over the issue of the loyalty oath, the more important business of the convention proceeded, with tempers occasionally flaring in the smoke and heat of the auditorium. Eleanor Roosevelt was given a fifteen-minute demonstration when she arrived, but seven southern states, including Virginia, refused to participate; Byrd reportedly left the hall. Almost overlooked was the passage of a watered-down civil rights plank that favored federal legislation to secure "equal opportunity for employment" and "full and equal participation in the nation's political life"; although it made no mention of the poll tax or a compulsory FEPC, it was still unacceptable to the South. Its mildness indicated that moderates, not liberals, were in control of convention machinery. Candidates Harriman, Kefauver, Russell, and Senator Bob Kerr of Oklahoma milled among the delegates, while backers of Governor Adlai Stevenson of Illinois maneuvered for a draft of their reluctant candidate. Russell had met with the Virginia delegation to reassure them that he was not in favor of repealing Taft-Hartley, only amending it. Satisfied with his explanation, they agreed to support him if given the opportunity.[15]

A little past noon on Thursday, July 24, nominating speeches for the many candidates began, while party leaders attempted to reach some compromise on the loyalty oath. In the morning caucus Byrd had been overheard to say, "They are trying to steamroller us . . . we won't sign on the dotted line." Not all Virginians agreed. It was estimated that about one-third of the delegates, having received reports from home that the Old Dominion was looking "reactionary" and acting like it had "a chip on her shoulder," preferred to compromise; other delegates were ready to walk out. At 7 P.M., with most of the nominations completed, permanent chairman Sam Rayburn recognized Louisiana, which yielded to Virginia in what was clearly a prearranged deal. Over the protests of several northern delegations, Rayburn permitted Governor Battle to address the convention. In brief but eloquent remarks, the tall, dignified Battle affirmed Virginia's law that required nominees of major parties to be on the ballot, but, he said, the Old Dominion objected to a pledge that might be construed as binding it to future action. Referring to Thomas Jefferson, "in whose county I happen to live—the great patron saint of this Party, who believed in freedom of thought and freedom of action," Battle declared, "We are not going to sign any pledge or any commitment which will abridge that freedom which we claim for ourselves and believe you would like for yourselves." Bill Tuck, who had followed Battle to the podium to support him, told him, "John, that was just the best speech heard anywhere by any man." Byrd likewise was effusive in his praise of the governor's speech. When the convention was over, he wrote Battle to commend the "magnificent leadership you gave us at Chicago. I was never more proud of anything in my life. You handled the whole thing superbly."[16]

But while Battle's remarks were applauded by Virginians, they seemed to have had little effect on the other delegates. Rayburn ruled that Virginia still could not participate, at which point Representative Lansdale Sasscer of Maryland moved that Virginia be seated officially since Battle's statement seemed in compliance with the reinterpreted Moody Resolution. Amid general confusion, Rayburn asked for a roll-call vote on the question; it consumed three hours, during which time two people fainted and a small fire broke out in the South Carolina delegation. The vote to seat Virginia was the crucial moment of the convention, but it had little to do with Battle's remarks or loyalty oaths. It was an intense political struggle between the Harriman-Kefauver forces, who were trying to keep the three conservative southern states out of the nominating process in order to improve their chances of winning, and the handlers of Governor Stevenson, who belatedly realized their opponents' strategy and switched sides. At one point a majority of votes had been cast against the Sasscer motion, but the cagey Rayburn kept the balloting going as states withheld or changed their votes. Finally, the Illinois delegation, which had earlier voted 45-15 to deny Virginia its seat, changed to support the motion, 52-8. The final vote was 615 in favor and 529 against. Very late in the evening, Battle moved that South Carolina and Louisiana also be seated, and after considerable parliamentary maneuvering, their delegations were accepted by a voice vote.[17]

The Old Dominion had won its point, but the bigger winner was Adlai Stevenson, who, with the open support of President Truman, defeated Kefauver and the others on the third ballot in the next day's canvass. Virginia cast its twenty-eight votes on each ballot for Senator Russell. In an effort to appease southerners, the convention selected Alabama senator John Sparkman as Stevenson's running mate, but it had little effect on Harry Byrd, who told Billy Prieur, "I think we did the very best we could under the conditions existing, but it was a very disagreeable situation, and I am glad it is over." To another correspondent he claimed that it would have been "calamitous" to have taken the loyalty pledge since it would have meant "endorsement of such things as compulsory FEPC, socialized medicine, etc. Such an action would have destroyed free thinking, the principle Thomas Jefferson most upheld."[18]

The senator, of course, was not blameless for the "disagreeable situation." He wildly exaggerated the implications of the loyalty oath, both during the convention and afterwards, to justify his obstinate efforts to get the convention to back down or throw Virginia out, a move that he had earlier admitted "a good many of us would welcome." In the words of one commentator, the three states "begged for eviction." The pledge in its final form was so innocuous that it hardly justified a fight; indeed, the loyalty pledge of Byrd's own Virginia Democratic party was much more stringent in what it demanded of its members. Having made "Trumanism" the main issue of his campaign against Miller, Byrd was so obsessed with defeating Truman and the Fair Deal that he was searching for a convenient way to break with the national party in order to choose whatever course he desired in the upcoming election. Yet his own hesitation about a walkout's consequences for the Organization, reinforced by the more moderate voices in the Virginia delegation, prevented the more precipitate action that Jimmy Byrnes had advocated.[19]

As the Virginians returned home from the convention, many expressed enthusiasm for the Stevenson-Sparkman ticket. Senator Robertson, looking ahead to his own reelection two years hence, called Stevenson a "Woodrow Wilson type of liberal and the ablest man the Democrats have nominated since Woodrow Wilson." Shortly thereafter, incumbent congressmen Hardy, Abbitt, and Smith registered their approval. Even Harry Jr. in the Winchester *Evening Star* applauded the Illinois governor for not becoming the candidate of Truman. However, his father, who was upset with Robertson's enthusiastic endorsement, merely said that he had no statement to make at the time; privately he told Bill Tuck that he was in a quandary about supporting a nominee who endorsed policies he found so offensive. Indeed, Byrd's voting record clearly demonstrated a greater affinity for the Republican position than for that of Stevenson. He had voted with Democrats on only 22 percent of the major Senate roll calls, the lowest figure for party unity in the body, which well explains why Virginia Republicans chose not to challenge his reelection to the Senate. As Lester Stovall succinctly put it, "He's the best Republican we've got." His only opposition would come from independent H. M. Vise, Sr., a seventy-year-old retired railroad engineer, and the Socialist candidate, Clarke Robb.[20]

Toward the end of August the presidential battle lines in Virginia were drawn more firmly. Governor Battle endorsed Stevenson, and the state committee indicated its intention to work for all Democratic candidates. However, Bill Tuck, who had been elected state chairman at the July convention, resigned, claiming that he could not commit to the party's nominee until his positions were more clearly delineated. At the same time a "Virginia Democrats for Eisenhower" group was formed. At this point, Byrd and Tuck seemed to have decided upon another "golden silence" similar to that of 1948.[21]

By mid-October it was not clear who was going to win the election, especially in Virginia, which increased the pressure on Byrd to declare his preference. Another strong endorsement of Stevenson by Governor Battle led to Byrd's announcement that he would have some comments on the subject on Friday, October 17. Democrats, Republicans, and Democrats for Eisenhower all waited expectantly, knowing that his nod would determine the results of the election in Virginia. Helped by his son, Byrd finished writing the speech at 4 P.M. on Friday afternoon and went off to the Senate gymnasium for a swim, telling Harry Jr. to polish it up. "But don't polish it too much," he said. "I want the people to understand what I'm talking about."

That evening over a statewide radio network, in a thirty-minute talk read in a "low, calm tone," Byrd castigated the administration and recited his long record of opposing government expansion and labor legislation. "Trumanism," he said, was the dominant issue in "the most momentous political campaign in the history of our nation"; the FEPC, the Taft-Hartley veto, and high taxes were all leading to socialism; and Stevenson had not moved to an independent position or repudiated the president. Unable to violate his primary pledges against these policies, Byrd concluded, "I will not, and cannot, in good conscience, endorse the Democratic platform or the Stevenson-Sparkman ticket. Endorsement means to recommend, and this I cannot do." While he did not recommend a vote for either candidate or indicate how he would vote, Byrd's intention was clear. Ending his "golden silence," he condemned to defeat the nominees of his own party. As he told his brother, "A change in Washington is the most essential thing."[22]

Reaction to the speech was mixed. The GOP hailed it, while stunned Organization leaders offered no comment. Ross Valentine in the *Times-Dispatch* trumpeted, "American Statesmanship is not dead." On the other hand, the Bristol *Herald-Courier* criticized Byrd for lacking the courage to make a real break with his party and endorse Eisenhower. "Antis," in particular, were vociferous in denouncing his betrayal of the party. In a speech in Radford ten days later, Robert Whitehead excoriated the senator: "We see a number of our high-ranking Democratic political officers, including the Generalissimo himself and his chief of staff from South Boston, all dressed up in the uniform of the Democratic Party, gaily bedecked with its medals and ribbons and parading under its colors, yet giving aid and comfort to the Republican party and its cause. . . . Democrats of Virginia, you are being politically betrayed. You are being politically betrayed by men who, while preaching political morality are practicing political immorality." Vice-President Alben Barkley later compared Byrd's unfaithfulness to that of a "housewife who dispensed her favors to the man next door but withheld them from her husband."[23]

While Old Dominion newspaper editors praised Byrd for his "devotion to principle," in reality politics had dictated Byrd's actions. Only when it appeared that Stevenson might win the state—delivering Byrd's leadership another defeat as in 1948—did he choose to break his silence. Pickens Miller reminded Byrd of his pledge signed the previous spring to support the nominees of the party, but in Byrd's mind time-honored opinions of various attorneys general had negated that stricture when it came to voting for presidential electors. Those opinions had originally been motivated by a desire to rebuild the Democratic party in state elections; now they were used to help elect Republicans in national elections. In both instances, however, perpetuation of Organization power was the objective. Even though Byrd may not have technically violated his pledge in the secrecy of the voting booth, he certainly had violated its spirit. A more forthright man would have switched parties, knowing that he and his party were no longer compatible. But Harry wanted it both ways. Attempting to blend principles and personal interest, he preferred Republican national victories that helped him preserve the status quo in the Commonwealth.[24]

On election day Eisenhower won an overwhelming national victory and took Virginia handily in a record turnout. Byrd thought the result was "magnificent," even though Democrats suffered defeat in three congressional races—the Sixth, Ninth, and newly created Tenth—the first losses to Republicans since 1930. M. M. Long, who lost in the Ninth, thought that Byrd's stand had cost him considerable support. The Republicans also narrowly seized control of Congress, costing the Democrats chairmanships and committee control. As Robert Whitehead said, "Party disintegration, like a contagious disease, is no respector of persons." Byrd, he claimed, had pulled "the temple down on the heads of the Democrats." In his own reelection bid, Byrd won effortlessly, but one-fourth of the vote went to two unknowns, indicative of the anti-Byrd sentiment in the state. Although it is likely Eisenhower would have carried the Old Dominion without Byrd's assistance because of his personal popularity and the dissatisfaction with Harry Truman, the senator's indirect support contributed to the size of his victory. Richmond attorney Lewis F. Powell, Jr., a Democrat who had defected to Eisenhower, wrote Byrd, "I believe your speech was a turning point in the campaign, as it influenced a number of other leaders as well as countless thousands of voters."[25]

In the days after the election, Byrd did some hunting with Frank Wysor in southwest Virginia and with Bob Taft on Bernie Baruch's estate in South Carolina, but his attention was focused on the important governor's race in 1953. The first order of business was healing the divisions within the Organization caused by the presidential campaign. To this end he approved the selection of Tom Blanton, a state senator from Bowling Green who had supported Stevenson, to be the next state chairman. At the invitation of Samuel Bemiss, Byrd attended a December harmony dinner in Richmond along with other Organization leaders and members of the Democrats for Eisenhower group. One old friend less favorably treated was Willis Robertson, who was singled out in an editorial in the Winchester *Evening Star* for having played politics as usual in his endorsement of Stevenson. Byrd Sr. did not comment on it, but observers believed the editorial forecast a purge effort in 1954 with Bill Tuck running for Robertson's seat. Robertson concurred, assuming that "young Harry would not have written so important a political article without his father's consent." Public criticism forced editor Byrd to retreat, but the relationship between the two senators had cooled.[26]

As Byrd contemplated the upcoming governor's race, he could take comfort in the Battle governorship. Fiscal conservatism had been practiced, while spending on school construction had increased as promised. He wrote the departing Battle, "As I look back upon your marvelous record as Governor there is not a thing which I can recall with which I have disagreed." Much to his pleasure, Harry Jr., who had been elected to the state senate in 1948, had introduced a tax reduction plan in 1950 to counter the tax increases pushed through during Governor Tuck's term. The bill reduced individual and corporation taxes if state surpluses exceeded anticipated revenues by a certain percentage. Since revenues were invariably underestimated to ensure that spending was kept in check, surpluses were the norm in Virginia, thus guaranteeing tax cuts under Byrd's proposal. Over the next three years Virginians received $20 million in refunds, although the largest number of them were for less than $5.[27]

During the same session the legislators had also approved a $45 million appropriation for school construction that attempted to deal with inadequate and crowded facilities, but the gains barely kept pace with population growth. Although state expenditures for education doubled during Battle's administration, teacher salaries and per pupil expenditures remained below national averages. The state was last in the percentage of its students attending high school and next to last in the percentage of its college-age children going to college. Faced with rising inflation and growing populations, localities were strapped for funds with which to provide basic services in education, health, and safety. While the state debt remained low, cities and counties had debts of over $200 million by 1952. Furthermore, Virginia ranked fortieth in appropriations for the care of the mentally ill, and its hospitals and sanatoriums were overcrowded. One official termed the state mental hospitals "a snake pit of the first order." Colgate Darden called these embarrassments the "harsh results of present policies."[28]

Dissatisfaction began to grow in the early fifties. During the 1950 legislative session an attempt to appropriate an additional $1 million for teachers' salaries was defeated largely for political reasons because the bill's architect was Robert Whitehead, who was a possible gubernatorial candidate in 1953. Behind the reform effort was a group of young Organization members, many of them veterans of World War II representing urban areas, who realized the need to change Virginia's tax and spending policies. Not content with the standpattism of the machine or the long apprenticeship of being seen and not heard, several of these "Young Turks" opposed the Byrd tax reduction plan and favored repeal of the poll tax, more equitable redistricting, and a more enlightened policy in dealing with racial segregation. But they faced an obstinate leadership, and the General Assembly acceded to none of their requests in the 1950 and 1952 sessions.

The legislature was still controlled by Byrd loyalists, traditionalists from the rural areas who were committed to maintaining fiscal solvency and who were insensitive to the changes that had been taking place in the Old Dominion since the end of the war: urban growth in the northern Virginia and Hampton Roads areas, migration into the state, the strengthening of the Republican party, and the rising black voice. Organization leaders believed that the poll tax was still necessary to safeguard a restricted electorate.[29] On redistricting, rural elements presumed that the balance of power in the Old Dominion should remain, in Charles Moses's words, "with the men who feed the hogs and milk the cows." Pressure from Pickens Miller in the 1952 primary forced Byrd to agree to a special legislative session to deal with redistricting in December 1952, but the result was far short of a fair apportionment for urban areas. As for race relations, the leadership judged them to be good and so rejected legislation introduced by Delegate Armistead Boothe of Alexandria to end segregation on all forms of transportation and to create a state civil rights commission. "Nonsegregation," Byrd wrote N. C. McGinnis of Kenbridge, "would be most unwise and I will certainly oppose it in every way I can." Faced with the prospect of federal action, the reactionaries within the Organization talked of closing parks and schools or turning them over to private firms in the event of desegregation.[30]

Byrd's problem was typical of political machines that hold power over a long period of time with limited competition; growing old and complacent, they atrophy. His longtime aides Ebbie Combs and Frank Wysor were in poor health, no longer fully involved in the affairs of the Organization, which cost Byrd the advice and information he had always relied upon. In light of the minirevolt in the assembly, he was getting more suggestions now about bringing young men and women into the Organization, giving them opportunities for service, and sharing patronage with them, but whether it was his distrust of youth, his own torpor, or preoccupation with Washington activities, Byrd continued to rely on traditional practices for rewarding supporters. According to William Spong, "New leadership was not nurtured or encouraged." There was no consideration of modifying the time-honored Organization policies of pay-as-you-go, low taxes, limited spending, and the poll tax. Colgate Darden put it best: "Organizations don't reform from within. An organization reflects the power of an individual and his friends. They are grouped together. They stay their day and go their way."[31]

In the selection of a new governor, Byrd gave the nod to another faithful retainer, although it may have been that a previous obligation tied his hands. For over a decade Byrd had turned Tom Stanley aside in favor of Darden, then Tuck, then Battle. An affable, wealthy businessman, Stanley had served nine terms in the House of Delegates—three as Speaker of the House—and three terms as a congressman from the Fifth District, but he was a bland politician, inarticulate and awkward in formal press conferences, and not very imaginative. As Billy Prieur told Byrd after the election, "If Tom had an idea no one knew it." Stanley had graciously stepped aside at Byrd's request in 1949, and there was little doubt that he would run in 1953 with Organization support. Combs remarked to Wysor, "Practically all our friends with whom I have talked lately are for Stanley." Byrd might have preferred a more dynamic figure, but none was acceptable to him. Lindsay Almond very much wanted to run, but his support of Truman and Stevenson and Martin Hutchinson's candidacy for the Federal Trade Commission had alienated Byrd; he chose to take another term as attorney general. Charles Fenwick of Arlington had likewise proved too independent. The death of Lieutenant Governor Preston Collins just before the presidential election removed another potential candidate. The least unpalatable of all the possibilities was Stanley, who had Bill Tuck's strong support and who offered the best chance of unifying the party after the divisive presidential election. Lulled into a false security by Battle's success in dealing with the assembly, Byrd hoped that the maintenance of such calm would enable Virginia to survive a Stanley governorship, and so he gave his blessing to the Henry County native shortly after the presidential election. With Whitehead choosing not to run, Stanley easily trounced Fenwick in a lackluster primary campaign.[32]

Coming on the heels of Republican successes in state and nation the preceding year, the gubernatorial election of 1953 was reminiscent of that in 1929. Although Hoover's coattails had proved weak in the twenties, Virginia Republicans were hopeful that Eisenhower's popularity would translate into victory. Their hopes were further buoyed by the selection of Ted Dalton of Radford as their nominee. A former Montgomery County commonwealth's attorney, state senator for ten years, and Republican national committeeman, Dalton was a popular and vigorous campaigner known for his candor on the issues. Generally supportive of Organization policies, he was a hunting companion of Frank Wysor and Harry Byrd, but he jokingly told Byrd to keep their contacts secret because he did not want his friends to know that he was hunting with a Democrat. Dalton immediately put Stanley on the defensive by calling for repeal of the poll tax, a voting age of eighteen, a review of absentee voter laws, and revisions to the state tax system. He appeared to be more flexible on public financing than Stanley and prudently suggested that Virginia be prepared to act when desegregation cases now before the Supreme Court were decided. Compensating for the dearth of grass-roots Republican organization and money, little of which was forthcoming from the national party, Dalton waged an issue-oriented campaign. Stung by such hard-hitting tactics, Stanley became evasive and often responded to reporters' questions with a simple "no comment." He and his handlers accused the Republicans of "pulling figures out of the air" and "using cry-baby tactics"; they even waved the flag of Black Reconstruction to frighten Old Dominion voters with memories of "carpetbaggers and Republicans." Late in the campaign Stanley finally endorsed a referendum on the poll tax, but this delayed gambit only confirmed his image as an inept, bumbling campaigner.[33]

Behind the scenes, a prophetic correspondence was going on between James J. Kilpatrick, editor of the Richmond *News Leader,* and Harry Byrd. Worried that the conservative but independent journalist might turn against the Organization, Byrd cautioned that defeat in 1953 would leave the party open to the "radicals"; he defended Stanley as "an honorable man who will adhere to . . . sound principles." Kilpatrick replied with a scathing critique of Stanley and the Organization:

> Throughout the whole year of campaigning . . . Tom never indicated the slightest ability to think for himself, to make tough decisions promptly, to speak knowledgeably about the State government. He has shown no imagination, no stature, no drive, nothing to recommend him to the voters. He has been wishy-washy, mealy-mouthed, half-hearted, equivocal; he has stumbled around over the simplest expression of opinion. He is not doing the Organization one damn bit of good. He isn't an asset, he's a liability, and Harry, damned if I think the Organization can afford a liability in the Governor's office for the next four years. . . . We've been coasting.

Kilpatrick criticized the machine for its perpetuation of a tired, inefficient bureaucracy and its inability to face the future by attracting "first class young people." When Byrd attempted to defend the honesty of Organization rule, the feisty editor responded that honesty was the minimum that should be expected of governments. Clearly there was concern in the minds of some about the immediate and long-range prospects of the Organization.[34]

The final blow to Democratic complacency came in mid-October when Sidney Kellam, Stanley's campaign director and longtime Byrd associate, was indicted with five others for conspiracy to avoid paying federal income taxes. Denying the charge, Kellam resigned his position, claiming that the Republicans had trumped up the case to embarrass the state's Democrats. Nothing ever came of it, and the indictment was withdrawn after the election, but, ironically, the Kellam incident, instead of harming the Organization, probably revitalized its efforts to defeat a suddenly formidable opponent. Harrison, Abbitt, and Harry Jr. were all brought into the campaign to replace Kellam. Abbitt made it clear that he would resign if Stanley said "no comment" one more time. At a meeting of the inner circle, Byrd exhorted Stanley to redouble his efforts. To dramatize his concern he wrote a check for several thousand dollars and demanded that the well-fixed furniture manufacturer commit more of his own funds to the race. Observers recalled a nervous Stanley filling out a check for more than twice the senator's contribution.[35]

As the campaign moved into its final stage, Dalton raised one issue too many. Seeking an alternative to raising gasoline taxes to pay for highways, Dalton offered a "pay-as-you-use" program for road building to be financed with special construction revenue bonds totaling $100 million over a five-year period. Senator Byrd, who had played an insignificant role in the campaign to that point, immediately branded the plan unconstitutional and said he would "oppose with all the vigor I possess this plan of Senator Dalton to junk our sound fiscal system based upon freedom from debt." Given the sorry state of the Stanley campaign, Byrd was itching to get into the fight, and Dalton's support for bonds gave him the perfect rationale to break his silence. Elated, he called his son: "Now we've got the reason. Meet me at the office tomorrow and we'll go to work. Let it sink in and then we'll issue a statement." Along with Battle and Tuck, Byrd jumped into the fray to repulse this attack on pay-as-you-go, the bedrock of Organization orthodoxy. Said one Seventh District Democrat, "Dalton couldn't have hurt himself more if he'd come out for licensed prostitution." With Byrd leading the way, Stanley swept to a 43,000-vote victory in the largest turnout in a gubernatorial election since 1889, but his 10 percent margin of success was the smallest ever for an Organization candidate seeking statewide office.[36]

Dalton, whom Wysor described as "utterly devastated," attributed his defeat to an error of conviction, but it is questionable whether his blunder changed the outcome. Many observers did believe that Dalton's support of bonds was the turning point in the campaign; in congratulating Byrd on his

Into The Home Stretch

THOMAS B. STANLEY

SENATOR HARRY F. BYRD

TED DALTON

10-26-53 To Senator Harry F. Byrd with my best wishes. Fred O. Seibel

FRED O. SEIBEL

success, Bill Tuck said that they had been "in a mighty tight squeeze" until the bond issue and the senator's speeches. Byrd's entry certainly stimulated vigorous debate and attracted many of his supporters to the polls, but it was Organization muscle and money, not issues, that decided the result. Bonds were no longer so critical an issue to Virginia voters as they had been in the 1920s. The diminished margin was mainly attributable to Stanley's "colorless and disappointing campaign" and to Ted Dalton's vigor. Byrd himself concluded, "If we had had a stronger candidate I believe we could have secured a normal majority." Bolstered by a temporarily reinvigorated Republican party, Dalton benefited from dissatisfaction that reflected the changing nature of Virginia society. Perhaps the real loser was Tom Stanley, who emerged a discredited politician, the figurehead of a political machine whose power seemed to be ebbing.[37]

Byrd feared that Stanley's poor showing would carry over to his governorship and adversely affect the Organization. He was particularly unhappy with Stanley's relationship with the press, believing his constant refusals to comment had irritated reporters. At one point, in frustration, Byrd sputtered, "If Stanley had two watches on either hand he wouldn't give you the time of day."[38] Relying on the good auspices of Bill Tuck and Howard Smith, he took special precautions to instruct the new governor on policies and appointments, but the unpredictable Stanley proved a difficult student. Shortly after the election he called for suspension of the tax reduction law for two years. An exasperated Byrd wrote Combs that such a maneuver would split the Organization and play into the hands of Dalton and Whitehead, both of whom favored repeal of the law. Urging Combs to rein in the headstrong businessman, Byrd sarcastically reminded his aide that Stanley had endorsed the law three times in the recent election, "about the only affirmative thing he said in the whole campaign." Combs agreed that suspension would be a serious mistake since the public might get the impression that Byrd was no longer in control. In the face of such formidable opposition, Stanley retreated.[39]

The new governor did not begin auspiciously. On a warm, damp January day, he pledged his allegiance to the Virginia constitution and then proceeded to violate his major campaign promise by calling for a one cent per gallon increase in the gasoline tax. The move not only confirmed the fears of some that the governor was indeed inept, but it may well have cost him much of his influence with the General Assembly. Louise Lacy told her boss, Ebbie Combs, then vacationing in Florida for his health, that there was a "slight gloom over the capitol.... People ... said they would not have voted for Stanley had they known he would do that." Little did they know that Stanley was only doing what Harry Byrd had told him to do. Advised by Highway Director James Anderson of the need for additional road funds, Byrd had conveyed this information to Stanley. He communicated back to Anderson, "I am very much pleased to hear that our friend is considering favorably the recommendation of an additional 1 cent gasoline tax." Surprised at the outcry against the increase, Byrd did not publicly come to the governor's rescue, and the bill went down to defeat, a result that reflected his diminished authority over the assembly. He lobbied hard from long distance for the tax increase but missed Combs's close supervision. He told his confidant, "I have done all I could but quite a few of our very strong friends are simply bitterly opposed to it." On the other hand, he was more successful in convincing legislators to defeat changes in the poll tax, fearing their impact on the elections in 1956 and 1957.[40]

The major issue of the 1954 session, however, was a renewed effort by the Young Turks to abolish the Byrd Automatic Tax Reduction Act—to get a start, said Senator Edward Breeden, on the things Virginia needed. Demanding larger appropriations for schools and hospitals, they introduced legislation to divert to these areas the estimated $7 million that would be returned to taxpayers. A bitter struggle ensued between these moderate Organization men, who had near control of the House, and their more conservative elders, who were dominant in the Senate. In an arduous final session that lasted thirty-seven hours, involved five conference committees, and required stopping the clocks in the legislative chambers, a compromise was finally arranged that permitted a diversion of $2.2 million of the $7 million for teachers' salaries and other educational expenditures. The assembly then adjourned, leaving the leadership to ponder its future.[41]

A major split over a cornerstone of orthodoxy associated with the Byrd name, a governor who would not or could not lead, and the narrow victory in the recent election all portended ill for the Organization. E. Ray Richardson warned the senator: "I am concerned with the present state of affairs here in our Virginia. This last session of our legislature confirms . . . impotent leadership. I heard it all through the session that things were badly confused at the top with no force and leadership. . . . There was a lot of bad decisions and timing and it is going to be felt from here on unless someone gets into the picture. The rank and file are not pleased and we are losing too many votes." Byrd acknowledged that the session had hurt the Organization, but he seemed powerless to respond except to retaliate against the Young Turks. Rather than acknowledge the legitimacy of their demands, Organization leaders chose to discipline them for their independence by denying them key committee assignments and support for statewide office. In the process they created a political opposition. Moreover, losses to the Republicans, more frequent changes in the congressional delegation, and the emergence of a more independent electorate suggested that the Organization was losing its control over Virginia politics. Only the emergence of the volatile desegregation issue would grant it an extended life.[42]

10. Senator Byrd with his longtime political ally Ebbie Combs in 1944

11. *From left*, Governor John Battle with Harry Byrd and Bill Tuck at the senator's 1951 picnic

12. Senator Byrd enjoys a laugh with Congressman Howard Smith and Senator A. Willis Robertson in 1958

13. Three Virginia governors, 1971; *from left,* Lindsay Almond, Albertis Harrison, and Colgate Darden

14. A "shocked" Senator Byrd looks at the 1958 federal budget.

15. Senator Byrd delivers his "Byrds-eye" view of the world at his 1960 picnic.

16. Senator Byrd with former president Dwight Eisenhower, President Lyndon Johnson, Mrs. George C. Marshall, and Ladybird Johnson at the dedication of the Marshall Library, Lexington, Virginia, in 1964

17. Senator Byrd confers with his aide, J. Heywood Bell, in his Senate office in 1961. Note the cartoons on the wall.

～ 17 ～

Massive Resistance

THE SPRING OF 1954 witnessed the making of significant history. The Army-McCarthy hearings were winding down; Dien Bien Phu, a little-known outpost in northern Vietnam, fell to the Communists of Ho Chi Minh; and on May 17 the Supreme Court of the United States reversed a fifty-eight-year-old decision that had legitimized racial discrimination in America. In *Brown* v. *Board of Education, Topeka, Kansas,* the Court held that racial segregation in public education was "inherently unequal" and, therefore, in violation of the Fourteenth Amendment to the Constitution. Kindling a revolution in American life, this landmark ruling transformed the Old Dominion into a firestorm of acrimony and demagoguery not witnessed in the state since the Funder-Readjustor clashes over the state debt in the 1880s. "Massive resistance" became the watchword of the Byrd Organization, dominating the political life of the state and diverting attention from more pressing needs. In the final analysis, however, it was the death knell of the machine, the sad last chapter of Harry Byrd's long reign.

The day after the Court's announcement was Governor Tom Stanley's finest in the governor's mansion. Calling for "cool heads, calm study, and sound judgment," he stated, "I am confident the people of Virginia will receive the opinion of the Supreme Court calmly and take time to carefully and dispassionately consider the situation before coming to conclusions on steps which should be taken."

He contemplated no immediate action but indicated that he would meet shortly with state and local leaders of both races to consider plans "in keeping with the edict of the court." He wrote Senator Byrd that he saw a "disposition to approach the situation calmly and work out an answer that would be acceptable to our people without . . . giving the appearance either of 'surrendering' or 'blustering.'"[1]

Although privately reported to have angrily exploded when he heard Stanley's statement, Senator Byrd publicly responded to the Court's decision in a restrained if somewhat critical way, warning that it was "the most serious blow that has yet been struck against the rights of the states in a matter vitally affecting their authority and welfare." Favoring "mature judgment after sober and exhaustive consideration," he advised Stanley to "proceed very slowly and cautiously."[2] He was not defiant, but neither was he conciliatory. Writing *News Leader* editor James J. Kilpatrick, Byrd applauded Stanley's words: "I think he is on the right track, but, in a matter of this kind, any Governor will need all the assistance and advice he can get. . . . I think all elements, regardless of politics, should combine in order to preserve our public school system and to make the best out of a bad situation." Immediately he began sounding out his advisers about a future course of action, asking Blackie Moore to join him and Combs and Wysor for a discussion at Skyland to "talk over the segregation problem." They were to meet several times over the next few weeks at the senator's Blue Ridge haven.[3]

Other politicians, editors, and school officials also commended the governor's moderation. Ted Dalton suggested the creation of a nonpartisan biracial commission to begin working out a program for Virginia, while Dowell Howard, state superintendent of public instruction, said he believed Virginia could solve the problem "gradually, calmly, and with an open mind." The editor of the Bristol *Herald-Courier* simply said, "Constitutionally we believe it was right morally and legally." Predictably, officials of the state NAACP hailed the verdict as a Declaration of Independence for black Americans.[4]

Such thoughts, however, were not universal in the Commonwealth. The Danville *Bee* predicted that the end of segregation would see white southerners "being brow-beaten into a repugnant way of life." Within days the governor's office was deluged with hundreds of letters protesting the decision, expressing fears of race mixing, and charging Communist plots. Said one, "The Parent Teachers Association of Crewe prefers, as the lesser of two evils, the end of public education, rather than unsegregated schools." Garland ("Peck") Gray, who was to figure prominently in the massive resistance movement, urged Stanley to make a fight against the decision or face the "destruction of our culture" and "intermarriage between the races." He warned the governor not to counsel with "educators, clergy, and Negroes."[5]

While informing his correspondents as well as the public that schools would remain segregated for the 1954–55 year, Stanley shied away from precipitate action. In spite of Peck Gray's warning, he met with a variety of interest groups on the subject, including the State Board of Education and prominent black leaders such as Oliver Hill and P. B. Young. The governor responded to Gray: "The Court's decision, of course, was unwelcome and distasteful. I do not agree with the decision, but I believe defiance of the Court would tend to aggravate the situation and deprive us of the chance of coming to some understanding that would minimize the effects of the ruling on our social and educational system."[6]

Such moderation did not last. Two weeks after a June meeting of southern governors in Richmond, where he seemed to side with the hard-line segregationists from the Deep South, Stanley declared that he would use all means at his disposal to continue a system of segregated education in Virginia; in lieu of that he suggested the possible repeal of section 129 of the state constitution, which provided for the maintenance of public free schools. Although Organization stalwarts supported the governor, many Virginians were shocked at the prospect of closed schools. Even Senator Byrd, who did not want to be portrayed as a school closer, told his son, "I think Stanley made quite a mistake when he came out to amend the Constitution to abolish the school system." Byrd knew the governor would have to be carefully instructed on what to say and do in the future since he would be perceived as the voice of the Organization.[7]

Governor Stanley did not shift to an obstructionist position on his own but was following the lead of more powerful voices in the Organization. Harry Byrd's decision to oppose school desegregation—what came to be known as "massive resistance"—was one of the most significant of his career for the Organization and Virginia. Its form did not take shape overnight but developed over many months and was influenced by many factors and individuals. As always, he consulted his advisers and his Senate colleagues, whose belligerence may have governed his response more than on previous occasions.

Part of the explanation for the development of massive resistance was an absence of enlightened leadership which allowed the forces of bigotry to overcome the voices of reason. President Eisenhower's failure to approve the Court's ruling publicly and to call for compliance was a tragic abdication of responsibility. With little sensitivity to the plight of black Americans, Eisenhower was loath to push desegregation, worried as he was about its political liabilities and the potential for violence. Furthermore, his philosophical conservatism favored gradualism. Without presidential leadership, a divided Congress likewise did nothing.[8] And the Supreme Court's failure to specify the timing or the method for carrying out its edict encouraged delay, evasion, and obstruction. In the South moral leadership was crucial. Where racial moderates governed and courageously spoke out, as in Kentucky, Florida, and North Carolina, reasonable progress was made. Where racial bigots fueled the fires of prejudice, as in Mississippi and Alabama, law and order broke down. Virginia lay somewhere in between. Although most white Virginians preferred segregated schools, the equanimity with which they accepted token integration five years later suggests that a similar course might have worked in 1955 or 1956; but they were not encouraged in that direction. The vacuum was filled by the demagoguery of racism.[9]

Traditional racial attitudes were certainly a factor in the creation of Virginia's response. Age-old customs and attitudes that had been legalized for half a century were being challenged by the *Brown* decision. The loudest voices defending the overturned separate-but-equal policy came from the Southside, the heartland of the Byrd machine, where the black percentage of the population was highest and where fears of race mixing were strongest.[10] The key representatives of this region—congressmen Watkins Abbitt and Bill Tuck and state senators Garland Gray and Mills Godwin—were highly placed Organization leaders whose views would become even more influential in the next few years. As politicians, they could not have been expected to deviate from the wishes of their constituents, but it was not merely their political futures they were thinking about. As Tuck told Byrd, "I would be perfectly willing to scuttle my own political life if that would be necessary to preserve the integrity of both the white and the colored races in Virginia."[11]

The economic and political changes taking place in Virginia—so evident in the last few years—forced Byrd to be attentive to Southside interests. He could not afford to antagonize his rural power base, and this gave the region and its racism an influence on policy making out of proportion to its population in the state. As Lindsay Almond said years later, "There would have been no hard, unyielding core of massive resistance in Virginia if there were no Southside. Virginia as a whole was opposed to racial mixing in the public schools, but outside of the Southside the state evinced more of a willingness to face reality."[12] Right after the Court decision, Garland Gray, who believed Byrd's leadership on the question was crucial, disclosed his concern to the senator and suggested a course of action that may have set the stage for future resistance. Pointing to the high percentage of blacks in his Southside region—which, he wrote, precluded whites from accepting integration—Gray sought to "circumvent" the decision. His solutions included repealing compulsory attendance laws, leasing schools to private corporations, and ending local support for public schools. Arguing that the senator and his friends in the Valley did not appreciate the "horrible potentialities" of the decision, Gray told Byrd that he was calling a meeting of local folks to discuss their problem. Gathering at a Petersburg firehouse on June 19, the group, which included Gray, Abbitt, Godwin, Albertis Harrison, and several other state legislators, recorded its "unalterable opposition to the principle of integration of the races in the schools" and pledged "to evolve some legal method whereby political subdivisions of the state may continue to maintain separate facilities for white and Negro students in schools." Their acknowledgment of the need for local control is notable, for in time they would demand that the entire state accept their "legal method." Within days of the firehouse meeting, citizens of the Fourth District descended on the state capital, and Governor Stanley's reversal followed.[13]

But more than racism was involved in the shift to radical obstructionism.

For years Virginia's leaders had disdained the racial demagoguery so common in the rest of the South. V. O. Key had written that the Old Dominion had "the most harmonious race relations in the South." The Ku Klux Klan had little clout, and racial violence was minimal thanks in large measure to the effective antilynching bill passed during Byrd's governorship. Moderate editorial voices praised the good relations between whites and blacks and supported improvements in the black community, albeit of the separate kind. Although poll tax requirements and a white electoral structure proved intimidating and kept participation low, blacks were allowed to vote in Democratic primaries.

Byrd himself had only rarely resorted to the race issue for political purposes, such as in the bitter 1928 campaign, and he did not use disparaging, condescending, or rabble-rousing racial language in his speeches or private correspondence. Invariably, his opposition to integration was couched in the rhetoric of states' rights. However, having lived his entire life in a segregated community, he had adopted its racial mores and believed that segregation was "essential to the maintenance of peaceful and friendly relationships between the races." Blacks were appropriately consigned to the positions that race and society had designated for them. His contacts with them as field laborers and servants reinforced that belief, but he treated them as employees, not as inferiors. Proud of the fact that he paid blacks the same as whites, he boasted, "I have always believed that the Negro had an honorable and most useful position in our nation." Harry Byrd's racism was of the genteel southern sort, based on a Darwinian sense of place and moderated by a paternalistic spirit.[14]

Why did the Old Dominion suddenly forgo its tradition of racial moderation? It appears that Byrd and other Organization leaders perceived race as an issue with which to maintain their political hegemony that had been so recently threatened by Miller, Dalton, and the Young Turks. Fears were expressed that if the Organization did not take a forceful stand on the issue, it would lose the initiative to moderates like Ted Dalton or Robert Whitehead. Massive resistance was designed, in effect, to revitalize a dying political machine. This is apparent in the attention given to Southside interests, in the use of the issue in political races, and in the gradual development of the final solution. The policy shifts and planning over a two-year period confirm the ulterior purpose. Had race prejudice alone been the primary motive, Virginia's resort to massive resistance would have been much more immediate and emotional, as it was elsewhere in the South. Throughout their time in power, Byrd and the Organization used race only when they were in political trouble. Now they would turn to it again in the fight over school desegregation.[15]

Race and politics were reinforcing elements in Organization thinking because black emancipation, particularly through increased political participation, threatened machine hegemony. Blacks would undoubtedly vote for Byrd's opponents. Opposing an amendment that would terminate the poll tax, Willis Robertson commented to Byrd, "Every man who knows anything about Virginia politics is bound to realize that if you suddenly give the vote to several hundred thousand who have not had it before, they are going to use it as directed by their group leader—labor or racial." Numerous postelection analyses found the Byrd hierarchy whining that its victories would have been much more substantial but for the black vote. Predictably, then, they fought changes in the poll tax or any civil rights legislation that promised to improve black voting opportunities. The Court's school decision was perceived as the first step in dismantling the entire Jim Crow system, including electoral control; it would have to be obstructed.[16]

Finally, Byrd also believed the Court's ruling was another dangerous example of federal interference in state affairs that would undermine the political and social status quo in Virginia, an act reminiscent of Civil War and Reconstruction. For Byrd, who had spent all of his Senate years fighting this federal octopus, the decision overturned legal precedent and time-honored custom and was another blow to states' rights; it was the final humiliation, and he reacted angrily and bitterly, his frustration producing an unreasonable and overwrought defiance. Elaborating on this point, Louis Rubin has suggested that the Court's decision "not only symbolized all the changes that were being forced upon Virginia . . . but it struck at the heart of the social and economic institutions that had seemed to make possible the old order and which reflected the values and attitudes embodied in the old order." A resolve to preserve this traditional way of life, along with political profit and racial conviction, dictated Byrd's response to desegregation.[17]

In August 1954 Governor Stanley appointed a thirty-two-man legislative commission on public education to devise a response to the *Brown* dictum. Despite advice to the contrary, Stanley included on his panel no educators, no blacks, and no "liberals" such as Dalton and Boothe who had counseled moderation. Almost half of its members were from the black belt, where the black population was high; six were from the Fourth District alone, one of whom—Garland Gray—was elected chairman. Byrd approved of Stanley's selections, hoping that the commission would produce a "workable plan." At Gray's suggestion he once again released his May 18 statement that emphasized his strong opposition to this "worst blow since Reconstruction."[18]

The Gray commission held one chaotic, nonsegregated open hearing on November 15, 1954, at the Mosque in Richmond that was attended by two thousand Virginians. More than one hundred speakers were heard; a majority of them favored retention of segregation, but several expressed support for local option and gradual integration. Emotions were high, and the commission never held another public forum, deliberating in private for another full year before releasing its report. In the interim a powerful new lobbying group that had been formed in October gave political and emotional support to the resisters. Founded in Blackstone but likely conceived in Farmville in Prince Edward County, the home of one of the original desegregation cases, the Defenders of State Sovereignty and Individual Liberties advocated maintenance of segregated schools through constitutional enforcement of states' rights. Its members eschewed violence and association with any Klan-like organization. Although it established chapters across the state, the Defenders were most powerful in the Southside.[19]

For the last months of 1954 and the better part of 1955, Harry Byrd chose a course of watchful waiting on the school question. The Court's implementation ruling on May 31, 1955, which called for desegregation with "all deliberate speed," respected the South's desire for delay and indirectly encouraged massive resistance. As Byrd interpreted it, "The emphasis should be on 'deliberate' rather than on speed." Late in the year he was off on a monthlong tour of European defense and CIA installations that took him to many NATO countries. He returned to face the recommendations of the Gray commission and the alluring siren of interposition.[20]

The long-anticipated Gray Plan was presented on November 12, 1955. It recommended a pupil assignment plan that permitted localities to assign students to schools for reasons other than race in order to keep race mixing to a minimum. The compulsory education law would be amended so that no child would be required to attend an integrated school. In the event of school closings or integration, the commission suggested the appropriation of tuition grants to enable children to attend private schools. Since the Virginia constitution forbade use of public funds for private schooling, the report asked for a special session of the General Assembly to initiate steps to permit such grants. Viewed within the context of the times, the Gray Plan struck a reasonable chord by allowing localities to integrate if they chose but advancing legislation to help them avoid it if they wished. Praising the work of the commission, Governor Stanley immediately called a special session of the assembly to approve a referendum on a constitutional convention that would consider an amendment allowing tuition grants for private education.[21]

Byrd made no public comment on the Gray Plan because he was out of the country, but the plan approximated an earlier proposal from Tuck and Abbitt for local referenda on integrating schools that he had endorsed as a "useful idea." Operation of public schools, Byrd had said, was founded on local self-government; parents should control them, and local taxes should pay for them. If the citizens of a locality voted for integration, then segregation could be abolished; if they opposed it, then the locality—with the backing of the state— could follow its best judgment. Clearly, in November 1955 the leaders of Virginia were comfortable with the idea of local option as a solution to the school crisis. The vote of Virginians two months later appeared to confirm this sentiment. But within a matter of weeks, the Old Dominion rejected this possibility and veered down the road of total noncompliance.[22]

The Gray Plan was not universally endorsed. Black Virginians labeled it another subterfuge to circumvent the law, while moderates such as Ted Dalton feared that tuition grants would undermine public education. The loudest objections, however, came from the segregationists, who argued that any integration in the state would be an intolerable invasion that could not be stopped once it was begun. The vehemence of their voices—including those of senators Gray and Godwin, who signed the report but disapproved of its moderation—undoubtedly carried great political weight with Byrd. In spite of the criticism of the Gray Plan, the assembly, meeting in early December, overwhelmingly passed legislation setting the referendum for January 9, 1956.[23]

Another voice of opposition, which may have had the greatest influence in converting Harry Byrd to massive resistance, was that of James J. Kilpatrick. A native Oklahoman with a degree in journalism from the University of Missouri, Kilpatrick had joined Douglas Southall Freeman's staff in 1941 and succeeded his mentor as editor of the *News Leader* eight years later. He had first met Byrd in 1943, but it was not until the 1950s that their friendship blossomed. Viscerally and intellectually opposed to governmental power that intruded on the rights of individuals, Kilpatrick wrote a series of crusading editorials in late November 1955 that urged adoption of "interposition" as a defense against integration. Resurrecting John C. Calhoun's concept of nullification and Jefferson's and Madison's defenses of states' rights in the Kentucky and Virginia resolutions of 1798–99, he argued that states could nullify undesirable federal action by interposing themselves between the central government and their citizens to protect their rights. Since he claimed that the recent Court decision was a usurpation of state sovereignty, states had the obligation to judge whether the decision was constitutional or not. With more zeal than logic, Kilpatrick drafted an interposition resolution for consideration by the General Assembly that would declare the *Brown* decision "null and void."[24]

The rhetorical flair, constitutional arguments, and historical foundations of Kilpatrick's editorials seduced Harry Byrd. Returning from his European tour, he wrote to the Richmonder that he had read and reread the editorial "Interposition Now" and had found it "beautifully written. . . . I wish we had gotten started on this sooner." He called it a "masterly exposition" of the fundamental principles of government and later credited Kilpatrick with arousing "the country to the evils of the Supreme Court's decision."[25] Kilpatrick gave Byrd the legal and intellectual foundation for state action against the federal government while appeasing the racist preferences of Virginians without the appearance of demagoguery. He made massive resistance "respectable," a prerequisite for the senator, who disdained emotional use of the race issue. While Kilpatrick remained somewhat skeptical about the ultimate success of interposition and eventually would advise its rejection, Senator Byrd never had such reservations. His obsession with the battle between federal power and states' rights—a hallmark of his Senate career—left him susceptible to a variety of constitutional arguments, some valid, others less so, in his search for a way out. With neither a lawyer's sense of the complexities of the constitutional issues raised by interposition nor the historian's understanding of the causes and results of the Civil War, Byrd wholeheartedly committed to interposition as a basis for any state obstruction of court-ordered desegregation. Such ignorance of the law—which even he acknowledged on one occasion—was to prove dangerous.[26]

Undoubtedly the editorials and suggestions touched a receptive nerve, for the senator immediately began reevaluating the implications of the Gray Plan and plotting a more vigorous attack on the Court's decision. He had the Legislative Reference Service of the Library of Congress search for examples of earlier congressional attempts to overcome Court objections to legislation. Referring to the proposals of the Gray commission, he urged his advisers to avoid committing to all the details. Desiring a mandate for action through the upcoming referendum, he was careful publicly to support the vote for a constitutional convention while privately counseling further deliberation on a final plan. "Let us proceed firmly and courageously, but . . . there is no occasion for precipitous action in the immediate future," he advised Virginians.[27]

On January 9, 1956, by a resounding two-to-one margin, Virginians approved a constitutional convention that would legalize tuition grants. Although the referendum was on a single provision of the Gray Plan, most observers believed that it was tantamount to a vote on the entire plan. But even as the votes were tallied, the limb was being sawed off behind those moderates who had strongly endorsed the Gray Plan.[28] The day after the election, spokesmen for the Defenders publicly talked of shelving the plan, while Senator Byrd, pointing out its weaknesses, privately told Stanley to go slow on implementation. So advised, the governor announced that additional school legislation would likely await a special session later in the year. It is clear that the Organization deceived the electorate into believing the referendum was for a "sound and moderate" approach to the school question and then used the vote as a mandate to pursue massive resistance. By that time moderates were confronted with a political fait accompli and the devastating charge that local option advocates were little more than integrationists in disguise. Massive resistance would allow no middle ground.[29]

The 1956 General Assembly was dominated by the desegregation issue even though the leadership had chosen not to take legislative action on that question. Influenced by the Kilpatrick interposition campaign, Delegate John Boatwright of Buchanan County submitted a resolution of nullification to the legislators. Somewhat watered down ("We pledge our firm intention to take all appropriate measures, legally and constitutionally available to us, to resist this illegal encroachment upon our sovereign powers"), it passed by huge margins in both houses. It is not clear what the legislators thought they were accomplishing other than sounding an emotional battle cry for continued defiance, a protest rather than a procedure. Many did not think it was a viable alternative, but because the issue had been given so much publicity, they bowed to political pressure from home. Attorney General Almond later ruled that the resolution posed no bar to integration, and Richmond attorney Lewis Powell privately called it "legal nonsense." Nonetheless, if interposition had little legal significance, it created a favorable climate for massive resistance. Robert Whitehead was mistaken when, in reference to interposition, he said, "The thunder roared, the lightening flashed and struck, and a chigger was killed." Reason and tolerance were dying as well.[30]

While the legislature was in session, Senator Byrd boldly put forward his idea of massive resistance. In Richmond to deliver a speech at the Jefferson-Jackson Day dinner on February 14, he offhandedly spoke of "passive resistance" to the Court's decision through Southern unity. Eleven days later in Washington, he adopted more aggressive rhetoric: "If we can organize the Southern States for massive resistance to this order, I think that in time the rest of the country will realize that racial integration is not going to be accepted in the South. . . . In interposition the South has a perfectly legal means of appeal from the Supreme Court's order."[31] Kilpatrick's doctrine had been digested. Interpreting the margin of victory in the recent referendum as a signal for total resistance, Byrd gauged the political climate to be favorable for a more forceful policy. It was apparent that any opposition could be portrayed as integrationist and easily defeated. Furthermore, the issue could be dramatized to overshadow other issues and so stifle dissenting opinion. Massive resistance would mean uniform resistance; it would mean recourse to all available means to prevent any integration in the Commonwealth. Organization leaders from the Southside, joined by vocal Defenders, jubilantly rallied behind his decision. As Bill Tuck arrogantly stipulated, "If they won't stand with us, then I say make 'em!"[32]

If Byrd needed additional encouragement to pursue this line of defense, he received it from other southern senators who were similarly captivated by Kilpatrick's arguments. Searching for measures that would preserve Jim Crow statutes, they were receptive to any legal labyrinth that promised success, however temporary.[33] When the Senate convened for the 1956 session, Senator Strom Thurmond of South Carolina proposed promulgation of a statement of southern resistance to the Court's decision. Being something of a Senate rene-gade, he sought the help of the respected Harry Byrd, who in turn broached the idea to Georgia's Walter George. At George's request, most of the southern senators met on February 8 to consider issuing a manifesto of principles. When a few colleagues voiced reservations, Thurmond and Byrd threatened to pro-ceed alone. To accommodate the competing views, senators Richard Russell, Sam Ervin, and John Stennis produced a restrained statement that condemned the *Brown* decision as an "abuse of judicial power" and recommended use of all lawful means to resist forced integration and reverse the decision. Released on March 12, the Southern Manifesto was signed by nineteen senators and eighty-two House members, including all of Virginia's representatives. Among the senators from the former Confederate states, only Albert Gore and Estes Kefauver of Tennessee and Lyndon Johnson of Texas declined to sign. Much like state declarations of interposition, the manifesto lacked legal standing, but it served as a rallying cry for southern segregationists in need of moral support. It initiated the counterrevolution against the Court and integration in the South.[34]

Byrd's perception of his role as a spokesman of and for the South strength-ened his commitment to massive resistance. As the originator of the slogan of the resisters, as an initiator of the Southern Manifesto, and, most importantly, as the leader of the Old Dominion, which was viewed as the pivotal state in the region, Byrd took on the role of regional standard-bearer. It would prove a difficult burden to lay down, for if Virginia conceded, it would be betraying its southern sisters; if Byrd capitulated, he would be betraying his southern col-leagues in the Senate and his friends at home. As he said at his annual apple orchard picnic some months later, "Let Virginia surrender to this illegal de-mand and you'll find the ranks of the other Southern states broken. . . . If Vir-ginia surrenders, the rest of the South will go down too."[35]

As the school crisis evolved, Byrd's references to Virginia's role as the leader of the South increased in frequency. So, too, did his own involvement. Years later his southern colleagues called him a "prominent" and "powerful" oppo-nent of civil rights legislation. Senator Thurmond said of his brother-in-arms, "He was active in supporting the Southern Manifesto and contributed to its creation." And Senator Fulbright, who reluctantly signed the manifesto, cred-ited Byrd with "asserting very strong leadership in stirring up the resistance of the South." They valued his national reputation for integrity and independence because it legitimated their efforts. Historian Frances Wilhoit has concluded that Harry Byrd, "more than any other single individual, determined the shape and style of the movement as it evolved in the decade after 1954." Putting it more negatively, Robert Whitehead in 1957 said that Byrd was "more responsi-ble for the present racial tension than anyone else in the whole South." Instead of channeling the South's frustration in a positive direction, he pushed it toward defiance. And he set the tone for Virginia's response as well. Bill Tuck reported to him, "Your leadership in the Manifesto matter has greatly augmented your strength in our section of the State, and I believe in the State as a whole."[36]

Organization leaders were active during the spring of 1956, plotting strategies and discussing constitutional interpretations, but it was not until June that they settled on a plan to combat the *Brown* decision. Slowed by a hernia operation in April, Byrd had not been able to give his full attention to the crisis.[37] The wishes of the Southside dictated the final solution. Mills Godwin wrote to the senator on June 8: "I am convinced we should not pass any State law which would permit integration even in those localities where some may desire it." He argued that doing so would be interpreted as compliance with the Court's decision, an action which most Virginians rejected and which was contrary to the concept of interposition. Calling for a statement of intentions in "unmistakable language," Godwin asked Byrd to convene a conference of interested parties on the subject. The "interested parties" seeking to meet with Byrd were seven members of the Gray commission from the Southside, who had declared their willingness to do anything to prevent integration anywhere in Virginia.[38]

The clandestine gathering of the "Southside Seven" with Senator Byrd, Governor Stanley, and congressmen Smith, Tuck, and Abbitt took place in Washington on July 2 in Howard Smith's Rules Committee conference room because the senator's office was too small. They determined the agenda for the upcoming special session of the assembly and set the course toward closing the schools. As noted by Representative Smith, whose constitutional expertise made him a key figure in devising a procedure to avoid compliance with the Court, the group agreed that Virginia would maintain a completely segregated public school system; that no state funds would go to any locality that attempted to integrate schools; that the right to sue local school boards would be repealed; and that pupil assignment authority would be transferred to the governor. As outlined earlier to Byrd by Smith, the conferees decided to shift control of the process from the localities to the state, thus reducing the number of suits filed and making the governor the official with whom the federal government would have to deal, which they hoped would lessen the likelihood of interference.[39]

The participants came away from the Washington conference confident that they had produced a workable plan to avoid integration. Aware of the legal problems involved, Byrd directed Smith, Tuck, and Abbitt to finalize the procedures. To Godwin he expressed his satisfaction with the "very fruitful" results but reminded him of the "difficult fight ahead." Godwin acknowledged the senator's effort: "I want you to know again, how much the people here appreciate your position and determination in this all-important matter. It is the most far-reaching problem of our time, and it is indeed reassuring to know you are on our side. . . . I left the meeting believing we can find a way to prevent integration in Virginia." Byrd replied, "I believe if the Southern States stand firm in massive resistance, we will win out."[40]

Over the summer Smith, Attorney General Almond, and Congressman Burr Harrison, in consultation with the governor, drafted the legislation that would be considered by the assembly. It conformed closely to the outline agreed upon in Washington. When he announced his intention to call the General Assembly into session on August 27, the governor outlined these proposals—now called the "Stanley Plan"—and claimed that he was responding to the "overwhelming sentiment of the people of Virginia" and to events threatening "to destroy our constitutional system." Abandoning the Gray Plan that he had called "splendid" just eight months before, Stanley urged a "total resistance line." At his annual picnic on the eve of the momentous session, Harry Byrd gave the Stanley Plan his blessing, exhorting the delegates to fight "with every ounce of . . . energy and capacity" against integration.[41]

Convened amid unfurled Confederate flags and heightened passions, the monthlong assembly session was an emotional, draining experience—"tense and unhappy days" in the memory of one participant. So many conflicting bills were introduced that neither side was ever clear on their intent and impact. Kilpatrick called it "the most shameful exhibition of legislative confusion I ever saw." Worried that the bill to cut off funds would lead to the school closings predicted by critics, the resisters placated the undecided by modifying the Stanley Plan to give the governor additional options before he withheld state funds from integrated schools. A three-man pupil placement board—under the governor's authority—would attempt to circumvent the courts by assigning pupils to schools on criteria other than race. If a school was integrated by court order, the governor was authorized to close it temporarily and then attempt to reopen it on a voluntarily segregated basis. State funds were to be cut off from any integrated school, and tuition grants, approved by the constitutional convention, would be available to those "forced" into attending private schools. Stanley acknowledged the possibility of school "interruptions" for a short time, but he said, "We've got to decide whether we want to pay the price." By shifting responsibility for school operations to Richmond and by creating new legal barriers, segregationists hoped that they could sidestep the sweeping nature of the Supreme Court decision; at the very least further litigation would delay the process. What the legislators produced was a maze of laws that proved contradictory, confusing, and cumbersome in implementation. In the final test of muscle, Organization forces won out, but more narrowly than they had hoped. Local option plans were defeated in the House, 59–39, and in the Senate, 21–17; the modified Stanley Plan was then passed by similar margins.[42]

As the weary delegates left Richmond—to less fanfare than they received on arrival—the opposition predicted school closings and court decisions that would find the legislation unconstitutional. Colgate Darden declared: "It's an illusion to assume that the bills will prevent integration. . . . They will simply close many schools in Virginia." Senator William Neff believed that what had been done would "heighten race tensions" as well as endanger the school system. He hoped early court decisions would clear the way for a "wiser approach."[43] Organization leaders, however, if somewhat restrained in their jubilation, were confident that they had done their duty to the Commonwealth. Byrd summarized the session, "Once again Virginia offers its peaceful leadership to the South, and I believe the offer will be accepted." He wrote Jimmy Byrnes: "I think Virginia showed up mighty well in the action the Legislature has just taken. What we have done is a strong defiance of the Supreme Court, and I do not think integration will occur anywhere in the State." Requesting a copy of the new laws, Byrnes praised the assembly for doing "a wonderful thing for the entire South." Massive resistance was now in force, a "defense in depth" against desegregation as *Time* labeled it.[44]

But the victory had been costly. More cracks were appearing in the Organization's armor. Many of the advocates of local option, who had been loyal soldiers in the machine, could not support legislation that threatened public education. An almost united Norfolk delegation, along with the local school board, preferred the Gray Plan to the Stanley Plan. Billy Prieur, longtime Organization whip in the port city, told Byrd that he was wrong on this one: "We can't support you." Byrd replied that Virginians would never accept desegregation and that he was "going to resist as long as I can."[45] Fitzgerald Bemiss, newly elected to the assembly from Richmond, recalled a similar conversation: "Senator Byrd talked to me . . . about the importance of resisting, referring to General Lee's long fight for his homeland in the face of clearly overwhelming force. As much as I liked and admired the Senator, I could not see that massive resistance made sense. . . . I was drawn to the logic and temperate leadership of much admired friends like Colgate Darden, Dabney Lancaster, and Lewis Powell." Darden frankly described massive resistance as "a sterile and barren program offering nothing but resistance" with "overtones of violence" in it. Another Organization leader who was slipping away was Willis Robertson, who had serious doubts about the school-closing plans. His independence from his longtime friend and colleague had been growing in recent years, as his exclusion from the crucial Washington discussions proved. Robertson would not desert his southern colleagues on any civil rights test in the Senate, but he was no longer obsequiously following the lead of his mentor, especially on national party politics.[46]

After the hectic presidential campaign that came on the heels of the legislative session, in which President Eisenhower once again soundly trounced Adlai Stevenson, the senator turned to the crucial gubernatorial election that he hoped would confirm his school policies. J. Lindsay Almond was not Byrd's choice for governor, but the attorney general, whom *Time* called "one of segregation's ablest legal advocates," preempted the field by announcing early and gathering pledges from courthouse officials and legislators whom he had served so well for so long. Almond had come up through the legal ranks: private practice in Roanoke, commonwealth's attorney, judge of the Roanoke hustings court. In 1945 he was elected to the House of Representatives and settled down for a long legislative career that abruptly ended when the state's attorney general died in 1948. Persuaded by Governor Tuck and Senator Byrd to take the position for the good of the Organization, Almond accepted and was elected to two full terms in 1949 and 1953.[47]

A fiery orator with a shock of waving white hair, Almond was a renegade who never quite won Byrd's trust. He was a faithful Organization man but demonstrated a streak of independence that precluded his entry into the inner circle. He had remained loyal to the Democratic party's national candidates and had endorsed Martin Hutchinson's nomination to the Federal Trade Commission, a move that "highly offended" Harry Byrd and may have cost Almond a chance for the governorship in 1953. To avoid being passed over again, Almond announced his candidacy on November 17, 1956, without seeking Byrd's approval. Analyzing his position, he concluded that he "had reached the end of the political road unless I went out on my own. . . . I made up my mind that if I was to be shelved, the people would have to do the shelving." He believed the position was fairly his: he had sacrificed his congressional career for the machine, had served as attorney general for eight years, and had aggressively defended Virginia's separate-but-equal system before the nation's highest court. A committed segregationist, Almond was a good enough lawyer to know that the Stanley Plan would not survive the legal test. Political expediency, however, along with those legal challenges, would make massive resistance the central issue of his campaign and his governorship.[48]

Failing to tempt Almond with a seat on the state supreme court, Byrd conceded, convinced that his preferred nominee, Garland Gray, could not defeat the attorney general. In his public declaration for Almond issued from his Berryville home, Byrd stressed the need to organize every precinct in the state, to qualify every Democratic voter, and to get out the full vote in November. He also lined up the rest of the ticket to avoid any factional primary strife that might weaken their forces before the crucial contest with the revitalized Republicans. At his request, A. E. S. ("Gi") Stephens stayed on as lieutenant governor, and attorney Howard Gilmer of Pulaski would run for attorney general.

Relieved that there would be no internal struggle, party members overwhelmed Almond with endorsements. Asking the candidate to meet with him and Combs in Washington, Byrd made it clear what the issue would be: "It is imperative that we hold our lines on the integration question, and especially is this important at the beginning of the school session next September." Anticipating that Ted Dalton would be the GOP nominee, Byrd believed that he would be weak on the integration issue because of his support for local option.[49]

Within a few weeks of these communications, Ebbie Combs was gone. "The Chief" died on January 5, 1957, leaving Harry Byrd grief-stricken. These two friends had dominated the politics of Virginia for thirty years, one from the outside, the other from the inside. A man to whom Byrd invariably turned for advice, Combs was an indispensable agent for the senator's success. It was no coincidence that his failing health in his last years paralleled the declining fortunes of the machine. Byrd felt his death professionally and personally. "I loved your father very dearly," he wrote to Combs's daughter.[50]

As if that were not stressful enough, Byrd lost his brother Richard two months later. The admiral died on March 11 at age sixty-eight, his heart weakened by his many exertions. The two brothers had remained very close over the years, the senator winning support for the aged explorer to make one last polar expedition in 1956, his fifth trip to the sub-continent. A grateful Dick wrote that he "could not have any more admiration or affection for a relative or friend than I have for you." Harry was pleased that he could help him "consummate a very wonderful career." The final personal blow came in September when his mother died at the age of ninety-four. The matriarch of the Byrd clan, she had remained healthy and clear-minded until her final years, as strong-willed as ever, living alone in the house on Amherst Street.[51]

Byrd did not allow these personal losses to interfere with his involvement in the gubernatorial election. Indeed, Combs's death probably spurred him into greater activity against "the radical element" that threatened Organization rule. Commending Kilpatrick on his recent defense of the South in his book *The Sovereign States,* he warned that they must "fight without compromise and have one session of the General Assembly after another" to prevent enforced integration. To a cheering crowd at a Kiwanis club luncheon in Richmond in March, Byrd urged a "no-surrender" fight against integration. "We have a right," he said, "to defy the Supreme Court if we do so without violence and do not try to overthrow the government. . . . Unyielding refusal to integrate may cause the Supreme Court to reverse itself again because they may find they've started something they can't finish." In a speech to the Hampton Roads

Maritime Association in May, Byrd presented his historical case for defiance of the Court: Lincoln's efforts to reverse the *Dred Scott* decision, Andrew Jackson's disavowal of John Marshall's decision on the Cherokee Indians, and Franklin Roosevelt's court-packing scheme, which, ironically, Byrd had opposed as unconstitutional. In his view massive resistance was an appropriate response to the *Brown* decision that had historical precedent. He had convinced himself that Armageddon was near, calling it "the greatest internal crisis since the War Between the States." To Virginius Dabney, he wrote: "Nothing in my life has worried me more than the integration problem. It is just as insoluble as the problem between the Jews and the Arabs in the middle East."[52]

Since Almond's opposition in the primary consisted only of Richmond's chattering gadfly Howard Carwile, his victory was assured, but a whiff of scandal threatened prospects for the fall contest with Republican Dalton. It was disclosed that attorney general nominee Gilmer had lent his name to a life insurance company promotion in violation of the state bar association's ethical code. It was a minor transgression of judgment, and his running mates advised Gilmer to ignore the publicity, but state newspapers, notably the *News Leader,* and Organization personnel, concerned with their reputation for incorruptibility, would not let the issue die. Likewise proud of the absence of major scandal in Old Dominion government during his leadership, Byrd felt compelled to remove Gilmer, confiding to Lloyd Bird, "We should not carry any more handicaps than are necessary in the next campaign." Praising Gilmer for his "manly and splendid" withdrawal, the senator quickly filled the position with Albertis Harrison of Brunswick County, who had managed his Senate race in 1952 and had been a loyal but moderate defender of massive resistance in the General Assembly.[53]

What little hope Ted Dalton had of defeating Lindsay Almond for the governorship was destroyed by the Little Rock, Arkansas, school crisis in September 1957. Byrd immediately condemned President Eisenhower's use of troops to integrate Central High School as "naked force," an "ill-advised and deplorable action," and a "usurpation of power" that was "clearly illegal." Privately he labeled it "one of the most dangerous things that has been done in our history."

Politicking as if his own Senate seat were on the line, Byrd toured the state with his message of massive resistance, equating the defeat of Dalton to a victory over the Court and federal authority. In an October speech in Halifax, he accused Dalton of trying to make integration legal in Virginia, tied him to the Republican administration responsible for Little Rock, claimed the Warren Court relied on the writings of "Swedish Socialists," and implied that the impeachment of Earl Warren would solve all these problems. To arouse people to the dangers involved, he addressed a letter to sixty close friends that put the issue succinctly: "This is undoubtedly the most important election we have had in Virginia since the Days of Reconstruction. The eyes of the whole nation will be upon us on November 5." And on Harry Byrd as well. The senator took this election as a test of his power in Virginia, of public support for his crusade of massive resistance, of his leadership of the South.[54]

Almond repeated Byrd's admonitions, if in somewhat more graphic language. His most memorable remark was one where he would raise his right arm and promise that he would lose the limb before he would allow a single black child to enter a white school. Warning of "racial amalgamation" if Dalton's local option plan was adopted, he painted a bleak vision of many "Little Rocks" in Virginia if Republicans were elected. But there was an air of resignation at times in Almond's speeches about the future of massive resistance. At one point he even hinted that some integration was likely. Others had similar reservations, warning Byrd of the possible consequences when the resistance plans were reviewed by the courts. But the senator never took these warnings seriously; defeat at one point was only a precursor to the next line of defense, which he was searching out with other attorneys. He traveled to Richmond to remind Almond that the choice was either accepting integration or resisting it. There could be no in-between.[55]

Not surprisingly, Almond's victory was substantial, nearly two to one. Dalton would have been in trouble anyway against an entrenched machine and a colorful campaigner like Lindsay Almond, but the voters' opposition to integration, the Court, civil rights legislation, and federal troops was responsible for the size of his defeat. As Dalton said, "Little Rock was not a little rock, it was a big rock."[56] There was no mistaking the election message. To the Norfolk *Ledger-Dispatch* it was "a sweeping endorsement of the program of 'massive resistance.'" In historian James Ely's words, "Almond and the Byrd Organization had successfully converted the gubernatorial campaign into a public referendum on the Supreme Court's integration edict." Describing the result as a statement to the South and the nation of "Virginia's determination to resist integration," the elated Byrd declared it would have a profound effect on Washington politicians.[57]

Byrd's rhetoric in the campaign and his unwarranted confidence that the *Brown* decision could be rolled back indicate the degree to which emotion had replaced reason in his thinking. His hyperbolic statements about villainous federal judges, a ruthless president, and an apocalyptic vision of the end of segregation were the delusions of an embittered, frustrated man whose world was collapsing around him. He sought support from friends, editors, and attorneys who could give him one last hope to cling to—a political forecast, a constitutional argument, a legal opinion—that only intensified his commitment and his eventual disappointment. Years later Almond explained the senator's mo-tives: "I think he was determined to preserve his power and his hold on the people of Virginia. He saw the seeds of the destruction of his organization."[58]

Almond's victory precipitated Senator Byrd's retirement from public life. He had mentioned such a possibility a decade earlier, but the challenges from the "antis" had compelled him to seek reelection in 1946 and 1952. He claimed that he had promised Sittie this would be his last term; her recent stroke, along with his increasing frustration over budget battles and the massive resistance campaign, reinforced his decision that was announced to a shocked nation on February 12, 1958. The outpouring of praise and distress over his departure was unprecedented. Old friends and total strangers exhorted him to stay on; his staff recounted the tearful cries of one caller who exclaimed: "My God! We can't do without him." In the General Assembly the speeches were eulogistic, with Mills Godwin proclaiming, "We shall never look upon his like again." The legislators passed a resolution of appreciation for his years of service to the Commonwealth, and then just as quickly they approved another resolution urging him to continue in office. The senator, in a deliberate isolation in Arizona, could not be reached for comment.[59]

Immediately a contest for Byrd's seat took shape. Bill Tuck had his announcement written and ready for release as soon as Byrd confirmed his intention not to reconsider. Having talked with the senator, Tuck was sure he would not retract. "If Harry Byrd ever told you anything," he said, "you could go to bed on it year after next." But rumors started that John Battle was also eyeing the seat and would likely have the support of Governor Almond in a struggle with Tuck. Confidentially, Battle told a friend that he would become a candidate if Byrd did not change his mind. Faced with the prospect of an Organization bloodletting and unable to choose between two friends, Byrd emerged from his seclusion with a letter from Mrs. Byrd stating that she would not stand in the way of the request of the legislature for her husband to continue. Harry Byrd was unretiring.[60]

Most public commentators believed his reversal was the result of the unexpected assembly request and the potential intraparty fight that would have weakened the Organization at a critical time in the massive resistance struggle. Byrd later said that the legislature's appeal was the most important consideration in changing his decision to retire. Colgate Darden believed Byrd's retirement would have destroyed the machine, a prospect that caused him to change his mind. But Darden also suggested that Byrd's actions may have been prearranged. He found it impossible to believe that Byrd was going to retire because politics was Byrd's life: "I don't know anybody who would have been more unhappy out of the United States Senate. He loved the panoply and the power and the fixings of politics. He just loved it—it was his life's blood. . . . Sitting around Winchester would have been awful punishment for him." Darden remembered Byrd calling him a few days after his retirement and asking him to get a statement from all the former governors requesting him to run again; he told Darden not to tell anyone of his solicitation. It is likely that Byrd was in a dilemma about his departure; he was sensitive to his wife's request but had no great enthusiasm for retiring. The public demonstrations of affection and the likelihood of a tough Tuck-Battle contest—both of which could have easily been predicted by a man with Byrd's political acumen—"convinced" him to stay and allowed him to escape his promise to Sittie. It is possible that he orchestrated the legislature's appeal just as he arranged the former governors' petition. It was not in his character to change his mind, and maybe he never did.[61]

Certainly Byrd was not concerned about his chances for reelection. He had no primary opposition, and in the general election the Republicans chose not to contest his seat, leaving the challenge to independent Louise Wensel, who had labor support, and Socialist Clarke Robb. Nonetheless, Byrd followed his election routine of using the lists to contact the local courthouse officials to urge them to get out the vote. He made few campaign speeches, choosing to rely on letters and circulars that emphasized his opposition to integration and organized labor while associating his opponents with those albatrosses. Byrd wanted another good turnout as a further test of Virginia's commitment to segregation. There was some fear that sizable black participation and liberal dissatisfaction with massive resistance would produce a large protest vote that would tarnish the senator's image, but the outcome was never in doubt. Byrd won with 70 percent of the total.[62]

The future of massive resistance, however, was more problematic. The 1958 General Assembly session had strengthened the massive resistance laws, but little could be done to intimidate federal judges. In July, Attorney General Harrison apprised Senator Byrd of the likelihood of an imminent confrontation with the courts. In Warren County, where there was no black high school, black children were being bussed and lodged outside the county, which paid for only two trips home a month. Harrison believed this case could be dragged out for another year, but "the problem is that our Federal Judges are going to put some Negroes into white schools. We are making a strenuous effort to prevent this but I am not optimistic that we will be successful."[63]

Harrison's prediction was off by a year. On September 8, 1958, over four years after the *Brown* decision, federal judge John Paul ordered the Warren County School Board to desegregate its high school. When the Fourth Circuit Court of Appeals upheld Paul's order, Governor Almond closed the school. He was forced to repeat this action only days later in Charlottesville and Norfolk, leaving nearly thirteen thousand students without public education in Virginia.

Returning from an Alaska vacation, Senator Byrd quickly rallied support for the closings, calling Judge Paul's decision "outrageous" and vowing to make a personal contribution to help pay the unemployed teachers of Warren. Surrender, he declared, was out of the question; local officials should be prepared to defy the law.[64]

Such defiance received unfavorable national publicity when a *Time* article revealed a face of bigotry in the Old Dominion. Byrd was quoted as calling for law enforcement "by the white people of this country." "We face," he said, "the gravest crisis since the War Between the States." The author described the Organization as "composed of the few, chosen by the few to make decisions for the many." It was an unflattering account that infuriated the senator, but Tuck consoled him: "Had it not been for you, many of the other leaders in Virginia would have surrendered to this unspeakable form of tyranny long ago."[65]

Byrd was now nearly hysterical on the issue. To Billy Prieur he predicted a class war in which white textile workers would attack blacks who were petitioning for integrating schools; and to Jack Kilpatrick he suggested that six-year-old children of both races would be "assembled in little huts before the bus comes, and the bus will then be packed like sardines. . . . What our people most fear is that by this close intimate social contact future generations will intermarry, as I am certain the Supreme Court will declare illegal the laws against inter-marriages." "A surrender in any form would have disastrous results," he told Lester Hooker.[66]

Byrd was greatly concerned that Lindsay Almond would give in. The governor and his attorney general had decided to initiate a suit in the state courts to test the validity of the school-closing laws. Fearing that the federal court currently considering a suit brought by the Norfolk Committee for Public Schools was going to overturn the Stanley Plan, they hoped either for a more favorable ruling in the state courts that would buy them more time or an adverse ruling that would prove to the people that the last alternative had been tried. If the highest Virginia court found school closings unconstitutional, the electorate might accept an end to massive resistance. Almond and Harrison knew that they had reached the end of the line. Their remaining options were limited and would be difficult to implement. Years later Harrison recalled: "Senator Byrd might have thought there was a possibility of altering the course of the Supreme Court. I didn't think so. I was an attorney and I knew what we were up against. But I also knew the effort had to be made. Too many people were demanding that that effort be made." Harrison attempted to prepare Byrd for this eventuality, but the senator wanted no part of that message. He thought the route through the state courts a mistake—a concession that did not have to be made—and having been told of the governor's "defeatist" attitude, he refused to meet with him.[67]

Lindsay Almond was caught in a terrible dilemma, but it was much of his own making. Throughout his political career he had alternated between the realistic lawyer and the demagogic politician. During the massive resistance years, he switched from one to the other with amazing rapidity and frequency, one moment acknowledging the permanence of the Court's ruling and the next second vowing defiance to the bitter end. Now in late 1958 he became somewhat reclusive, waiting for the predicted storm. Despondently, he wrote to Byrd: "I feel I must ride with Virginia's law as long as a piece of it is left. After that we must take some definite action legislatively." He denied rumors of a break with the senator, but his lack of ardor for the cause drew criticism from the extremists, who wanted reassurances that the governor would never give in to federal dictates. For them, schools should be shut down and reopened on a segregated basis, or they should be shut down for good.[68]

But the governor was also hearing different voices. Parent and teacher groups across the state were expressing concern over the closings. Several prominent state newspapers that had been staunch defenders of massive resistance, including the Richmond papers, now counseled moderation. Convinced that massive resistance was no longer appropriate, publisher D. Tennant Bryan and editors Kilpatrick and Dabney drove to Berryville to tell Senator Byrd of their new editorial position. He was not happy and informed them that he and other Virginians were not ready to quit. "Virginia is the keystone to this whole fight," he declared, "and as long as we hold out we can win."[69]

Most importantly, civic and business leaders in Richmond began to sound out the governor on other possibilities. In early December, Almond and Harrison met at the Rotunda Club with several prominent Richmond citizens, who urged a more flexible attitude on schools. Months later, when he was justifying his change of course, Almond mentioned the negative impact that the school closings were having on Virginia's economy. When Senator Byrd insisted on documented evidence that businesses were refusing to locate in Virginia because of massive resistance, Almond said he had no such facts but stated that many businessmen had written to decry "our attitude in the matter of integration. . . . I have been advised by individuals connected with great industries in Virginia that this would have a most deleterious effect on the operation of existing industries and the attraction of new industry."[70] James Ely has said the industrialists' fears were "extravagant," but they were fears nonetheless. The Advisory Council on the Virginia Economy announced that not a single dollar for new industry had been spent in Virginia in 1958 while North Carolina, where token integration had occurred, had received a quarter of a billion dollars in new investments. Furthermore, the existence of a sizable school bond debt concerned bondholders, who feared the possibility of defaults with the closing of schools. Thomas Boushall, a leading Richmond banker, said of mas-

"I CAN'T UNDERSTAND IT....IT USED TO RUN SO SMOOTH!"

sive resistance: "It was a waste of everyone's energies. . . . I thought he [Byrd] had more sense than that."[71]

On January 19, 1959—Robert E. Lee's 152d birthday—both the Virginia Supreme Court of Appeals and a federal district court ruled that Virginia's school-closing laws were unconstitutional because they violated section 129 of the state constitution requiring the state to maintain free schools and the equal protection clause of the Fourteenth Amendment to the United States Constitution.[72] The day after the rulings, Lindsay Almond became a demagogic ranter for the last time. In a blistering, near-hysterical attack on the federal courts and integration generally, he vowed to continue the fight: "To those who defend or close their eyes to the livid stench of sadism, sex immorality and juvenile pregnancy infesting the mixed schools of the District of Columbia and elsewhere; to those who would overthrow the customs, morals and traditions of a way of life which has endured in honor and decency for centuries . . . Let me make it abundantly clear, . . . I will not yield to that which I know to be wrong and will destroy every rational semblance of education for thousands of the children of Virginia." He left the impression that new strategies were available to block integration, promising Congressman Tuck that he was "going to do my best to hold the line." Senator Byrd could not have been happier. Publicly and by telegram he commended Almond for his "notable speech" that "will do much to strengthen the resistance not only in Virginia but all through the South." The governor thanked him and expressed the hope that "we can talk soon concerning some of the problems we are facing."[73]

Almost immediately, Almond regretted making "that damn speech." He later said that he was "distraught" and had "succumbed to inner frustration," fearing "friendships melting away." Nevertheless, he was to pay dearly for his indiscretion, for those whose hopes he had raised saw his subsequent actions as the ultimate betrayal. Seeking advice from Byrd, he met secretly with the senator and congressmen Tuck and Abbitt in the "catacombs" of the United States Capitol. Supported by Harrison, Almond said he had no authority to override a federal court decree, to which Byrd replied that Virginia should hold the line. According to Almond, the senator was worried about "what his Senate colleagues would think if Virginia gave up." When the governor inquired how he might resist, Tuck said he could go to jail. Almond rejected that suggestion.[74]

Almond's subsequent attempts to contact Byrd failed. Wanting no direct association with any new plans, the senator conveniently could not be found at his office or home. "He hid from me," Almond recalled. Needing Byrd's direction, the governor consulted with Lieutenant Governor Stephens and Speaker Blackburn Moore, Byrd's closest adviser in the House of Delegates, who suggested a conference with senior legislators preparatory to a special session that would enact stopgap legislation to prevent integration. Moore promised to contact selected delegates while Stephens wired the senators, but within hours the Speaker said he was unable to reach his fellow assemblymen and advised Almond to call off the meeting. Senator Lloyd C. Bird, whom Stephens had invited, offered the lieutenant governor a succinct explanation: "Blackie had a reason—a big one—for his decision." It takes little imagination to see the hand of Harry Byrd in this. As Mills Godwin declared, "One would never listen to anything Blackie was saying without knowing full well that he was speaking the sentiments of Senator Byrd."[75] The senator was aware of cracks in the massive resistance facade and was wary of an uncontrollable assembly. He preferred to let the governor take the heat by using all the machinery available to him to keep the schools closed, perhaps even risking a contempt citation and a jailing as a final act of defiance. Byrd later told columnist Charles McDowell that "Lindsay should have gone to jail. The people of Virginia would have come to the jail and serenaded him and brought him good things to eat."[76]

At this point Almond decided to call the legislature into session on January

28. Apparently wanting to know what the governor planned, Byrd broke his silence and contacted him. Almond recalled a difficult phone conversation in which he admitted that resistance was over: "I said that the only way to prevent integration was to close down every public school in Virginia, and that I could not do. . . . I asked him for his views, and he told me that Speaker Moore represented his thinking on the subject. I said that I had talked to Mr. Moore and still didn't know what those views were. . . . I could tell that he was upset at me."[77]

But not so upset as he would be after Lindsay Almond's public capitulation on massive resistance. Addressing the General Assembly in somber tones and near-funereal garb, the governor acknowledged defeat. Virginia, he said, was now powerless to defy federal decrees. He reviewed his record of maintaining Virginia's rights and saving its public schools, directed sarcasm toward those who advocated further resistance or closing of schools, and announced formation of a commission, to be headed by Senator Mosby Perrow of Lynchburg, to deal with the specifics of a new plan that would limit the degree of integration. The resisters sat in stunned silence, not believing the defection of the man who once had vowed to cut off his arm before acceding to integration. "He left us hanging out on a limb," recalled Mills Godwin. Judge Smith said of Byrd's reaction, "He never forgave Almond entirely for what he considered a defection from the ranks of the resisters." After inquiring if Almond still had his arm, Byrd reaffirmed his opposition to school integration and encouraged his friends in the assembly to press for legislation that would obstruct integration to the point of closing all schools. But Almond, who had previously consulted with moderate legislators, had correctly judged the rising tide in favor of public education and had counted his votes well. His proposals passed, and those of the resisters were defeated. As the legislators sat, the first black children entered formerly all-white schools in Norfolk and Arlington. Massive resistance was dead.[78]

But the senator would not admit defeat. In an effort to nullify the *Brown* decision, Byrd joined other senators to offer a constitutional amendment that would have vested control of public schools exclusively with the states and their political subdivisions. He was also working to gain tax exemptions for donations to private schools and to cancel the tax-exempt status of the NAACP, which he had always blamed for stirring up this trouble. Corresponding with Albertis Harrison, Byrd criticized Almond and pressed for legislation that would maintain the barriers of segregation. Harrison, as gently as he could, defended the governor and the shift toward accommodation. As long as the Court's decision was standing and enforced, he wrote, "we cannot write a state law that will wholly avoid its effect. There are many people who do not know or will not admit this. . . . In truth, Senator, there is simply no ready or easy solution to this problem."[79]

It took considerable courage for Lindsay Almond to challenge Senator Byrd and the resisters. He could have kept the schools closed or resorted to other delaying tactics that would have satisfied the resisters and retained their support. Instead he chose, however hesitantly, to move Virginia in a different direction, alienating Organization forces who had anticipated continued opposition. Although this terminated Lindsay Almond's career in the machine, it also signaled the end of Organization authority and Harry Byrd's control of Virginia politics. Neither occurred immediately, but the division between those who now placed a greater priority on public education over continued segregation and those who supported continued resistance at the expense of the schools would grow. The economic and social changes that had been taking place in the Old Dominion over the last decade had finally produced a political revolution as well, all of it coming to a head with the school crisis. Moderate leadership, which would include many business leaders and some of the staunchest members of the Byrd hierarchy such as Almond and Harrison, would begin to face forward and develop the resources of the Commonwealth to their fullest. Members of the Old Guard like Bill Tuck, who demanded that they "never surrender," lost their mandate to lead. In historian Numan Bartley's view, the Organization "battled for the principle of massive resistance far beyond the dictates of political wisdom."[80]

The extent of this political transformation was apparent in the subsequent special session of the General Assembly in April 1959 that considered the recommendations of the Perrow commission. Unlike the earlier Gray commission, this education commission included four members from each congressional district, most of whom clearly favored the Almond position. By a 31–9 margin, it recommended a local-option desegregation plan that included new pupil placement laws, a new compulsory attendance law, and tuition grants that would keep integration to a minimum. The euphemism "freedom of choice" was applied to a program whose similarities to the old Gray Plan were striking.

Despite lobbying by a Capitol Square crowd of five thousand Southsiders, who on the eve of the session condemned the governor for his betrayal, the legislators adopted the commission report by a narrow margin. Fearing that the key pupil placement bill would be blocked by Byrd partisans in the senate's Education Committee, the Almond allies, by a 20-19 vote, resolved the senate into a committee of the whole and passed the package by a similar vote. Passage in the house was less controversial, but the delegates defeated a proposal to repeal section 129 of the constitution by a vote of only 53–45, which demonstrated that there was still a sizable opposition that preferred closing the schools to integration. Kilpatrick wrote Byrd that he was "disgusted" with the General Assembly for capitulating too soon instead of adopting a "flexible, shifting guerrilla defense" for the future. A different assessment came from Francis

Pickens Miller, who told Governor Almond that the session marked "the beginning of a new chapter in the political history of Virginia." Although the pace of integration over the next few years would be glacial, the process had begun. Significantly, the massive resistance lines began to crumble across the rest of the South as well.[81]

The session left an irreparable rift in the Organization, embittering old friends toward one another. Almond and Stephens, whose ruling had permitted creation of the committee of the whole, would never again have the regime's support. Mosby Perrow believed that an audit of his tax returns by the IRS after the 1959 session was more than coincidental. Even the wives of the antagonists were not speaking to one another.[82] Byrd himself had remained silent during this special session; had he spoken out forcefully on the issue, he might have swayed several key legislators away from the Perrow proposals. It was not due to a lack of interest. Years before, to avoid charges of dictatorship, he had adopted the policy of not interfering publicly in the deliberations of the assembly, preferring to use confidants such as Combs, Moore, and his son to convey his thoughts on legislation and appointments. He had also adhered to the rule of avoiding association with failure; as Almond described it, "If there is failure, he [Byrd] can separate himself from the responsibility for it. If there is success, and it is popular, the organization claims credit [and] it becomes obvious to whom that credit redounds." Byrd's reticence on this occasion contributed to the most significant defeat of his career.[83]

During the summer of 1959 the Virginia electorate was treated to an unusual spectacle: Organization Democrats fighting among themselves for seats in the next General Assembly. The closeness of the votes in the special session suggested that control of the 1960 legislature was in doubt. This led to a bitter struggle between the Almond and Byrd factions in many primary contests where the issue was simply schools versus segregation. Both sides claimed victory. Senator Byrd commented that the election "turned out fairly well," with both houses about the same as before, but in reality that was a defeat, for it left the Almond coalition with a slight majority. There would be no turning back the clock to massive resistance. Nevertheless, at his annual picnic a few weeks later, Senator Byrd proclaimed, "I stand now as I stood when I first urged massive resistance." The numbers who had stood with him were fast diminishing.[84]

Massive resistance was a sorry spectacle for Harry Byrd and Virginia. Ralph McGill's epitaph stands: "The worst of the demagogues, the ugliest of passions and prejudices were given dignity and status by the stand of the Byrd machine."[85] There are ample explanations for this behavior, but none justify what was done. Massive resistance was not inevitable or necessary. Different choices by Virginia's leaders could have produced a different result.

Apologists for the Organization claim that they were merely following the wishes of the electorate in defying the Court's decision. Albertis Harrison vividly recalled the mood: "I was there; I heard the clamor. Your own intimate friends, people you played golf with, drank whiskey with, went to parties with—you didn't hear anything but talk of integration. . . . I saw 5,000 of them out in front of the capitol; they came from everywhere and were not solicited to come. . . . We knew we were up against a stone wall, but you had to make the effort or they would throw you out and put someone else in who would make the effort."[86] In his excellent history of massive resistance, James Ely has emphasized the commitment of white Virginians to segregation as an important component of the decision to resist, but he exaggerated the depth of that commitment. They were segregationists, but, except for the Southsiders, not at any price. Several key votes by the electorate and the legislature indicated a willingness to compromise, to pursue token integration or local option to avoid closing the schools. When Delegate Armistead Boothe polled his fellow legislators in the summer of 1954 on the desegregation of schools, he discovered that, of the one-third who replied, a surprising number were ready to accept a degree of integration. The moderates, many of whom believed in racial separation but not at the cost of closing schools or restricting economic development, lost out to the resisters because they lacked unity, were the victims of emotional racist rhetoric, and did not have friends in high places. They started with public support, lost it in the heat of demagoguery, and recaptured it when Virginians became aware of the threat that massive resistance posed for public education.[87]

But the debate over popular sentiment—over who had more votes—is not the significant question. The important issue is leadership, the necessity of having wise and moral leaders in a democratic society who will defy popular emotions when the issue demands it. During the 1950s, Virginia's leaders all too often appealed to the basest of human emotions, used the politics of race to achieve their objectives, or, abdicating their responsibility, deferred to the racists. Their perspective was limited by their political horizons, not informed by an understanding of opinion across the Old Dominion or of the broader currents of change occurring in state and nation. Ironically, massive resistance was not necessary to sustain the machine. Virginians would have tolerated a variety of responses to *Brown*, including gradualism or local option, knowing Harry Byrd was at the helm. He could have led them in a different direction than he did and still retained his authority.[88]

Defenders of the resisters also justify their actions on constitutional grounds, arguing that they were fighting to preserve states' rights from a grasping federal tyranny. Yet historical analysis reveals that states' rights has frequently been a cry to defend special interests, not the rights of all citizens. It has been a facade to conceal individual prejudice and state discrimination as was the case in the South during the Civil Rights movement. States' rights in the defense of immoral purposes has no validity.

Years later all of the resisters justified the policy of massive resistance as a play for time, to give Virginians the opportunity to adjust to a new condition. Godwin and Harrison both believed the people would not have accepted integrated schools without some effort to prevent them. As Harrison remembered, "We had to convince the people that this law which had been the law for over a hundred years wasn't the law any more and that we had to abide by [the new law]. And the only way you could convince them was to test it, and by the time we got through fighting those cases before federal judges, people in the hinterlands knew we were trying and when it was over it was over." This may have been true of Harrison, who was a legal realist, but the actions of many others undermined their defense of playing for time. Instead of channeling the change in positive directions, they were building walls to hold back the tide altogether. They had shifted away from the moderation of the Gray Plan, and even after the January 1959 court decisions, they were still insisting on closing the schools rather than submitting. As Jack Bass and Walter De Vries have pointed out, "Raising false hopes and intensifying voters' emotions hardly fostered a climate for acceptance." William Spong, who was in the General Assembly at the time, concluded: "I believe the same time would have been available to Virginians had we proceeded with the recommendations of the Gray Commission and the implementing legislation drafted by David Mays. North Carolina bought the Mays plan, gave it a different name, and avoided the trauma caused by school closings and the bitter divisions that took place in the Virginia Senate."[89]

A more reasonable argument of the resisters is that their policies avoided violence in the Old Dominion. When one looks at events elsewhere in the South, this was no small achievement. It is possible that an early adoption of local option would have been so vigorously opposed in the Southside that violence would have ensued, but that was unlikely. Since resistance leaders, including the Defenders, were so adamant against the use of physical force, they could have prevailed upon their constituents to abstain from it. Furthermore, under local option the segregationist communities would have been allowed to continue separate but equal facilities at least as long as they had a choice, thus defusing immediate concerns. Indeed, there was not much emotion on this issue in the Old Dominion outside of the Southside until the leadership whipped it up under the banner of massive resistance. Nor should this defense conceal the intimidation, racial epithets, cross burnings, and anti-NAACP laws—more subtle forms of force—that took place in the state. What Virginia endured was not a clean, gentlemanly act of courtroom dueling.[90]

While massive resistance may have produced a few more election victories, it did not prolong the life of the Organization but contributed to its demise by further dividing the Democratic party, stimulating black political participation, and encouraging more federal interference. It also tarnished the image of the Old Dominion and complicated what was truly inevitable: the end of state-imposed racial discrimination. Virginia did not need time; it needed leaders with vision and a sense of justice. Lenoir Chamber, the editor of the Norfolk *Virginian-Pilot,* one of the few Virginia newspapers to stand against massive resistance, put it simply, "There is no justification in injustice, no rightness in moral wrong, and no need for extreme measures when simple measures are at hand."[91] The failure of leadership—the absence of flexibility, foresight, and moral sensitivity—is the real lesson of massive resistance. It is a failure for which Harry Byrd must assume responsibility. The only apology that suffices is that he and his friends were doing what they had been doing for years and could not have been expected to change. To that extent, massive resistance was inevitable.

～ 18 ～

"Mr. Republican"

OR HARRY BYRD the years of massive resistance were tempered by the presence of a friendly face in the White House. The arrival in Washington of a Republican administration in 1953, reputedly committed to balanced budgets and cutbacks in federal spending, augured well for Byrd. He wrote Douglas Freeman, "I see now the first ray of hope we have had for many years to halt these things that have been leading to the destruction of our system of government."[1]

Immediately after the 1952 election, Byrd publicly declared that Eisenhower could count on southern Democrats to pass sound measures, and he informed the president-elect through a third party how pleased he was with his triumph; Ike reciprocated by offering him the position of secretary of the treasury. Because Eisenhower needed an immediate response, Byrd declined, unsure of the demands of the new position. The offer may have been only a gesture of appreciation for Byrd's support in the campaign, but it reflected Eisenhower's agreement with the Virginian's philosophy of government. He wrote the senator: "I hope further that our association in the governmental service can be as close as the circumstances of politics will permit. On my part your record in the Senate and your philosophy of government, so far as I understand it, both appeal to me mightily."[2] Byrd had no regrets over not taking the Treasury Department job and was pleased with the appointment of George Humphrey, a Cleveland industrialist, whom he had known since his governorship. Sometimes hunting companions, they were in near-total accord on fiscal policy.[3]

Byrd was less enamored with the selection of Charles E. Wilson to be secretary of defense. He had no personal objections to the president of General Motors, but the senator perceived a major conflict of interest in Wilson's retaining control of $2.5 million of GM stock while supervising the defense establishment that undoubtedly would enter into multimillion-dollar contracts with the automobile giant. In the confirmation hearings before the Senate Armed Services Committee on January 16, Byrd, who over the years had fought several nominations over conflicts of interest, claimed that it was "sound public policy to ask government officials to divest themselves of substantial holdings in any business they would have to deal with as officials." When Wilson resisted, Byrd applied more pressure; he met personally with the automotive executive and had memos from the Senate legislative counsel placed in the *Congressional Record* citing laws barring government officers from doing business with companies with which they were directly involved. A few days later, at Eisenhower's insistence, Wilson offered to sell his stock, and his nomination was quickly approved. Only after the proceedings did Byrd reveal that he had tipped off the administration about the conflict of interest, not for any political gain but to ward off embarrassment for the president.[4]

He need not have worried about GOP retaliation. His tacit support of Eisenhower in the fall was rewarded with re-appointment as chairman of the Joint Committee on Reduction of Non-essential Federal Expenditures, just as in 1946 when the Republicans also won control of Congress. Although Byrd offered to resign the chairmanship, Senate leader William Knowland asserted that he was "doing a fine job." It was also common knowledge that Byrd, much to the chagrin of state Republicans, would be consulted by the administration on patronage in Virginia. When T. Coleman Andrews, a conservative Virginia Democrat who had served as state auditor under Governor Pollard, was appointed to head the Internal Revenue Service, Virginia GOP leaders were dumbstruck. Groused Walter Johnson:

> The choice of a Democrat for high position in a Republican administration threatens the two party system. . . . Here in Virginia it has been publicly proclaimed and not denied that Senator Byrd will be "consulted" on patronage, and that means he will control. Patronage control is party control and this means that the Republican party of Virginia has been reduced to control by the boss of the Democratic party of Virginia. . . . Certainly Virginia Republicans who struggled so many years against heavy odds never expected that winning an election would merely win their party a place subordinate to Senator Byrd.[5]

Such parochial concerns did not worry Eisenhower, whose respect for the Virginian outweighed any party loyalty, which for him never ran very deep. The two developed a very cordial relationship over the course of Ike's presidency. Byrd was not one of the president's close associates or advisers, but he had easy access to the White House, particularly through his friendship with George Humphrey. In the flush of the 1952 victory, amid the promises of turning back twenty years of the New Deal, the senator's influence seemed more significant than it actually was. He was seated next to the president at a White House luncheon—the first time Byrd had been to the executive mansion in eight years—and also at a Washington's Birthday service at Christ Church, Alexandria. Later in 1953 he accompanied Eisenhower on the presidential yacht to Williamsburg where the president received an honorary degree from the College of William and Mary.[6]

Celebrating twenty years in the Senate, Byrd now ranked fourth in seniority behind senators Carl Hayden, Walter George, and Richard Russell. Although Democrats had lost control of the Senate, southerners were least affected by the shift since their conservative inclinations matched those of the GOP. An example of the close alliance between Senate Republicans and southern Democrats was the overwhelming defeat of proposals to change the filibustering provisions that protected the South from passage of civil rights legislation.[7]

Befitting a Republican administration, Eisenhower pursued cuts in spending, a balanced budget, and restraint in the use of federal power; voluntarism in the mode of Herbert Hoover was his governing principle. While this commended him to Harry Byrd, the president and his economic advisers proved more flexible than Byrd would have wished, following a middle road on fiscal matters that reflected the president's own nonideological bent and the narrow Republican majority in Congress. Confounding conservative Republicans such as Senator Taft, the administration agreed with Byrd that tax cuts would aggravate the federal deficit and so rejected them for the moment; but at the same time, faced with continued military and social needs, Ike refused to pare federal spending to the bone. He did cut Truman's budget by $5 billion, mostly in defense expenditures, but this was only half of what Byrd demanded. Furthermore, a new cabinet position, the Department of Health, Education, and Welfare (HEW), was created, which Byrd saw as another example of an expanding bureaucracy. When a recession occurred later in the year, caused by the end of the Korean War and tight Federal Reserve credit policies, Eisenhower authorized some modest pump priming and tax reform to encourage economic growth. By the end of 1954 the economy was expanding vigorously, producing a small budget surplus the following year that warmed Harry Byrd's heart, even though it had been achieved by methods not entirely to his liking.[8]

Byrd usually could be counted on to support administration positions, notably the extension of a reciprocal trade act, passage of the tidelands oil bill, which gave states ownership of the oil underlying coastal waters, and the creation of a new Hoover commission to consider another government reorganization. He rejoiced at the death of the Reconstruction Finance Corporation, reminding his listeners that in 1940 he had been the only senator to vote for its termination. At the end of the first legislative session, President Eisenhower, in obvious reference to Truman's famous remark, wrote to the Virginian: "Hurrah for the Byrds. We need more of them." His gratitude was more than justified, for Byrd was the only Democrat among seven senators who had voted for all of the administration's major legislative proposals.[9]

On one issue, however, Byrd would not relent: the debt ceiling. Forecasting a weak economy, Secretary Humphrey asked for a $15 billion increase in the debt limit that was then at $275 billion. Labeling the request a "grave mistake" and an "invitation to extravagance," Byrd fought it in a private meeting with Humphrey and Eisenhower at the White House and in the Finance Committee hearings. Although passed by the House of Representatives on the eve of the August adjournment, the issue died in the committee, 11–4, upon Byrd's motion.[10]

During the summer of 1953, the Korean War ended after three long years of battlefield stalemate and drawn-out negotiations. General war weariness on all sides and the threatened use of nuclear weapons produced a truce agreement on July 26. Korea had become a very unpopular war: a limited war seemingly without objectives and without end, a divisive issue in American politics through the ongoing Red Scare. In March, Byrd had become embroiled in another incident which confirmed in the public mind the incompetence with which the war had been fought. In testimony before the Armed Services Committee, former Eighth Army commander General James Van Fleet claimed that his troops had been handicapped by a shortage of ammunition. Byrd, who said he had never heard more shocking testimony in his twenty years in the Senate, immediately called on Defense Secretary Wilson to punish those responsible for this "criminal inefficiency." Van Fleet's report was challenged by Wilson and other military officials, who insisted that there were satisfactory levels of ammunition available and that no operations had been affected. When Byrd released data showing that only 40 percent of the ammunition for which Congress had appropriated funds had been delivered, the Armed Services Committee authorized a full inquiry by a subcommittee that included him as a member.[11]

The resulting investigation rehashed the long debate over the objectives of the Korean War. Van Fleet, a disciple of Douglas MacArthur, claimed that the shortages had hampered the army's effort to win battlefield victories, while the top army brass, defending President Truman's limited war strategy, denied the charges. They did acknowledge that there had been shortages at times, but not at alarming levels or on the front lines. While the inquiry uncovered much Defense Department red tape that slowed ammunition procurement, its major bombshell was the revelation of a September 1950 decision by Truman and his military advisers to reduce budgetary shortfalls by cutting back military purchases. Based on predictions of a short war, that decision resulted in no substantial ammunition production for the next two years. Castigating the Truman administration for miscalculating Communist aggression, the subcommittee report concluded that shortages existed that adversely affected the operation of the war and went so far as to suggest that there had been "needless loss of American lives" because of the deficiency. Since the war was coming to a close, the report had no impact, but it did reinforce the general perception of Korean War ineptitude. Despite the political ramifications of the investigation—for Byrd truly relished the chance to snipe at Harry Truman one more time—the senator won praise for his performance, which, as always, demonstrated his keen nose for waste and incompetence in government.[12]

The summer of 1953 also witnessed Harry Byrd going up against Senator Joe McCarthy. McCarthy had continued his assault on Communists in the government, but with the Republicans now in power and the Korean War winding down, the Red Scare was losing its appeal, forcing McCarthy to search more widely for new evidence of communism with which to keep his name in the spotlight. In July one of his aides, J. B. Matthews, charged that the American clergy was being infiltrated by Communists. Up to this point, Byrd had remained friendly with McCarthy and had refrained from any criticism of his work or that of his assistants, even when he had impugned the loyalty of General George Marshall. But now, emboldened by a change in the public reaction to McCarthy's activities and the assurances of J. Edgar Hoover that the FBI had not found a single churchman who could be prosecuted as a Communist, Byrd challenged Matthews's "irresponsible attacks on religious leaders." He demanded that he provide names to support his charges or "stand convicted as a cheap demagogue, willing to blacken the character of his fellow Americans for his own notoriety and personal gain." He was particularly incensed by Matthews's indirect reference to his good friend G. Bromley Oxnam, Methodist bishop of Washington, D. C., as one who had aided the Communist cause by speaking out against those who were trying to combat it. Lyndon Johnson remarked to Hubert Humphrey that Matthews's attack was "a fatal mistake" for McCarthy. "You can't attack Harry Byrd's friends in this Senate," he said. "Mark my words, he's in trouble."[13]

A year later McCarthy was, indeed, "in trouble," facing the censure of his colleagues. Continuing to overreach, he began a new round of hearings in early 1954 into his charges that the United States Army was coddling Communists. Army countercharges led to the televised Army-McCarthy hearings that revealed to the American people the smear tactics of the Wisconsin senator. A Senate inquiry into his conduct produced a resolution of condemnation for obstructing the constitutional processes of the Senate, acting contrary to its traditions, and abusing members of the investigating panel. Byrd, who at one point had been considered for membership on the panel, voted for the resolution, but he played little role in the debates. He disapproved of McCarthy's methods but had no stomach for the public censure of a senator. To avoid any misinterpretation of where he stood on the larger issue, he immediately joined others in introducing a resolution endorsing Congress's power to investigate communism. Three years later when McCarthy died of alcoholism, Byrd benevolently praised his colleague's patriotism, family devotion, and religious faith. Admitting McCarthy's errors of judgment but his sincerity of purpose, Byrd queried, "Could it be that the great objectives of his principal work required practices he deplored?"[14]

As always, Byrd was preoccupied with fiscal matters in 1954. Foreseeing "a pivotal year" in budget balancing, he was disappointed when President Eisenhower requested an increase in the debt limit, greater social security benefits, a new farm program with flexible price supports, and the vote for eighteen-year-olds. Unlike the year before, Byrd now opposed almost everything the president proposed. Insisting that deficits forbade any tax cuts, he was one of only eight senators to vote against a reduction in excise taxes. He was also in the minority in opposing the president's tax reform bill that provided modest deductions for medical expenses and child care and lower taxes on dividends. Despite his membership on the Finance Committee and on the joint conference committee to settle differences between the Senate and House bills, Byrd was unable to modify the major elements of the bill, and it passed in August. On the debt ceiling, Byrd again contested Secretary Humphrey's request for a $15 billion increase. "To avoid embarrassment to the Treasury," he arranged a compromise that permitted a temporary $6 billion increase until June 1955. The senator also found himself on the losing side of social security increases. Rejecting a significant expansion of the security rolls because of costs, he led the effort in the Finance Committee to trim the administration's request to extend coverage to ten-and-a-half million Americans, but he was unsuccessful in defeating the larger figure on the Senate floor.[15]

The president and the senator also crossed swords on several other issues with mixed results. Byrd vehemently opposed Hawaiian statehood because the racially mixed population, whose ways of thinking were not "typically American," might "send to the United States Senate a Chinese or a Japanese Senator— or both." He argued that they did not have the same feelings and traditions of the people who settled Virginia and the other states. Faced with such prejudice and politics, Alaska and Hawaii would have to wait until 1958 and 1959, respectively, before becoming the forty-ninth and fiftieth states, although even then the senators from Virginia voted against their entry.[16] On giving the vote to eighteen-year-olds, Byrd joined the minority who prevented the amendment from receiving the necessary two-thirds approval, but he was unable to sidetrack the St. Lawrence Seaway bill that he believed would detour trade away from Hampton Roads. Nor did he see eye-to-eye with Ike on foreign aid and public housing. Over Eisenhower's objections he supported the Bricker amendment that would have limited the president's treaty-making power; it failed to pass by only one vote. At the end of the session, the *Congressional Quarterly* reported that he had backed the president on only 44 percent of the key votes during the entire Eighty-third Congress.[17]

Byrd's vote against the public housing bill reflected not only his perpetual opposition to such spending but his current involvement in an investigation of Federal Housing Administration (FHA) practices. Tipped off several months earlier by IRS chief Andrews, who was probing FHA-approved loans, Byrd initiated April hearings into the windfall profits that housing promoters were reaping through these loans that often were larger than the cost of the project and were covered with very little private capital. His joint committee on government spending, which had a budget of only $20,000 for all of its work, did not have the resources to carry out a full-fledged investigation on its own, but that did not prevent its chairman from undertaking his search for misdeeds. His publicity forced the Senate Banking Committee to begin its own probe into the scandal and coerced FHA officials to be more forthcoming with information on their procedures.[18]

As the many investigations continued, Byrd called the FHA loan program "one of the most scandalous in the history of our government's operations," likening it to Teapot Dome in the twenties. There was, he said, "an unsavory concentration of malfeasance, greed, collusion and graft." Billions of dollars of loans were made without appraisals by the lending institutions, and gift giving and favor taking by FHA employees were common practices. Reporting that lenders had filed claims of $150 million on defaulted government-insured home repair loans, Byrd cynically remarked that everyone was insured except the taxpayers. As a result of the investigations, many FHA officials were fired, and the Justice Department, which had been urged into action by Byrd, was looking into scores of cases of fraud, collusion, and other irregularities. Remarkably, despite all of the revelations, a much-weakened housing bill creating 140,000 new units over the next four years easily passed Congress. Byrd had to wonder if playing watchdog to the people's tax dollars was worth the effort when his amendments to tighten rules were rejected or watered down.[19]

Byrd's legislative efforts became more focused after 1954. The off-year elections returned the Democrats to power by a narrow margin and elevated him to the chairmanship of the important Finance Committee, a vacancy created when Walter George, who had been the ranking Democrat on the committee, chose to become chairman of the Foreign Relations Committee. It would be the ultimate achievement of his Senate career, propelling him into a position of visibility and influence. Fully aware of the significance of the job, he devoted all of his energies to a full and fair consideration of all the crucial legislation for which the committee had responsibility: tax policy, social security, foreign trade, health care, and veterans benefits. For the last decade of his career, he was in the maelstrom of controversy. As the nation moved leftward in its pursuit of greater social justice and liberal economic policies, Byrd did his best to slow the process, but it was a losing proposition.

The Democrats' return to power occasioned no great changes in the legislative process or the relationship between the two branches. Texans Lyndon Johnson and Sam Rayburn established a good working relationship with the president, and as majority leaders over the next six years, they would achieve an unparalleled record of bipartisan cooperation in passing legislation. Eisenhower had a high regard for southern Democrats, "the kind of men that we should have in Washington." As he wrote in his memoirs, "I could count on Byrd and George on critical votes." He frequently sent Byrd short notes thanking him for his support or for the apples he had sent. Much to Byrd's regret, he never managed to attend one of the senator's spring luncheons at Rosemont.[20]

Byrd's friendship with Lyndon Johnson also blossomed in these years. Having served as a legislative assistant and congressman before coming to the Senate in 1949, Johnson knew the mechanisms by which the upper house operated, easily balancing a regard for tradition and seniority with an insistence on getting legislation passed. A nonideological politician, the burly Texan was a virtuoso in practicing the art of compromise, trading votes, massaging egos, and dispensing favors and committee assignments to achieve his ends; it was called "the treatment." Ingratiating himself with southern colleagues by opposing civil-rights legislation while at the same time appeasing the New Deal liberals, Johnson garnered enough support, notably that of Richard Russell, to win election as Senate minority leader in 1953, a remarkable accomplishment for such a novice. His elevation to majority leader in 1955 was a mere formality.[21]

His first contact with Harry Byrd was not friendly. Serving with Johnson on a House-Senate Armed Services conference committee, Byrd criticized the position that Johnson was defending, causing the Texan to demand an apology. Flustered, Byrd conceded the request, but he did not allow the incident to precipitate a hostile relationship. Johnson knew of Byrd's prestige among his colleagues and cultivated his friendship in a series of small dinner parties for Senate leaders at his Northwest Washington apartment. In 1952 Johnson was one of a few senators who attended Westwood's funeral, a gesture that probably cemented their high regard for one another. At the end of one Senate session, Johnson thanked Byrd for his support, calling him "a gentleman, a statesman, and one of the best friends I have ever had." Byrd could be counted on to support Johnson on many occasions over the next decade.[22]

Despite the friendly relations between the major Washington players, the changing of the guard on Capitol Hill was not accomplished without partisan controversy, and several of Eisenhower's major initiatives in 1955 were sidetracked. One of these, which later proved to be a cardinal achievement of his administration, was the creation of an interstate highway network. Postwar economic growth and urban sprawl had created a chaotic transportation system in the country; road building, despite increased federal and state spending, had not kept pace with the explosion in the number of cars and the expansion of the cities into the suburbs. The result was more accidents, congestion, and higher business costs.

In August 1954, Eisenhower created an advisory committee on national highway development and appointed his wartime buddy General Lucius Clay to command it. The committee recommended a 40,000-mile network linking the country's major cities to be funded by a $25 billion bond issue that would be repaid with the federal gasoline tax; the government would pay 90 percent of the cost, and the entire operation would be controlled by a federal highway corporation. When the plan was released in early 1955, it generated considerable criticism. Farm groups disliked the attention given cities at the expense of rural roads; others complained about the means of payment, particularly the cost of interest on the bonds; and many opposed the creation of another federal agency. It was not surprising that the leading critic was Harry Byrd, the old farm-to-market road advocate, pay-as-you-go defender, and opponent of a larger federal bureaucracy.[23]

In a formal statement released in January, Byrd branded the road program "thoroughly unsound," arguing that it would cost taxpayers fifty-five cents on every borrowed dollar and destroy the budget and the debt limitation. Privately he told Herbert Hoover that it was "a disaster of the first magnitude." He foresaw additional proposals following this example that would finance other public services. Another objection was federal control. "Every Federal grant," he warned, "elevates the control of the Federal government and subordinates the authority of the States. Nothing is truer than the rule that power follows the purse. . . . Time and time again I have seen the iron hand of the Federal bureaucracy compel the States to do things that they did not desire to do, because of grants made by the Federal government." He recommended that the federal tax on gasoline be repealed so that the states might reimpose it as their own tax. The government would then continue its funding of roads through its traditional matching system, abetted by continuing the tax on lubricating oil and imposing a new half-cent gas tax. This, he believed, would get the highways built without breaking the budget.[24]

Although he was just one of many critics of the plan among conservatives and liberals alike, Byrd's reputation on fiscal matters and his chairmanship of the Finance Committee through which any tax proposals had to travel made him a key participant in the negotiations. As Pennsylvania's Senator Edward Martin said of the plan, "I think it will work. But when you get men the caliber of Harry Byrd objecting, it gives you pause." Appearing before the Senate public roads subcommittee—the first time he had gone before a committee to testify on legislation—Byrd condemned the administration's highway plan as "dictatorial" and funded by "financial legerdemain." One senator concluded that Byrd had "put the last nail in the coffin" of the proposal. Both the Clay bill based on bonds and a House bill that would have increased the federal gas tax to fund the roads were killed and the proposal rolled over to the next term, a victim of politics, competing interest groups, and Harry Byrd.[25]

Even as the dust settled on the road bill, however, Byrd was moving to a more conciliatory position. Acknowledging the need for highways, he indicated a willingness to support any pay-as-you-go plan, even if it included higher gas taxes. Early the next year Eisenhower capitulated and told aides that Byrd was "to be consulted as to the most desirable procedures for expediting the bill." A bill emerged from the House that more fairly distributed the road allocations, set national road standards, and funded the system through increased gas, tire, and truck user fees, which were to be collected in a highway trust fund. The Finance Committee approved the new taxes, and a Byrd amendment was tacked on prohibiting trust fund deficits in the early stages of the construction. The final bill passed in June 1956, with Byrd rightly sharing credit for its final form. Certainly the funding mechanism, as he said, was "right down my alley," but that approach had its limitations. Soaring gas tax collections, fueled by an expanding economy and an increasingly mobile population, ensured that the interstates would be built—and without interest costs—but parsimony and petty bickering delayed their beginning by a year and then slowed down construction. Senator Russell Long, who said he reluctantly "voted with Harry," estimated that pay-as-you-go delayed completion of the system by ten to fifteen years.[26]

Adhering to his traditional positions, Senator Byrd also opposed administration initiatives in foreign aid and federal aid to education in 1955, but he supported the president on several other issues, most notably helping to defeat a Democratic effort to legislate a $20 income tax cut for all Americans. Leading the effort against it in the Finance Committee, Byrd said it would cost the treasury $1.5 billion a year and increase the deficit. "We are enjoying the greatest prosperity in our history," he argued. "We are not engaged in war. If we cannot balance the budget now, I ask when can we balance it? Are we on a chronic deficit basis?" In March the Finance Committee voted against the tax cut, 9–6, with Byrd and Walter George joining seven Republicans in opposition, but a narrow victory in the House forced the issue onto the Senate floor where the old budget balancer led the debate against it. He suggested that the tax cut amounted to only thirty-eight cents a week for each taypayer, a paltry and senseless sum for which the debt would be increased $1.5 billion. In the final debate Byrd called the legislation "a Coca-Cola proposition [that] would give a taxpayer about six cents relief a day—about the price of a soft drink." Majority leader Johnson, a leading sponsor of the bill, responded, "Not until now did I realize that some persons begrudged the needy even one little Coca-Cola." Five southern Democrats, including senators Byrd and Robertson, joined with the Republicans to defeat the proposal, 50–44.[27]

The senator also affirmed his friendship with the administration through his support of a new trade bill that extended reciprocal trade agreements and obliged the United States to join international organizations pursuing more open trade arrangements. Byrd favored free trade, but he objected to the association with international groups that might commit the country to undesirable policies. Protectionist senators were using this latter argument in an attempt to defeat the entire bill. To obtain passage of the trade provisions, Byrd separated the two issues, whereupon the Finance Committee approved the Reciprocal Trade Agreement Act for three years, giving the president authority to reduce tariffs up to 15 percent and curb imports in the interest of national security. His efforts in rewriting the legislation silenced its opponents and produced an overwhelming victory in the Senate. Representative J. Vaughan Gary of Virginia's Third District credited Byrd with a "magnificent job in steering the measure through his committee and through the Senate."[28]

Apart from his interest in foreign trade and his contempt for foreign aid, Byrd had given little attention to global concerns over the years. Now with a former military hero in the White House, he deferred even more to executive authority. He approved of Eisenhower's defense cutbacks, voted for the controversial Charles Bohlen as ambassador to Russia, and backed the Southeast Asia Treaty Organization (SEATO) that was created to contain communism in Vietnam. The major foreign crisis of 1955 was the Chinese Communists' attempt to seize the offshore islands of Quemoy and Matsu then held by Chiang Kai-shek and his nationalist forces on Formosa (Taiwan) one hundred miles away. The islands were of negligible military value, but they became symbols of America's willingness to defend its allies and thus were deemed critical to the containment policy. Pressed by Chiang and the China Lobby for a show of support, Eisenhower asked Congress to approve the president's use of military force in the defense of Formosa and "such related positions and territories of that area now in friendly hands." Harry Byrd was among those who doubted the wisdom of such an open-ended grant of power to the chief executive. Calling the resolution "a pre-dated declaration of war on the part of Congress," he feared the prospect of war over bits of territory of questionable worth. Having little affinity for Chiang's corrupt regime, Byrd preferred language that would have placed the islands near the China coast outside the defense perimeter of the United States, and he backed the defeated Lehman amendment to that effect.[29] In the final analysis, however, he supported the Formosa Resolution because he had "great confidence in President Eisenhower. I respect his military decisions. He is the outstanding military man of his age. I am firmly convinced that he sincerely wants to keep us out of war." Fortunately, the Chinese made the resolution a dead issue by ending their aggressive behavior in the area for the moment.[30]

The 1955 congressional session was a difficult one for Byrd. Chairmanship of the Finance Committee imposed new time-consuming duties on him. The committee had many bills before it, and colleagues George and Millikin were not in good health, leaving the chairman to assume much work. His attendance on roll-call votes was his highest in seven years: 88 percent. In addition to tending to tax and trade legislation, the senator continued to head the Joint Committee on Reduction of Non-essential Federal Expenditures. Since no senator was supposed to chair two committees at once, he had offered to step down, but his colleagues rejected his resignation. Although he still proudly pointed to the billions the committee was saving the country, it was doing little more than publishing statistics on government spending, unexpended balances, and federal employment. With relief, he left for Winchester and the apple harvest at session's end.[31]

For Byrd, 1956 was the same old story: an uphill struggle against tax cuts and social programs. Even when Eisenhower presented a balanced budget, Byrd called it "alarming," seeing the $400 million surplus as too "fragile" in light of increased spending. He claimed the administration was overestimating revenues and counting on a continuation of the current economic boom. In fact, in a letter addressed to Virginia's senior senator in the year 2056—to be placed in a time capsule in Bristol, Virginia—Byrd wrote clairvoyantly, "I have prophesied that this colossal debt, and the interest therein, will plague generations to come and will be the greatest domestic problem with which future Americans will be confronted." Byrd did have the satisfaction of seeing the temporary debt ceiling lowered to $278 billion later in the year, and he won the thanks of President Eisenhower and Treasury Secretary Humphrey for his "skillful handling" of the tax bill which avoided major revenue losses.[32]

Voting more like a Republican than ever before, Byrd, in the face of opposition from some farm organizations, rejected the fixed high price supports in the Democratic farm bill that the president vetoed and supported the administration's bill that included a soil bank and more flexible price supports. He helped Republicans kill the proposed Hells Canyon Dam on the Snake River, lost the fight to limit funding for the air force, and carried the case in committee against expanded social security provisions for the disabled. But on the latter bill he could not stem the election-year tide. The Democratic leadership sought reduction of the retirement age for women from sixty-five to sixty-two and disability benefits starting at age fifty instead of sixty-five. Byrd thought the latter provision a budget buster, "an entering wedge for a greatly expanded system at tremendous costs and onerous taxes." In his gentlemanly way he did not smother these provisions in committee, but when the bill emerged, it was without these two features, as the administration wished. However, a vigorous lobbying effort by majority leader Johnson, backed by renegade committee members Long, Kerr, and George, restored both items, the disability provision by the narrow margin of 47–45. In spite of a final Senate vote of 90–0 in favor of the legislation, Harry Byrd labeled it "a sloppy pension bill." A week later Congress adjourned in favor of the upcoming presidential race.[33]

Although Byrd was preoccupied with Finance Committee business as well as the fight against integration in Virginia, he could not afford to neglect the election, if only to keep the opposition at home in check and to dramatize the South's beleaguered racial situation.[34] His preference for the Democratic nomination was Lyndon Johnson, whose major appeal in this year of massive resistance was his supposed opposition to integration; he was the only candidate in Byrd's view with such credentials. To avoid a potential division in Organization ranks among followers of Johnson and Adlai Stevenson, Byrd arranged for an uninstructed Virginia delegation to the national convention. With the delegation bound by the unit rule, he hoped to win a majority for Johnson in Chicago and commit Virginia's entire vote to the majority leader.[35]

Unfortunately for his plans, Sittie suffered another heart attack that left her partially paralyzed and forced him to postpone his vacation and give up the Chicago convention. He instructed his son to stick with Johnson to the end, but without the senator's influential presence, the Virginia delegation could not resolve its differences and so cast the state's ballots for former governor John Battle. Stevenson won a surprisingly easy first-round victory, but when he threw open the vice-presidential nomination to the convention, a heated contest ensued between Estes Kefauver and John Kennedy, the young senator from Massachusetts. Animosity toward the liberal Tennessean caused many southern delegates to vote for Kennedy, but he lost on the third ballot, much to the chagrin of Harry Byrd, who was much impressed with the future president. Kennedy had a more moderate Senate record than his later image suggested, and he had ingratiated himself with Byrd, who had twice read his book, *Profiles in Courage*, and had loaned him the use of his personal hideaway off the Senate floor when Kennedy was recovering from back surgery.[36]

Byrd was totally disappointed by the results of the Chicago convention. Not only were Johnson and Kennedy rejected, but the civil rights plank pledged the Democrats to fight discrimination and oppose attempts to interfere with the courts, exactly the opposite of what Byrd and the General Assembly would be doing in a matter of days. Even though Stevenson's personal position was more moderate, he committed himself to the platform, which likely cost him

Virginia's vote at the convention. More importantly, he lost Harry Byrd's endorsement for the election.[37]

The special assembly session that was working on Virginia's school-closing laws delayed the presidential campaign in Virginia until October, but its tone had been set weeks earlier at Harry Byrd's annual picnic just after the Chicago meeting. These picnics, begun as gatherings for apple growers, had become political happenings. Spread over the grounds of the Berryville cabin, seated on old apple crates, eating fried chicken and Byrd applesauce, thousands of Organization friends listened to the senator, who, decked out in his finest white linen suit, presented his "Byrd's-eye" view of the world. Speaking from a flat-bed truck, he defended his votes and berated his enemies, often with a twinkle in his eye and a humorous jab at his foes.

The big news of the 1956 picnic was Byrd's refusal to commit to a candidate. Using language that marked his position in all subsequent presidential elections, he explained that sometimes the best advice is "silence is golden."[38] The Democratic platform was anathema to him, and the Republicans offered little better. Although he undoubtedly preferred that Virginia cast its vote for Eisenhower in this year of massive resistance, he did not want to reward the president's missteps on civil rights with an outright endorsement. Byrd blamed Eisenhower for the appointment of Earl Warren to the Supreme Court and for the Justice Department's activism in prosecuting civil rights cases, something he had asked Ike not to pursue. Nor would he consider defecting to the Republicans, fearing the impact such a shock would have on the Organization in this already traumatic year. Although the Washington *Post* reported that Byrd would support Eisenhower, he was truly going to sit this one out.[39]

These "golden silences" reflected the dilemma that southern Democrats faced as their party became more liberal, especially on the question of racial discrimination. The old order that had permitted one-party rule was crumbling. In reacting to these events, Byrd—unlike other southern politicians who were not so encumbered—had to consider the consequences of his behavior on the survival of his political machine. He chose to walk a tightrope between preserving the hegemony of the Democratic Organization in the state—always his highest priority—and advancing his conservative principles through the election of Republicans at the national level. It was an extension of the decision he had made in 1948 to separate the state party from the national party. He believed endorsement of either party's presidential candidate would undermine the machine. Lining up behind liberal Democrats—an objectionable act in itself—would encourage defections among his conservative allies to the state Republicans; supporting the GOP would drive many Democrats into the ranks of the "antis" or Young Turks. However, by not endorsing the Democratic candidate, he implicitly indicated a preference for the more conservative Republi-

Sphinx Under The Apple Tree

IKE ADLAI

ANDREWS

SENATOR
HARRY F. BYRD

WINCHESTER
VIRGINIA

10-18-56   To Senator Harry F. Byrd
with my best wishes
Fred O. Seibel

FRED O. SEIBEL

can nominee. For him, silence seemed the best policy for maintaining the political status quo in Virginia. But silence had its liabilities as well, alienating loyal Democrats and frustrating those who looked to Byrd for leadership, thereby weakening the bonds of loyalty to party and machine. His strategy appeared to work throughout the fifties because Virginia Republicans remained impotent and the fears generated by massive resistance sustained traditional party fealty. But with the termination of massive resistance and the establishment of a viable Republican alternative, "golden silences" contributed to further division within the machine and its eventual death in the sixties. As Robert Whitehead commented to Watt Abbitt, "Telling Democrats it's all right to vote Republican in national elections will backfire; soon they will ask why they can't do that in state elections."[40]

Indeed, Byrd's stand in 1956 generated considerable consternation among Virginia Democrats. Fearful that continued erosion to the Republicans would mean, in Howard Smith's words, "the end of the Virginia Democratic Organization as we have known it," many leaders rallied behind Stevenson and gingerly encouraged Byrd to endorse the party. But their arguments about the potential threat to the Organization and its chances in next year's governor's race did not dissuade him. He apologized for any embarrassment he might be causing them, contributed to their campaigns, and publicly endorsed their reelections; but, citing the liberalism of the party and its nominee, he remained silent. As he told Smith, he found Stevenson's remarks about social security extensions, federal aid to education, and repeal of the Taft-Hartley Act "repulsive." Byrd's close friends knew of his difficult position and did not press the issue, but other party members were less sympathetic, concerned that his silence was giving strength to the "antis" as well as the Republicans, who were benefiting from the reemergence of "Virginia Democrats for Eisenhower."[41]

The results of the 1956 election confirmed the political wisdom of Byrd's actions. Eisenhower steamrollered Stevenson once again in both state and nation; but all the Virginia Democratic congressmen were returned to office, and Congress remained in the hands of the Democrats, though by a very narrow margin in the Senate. Byrd even won a handful of votes for the presidency himself. Without his authorization he had been placed on the ballot in South Carolina, Kentucky, and Mississippi as a States Rights candidate. He received over 80,000 votes in South Carolina, 29.4 percent of the vote, placing him ahead of Eisenhower in the state, and 43,000 votes in Mississippi, 17.3 percent of the vote. Secure in the preservation of his power base and enjoying the accolades of southern conservatives, Byrd looked forward to more budget fights and the crucial gubernatorial election that he hoped would confirm his school policies.[42]

Eisenhower's reelection forecast a continuation of "Modern Republicanism"—a modicum of social progress and vigorous anticommunism at acceptable cost—but faced with Democratic control of Congress, the aging president pursued few new domestic initiatives and focused instead on balancing budgets to avoid inflation. The result was a second term noted for its drift, a re-hashing of many of the same issues of the first four years without clear direction. Meanwhile, events abroad consumed much of his time.[43]

The 1956 election had been disrupted at its close by two significant international crises: the revolution in Hungary and the war over the Suez Canal. Senator Byrd had no comment on these events, likely agreeing with his president that neither one justified American participation, costly as that would have been. However, to fill the vacuum created by the Suez affair and to thwart further Soviet penetration in the Middle East, the administration sought congressional approval of another "area" resolution. Dubbed the "Eisenhower Doctrine," it authorized the president not only to use force in the region but also to send military and economic aid to Arab states that were threatened by communism. Briefed by the president and Secretary of State John Foster Dulles on the situation, Byrd feared that intervention might escalate into war; he also had serious reservations about the $400 million two-year aid package. The president's program, he said, "remains cloudy and confused. We have never been able to get any clear explanation of how or where they expect to spend the assistance funds. . . . I am going to fight to separate the military and economic aspects and I think there is strong support for this move within the committees." In final action the joint Foreign Relations and Armed Services committees defeated Byrd's proposal to divide the resolution, 17–11. His amendment to strip the economic aid from the resolution was likewise killed, 58–28, and the Mideast Resolution passed, 72–19, with Byrd in the minority on both votes. The Eisenhower Doctrine proved of questionable value. The president used it to justify a military action in Lebanon the following year with inconsequential results except for an increase of anti-Americanism in the region. Perhaps Byrd had been right, if for the wrong reasons.[44]

As the Eighty-fifth Congress got under way, Byrd continued his squabbles with Eisenhower over the budget. A well-publicized photograph showed Byrd reacting to the $72 billion document, his eyes popping out of his head. The senator claimed this "largest peacetime budget in our history" could only be balanced with "increased inflation." He was particularly critical of proposals to support school construction and health insurance programs that "will open up a pandora's box of federal spending. . . . They start as a mouse and quickly grow into the size of an elephant."[45]

Using his traditional forums of speeches to national business groups and articles in news magazines, Byrd took his economy message to the nation, attempting to orchestrate a public response. In a speech to a conference on government reorganization, Byrd questioned: "How long can we continue to tax and tax and spend and spend—and at the same time continue our progress and preserve our solvency? . . . I am convinced that the time is ever close for substantial tax reduction. But I could not support any tax reduction unless the expenses of government are reduced to a level which would make a tax reduction possible on a sound basis. I know of no more certain road to financial suicide than to reduce taxes and thereby create deficits and debts." Calling for deep budget cuts, he found useful allies among congressional Republicans and Treasury Secretary Humphrey, who warned of "a depression that will curl your hair" if spending levels kept rising.[46]

Flush with unexpected political and public support for his efforts, Byrd grabbed for the brass ring and offered his "Byrd Budget" totaling $6.5 billion

Sharpening His Axe Again

in cuts: $1.5 billion in nuclear programs, $2 billion in foreign aid, and $3 billion in domestic programs, reductions that were far too deep for Eisenhower.[47] Reflecting the changed climate, the *Times-Dispatch* editorialized: "Judging from the current Congressional race for budget cutting honors, Mr. Byrd's perennial efforts have not been in vain. His position as chairman of the Senate Finance Committee, and his bipartisan reputation for integrity give direction and momentum to the sudden 'economy drive.'" Other editorials across the country hailed the senator for his efforts. Said the Pontiac, Michigan, *Press:* "Senator Harry Byrd has been one of the most forthright men in government over an extended period of years. If any Congressman in Washington has endeavored to serve the United States of America first and his party and himself second, that man is Sen. Byrd. . . . one of the greatest friends the common man has in Washington, or anywhere else." The Tax Foundation, a national clearinghouse for state and local taxpayer organizations, lauded Byrd's "wonderful leadership in fiscal affairs." He emerged as that selfless public servant beholden to no one, who, wrote columnist Ray Tucker, "shows utter disregard to politics or personal friendships," including those of the president and his treasury secretary.[48]

Without question, Harry Byrd was one of the most honest politicians Washington has ever seen. He treated taxpayers' money with the same parsimonious care he gave his own. If he said no spending, that meant on himself and Virginia, too. He took no junkets abroad; he was no pork-barreler; he accepted no federal subsidies for his apple business. While others looked after their states, Byrd was content to let the Old Dominion's location speak for itself. This consistency between preachment and practice is what won Byrd the respect of his colleagues and constituents. In fact, one woman had so much "confidence in his patriotic wisdom" that she left him $110,000 in AT&T stock to do with it what he thought would be best for the country.[49]

At no other time in his long Senate career had Byrd received the applause tendered him during the budget fight of 1957, and it pushed him to rhetorical excess in making greater demands for economy. He accused the administration of "spending sprees" and "luxury budgets," of switching from "frugality in government to big government," of submitting "the most irresponsible budget . . . in my day," and of making unsound estimates of revenues; he called Eisenhower's proposed budget cuts of $1.8 billion "totally inadequate" and asked for still deeper cuts of $8 to $9 billion; and he won Finance Committee approval of a full investigation into the nation's financial condition. When the president appealed to the country for support of his budget, Byrd challenged his right to do so. When Eisenhower disputed Byrd's contention that nondefense spending could be cut by $5 billion, Byrd retorted: "I'm not worrying. I am sticking to my guns. We've got a prairie fire started among the people in favor of cutting the budget." Week by week Congress reduced the amounts requested in most appropriations bills; money for school construction was lost, and a big chunk was taken out of foreign aid. Eventually $4 billion was excised: a personal defeat for the president and a day of jubilee for Senator Byrd. How was it possible?[50]

Byrd rode the crest of a popular wave demanding less federal spending during a period of booming prosperity. Tired of the sacrifices demanded by depression and war, Americans now were content with the status quo as long as their bank accounts kept growing. There was no need for an expansion of federal social programs in this "affluent society." Anger in the South at the Supreme Court's desegregation decision intensified opposition toward additional federal intervention. Southern Democrats and Old Guard Republicans, apprehensive over Eisenhower's seeming endorsement of New Deal programs, united in one last attempt to turn back the clock. For Byrd, it was, in William S. White's words, "the last opportunity for the vindication of the philosophy of conservatism in government." The president, of course, had not embraced the New Deal, but neither was he willing to ignore the problems generated by modern society. "I believe," he said, "that unless a modern political group does look these problems in the face and finds some reasonable solution, . . . then in the long run we are sunk." For the moment, few were willing to listen, but this would be the last victory for fiscal conservatives for years to come.[51]

The long-awaited probe into the nation's financial health got under way in late June with George Humphrey, just retired as treasury secretary, as the featured witness. Byrd claimed that it would be the most comprehensive review since the Aldrich investigation of 1908, which ran for four years and proposed far-reaching changes in the nation's economy; but it achieved no such eminence, proving to be little more than another platform for Byrd's doomsday prophecies about the nation's fiscal future and his usual flood of figures about debt and taxes. Although accused by administration spokesmen of conducting a partisan inquiry, the senator played no political favorites. His target was inflation and the government spending that contributed to it, regardless of which party or president was responsible, and he sparred good-naturedly with Humphrey on the Eisenhower administration's contribution. After fourteen days of tough questioning, the secretary stepped down, grateful that he was leaving Washington. As the hearings recessed, falling far short of the chairman's estimate of their importance, Byrd claimed credit for the administration's shift toward spending cuts, all the while demanding even greater reductions.[52]

The Finance Committee investigation, however, faded to the back pages of the newspapers in the face of the bitter debate over the civil rights bill. Next to the budget fight, it consumed the most time and rhetoric of any legislation in 1957. Over the last three years, Supreme Court decisions, bus boycotts, southern obstructionism and acts of violence, and increased black political participation in the North had generated support for legislation that would advance the rights of black citizens. The bill presented by the administration would create a civil rights commission and expand federal involvement in cases of civil rights violations, particularly in the field of voting. Labeling this "a punitive measure aimed to humiliate and destroy the South" for the "ignoble purpose of collecting Negro votes," Byrd specifically challenged the "tyrannical procedure" that would allow federal judges rather than juries to decide criminal contempt cases in suits involving civil rights violations. (This feature was deemed necessary to combat all-white juries that refused to convict those who interfered with the rights of blacks.) Claiming that this infringed on a basic American freedom, he and senators Eastland and Thurmond proposed an amendment to ensure jury trials in such proceedings.[53]

Southern legislators also protested that the broad powers granted the attorney general to bring suit in civil rights cases involved more than voting rights; they charged that this would permit introduction of federal troops in school desegregation cases. Byrd made this point in another address in July. Virginia, he said, wanted no part of the "heavy heel of federal dictatorship on our throat" that it had once experienced. Referring to President Eisenhower's disingenuous statement that he did not know what was in the section of the bill that authorized the use of troops (section 3), the senator, his rhetoric rising to a fever pitch, claimed that no one else knew except "the modern Thaddeus Stevens, now cloaked in the robes of the Chief Justice of the United States Supreme Court, . . . the NAACP, one of the principal beneficiaries of his official acts, . . . the ADA [Americans for Democratic Action], the NAACP's gold dust twin, . . . [and] the Attorney General—of whom this bill would make a 20th Century American Caesar." Surprised by the fury of his oratory, several of his colleagues rose to challenge his condemnation of Chief Justice Warren, while the Dixie legislators applauded his efforts.[54]

Although Byrd's speech had some shock value, it was Senator Russell's address on this issue two weeks earlier that created considerable publicity and caused the president to withdraw his support from section 3, which was eliminated by the Senate on July 24. However, Eisenhower remained adamant in his opposition to Byrd's jury trial amendment, and when the Senate approved this provision, 51–42, it appeared that the entire bill might be lost, much to the glee of the southerners. But majority leader Johnson, with presidential ambitions in mind, engineered a compromise that permitted a federal judge to deny a jury trial in voting rights cases by reducing the penalties applied. The House, which had earlier passed the entire package, approved the modifications, as did the Senate on August 29, after a record-breaking filibuster by Senator Thurmond. Although on the losing end of the 60–15 vote, southern senators felt a sense of relief. They had done their best to dilute the bill to the point that it created little more than a Civil Rights Commission with limited authority. And one of their own, John Battle, would soon be appointed to the commission, an appointment that "delighted" Byrd and assured him that there would be no radical action by the new agency. At his apple picnic two days later, Byrd claimed the civil rights bill was "a tremendous victory for the South." It was not quite that. Although greatly weakened and lacking enforcement power, the 1957 Civil Rights Act, the first since Reconstruction, symbolized the dawning of a new era in the government's effort to end racial discrimination. The Little Rock incident within the month was proof of that.[55]

During the 1958 session Byrd was preoccupied with his announced retirement, quick change of heart, and reelection, and so gave less attention to his senatorial duties. The congressional elections that year indicated a forthcoming change in the mood of the nation. Influenced by a recession and the launching of "Sputnik," Americans registered their dissatisfaction with the Eisenhower administration by returning large Democratic majorities to both houses of Congress. The Republican Old Guard—the ultraconservative class of '46—was decimated by retirements and electoral defeats. Liberals such as Edmund Muskie, Eugene McCarthy, Phil Hart, and Gale McGee entered the Senate ready to contest the leadership for a greater say in legislative proceedings. The tilt toward liberalism promised a more contentious political field over the next two years as the parties and potential candidates jockeyed for advantage in the 1960 presidential election.[56]

The changed political climate was demonstrated in the struggle to confirm the nomination of Admiral Lewis Strauss as secretary of commerce. The longtime chairman of the Atomic Energy Commission, Strauss had declined reappointment because of a simmering feud with Senator Clinton Anderson, who had been the chairman of the Congressional Joint Committee on Atomic Energy and who was to assume that position again. In spite of this, Eisenhower recognized Strauss's ability and service by awarding him a recess appointment as commerce secretary in October 1958. A native Richmonder and resident of Virginia, the admiral, although a Republican, had the total endorsement of his longtime friend Harry Byrd.

When the long-delayed hearings began, it was clear that Strauss was in trouble. Senator Anderson was particularly vehement in denouncing him for his lack of cooperation with the joint committee and for withholding information from Congress. Combative in his defense, Strauss alienated many Democratic senators, who were under increasing political pressure to vote against him. Byrd, who was encouraging his newspaper friends to write favorably about Strauss's nomination, told James J. Kilpatrick that "a contemptuous and malicious campaign" was being waged against the nominee. On June 18, as the final debate on confirmation droned into the evening, Byrd and Anderson discussed their prospects, Anderson claiming victory by three or four votes and Byrd arguing that he would lose by that margin. The senator from New Mexico concluded, "Harry, you really know how to grow good apples, but you sure don't know how to count votes." Shortly after midnight the Senate rejected Strauss, 49–46, the first defeat of a cabinet nominee since 1925. Eisenhower was livid, recalling it as "one of the most depressing official disappointments" of his presidency, a partisan vote for which there was no justification. Byrd echoed those same thoughts in consoling Strauss.[57]

The growing liberalism of the Democratic party forced Byrd back toward his alliance with the administration in 1959, and he voted with a grateful president to maintain a budget surplus by opposing Democratic initiatives in housing, area redevelopment, water pollution control, airport construction, and youth employment. The recession had produced the largest peacetime deficit in American history—$12 billion—encouraging Ike to pursue budget balancing with a vengeance. Unfortunately for the Republicans, his spending cuts curtailed the recovery and led to another recession just as the election occurred in 1960. In return for southern support on budget issues, Eisenhower did not push for additional civil rights legislation, except to extend the Civil Rights Commission.[58]

Senator Byrd continued to enjoy the adulation of the conservative community as he moved into the twilight of his career. The United States Chamber of Commerce selected him for its "greatest living Americans" award. The citation recognized his "constant and courageous efforts in the Senate to close the floodgates of profligate spending, his fidelity to public duty, and his wise and patient statesmanship." The American Farm Bureau Federation also gave him its distinguished service award. Both on the occasion of his seventy-second birthday and on the day he set a record for Senate service for a Virginian, he was extolled by his colleagues for his exceptional service and integrity.[59]

With the presidential election on the horizon, Democrats and Republicans alike supported new social programs in 1960 that they hoped would translate into victory in the fall—aid to education, medical care for the aged, a higher minimum wage, and a tougher civil rights bill—but differences in content and conservative opposition thwarted passage of much of this legislation. Distracted by deteriorating relations with the Soviets brought on by the U-2 incident, in which an American spy plane was shot down over Russia, Eisenhower offered little leadership in the domestic field.

The administration's civil rights bill, taken over by the Democratic leadership, provided for federal referees to investigate discrimination in voting, stronger powers for the Civil Rights Commission, and tougher penalties for rights violations. There were several counties in the Deep South where thousands of blacks resided but not one was registered to vote. Majority leader Johnson and House Speaker Rayburn, working with Republican minority leader Everett Dirksen, cagily crafted procedural changes that would prevent the legislation from being tied up in committee, but Johnson could not avert the expected filibuster in the Senate. Along with his southern brethren, Byrd promised to fight "to the last ditch the iniquitous civil rights proposals which in my judgment are unconstitutional and would result, if adopted, in the destruction of the rights of states."[60]

As the southerners organized their forces, Johnson promised to keep the Senate in session around the clock in order to break the filibuster, but his tactic backfired. Relying on frequent quorum calls that required a majority of senators to appear on the floor to avoid adjournment, the southerners outlasted their tired colleagues, who were sleeping on office cots to meet the late-night quorum calls. Starting on February 29, the filibusterers, led by Senator Russell, spoke for ten days; the seventy-two-year old Byrd shared the burden, speaking up to four or five hours at a time against the Warren Court, the NAACP, and a new fair employment commission. Failing on a vote for cloture, Johnson called off the continuous sessions, and the filibuster ended as both sides sought a compromise position. The result was another watered-down civil rights bill that retained the provision for voting referees but little else. Sections dealing with employment, school integration, and public accommodations were deleted. Byrd was again elated, claiming a victory for "courageous massive resistance." "With our backs to the wall," he proudly declared, "the Southerners withstood the power of the federal government, the political pressure of those states appealing to the Negro vote, and the propaganda of the facilities available to the NAACP. The more vicious proposals and the worst features of the administration bill were eliminated." He was particularly pleased that they had removed the statement proclaiming the Supreme Court's decision against school segregation to be the law of the land. Coincidentally, lending an air of urgency to the debates in Washington, the first sit-ins aimed at desegregating public facilities took place in Greensboro, North Carolina. Spreading like wildfire across the South, they inaugurated a new era of activism in the civil rights movement that culminated in more far-reaching legislation four years later.[61]

The Democrats were no more successful in pushing through a broad-based health care program. Since 1945, when President Truman had first asked for medical insurance for the aged, there had been no progress in this field, but the rising medical costs of the elderly demanded attention. Liberals favored a compulsory health insurance plan financed through social security (the Forand bill); labeling this "socialized medicine," conservatives, including President Eisenhower, preferred a smaller federal role that would provide voluntary coverage through insurance with private companies. The president had offered such a modest program in 1954, but it had been overwhelmingly defeated. The two competing approaches were debated in the 1958 and 1959 sessions without resolution, but in this politically charged election year a compromise was arranged: the Kerr-Mills bill, which combined features of both plans. Following the lead of Harry Byrd, who was hostile to any tampering with the social security payroll system, Senator Kerr advocated matching federal and state grants to pay the medical costs of poor people over sixty-five who could pass a means test— a public welfare approach to the problem. When Senate liberals fought to expand the concept to include all elderly over sixty-eight, the Finance Committee, by a vote of 12–5, rejected tying health care to social security and approved the compromise bill. Chairman Byrd declared: "I'm against the Forand Bill and you can quote me on that. It is socialized medicine." Byrd thought the compromise "a realistic and workable plan to help millions of aged persons who are unable to pay their medical bills when illness occurs or continues." A further attempt to amend the bill on the Senate floor was defeated, and the Kerr-Mills proposal became law, a modest beginning for national health care.[62]

For Harry Byrd the election of 1960 bore interesting similarities to the three previous presidential elections: support for a southern candidate, defeat at the national convention, and a "golden silence" during the campaign. Once again he endorsed his fellow southerner, Lyndon Johnson, in spite of the majority leader's support of the civil rights bill. As he wrote Walter Sillers of Mississippi,

> I do not agree with all of his votes, but I can say this for him that he is a man of great ability, and you can rely absolutely upon his word. In the Civil Rights legislation recently before the Senate he made a very bad error in attempting to attach the Civil Rights to a minor bill. . . . yet, in the final analysis, it was the influence of Lyndon Johnson that defeated the most iniquitous parts of the proposed bill. The other two Senatorial candidates for the Presidency [John Kennedy and Stuart Symington] signed the cloture petition, voted for cloture, and, on the same day, voted to take away the right of trial by jury in Civil Rights cases."[63]

Byrd had a soft spot for Jack Kennedy, the youthful and wealthy senator from Massachusetts, but his pro-labor positions, especially on right-to-work laws, were unacceptable to conservative Virginians.

Governor Almond's position complicated Byrd's planning. Having broken with the Organization leadership over school closings, Almond was embittered by the defeat of his legislative program and sales tax proposal in the 1960 General Assembly at the hands of those same leaders. Although Almond had indicated that Johnson was his choice, Byrd was suspicious of the intentions of the governor, who by tradition headed the delegation to the national convention; therefore, the senator insisted that the state convention instruct the Virginia delegation to vote for Johnson rather than risk letting the governor lead a bandwagon for Kennedy. The convention also authorized its own recall by the state Democratic Committee if the situation warranted it. Byrd was delighted with the result, but the level of dissent against an instructed delegation revealed a growing independence among Democrats that portended a weakening of Organization control.[64]

Certain that the results of the Democratic convention in Los Angeles would be unsatisfactory to him, Byrd and Blackie Moore went off to Switzerland in July for a three-week vacation. While the convention was in session, Peachy Menefee reported to Byrd almost daily on its proceedings. Confirming his worst fears, the platform included the strongest civil rights plank in the party's history; it called for an end to segregation in schools, housing, jobs, and public facilities, full compliance with the *Brown* decision, and creation of a fair employment practices commission. It also demanded repeal of the right-to-work provisions of the Taft-Hartley Act. Over the objections of the Virginians, Kennedy, who had dominated the primary campaign, was nominated on the first ballot and pledged his support for the platform. His selection of Lyndon Johnson as his running mate was small consolation to Harry Byrd, who upon his return to Washington issued a "no comment" when asked about the nominees.[65]

Six weeks later at his apple picnic, Byrd announced that he would once again follow a "silence is golden policy" in the forthcoming contest between Kennedy and Vice-President Nixon, who, with the lukewarm blessing of President Eisenhower, had won the Republican nomination. The senator was lobbied hard by Kennedy and Johnson, who realized that his support was crucial to winning the Old Dominion in what promised to be a very close race; but having been told by Dick Russell that Kennedy would go beyond the platform on civil rights legislation, Byrd could not go along.[66] The key consideration behind Byrd's decision not to endorse any candidate was, as always, the impact of the election on the Organization. A victory for Kennedy would enhance the position of Governor Almond, who had enthusiastically endorsed the ticket, and lead to a major struggle for the governorship in next year's primary. But fence-sitting had its liabilities as well, further dividing a party already fractured by years of massive resistance. As Albertis Harrison, a potential candidate for governor, said, "Frankly, Senator, we are in a mess."[67]

Other Democrats proved more loyal to the party. In addition to Governor Almond, Senator Robertson, former governor Battle, Representative Abbitt, and a majority of Democrats in the General Assembly came out for Kennedy, whose campaign in the state was led by Battle's son, William, a Charlottesville attorney who had skippered PT boats with Jack Kennedy in the South Pacific during World War II. Attempts were made, with little success, to coordinate efforts with the remnants of the "antis," who remained suspicious of the Kennedy camp's ties with members of the Byrd machine. For some members of the Organization, choosing between loyalty to Byrd and their political futures was difficult. Attorney General Harrison reluctantly told Byrd that he would have to support the Democratic nominees in order to maintain party unity in Virginia, even if it did antagonize their conservative friends.[68]

As the campaign progressed, Byrd indicated a preference for a Republican victory, particularly as Kennedy surged in the Old Dominion after his televised debates with Nixon and his skillful neutralization of the religious issue. Byrd's continued criticism of the platform's labor plank, copies of which he was distributing around the state, was clearly directed at Kennedy's labor record. The senator also orchestrated a visit by President Eisenhower to the Woodrow Wilson Birthplace in Staunton where he praised the chief executive's eight-year record in office. Calling the two friends "ideological soul-mates," the *Times-Dispatch* concluded, "If there was ever any doubt that Senator Harry F. Byrd is opposed to the presidential candidacy of Senator John F. Kennedy . . . events of this week have removed it."

Byrd's final effort on behalf of the Republicans was his use of the race issue to counter Kennedy's surge and to rebut remarks made by Nixon's running mate, Henry Cabot Lodge, that Nixon, if elected, would appoint a black to his cabinet. On the eve of the election, Blackie Moore wrote Bill Battle about the possibility of Kennedy appointing blacks to federal court vacancies in the South, which, he believed, would produce "chaos" in the region. The letter was released to the press and then circulated across Southside Virginia. It is inconceivable that Moore would have done this without checking with Byrd; indeed, Byrd may have helped draft the letter, for he had asked Jimmy Byrnes to send him material about Kennedy's earlier statement on federal judges. Elated, Byrd wrote to Eisenhower's aide General Wilton Persons, "This has gone all through the South and I think is enormously effective." But he instructed Persons: "It is imperative that neither of your candidates make any statements in favor of Negro Federal Judges. . . . I hope you will contact the proper persons to avoid such statements."[69]

Although both sides utilized the race issue for the remainder of the campaign, the Moore letter undoubtedly slowed the momentum for Kennedy that had been building in the state. He lost Virginia to Nixon by 42,000 votes, but squeaked into the White House by the narrow margin of just over 100,000 votes nationwide. His electoral victory was more substantial, 303 to 219. Harry Byrd received the remaining 15 electoral votes: 8 from Mississippi, 6 from Alabama, and 1 from Oklahoma. The election was so close that Byrd's influence with these disaffected electors at one point was considered crucial in determining the victor. The day after the election, with Kennedy's victory still in doubt, the White House called Byrd to request that Mississippi's electors remain uncommitted until the final results were in. Although Howard Smith got assurances from Representative William Colmer that Mississippi would make no commitments until the outcome was decided, Kennedy's razor-thin majorities in Illinois and Texas obviated the need for Byrd's votes.[70] The Democratic defeat in the Old Dominion was attributable to Harry Byrd's public "silence" and his behind-the-scenes maneuverings against Kennedy, but this was hardly grounds for joy within the Organization. There was growing dissatisfaction among many Democrats that their leader's continued apostasy was harming the party and no longer could be tolerated.[71]

The changing of the guard in Washington terminated Harry Byrd's brief fling with influence in the halls of power. Although never an insider and frequently in opposition to the Eisenhower administration, he had enjoyed an association with the chief executive that he had not experienced before and would not thereafter. In their commitment to balanced budgets and reduced spending, Ike and Harry were, indeed, "ideological soulmates." As Congress became more liberal, Harry could count on Ike to veto undesirable legislation and Ike could depend on Harry to help sustain his vetoes. With Eisenhower there was always hope that Byrd's world might be reincarnated. With Kennedy, and then Johnson, his was a forlorn cause.[72]

❧ 19 ☙

"He Gives Us Fits"

AMERICA IN THE 1960s was in the grip of social revolution. The election of more liberal presidents, who pushed for comprehensive social welfare legislation, the new activism of the civil rights movement, which in turn inspired women and other minority groups, and a youthful cultural rebellion spurred by the complacency of the Eisenhower years combined to produce an environment uncongenial to Harry Byrd. He would be no more successful now than he had been during the depression and postwar period in turning back the clock, but that did not prevent his trying.

His first confrontation with the new order came after the election when Senator Joseph Clark of Pennsylvania proposed stripping party privileges, including committee chairmanships, from any Democratic senator who had not supported the party ticket and platform. Since Byrd was the only Democrat chairing a major committee who had not supported the candidates, Clark's target was obvious. Blaming party liberals for this effort, Byrd retaliated at once in a frank public letter to the Pennsylvanian in which he reiterated his opposition to much of the party platform. Referring to Thomas Jefferson, his constitutional oath, and his allegiance to the people of Virginia, Byrd queried:

> Am I to be purged as chairman of the Finance Committee because I refuse to support measures which I believe to be dangerous to the Republic I pledged myself to serve faithfully and to the best of my ability? . . . I recognize no control over my votes in the Senate from any outside influence including the national Democratic convention and a caucus of my Democratic colleagues in the Senate. I think it would be very wholesome if you would bring your proposal to the Floor of the Senate because many fundamental principles are involved. Southerners frequently have been threatened with loss of committee assignments or other prerogatives unless they support measures obnoxious to them and their constituents. Personally, I resent this. . . . I will submit to no coercion such as you propose in performing my duties as a Senator from Virginia.[1]

He pledged to support President Kennedy when he could but not when it conflicted with his conscience.

His letter was a moving defense of senatorial independence, but it ignored the issue of party loyalty, which he had defined so well thirty-six years earlier.[2] Clark was not denying Byrd's right to vote his conscience, only the rewards that come with service to the party. He replied to Byrd, "I merely ask that you sail under the colors which you fly on the Democratic masthead if you wish to be an officer of the Democratic senatorial ship." He reminded him that a committee chairman "is chosen not by the people of any one state, but by his colleagues in his party in the Senate." Challenging the time-honored precedent of seniority, Clark received little support, and in a vote on the Senate floor, even the Republicans backed Byrd's reassignment as chairman of the Finance Committee, with Clark casting the only dissenting vote.[3]

Although Byrd had a personal fondness for the new president, that did not alter his standards for cabinet officers or his attitude on the legislation Kennedy presented to Congress. Just as he had done with Eisenhower's nominee for secretary of defense, Byrd forced Kennedy's selection, Robert McNamara, president of Ford Motor Company, to divest himself of stock in companies with which the Defense Department did business. When C. Douglas Dillon came up for confirmation as treasury secretary, Byrd asked him for a list of his stock holdings. "I will put it in that little safe and I will destroy it when your tour as Secretary is completed," he explained, believing that this position was quite different from that of defense secretary. A conservative investment banker who had served in the Eisenhower administration, Dillon had the backing of George Humphrey, who urged Byrd to help his successor cope with the demands for more deficit spending. When Dillon asked Virginian Henry Fowler to serve as his undersecretary, President-elect Kennedy warned him that Senator Byrd might not approve because Fowler was friendly with the anti-Organization crowd. With trepidation Dillon approached Byrd on the matter; after a moment of reflection, the senator replied, "If you and Kennedy want Fowler, there will be no trouble from me." A few years later Byrd supported Fowler as Dillon's successor.[4]

Taking a dim view of Kennedy's proposals for increases in unemployment benefits and the minimum wage, aid to education, and medical care for the elderly, Byrd got first crack at the proposed extension of unemployment compensation payments after it passed the House. Although critical of its financing, he promised the president early hearings. The bill emerged from the Finance Committee with a major revision suggested by Byrd. Instead of a pooling arrangement that he claimed would federalize the system and favor the larger industrial states, he proposed that employers in each state pay for that state's benefits. Mounting an all-out fight against the Byrd amendment, the president's forces narrowly defeated it, 44–42, and then passed the final bill, 84–4, with Senator Byrd in opposition. This skirmish immediately raised rumors of a feud between Kennedy and Byrd that required an unusual denial by Senate majority leader Mike Mansfield of Montana, who praised Byrd as a "fair minded, equitable, just man.... He may oppose legislation,... but he has never held up legislation because he didn't like it." Other senators on both sides of the aisle rose to commend the Virginian, who listened in silence to the tributes.[5]

Mansfield's tactic was part of an administration effort to appease the nettlesome chairman of the Finance Committee. Kennedy reportedly once told Adlai Stevenson that Byrd was one of the "greatest phonies" in the Senate, but if he believed that, he never showed his disrespect publicly; certainly he had high regard for Byrd's power.[6] Knowing that Byrd's influence could make or break tax legislation, he curried the Virginian's favor, inviting Byrd to his Florida compound for discussions right after the inauguration and helicoptering to Rosemont for the senator's 1961 spring luncheon, the first chief executive to accept this annual invitation. The senator was beside himself with pride as the president chatted with the guests and gave out autographs to the servants.[7] But such stroking did not change Byrd's votes or his handling of legislation. He was not an obstructionist in the mold of Howard Smith, but he could delay legislation by waiting until action by the House had concluded and then holding drawn out hearings on matters already fully discussed in public forums. This was often the case in Kennedy's first two years, when the president's own hesitancy and conservative inclinations limited his leadership on key bills. His slim margin of victory in the 1960 election, his wariness of alienating southern Democrats, and his preoccupation with reelection in 1964 precluded more forceful action. Furthermore, Lyndon Johnson's promotion out of the Senate left it disorganized and more independent. As vice-president Johnson declined to practice his "treatment," which had proved so effective in lining up votes in the past. Mansfield was too mild-mannered an individual for such arm-twisting techniques, and so the southern "barons," who chaired key committees, were free to pursue their own agendas.[8]

In his quest to control tax and welfare legislation, Chairman Byrd could be a persuasive advocate of his positions, using his authority and his personal integrity to influence members of the executive branch and senators alike. He enjoyed telling the secretary of state what kind of tariff authority the administration could have or stipulating to the secretary of the treasury what the debt limit should be. When Secretary Dillon, whom Byrd liked, sent his assistant to Capitol Hill to discuss tax policy, Byrd declared it an affront to the Congress and insisted that there would be no legislation until Dillon himself appeared. He could be just as difficult with his colleagues. On one occasion he obstructed Senator Fulbright's efforts to advance two minor bills that revised tax rates for small businesses. Fulbright won Byrd's acquiescence to appear before the Finance Committee, but his subsequent requests for additional hearings or for attaching the bills as amendments to related legislation met a stone wall. Fulbright appealed to Senator George Smathers to press the issue in committee, but Smathers told him, "I have experienced a similar situation with respect to tax legislation introduced by me, and knowing the results I have had, the situation with respect to obtaining hearings on our tax bills is none too optimistic." When Byrd finally responded to his colleague from Arkansas, he blamed the delays on a recent stay in the hospital and the committee's heavy workload. Fulbright pleaded with then majority leader Johnson to permit Senate consideration of his bills, quoting committee testimony and the *Congressional Record* to prove that Byrd had promised him full hearings, but Senate bill 3129 did not come up for a vote.[9]

Nevertheless, Byrd generally relied upon a "courtly code" in overseeing his committee. Dillon believed that Byrd's control was "absolute," but that he "exercised his power gently." He reported: "Senator Byrd had a good sense of Adam Smith economics but would have no truck with Keynesian theories. . . . He was a very good judge of character and would rely on those who had earned his trust."[10] Finance had no subcommittees and had the smallest staff of any major committee in Congress, with only two professional economists on it. No Treasury Department experts were consulted during the committee's drafting sessions. To keep his committee's expenses down while obtaining information relevant to legislation being considered, Byrd relied on his friendships with the treasury secretaries and the staff of the Joint Committee on Internal Revenue Taxation, whose director was the fiscally conservative Colin Stam. He often left the details on tax law to the House Ways and Means Committee, which weakened the Finance Committee's position if there were substantial differences between the two groups. Indeed, Wilbur Mills, chairman of the Ways and Means Committee from 1958 to 1974, was the congressional power behind tax legislation. This left the Senate Finance Committee as a "court of appeals," a second chance for interest groups to modify the bills coming over from the House. Members of the committee would add amendments to the bills to satisfy constituents, knowing that in conference they would likely be removed. Referring to Byrd, one senator commented: "The old man won't begin a bill unless it's sent over by Ways and Means. He's a stickler on this. Of course, one of the reasons is that he's opposed to doing anything anyway."[11] Believing that there was entirely too much legislation being submitted, Byrd acknowledged that no one had "offered fewer bills than I have." His view of his role as a senator was "to oppose bills which may be injurious to the future of our country."[12]

With little professional expertise, fickle leadership, and limited time for consideration of tax legislation, the Finance Committee during Byrd's chairmanship was an undisciplined, freewheeling group of senators whose votes were not always determined by party or philosophy. Preferring ideological consistency to party regularity, Byrd permitted contentious debate without taking strongly partisan positions himself. The senator best expressed it: "What I try to do is to ignore party lines completely and vote my best judgment. I don't claim to have any special virtues at all. I just vote for what I think is right." Consequently, in Douglas Cater's words, the Finance Committee had "tendencies toward . . . anarchy," primarily because its chairman, preferring inaction to action, sought no consensus among the senators. Senator Albert Gore of Tennessee thought that "working conditions on the committee were almost impossible."[13]

Committee meetings were often a seething tide of acrimonious debate between Russell Long and Bob Kerr, whose primary interest was protecting the oil depletion allowance, and Paul Douglas and Gore, who had been kept off the committee for several years because of their opposition to the allowance. Byrd and the Republicans could generally be counted on to vote their conservative preferences on tax and welfare legislation, with liberals Douglas and Gore in opposition to them, but Long, Kerr, Clinton Anderson of New Mexico, and Eugene McCarthy of Minnesota were more unpredictable. Byrd, Douglas, and John Williams of Delaware were the sticklers on waste in government and strict personal integrity for government officials, but the conservative Williams would join Douglas and Gore in voting against the oil depletion allowance.[14]

No matter what their political views, however, members agreed about Harry Byrd's open and impartial handling of legislation before the committee. Eugene McCarthy remembered the Virginian as "a stern conservative, a watchdog of the treasury, and an unrelenting segregationalist," but as chairman of the Finance Committee, he was "unaggressive, considerate, and above all, . . . utterly fair, the fairest chairman of the ten or twelve under whom I served in both the House and the Senate." McCarthy particularly liked Byrd's rule for maintaining open committee work: that any action in closed session could be subject to a roll call at the request of a single member of the committee with the results announced to the press and public at the end of the executive session. This permitted both liberals and conservatives to disclose the voting preferences of their opponents. The Minnesotan was so impressed with Byrd's fairness that he told Byrd he would resign from the committee if anyone tried to take Byrd's chairmanship from him.[15]

Russell Long also remembered Byrd as a very fair and courteous chairman who gave everyone a chance to present amendments and discuss the strengths and weaknesses of legislation, but "if he didn't want something to happen it usually didn't and vice versa," the mark of an effective chairman. This was especially true in the early Kennedy years when Byrd believed the country would be better off without liberal legislation. Although he did not always agree with

Byrd's conservative philosophy, Long thought this viewpoint deserved to be represented because the government needed a watchdog on waste. He did not approve, however, of Byrd's parsimonious operation of the committee, recalling that there were only two telephones available for the committee's work, one for the chairman and one for everyone else. Finance had the second-lowest expenditures of any Senate committee; it funded no foreign trips and never exceeded $300 a year in stationery costs.[16]

Senators Douglas and Gore both had a similar assessment of Byrd. Douglas said he "had a rugged personal honesty and a genial air of courtesy toward his opponents, except when severely pressed." Gore referred to him as "one of the kindest men who ever lived, and a gentleman," but "a little antediluvian in his social and political views" and in his "dotage" at the end. Both thought Byrd, Kerr, Long, and Herman Talmadge of Georgia were guilty of "tax favoritism" toward the rich. Their most notable dispute with the chairman on this issue came in September 1961 over the Du Pont tax bill, designed to ease the tax burden of Du Pont stockholders after the Supreme Court ordered the chemical company to divest itself of General Motors stock. The two liberals accused Byrd of rushing the measure through the committee at an evening session called one hour beforehand. On the Senate floor Byrd angrily retorted that this statement was "untruthful and a personal reflection upon the chairman of the Senate Finance committee and the 13 other members thereof who voted to report favorably." Gore and Douglas said they meant no personal attack but insisted that the meeting had been called in haste. In January, the Du Pont bill, defended by Byrd as a protection of the small investor against unfair taxation, easily passed Congress over the protests of the liberals.[17]

The issue occasioned another bitter exchange between Byrd and columnist Drew Pearson, who wrote a column entitled "Byrd Champions Relief for Rich." Summarizing the charges of Gore and Douglas that the bill was a tax dodge for the wealthy, Pearson said that the Du Ponts were the biggest contributors to the Republicans with whom Byrd was frequently aligned. Citing "numerous misstatements" by the journalist, Byrd quickly responded by asking for space in the newspapers to reprint editorials in the Washington *Post* and Washington *Star* that defended the legislation. "I called Drew Pearson a liar," he wrote Fred Kienel, "and I have a letter from him saying that he will sue me unless I apologize. I certainly hope he will do so."[18]

If there was a threat to Byrd's leadership of the committee, it came from Bob Kerr, the wealthy oil-cattleman from Oklahoma whom many considered the "uncrowned king of the Senate." A tall, self-assured, take-charge politician, Kerr became powerful through his willingness to make any trade that gave him leverage on future votes. As chairman of the Public Works Committee—the infamous "pork barrel" committee—he was in position to make many trades.

When asked if he was porkbarreling with public works for Oklahoma, Kerr responded, "I call that bringing home the bacon."[19] He was best known for his defense of oil and gas interests, but he also supported expanded social security benefits and medical care for the aged, which brought him into conflict with Byrd. President Kennedy sought to capitalize on this disagreement by supporting Kerr's pet projects in return for his influence on legislation coming before the Finance Committee.[20] Kerr, who hoped to be chairman some day, tried to arrange afternoon committee meetings when the aging Byrd tended to tire so he could ram through what he wanted. Their sparring generated some friction, but the Oklahoman's premature death in January 1963 ended the threat. Russell Long then assumed a more prominent position on the committee, and he would replace Byrd as chairman when Byrd retired in 1965.[21]

Throughout the summer of 1961, despite frequent consultations with the White House, Senator Byrd continued to oppose the legislative initiatives of President Kennedy. He denounced the new housing bill as the "worst bill on this subject ever proposed," contested extension of the minimum wage, and ridiculed Kennedy's education bill as a step toward federal control of schools. Thanks to the controversy over aid to parochial schools and the president's clumsy handling of the legislation, the latter bill died in the House Rules Committee. Byrd gloated, "I'm glad to see that Howard Smith has re-established control of his committee at least for these school bills." Although he supported another expansion of social security benefits, Byrd tied up the tax bill in committee and cast a vote against Virginian Spottswood W. Robinson for a position on the Civil Rights Commission; Robinson, a black lawyer for the NAACP who had been active in the fight for desegregation in the Old Dominion, was confirmed, 73–13.[22]

Kennedy's first year proved disappointing. Some programs were approved, but several of the most significant pieces of legislation were defeated, delayed, or watered down. No new initiatives were pursued in civil rights, as the freedom riders challenged segregated bus facilities in the South, only to be beaten for their efforts. Missteps in foreign policy left the president struggling for ways to reassert his control of situations in Cuba, Berlin, and Southeast Asia. But for Harry Byrd, the disappointment was not the failure to address new problems but the inability to reduce spending and keep budgets balanced. Predicting continuing federal deficits, he criticized the administration for not curtailing domestic spending, including the proposed trips to the moon, which Byrd said should be pursued on a pay-as-you-go basis. "Administration spokesmen," he said, "seem to justify the continuance and enlargement of domestic programs on the basis of their belief that America's economic capacity is sufficient to support both added social measures as well as added defense measures. I do not agree with this position." He did not agree with the president on much of anything, for he had voted with the Democrats only 19 percent of the time in 1961.[23]

Interspersed with Byrd's sparring with the administration was his ongoing debate with the NAACP and the federal government over desegregation in Virginia. Still bruised by the defeat of massive resistance, he never missed an opportunity to criticize the Warren Court or the "ruthless federal bureaucrats" for their interference in state affairs. The focal point now was the closing of schools in Prince Edward County. Rather than submit to court orders directing integration of their schools, county leaders had chosen to terminate public education in 1959, the only locality in the country to take this step. White citizens of Prince Edward, under prearranged plans, immediately opened a private academy for their children and offered to do the same for black children. Black parents, who had challenged the segregated public system, were not about to settle for segregated private schools and, with the advice of the NAACP, took the county board of supervisors to court. It took five years of litigation before the Supreme Court determined that the closed schools violated the plaintiffs' right to an education, during which time most of the county's black children received no instruction at all. For Harry Byrd it was a question of state or local rights versus a tyrannical federal government. "The gallant little county of Prince Edward," he declared, "is fighting against great odds to protect a principle it believes to be right." In a well-publicized address in neighboring Buckingham County in May 1961, Byrd called the Warren Court's *Brown* decision "an infamous blot on our history" and blamed the NAACP for "the fact that 1,700 colored children in Prince Edward county are not now attending good schools with qualified teachers." He also castigated the Justice Department's recent attempt to intervene in the case as "another black day" in Virginia history that ranked with the use of troops in Little Rock. Byrd's words brought an immediate response from Roy Wilkins, executive director of the NAACP, who said the school closing was the ultimate result of the massive resistance policy initiated by Harry Byrd that had "substituted racism for Americanism."[24]

The only respite Byrd had during the trying summer of 1961 was a vigorous hike up Old Rag Mountain on his seventy-fourth birthday to dedicate a shelter he was donating to the National Park Service. Explaining his gift, Byrd said, "I've been caught up here too damn many times in the rain without shelter." Old Rag was his favorite mountain; protruding out from the rest of the Blue Ridge like a silent sentinel, it may have reminded him of the lonely independence of his own life. He had been climbing it since he was sixteen. However, as columnist Guy Friddell noted, Byrd "does not climb a mountain, he charges it." On his birthday he briskly ascended the steep, rocky 1.5-mile trail to the top, leaving younger souls panting by the wayside. A year later on his seventy-fifth birthday, after another hike and camp-out, he donated a second Adirondack shelter to the park, this one on Hawksbill Mountain. Byrd made these affairs real excursions. Invited guests spent the night on the mountain with the senator, courtesy of the Park Service, which provided the tents, cots, sleeping bags, steaks, and several bottles of good whiskey.[25]

The senator had maintained an active walking program to strengthen an arthritic left knee that he had injured in a fall on the ice some years before. Rejecting a physician's advice to have an operation that would remove the knee-cap and limit his mobility, he resolved to combat the disease with further exercise and weight reduction; but as he grew older the pain intensified, and he resorted to heavy doses of Anacin. Byrd had been in good health for most of his life. He had had minor surgery for a kidney stone in 1936, major surgery for removal of another stone in 1952, and an operation for a hernia in 1956.[26]

Because he loved the out-of-doors, Byrd supported many conservation issues, including clean water acts, wilderness preservation legislation, and efforts to save the California redwoods, but his prodevelopment, antiregulation attitude did not make him a favorite among environmentalists. He did, however, have a "fiscal soft spot" for the national parks. Claiming the parks returned a $1.20 value for every dollar spent, he invariably voted to increase their meager budget. He especially enjoyed the magnificent mountains of the West and frequently took his vacations there. He visited Yosemite four times, where in 1959 he was given a park ranger's badge. Usually accompanied by Blackie Moore, sometimes by his sons or park officials, Byrd would spend a couple of weeks touring the sites, often on foot, carrying a pack.

Following the fatiguing session of 1961, Byrd and Dr. George Ruhle, a naturalist with the Park Service, embarked on a 30,000-mile, five-week around-the-world trip whose highlights included Rome, a climb up Mount Vesuvius, the Taj Mahal by moonlight, Nepal, and Hong Kong. His only disappointment was that he did not find a satisfactory eating apple anywhere along the way. A stop in Vietnam led to an excursion into the backcountry where a guerrilla war was being waged; prophetically, Byrd concluded: "The communists are seeping in there, and it will be difficult to stop them in that country. It's all swamps and mountains. You could send in troops and they might never find the enemy."[27]

Preparing for a new legislative session in 1962, Byrd faced not only the perennial issues of budget and poll taxes but also important tax, trade, and health care legislation that would have to travel through the Finance Committee. When queried whether he would tie up the president's programs in committee, Byrd replied: "I am going to cooperate with the President all I can. I am not going to support a lot of this stuff, but I am going to get it to a vote in the committee. There is no object in trying to smother important bills in committee. I may try to amend a bill to make it the best I can, and I may vote against it myself, but I won't try to smother it." On foreign trade, he worried about new world economic conditions that put the United States at a competitive disadvantage with cheap foreign labor in a free trade situation. "I've never been a high tariff man," he confessed, "but I want to hear a lot more about this thing. I'll keep an open mind." Less hesitantly, he immediately rejected Kennedy's proposal to change the tax rates. When the president urged Byrd to speed up the process by holding public hearings on the tax and trade bills before their passage by the House, the senator resisted, saying that they would only have to repeat the process when the final bill arrived from the House. It would not be an easy sell for the president, whose problems were compounded by the death of Speaker Sam Rayburn, a powerful and sympathetic ally.[28]

Early in 1962 Kennedy met with senators Mansfield, Humphrey, and Russell to discuss ways of getting around the uncooperative Finance Committee chairman. He decided to rely upon Bob Kerr to make sure the bills got to the Senate floor. To this end he made concessions to Kerr to maintain the oil depletion allowance and to support the Arkansas River Project. This move proved of little help on the medicare bill. Kennedy attempted to revive the Forand plan that had been defeated in 1960, but Kerr, defending his own Kerr-Mills plan, led the fight on the Senate floor to defeat the bill, 52–48. Byrd called it the "wise and proper action to take."[29]

Kerr was more helpful on the tax bill. Backing away from any change in the tax rates in the face of Byrd's opposition, the administration put forward an investment tax credit for business and a withholding tax—collected at the source—on interest and dividends. The senator was not mollified. He labeled the tax credit "a subsidy and . . . a gimmick." In open hearings with Secretary Dillon as a witness, Byrd denounced the plan, calling it "a remarkable indictment of the American economic system" for the Treasury Department to insist that American companies be provided tax incentives to buy new machinery and equipment. Furthermore, he said, the credit would jeopardize a balanced budget and was not large enough to stimulate growth. Byrd and John Williams joined an unlikely alliance with Gore and Douglas to try to kill the investment incentive, but Kerr, whom Gore called "the most influential Senator on tax matters in our history," led the fight to retain it.[30]

Byrd also made clear his opposition to the withholding feature of the bill, against which banks and building and loan associations were vigorously lobbying. He said it "would be complex if not unworkable" and would overtax the people. Senator Douglas, its leading defender, argued that the government was losing over $1 billion on unreported dividends and $3 billion on unreported interest. With obvious delight he indirectly chided Byrd for his opposition: "I am absolutely amazed that many of the same individuals and same groups who are constantly criticizing the size of the national debt, who are demanding that the budget be balanced, and who appeal for fiscal soundness are fighting this proposal. The test of their real concern about financial soundness will come when we vote on the withholding provision." The scolding hit home, for while Byrd disliked compulsory withholding, he was disturbed by the lost revenue. Following up an earlier suggestion, he introduced a bill that required financial institutions to report to the government the names and social security numbers of those earning interest and dividends. The Kennedy withholding provision was defeated in the Finance Committee, 10–5, but Byrd's suggestion was incorporated into law.[31]

The demands on Byrd from the crush of legislation and pressure from the White House intensified. He assessed the workload as "the worst I've seen in my 29 years in the Senate. I don't know how we're going to work our way out of it." His meetings with the president were cordial but produced little change in his positions. After one conference Kennedy, tongue in cheek, said, "Senator Byrd and I have agreed on everything," but privately Byrd's hostility was no joking matter to him. The senator delayed the progress of the tax bill for three months by postponing hearings and twice having it read aloud in committee. A *Time* cover story on Byrd in late summer portrayed him as the major obstacle to Kennedy's legislative program, attributing his effectiveness to the absence of executive or congressional leadership and the popularity of the senator's position. Kennedy told the reporter, "Harry Byrd is the most gracious person you'd want to meet, but he does give us fits." *Time*, however, overestimated Byrd's authority when it contended that he had "arrived at a crest of effective power and influence." He was one of many conservatives obstructing the president's programs, and at times he was not even in control of his own committee. More accurately, an administration official concluded: "Byrd was like a yellow blinker. You had to slow down when you got to him."[32]

Despite his opposition the tax bill proceeded on its course. Acknowledging its likely passage, Byrd amended the tax credit provision so that it would not apply to machinery or equipment destroyed or damaged by fire, hurricane, or other such causes that were covered by insurance. With this action he deprived himself of a tax windfall, for the 7 percent credit on the $300,000 replacement cost for his insured Berryville cannery that had been destroyed by fire would have entitled him to $21,000. "I didn't think that would be fair," he boasted. For one of the few times in his twenty-nine years on the Finance Committee, Byrd found himself in the minority on a major piece of legislation reported by the committee. Although he continued to argue against the investment credit after his amendment to delete it was defeated, he concluded that the good features of the bill outweighed the bad, and he voted for it. It passed the Senate in early September, 59–24. Similarly, Byrd decided to support the trade expansion bill despite his "very strong reservations" about some of its features. With another assist from Bob Kerr, the bill emerged from the Finance Committee on a unanimous vote and passed Congress at the end of another long session.[33]

On other legislation Byrd was less agreeable, voting against aid to education, a constitutional amendment outlawing the poll tax in federal elections, and creation of a new department of urban affairs and housing, which he labeled "a department of backdoor spending and contingent liabilities." Responding to Kennedy's belated effort to integrate the University of Mississippi, Byrd declared the use of federal troops "offensive to our form of government."[34]

Late in 1962 Byrd became quite ill. The lengthy legislative session had weakened him, and he contracted a virus which did not respond to treatment. He traveled to Europe with Harry Jr. for a NATO meeting but returned a very sick man, having lost eight to ten pounds and still carrying the fever. Hospitalized, he was given intensive antibiotic therapy and spent Christmas Day at his physician's home in Baltimore. Discharged after the holidays, he continued his recovery at Rosemont.[35]

The major confrontation between Byrd and President Kennedy during the first session of the Eighty-eighth Congress in 1963 was over a new tax bill that provided deep tax cuts to stimulate the economy. From the beginning of Kennedy's administration, Walter Heller, chairman of the Council of Economic Advisers, had urged a Keynesian solution for economic growth. The president had been loath to upset the conservative business community with an incurred federal deficit, but the continuing sluggishness of the economy, highlighted by a steep drop in the stock market the previous May, convinced him that a more dramatic tactic had to be pursued. In a commencement address at Yale University on June 11, 1962, Kennedy had broached the possibilities of new economic thinking. Speaking as if Harry Byrd were in the audience, the president said: "The budget is not simply irrelevant; it can be actively misleading. And yet there is a mythology that measures all of our natural soundness or unsoundness on the single simple basis of this same annual administration budget." After making appropriate peace overtures to businessmen, he concluded with a call for "new words, new phrases, and for the transfer of old words to new objects." Praising Kennedy's speech, columnist Walter Lippmann foresaw the next problem: "With rare exceptions the leaders of both parties hold to economic doctrines that have long since been abandoned as antiquated by all the progressive and advanced countries of the world. . . . men like General Eisenhower and Senator Byrd talk as if they had never read a book on economic matters that has been written since the great depression of 1929. . . . the administration will have to do a mighty job of public re-education."[36]

Any reeducation of Harry Byrd, who believed Keynesian economics was heresy, would prove difficult if not impossible. Columnist Douglas Cater predicted that Byrd, "a man of quite ordinary ability," who "never bothered to master the technical details" of legislation, would approach the tax cut "with a closed mind and a confused committee." Senator Long surmised that Byrd did not believe large deficits could lead to economic growth; the idea was too speculative. He was, said Long, "blind to charts. He could understand a column of figures but not charts and graphs." A month after Kennedy's address, the senator responded to the new economics with old words. Big government and deficits, he said, were not myths. The ideas that debt was not bad and that budgets could be balanced over a cycle were "illusions that prevent actions." The president was disguising reality with his words; gold reserves were declining, and deficits were inflationary. "When will the breaking point come?" he asked. The senator also got into a running debate with the United States Chamber of Commerce, which had come out in favor of the tax cut. Calling that stand "fiscally irresponsible," Byrd said he was "astonished, dismayed, and shocked" that the Chamber, which for "fifty years has been a bulwark for fiscal responsibility in the federal government," should adopt such a position. He cited support for his views among conservative economists, but as Senator Douglas concluded, "the compensatory theory of public finance was winning out among economists and progressive businessmen," and only the "die-hard group" still clung to annual balanced budgets. Nevertheless, the "die-hards" carried clout. Deciding not to pursue the broader tax cut in 1962, Kennedy told Wilbur Mills, "Harry Byrd would screw us even if you put it through the House."[37]

In January 1963, however, President Kennedy presented his new budget with the $13.6 billion tax cut included. Forewarned of the bill's particulars by Treasury Department officials Dillon and Fowler at a December meeting at Rosemont, Byrd forecast an even greater shortfall than the estimated $10 billion deficit. Concurring with former Treasury Secretary George Humphrey that the Kennedy deficits only "disguise plain stealing from our grandchildren," he offered his own "Byrd Budget" that would cut government spending by $7 billion and leave a balanced budget if no tax cuts were voted.[38]

The death of Bob Kerr and a failed administration effort to enlarge the Finance Committee strengthened Byrd's obstructionist hand. With widespread conservative support—Byrd claimed he received hundreds of letters opposing the tax bill and almost none in favor—he continued to snipe at the president's proposal and delayed taking it up until the House had finished with it. That did not occur until September 30, which left no time for full congressional action. Secretary Dillon sought to speed the bill through committee, but Byrd claimed that he needed ten days of staff briefings, four weeks of testimony, and another two weeks to create a Senate version of the bill. He offered Dillon a deal: a delay until January when, in return for a reduced budget, he would

Bobbing For The Apple

"personally guarantee" the tax cut would pass and be made retroactive. Dillon rejected the offer.[39]

Over the objections of the liberals, a majority of the committee supported the chairman's decision to hold "comprehensive and lengthy hearings." Byrd did not vote on speeding up the procedure because, as he said, "I felt I was the issue. Besides, my vote wasn't needed." Perhaps revealing the true intent behind his delay, he warned Kennedy that public concern with national insolvency might be reflected in next year's presidential election. "The people," he said, "are awakening to the fact that after having deficits for most of thirty years, we've gone about as far as we could go in adding to the debt." Following the very deliberate schedule established by the chairman, the Finance Committee conducted its hearings until near the end of the year, when, Byrd hoped, new budgetary figures might require another year of debate or prove the need for a balanced budget. By this time the senator was receiving many bitter letters blaming him for obstructing the tax cut bill. When Senator Robertson consoled him by saying Kennedy's legislative program might wreck the country, Byrd replied, "I am not too sure he hasn't already wrecked it." It was a trying time for Byrd, who reminded one audience of his loyalty to the original New Deal: "I have experienced combat fatigue at times; I have taken some shell shock; and I am a battle-scarred veteran from fighting for the promised New Deal. But somehow I have survived, and I am still here defending fundamentals of our great system."[40]

Byrd was not solely responsible for the failure of the Kennedy tax cut to pass in 1963. The introduction of new civil rights legislation and the negotiation of a nuclear test ban treaty with the Soviets took up valuable time in Congress and preoccupied the president. In April, Martin Luther King, Jr., had taken his civil rights crusade to Birmingham, Alabama, where the use of police dogs and fire hoses against the demonstrators shocked the nation and compelled President Kennedy to go before the country on national television to ask for justice and equal treatment for its black citizens. Up to this point Kennedy had been reluctant for political reasons to support forcefully the efforts to end segregation, but on June 19 he submitted a strong civil rights bill to the Congress.

Once again Harry Byrd was quick to blame the federal government and black activists for the disorders, ignoring the legitimate demands of the protesters and the violence perpetrated by local law enforcement officials. He told D. Tennant Bryan of the Richmond *Times-Dispatch*, that Attorney General Robert Kennedy "seemed to think the only way to prevent this was to yield to the demands of the Negroes and pass legislation as quickly as possible. In other words, we should submit to blackmail." Asked about the recent integration of southern universities, Byrd said that he did not believe in telling other people what to do but predicted that the nation was "on the verge of serious trouble not only in the South but in the North" on the racial issue. Not above practicing a little "blackmail" himself, he suggested that a Senate filibuster on civil rights would jeopardize the president's tax bill.

After the August March in Washington by 250,000 civil rights protesters, who listened to King's "I have a dream" oration, the senator said he would not be intimidated by marchers and demonstrators. The only reason the march had been orderly, he said, was because "8,000 soldiers and police were on hand." Of the marchers' demands for action, he estimated that "80 percent are unconstitutional and the other 20 percent are unworthy." With a smile he declared that thousands of words would be spoken by southerners before any action would be taken on the civil rights bill. On the issue of civil rights, Harry Byrd was an immovable object, totally insensitive to the discrimination against black Americans. The opposition of Byrd and other southern representatives to Kennedy's proposed public accommodations bill would require a massive public relations campaign and adroit political arm-twisting by the administration, which necessarily delayed action on it until the following year.[41]

The test ban treaty was a by-product of the Cuban missile crisis of the previous fall when the United States and the Soviet Union came to the brink of nuclear annihilation. Chastened by the experience, Kennedy and Soviet premier Nikita Khrushchev entered into negotiations to reduce the nuclear threat and signed a modest treaty in July 1963 that stopped atmospheric testing of nuclear weapons. Senator Byrd attended all the Armed Services Committee meetings on the subject to familiarize himself with the technical information about testing and detection. Acknowledging the difficulty of the decision, he said, "I do not believe entering such a treaty as it stands . . . would serve national security. I am fearful that it will weaken if not undermine, our defense. . . . I cannot within my conscience and my duty, as I see it, vote to ratify the treaty without effective inspection while the Soviets are in possession of such vast nuclear power." The treaty passed easily in late September, 80–19, with Byrd in the small company of conservative Republicans and southern Democrats who made up the opposition. Once more, he was shortsighted. The treaty was an important first step in easing tension between the United States and the Soviet Union and addressing the problem of nuclear proliferation. It was a major achievement of the Kennedy administration and contributed to the highest approval ratings of his presidency.[42]

In spite of Kennedy's charisma and growing popularity, Byrd's prestige also remained high. It was not because he was preferential to businessmen, for many of his votes on the recent tax legislation, such as opposition to the tax credits for investment and his support for tightening overseas tax havens, were not in their interests. His greatest weapon was his public reputation. Personal integrity and consistency in thought were the cornerstones of his popularity. The Virginian could be depended upon. He received the distinguished service award from Americans for Constitutional Action for his 94 percent rating on legislation between 1955 and 1961. His friendships with conservative editors and publishers, among them Harry Guggenheim of *Newsday*, Francis Drake of *Reader's Digest*, and David Lawrence of *U.S. News and World Report*, guaranteed an accessible medium for promulgation of his views. Raymond Moley, one of FDR's initial brain trusters and now an editor at *Newsweek*, referred to pictures of Byrd and Jimmy Byrnes on his office wall as "my inspiration in everything I write and every position that I take." Byrd frequently taped short talks for radio distribution, but he shied away from television talk shows, fearing their spontaneity and their liberal bias. His formal speeches and articles, although still strewn with facts and figures, now emphasized principles of conservatism, most notably states' rights, the separation of powers between the branches of government, and the threat to liberty posed by an authoritarian federal government. "Conservatism, as we understand it in Virginia," he proclaimed at one of his August picnics, "means to accept responsibility for preserving and protecting our basic principles and institutions while exercising the privilege of using them. . . . Virginians are not reactionaries. We do not turn back the hands of the clock. We do not necessarily defend the status quo. But neither do we assume that change is necessarily progress. We want progress but we want sound progress. . . . In Virginia we believe sound progress is built on fiscal conservatism, and we have the record to prove it." Defending his voting record, he declared, "I think a senator should represent his state and I believe that Virginia still is among the most conservative states in the union."[43]

Politics, however, took a holiday on the occasion of Senator Byrd's thirtieth anniversary in the United States Senate. On the Senate floor friends and enemies alike rose to praise his contributions. Testifying to Byrd's authority, one congressman said there were three parties in the Senate: "the Democrats, the Republicans, and the party of Harry Byrd—the Byrd-Democratic Party."[44] At a dinner hosted in his honor by the publishers of *Reader's Digest* at the National Press Club and attended by three hundred of the senator's friends, the congratulatory testimonials flowed from everyone, including former president Truman, who wrote: "One of my greatest privileges was to know you. While we didn't always agree, we each knew the other had honest convictions. May good luck and a long life of public service be yours from now until the Almighty decides you have done your share." Responding to this letter, Byrd called Truman "a man of great courage." Chuckling over Truman's remark about there being too many Byrds in the Senate, a forgiving and forgetful Byrd said it "never affected our friendship" and "actually helped me get re-elected." President Kennedy also sent a tribute: "There have been few men in the history of the Congress who have worked so consistently and persistently for the principles which have guided their public life."[45]

Despite their many disagreements over policy, Byrd was shocked and saddened by the assassination of the president in November. The next day he recalled his associations with Kennedy and eulogized him as a man of courage and independence, bold and "gifted in the art of government." But even tragedy would not mollify Harry Byrd when it came to JFK's legislative program. When the newly sworn-in president Lyndon Johnson spoke to Congress and asked it to pass the civil rights and tax bills as a tribute to the slain leader, Byrd termed it an "eloquent speech" but rejected the plea, declaring, "I think any legislation should be passed on its merits and not on the basis of being a memorial to any person living or dead."[46]

Lyndon Johnson and Harry Byrd had been friends for years. The new president had regularly attended the Berryville luncheons; as majority leader he had allowed Byrd free rein in the Finance Committee, carefully stacking its membership to assure a conservative and friendly majority for the Virginian; he had also cleverly watered down civil rights legislation, making it more palatable for most southern legislators. Even though Johnson was more liberal than they were, southern senators saw him as one of their own and maintained their friendships with him. But motivated by personal and political conviction, Johnson shifted his agenda leftward to endorse more liberal social experimentation, including passage of Kennedy's civil rights and tax bills. To accomplish this he had at his disposal sympathy for the assassinated president and his own unsurpassed legislative skills. The master of political lobbying and consensus building now turned his charms on Harry Byrd, who some believed controlled the destiny of the tax bill.[47]

Only two weeks after assuming the presidency, Johnson had an extended White House luncheon with Byrd at which they apparently agreed to defer any action on the tax cut until the new federal budget was submitted in January. In return the president won a pledge from the senator to facilitate eventual action on the bill and make any enacted tax cuts retroactive to January 1, 1964. Johnson did not expect Byrd to support the bill, but he pressured his old friend not to bottle it up in committee as he had done the previous year. To this end he appeased Byrd by cutting the budget. He told Walter Heller, "I can defend $101.5 billion [the size of Kennedy's last proposed budget], but you'll have to take on Senator Byrd. If you don't get it down to $100 billion you won't pee one drop." In early January he called Byrd to his office: "I've got a surprise for you Harry. I've got the damn thing down under $100 billion . . . way under. It's only $97.9 billion. Now you can tell all your friends that you forced the President of the United States to reduce the budget before you let him have his tax cut." Criticized for his obstructionist tactics, flattered by the attention, and appreciative of the budget cuts, Byrd was falling under Johnson's sway. Secretary Dillon remembers passing the same information to Byrd and winning his promise to release the bill from committee; nevertheless, the senator predicted, "Douglas, mark my words, Lyndon Johnson will be the biggest spender we have ever had in the White House."[48]

The "treatment" continued with a late-night session at the White House following the Gridiron dinner a few days later. As Hubert Humphrey recalled it, LBJ told him to get Byrd over to the executive mansion for a nightcap. After they arrived, Humphrey, at Johnson's orders, fixed "two fingers of Old Grand-

Dad" for the Virginian, and the three of them sat parleying and sipping. The president then said, "Harry, before you go home I think you ought to visit with your girl friend," at which point he called Lady Bird Johnson from an adjacent bedroom: "Lady Bird, your boy friend Harry is out here." She entered, clad in a dressing robe, and chatted with Byrd, who, in Humphrey's words, had become "more animated." After a few moments LBJ dismissed her and turned to Byrd and said: "Whenever I can't find Lady Bird, I know she's with Laurence Rockefeller, Hubert, or you. That's why I don't dare leave town too much." Then he abruptly changed the subject. "Harry," he opportuned, "I know you're opposed to that tax reduction, but I've got to have that bill out of committee. We owe it to the late president. I know you can't vote for it, but don't bottle it up. Will you give me your word that you'll report it out?" The senator replied, "Lyndon, if you want that bill out, I'll do nothing to stop it." After he left, Johnson told Humphrey to remind Byrd every day of what he had said.[49]

Russell Long insisted that up to that time Byrd, who rejected the economic philosophy behind the tax cut, was not going to permit the bill to pass and had been encouraging John Williams and others to offer obstructive amendments. "Johnson," he said, "gave Byrd the million-dollar selling job." Other committee members believed Byrd operated on his own timetable. Said one: "It is just not in Harry's makeup to stall a bill he dislikes or to rush through the committee a bill he's for. He knows that millions of dollars can ride on a misplaced comma in a tax bill, and nobody is going to persuade him to telescope hearings." Byrd did not change his mind on the bill because of Johnson's political massaging, but he likely became more compliant on the procedure.[50]

The senator was good on his word, but other members of the Finance Committee almost upset the arrangement. An amendment to repeal the excise taxes threatened to unbalance the budget. On the afternoon of January 23, LBJ phoned all seventeen members of the committee and urged them to work on each other in holding the line. When Senator Vance Hartke of Indiana said he wanted to eliminate the tax on musical instruments, Johnson exploded: "The goddamned band and musical instruments; they won't be talking about them next November. They're going to be judging us by whether we can pass a tax bill or not, and whether we got prosperity." He asked Byrd to get the excise tax amendment eliminated. "If you'll go along with me on that, we can do it." He advised him to do it on a general motion in order to overcome the special interests. Byrd replied, "I'll do the best I can." Late that afternoon, on a vote of 9–8, the committee defeated the excise tax cuts passed that morning. Lyndon Johnson was profoundly grateful. Calling Byrd back, he gushed, "You're a gentleman, and a scholar, and a producer, and I love you." A dazzled Byrd responded: "Well, it was only one vote. We got by." "I know it," said the president. "That Harry Byrd though, he can do anything. You've learned to count since I left up there. I used to do your counting. But when you can beat them nine to eight, you're doing all right."[51]

The committee gave final approval to the $11.5 billion tax cut bill, 12–5, with Byrd among those opposed. "I don't feel it is the right thing to do to cut taxes without a greater reduction in expenditures," he explained. "That has been my position from the beginning." He reported the bill out but turned its floor management over to Senator Long, who was fast becoming the new leader of the Finance Committee. Making clear his objections to the tax cut, Byrd told Humphrey, "Now you tell the President that I kept my word—that I've reported out the bill, that I've made my speech, and now I'm leaving." Since he had little desire to manage legislation or participate in debate, Byrd probably did not mind deferring to Long on a bill he had no love for. Despite his reputation as an expert on taxes and budgets, most observers did not think he had that kind of expertise. One Treasury Department expert was quoted as saying, "Senator Byrd confines himself to the broader issues and doesn't go far beyond." Byrd would usually make one speech on the subject, as he did this time, and then fade into the background. Within the week the Senate passed the bill, 77–21, with Senator Byrd voting with the minority. In spite of this, when President Johnson signed it into law on February 26, he praised Harry Byrd for his contribution. Eric Goldman has said that this was "no doubt the only bill-signing ceremony at which a President has lauded a congressman who voted against the legislation." Although Byrd deserves credit for not destroying this bill, history records another misguided vote by the Virginian, for the tax cut contributed to one of the longest economic expansions in American history.[52]

When Johnson tackled his next priority, the public accommodations bill, it was not Harry Byrd to whom he turned. The senator and his southern colleagues were preparing for a final filibuster of a bill that would remove most of the last vestiges of legalized racial discrimination in America. Already passed overwhelmingly by the House of Representatives, the legislation would empower the federal government to prohibit discrimination in hotels, theaters, and other public accommodations, cut off federal funds from programs where discrimination existed, create an equal employment opportunity commission, further desegregate public schools, and advance black voting. The southern senators, as they had done eleven times since 1938, hoped to attract enough conservative Republicans to defeat the vote on cloture and force a compromise. It would be a difficult chore. The issue had attracted national attention and support, and black organizations and voters were enjoying increased political influence. The Senate had become younger and more liberal, its members more in tune with current social and political trends and less bound by the customs of the chamber. The ranks of the southerners were ravaged by age and the defections of those on the periphery in Texas and Tennessee. Finally, the chief executive had added his powerful voice to those in favor of equal opportunity. Nevertheless, history demanded that the southerners try, and they entered the fray with the same vigor and determination that they had displayed on previous occasions.[53]

Senate leaders Humphrey and Mansfield permitted a lengthy filibuster in order to build support for the cloture vote rather than repeat the 1960 strategy of around-the-clock sessions that exhausted the senators. Winning an early vote not to send the bill back to committee, they forced the southerners to start their filibuster on March 9. For the next three months, pausing for numerous quorum calls and a few short recesses, the senators from Dixie battled on toward another Appomattox. Byrd's arguments, the same as those advanced by his colleagues, were ancient and predictable. Speaking in a barely audible voice, he warned against the invasion of individual rights by an oppressive federal government: the rights to determine whom you will hire, whom you will serve, and with whom you will associate. He argued that the bill would create an enormous mountain of red tape, as "employers will have to keep cradle-to-grave records on every employee to justify pay raises, promotions, transfers, and so forth." Even during the brief recesses, Byrd continued his attack. At the annual Wakefield shad planking in April, Byrd warned his listeners that the bill applied not only to businesses but to churches, cemeteries, private hospitals, doctors, dentists, and lawyers and "will extend federal control over private clubs if they offer any courtesies to guests of hotels. . . . [It is] a monstrous grab for federal power. . . . It is the worst legislation ever introduced." In May he lambasted the recent Supreme Court decision that reopened public schools in Prince Edward County, calling it "tyrannical" and a "usurpation of power." He urged the county board of supervisors not to levy the taxes necessary for a reopening of schools.[54]

The major breakthrough in the Senate came on May 19, when Illinois senator Everett Dirksen, the minority leader, announced his support for the bill. Quoting Victor Hugo, he proclaimed, "No army is stronger than an idea whose time has come." Having been lobbied hard by Johnson and the Democratic leadership, the mellifluous Dirksen carried many undecided Republicans with him. On June 10 the longest filibuster in Senate history came to an end on a 71–29 vote to invoke cloture. With the deadlock broken, the bill passed a few days later, 73–27. In a historic White House ceremony, President Johnson signed it into law on July 2, distributing the seventy-one signing pens to the beaming legislators and civil rights leaders who had been most responsible for its passage. The most significant piece of civil rights legislation since Reconstruction was the result of strong presidential leadership, Dirksen's crucial conversion, vigorous lobbying by civil rights groups and churches, and the black protest movement: its time had come.[55]

Harry Byrd was unrepentant, undeterred, and ignorant of the majesty of the moment, labeling the new act "unconstitutional and unworkable." He was satisfied with the effort that he and his southern colleagues had made against overwhelming odds. In an address to Virginia's commonwealth's attorneys a month later, he cautioned against violence, but declared that noncompliance with the civil rights law "is no more illegal than sit-ins, lie-ins, and other demonstration practices in violation of other laws." Since the law did not define what discrimination is, he conjectured that it would be left to federal bureaucrats and Supreme Court justices to define it by "amending the Constitution . . . and usurping legislative authority" in the process. Byrd, as always, had a point, but it paled in significance to what had been accomplished. Rarely do legislators confront a bill that tests their understanding of history and the moral forces at work in the world. The Public Accommodations Act of 1964 was such a bill, and Harry Byrd failed the test.[56]

Byrd found himself at odds with LBJ on one other major piece of social engineering in 1964, the antipoverty program. President Kennedy, moved by Michael Harrington's book *The Other America,* had initiated a study of a broad-based program to attack poverty in the nation. Johnson, harking back to his New Deal roots and his association with FDR's struggle against the depression, enthusiastically supported the idea and turned it into the major objective of his administration. He proposed a new agency, the Office of Economic Opportunity, to oversee the new programs that included a community action program, a job corps for training youth, work-study funds for college students, and VISTA, a program for volunteers willing to work with the poor.[57]

Senator Byrd was understandably upset with this liberal agenda and told LBJ so. His primary concern, naturally, was budgetary; in light of the new tax cut, the country needed to reduce spending in order to keep the deficit manageable. He recommended abandoning the $962 million antipoverty program as well as cutting appropriations for civil defense, vocational education, community health centers, work-training programs, and mass transit. He also asked for minor cuts in defense spending and in foreign aid. Although the president knew converting the Virginian was impossible, he invited Byrd to accompany him to the dedication of the George Marshall Library at VMI. When they stepped onto the parade grounds, Johnson quipped to Governor Albertis Harrison, "I've been trying to borrow some money from Harry all the way down here but I haven't had much luck." To which Harrison responded, "It might be easier to borrow some apples from him, Mr. President." Byrd was among the one-third of the senators who voted against the economic opportunity bill when it passed the Senate in late July. As with the civil rights act, he called the poverty program "unworkable"; this time he would be closer to the truth.[58]

The senator did not oppose Johnson on all of his legislation. Despite missing a large number of roll calls, he supported a new wheat price-support bill and a land and water conservation act, backed the preservation of wilderness areas, and along with every senator but two favored the Tonkin Gulf Resolution authorizing the president to use whatever force was necessary to deter aggression in Southeast Asia. Byrd's apprehension over the growing American presence in Vietnam was long-standing, going back before the Dien Bien Phu disaster in 1954. Along with Senator John Stennis, he had voiced dissatisfaction with the Eisenhower administration for sending air force mechanics to Indochina without congressional approval. Now ten years later he lamented to K. V. Hoffman, "Conditions are certainly rapidly deteriorating from every standpoint." Like many congressmen, he was wary of an escalating commitment but could not bring himself to vote against the president and the ostensible struggle against worldwide communism.[59]

Shortly after the Tonkin Gulf vote, Senator Byrd suffered a devastating personal loss when Sittie died of a heart attack on August 25. A near invalid in her final years, she had moved her bedroom to Rosemont's ground floor to avoid stairs and often required an ambulance to travel between Washington and Berryville. Sometimes she could not make the trip, which increased the senator's loneliness in Washington. Although he had not allowed her illnesses to interfere with his business and political interests, theirs had been a loving relationship. A year earlier they had celebrated their fiftieth wedding anniversary with a quiet family dinner during which he affectionately toasted her for her years of loyal support. He never fully recovered from her loss.[60]

In a demonstration of respect for his friend, President Johnson, who was preparing to fly to Atlantic City to receive the nomination of his party for the presidency, issued a public statement of condolence and attended the funeral at Christ Episcopal Church where the Byrds had been married. There, in an act of genuine sympathy, he kissed the hand of Senator Byrd. A photographer caught the gesture and it was flashed across the country, angering the president, who believed it might be taken as an effeminate act or, worse, a crass political attempt to woo Byrd and Virginia to his column in the fall election. His fears were realized when the Knoxville *Journal* called the gesture a "high point in cynicism and hypocrisy." Ordinarily that might have been an accurate appraisal of LBJ's political behavior, but in this case it was an unfair assessment, for Johnson had enjoyed a long friendship with Byrd and was known to get very emotional at weddings and funerals.[61]

What gave credence to the stories about Johnson's graveside politicking—

in addition to his reputation as a political manipulator—was Harry Byrd's "golden silence" in another presidential election year. Speaking only days before Sittie's death to an audience of four thousand at what would be his last annual picnic, he objected to LBJ's legislative agenda and strongly castigated the "wild political platform" he expected from the Democratic national convention. He made no mention of what he would do in the forthcoming campaign, but it was clear that he would run for reelection on his record and ignore what was happening elsewhere. Johnson very much wanted Byrd's endorsement, knowing that it would secure Virginia for him, but rather than wait for what might not come, he chose to cultivate other elements of the party in the Old Dominion. His success in this effort revealed the extent to which Byrd's machine was moribund.[62]

20

"His Face against the Future"

Harry Byrd's final years in public service were not happy ones. Not only was he being outflanked by liberals on the national scene, but his control of politics in Virginia was ebbing. The state Democratic Party was in transition. The liberalization of a growing electorate, the acrimony of the massive resistance fight, and the challenge from the Republicans had generated dissension within the Organization, particularly among those dissatisfied with the policies and practices of the Old Guard. The gubernatorial election of 1961 and the presidential election of 1964 revealed the new currents in Old Dominion politics.

Lieutenant Governor Gi Stephens, a longtime member of the Organization, had sounded Byrd out about running for governor as early as 1959, but since he had supported Governor Almond in the school fight, he was not in good favor with the senator and others in the inner circle. Garland Gray told Byrd that "a Stephens victory would be disastrous" for the Organization. Announcing his candidacy in December 1960, the two-term lieutenant governor wrote again to Byrd to ask for his support, but the senator declined to give his nod.[1]

With Stephens unacceptable to the machine leadership, attention turned to state senator Harry Byrd, Jr., who had strong support within the Organization. But after consulting his father, the younger Byrd decided to withdraw his name from consideration, claiming that it would be inappropriate for two Byrds to hold top elective positions simultaneously. More likely, they feared a bitter primary fight that they might lose or that might divide the Organization irreparably. Byrd Jr. was so identified with massive resistance that his candidacy would have resuscitated the school-closing issue and turned the race with Stephens into a Byrd versus anti-Byrd affair. As Mills Godwin wrote Watt Abbitt, Harry might win, but it would be a difficult campaign that would leave scars on the Organization and perhaps deny them control of the assembly. Byrd Jr.'s withdrawal shifted Organization support to Albertis Harrison, the silver-haired attorney general whose moderate counsel in the school crisis—albeit in defense of massive resistance—had won praise from all segments of the machine,

Young Turks and Old Guard alike. Missing the advice of Ebbie Combs and weary from his Senate battles, the elder Byrd acquiesced to Harrison's bid, thus setting up a bitter fight with Stephens, who was being supported by the remnants of the "antis."[2]

Announcing his candidacy early in 1961, Harrison received the endorsement of state senator Mills Godwin of Chuckatuck, a staunch massive resister, who decided to run for lieutenant governor. They agreed to run as a ticket and asked state senator Robert Button of Culpeper to join them as the candidate for attorney general. The threesome made the obligatory trips to Washington to discuss the campaign with the senator, who remained uninvolved in the race until Stephens, like Miller and Dalton before him, made a slip that enabled Byrd to make his preference known publicly.[3]

Having lost the support of most Organization officials, Stephens's campaign floundered until Armistead Boothe entered the race for lieutenant governor against Godwin. Much like Harrison and Godwin, the two agreed to form a ticket to better combat their opponents, and for the first time since Byrd's campaign against Miller in 1952, Virginians had a real choice in the Democratic primary. Stephens began to attack the machine for its high-handed and reactionary ways, but in disassociating himself from the Organization, he remarked that he had "not at any time solicited the support of Senator Byrd." That brought forth from Byrd's office a copy of the letter in which Stephens had stated that he was "hopeful of being the recipient of your most valuable support in the gubernatorial campaign of 1961." Admitting that he had made the request, Stephens insisted that he had made no compromises with Byrd, asserting that the letter's release "clearly demonstrates that I am not running against Albertis Harrison but that I am opposing the head of a machine who would be United States Senator and Governor at all times." Humorously, he concluded: "This is a primary of pen pals. I write the letters. Senator Byrd releases them to his pals." The revelation of the letter indicated Byrd's preference in the primary and shattered Stephens's hopes. Harrison said that the lieutenant governor's comments were "just like lighting a fuse; I never welcomed a speech as much in all my life as I did that one." Harrison and Godwin won easy victories in the July primary, but their margins of victory were considerably lower than previous Organization tallies. It was, J. Harvie Wilkinson has said, "the last statewide race in which the classic Byrd coalition was able to win in style."[4]

Harrison's governorship was a calm transition between the plodding mediocrity of the old regime and the progressivism of Mills Godwin's subsequent governorship. At the time of Harrison's inauguration, Virginia ranked last in the country in per pupil expenditures for schools in relation to per capita income and last in per capita expenditures for welfare programs. Even its much-acclaimed highway spending ranked only thirty-sixth. The state tax burden was the lowest in the nation, but the Old Dominion was in need of additional revenues with which to balance the budget. The new governor did little to improve this sad record, but he did prepare the way for what was to follow. His congenial demeanor mended the political fences between conservatives and moderates that had been demolished by massive resistance, and he worked assiduously to promote industrial development in the Commonwealth, encouraged increases in educational expenditures, and maintained racial calm during the turbulent protest years.

Reluctantly, as always, the General Assembly dragged its heels on reapportionment. Only under court order in 1964 did it redistrict the state to reflect the urbanization that was transforming the Old Dominion economically and politically. The declining importance of the rural areas in state politics was a key element in the demise of the Organization because it diminished the ability of the "courthouse crowd" to control the vote. Legislative districts in the urban areas no longer corresponded with county lines, and county officials had become little more than administrative bureaucrats, a far cry from their former roles as political agents. As Governor Harrison remarked years later, the local officials—the treasurers and clerks—were no longer the people one would ask about issues and candidates; thus, the internal network of the machine was gone.[5]

Byrd's involvement in policy matters was now superficial at best. Through his son and Blackie Moore he learned of assembly deliberations, but he made little attempt to influence them. Harrison has said that the senator only called him a half-dozen times about appointments or legislation, a vast change from the frequent communications he had maintained with previous governors. Old friends in the legislature and at the courthouses had retired or died and he made no effort to get to know the newcomers. At party gatherings, such as the Jefferson-Jackson Day dinner or his annual picnic, Byrd would whale away at the federal government and reminisce about old times, but he had few comments to make about the state of affairs in the Old Dominion. Potential candidates still went to see him because his blessing carried much weight, but their candidacies were no longer dependent upon receiving the nod. He had lost his grasp of Virginia politics.[6]

The senator's most significant intervention in Virginia affairs during the sixties was an act of vengeance. He could not forgive Lindsay Almond's betrayal. He thoroughly enjoyed the way Harry Jr. and Blackie Moore had engineered the defeat of Almond's request for a sales tax in the 1960 assembly. Referring to Jim Latimer's comment that Moore was torpedoing the governor's plans, Byrd snidely remarked to the Speaker, "I can hardly credit this, as you are such a kind man. . . . After your very arduous efforts and hard work for the beloved Governor of Virginia, I think you need a vacation."[7] The rift widened during the 1960 presidential campaign when Almond enthusiastically backed Jack Kennedy, and it ruptured permanently on the eve of Almond's departure from the governor's mansion in 1962, when he commented on his private discussions with Byrd over the school closings, which brought forth a heated rebuttal from the senator.

It was no surprise then that Byrd obstructed Kennedy's nomination of Almond to the United States Court of Patent Appeals in April 1962, despite having given initial assurances to the administration that he would not block his nemesis. Disingenuously, Byrd claimed that the appointment was obviously political and that he had always been opposed to such appointments for judges. Although Almond was given a temporary interim appointment to overcome Byrd's stalling tactics, he was not confirmed in the post for over a year. Most observers labeled Byrd's behavior an act of petty vindictiveness, which hurt his reputation as a statesman and further undermined Organization authority.[8]

The senator also foolishly continued his efforts to prevent elimination of the poll tax in Virginia. The Twenty-fourth Amendment repealing the tax for voters in federal elections had finally passed Congress over his objections, and a special session of the General Assembly was called to consider a replacement. Harrison and Godwin traveled to Washington in September 1963 to convince Byrd that there was no sense in obstructing this in the legislature. In the presence of the old inner circle—Blackie Moore, Harry Jr., Bill Tuck, Howard Smith, and Watt Abbitt—Byrd went into a tirade about retaining the tax. He apparently had had too much to drink, and had it not been for the conciliatory efforts of Judge Smith, it would have been a disastrous meeting. Still, his position carried the day. Convening in November, the assembly chose to retain the tax for state elections; and for those who desired to vote in federal elections without paying it, the legislators imposed an annual residency certification. Bill Tuck chortled to Byrd, "If these dead beats are required to go to the court house and register personally, it will cost them much more than it would to pay the poll tax." The certification requirement was the defiant act of a dying machine that had lost touch with the political currents running in Virginia. Although they had both participated in its creation, congressmen Smith and Burr Harrison warned Byrd of the likelihood of this provision being overturned by the federal courts, an action that quickly followed. The ratification of the Twenty-fourth Amendment in January 1964 produced an increase of almost a quarter million registered voters in Virginia over the next few months, many of them black.[9]

Almost leaderless and no longer representative of the new Virginia, the Organization slowly disintegrated. Its defenses of massive resistance and the poll tax were major liabilities among a younger, less white, less native, more urban electorate. It was facing serious competition in Norfolk and in the Ninth and Tenth districts. From the port city Billy Prieur was urging Byrd to eliminate the state poll tax because it was being used against them by more liberal candidates who were challenging Organization control. These political differences came to a head in the 1964 presidential election.[10]

Given recent Republican successes, many Organization Democrats desired a stronger affiliation with the national party to prevent further erosion. They went to the state convention in July 1964 intending to endorse President Johnson in spite of their differences with him on many issues. Harry Byrd and his friends were adamantly opposed. When Byrd heard of Governor Harrison's proposal to back Johnson, he threatened to argue against it personally on the floor of the convention. During a late-night session at the Hotel John Marshall in Richmond, he was unyielding, and the word went forth that the delegation to the national convention should be uninstructed. Howard Smith reportedly remarked, "You just can't reason with him." Nevertheless, the next day at the Mosque the delegates voted 633.5 to 596.5 to endorse Lyndon Johnson; it was a major defeat for the senator.[11]

In the ensuing campaign the divisions continued. Byrd remained silent, and his closest friends followed his lead. But Governor Harrison, Lieutenant Governor Godwin, most of the Virginia congressmen, and Organization stalwart Sidney Kellam, who managed Johnson's campaign in the Old Dominion, literally jumped on the president's train. The Lady Bird Special was to carry the first lady on a whistle-stop tour of the South in early October; boarding the train would be a clear indication of one's preference in the election. Lady Bird called her "boy friend" Harry Byrd to invite him to join her, but he excused himself and his sons on account of the recent death of his wife. Looking for any kind of political advantage, the first lady approached Helen Byrd, the senator's daughter-in-law, who was very excited about the prospect. Her husband, Dick, however, told her to check with his father, who made it clear that she would have to refuse. "Helen," he said, "I know you can't understand this, but your presence on that LBJ special would send a message to the world, to the whole country; I have always sent my messages with silence or with subtle ways; it would be interpreted that I was backing Johnson by sending you on that train; I can't afford to do that." So advised, Helen decided not to ride, but many of Virginia's leaders did. Mills Godwin believed his decision to board the train—at Kellam's and Harrison's suggestion—secured for him the Democratic nomination for governor the following year. Knowing of Byrd's likely response, he did not inquire of the senator whether he should join the entourage.[12]

Isolated in his silence, Byrd concentrated on his own reelection. He had delayed his decision to run again, considering his advancing age, the poor health of his wife, and the ever-longer congressional sessions. Virginia Democrats expected some announcement at the Jefferson-Jackson Day dinner in late

February, but the amiable senator laughed off reporters' questions and smiled and waved to the audience. Three weeks after the dinner, he announced his bid for a sixth full term. Reaffirming his allegiance to the people of Virginia, he stated that his platform would be "my record of nearly fifty years of public service."[13]

Surprisingly, the Republicans decided to contest his reelection for the first time since 1946. Claiming Byrd's pride was exceeding his prudence, state chairman Horace E. Henderson said that the senator was too old, his basic rural orientation out of place in a state that was rapidly urbanizing, and his political philosophy, although at one time admirable, was now outdated. "The world and Washington have changed much in spite of the senior senator and he no longer represents today's people and problems in Virginia," said Henderson. "Virginia and the nation require more than total negativism in Washington if we are to preserve our Constitution and secure our national freedom." Although the party had been successful in capturing Virginia in recent presidential elections, it remained a skeleton operation on the state scene and no threat to Byrd. Indeed, Republican congressman Joel Broyhill of the Tenth District argued that a futile effort against the man who had proved so friendly to the GOP would make the party appear even weaker. Only with great difficulty did Republicans find someone to make the sacrificial race against the senator.[14]

Despite the opposition Byrd hardly bothered to campaign. A few speeches and statements, usually a compilation of threadbare slogans and clichés, were the extent of his effort. He undertook a modest letter-writing campaign, but for the most part he relied on the old network of local managers and the speeches of Tuck, Abbitt, and Smith, who were running for reelection to Congress, to spread the word for him. He declined all joint appearances with his opponent, Richard A. May, a retired General Motors executive and former Lend-Lease administrator who was now raising cattle in Gloucester County. Byrd raised $11,097—the largest sums from three old friends in the New York business community—and spent only $6,539 in a race that saw him win 64 percent of the vote.[15]

During Byrd's campaign Republicans and Democrats unsuccessfully tried to get him to express his preference in the national race. Captured by its conservative wing, the Republican party had nominated Arizona senator Barry Goldwater, Byrd's philosophical soul mate, to contest President Johnson, but his reservations about social security and his reputation as a warmonger jeopardized the national GOP's winning streak in the Old Dominion. The controversial nature of the candidates and the issues, along with the concurrent presidential and Senate races, made for some interesting campaign affiliations. Byrd appreciated the support of "Virginia Democrats for Goldwater and Byrd," the same group that had campaigned for Eisenhower and Nixon, but he refused their invitation to speak out. He also received support from "Republicans for Byrd." Straight-ticket Democrats criticized Goldwater for his votes against the antipoverty bill, the tax cut, the civil rights act, and the test ban treaty and then praised Senator Byrd, who had also voted against all of them.

Unlike the previous three elections, Virginians chose not to follow Byrd's lead in 1964, another signal of his declining influence in the state. Johnson won a handsome majority in the Old Dominion to enhance his landslide nationwide. Observers attributed his victory to the endorsement of key Organization leaders, the managerial skills of Sidney Kellam, the extremism of Goldwater's image, and the new electorate. His strongest support came in urban areas and black precincts where voter registration drives had proved effective. Byrd's opponent Richard May exaggerated only slightly when he said, "I feel like it's no longer the Byrd Machine now. It's the Kellam Machine." Sidney Kellam would not assume such prominence, but Harry Byrd's reign had ended.[16]

Indeed, the 1964 election forecast a new era in Virginia politics. Astutely judging the changing scene, Mills Godwin closed the door on his past handiwork and began working to maintain the fragile coalition of conservative, moderate, and liberal Democrats by stressing the need for better state services and new sources of state income. "My philosophy is in tune with Byrd-type conservatism," he said. "But I don't think the status quo can or ought to be maintained."[17] Godwin had no competition for the party's gubernatorial nomination in 1965, as Harry Byrd, Jr., once again declined to enter the race. Much like Harrison before him, Godwin did not feel obliged to consult the elder Byrd on his candidacy, but he welcomed his public support. That assistance came so late in the campaign that some believed Byrd preferred the Conservative party candidate because of Mills's train ride. Only some gentle arm-twisting by old friends extracted from the senator a modest endorsement of the Organization's candidate, who, he said, "stands for sound progress built on fiscal conservatism." Godwin defeated Republican and Conservative party opponents in the general election, but only by a plurality, which indicated the weakness of his coalition. Many conservative Democrats, upset with the liberalization of the national party and Godwin's apparent obeisance to it, deserted the Organization. Godwin's progressive governorship, during which he won passage of a sales tax and bond-funded increases in educational expenditures, further alienated Old Guard Democrats. Four years later, signifying a total party realignment, many of them helped elect Linwood Holton governor, the first Republican to hold that office since Reconstruction. Final fragmentation of the Byrd Organization—and the final irony—came in 1973 when Mills Godwin won a second gubernatorial term, this time as a Republican.[18]

The legacy of Byrd's forty-year rule in Virginia was mixed. The senator always liked to say that he was a progressive conservative who favored "sound progress" within the bounds of fiscal restraint. His own solid governorship reflected this philosophy. His greatest gift to the state was a debt-free government that honestly and efficiently provided basic services to its citizens: good roads, law enforcement, and economic development. But as rapid changes engulfed the Old Dominion, Byrd did not keep pace. Honest and frugal government, while commendable, was not enough. Policies that helped Virginia through the depression became obsolete by the fifties, retarding development. In William Chapman's words, "sound progress" became "sound budgets and limited progress." And massive resistance was a discredited and dishonorable course that further obstructed advancement.[19]

No one was more dedicated to Virginia than Harry Byrd. Said Albertis Harrison, "His passion was the Commonwealth of Virginia and the welfare of the people and the soundness of the government. . . . He never did a thing in his life that he didn't think was in the best interests of this Commonwealth." But Byrd erred in equating the interests of the Commonwealth with his own political fortunes and the financial interests of the wealthier classes. He ignored the majority of Virginians. According to Chapman, a record of "cash-drawer honesty" disguised a "legacy of crowded colleges, inadequate mental hospitals, and neglected social services," not to mention racial intolerance. Byrd was so committed to limited government that it never occurred to him that something more might be needed. While Virginia was changing, he was clinging to a time when life was simpler, goods and services were cheaper, and white males held sway. His loyalty was to an Old Dominion that no longer existed. Fitzgerald Bemiss, who served in the General Assembly for twelve years, put it plainly: "The old men of the organization failed the test which the young men put them to; they made opponents of men they should have embraced as their natural successors and thereby became protesters rather than directors of inevitable change. No more than the Bourbons, the Hapsburgs, and Romanoffs were the Byrds able to see what lay ahead and to interrupt the progress of the revolutionary cycle."[20]

But regardless of how one assesses Byrd's contribution to his state, there is no denying that he made a difference. Virginians likely would have selected leaders with a philosophy similar to his, but no one could have matched his ingratiating yet forceful personality, his single-mindedness and decisiveness on basic issues, his organizational skills, and his energetic involvement in the daily affairs of the Commonwealth. He was without a peer in building and maintaining a political organization that dominated the state for forty years. He wrote the script, created the set, chose the actors, and directed the play. For nearly half a century, Virginia—or at least the part that was politically active and economically well-off—was Harry Byrd. Yet Harry Byrd was also Virginia. He was a product of its conservative political heritage, a white, male-dominated aristocracy that ruled its domain with a selfish but paternalistic hand. Wanting no social revolution, these gentlemen cavaliers feared the hand of big government in their pockets and the power of an expanded electorate at the polls. Byrd gave them the leadership they desired. Society and individual were compatible. Years later, at a time when the General Assembly confronted a nettlesome issue, Senator William Stone of Martinsville reminisced: "It makes you appreciate Harry Byrd. He really knew how to run things."[21]

Byrd's last year in the Senate was marked by continued deterioration in his health, which affected his control of the Finance Committee, and further defeats at the hands of Lyndon Johnson, who had been strengthened by his election victory and the addition of many liberal Democrats in Congress who were beholden to his coattails. Preparing for the new Congress, Johnson told his aides: "Every day while I'm in office, I'm going to lose votes. I'm going to alienate somebody. . . . We've got to get this legislation fast. You've got to get it during my honeymoon. . . . I want to see a whole bunch of coonskins on the wall."[22] Pursuing the "Great Society" that he hoped would make him the Franklin Roosevelt of his time, Johnson introduced an array of programs that were directed at every conceivable social ill.

The flagship of Johnson's Great Society fleet was medicare, a health insurance plan for the elderly. Ever since passage of the Kerr-Mills Act in 1960, congressional liberals had unsuccessfully attempted to broaden its coverage and fund it out of increased social security taxes. The election of 1964 changed not only the membership of Congress but also the political climate. The obstructionist voice of the American Medical Association was losing out to the higher costs of health care and the growing power of retired Americans. Realizing that passage of President Johnson's medicare program was inevitable, Wilbur Mills moved from an adversarial position to advocacy of a stronger bill that provided compulsory hospital insurance funded by social security, voluntary insurance to cover other fees, and a new program called medicaid for indigent persons under the age of sixty-five. With Mills's support, the bill easily cleared the House in April 1965.

To ensure that Harry Byrd would not block the bill, the president applied another dose of the "treatment" to the Finance Committee chairman. Inviting the senator to the White House on March 26, ostensibly for a medal ceremony for astronauts Gus Grissom and John Young, Johnson proceeded to hold a meeting with House and Senate leaders on the medicare bill, after which he moved the gathering to the Cabinet Room where newsmen and television cameras awaited them. Asked by the president for his observations on the bill, a somewhat flustered Byrd said that he could not make any comments before the bill got to his committee where, he assured Johnson, he would hold "adequate and thorough hearings." Johnson persisted: "And you have nothing that you know of that would prevent that coming about in reasonable time, not anything ahead of it in the committee?" "Nothing now," commented the senator, who said later that if he had known he was going to be on TV, he would have dressed more formally. At that point the president applied the coup de grâce: "So when the House acts and it is referred to the Senate Finance Committee, you will arrange for prompt hearings and thorough hearings?" To which Byrd in a barely audible voice replied, "Yes." Speaker Carl Albert said afterwards, "That was the best example of 'the treatment' in public that anyone ever got." Although accorded the opportunity to shake hands with the astronauts, Byrd was angry at LBJ for the deception.[23]

Behind Byrd's back White House aides were also working with Senator Long to ensure that enough committee members would support the bill. Senator Anderson got Byrd to limit the number of witnesses called, and the hearings proceeded expeditiously, with Byrd keeping his promise to LBJ not to delay matters. The legislation emerged from committee on a 12–5 vote with Byrd and four Republicans in the minority. Having aggravated the arthritis in his knee on his birthday walk to dedicate Byrd's Nest shelter no. 4, Byrd was absent from the floor debate on the bill. After a twenty-one-day convalescence at Rosemont, he returned for the final vote on medicare, lamenting: "There won't be many of us against it. And I wanted to be sure to be here." In his statement of opposition, he cited its costs, the harm it would do to the private insurance system, and the objections of the medical profession. Like a Hooverian ghost moaning for rugged individualism, Byrd claimed that there was a need for more self-responsibility in taking care of one's health. Over such protests the bill easily passed the Senate in July, 68–21. To dramatize the significance of the health care legislation, President Johnson flew to Independence, Missouri, and signed it in the presence of Harry Truman, who had initiated the idea twenty years before.[24]

Nothing else in Lyndon Johnson's legislative program pleased the Virginian, whose last "Byrd Budget" called for massive cuts in federal spending for poverty programs, vocational education, manpower training, and area development. To his credit he was asking the right questions: what are the goals of the poverty program and how long will it take to achieve them? He opposed extension of the Economic Opportunity Act, all federal aid to education, another housing bill, an increase in the debt limit, home rule for the District of Columbia, highway beautification, even a veterans bill. Although voting for the defense appropriation and a supplemental appropriation for the expanding war in Vietnam, he continued to condemn foreign aid. His only real satisfaction came through his support of a successful filibuster to defeat Johnson's attempt to repeal the right to work provision of the Taft-Hartley Act.[25]

Once more he took up the fight against another civil rights bill. Martin Luther King's crusade in Selma, Alabama, to dramatize the denial of the ballot to black southerners—highlighted by the march from Selma to Montgomery—produced a quick request from President Johnson for the passage of voting rights legislation. The bill required the direct intervention of federal registrars in states where literacy tests were used and where fewer than half of the eligible voters voted, which included Virginia. Bitterly denouncing this "vicious" bill, Byrd declared its provisions "iniquitous in effect and contemptible in design. . . . [and] grossly offensive to Virginia." Although Byrd reportedly told *Newsweek* journalist Sam Shaffer that blacks could not be denied "a basic constitutional right to vote," he said he was obliged to obstruct the bill. Hampered by the ill health of Senator Russell, the weak southern filibuster was easily overcome, and the voting rights act of 1965—the last significant victory of the civil rights movement—was enacted into law in August over Senator Byrd's objections. Within a year over 400,000 new black voters were added to the registration rolls.[26]

Not since the heady days of the New Deal had Harry Byrd been so out of step with the Congress and the country. And it was clear the senator no longer commanded the attention of his colleagues, in part because of his declining health, in part because he seemed like such a political dinosaur. A year earlier one congressman said of him, "Harry is like the lonesome right end on the football team. We need him on the team, but I can't see him catching a touchdown pass anymore." Another was less generous: "Byrd and his friends already have the dead hand of the past on us. What he keeps trying to do with his talk of mortgaging our children is to use the unborn hand of the future to put brakes on our progress now."[27] For the longest time, even when so frequently in the minority, Byrd could rationalize his activity with the thought that things would be worse without him. But now he was overwhelmed by the liberal majorities in Congress and the revolutionary temper of the sixties. He was an old man whom time had passed by. Senator Robert Kennedy affectionately wrote him in August 1965: "I was sorry to hear that you were not feeling well. We need you back here to keep a check on us young liberals who will get away with everything without you to keep on eye on us." Unfortunately for Byrd, the cookie jar was almost empty.[28]

On November 11, 1965, Harry Byrd retired from the United States Senate after nearly thirty-three years of service. It was not unexpected. Billy Prieur had been to Skyland to visit him in late October and reported to Peachy Menefee that something had to be done to save the senator embarrassment down the road. The knee was giving him constant pain, and he no longer had the vitality he had been so famous for; the twinkle had left his eyes, and he was dozing off in committee meetings. In his brief letter of resignation to Governor Harrison, Byrd said the painful arthritis and the advice of his physicians had led him to conclude that he should make way for "someone younger to bear these burdens and shoulder these responsibilities" of representing Virginia in Washington. Certainly not far from his mind was the memory of Senator Glass clinging to his seat when he could no longer serve. The governor quickly appointed Harry Jr. to his father's seat.[29]

The announcement of Byrd's retirement brought forth the customary eulogies. Journalist David Lawrence cited him for "courage and integrity amid the hypocrisies of political life today." Senate colleagues on both sides of the aisle were quick to commend his service. Archenemy Hubert Humphrey stated: "The Senate is losing one of its most distinguished members. My friend Harry Byrd has given a lifetime of service to the state and nation. He is a man of sincere conviction, always a gentleman, and ever a patriot." Fellow Finance Committee member Eugene McCarthy praised Byrd's chairmanship: "Those who have served with him . . . will remember him for his dedication, for his great courtesy and absolute fairness to members of the committee and committee staff, to government witnesses and to all others who appeared before his committee." Everett Dirksen simply said: "Byrd was one of the great senators who came to the Senate. He stoutly maintained the ideals of Virginia and the country. Byrd was unrelenting in his views, but think of the leavening effect he had on this country."[30]

The tributes emphasized the man, for there could be no denying Byrd's rock-solid integrity and devotion to duty as he saw it, but critics looked more carefully at the record. In reality, Dirksen exaggerated his influence, for there had been little leavening, only a warning. Byrd had not been a major player in the United States Senate. References to him in histories of the period or in the memoirs of the presidents with whom he worked are infrequent. His rock-ribbed conservatism won him a loyal following among segments of the media and business community, but that did not translate into power. Protective of his own independence, he made little effort to pressure others into voting his way, not even his Virginia colleagues. He once said of Bob Kerr, who was known for his political machinations, "I don't criticize him for it, but I just can't operate that way."[31] Furthermore, his own inflexibility on the issues did not permit him to become a horse trader like Kerr. Instead, he used his personal integrity, his consistency, his public image as a conservative spokesman, his stature and his longevity in a forum laden with tradition, and his chairmanship of the Finance Committee to try to modify that which he could not defeat. Introducing no significant legislation during his career, he was primarily an obstructionist—a gadfly—and not the most noted one at that because of his limited debating skills. He was not even preeminent among his southern colleagues and had little authority in his own party. When he became chairman of the Finance Committee, he assumed a more prominent role in the legislative process that considered tax and social welfare bills, but even there he could only slow the speed with which they were enacted. At the end Byrd was little more than an elder statesman and a conservative icon, one of the old Southern barons who had outlived his usefulness but whose courtliness and honesty warranted condescending attention.

Byrd entered the Senate at a time when his America of farms and small towns, formerly insulated from the shocks of world affairs and modernization, was dying. Rather than adjust to the revolutionary changes that occurred over the course of his lifetime, he chose to contest their inroads, becoming a cipher whose predictable negativism made his position inconsequential and whose votes against civil rights and welfare legislation revealed a parochialism that bordered on meanness and miserliness. Driven by a desire to preserve the old order, Byrd spent over thirty years fighting ever-increasing federal bureaucracies and budgets, protecting states' rights from intrusions by Washington, and defending racial segregation. Focusing attention on waste in government and pressing for reductions in federal spending, he won some minor skirmishes, but he lost most of the battles. His political philosophy of unregulated individualism and limited government was no longer appropriate for the modern world. Much of his personal value system remained sound—hard work, thrift, initiative, and responsibility—but the demands of the highly technological, mass consumer, global society called for modifications to this individualistic ethic through community planning, resource management, public assistance for the dependent, aid to education, and international commitments. Without a political opposition that might have forced him to reevaluate his position, Byrd could not overcome the limitations of his upbringing and his experience. He remained caught in the time warp of the early twentieth century when the nation was still closely tied to the libertarian principles of the old yeomanry. In the words of the New York *Times,* "A talented man, Byrd chose to stand outside the broad currents of his time and to set his face against the future. . . . He began as a force and ended as an anachronism."[32]

Nevertheless, there was merit in the manner of the man and the portent of his prognostications. His major contribution as a senator was his repeated warning about the dangers of excessive federal spending, a warning that had more substance twenty years after his retirement than it did during the prosperous post–World War II years. There are limits to what government can accomplish, dangers in long-term unbalanced budgets, and liabilities in dependence on the welfare state—for rich and poor alike. Byrd's flaw was that he did not translate these forebodings into imaginative solutions to the problems of modern society but instead fell back on old clichés and a narrow individualistic ethic that was no longer serviceable, a sterile legacy to show for thirty years of service.[33]

Harry Byrd's retirement was short-lived. A few months later, as his condition deteriorated, he was diagnosed as having an inoperable brain tumor. He spent his remaining days at Rosemont, mostly bedridden, but not without having one last small impact on Virginia politics. On the eve of his son's reelection bid, he lapsed into a coma, and out of respect for him, the campaign was halted. Days later, Harry Jr. won a narrow victory over Armistead Boothe in the Democratic primary, but Willis Robertson and Howard Smith went down to defeat. The Old Guard had passed. On October 20, 1966, Harry Flood Byrd died in the same room where his wife had died two years earlier. He was buried next to her on a hill overlooking Winchester and the Valley and mountains he loved so much.[34]

Notes
Bibliography
Index

Notes

Abbreviations

BEP   Harry Flood Byrd Executive Papers, Library of Virginia
BP   Harry Flood Byrd Papers, University of Virginia Library
br   business records in Byrd Papers
CR   *Congressional Record*
HFB   Harry Flood Byrd
LV   Library of Virginia
NYT New York *Times*
RTD Richmond *Times-Dispatch*
UVL University of Virginia Library
VMHB *Virginia Magazine of History and Biography*
WES Winchester *Evening Star*

1. Legacies and Opportunities

1. Foster, *Ghosts of the Confederacy,* 38–39, 128; DeLauter, *Winchester in the Civil War,* 94–95; *Southern Historical Society Papers* 7 (1879): 349–52, 22 (1894): 41–48; *NYT,* Oct. 26, 1866; *WES,* June 7, 1907.

2. Morton, *Story of Winchester in Virginia,* 243–44; *RTD,* April 14, 1946. Winchester's population in 1890 was 5,196; in 1910, 5,864; in 1930, 10,855. John Lupton was the first large commercial apple grower in the area, beginning his operations around 1883. Ebert and Lazazzera, *Frederick County, Virginia,* 132, 186; *WES,* Nov. 6, 1908.

3. Hatch, *Byrds of Virginia,* 3–225; see also Marambaud, *William Byrd of Westover,* and Tinling, *Correspondence of the Three William Byrds of Westover.*

4. Interviews with Harry Byrd, Jr., Dick Byrd, Beverley Byrd; HFB to August Dietz, April 13, 1942, box 430, BP.

5. Hatch, *Byrds of Virginia,* 225–34. Richard Byrd was born in 1860; he had three brothers and four sisters. Harry Byrd, Jr., to author, Jan. 15, 1991.

6. Hatch, *Byrds of Virginia,* 234–36; *Proceedings of the Thirty-Sixth Annual Meeting of the Virginia State Bar Association* 1926:158, 160–61; *RTD,* Oct. 25, 1925; Freeman to HFB, May 2, 1951, box 423, BP.

7. Quarles, *Some Worthy Lives,* 55; Hatch, *Byrds of Virginia,* 234, 406; Tyler, *Men of Mark* 1:28–29; interview with Joseph and Teresa Massie.

8. Joel Flood to HFB, Jan. 2, 1958, box 243, BP; Kaufman, "Flood," 10.

9. Treon, "Flood," 44–64; Harry F. Byrd, Jr., to author, Jan. 15, 1991; Hatch, *Byrds of Virginia,* 237, 245; Quarles, *Some Worthy Lives,* 54; Joel Flood, Flood Family History, in possession of Mr. and Mrs. Francis E. Tyler of Eldon; interviews with Byrd's sons and Joe and Teresa Massie; Green, "Mother of Tom, Dick, and Harry," 143–45.

10. Harry Byrd, Jr., to Jane Wegner, Dec. 18, 1950, box 265, BP; Hawkes, "Career of

Byrd," 5–6; Hatch, *Byrds of Virginia,* 245–48, 405–6; *RTD,* June 8, 1941; interview with Harry Byrd, Jr.; memoirs of Mrs. J. A. Massie, Jr., "When I Was Very Young," in possession of Joe and Teresa Massie (Mrs. Massie claimed she verified her facts with Senator Byrd before giving this talk to the Winchester Century Club in the early 1960s); Green, "Mother of Tom, Dick, and Harry," 144–45.

11. Massie memoirs; Door, "The Man Who Set Virginia One Hundred Years Ahead," 52.

12. HFB to Hunsdon Cary, Aug. 3, 1946, box 403, BP.

13. Interview with Dick Byrd; Massie memoirs; Hawkes, "Career of Byrd," 7–9; Hatch, *Byrds of Virginia,* 406–7; Strother, "Youth Takes the Helm," 142–43; McCardle, "Lone Crusader for Thrift."

14. *WES,* Jan. 5, 26, April 27, May 6, 1907; Hatch, *Byrds of Virginia,* 407; Massie memoirs; interview with Harry Byrd, Jr.; Cappon, *Virginia Newspapers,* 226–28.

15. *WES,* Nov. 26, 27, 1907, Nov. 6, 1908.

16. Massie memoirs; Hawkes, "Career of Byrd," 10; *WES,* April 3, 1907; HFB to Flood, Jan. 10, 1906, Flood to HFB, Jan. 12, 1906, box 30, Hal Flood Papers, Library of Congress; J. W. Crews to HFB, March 7, 1907, box 66, BP.

17. Byrd address, *Virginia Record,* Sept. 1956, copy in box 299, statement, box 79, records, box 65, BP; Hawkes, "Career of Byrd," 12.

18. Byrd biographical material, box 168, BP; "Appomattox's Hal Flood," *Virginia and the Virginia County* 5 (Jan. 1951): 66; *Eastern Fruit Grower* 20 (Aug. 1956): 6–37; Massie memoirs; interviews with Harry Jr. and Beverley Byrd; Hatch, *Byrds of Virginia,* 409.

19. Massie memoirs; Hatch, *Byrds of Virginia,* 242, 410–11.

20. Interview with Harry Byrd, Jr.; Massie memoirs; Hatch, *Byrds of Virginia,* 409; Moger, *Virginia,* 344.

21. HFB to Elgin, Sept. 28, 1957, box 243, BP; *WES,* April 12, 1910; Door, "The Man Who Set Virginia One Hundred Years Ahead," 52.

22. Hawkes, "Career of Byrd," ii, 14–15; *WES,* Oct. 2, 25, Dec. 14, 1907, Jan. 21, 1908.

23. See Grantham, *Southern Progressivism,* and Moger, *Virginia,* 231–64.

24. Reeves, "Thomas S. Martin," 344–51; Moger, *Virginia,* 103–21; Readnour, "Fitzhugh Lee," 117–18; Martin to Flood, Sept. 9, 1893, William M. Murrell to Hal Flood, Oct. 14, 1893, box 2, Flood Papers.

25. Kaufman, "Flood," 2–24; Treon, "Flood," 46–56.

26. Kaufman, "Flood," 82–94.

27. Moger, *Virginia,* 120–22, 157–98; Treon, "Flood," 44–55; Kaufman, "Flood," 14, 66–111; Larsen, "Montague," 161–62; Horn, "The Growth and Development of the Democratic Party in Virginia since 1890"; Pulley, *Old Virginia Restored,* 23, 83–91, 114. The number of Virginians voting in the presidential elections declined between 1900 and 1904 from 264,095 to 129,929; black voting may have been reduced by over 80 percent. Moger, *Virginia,* 192

28. Pulley, *Old Virginia Restored,* 118–31, 153–56; Treon, "Flood," 55–56; Moger, *Virginia,* 165, 250–68; Ferrell, "Swanson," 172–79; Kaufman, "Flood," 57, 121–23, 159, 261.

29. Ferrell, *Swanson,* 73; Moger, *Virginia,* 114, 120, 230, 330; Tyler, *Encyclopedia of Virginia Biography* 5:29–30.

30. Moger, *Virginia,* 297–304; Ferrell, *Swanson,* 91–92; Pearson and Hendricks, *Liquor and Anti-Liquor in Virginia,* 252, 262, 264; Rhodes, "Mann," 186–88.

31. HFB to R. E. Byrd, March 18, 1910, R. E. Byrd to Flood, March 18, 1910, box 79,

Flood Papers; Treon, "Flood," 57–59; Kaufman, "Flood," 170–75; Ferrell, *Swanson,* 92–95, 103, 111, 136–48; Moger, *Virginia,* 221.

32. Flood to M. W. Paxton, July 4, 1912, box 44, Flood Papers; Moger, *Virginia,* 277–91; Kaufman, "Flood," 185–219; Kaufman, "Virginia Politics and the Wilson Movement"; Ferrell, *Swanson,* 101–4; Holt, "Martin and Democratic Floor Leadership," 10–19; *Proceedings,* 159–60.

33. Moger, *Virginia,* 306–13; R. E. Byrd to Flood, Jan. 23, 1914, Flood to R. E. Byrd, Jan. 26, 1914, box 70, Flood Papers.

34. Byrd was appointed by the council to complete the term of the late W. H. Smith. *WES,* June 2, 1909.

35. Ibid., July 24, 1907, Dec. 8, 1909, Jan. 5, April 6, 22, May 18, June 15, 1910, April 21, 1915.

36. Interviews with Byrd's sons and Joe and Teresa Massie; Hatch, *Byrds of Virginia,* 411–13.

37. *WES,* Feb. 2, 5, 6, May 11, 1915; R. E. Byrd speech, July 30, 1913, box 424, BP.

38. *WES,* Aug. 3, 27, 30, Oct. 12, 1915.

39. Ibid., Sept. 24, 27, 1915; campaign statement, box 65, BP.

40. HFB to Kingree, Oct. 21, 1915, box 65, BP; HFB to Richard Wright, Sept. 24, 1917, quoted in Hawkes, "Career of Byrd," 21.

41. *WES,* Oct. 12, 26–29, Nov. 1, 3, 6, 1915. Byrd received 3,090 votes; Haldeman, 2,295.

2. The Apprenticeship

1. Hawkes, "Career of Byrd," 22–24; *RTD,* Jan. 15, 1916.

2. Goode, "Distribution and Disposition of Highway Funds in Virginia," 15–25; Willis, "Out of the Mud," 425–27.

3. *RTD,* Jan. 3, 12–16, 19, 20, 26, Feb. 5, 9, March 4, 12, 1916; Hawkes, "Career of Byrd," 30–33.

4. Hawkes, "Career of Byrd," 22–23; *RTD,* Feb. 16, 1958.

5. For Harry's concern about his father's drinking problem, see HFB to Carter Wormeley, July 20, 1922, box 4, Carter Wormeley Papers, Virginia Historical Society.

6. *RTD,* Feb. 10, 19, 25, March 4, 12, 1916. The Mapp Act that implemented prohibition was written by Senator G. Walter Mapp of Accomac with assistance from the Reverend Mr. Cannon; outlawing the manufacture and sale of spiritous liquors inside the state, it permitted residents to acquire a quart of whiskey, a gallon of wine, or three gallons of beer each month from outside the state. Moger, *Virginia,* 313.

7. Kirby, "Westmoreland Davis," 209–15; Kirby, *Davis,* 43; HFB to Ellyson, Aug. 1917, BP.

8. HFB to H. B. Sproul, Nov. 6, 1917, to Joe Bauserman, Nov. 10, 1917, Harry Garfield to HFB, Nov. 6, 1917, box 68, HFB to Governor Henry C. Stuart, May 17, 1917, box 66, BP; Ferrell, "Democratic Party Factionalism," 162; interview with Harry Byrd, Jr.

9. *WES,* Nov. 10, 1917; *RTD,* Nov. 28, 1917; Fuel Administration records in box 68, BP; HFB to Flood, Nov. 21, 1917, box 72, Flood Papers. Byrd's staff of secretaries and bookkeepers were salaried; at the end of the war, he received a commemorative $1 check

for his services as fuel administrator and later was paid a $4 per diem rate for expenses. HFB to Harry Garfield, Feb. 3, 1919, box 68, BP.

10. *WES*, Jan. 19, 1918; *RTD*, Dec. 2, 16, 20, 27, 30, 1917, Jan. 17–22, 1918.

11. Bulletin to local commissioners, May 14, 1918, box 67, BP.

12. Fuel Administration records, box 68; Joe Bauserman to HFB, May 17, 1918, box 65, HFB to Robert Angell, Sept. 30, 1918, to John C. Dillon, Oct. 23, Dec. 9, 1918, other records, box 68, BP.

13. Letters about an officer's commission, box 66, HFB to John Stuart Walker, Sept. 30, 1918, to Reed, Sept. 19, 1918, box 68, BP; Glass to Hal Flood, Sept. 13, 1921, box 169, Carter Glass Papers, UVL; Hawkes, "Career of Byrd," 24.

14. *RTD*, Jan. 11, 16, 24, Feb. 28, March 1, 1918; Hawkes, "Career of Byrd," 34–35; HFB to James Dushare, March 2, 1918, box 66, BP.

15. *RTD*, Jan. 30, Feb. 20, 1918; HFB to Davis, Feb. 12, 1918, box 66, to Directors of Valley Turnpike, Feb. 11, 1918, to William Renalds, Feb. 12, 1918, box 5, to E. D. Newman, March 12, 1918, box 4br, to Joe Bauserman, Feb. 7, 1918, box 65, BP.

16. *RTD*, Jan. 11, 17, 25, Feb. 2, 12, 16, 20, 26, 28, March 5, 11, 1918; Kirby, *Davis*, 79.

17. Cather to HFB, Jan. 14, 1918, Byrd to Cather, Jan. 16, 1918, box 65, BP.

18. HFB to F. E. Clerk, Jan. 5, 1920, box 69, to Mrs. Cora Williams, Feb. 6, 1918, box 66, to C. V. Shoemaker, Sept. 1, 1919, box 67, BP.

19. Kirby, *Davis*, 81–86; *RTD*, March 19–22, 1918.

20. R. E. Byrd to Martin, Jan. 31, 1919, box 72, Flood Papers.

21. HFB to Henry Stuart, Oct. 7, 1918, box 66, to J. N. Brenaman, Jan. 16, 1919, to Harrison, Jan. 18, 1919, box 67, to R. E. Byrd, Feb. 1, 1919, box 423, BP.

22. HFB to William Carson, Feb. 16, 1920, box 69, to Davis, Oct. 16, 1922, Byrd's printed defense, box 79, BP; Davis to HFB, Nov. 2, 1922, Box 82, Westmoreland Davis Papers, UVL.

23. HFB to R. E. Byrd, Aug. 30, 1917, R. E. Byrd to HFB, Oct. 19, 1918, box 423, HFB to Joe Bauserman, Dec. 2, 1918, box 65, to Newman, March 15, 1919, to C. V. Shoemaker, June 6, 1919, box 67; BP; *RTD*, Aug. 6, 1919.

24. HFB to Frank Tavenner, May 29, 1919, C. O'Conor Goolrick to HFB, July 5, 1919, box 67, BP; Kirby, *Davis*, 89–93; *RTD*, Aug. 10, 14, 27–30, Sept. 6, 1919.

25. HFB to T. W. Harrison, Dec. 4, 1919, box 67, BP; T. W. Harrison to HFB, Dec. 6, 1919, box 55, Flood Papers; *RTD*, March 6, 1994.

26. HFB to Smith, Dec. 18, 1919, box 67, BP.

27. Anonymous interview; *RTD*, Feb. 6, 7, 19, 21, March 14, 1920; Flood to J. E. West (copy to Byrd), Feb. 14, 1920, to Mrs. R. E. Byrd, March 15, 1920, box 56, Flood Papers; HFB to Smith, April 26, 1921, box 73, BP. Flood had voted against the suffrage amendment in the House, as had all Virginia Democratic representatives. The lone Republican, Bascom Slemp, had voted for it. In 1952 the General Assembly finally ratified the Nineteenth Amendment. *RTD*, Jan. 17, 1918, March 4, 1990.

28. *RTD*, Jan. 22, Feb. 11, March 11, 1920; Hawkes, "Career of Byrd," 39–40.

29. Kirby, *Davis*, 123–35; Moger, *Virginia*, 324–25.

30. Kirby, *Davis*, 137.

31. Pulley, *Old Virginia Restored*, 83–84, 102–3; Kirby, *Davis*, 140–41, 150–52; Ferrell, *Swanson*, 127–32; Moger, *Virginia*, 222, 292, 317, 325–27.

32. Moger, *Virginia*, 327; Flood to Sam Ferguson, June 17, 1920, box 74, Flood Papers; HFB to Joseph Myers, June 7, 1920, to Willis Robertson, Sept. 30, 1920, box 70, Flood to T. Freeman Epes, Dec. 4, 13, 1920, Claude Kitchin to Flood, Nov. 15, 1920, box 434, BP.

33. Kirby, *Davis*, 153; Willis, "Trinkle: Prelude," 224–25; Willis, "Trinkle and the Virginia Democracy," 68; HFB to Trinkle, Dec. 24, 1920, box 70, to Carroll Menefee, Jan. 24, 1921, box 72, to Logan Fay, Jan. 10, 1921, box 13, R. E. Byrd to HFB, no date, box 423, BP.

34. Kaufman, "Flood," 253–55; Treon, "Flood," 64; Robertson to HFB, Aug. 13, 1921, box 72, BP; Carson to Flood, Aug. 8, 1921, Flood to George Denny, Aug. 23, 1921, Flood to R. E. Byrd, Aug. 11, 1921, HFB to Flood, Aug. 15, 1921, box 72, Flood Papers; Glass to Flood, Sept. 13, 1921, box 169, Glass Papers.

35. Brenaman to HFB, Dec. 13, 1921, HFB to Brenaman, Dec. 14, 27, 1921, Joe Bauserman to HFB, Dec. 15, 1921, box 71, BP; Ferrell, *Swanson*, 136; Ferrell, "Democratic Party Factionalism," 156–57; *RTD*, Feb. 1, 1922.

3. Roads to Richmond

1. HFB to Joe Funkhouser, April 8, 1921, box 13, BP. A memo in Westmoreland Davis's papers states that Byrd voted for bonds for city improvements, county roads, and schools 186 times when he was in the senate. Box 102, Davis Papers.

2. Miller, "Giving Them Fits," *Time* 80 (Aug. 17, 1962): 11.

3. Interview with Harry Byrd, Jr.; HFB to Ferguson, Oct. 23, 1920, box 69, BP.

4. HFB to Bauserman, Oct. 23, 1920, box 69, to Joe Funkhouser, May 3, 1921, to George Coleman, Sept. 9, Oct. 12, 1920, box 69, to Wade Massie, Oct. 16, 1920, box 70, to Hal Flood, April 28, 1921, box 71, BP; Hawkes, "Career of Byrd," 35–42; Willis, "Trinkle and the Virginia Democracy," 96; Willis, "Out of the Mud," 428–29.

5. Kirby, *Davis*, 105–22; Ferrell, *Swanson*, 139; *Virginia Farm Statistics* 15 (1949): 9–20, 150; *Virginia Farm Economics*, no. 42 (July 1942): 688.

6. HFB to Flood, April 28, 1921, to D. H. Barger, Dec. 15, 1921, box 71, Trinkle to HFB, Nov. 21, 1921, HFB to Trinkle, Dec. 6, 31, 1921, box 73, BP; Willis, "Out of the Mud," 430; Hawkes, "Career of Byrd," 45–46; *RTD*, Jan. 9, 15, 18, 20, Feb. 2, 1922.

7. For Byrd's belief that fear of Coleman kept some witnesses away, see HFB to D. H. Barger, April 14, 1922, box 74, BP.

8. *RTD*, Jan. 14, 19, 26, Feb. 4, 10, 14, 17, 21, 1922.

9. Willis, "Out of the Mud," 431–34; Hawkes, "Career of Byrd," 50; *RTD*, Feb. 16, 23, 24, March 4, 1922.

10. Ibid., Jan. 13, Feb. 18, 25, 28, March 8, 11–13, 1922.

11. C. C. Louderback to HFB, April 12, 1922, box 76, HFB to Trinkle, March 21, 27, 31, May 8, 1922, Trinkle to HFB, March 24, 1922, box 77, HFB to R. E. Byrd, June 24, 1922, box 423, BP, Willis, "Out of the Mud," 430, 434.

12. Trinkle to HFB, March 24, 1922, box 77; HFB to Joe Bauserman, March 21, 1922, box 74, BP.

13. HFB to Swanson, May 1, 1922, box 77; HFB to Massie, Dec. 21, 1921, box 72, April 17, 1922, box 76, Sam Ferguson to HFB, April 28, May 15, 1922, box 75, BP; Willis, "Out of the Mud," 434–36; Ferrell, *Swanson*, 136–37. On appointments of Massie and Sproul, see correspondence in box 77, BP.

14. Joel Flood to HFB, March 31, 1922, HFB to Joel Flood, April 11, 1922, box 71, Lester Arnold to HFB, Aug. 30, 1922, box 435, HFB to R. Gray Williams, president of the Handley Schools Board, Dec. 26, 1922, box 71, materials, box 71, HFB to Richard Byrd, Jr., March 31, 1921, box 425, R. E. Byrd to Collector of Internal Revenue, March 6, 1924,

HFB to Internal Revenue Commissioner, March 7, 1925, box 422, BP; interview with Harry Byrd, Jr.

15. Associated Press to HFB, April 16, 1919, box 66; HFB to George Conrad, June 12, 1922, box 66; to Crown, Sept. 24, 1925, box 82, materials, box 17br, BP.

16. Hawkes, "Harry F. Byrd," 236; Hawkes, "Career of Byrd," 51–53; Moger, *Virginia*, 331; Ferrell, *Swanson*, 138; HFB to Joseph Button, Dec. 15, 1921, box 71, J. N. Brenaman to HFB, April 1922, HFB to William T. Reed, June 8, 1922, to C. C. Carlin, Dec. 23, 1922, box 74, to James Hayes, Aug. 22, 25, 1922, box 76, BP.

17. Election correspondence and reports, boxes 69, 74, and 77, BP; Hawkes, "Career of Byrd," 53; Hathorn, "Slemp," 250.

18. Fry, "Peery: Byrd Regular," 263.

19. Combs to Ervin, April 27, 1922, box 1, E. R. Combs Papers, UVL; to HFB, Oct. 12, 1922, box 74, BP.

20. HFB to Morison, May 11, 1922, HFB to Hayes, Aug. 22, Oct. 9, 1922, box 76, BP.

21. Fry and Tarter, "Redemption of the Fighting Ninth," 359–68.

22. HFB to Peery, Nov. 10, Dec. 22, 1922, box 76, Combs to HFB, June 22, 1922, HFB to Combs, July 5, 1922, box 74, to S. A. Minter, Nov. 14, 1922, letters, box 76, BP; HFB to Combs, Nov. 10, 14, 1922, box 11, Combs Papers.

23. Willis, "Out of the Mud," 437–39; HFB to Ozlin, Sept. 9, Nov. 13, 1922, Ozlin to HFB, Sept. 11, Nov. 21, 1922, HFB to Epes, Oct. 24, Dec. 8, 12, 1922, box 79, BP.

24. Ferguson to HFB, Jan. 15, 1923, HFB to Swanson, Jan. 15, 1923, box 78, to Epes, Jan. 6, 1923, Epes to Ferguson, Jan. 6, 1923, box 79, BP; *RTD*, March 1, 1923; Hawkes, "Career of Byrd," 57–58.

25. *RTD*, Feb. 25, 28, March 1, 2, 9, 13–19, 22–24, 1923; Hawkes, "Career of Byrd," 60–61; Willis, "Out of the Mud," 442–44.

26. HFB to Trinkle, March 27, Aug. 14, 1923, Trinkle to HFB, May 1, 1923, Byrd circular, April 4, 1923, box 13, Trinkle Executive Papers, LV; HFB to Combs, Sept. 24, 1923, box 11, Combs Papers.

27. Willis, "Out of the Mud," 444–48; Hawkes, "Career of Byrd," 61–62; HFB to Trinkle, May 10, 1923, box 13, Trinkle Executive Papers; HFB to Combs, Sept. 22, 1923, box 2, Combs Papers.

28. Byrd address, *Virginia Record*, Sept. 1956; HFB to Trinkle, Nov. 21, 1923, box 13, Trinkle Executive Papers; Willis, "Out of the Mud," 448–51; Hawkes, "Career of Byrd," 63–64.

29. Ferrell, *Swanson*, 139; E. R. Combs to George Peery, Nov. 20, 1923, box 2, Combs Papers; Claude Swanson to W. E. Carson, Feb. 7, 1923, box 79, HFB to Beverley, Jan. 13, 1923, box 78, BP.

30. Ozlin to HFB, Nov. 19, 1923, HFB to Ozlin, Nov. 21, 1923, box 78, BP; HFB to Carter Wormeley, Aug. 23, 1923, box 4, Carter Wormeley Papers; HFB to Trinkle, June 2, 1923, box 13, Trinkle Executive Papers; *RTD*, Jan. 9, March 22, 1924.

31. HFB to Trinkle, Nov. 21, 1923, box 13, Trinkle Executive Papers; Epes to HFB, Nov. 25, 1923, box 79, BP.

32. Letters to legislators, HFB to Ferguson, Nov. 14, 1923, Ozlin to HFB, Nov. 19, 1923, HFB to Ozlin, Nov. 23, 1923, to J. R. Horsley, Nov. 27, 1923, to R. E. Byrd, Dec. 27, 1923, box 78, BP.

33. *RTD*, Jan. 17–23, 1924; Willis, "Trinkle and the Virginia Democracy," 134–43; Willis, "Trinkle: Prelude," 230; HFB to Walter Addison, Feb. 2, 1924, box 81, BP.

34. Treadway, "Sarah Lee Fain."

35. *RTD*, Jan. 9, Feb. 1, March 1, 3, 8, 9, 17, 1924; Hawkes, "Career of Byrd," 64–66.

36. Willis, "Trinkle and the Virginia Democracy," 150–52; HFB to Swanson, Oct. 6, 1924, box 80, Willis Robertson to HFB, Dec. 30, 1925, box 90, BP.

37. Lists in boxes 134 and 135, letters, boxes 76, 77, 78, HFB to Charles Callahan, Oct. 22, 1934, box 133, to H. H. Watson, May 22, 1923, to Thomas Lion, July 5, 1923, box 78, to E. Lee Trinkle, Dec. 22, 1922, box 79, to Robert Sultice, Aug. 23, 1924, statement on voting Republican, July 27, 1924, box 80, BP.

38. HFB to Paschal Reeves, March 12, 1958, box 249, BP; Heinemann, *Depression and New Deal in Virginia*, 135, Moger, *Virginia*, 334, 351–53.

39. Interview with Mills E. Godwin, Jr.; Moger, *Virginia*, 360–61.

40. *RTD*, June 10–12, 1924. Richard Byrd had written an anti-McAdoo editorial for the *Evening Star*, which Glass feared would turn the McAdoo people against him. The Byrds may have opposed McAdoo because he had had a minor falling out with President Wilson during the 1920 campaign. Harry also disapproved of his administration of the railroads during the war. Glass to R. L. Ailworth, June 4, 1924, box 1, Glass Papers; Ferrell, *Swanson*, 140.

41. Murray, *The 103rd Ballot*, 191.

42. Glass to Henry Stuart, July 9, 1923, box 145, to R. L. Ailworth, June 2, 1924, box 1, Glass Papers; *RTD*, June 24, July 1–11, 1924.

43. Harbaugh, *Lawyer's Lawyer*, 211–16.

44. Ferrell, *Swanson*, 140; Glass to HFB, July 22, 1924, Glass to Dr. F. S. Hope, July 20, 1925, HFB to Glass, Aug. 1, 1924, box 1, Glass Papers.

45. John Hopkins Hall to HFB, Nov. 8, 1924, HFB to Adams, Oct. 18, 1924, box 81, BP.

46. Letters, box 80, Combs to HFB, Oct. 18, 1924, box 81, BP; Combs to Bowden, March 17, 1925, box 3, May 28, 1925, to Peery, May 28, 1925, Bowden to Combs, June 24, 1925, box 5, Combs Papers.

47. HFB to Swanson, Sept. 19, 1924, box 80, to William Reed, Nov. 5, 1924, box 81, BP.

48. HFB to Douglas Southall Freeman, May 15, 1951, box 104, Douglas Southall Freeman Papers, Library of Congress.

49. HFB to William Carson, Jan. 31, 1923, Carson to HFB, Feb. 14, 1923, box 78, HFB to R. E. Byrd, Nov. 23, 1923, box 423, BP. When Byrd asked Carson to sound out Senator Swanson about his candidacy, he cautioned, "Of course state that you are doing it at the request of a number of the people throughout the Valley."

50. HFB to W. E. Carson, Nov. 12, 1924, box 81, Reed to HFB, Nov. 10, 1924, HFB to Reed, Nov. 12, 1924, box 88, BP.

51. *RTD*, Nov. 23, 25, 1924; biographical sketch, box 11, Combs Papers.

52. *RTD*, March 6, April 22, 1925; HFB to Combs, Nov. 20, 1924, box 11, Jan. 16, 1925, box 12, Combs Papers; Horan, "Will Carson," 392–94.

53. HFB to George Keezell, Dec. 29, 1924, sec. 104, Henry A. Wise Family Papers, Virginia Historical Society.

54. *RTD*, Dec. 13, 1924, Feb. 12, March 6, 11, 27, June 13, 1925; Moger, *Virginia*, 339–40.

55. Havilah Babcock to HFB, April 17, 1925, box 88, HFB to Bryan, Jan. 12, 1925, Bryan to HFB, Jan. 20, 1925, BP.

56. HFB to R. E. Byrd, Oct. 20, 1922, box 79, to Havilah Babcock, April 18, 1925, box 88, to William Reed, Dec. 16, 1931, box 108, BP; Gray Williams to Reed, July 5, 1928, box 23, William T. Reed Family Papers, Virginia Historical Society.

57. *RTD*, Jan. 27, Feb. 1, March 27, April 3, 10, 27, 1925; Hawkes, "Career of Byrd," 68–71.

58. *RTD*, April 22, May 12, 16, 19, June 4, 10, 16, 23, July 2, 9–14, 22, 1925; Hawkes, "Career of Byrd," 71–73; HFB to Otho Mears, Dec. 4, 1924, box 84, to Louis Epes, June 11, 1925, box 88, BP.

59. *RTD*, July 8–18, 1925; HFB to F. F. Lewis, June 17, 1925, box 83, to Bernard Jones, June 25, 1925, box 88, BP; Hawkes, "Career of Byrd," 71–73.

60. *RTD*, May 26, July 3, 23, 24, 1925; campaign materials, boxes 84–88, BP.

61. *RTD*, May 17, July 25, Aug. 2, 4, 1925; Combs to HFB, May 1, 30, 1925, box 12, to C. W. Bondurant, June 11, 1925, to R. W. Ervine, April 24, 1925, box 5, Combs Papers; A. Plummer Pannill to HFB, June 18, 1925, HFB to Pannill, June 19, 1925, to H. B. McLemore, June 17, 1925, box 86, BP.

62. Interview with Harry Byrd, Jr.

63. Campaign materials, box 86, Rawlett to HFB, March 10, 1925, box 87, Hall to F. S. Hope, July 22, 1925, Hall to HFB, May 7, 1925, box 88, Byrd to Miller, July 7, 1925, box 86, Leon Beardsley to HFB, May 15, 1925, HFB to Beardsley, May 18, 1925, box 88, BP.

64. HFB to Kern, July 29, 1925, Munford to HFB, June 29, 1925, box 88, Lineweaver to HFB, July 23, 1925, box 86, BP.

65. *RTD*, Aug. 5, Oct. 6, 1925; *WES*, Aug. 5, 7, 1925.

66. HFB to J. Murray Hooker, Sept. 23, 1925, box 89, to Combs, Sept. 21, 1925, box 82, Ozlin to HFB, Sept. 11, 1925, HFB to Morrissett, Sept. 18, 22, 1925, W. D. Jenkins to HFB, Nov. 13, 1925, box 90, E. Warren Wall to HFB, Oct. 6, 31, 1925, HFB to H. C. Stuart, Oct. 5, 1925, box 91, BP.

67. *RTD*, Sept. 6, 20, 22, 1925; Hooker to HFB, Sept. 21, 1925, box 89, BP.

68. HFB to Combs, Oct. 8, 1925, box 82, to Hooker, Oct. 5, 1925, box 89, BP.

69. HFB to R. E. Byrd, April 6, 1920, and other letters, box 423, BP; HFB to Reed, Oct. 28, 1925, box 4, Reed Papers; *RTD*, Jan. 25, Feb. 3, 1922, Oct. 20, 24, 25, 1925; *WES*, Oct. 24, 1925. The cause of Richard Byrd's death was given as "complications of diseases"; it may have been attributable to liver damage caused by his heavy drinking, or it may have been a result of exhaustion produced by the strenuous primary campaign.

70. *RTD*, Oct. 31, Nov. 1, 5, 1925; Eva Bell to HFB, Nov. 11, 1925, box 82, HFB to his mother, Nov. 4, 1925, box 430, BP. Coincidentally, forty-one years later, Byrd would die on the eve of Harry Jr.'s first election to the United States Senate.

71. *RTD*, Nov. 10, Dec. 16, 21, 22, 1925; HFB to Hugh Sproul, Nov. 27, 1925, box 91, to Louis Epes, Nov. 9, 1925, box 83, Adams to HFB, Nov. 30, 1925, box 82, HFB to Hutchinson, Dec. 23, 1925, box 89, other letters, boxes 90, 91, BP.

4. Chief Executive

1. *RTD*, Dec. 25, 1925, Jan. 5, 1926; Richmond *News Leader*, Feb. 26, 1926.

2. HFB to H. C. Stuart, Oct. 5, 1925, box 91, to E. R. Combs, Dec. 1, 1925, box 82, BP; HFB to J. P. Buchanan, Nov. 13, 1925, box 61, BEP.

3. HFB to Combs, Nov. 2, 1925, box 12, Ferguson to Combs, Nov. 11, 1925, box 6, Combs Papers; Ozlin to HFB, Sept. 11, 1925, Nov. 14, 1925, box 90, BP; *RTD*, Jan. 13, 1926.

4. Ibid., Jan. 5, 1926; Seale, *Virginia's Executive Mansion*, 136–39.

5. Mrs. Byrd arrived for the inaugural ceremonies but left the next evening to be with her father, who died three weeks later; Sittie would also lose her mother in April 1928. *RTD*, Jan. 30, Feb. 1, Feb. 22, 1926, May 1, 1928.

6. The farmer thought high office would turn Byrd's head and cause him to reject his rural roots; "I'll bet you'll wear a stovepipe hat in the inaugural parade," he told Byrd. Dabney, "What We Think of Senator Byrd's Machine."

7. *RTD*, Feb. 2, Jan. 27, 30, 1926; Reed to Byrd, Jan. 19, 1926, box 4, Reed Papers.

8. *RTD*, Feb. 2, 1926; Hawkes, "Career of Byrd," 79–82; McDonald Lee to HFB, Feb. 2, 1926, box 47, BEP.

9. *RTD*, Dec. 21, 1925, Jan. 18, Feb. 3, 1926; Hawkes, "Career of Byrd," 82–85, 91; HFB to Junius Fishburne, Nov. 9, 1925, box 83, BP.

10. *RTD*, Feb. 4, 1926; Spicer, "Political Chief," 101.

11. Hawkes, "Career of Byrd," 86. See also Spicer, "Political Chief," 95, 98; Lipson, *American Governor,* 64.

12. Lipson, *American Governor,* 88; Hawkes, "Career of Byrd," 87–90; *RTD*, Feb. 4, 1926.

13. Ibid., Feb. 9, March 14, 20, 1926; Hawkes, "Career of Byrd," 91–95; Combs to J. N. Bosang, Jan. 5, 1926, to C. J. Duke, Feb. 16, 1926, box 12, Combs Papers.

14. *RTD*, Feb. 8, 11, 12, March 14, 16, 1926; Hawkes, "Career of Byrd," 93–96.

15. *RTD*, Jan. 15, March 13, 1926.

16. Sherman, "'Last Stand'"; Sherman, "'Teachings at Hampton.'"

17. Ibid., 294, 295, 299; *RTD*, March 14, 1926.

18. Suggs, *P. B. Young,* 61, 96; HFB to Tunstall, Nov. 29, 1926, box 16, BEP. A United States District Court judge in 1929 ruled that the Virginia primary law excluding blacks from voting was unconstitutional and blacks could no longer be excluded from the Democratic primary. The decision was not appealed, and one barrier to black voting was removed. *RTD*, June 6, 1929.

19. Dabney, "Americans We Like," 632–34; letters, box 24, BEP; Lipson, *American Governor,* 147.

20. Adams to HFB, Aug. 13, 1926, box 65, HFB to Shirley, April 21, June 30, 1926, to Hugh Pierce, April 21, 1926, box 24, to Wade Massie, March 4, 1927, to Cecil Connor, March 2, 1927, box 25, BEP; HFB to R. E. Byrd, May 29, 1922, box 423, BP.

21. *RTD*, March 20, May 13, June 4, July 29, 1926; HFB to Willis Robertson, April 9, 1926, to J. T. Penn, April 4, 1926, to President Calvin Coolidge, June 1, 19, 1926, to Governor Alvan Fuller of Massachusetts, June 14, 1926, box 19, BEP; Hawkes, "Career of Byrd," 98–99; Dabney, "Americans We Like."

22. Ibid.; *RTD*, July 29, Aug. 1–3, Sept. 1, 2, 1926, Jan. 21, March 22, April 10, 1927; Adams to HFB, Aug. 13, 1926, HFB to John Saunders, Sept. 1, 1926, box 65, BEP.

23. *RTD*, June 18, Oct. 6, 9, 1926.

24. Ibid., March 23, April 1, May 19, June 15, 16, 1926; Carl Gunderson, Governor of South Dakota, to HFB, April 12, 1926, HFB to Gulick, May 1, 1926, Gulick to HFB, May 3, 4, 1926, box 60, BEP.

25. Materials, box 51, BEP; *RTD*, April 25, June 12, 1926.

26. Ibid., June 26, 1926; Hawkes, "Career of Byrd," 104–6.

27. Fry, "Senior Advisor to the Democratic 'Organization'"; HFB to Reed, Oct. 28, 1925, Reed to HFB, Jan. 4, 1926, box 4, Reed Papers; HFB to Williams, April 27, 1926, box 81, BEP.

28. HFB to Reed, Aug. 6, 1926, Reed to HFB, Sept. 25, Oct. 23, 1926, box 4, to Gulick, June 30, Oct. 23, 1926, box 11, Reed Papers.

29. *RTD*, April 11, May 18, 19, 23, 1926.

30. Ibid., April 16, May 15, 16, June 14, 18, July 5, Oct. 15, Nov. 6, 1926.

31. HFB to George Orlady, June 1, 1926, James Davis to Mrs. E. C. Brooks, May 14, 1926, box 6, papers, box 7, BEP; *RTD*, April 20, 1926.

32. HFB to Combs, Sept. 17, 1926, box 1, BEP; *RTD*, April 21, May 6, 1926, April 29, 1927, May 3, 1928, April 19, 1929.

33. Interviews with Byrd's sons; *RTD*, Dec. 21, 25, 1926, Feb. 9, 1927; HFB to Gray Williams, Dec. 23, 1926, box 12, to Mrs. F. C. Beverley, May 12, 1926, July 25, 1927, box 70, BEP.

34. Rodgers, *Beyond the Barrier*, 23–24; *RTD*, Aug. 24, Sept. 24, 1926.

35. Hoyt, *Last Explorer*, 20–31; Richard Byrd to HFB, Aug. 11, 1919, box 425, BP.

36. Richard Byrd to HFB, March 31, 1925, box 425, BP; Hatch, *Byrds of Virginia*, 282.

37. There remains some doubt whether Byrd and Bennett actually made the Pole. Rodgers, *Beyond the Barrier*, 8, 291, 294.

38. Ibid., 1–9; *RTD*, May 10, June 24, 25, 1926; HFB to Richard Byrd, April 30, 1930, box 425, BP.

39. *RTD*, July 22–24, Aug. 16, 31, Sept. 10, 18, 25, 27, 1926; Hawkes, "Career of Byrd," 137.

40. *RTD*, Sept. 13–15, 24, 28, 29, Oct. 12, Nov. 10, 1926; Henderson to HFB, Sept. 14, 1926, Feb. 8, 1927, HFB to Henderson, Feb. 3, 15, 1927, box 15, BEP.

41. *RTD*, Jan. 1–7, 25, 1927; J. Vaughan Gary to HFB, Dec. 7, 1926, HFB to Walter L. Kerr, Jan. 22, 1927, box 21, BEP.

42. See Commission on Simplification and Economy folder, Reed Papers; Fry, "Reed," 455–56; *RTD*, Jan. 21, 23, 27, 1927.

43. *RTD*, Feb. 4, 13, 14, March 8, 1927; memo to Byrd, Jan. 10, 1927, box 52, BEP; Hawkes, "Career of Byrd," 107–8; Lipson, *American Governor*, 90–109; Fry, "Reed," 456.

44. HFB to Reed, March 4, 1927, box 60, BEP; Reed to Gulick, Feb. 19, 1927, Gulick to Reed, Jan. 5, 1927, box 11, Reed Papers. The final cost of the bureau's work was over $19,000, exceeding its estimate by $3,000 but still under the appropriated amount of $25,000.

45. HFB to Robert Hughes, Jan. 17, 1927, to William M. Fletcher, Feb. 1, 1927, box 12, to Prentis, Feb. 14, 1927, box 52, BEP.

46. *RTD*, Jan. 7, Feb. 15, 18, 23, 1927.

47. Ibid., Feb. 23, 1927; Hawkes, "Career of Byrd," 111.

48. HFB to Andrew Montague, March 1, 1927, box 52, Swanson to HFB, March 8, 1927, box 53, BEP; see folder on Commission on Simplification and Economy, Reed Papers; *RTD*, March 10, 11, 16, 1927.

49. Ibid., March 17, 19, 29, April 1, 2, 8, 1927; HFB to J. Murray Hooker, April 19, 1927, box 52, BEP.

50. Hawkes, "Career of Byrd," 115–16; *RTD*, March 3–9, 23, 29, April 1–9, 1927; Reed to D. H. Barger, April 12, 1927, box 2, Gulick to Reed, April 2, 1927, box 11, Reed papers.

51. *RTD*, March 28, April 10, 19, 1927; Reed to Gulick, Nov. 9, 1926, box 11, HFB to Reed, June 10, 1927, box 4, Reed Papers.

52. HFB to Douglas Freeman, May 5, 1927, box 9, Freeman Papers; papers, box 25, BEP; *RTD*, Feb. 17, April 8, 29, May 5, 29, June 3, July 13, Nov. 10, 1927; Hawkes, "Career of Byrd," 124–25; Goode, "Highways," 86.

53. *RTD*, April 17, 25, 27, May 6, 9, 12, 21, 22, June 10, 12, 15, 30, July 1, 18, 1927; Richard Byrd to HFB, May 14, 1927, box 425, BP.

54. Newsclippings, BP; *RTD*, Aug. 20, 31, Sept. 9, Dec. 3, 1927; Charles McDowell, Jr., "The Governor Went by Blimp," ibid., Sept. 15, 1963.

55. HFB to Du Pont, June 7, 1929, box 14, BEP; *RTD*, Sept. 30, Oct. 1, 1927, Aug. 2, 1928; Sam Ungerleider to HFB, Feb. 6, 1958, scrapbooks, box 94, BP.

56. *RTD*, Sept. 10, 16, Oct. 15, 16, 18, Dec. 1, 3, 1927; HFB to William J. Fields, Governor of Kentucky, Dec. 1, 1927, box 43, BEP.

57. Combs to HFB, April 27, 1926, HFB to Combs, July 22, 1926, to Combs, no date, box 12, Combs Papers; *RTD*, Oct. 2, 7, 1927; HFB to Douglas Freeman, Oct. 4, 1927, box 9, Freeman Papers; Weisiger, "Combs," 37–44.

58. *RTD*, Dec. 6, 1927.

59. Letters, box 49, Carter Glass to HFB, Dec. 12, 1927, box 12, Tuck to HFB, Dec. 10, 1927, box 75, BEP.

60. *RTD*, Jan. 12, 13, 17, 1928; Hawkes, "Career of Byrd," 120–22.

61. *RTD*, Dec. 31, 1927; Hawkes, "Career of Byrd," 127–29.

62. *RTD*, Jan. 17, 1928; HFB to General J. A. Lejeune, Feb. 27, 1930, box 98, BP; W. H. Cocke to HFB, Jan. 23, 1928, box 20, BEP; HFB to Combs, Jan. 4, 1926, Combs to HFB, Jan. 7, 1926, box 12, Combs Papers.

63. *RTD*, Jan. 17, March 1, 7, 11, 1928; Hawkes, "Career of Byrd," 127–30.

64. Walton, "Analysis of Expenditures for Public Schools in Virginia from 1909 to 1939," 135.

65. *RTD*, Jan. 17, 1928, Jan. 1, 1929.

66. Jaffe to HFB, Aug. 30, 1926, Oct. 26, Dec. 1, 1927, Feb. 3, 1928, HFB to Jaffe, Oct. 31, 1927, to Edwin Alderman, Jan. 28, 1929, James S. Barron to Alderman, Jan. 25, 1929, box 2b, Louis Jaffe Papers, UVL; HFB to Edith K. Wriggins, Nov. 3, 1934, box 154, BP; Brundage, *Lynching in the New South*, 187–89.

67. Reed to HFB, Sept. 26, 1927, HFB to Reed, Sept. 27, 1927, box 4, Luther Gulick to Reed, Sept. 23, 1927, box 11, Reed Papers; Hawkes, "Career of Byrd," 132–35; HFB to Gulick, Feb. 3, 1928, box 46, to Gee, Jan. 24, 1929, BEP.

68. Hawkes, "Career of Byrd," 132–36; F. H. Combs to E. E. Smith, July 23, 1928, C. Lee Moore to HFB, May 29, 1929, box 14, BEP; *RTD*, Feb. 1, 1928; Egger, "Governmental Reorganization and Intergovernmental Relations," 183; Reed to HFB, March 7, 1930, box 99, BP. Not surprisingly, an audit of local accounts done after Byrd left office revealed that thirty-nine of one hundred county treasurers were deficient in their accounts. Pate, "State Supervision of Local Fiscal Officers," 1005–6.

69. *RTD*, Feb. 3, 9, 14, 17, 25, March 6, 9, 11, 1928; Freeman to Bryan, March 8, 1928, box 9, Freeman Papers.

70. *RTD*, March 9, 11, 13, 18, 1928.

71. Ibid., July 27, Aug. 7, Dec. 11, 1927; Door, "The Man Who Set Virginia One Hundred Years Ahead," 52; HFB to Douglas Gordon, March 21, 1928, to local officials, March 28, 1928, box 20, articles in boxes 20 and 46, BEP.

72. Reed to Allen, March 15, 1927, box 1, Reed Papers.

73. *RTD*, March 6, May 10, 1928; HFB to H. P. Brittain, May 24, 1928, box 12, BEP.

74. *RTD*, March 15, 25, April 1, 15, 19, 24, 28, May 6, June 1, 1928; Peter Saunders to Suffolk *News Herald*, April 23, 1928, box 1, BEP; Hawkes, "Career of Byrd," 143–44.

75. *RTD*, March 17, May 1, June 3, 1928; Hawkes, "Career of Byrd," 142; Byrd statement, June 3, 1928, box 1, BEP.

76. *RTD*, May 24, 25, 30, June 8, 9, 1928; see also Alleghany Klan no. 49 to HFB, June 5, 1928, box 52, BEP.

77. *RTD*, May 30, June 10, 17, 18, 20–22, 30, 1928; Hawkes, "Career of Byrd," 141–44.

78. Shirley to HFB, June 21, 1928, box 52, HFB to Robert H. Tucker, July 19, 1928, box 81, BEP.

5. "Rum, Romanism, and Rebellion"

1. Hawkes, "Career of Byrd," 145–46; *RTD*, Jan. 1, 15, 1928.

2. Ibid., Oct. 15, Dec. 29, 30, 1927, Jan. 4, 10, 1928.

3. *Ibid.*, Jan. 14–18, 1928. A seafood commission created by the assembly in 1927 recommended a new survey and a tax on oysters that would fund replenishment of the public rocks. Hawkes, "Career of Byrd," 147–49.

4. *RTD*, Jan. 4, 12, 30, Feb. 3, 5–10, 21, June 21, Sept. 15, 17, 20, 23, Oct. 10, 1929, Jan. 9, 1930; Charles Smith to HFB, Feb. 7, 1929, Catesby G. Jones to Harry Houston, Sept. 10, 1929, HFB to Judge Claggett B. Jones, Sept. 11, 1929, to Adjutant General, U.S. Army, Sept. 13, 1929, box 17, BEP; Hawkes, "Career of Byrd," 145–49.

5. *RTD*, Aug. 31, 1928, April 16, Aug. 27, 1929; HFB to J. M. Doran, Feb. 27, 1929, box 49, to L. T. Christian, May 17, 1927, box 48, BEP. A new system of corrections and a parole system would not be adopted until 1942.

6. *RTD*, April 30, 1926, April 15, 1927, June 1, 1929; E. G. Dodson to HFB, Sept. 28, 1926, C. Lee Moore to HFB, May 29, 1929, box 14, BEP.

7. HFB to Robertson, May 23, 1928, box 31, BEP; Robertson to HFB, Dec. 14, 1931, box 108, BP.

8. HFB to R. E. Byrd, July 7, 1922, box 423, BP.

9. Simmons, "Establishment of Shenandoah National Park," 387–93; *RTD*, Dec. 14, 1924, Jan. 20, Sept. 1, 1925.

10. Simmons, "Establishment of Shenandoah National Park," 393–94; *RTD*, Jan. 15, 1926.

11. Quoted in Horan, "Will Carson," 398.

12. Carson to HFB, Sept. 9, 1927, Jan. 21, 1929, box 9, BEP; Carson to HFB, March 15, 1930, box 93, BP; *RTD*, Feb. 16, 1926, Aug. 18, Sept. 13, 1929; Simmons, "Establishment of Shenandoah National Park," 395–98, 404; Simmons, "Creation of Shenandoah National Park," 39–58, 64–88; Horan, "Will Carson," 397–99, 402–3.

13. Horan, "Will Carson," 395–97; minutes of commission meetings, boxes 8–10, BEP. Although Byrd did not initiate the restoration of Williamsburg, he had several contacts with John D. Rockefeller, Jr., in 1926 and 1927 and undoubtedly encouraged his effort. *RTD*, April 2, 1926, Dec. 10, 1927, June 13, 1928.

14. HFB to Carson, Oct. 11, 1929, box 10, BEP; Carson to HFB, Oct. 17, 1929, HFB to Carson, Jan. 14, 1930, box 93, BP.

15. HFB to Carson, Feb. 12, March 5, 1930; Carson to HFB, March 3, 1930, box 93, Ozlin to HFB, Feb. 13, March 3, 1930, box 99, BP; Horan, "Will Carson," 406–15; see also E. Griffith Dodson Papers, LV.

16. *RTD*, June 25, 29, 30, 1928; Ferrell, *Swanson*, 145–46; Dabney, *Dry Messiah*, 177–79; Davenport, "Virginia Reel," 12.

17. *RTD*, July 1, 18, 1928; Hooker to Robinson, July 19, 1928, box 417, Glass Papers. Governor Byrd had been mentioned for the vice-presidency, but Senator Robinson of Arkansas was nominated.

18. *RTD*, July 12, 20, Aug. 5, 1928; Smith and Beasley, *Glass,* 283; Sweeney, "Campaign of 1928," 408–9.

19. Davenport, "Virginia Reel"; Smith to HFB, Aug. 13, 1928, scrapbooks, BP; Glass to HFB, Aug. 16, 1928, box 1, Glass Papers.

20. Sweeney, "Campaign of 1928," 409–10; Dabney, *Dry Messiah,* 179.

21. *RTD*, Aug. 24, Sept. 30, 1928; Sweeney, "Campaign of 1928," 414–15.

22. *RTD*, Oct. 1, 8, Nov. 2, 3, 1928; Sweeney, "Campaign of 1928," 419–20, 424; HFB to Reed, undated, box 4, Reed Papers.

23. *RTD*, Sept. 26, Oct. 2, 7, 12, 16, 19, Nov. 1, 4, 1928; Sweeney, "Campaign of 1928," 415–25.

24. *RTD*, Nov. 7, 8, 1928.

25. Jaffe to HFB, Jan. 1, 1929, box 2b, Jaffe Papers.

26. Sweeney, "Campaign of 1928," 426–27; HFB to H. F. Hutcheson, May 23, 1931, box 106, BP; Glass to Bernard Baruch, Nov. 8, 1928, box 1, Glass Papers.

27. HFB to Douglas Freeman, Nov. 9, 1928, box 9, Freeman Papers.

28. HFB to Glass, Nov. 18, 26, 1928, box 250, Glass Papers; Hopewell, "Outsider Looking In," 145; Tuck to HFB, Nov. 7, 1928, scrapbooks, BP; Dabney, *Dry Messiah,* 213.

29. RTD, Jan. 5, 1929; Heinemann, *Depression and New Deal,* 8–9; Hawkes, "Career of Byrd," 131–32; see also Hurlburt, "Significant Trends in Virginia Agriculture."

30. *RTD*, Jan. 13, Feb. 16, Dec. 28, 1929, Jan. 9, 1930; papers, box 2, HFB to Stuart Moffett, Feb. 28, 1929, box 12, BEP.

31. *RTD*, Feb. 1, 1929; Latimer, "Virginia Politics, 1950–60," 30–31; see also Sabato, *Democratic Party Primary,* 40–41.

32. *RTD*, Feb. 1, 2, 6, 1929; Dabney, *Dry Messiah,* 192–94, 213.

33. Pollard to HFB, Aug. 17, 1925, March 26, 1926, folder 141, John Garland Pollard Papers, College of William and Mary Library; Hopewell, "Pollard," 247–53; Hopewell, "Outsider Looking In," 110, 116, 153; Weisiger, "Combs," 48; Hall, "Campaign of 1929," 280–83; *RTD*, March 3, 1929.

34. *RTD*, March and April 1929, July 30, 1929; Ferrell, *Swanson,* 148; Hall, "Campaign of 1929," 284; Hatch, *Byrds of Virginia,* 433; Hopewell, "Outsider Looking In," 152–55; HFB to Mrs. Charles Duke, Jan. 11, 1960, box 243, BP; Pollard to Glass, May 7, 1929, box 105, Glass Papers.

35. Hall, "Campaign of 1929," 286; Hawkes, "Career of Byrd," 154–56; Dabney, *Dry Messiah,* 194–95.

36. *RTD*, June 18, July 2, 6, 11, 12, 17, 1929; Hall, "Campaign of 1929," 292–96; Hawkes, "Career of Byrd," 160.

37. Hall, "Campaign of 1929," 285–91; Hopewell, "Outsider Looking In," 172–73; *RTD*, May 2, June 19, 27, 1929.

38. Hall, "Campaign of 1929," 290–91; Dabney, *Dry Messiah,* 195–212; Sweeney, "Campaign of 1928," 430. For a kindlier view of Cannon, see Hohner, "Dry Messiah Revisited."

39. *RTD*, Aug. 3, Sept. 14, 19, Oct. 7, 8, 22, 26, 28, 1929; Hall, "Campaign of 1929," 296–300; Hopewell, "Pollard," 253.

40. *RTD*, June 29, Sept. 18, 20, Oct. 3, 5, 15, 24, 29, 1929; Hall, "Campaign of 1929," 298–300.

41. *RTD*, Nov. 6, 7, 1929; Hall, "Campaign of 1929," 301; Hopewell, "Outsider Looking In," 213–14.

42. *RTD*, May 19, July 18, 1929; papers in boxes 6, 14, and 23, BEP.

43. Richard Crane to HFB, May 26, 1927, HFB to Crane, May 28, 1927, box 72, to Roosevelt, Jan. 9, 1929, box 78, BEP.

44. *RTD*, Nov. 10, 20–25, 1929; HFB to Guggenheim, Sept. 10, 1929, Shirley to HFB, Oct. 24, 1929, box 5, BEP.

45. *RTD*, Nov. 6, Dec. 3, 1929, Jan. 1, 1930; Hoover to HFB, Nov. 23, 1929, HFB to Hoover, Nov. 25, 1929, box 42, John Q. Rhodes to HFB, Dec. 16, 1929, HFB to Brown, Dec. 10, 1929, box 22, BEP; Hawkes, "Career of Byrd," 165.

46. *RTD*, Jan. 9, 11, 16, 1930. Cartoon 2 remained Byrd's favorite Seibel cartoon. HFB to Seibel, March 8, 1960, box 243, BP.

47. Glass to HFB, Nov. 21, 1929, box 1, Glass Papers; *RTD*, Jan. 4, 16, 1930.

48. Strother, "Youth Takes the Helm."

49. Tindall, "Business Progressivism"; Cobb, "Beyond Planter and Industrialists"; Preston, *Dirt Roads to Dixie*, 3–6; see also Grantham, *Southern Progressivism*; Blanton, "Virginia in the 1920's," 63, 107.

50. Strother, "Youth Takes the Helm," 146–48; Door, "The Man Who Set Virginia One Hundred Years Ahead," 52; Tindall, "Business Progressivism," 100.

51. Spicer, "Political Chief," 100.

52. Strother, "Youth Takes the Helm"; Spicer, "Political Chief," 101, 118; see also Dabney, "Americans We Like."

53. Hawkes, "Harry F. Byrd," 243–44; Moger, *Virginia*, 343–44; Buck, *Reorganization of State Governments*, 242–45.

54. Bass and De Vries, *Transformation of Southern Politics*, 342; Lipson, *American Governor*, 101, 113–14.

55. Hawkes, "Harry F. Byrd," 241–44; Hawkes, "Career of Byrd," 131, 134, 166–69; Strother, "Youth Takes the Helm," 144; Pulley, *Old Virginia Restored*, 183.

56. Gottmann, *Virginia at Mid-Century*, 555; Pulley, *Old Virginia Restored*, 186–88.

6. "Retirement"

1. Farland and Greenhalgh, *In the Shadow of the Blue Ridge*, 66; interview with Joe and Teresa Massie.

2. Interviews with Dick Byrd and Harry F. Byrd III.

3. HFB to Flood, March 24, 1931, box 105, BP; interviews with Byrd's sons.

4. Interview with Harry Byrd, Jr.

5. HFB to Willis Robertson, May 29, June 8, 1931, box 108, Byrd Jr. to Byrd Sr., March 18, 1936, box 428, John Crown to HFB, July 13, 1935, box 430, BP; Garrard, "Story of Harry Byrd, Jr."

6. HFB to Westwood, Feb. 5, 1932, box 112, Dec. 3, 1931, box 430, to Beverley, Oct. 8, 11, 1934, box 430, to General L. R. Gignilliat, Aug. 2, Sept. 11, 1939, to John Page Williams, Sept. 6, 1940, box 430, BP; interview with Dick and Helen Byrd.

7. HFB to Joseph Bauserman, Dec. 2, 1918, box 65, to Guggenheim, Jan. 31, 1933, box 139, to Reed, July 11, 1934, box 148, to Guy McConnell, Oct. 9, 1956, box 236, BP; Reed to Guggenheim, Jan. 23, 1933, Feb. 10, box 11, Reed Papers.

8. Interview with Dick Byrd.

9. Interviews with Elizabeth Wyeth, Joe and Teresa Massie, Byrd's sons, and Harry Byrd III.

10. Massie memoirs; interviews with Byrd's sons and Watkins M. Abbitt; Virginius Dabney to HFB, Dec. 27, 1963, box 265, BP.

11. Interview with Harry Byrd III; correspondence, boxes 121, 139, 199, HFB to Reed, July 30, 1932, box 121, to Burr Harrison, Dec. 4, 1952, box 199, BP; Reed to Willis Robertson, Feb. 15, 1927, box 19, Reed Papers.

12. Correspondence, boxes 65, 96, 102, HFB to T. McCall Frazier, June 16, 1930, box 96, BP.

13. HFB to Williams, Jan. 12, 1943, box 178, Wickham to HFB, Oct. 3, 1940, box 167, BP.

14. Weisiger, "Combs," 2–31; Combs to Henry Stuart, Feb. 2, 1925, box 3, Byrd to Combs, Aug. 21, 1925, box 12; Combs Papers.

15. Weisiger, "Combs," pp. 33–46; Stuart to Byrd, June 25, 1927, box 12, Combs Papers.

16. Fry, "Reed"; Shirley Carter to Reed, Jan. 12, 1932, Reed to Carter, Jan. 18, 1932, box 6, HFB to Reed, March 11, 1930, box 4, Reed Papers; Reed to HFB, Jan. 13, 1930, box 99, BP.

17. HFB to Glass, April 23, 1930, box 147, Glass Papers; to Glass, Oct. 13, 1931, Glass to HFB, Oct. 15, 1931, box 106, BP.

18. Joe Smith to HFB, Aug. 9, 1932, other letters, box 123, HFB to Alderman, March 1, 1930, box 92, BP.

19. Julian Burruss, President of VPI, to HFB, June 17, 1930, box 92, R. R. Moton to HFB, Jan. 18, 1930, box 93, Arthur Wright to HFB, Dec. 11, 1933, box 153, BP.

20. HFB to Scott, Dec. 11, 1931, box 109, to Williams, Dec. 19, 1932, Williams to HFB, Dec. 22, 1932, box 124, BP.

21. HFB to Scott, Sept. 9, 1931, box 109, March 1, 1933, box 149, Sept. 18, Oct. 3, 1933, to William Stuart, Sept. 27, 1933, box 152, to Beverly Tucker, Oct. 30, 1939, box 155, Scott to HFB, Dec. 27, 1932, box 149, BP; Tarter, "Newcomb and the University of Virginia."

22. C. G. Maphis to HFB, July 3, 1930, box 98, HFB to H. Hiter Harris, April 20, 1948, box 192, to W. H. Schwarzschild, June 13, 1949, to Darden, June 24, 1949, Jan. 23, 1951, Darden to HFB, Feb. 4, 1950, Kenneth Chorley to HFB, Jan. 15, 1951, box 228, BP.

23. *Country Home Magazine,* Dec. 1939, copy in box 294, BP.

24. William T. Reed, Jr., to HFB, Oct. 15, 1964, box 278, HFB to Arnold, Jan. 15, 1933, Jan. 19, 1934, box 128, BP.

25. HFB to H. B. Slaven, March 29, 1932, Dec. 10, 1932, box 120, Dec. 11, 1934, box 135, to Williams, Nov. 2, 1935, box 153, to Frank Fuller, Aug. 12, 1932, box 116, to W. J. McCambridge, Aug. 3, 1932, box 119, BP.

26. Richard Byrd to HFB, Sept. 17, 1931, HFB to Richard Byrd, Nov. 29, Dec. 17, 1930, box 425, BP.

27. Reed to HFB, Feb. 5, 1930, box 4, Reed Papers; Reed to HFB, June 30, 1930, box 99, N. B. Early to HFB, March 19, 1930, box 96, HFB to Ralph Bader, March 11, 1930, box 92, BP.

28. Combs to HFB, April 11, 1930, HFB to Combs, July 8, 1930, box 93, to John Fishburne, May 21, Oct. 15, 1930, box 96, BP.

29. HFB to Reed, Feb. 6, 1930, box 99, Combs to HFB, Feb. 10, 1930, box 93, Ferguson to HFB, Jan. 20, Feb. 12, 1930, box 96, BP.

30. Hopewell, "Pollard," 260; Hopewell, "Outsider Looking In," 272; Pollard to HFB, Dec. 26, 1930, box 99, July 15, 1931, box 108, BP.

31. HFB to Pollard, March 31, 1931, box 108, BP.

32. Hawkes, "Career of Byrd," 173–75; HFB to Pollard, Feb. 17, March 3, 18, 1930,

Pollard to HFB, April 17, May 12, 21, 1930, box 99, Ferguson to HFB, March 13, 1930, box 96, BP; Hopewell, "Pollard," 254; Hopewell, "Outsider Looking In," 238–76.

33. HFB to Reed, July 14, 26, 1930, box 4, Reed Papers; to George Thomas, July 22, 1930, box 100, HFB to John Hutcheson, Nov. 5, 1930, box 94, BP.

34. Heinemann, *Depression and New Deal,* 5; HFB to Reed, Aug. 12, 19, 1930, Reed to HFB, Aug. 13, 1930, box 4, Reed Papers; HFB to Pollard, Aug. 11, 1930, box 99, BP; Hawkes, "Career of Byrd," 176.

35. Heinemann, *Depression and New Deal,* 4–5; HFB to Ellerson, Sept. 6, 1930, box 94, BP.

36. Reed to HFB, Dec. 2, 1930, box 4, HFB to C. W. Warburton, Secretary of the Federal Relief Committee, Oct. 16, 1930, box 41, Reed Papers; Tom Ozlin to HFB, Nov. 26, 1930, HFB to Tom Ozlin, Nov. 24, 1930, box 95, to Pollard, Dec. 18, 1930, box 99, BP; Heinemann, *Depression and New Deal,* 4–5; *RTD,* Oct. 18, 1930.

37. HFB to Moore, Dec. 29, 1930, to John Barton Payne, Dec. 12, 1930, box 95, to James Aswell, Nov. 26, 1930, box 94, BP; Hamilton, "Hoover and the Great Drought."

38. Communiqué of Nov. 20, 1930, meeting sent to Virginia Drought Relief Committees, box 95, BP.

39. HFB to Glass, Dec. 18, 1930, box 147, to Aswell, Nov. 24, 1930, Aswell to HFB, Nov. 25, 1930, box 94, R. Walton Moore to HFB, Dec. 19, 1930, box 95, BP; Glass to Walter Harris, Feb. 18, 1931, box 4, Glass Papers.

40. C. W. Warburton to HFB, Jan. 30, 1931, box 104, HFB to Reed, Feb. 21, 1931, box 108, BP.

41. Heinemann, *Depression and New Deal,* 6; Report of the Drought Relief Committee to Pollard, July 31, 1931, box 104, BP.

42. Pollard to HFB, Aug. 20, 1931, HFB to Pollard, Aug. 24, 1931, box 108, BP; HFB to Pollard, Aug. 15, 1931, Pollard Executive Papers, LV; Fry, "Reed," 461.

43. Heinemann, *Depression and New Deal,* 173–77; *NYT,* March 15, 1931.

44. With the approval of AFL President William Green, Byrd had offered his services in settling the strike at Dan River Mills, but he had been rejected by management. Norfolk *Virginian-Pilot,* Dec. 31, 1930; Ferrell, *Swanson,* 149.

45. Heinemann, *Depression and New Deal,* 6–13; Bryant to T. G. Burch (with copy to Glass), Oct. 27, 1931, box 280, Glass Papers.

46. HFB to Henry Stuart, May 27, 1931, box 109, BP; to Reed, May 26, 1931, box 4, Reed Papers.

47. Reed to Lee Long, Oct. 21, 28, 1931, box 15, Reed to Angell, Oct. 23, 1931, box 1, Reed to HFB, Sept. 5, 8, 1931, box 4, Reed Papers; Reed to HFB, Aug. 8, 31, Oct. 26, 1931, box 108, BP; Fry, "Reed," 461–64; Heinemann, *Depression and New Deal,* 11–13; Hopewell, "Pollard," 255.

48. HFB to Reed, Sept. 7, 1931, box 4, Reed Papers.

49. Byrd, *Country Home Magazine;* HFB to Frederic Scott, July 1, 1931, box 109, BP.

50. HFB to Scott, June 3, 1931, box 109, Pollard to HFB, May 13, 1931, box 108, BP.

51. HFB to Reed, May 26, July 23, Aug. 7, 1931, box 4, Reed Papers; HFB to Shirley, June 17, 1931, box 109, BP.

52. HFB to Combs, Oct. 5, 1931, box 103, HFB to Reed, Sept. 7, 1931, box 108, BP; Hopewell, "Outsider Looking In," 284–86.

53. HFB to Pollard, Oct. 13, Dec. 23, 1931, box 108, BP; Dec. 30, 1931, folder 144, Pollard Papers.

54. Ferguson to HFB, Nov. 7, 17, 1931, HFB to Ferguson, Nov. 13, 27, 1931, box 105, BP.

55. Hatch, *Byrds of Virginia,* 402.

56. HFB to Combs, July 28, 1932, box 113, to Reed, July 9, 1931, box 108, BP.

57. Weisiger, "Combs," 50–52; HFB to Combs, June 3, 1931, box 103, to Reed, Dec. 16, 1931, box 108, BP.

58. HFB to Reed, Feb. 4, 1932, box 5, Reed Papers; Heinemann, *Depression and New Deal,* 14; *RTD,* Feb. 7, 1932; HFB to Louis Jaffe, Feb. 4, 1932, box 2b, Jaffe Papers; to Charles Hasbrook, Feb. 4, 1932, box 121, to H. C. Stuart, March 4, 1932, box 123, to Epes, Feb. 8, 1932, box 115, BP.

59. Hawkes, "Career of Byrd," 181–86; *Virginian-Pilot,* Feb. 13, 1932; Byrd address, *Virginia Record,* Sept. 1956; *RTD,* March 30, 1932. Tax Commissioner C. H. Morrissett may have been the originator of the road plan, knowing as he did of the growing number of tax delinquencies; ten months later Byrd wrote to Morrissett, "The credit is due you for the new road system." HFB to C. H. Morrissett, Feb. 8, Dec. 24, 1932, box 119, BP.

60. HFB to Combs, Jan. 25, 1932, Combs to HFB, Jan. 25, 1932, box 113, HFB to Reed, March 12, 1932, box 121, BP; to Pollard, April 4, 1932, folder 144, Pollard Papers; Freeman to John Stewart Bryan, Feb. 26, 1932, box 15, Freeman Papers; Heinemann, *Depression and New Deal,* 14–15.

7. The Apple King

1. Johnson, "Senator Byrd of Virginia," 82.

2. Statement, box 128, HFB to George Michie, Jan. 16, 1932, box 119, BP.

3. Byrd biographical material, box 168, HFB to Frank Tavenner, May 20, 1919, box 67, BP; *Eastern Fruit Grower* 20 (Aug. 1956): 6–37; Morris, "3,000,000 Apples"; Massie memoirs; interview with Beverley Byrd.

4. Biographical materials, box 168, HFB to Hamilton Orchard Heating Co., Feb. 3, 1914, box 1br, to Orlando Harrison, Dec. 16, 1919, box 7br, to W. J. Schoene, Feb. 15, 1921, box 73, G. S. Ralston to HFB, Nov. 29, 1918, HFB to Ralston, Dec. 2, 1918, box 5br, BP.

5. S. P. Calkins and Co. to HFB, Sept. 24, 1920, box 10br, HFB to E. N. Loomis, May 24, 1920, to Loeb-Apte Co., Oct. 31, Dec. 1, 1919, box 7br, Sept. 20, 1920, box 11 br, BP.

6. Interview with Harry Byrd III.

7. Madison Cooper to HFB, Oct. 18, 1907, box 1br, HFB to Edward Loomis, May 21, 1917, box 4br, to E. V. Weems, Aug. 21, Sept. 20, 1917, box 5br, to J. Homer Copp, July 26, 1917, box 3br, to John Nix, March 23, 1917, box 4br, BP.

8. HFB to Melvin Green, April 9, 16, 1917, to Electric Machinery Co. June 28, 1917, to Van R. H. Greene, Aug. 1, 1917, Byrd form letter, Sept. 17, 1917, box 3br, HFB to C. M. Shannon, Jan. 5, 1920, box 70, BP.

9. HFB to Bureau of Markets, May 12, 1919, Frame Brown to HFB, Sept. 16, 1919, box 6br, HFB to M. C. Kennedy, Sept. 30, 1920, box 10br, speech, box 6br, BP.

10. HFB to R. E. Byrd, April 24, 25, 1922, box 423, to Richard Byrd, March 31, 1921, box 425, to Jacinto Alfonso, May 30, 1922, box 16br, BP; interview with Beverley Byrd.

11. Interviews with Harry Byrd III and Beverley Byrd; HFB to W. L. Dechert Co., June 10, 1930, box 18br, to W. T. Reed, Aug. 10, 1934, box 148, BP.

12. HFB to Harrison, May 24, 1917, Harrison to HFB, May 27, 1917, HFB to M. C. Kennedy, July 2, 1917, box 4br, BP.

13. C. R. McCann to Shirley Carter, Nov. 27, 1918, box 5br, HFB to John Nix, Jan. 13, 1919, box 7br, to Thomas Kennedy, Dec. 2, 1918, box 4br, to Senator Thomas Martin, Dec. 13, 1918, box 66, BP.

14. HFB to William Armstrong, March 12, 1918, box 2br, to W. H. Bates, Sept. 15, 1919, box 6br, to N. F. Pennington, Aug. 31, 1917, box 4br, BP.

15. HFB to William Massey, Feb. 22, 1918, box 66, to W. J. Schoene, Feb. 20, 1918, box 5br, BP.

16. HFB to Floyd Bowman, Jan. 3, 1923, box 16br, to E. M. Waylands, Dec. 1, 1925, box 91, C. R. Willey to HFB, April 22, 1930, box 99, HFB to Loudoun County Board of Supervisors, March 15, 1920, to George Coleman, Feb. 16, 1920, box 67, BP.

17. HFB to George Coleman, Dec. 26, 1919, July 12, 1920, to T. W. Harrison, Aug. 11, 1919, box 67, to W. E. Carson, Jan. 6, 1921, box 71, to R. E. Byrd, Dec. 10, 1918, box 419, Aug. 27, 1919, box 423, R. E. Byrd to HFB, Oct. 28, 1919, box 423, BP.

18. HFB to William Massey, Dec. 20, 1917, to Hal Flood, April 22, 1918, box 66, to W. J. Schoene, Feb. 20, 1918, box 5br, to A. B. Thornhill, June 28, 1922, box 77, to Henry Shirley, Aug. 23, 1933, box 149, J. H. Meek to HFB, Feb. 24, March 14, 1932, box 119, BP.

19. HFB to G. S. Ralston, Jan. 7, 1922, box 16br, to H. B. McCormac, May 1, 1917, box 4br, statement, box 128, BP; Hatch, *Byrds of Virginia*, 441.

20. Interview with Harry Byrd III; "5,000 Acres of Apples," *Service*, Oct. 1956, 26.

21. HFB to Produce Reporter Co., Sept. 6, 1920, box 11br, to Shirley Carter, Oct. 14, 1920, box 10br, Jan. 29, 1921, box 13br, Dec. 29, 1917, box 65, BP.

22. S. L. Ferguson to HFB, Dec. 21, 1920, box 67, BP; Newman, "Master Orchardist."

23. Speech, Jan. 28, 1925, box 423, BP.

24. Letters, box 2, BEP; pamphlets of Shenandoah Apple Blossom Festival.

25. HFB to R. L. Ailworth, Sept. 21, 1925, box 82, to E. Lee Trinkle, Sept. 8, 1919, box 67, BP; to Mrs. Charles Lee, July 20, 1928, box 18, BEP.

26. HFB to George Johnson, Feb. 18, 1927, box 2, BEP; interview with Harry Byrd, Jr.

27. *Eastern Fruit Grower;* interviews with Dick and Beverley Byrd; *RTD*, June 8, 1941, Feb. 25, 1968; Newman, "Master Orchardist."

28. *Eastern Fruit Grower;* interview with Beverley Byrd.

29. *Eastern Fruit Grower;* interview with Beverley Byrd; Newman, "Master Orchardist"; list of expenses in box 20br, BP.

30. HFB to Henry Stuart, Dec. 14, 1930, box 95, to E. C. Auchter, June 18, 1931, box 101, to H. H. Gordon, Nov. 17, 1932, box 116, to Tom Byrd, April 16, 1934, box 128, materials in boxes 93, 103, 123, BP; interview with Beverley Byrd; *RTD*, Dec. 14, 1930.

31. HFB to Reed, June 3, Sept. 9, 14, 1931, box 108, BP.

32. HFB to managers, Aug. 31, 1931, box 20br, statement, 1933, box 128, BP.

33. HFB to Melvin Green, Jan. 27, 1921, to Jacinto Alfonso, Sept. 16, 1921, box 13br, to Ferguson, Sept. 26, 1931, box 105, BP; Morris, "3,000,000 Apples."

34. Claude Swanson to HFB, Feb. 20, 1931; HFB to W. Van Bokkelen, May 28, 1931; J. Oliver to Tom Byrd, Aug. 1, 1930, box 18br; HFB to William Reed, July 11, 1930, box 99, to Swanson, July 25, 1930, box 100, to Carson, July 1, 1931, box 103, BP.

35. HFB to W. S. Campbell, secretary of the Virginia Horticultural Society, March 29, June 13, 1930, box 93, Herbert to HFB, Feb. 24, 1931, box 20br, BP.

36. HFB to Edmund Waterman, July 28, 1931, Walter Thurston to Byrd, Aug. 29, 1931, box 19br, HFB to Swanson, June 28, 1930, box 100, to Edge, Aug. 12, 1932, box 115, to Hull, Dec. 23, 1933, box 141, May 13, 1936, box 36, to FDR, Dec. 23, 1933, box 148, Roper to HFB, Jan. 13, 1934, box 149, HFB to Edmund Waterman, March 3, 1934, box 152, BP; letters, HFB to Glass, box 147, Glass Papers.

37. Byrd, *Virginia Fruit;* F. A. Motz to HFB, Jan. 28, 1931, HFB to Motz, Feb. 10, 1931, box 107, BP.

38. HFB to Ralston, Aug. 27, 1931, box 19br, June 16, 1932, box 121, Ralston to HFB, Sept. 24, Oct. 16, Dec. 14, 1931, box 21br, May 9, 17, Sept. 15, 1932, box 121, BP.

39. Ralston to HFB, Dec. 14, 1931, box 21br, papers, box 19br, BP.

40. HFB to John Miller, March 26, 1930, box 98, BP; interview with Harry Byrd III.

41. HFB to Miller, Oct. 10, 1931, box 107, July 21, 1932, box 119, Feb. 10, 1933, Miller to HFB, Feb. 9, 1933, box 144, BP.

42. HFB to H. D. Fuller, April 5, 1921, box 13br, to H. B. Sproul, Jan. 15, 1923, Drewry Smith to HFB, Jan. 26, 1923, box 17br, Michie to HFB, July 13, 1932, HFB to Michie, July 14, Oct. 3, 1932, box 119, to John Miller, Nov. 11, 1933, box 144, BP.

43. Interviews with Byrd's sons, Helen Byrd, and Harry Byrd III; HFB to C&P Telephone Co., n.d., box 3br, Byrd to T. M. Hamilton, Oct. 17, 1931, box 106, BP.

44. Interview with Dick Byrd; papers on RFC loan, box 27br, HFB to Arnold, Jan. 13, 1936, box 128, to Charlie Bolen, April 11, 1959, box 242, BP; Washington *Post,* Oct. 1, 1950.

45. HFB to John Livengood, Dec. 13, 1930, box 98, Aug. 19, 1930, to R. T. Osborn, June 20, 1931, box 18br, Tom Byrd to Robert Thornton, Jan. 26, 1933, HFB to Livengood and Neurdenburg, Feb. 22, 1933, to H. B. McCormac, March 31, 1933, box 24br, to Henry Gilmer, Aug. 16, 1932, box 116, BP.

46. In May 1937 Byrd was paying his workers only $1.50–$1.75 for a ten-hour day; Tom Byrd to H. B. McCormac, May 17, 1937, box 30br, HFB to William Nelson, April 12, 1938, box 166, BP; Tugwell, *Democratic Roosevelt,* 444. For Drew Pearson's personal attacks on Byrd and Byrd's reactions, see Washington *Evening Star,* Oct. 24, 1961, Jan. 17, 1962, and letters, boxes 203, 249, BP.

47. Interviews with Byrd's sons; HFB to Harry Byrd, Jr., Oct. 8, 1942, box 428, to Freeman, Oct. 30, 1944, box 176, BP.

48. Interview with Harry Byrd III; Morris, "3,000,000 Apples"; "5,000 Acres of Apples"; Carrol Miller to HFB, April 7, 1961, HFB to Miller, April 10, 1961, Charles Toan to HFB, June 3, 1964, box 290, BP.

49. Interview with Dorsey.

50. Reed, "Sporting Venture"; HFB to Bank of Clarke County, Feb. 15, 1935, box 131, Lester Arnold to HFB, May 22, 1936, box 128, BP. The percentage of Byrd's crop shipped abroad dropped to less than 10 percent in the 1950s; yet he was still exporting 150,000 barrels in 1964 because it was "good to keep up these connections." Morris, "3,000,000 Apples"; *Eastern Fruit Grower;* HFB to Arnold, March 24, 1964, box 36br, BP.

51. *Eastern Fruit Grower;* Reed, "Sporting Venture"; interviews with Harry Byrd III and Dick Byrd.

52. Interviews with Dick Byrd and Ralph Dorsey; HFB to W. E. Elmore, Nov. 13, 1950, box 199, to E. B. Bonham, April 24, 1962, box 35br, records, box 31br, BP; Morris, "3,000,000 Apples."

53. HFB to Beverley Byrd, July 13, 1953, letters, box 31br, BP; *Eastern Fruit Grower.*

54. Interviews with Byrd's sons and Ralph Dorsey; *Eastern Fruit Grower.*

55. Morris, "3,000,000 Apples"; materials, box 36br, BP.

56. Interviews with Byrd's sons and Harry Byrd III.

8. A Presidential Campaign

1. Heinemann, "Byrd for President"; HFB to Reed, Oct. 7, 1930, Reed to HFB, Oct. 9, 1930, box 99, BP.

2. Reed to HFB, Feb. 5, 1930, box 4, Reed Papers; Gardner to HFB, Feb. 28, 1930, box 96, Taylor to HFB, Aug. 13, 1930, box 100, Oct. 1, 1930, box 96, BP; Morrison, *Gardner*, 88.

3. Heinemann, "Byrd for President," 30; Richard Byrd to HFB, Aug. 11, 1919, Jan. 29, 1931, March 21, 1931, HFB to Richard Byrd, Feb. 11, box 425, BP.

4. Tarter, "Flier," 282–83; HFB to Roosevelt, Feb. 27, 1931, Roosevelt to HFB, March 2, 1931, box 108, HFB to Josephus Daniels, March 11, 1931, box 105, to George Milton, March 11, 1931, box 107, to Glass, Feb. 27, 1931, box 106, to Reed, July 21, 1932, box 121, BP.

5. Bailey to HFB, June 26, 1931, Chandler to HFB, Feb. 12, 1931, box 102, Thomson to HFB, June 23, 1931, box 110, BP.

6. Pollard to HFB, July 15, 1931, box 108, Epes to HFB, Feb. 2, 1931, HFB to Epes, Feb. 19, 1931, box 105, BP.

7. Reed to W. R. Perkins, Oct. 20, 1931, box 17, Reed Papers; Reed to HFB, March 27, 1931, box 108, BP.

8. HFB to Reed, June 27, 1931, July 9, 1931, box 4, Reed Papers; to Reed, March 10, 1931, Aug. 7, 1931, to Raskob, July 13, 1931, box 108, to Stuart, June 29, 1931, box 109, to Sam Ferguson, March 27, 1931, to W. E. Carson, July 15, 1931, box 103, to Pat Drewry, July 28, 1931, box 104, BP; Tarter, "Flier," 284–85.

9. Breckinridge to HFB, Oct. 6, 27, 28, 1931, box 102, HFB to Reed, Oct. 13, 1931, box 108, BP; Reed to Breckinridge, Dec., 1931, letters, box 3, Reed to Robertson, Oct. 19, 1931, box 19, Reed Papers.

10. Breckinridge to A. P. Staples, Dec. 2, 1931, box 111, Breckinridge to HFB, Oct. 20, 1931, box 102, HFB to Reed, Oct. 13, 1931, box 108, BP.

11. Heinemann, "Byrd for President," 31; Milton to HFB, Dec. 2, 1931, box 108, BP; Reed to H. C. Stuart, July 25, 1931, box 21, Reed Papers.

12. Richard Byrd to HFB, Nov. 3, 1931, box 425, BP.

13. *RTD*, Jan. 6, 9, 1932; Farley, *Behind the Ballots*, 75.

14. Farmville *Herald*, Jan. 8, 1932; *RTD*, Jan. 14, Feb. 8, 1932; Tarter, "Flier," 288; Heinemann, "Byrd for President," 31; HFB to Reed, Jan. 15, 1932, box 5, Reed Papers; HFB to Harkrader, Feb. 3, 1932, Charles Harkrader Papers, UVL; HFB to Breckinridge, Nov. 14, 30, 1931, box 102, to Reed, Dec. 16, 1931, box 108, to Williams, Jan. 6, 1932, box 124, BP.

15. HFB to Flannagan, Feb. 3, 1932, box 115, Reed to HFB, Jan. 25, 1932, box 121, Tyre Taylor to HFB, Feb. 7, 1932, box 123, BP; Reed to Breckinridge, Jan. 1, 1932, box 3, HFB to Reed, Jan. 23, 1932, box 5, Reed Papers; *Virginian-Pilot*, Feb. 12, 1932; *RTD*, Feb. 12, 1932.

16. *RTD*, Feb. 6, 19, 1932; Heinemann, "Byrd for President," 32; Reed to Robertson, March 1, 1932, box 19, Reed Papers; HFB to Breckinridge, Feb. 11, 1932, box 111; HFB to Reed, Feb. 29, 1932, box 121, BP.

17. Richard Byrd to HFB, March 8, 1932, box 425, HFB to Flannagan, March 9, 1932, box 115, BP; HFB to Reed, March 17, 1932, box 5, Reed Papers.

18. Tarter, "Flier," 290–91; Heinemann, "Byrd for President," 32.

19. Tarter, "Flier," 291–92; *RTD*, April 5, 1932; Rosen, *Brains Trust*, 219, 221.

20. *RTD*, April 14, 1932; Heinemann, "Byrd for President," 32; Tarter, "Flier," 292–93.

21. Heinemann, "Byrd for President," 33; HFB to Breckinridge, May 13, 1932, box 111, W. L. McCann to HFB, May 3, June 13, 1932, box 119, HFB to Reed, May 3, 1932, box 121, to Flannagan, April 29, 1932, box 115, BP; *New Yorker*, May 21, 1932; HFB to Reed, May 14, 1932, Reed to HFB, May 16, 1932, box 5, Reed Papers.

22. HFB to Flannagan, May 24, 1932, Flannagan to HFB, April 18, 1932, box 115, BP; Flannagan to Reed, Feb. 20, April 21, 1932, box 10, Reed Papers.

23. HFB to Combs, April 2, 20, 29, June 11, 1932, box 113, to Parke Deane, May 3, 1932, box 114, to Emory Elmore, April 20, 1932, box 115, BP.

24. HFB to Flannagan, May 19, June 1, 1932, box 115, to Reed, June 14, 1932, box 121, to John Hanes, June 15, 1932, box 116, BP; Crane to Roosevelt, May 17, 1932, box 754, Franklin D. Roosevelt Papers, Franklin D. Roosevelt Library.

25. Combs to HFB, June 13, 1932, box 113, Josiah Bailey to John Miller, June 21, 1932, box 119, HFB to Reed, June 14, 1932, box 121, BP; Breckinridge to Reed, July 7, 1932, box 3, HFB to Reed, June 22, 1932, box 5, Reed Papers; HFB to Combs, June 17, 1932, box 1b, Combs Papers.

26. *RTD*, June 23, 26, 27, 1932.

27. Interview with Harry Byrd, Jr.

28. *RTD*, June 29, 30, 1932; Tarter, "Flier," 297–98.

29. *NYT*, July 1, 1932; *RTD*, July 1, 1932.

30. Arthur Krock, quoting Jackson's diary, *RTD*, April 11, 1952. Willis Robertson claimed that Farley offered Byrd the vice-presidency. Charles Harkrader said Homer Cummings asked Byrd to switch to Roosevelt and offered his brother the War or Navy Department. Farley said he offered the vice-presidency to Byrd through Richard Byrd. Hatch, *Byrds of Virginia*, 443–45; Archer Jones to author; Farley, *Jim Farley's Story*, 19.

31. Heinemann, "Byrd for President," 35; Tarter, "Flier," 300–302; Rosen, *Brains Trust*, 32, 219.

32. *RTD*, July 2, 4, 1932; Heinemann, "Byrd for President," 35–36; Tarter, "Flier," 302–3.

33. Governor Murray of Oklahoma to HFB, July 25, 1932, box 119, BP. Raskob later told Reed that he regretted Smith did not withdraw in favor of Byrd as soon as McAdoo made his speech. Raskob to Reed, July 11, 1932, box 18, Reed Papers.

34. *RTD*, June 27, July 4, 1932; interview with Harry Byrd, Jr.; Heinemann, "Byrd for President," 37.

35. HFB to Tom Ozlin, July 6, 1932 box 120, BP. Farley thought he had a commitment from Byrd to deliver Virginia's twenty-four votes when needed; Arthur Mullen, a national committeeman from Nebraska, confirmed Farley's view. Davis, *FDR: The New York Years*, 321; Mullen, *Western Democrat*, 274.

36. HFB to Reed, July 7, 1932, box 5, Reed to Breckinridge, July 8, 1932, box 3, Reed Papers.

37. HFB to Chandler, July 13, 1932, box 112, BP; Baker to Glass, Sept. 6, 1932, box 299, Glass Papers; Rosen, *Brains Trust*, 257, 262; see also HFB to Scott, July 27, 1932, box 122, Richard Byrd to HFB, Aug. 4, 1932, box 425, BP.

38. Total expenditures for the Virginia Byrd Committee were $9,125, two-thirds of which went for mailing and printing expenses; Reed contributed $7,400, Frederic Scott, $1,225, and Byrd, $500. Byrd's personal campaign expenses were $1,618, most of which was spent at Chicago. Byrd actually left Chicago without paying his hotel bill, thinking that as a member of the Arrangements Committee his bill would be paid by the Democratic National Committee. He later paid it. HFB to Flannagan, July 12, 1932, account of Virginia Byrd Committee, box 115, HFB to Robert B. Howell, Oct. 19, 1932, box 117, Ewing Laporte to HFB, July 21, 1932, box 118, BP.

39. Richard Byrd to HFB, June 9, 1932, box 425, BP; *RTD*, May 28, 1932; Heinemann, "Byrd for President," 37.

40. Heinemann, "Byrd for President," 37; HFB to Reed, July 6, 7, 21, 1932, Reed to HFB, July 18, 1932, box 5, Reed Papers.

41. Breckinridge to Reed, July 7, 1932, HFB to Reed, Aug. 18, 1932, box 121, Breckinridge to HFB, July 6, 12, 1932, HFB to Breckinridge, July 7, 1932, box 111, BP.

42. HFB to Reed, July 29, 1932, box 121, BP.

43. HFB to Reed, July 7, 1932, Reed to HFB, July 8, 1932, box 5, Reed Papers; HFB to Shirley, correspondence, box 122, Combs to HFB, July 27, 30, 1932, HFB to Combs, July 28, 1932, box 113, BP.

44. HFB to Roosevelt, July 9, 1932, box 121, materials in box 120, HFB to Pollard, Sept. 8, 1932, box 120, to J. Murray Hooker, Sept. 8, 1932, box 117, to W. Forbes Morgan, Sept. 26, Oct. 15, 1932, Morgan to HFB, Nov. 10, 1932, box 119, BP.

45. HFB to Willis Robertson, Oct. 18, 1932, to Reed, Oct. 4, 1932, to Roosevelt, Nov. 9, 1932, Roosevelt to HFB, Dec. 1, 1932, box 121, BP; *RTD,* Oct. 26, Nov. 10, 1932.

46. HFB to Reed, Dec. 19, 1932, box 5, Reed Papers; to Walter Davenport, Dec. 11, 1932, to H. W. Ellerson, Nov. 22, 1932, box 113, to Richard Byrd, Dec. 13, 1932, box 425, BP.

47. Ferrell, *Swanson,* 144–48, 192–98; Reed to HFB, March 28, 1931, box 108, BP.

48. HFB to Reed, Aug. 18, 1932, box 5, Reed Papers.

49. Ferrell, *Swanson,* 197–98; HFB to Reed, July 29, 1932, box 121, Truxton to HFB, Sept. 27, 1932, box 123, BP.

50. HFB to Reed, Dec. 12, 1932, box 5, Reed Papers; to Reed, Dec. 10, 27, 1932, box 121, to Combs, Dec. 10, 1932, box 113, BP; Hatch, *Byrds of Virginia,* 447.

51. HFB to Richard Byrd, Nov. 29, Dec. 13, 1932, box 425, to Reed, Dec. 16, 31, 1932, box 121, BP.

52. Davis, *FDR: The New York Years,* 439; Freidel, *Roosevelt: Launching the New Deal,* 148–50.

53. Ferrell, *Swanson,* 199; Hawkes, "Career of Byrd," 200; HFB to Glass, Jan. 30, 1933, box 139, BP.

54. HFB to Reed, Dec. 27, 1932, Robertson to HFB, Dec. 1, 1932, box 121, BP; Hawkes, "Career of Byrd," 202.

55. HFB to Richard Byrd, Dec. 19, 1932, box 425, Jan. 26, 1933, Richard Byrd to HFB, Jan. 24, 28, 1933, box 426, BP.

56. HFB to Breckinridge, Jan. 25, 1933, box 129, BP.

57. Glass to Roosevelt, Feb. 7, 1933, Glass to HFB, Feb. 4, 1933, box 6, Glass Papers.

58. HFB to Richard Byrd, Feb. 10, 1933, box 426, to Breckinridge, Feb. 27, 1933, box 129, to Farley, Feb. 25, 1933, box 138, BP. The final chapter in the feud came six years later at Swanson's death when his second wife unsuccessfully tried to prevent Harry Byrd from serving on the funeral committee. Ferrell, *Swanson,* 218; Robert Ferrell, *Dear Bess,* 414.

9. New Deals

1. See Heinemann, *Depression and New Deal,* 1–43.

2. *RTD,* March 5, 8, 9, 1933.

3. Heinemann, *Depression and New Deal,* 46–47.

4. Henry Hyde diary, April 24, 1933, UVL.

5. HFB to Fred Switzer, March 18, 1933, box 1, G. Fred Switzer Papers, UVL; interview with Harry Byrd, Jr.

6. Heinemann, *Depression and New Deal,* 46–47; *NYT,* June 14, 1933; HFB to William O. Bailey, July 5, 1933, box 152, BP; to Reed, June 16, 1933, box 5, Reed Papers. Reed was warning Byrd about the foolishness of Roosevelt's proposals, but it did not seem to have any effect. Reed to HFB, April 4, 15, May 23, 1933, Reed Papers.

7. Heinemann, *Depression and New Deal,* 50–51; HFB to Associated Press, Sept. 8, 1933, box 128, radio speech, Aug. 27, 1933, box 359, BP.

8. For Byrd's voting record on New Deal legislation, see Hilty, "Voting Alignments."

9. Tuck to HFB March 28, 1933, HFB to Tuck, March 29, 1933, box 151, BP.

10. Tarter, "Freshman Senator," 28–32, 37; *RTD,* Oct. 22, 1933.

11. Ibid., Feb. 26, 1933; HFB to Glass, Feb. 11, 1933, box 139, Hargis to HFB, Jan. 14, 1933, HFB to Hargis, Jan. 25, 1933, box 140, BP.

12. HFB to Breckinridge, Feb. 2, 1933, box 129, to A. C. Pleasants, Oct. 11, 1934, box 147, to Reed, Aug. 21, 1933, box 148, BP; to Reed, undated, June 19, 1933, box 5, Reed Papers.

13. Glass to HFB, Oct. 12, 1933, box 147, Glass Papers; HFB to Early, Oct. 4, 1933, box 137, to Reed, Aug. 14, 1933, box 148, BP. See also Bill Tuck to HFB, Sept. 14, 1933, folder 2776, William Tuck Papers, College of William and Mary Library.

14. HFB to Reed, July 29, 1932, box 121, BP; Frazier to Glass, May 6, 1933, box 345, Glass Papers.

15. Fry, "Peery: Byrd Regular," 264–65; Reed to HFB, Aug. 19, 1932, box 121, BP.

16. HFB to Reed, March 1, 1933, box 148, to Peery, Feb. 6, 15, 1933, box 146, to Pollard, Feb. 2, 1933, box 147, to Louis Epes, Feb. 2, 1933, box 137, BP; to Lou Jaffe, Feb. 22, 1933, box 2b, Jaffe Papers.

17. HFB to Peery, March 1, 1933, Peery to HFB, April 1, 1933, box 146, HFB to Conrad, July 5, 1933, box 132, BP.

18. James Latimer interviews with Bill Tuck and Colgate Darden, 1975; Tuck to HFB, July 3, 1933, box 151, BP.

19. Hopewell, "Pollard," 258–59; Fry, "Peery: Byrd Regular," 267; HFB to Combs, Sept. 18, 1933, box 132, to Pollard, Aug. 7, 1933, Pollard to HFB, July 13, 1933, box 147, BP.

20. Woodrum to HFB, July 22, 1933, box 153, Goolrick to HFB, April 7, 1933, box 139, HFB to Peery, May 29, June 9, 1933, box 146, to Sidney Barham, June 26, 1933, box 128, BP; Fry, "Peery: Byrd Regular," 267.

21. Flier from Military Order, J. M. Harrison to *Virginian-Pilot,* Sept. 25, 1933, box 152, HFB to F. B. Waters, Aug. 9, 1933, box 153, to George Doughty, Sept. 9, 1933, box 136, BP; *Virginian-Pilot,* Nov. 8, 1933.

22. HFB to Peery, Dec. 21, 26, 1933, box 146, Jan. 6, 1934, box 132, to Reed, Jan. 1, 1934, box 148, BP.

23. Fry, "Peery: Byrd Regular," 268–69, 274; Heinemann, *Depression and New Deal,* 130; *RTD,* March 11, 1934; HFB to Reed, Nov. 28, 1933, box 148, HFB to Bryan, March 31, 1934, box 130, BP.

24. Heinemann, *Depression and New Deal,* 107–8; *RTD,* March 21, May 23, 29, June 7, 14, 17, 1934; speech, box 359, HFB to Scott, June 21, 1934, box 149, BP. As a tobacco manufacturer opposed to the AAA processing tax, Billy Reed reinforced Byrd's sentiments on the farm program. Reed to HFB, April 20, 1934, box 148. BP.

25. HFB to Glass, Feb. 15, 1933, box 139, BP; *RTD,* June 9, 15, 1934.

26. *RTD,* June 13, 1934; Robert Hopper to Tugwell, June 15, 1934, Department of Agriculture Records, record group 16, National Archives.

27. *Southside Virginia News* (Petersburg), June 14, 1934; Heinemann, *Depression and New Deal,* 109–10.

28. Articles in box 293, HFB to L. D. Arnold, Feb. 10, 1935, box 293, to Frederic Scott, July 1, 1931, box 109, BP.

29. HFB to Reed, July 6, 1934, box 148, BP; Moore, *Bailey,* 105.

30. HFB to Harkrader, July 9, 1934, Harkrader to HFB, July 14, 28, 1934, Harkrader Papers; HFB to Harkrader, Aug. 13, Sept. 5, 1934, Harkrader to HFB, Sept. 2, 1934, box 140, Robert Pennington to HFB, July 18, 1934, HFB to Pennington, July 19, 1934, box 146, BP.

31. HFB to Glass, July 14, 1934, box 320, Glass Papers.

32. Farley to HFB, July 6, 1934, box 138, HFB to Emory Elmore, Oct. 11, 1934, box 135, to Hubert Bennett, Aug. 11, 1934, box 130, to Allan Epes, Oct. 13, 1934, box 137, to William Trotter, Oct. 8, 1934, box 152, Tuck to HFB, Aug. 13, 1934, box 151, BP; Tarter, "Freshman Senator," 60; *RTD*, Jan. 28, March 29, June 5, 12, Nov. 6, 9, 1934.

33. Heinemann, *Depression and New Deal*, 139–40; Bainbridge Colby to Glass, Aug. 8, 1934, Glass to Colby, Aug. 10, 1934, box 320, Glass Papers; HFB to Breckinridge, Aug. 9, 1934, Breckinridge to HFB, Aug. 20, 1934, to Reed, July 23, 1935, box 129, Taylor to HFB, Oct. 15, 1935, box 151, BP; Portsmouth *Star*, Aug. 24, 1934.

34. Heinemann, *Depression and New Deal*, 69–70.

35. Hopkins to Williams, Feb. 10, 1934, to Peery, March 6, 1934, box 298, Johnstone to Williams, March 7, 1934, box 300, FERA records, record group 69, National Archives; *RTD*, March 7, 1934.

36. Byrd quoted in Creel, "Byrd Song"; HFB to Reed, Oct. 6, 1934, box 148, BP.

37. *Virginian-Pilot*, April 14, 1935; Fry, "Peery: Byrd Regular," 270; *RTD*, Dec. 16, 1934; for a more detailed account of this controversy, see Heinemann, *Depression and New Deal*, 77–86.

38. Reed to HFB, Nov. 15, 1934, box 148, BP.

39. *RTD*, Jan. 25, Feb. 7, 21, 28, March 19, 20, 24, 1935; HFB to C. M. Shannon, March 7, 1935, to James L. Hamner, Aug. 9, 1934, box 134, BP.

40. Heinemann, *Depression and New Deal*, 88–104; HFB to Williams April 21, 1936, WPA records, record group 69, National Archives; Harry Byrd, Jr., to HFB, March 18, 1936, box 428, BP.

41. HFB to Bailey, Oct. 4, 1934, box 129, BP.

42. Geddes, *Trends in Relief Expenditures*, 91–92; Heinemann, *Depression and New Deal*, 156; *RTD*, Jan. 25, 1935.

43. *RTD*, Jan. 24–31, March 31, April 11, June 20, 1935; *Virginian-Pilot*, April 21, 1935; G. W. Snodgrass to HFB, Nov. 7, 1934, box 151, BP; Altmeyer, *Social Security*, 39, 59.

44. HFB to Combs, Oct. 10, 1935, box 133, to Peery, Oct. 22, 1935, box 146, C. H. Morrissett to HFB, Oct. 10, 1935, HFB to Morrissett, Oct. 11, 22, 1935, box 144, BP; Heinemann, *Depression and New Deal*, 156–61.

45. *RTD*, May 17, 21, 22, 28, 1935, April 4, 1937; Heinemann, *Depression and New Deal*, 58–59; HFB to M. M. Henley, May 27, 1935, box 152, BP; Hilty, "Voting Alignments," 1:95, 2:A46–69.

46. *RTD*, April 17, July 11, 16, 21, 24, 1935; Heinemann, *Depression and New Deal*, 109–10; HFB to Arnold, April 25, 26, 1935, box 128, BP; *Time*, May 13, 1935.

47. Simmons, "Creation of Shenandoah National Park," 76–125, 149–59, 179–85; Horan, "Will Carson," 408–15; *RTD*, March 3, 5, 13, 1935; Jolley, *Blue Ridge Parkway*, 23–56, 112; HFB to Pollard, Oct. 19, 1933, box 147, BP; James, "National Domain," 10.

48. Speeches in boxes 359, 360, BP; *RTD*, March 15, 1935. Byrd was inducted into Phi Beta Kappa at William and Mary a year later. Donald Davis to Byrd, Nov. 20, 1936, box 135, BP.

49. *RTD*, Oct. 30, 1935.

50. Heinemann, *Depression and New Deal*, 132, 178–79.

51. *RTD*, April 24, June 12, Aug. 16, 30, Sept. 3, 1935; Brooklyn *Eagle* to HFB, June 2, 1936, box 131, John Hanes to HFB, June 30, 1936, box 140, M. M. Neely to HFB, July 8, 1935, box 146, BP.

52. Woodrum to Hutchinson, Aug. 30, 1934, box 2, Martin Hutchinson Papers, UVL.

53. Radio speech, Oct. 13, 1936, box 130, Glass to HFB, Oct. 5, 1936, box 139, BP.

54. Noah Power to Combs, April 23, 1936, HFB to George Coleman, April 7, 1936, box 133, BP; *RTD*, April 5, June 17, Aug. 5, 1936.

55. HFB to Roosevelt, Nov. 4, 1936, box 148, BP; Heinemann, *Depression and New Deal*, 142–45; Tuck to T. G. Burch, Aug. 17, 1935, folder 2780, Tuck Papers.

56. Lynchburg *News*, Feb. 7, March 10, 1937; *RTD*, Feb. 6, March 4, 24, 30, May 29, July 23, 1937; HFB to Tuck, Feb. 8, 25, 1937, Tuck to HFB, Feb. 12, 1937, folder 2782, Tuck Papers; Heinemann, *Depression and New Deal*, 145–46.

57. Wheeler, *Yankee from the West*, 322; Moore, *Bailey*, 130.

58. Ibid., 150–59; see also Patterson, *Congressional Conservatism*.

59. *RTD*, Jan. 10, 12, Feb. 25, 1936.

60. Radio speech, box 165, BP.

61. "Senator Byrd Talks about 'Presidents I Have Known,'" *U.S. News and World Report* 53 (Sept. 10, 1962): 84.

62. *RTD*, Jan. 13, 15, 1937; Porter, *Congress and the Waning of the New Deal*, 89; Polenberg, *Reorganizing Roosevelt's Government*, 31–35; Polenberg, "Roosevelt, Carter, and the Executive Reorganization," 37, 42; Mulder, *Insurgent Progressives*, 253; Ickes, *Secret Diary* 2:55.

63. Speech, May 28, 1937, box 360, BP.

64. Heinemann, *Depression and New Deal*, 147; *RTD*, May 29, June 2, 1937, March 25, 29, April 9, 1938; Polenberg, "Roosevelt, Carter, and the Executive Reorganization," 37.

65. Conkin, *Tomorrow a New World*, 113, 163–67, 224, 333; Baldwin, *Poverty and Politics*, 111, 319, 347–56; *RTD*, May 24, 27, Aug. 2, Sept. 3, Dec. 15, 1937; Davis, "Fourth Term's Hair Shirt."

66. A. J. Cahn to HFB, March 19, 1940, box 157, BP.

67. Heinemann, *Depression and New Deal*, 152–54.

10. Rebellion in Richmond

1. Fry, "Reed," 445.

2. HFB to Pleasant Reed, Nov. 2, 1935, box 148, William Reed to HFB, Aug. 8, 1931, box 108, BP.

3. HFB to W. D. Smith, Sept. 22, 1936, box 143, to Joel Flood, Nov. 2, 1936, box 138, Harry Jr. to HFB, March 18, 1936, box 428, HFB to Battle, Oct. 21, 1937, box 156, BP; interview with Harry Byrd, Jr.

4. HFB to Combs, Dec. 11, 1933, box 1b, Combs Papers; Reed to HFB, Dec. 20, 1933, box 148, Wysor to HFB, March 11, 1934, box 153, BP; Weisiger, "Combs," 58–67; *News Leader*, Aug. 8–13, 1955.

5. Whitehead to editor, *RTD*, Aug. 25, 1937, box 18, Robert Whitehead Papers, UVL.

6. *RTD*, July 16, 1936.

7. Byrd even worried about a few Republicans, telling Combs to get rid of all of them in the Richmond Internal Revenue Office. HFB to Combs, Dec. 5, 1934, box 132, BP.

8. Heinemann, *Depression and New Deal*, 134, 142.

9. Hall, "Price: New Dealer," 278–80; HFB to John Rust, Nov. 5, 1935, box 148, to Abe Schewel, Nov. 23, 1935, box 149, to Combs, Sept. 24, 1935, box 133, Combs to John Henry Smith, Sept. 4, 1935, box 133, BP.

10. Albert Sidney Johnson to HFB, Feb. 10, 1936, box 142, BP.

11. Hosier to HFB, Aug. 5, 1935, box 141, BP.

12. Hutchinson to Trinkle, Aug. 13, 1935, to Curry Hutchinson, Oct. 26, 1935, box 2, Hutchinson Papers; state senator quoted in Hall, "Price: New Dealer," 281; Koeniger, "New Deal and the States," 880–81.

13. HFB to Burch, Nov. 4, 7, 1935, C. S. Bennett to HFB, Dec. 8, 1935, box 130, Schewel to HFB, Nov. 18, 1935, June 17, 1936, box 149, HFB to Combs, Oct. 10, 1935, Combs to HFB, Nov. 11, 1935, box 133, T. McCall Frazier to HFB, Nov. 15, 1935, Roy Flannagan to HFB, Jan. 14, 1935, box 138, HFB to Battle, Dec. 30, 1935, box 129, BP.

14. Interview with Harry Byrd, Jr.; HFB to Combs, Dec. 26, 1935, box 133, Junius Fishburne to HFB, Jan. 9, 1936, box 159, James Woods to HFB, Feb. 8, 1936, box 153, HFB to Jaffe, Jan. 14, 1936, box 142, BP; Lou Jaffe to HFB, Jan. 13, 1936, box 2b, Jaffe Papers.

15. Tuck to HFB, June 8, 1936, box 151, Harry Jr. to HFB, April 8, 1936, box 428, BP.

16. Hall, "Price: New Dealer," 281; *RTD*, Dec. 24, 1936; Hutchinson to Pearne Ketron, Nov. 19, 1936, to Trinkle, Dec. 27, 1936, box 2, Hutchinson Papers.

17. Syrett, "Ambiguous Politics," 456–59; HFB to Glass, April 12, 1937, box 345, Glass Papers.

18. Combs to HFB, April 1, 1937, Preston Collins to HFB, June 17, 1937, box 157, HFB to W. N. Chinn, July 15, 1937, box 158, Holt to HFB, Aug. 14, 1937, box 160, Tuck to HFB, Aug. 3, 1937, box 165, BP; HFB to Glass, April 29, 1937, box 345, Glass Papers; *RTD*, Aug. 4, 1937.

19. Hall, "Price: New Dealer," 282–84; Syrett, "Ambiguous Politics," 461–63; Heinemann, *Depression and New Deal,* 149–50; Tom Ozlin to HFB, Dec. 15, 1937, box 163, Combs to HFB, Jan. 11, 12, 14, 1938, HFB to Combs, Feb. 8, 1938, C. S. Carter to Combs, Jan. 13, 1938, box 157, HFB to B. Redwood Councill, Feb. 14, 1938, box 158, BP.

20. Hall, "Price and Virginia Politics," 185–192; Weisiger, "Combs," 74–75; Bolling Handy to Combs, Dec. 30, 1925, Price to Lee Long, Dec. 2, 1925, box 6, Combs Papers; Moore to Price, Nov. 28, 1938, Price to Moore, Nov. 30, 1938, R. Walton Moore Papers, Roosevelt Library; Syrett, "Ambiguous Politics," 459–67.

21. Ozlin to HFB, Jan. 31, 1938, box 163, Combs to HFB, Feb. 24, 1938, box 157, Tuck to HFB, Feb. 26, 1938, box 165, BP.

22. Interviews with Harry Byrd, Jr., and Watkins Abbitt; Syrett, "Ambiguous Politics," 462–67; *RTD*, March 8, 1938; Roy Flannagan to HFB, Feb. 21, 1938, box 159, W. Stuart Moffett to HFB, March 1, 1938, box 162, Tuck to HFB, March 14, 1938, box 158, BP.

23. Hall, "Politics and Patronage," 339; Farley, *Jim Farley's Story,* 163–64.

24. Koeniger, "New Deal and the States," 882–86; Heinemann, *Depression and New Deal,* 147–48; Glass to Farley, Aug. 20, 1937, Farley to Glass, Aug. 21, 1937, box 380, Glass to HFB, July 5, 1938, box 383, Glass Papers; HFB to Colgate Darden, Jan. 12, 1938, box 158, BP; Syrett, "Ambiguous Politics," 471.

25. Glass to HFB, May 31, 1938, box 345, Glass to George Peery, June 11, 1938, box 398, Glass Papers; Hall, "Politics and Patronage," 337–40; Koeniger, "New Deal and the States," 882–87; memo, July 5, 1938, box 43, James Farley Papers, Library of Congress; Farley, *Jim Farley's Story,* 161.

26. Hall, "Politics and Patronage," 340–43; interview with Beverley Byrd; *RTD*, July

1, 1938; Koeniger, "New Deal and the States," 888–89; HFB to Glass, July 27, 1938, Dec. 2, 1938, Glass to HFB, July 28, Nov. 28, 1938, box 402, Glass Papers.

27. Watson to Missie LeHand, March 14, 1939, box 9, Edwin M. Watson Papers, UVL; Hall, "Politics and Patronage," 343–48; *NYT*, Feb. 2, 7, 10, 1939.

28. Patterson, "Eating Humble Pie"; Koeniger, "New Deal and the States," 892–95; Hall, "Politics and Patronage," 348–49; see also memos from Edwin M. Watson regarding patronage, Glass to Watson, Nov. 3, 1939, boxes 9, 10, Watson Papers; *RTD*, May 17, 1939.

29. Heinemann, *Depression and New Deal*, 151; Hall, "Price and Virginia Politics," vii.

30. Combs to HFB, Feb. 7, 1939, to J. B. Wampler, June 27, 1939, box 158, BP; *RTD*, Feb. 26, 1939; Martin Hutchinson to Price, Aug. 7, 1940, box 4, Hutchinson Papers; HFB to Bradford, Feb. 16, 1939, box 155, BP.

31. Ozlin to HFB, Jan. 31, 1939, HFB to Ozlin, Feb. 3, 1939, box 163, to G. H. Branaman, Feb. 15, 1939, box 156, Tuck to HFB, Jan. 9, 1939, box 166, BP.

32. Harkrader to Hutchinson, Jan. 7, 1939, box 3, Hutchinson Papers. Harkrader was defeated for the state senate seat by a Republican in the November election.

33. Weisiger, "Combs," 79; Combs to HFB, April 26, June 21, July 6, 1939, HFB to Combs, Feb. 20, 27, 1939, H. B. Chermside to HFB, Jan. 19, 1938, HFB to Chermside, Feb. 13, June 24, 1938, box 157, Peery to HFB, March 2, 1939, box 163, BP; *RTD*, May 2, June 12, 20, 1939.

34. *RTD*, Aug. 2, 3, 1939; Combs memo to HFB, June 15, 1939, box 157, HFB to Tom Ozlin, Aug. 5, 1939, box 163, BP; Syrett, "Politics of Preservation," 439–52.

35. *RTD*, Aug. 8, 9, 18, 1939; HFB to Menefee, Nov. 30, 1939, box 4, Marvin Menefee Papers, UVL; HFB to Combs, Oct. 30, 1939, C. S. Carter to Combs, Dec. 27, 1939, box 157, BP.

36. Leonard Muse to Hutchinson, Jan. 5, 1940, box 4, Hutchinson Papers; C. C. Reed to HFB, Jan. 10, 1940, box 163, BP; Weisiger, "Combs," 80.

37. Syrett, "Politics of Preservation," 457–58; *United States News*, Feb. 2, 9, 18, 1940; *RTD*, Feb. 3, 6, 1940; Leib's correspondence, box 398, Glass to Combs, Feb. 12, 1940, Combs to Glass, Feb. 14, 1940, box 398, Glass Papers; HFB to William T. Reed, Jr., Jan. 31, 1940, box 163, BP.

38. *RTD*, Feb. 1, March 10, 12, 1940; Fletcher to HFB, Feb. 5, 1940, Ozlin to HFB, Feb. 3, 1940, box 159, BP; Leonard Muse to Hutchinson, March 11, 1940, H. C. Coleman to Price, March 5, 1940, box 4, Hutchinson Papers; Hall, "Price: New Dealer," 285–87.

39. HFB to Freeman, March 16, 1940, Freeman to HFB, March 18, 1940, box 35, Freeman Papers.

40. HFB to John Stewart Bryan, March 1, 1940, box 156, to Raymond Bottom, March 12, 1940, to Robert Lancaster, Feb. 12, 1940, to Foots Dettor, Feb. 15, 1940, box 165, BP; *RTD*, March 12, 14, 1940; Hart to Hutchinson, May 24, 1939, box 3, Hutchinson Papers; Syrett, "Politics of Preservation," 459–62. Responding to one critic, Byrd said the references to "Byrd Forces" should not be confused with his personally directing those forces. HFB to G. M. Gilkeson, March 16, 1940, box 165, BP.

11. A National Reputation

1. J. Heywood Bell on Byrd's staff was likely the primary author of these pieces: "Lumping Debts on Uncle Sam," *Christian Science Monitor*, Oct. 20, 1937; "The Cost of

Our Government," *Atlantic Monthly,* April 1938; "Pump Priming a Failure While Deficits Mount," *Manufacturers Record,* June 1938; "Uncle Sam's Cash Register," *Commentator,* June 1938; "Government Reorganization," *Country Gentleman,* Oct. 1938; "Waste and Its Effects, *Farm Journal,* Oct. 1938, copies in box 294, BP.

2. *RTD,* Dec. 11, 1938.

3. Link, *American Epoch,* 427–30; Eccles, *Beckoning Frontiers,* 252; *RTD,* Dec. 1, 1937, April 11, 15, May 13, June 4, 1938; Lekachman, *Age of Keynes,* 113, 122–23, 138; Leuchtenburg, *Roosevelt and the New Deal,* 243–46, 264; Roose, *Economics of Recession and Revival,* 238–39; HFB to Marshall, April 21, 1938, box 166, BP.

4. *RTD,* Dec. 26, 1938.

5. Ibid., Jan. 16, 1939; *NYT,* Jan. 16, 1939.

6. See articles by Thomas Ferguson, Steve Fraser, and Alan Brinkley in Fraser and Gerstle, *Rise and Fall of the New Deal Order;* Hogan, *Marshall Plan,* 2–4; Hawley, "The Discovery."

7. Frank DeFriece to HFB, Aug. 5, 1939, box 159, Atlanta *Georgian,* June 21, 1939, copy in scrapbooks, box 24, Baumgartner to HFB, Dec. 21, 1939, HFB to Baumgartner, Dec. 22, 1939, box 156, BP.

8. *CR* 84, pt. 3: 2905–7, March 17, 1939.

9. Porter, *Congress and the Waning of the New Deal,* 90–106; *CR* 84/3/2949, March 20, 1939, 84/3/3050, March 21, 1939; *RTD,* March 7, 18, 23, April 27, 1939; *NYT,* March 18, 1939. For Harold Ickes's claim that Byrd told him he was supporting Wheeler only for political reasons, see Ickes, *Secret Diary* 2:338.

10. Porter, *Congress and the Waning of the New Deal,* 6–19, 44; *RTD,* March 25, May 6, 13, Aug. 11, 1939; *CR* 84/6/6158, May 25, 1939.

11. *NYT,* June 24, July 23, 27, 1939; *RTD,* July 28, 29, Aug. 1, 2, 1939.

12. *NYT,* July 13, 1939; *RTD,* July 14, 1939; *CR* 84/8/8902–11, July 12, 1939.

13. Bailey to HFB, Aug. 29, 1939, scrapbooks, box 25, BP.

14. See Kirby, *Rural Worlds Lost.*

15. Platt, *Virginia in Foreign Affairs,* 63–69; *RTD,* Jan. 19, 1940.

16. Platt, *Virginia in Foreign Affairs,* 49–50, 84, 96–98, 127, 167; Porter, *Seventy-sixth Congress,* 114, 150, 204.

17. Divine, *Reluctant Belligerent,* 22.

18. Speech, June 10, 1935, box 359, BP; *RTD,* Oct. 7, 1951. Byrd may have been influenced by a 1928 article on his governorship which compared him to Mussolini in activist style; see Door, "The Man Who Set Virginia One Hundred Years Ahead," 52.

19. Platt, *Virginia in Foreign Affairs,* 127–28; *RTD,* Feb. 22, 1939.

20. Platt, *Virginia in Foreign Affairs,* 136–47, 194; HFB to Freeman, April 11, 1939, box 28, Feb. 18, 1947, box 76, Freeman Papers.

21. Platt, *Virginia in Foreign Affairs,* 167–68; Lindbergh to HFB, June 7, 1940, scrapbooks, box 30, BP; Lindbergh, *Wartime Journals,* 202, 218, 261, 263, 382.

22. *RTD,* May 31, Aug. 29, 1939; speech, box 362, BP.

23. HFB to Bailey, Sept. 9, 1939, quoted in Patterson, "Eating Humble Pie," 413.

24. *RTD,* Sept. 16, 22, 28, Oct. 14, 16, 1939; *NYT,* Oct. 16, 1939; Divine, *Reluctant Belligerent,* 64–78; Lindbergh, *Wartime Journals,* 261, 263, 273.

25. Speeches, Nov. 7, 1939, Feb. 1, 1940, March 16, 1940, box 362, BP; *RTD,* Nov. 9, 1939, Jan. 16, 20, Feb. 2, 1940; Platt, *Virginia in Foreign Affairs,* 169.

26. Statement, May 15, 1940, speech, May 28, 1940, box 362, BP; *NYT,* May 31, June 3, 10, 1940; *RTD,* May 17, June 12, 13, 19, 1940.

27. G. H. Branaman to HFB, June 13, 1940, HFB to Branaman, June 21, 1940, BP.

28. *RTD*, Oct. 30, 1939, June 2, 15, 23, July 4, 1940; Platt, *Virginia in Foreign Affairs,* 163–71.

29. Donahoe, *Private Plans and Public Dangers,* 21, 117; HFB to George Sloane, Feb. 22, 1940, box 165, BP; to Robertson, Aug. 19, 1939, drawer 108, folder 55, A. Willis Robertson Papers, College of William and Mary Library.

30. HFB to Bruce, Nov. 6, 24, 1939, Bruce to HFB, Nov. 21, 1939, box 156, BP.

31. Byrd/Combs correspondence, 1940, box 158, BP; *RTD*, June 15, 1940.

32. *RTD*, July 18, 1940, Oct. 22, 1944; Davis, "Fourth Term's Hair Shirt."

33. Donahoe, *Private Plans and Public Dangers,* 177; Lindbergh, *Wartime Journals,* 382; *RTD*, Aug. 4, 6, Nov. 4, 1940; *NYT*, July 16, 1940; Combs to HFB, July 22, 24, 1940, box 158, John Laylin to HFB, Aug. 28, 1940, box 162, HFB to C. C. Reed, Aug. 7, 1940, box 163, to Oren Root, June 18, 1940, box 164, to J. Alfred Tyler, Aug. 1, 1940, box 165, to N. E. Clement, Nov. 11, 1940, box 157, BP.

34. *NYT*, Aug. 25, 1940; *RTD*, Aug. 16, 25, 1940.

35. *RTD*, Aug. 25, 28, 29, 1940; *NYT*, Aug. 27, 1940.

36. Divine, *Reluctant Belligerent,* 105–6; Polenberg, *War and Society,* 6–8; *RTD*, Oct. 13, 1940.

37. *CR* 84/2/2285, March 6, 1939; Hilty, "Voting Alignments," 2:399–462, 470; HFB to Gerry, Dec. 9, 1940, box 159, BP.

38. Carey Martin to HFB, Aug. 28, 1940, box 162, BP. Byrd's inquiries failed to identify "Carey Martin," leading him to conclude it was a pseudonym.

39. *NYT*, Dec. 22, 29, 1940; Platt, *Virginia in Foreign Affairs,* 172–73; HFB to Freeman, Dec. 27, 1940, Freeman to HFB, Dec. 30, 1940, box 35, Freeman Papers; Menefee to HFB, Dec. 21, 1940, box 4, Sept. 9, 1941, box 5, Menefee Papers.

40. Truman, *Harry S. Truman,* 138–40; Ferrell, *Truman and the Presidency,* 34–35; McCullough, *Truman,* 264–88.

41. Kimball, *Most Unsordid Act,* 211–20; *CR* 87/2/1803, March 5, 1941; Hatch, *Byrds of Virginia,* 470; *NYT*, June 1, Aug. 19, 1941.

42. Senate speech, March 27, 1941, box 363, BP; Polenberg, *War and Society,* 165; *RTD*, March 20, 30, April 3, 7, 1941; Platt, *Virginia in Foreign Affairs,* 171.

43. *NYT*, April 22, 26, 1941; Senate speeches, April 25, May 26, 1941, box 363, BP.

44. *RTD*, May 16, 26–28, 1941.

45. *CR* 87/7/7209–12, Aug. 19, 1941; *NYT*, Aug. 20, 1941; *RTD*, Sept. 6, 1941.

46. *NYT*, Aug. 23, Sept. 5, 1941; *RTD*, Aug. 29, Sept. 2, 1941.

47. *NYT*, Aug. 29, 1941; *RTD*, Sept. 6, 7, 1941; White, "Meet the Honorable Harry (the Rare) Byrd."

48. *RTD*, Oct. 30, Dec. 26, 1941; committee report, Dec. 24, 1941, box 363, BP; *CR* 87/9/10109–16, Dec. 26, 1941; Glass to HFB, Sept. 19, 1941, HFB to Glass, Sept. 22, 1941, box 246, Glass Papers.

49. Wendell Willkie to Byrd, Oct. 28, 1941, box 294, BP; Lilienthal, *Journals* 1:408.

50. Miller to Dabney, Aug. 29, 1941, box 7, Virginius Dabney Papers, UVL.

51. Key, *Southern Politics,* 27.

52. Byrd, "Waste—The Enemy at Home," *Reader's Digest,* Sept. 1942; speech, Nov. 19, 1941, box 363, BP.

53. HFB to Cox, July 7, 1941, box 173, BP; *RTD*, Sept. 5, 16, Oct. 5, 18, 19, Nov. 1, 8, 13, 14, 1941; Divine, *Reluctant Belligerent,* 137–41, 147–53.

54. *RTD*, Oct. 28, Nov. 2, 13, 14, 1941; Platt, *Virginia in Foreign Affairs,* 180, 189–90;

Dierenfield, *Keeper of the Rules*, 70; HFB to Kump, Nov. 4, 1941, box 177, to Reed, Nov. 21, 1941, box 174, BP.

55. *NYT*, Aug. 20, 1941.

12. The War Years

1. Interviews with Dick and Beverley Byrd.

2. *RTD*, Jan. 7, 8, 1942; Polenberg, *War and Society*, 10–35.

3. *NYT*, Feb. 13, 1942.

4. *RTD*, Feb. 20, 25, March 10–14, April 11, 1942; Blum, *V Was for Victory*, 224–25.

5. *NYT*, May 3, 1942; *RTD*, May 3, 1942; Kent column, *CR* 88/9/A1786, May 15, 1942.

6. *RTD*, Aug. 15, 1943; *CR* 88/3/4224–52, May 15, 1942; McCardle, "Lone Crusader for Thrift."

7. *RTD*, June 21, July 1, 12, 27, 28, 1942, Aug. 15, 1943; Fite, *Russell*, 153–57; *CR* 88/3/ 4270–73, May 18, 1942, 88/5/6625, July 27, 1942.

8. *NYT*, May 13, 29, June 26, 1942.

9. *RTD*, July 15–17, 31, Oct. 10, 1942; *NYT*, July 17, 30, 1942; Polenberg, *War and Society*, 26–33.

10. *CR* 88/7/9264, Dec. 3, 1942.

11. *RTD*, Nov. 16, 18, 23, 1942; Polenberg, *War and Society*, 20–22; McCardle, "Lone Crusader for Thrift."

12. McCardle, "Lone Crusader for Thrift."

13. "Waste Goes On," *American Magazine*, Jan. 1943; "U.S. versus the Frankenstein Monster," *Reader's Digest*, July 1943; "Are We Losing Our Freedom?" *American Magazine*, Aug. 1943; other articles in box 295, BP; *Saturday Evening Post*, April 24, 1943.

14. *RTD*, Dec. 5, 13, 1942, Feb. 19, July 4, 1943; *NYT*, Dec. 11, 13, 1942, May 15, June 10, 1943; Blum, *V Was for Victory*, 235–40; Polenberg, *War and Society*, 81–89; speech to bankers, May 14, 1943, box 365, letter defending Byrd's FSA vote, box 415, BP.

15. Polenberg, *War and Society*, 156–75; Dulles, *Labor in America*, 334–51; *NYT*, March 2, 1943; *RTD*, April 29, 1943; Senate speech, March 1, 1943, box 365, BP.

16. *NYT*, April 8, May 15, Nov. 4, 1943; *RTD*, May 15, June 5, 24, 26, 1943, April 27–29, 1944; Dierenfield, *Keeper of the Rules*, 95–101; Byrd Senate speeches, June 24, 1943, April 28, 1944, boxes 365–66, BP; *CR* 89/3/3029, April 7, 1943.

17. *NYT*, June 17, 30, July 1, Oct. 9, 28, 1943; *RTD*, July 9, 18, Aug. 15, 22, Oct. 19, Nov. 6, 1943; Davis, "Fourth Term's Hair Shirt."

18. HFB to Glass, Nov. 21, 1942, box 423, Glass Papers.

19. *RTD*, Nov. 13, 21, 1943; HFB to Mrs. Richard Loper, March 19, 1942, box 177, BP.

20. *RTD*, Aug. 26, Oct. 14, Nov. 10, 17, 24, 1942, Dec. 4, 1943; HFB to Glass, Oct. 13, 1942, box 423, Glass Papers; Moore, *Bailey*, 215–16.

21. *RTD*, Dec. 5, 8, 1943; *CR* 89/8/10344–46, Dec. 7, 1943; *NYT*, Dec. 8, 1943.

22. Polenberg, *War and Society*, 195–97; *RTD*, Dec. 9, 14, 1943; *NYT*, Dec. 27, 1943; *CR* 90/1/1062–68, Feb. 2, 1944.

23. Wolfe, "Virginia in World War II," 75–80; *RTD*, Feb. 20, March 4, 10, Nov. 21, Dec. 15, 16, 1944, May 4, 1945.

24. *Look* ranked Byrd as the eleventh most useful man in public life in 1944. HFB to Harry Byrd, Jr., May 10, 1944, box 428, BP.

25. Letters to Harry Jr., box 428, BP.

26. HFB to Beverley, June 27, 1945, to Dick, June 30, 1945, box 431, other letters to Beverley, boxes 430–431, BP; interview with Beverley Byrd.

27. Letters to Dick, boxes 430, 431, BP; interview with Dick Byrd.

28. *News-Virginian* quoted in *RTD,* Feb. 11, 1945; *RTD,* Feb. 5, 1945; Combs to HFB, Sept. 29, 1942, HFB to Colgate Darden, Dec. 23, 1942, box 173, to Billy Prieur, Dec. 21, 1943, box 176, to Powell Glass, March 19, 1945, box 186, to Joseph Jett, Oct. 29, 1945, box 187, BP.

29. *NYT,* Dec. 10, 1943.

30. Katznelson, Geiger, and Kryder, "Limiting Liberalism," 284; Savannah *Morning News,* April 23, 1944, copy in scrapbooks, box 49, BP.

31. Garson, *Democratic Party and the Politics of Sectionalism,* 10–90; Grantham, *Life and Death of the Solid South,* 112–17; Farley to Garner, Dec. 17, 1943, box 18, Farley Papers.

32. Hutton to Shephard, Aug. 5, 13, 1943, box 170, BP.

33. HFB to Willis Swift, June 24, 1942, other letters, box 169, BP.

34. HFB to Erwin H. Will, July 10, 1943, box 169, BP; *RTD,* July 2, Oct. 22, 1943.

35. Thomson was the uncle of Gretchen Thomson Byrd, who had married Harry Jr. in 1941.

36. Adler to Thomson, July 3, 1943, Coghlan to Thomson, July 2, 1943, other letters, box 171, BP.

37. *RTD,* June 5, 1943; HFB to Knight, July 19, 1943, box 169, Hutton to Gannett, April 22, 1943, box 170, BP.

38. Archer to HFB, Aug. 18, 29, Sept. 3, 14, 1943, HFB to Archer, Aug. 27, 30, Sept. 9, 1943, boxes 169 and 170, BP.

39. HFB to McLemore, July 14, 1943, box 178, BP; Fraser and Gerstle, *Rise and Fall of the New Deal Order,* xii-xvi; see also Collins, *Business Response to Keynes.*

40. Materials, box 170, newspaper editorial comment, scrapbooks, box 47, BP.

41. Woodring to HFB, Oct. 8, 1943, HFB to Woodring, Nov. 2, 1943, box 170, BP. Woodring headed one of several conservative organizations that were seeking to topple Roosevelt.

42. HFB to Dick Byrd, March 9, 1943, box 430, to Watts, April 5, 1944, box 182, Woodring to HFB, Feb. 16, 1944, scrapbooks, box 48, BP.

43. *RTD,* March 1, 23, 25, 30, 31, April 1, 6, 11, 12, 15, 1944; W. T. Reed, Jr., to Walter Sams, March 29, 1944, box 179, Combs to HFB, April 7, 1944, HFB to Combs, April 8, 1944, box 173, to Arnold, April 7, 1944, box 168, BP. Byrd was irritated with the *Times-Dispatch* for publishing the low attendance figures, for which he was primarily responsible. HFB to Virginius Dabney, April 10, 1944, m3, Dabney Papers.

44. Farley to Garner, April 19, 1944, box 18; memos, April 15, June 29, Nov. 10, 24, 1943, March 20, 1944, box 45, Farley Papers; Combs to HFB, April 20, 1944, box 173, HFB to Harry Byrd, Jr., April 27, 1944, box 428, BP.

45. *RTD,* March 31, April 9, 12, 1944.

46. *RTD,* April 18, 19, 27, 1944; Zach Cobb to Colgate Darden, June 12, 1944, Cobb to HFB, May 15, 1944, box 171, BP; Davis, "Fourth Term's Hair Shirt."

47. HFB to Colgate Darden, May 19, 1944, box 175, Crowley to HFB, June 13, 1944, HFB to R. B. Stephenson, June 1, 1944, box 181, Lewis Brown to HFB, June 2, 1944, box 172, HFB to C. S. Carter, June 13, 1944, BP.

48. HFB to William T. Reed, Jr., April 5, 1944, box 179, to W. F. Wynn, June 28, 1944, box 183, to Karl Crowley, June 28, 1944, box 173, BP.

49. *RTD*, March 31, April 10, May 1, June 21, 24, 25, 1944; Garson, *Politics of Sectionalism*, 108–11; HFB to J. E. McDonald, June 30, 1944, Marrs McLean to HFB, June 10, 1944, box 178, HFB to Harry Byrd, Jr., June 9, 23, 1944, box 428, BP.

50. *RTD*, July 12, 1944; Garson, *Politics of Sectionalism*, 113; HFB to J. Mark Wilcox, June 9, 1944, box 171, BP.

51. *RTD*, June 4, 25, July 9, Oct. 22, 1944; Willis Robertson to Colgate Darden, June 10, 13, 22, 1944, drawer 108, folder 27, Robertson Papers; Robinette to Martin Hutchinson, July 10, 1944, box 6, Hutchinson Papers; HFB to Smith, July 17, 1944, box 180, speech, July 8, 1944, box 366, BP.

52. *RTD*, July 18, 19, 21, 1944; *NYT*, July 21, 1944; Garson, *Politics of Sectionalism*, 118–19.

53. Blum, *V Was for Victory*, 289–92; Byrnes to HFB, Aug. 3, 1944, scrapbooks, box 55, HFB to Beverley and Dick Byrd, July 26, 1944, box 431, BP; Moore, "Unrewarding Stone," 21; Latimer interviews with Tuck and Darden; *RTD*, July 22, 1944; *NYT*, July 22, 1944; Johnson, "Senator Byrd of Virginia"; Mitchell, South Dakota *Republic*, July 25, 1944, copy in scrapbooks, box 50, BP.

54. *RTD*, July 28, 1944; John Barr, "Draft Byrd for President Campaign," June 1, 1944, HFB to Cobb, Aug. 21, 1944, box 171, BP.

55. HFB to W. B. Bogart, Sept. 28, 1944, box 172, to Junius Fishburne, July 25, 1944, box 175, to Combs, July 28, 1944, box 173, to Crowley, Oct. 4, 1946, box 171, to Richard Byrd, Aug. 4, 1944, box 426, BP.

56. HFB to Wysor, April 6, 1944, box 183, BP.

57. HFB to Lloyd C. Bird, Aug. 10, Sept. 25, 1944, box 168, BP.

58. Efforts to line up independent electors were underway in Texas, Florida, Mississippi, and South Carolina; see E. H. Ramsey to John Barr, Aug. 29, 1944, Karl Crowley to HFB, Sept. 18, 1944, box 171, HFB to Combs, Sept. 29, 1944, other correspondence, box 173, James Eastland to HFB, Nov. 6, 1944, box 175, BP.

59. *RTD*, Oct. 19, 22, 24, 29, Nov. 4, 5, 21, 1944; Frank Kent, Baltimore *Sun*, Nov. 17, 1944, copy in box 177, Mrs. Richard Loper to HFB, Oct. 31, 1944, box 177, HFB to Rhodes, Oct. 31, 1944, box 179, to Richard Richardson, Nov. 14, 1944, box 180, BP; to Willis Robertson, Oct. 10, 1944, drawer 108, folder 27, Robertson Papers; Dabney to Byrd Jr., Nov. 11, 1944, Byrd Jr., to Dabney, Nov. 21, 1944, N5, Dabney Papers.

60. *RTD*, Nov. 8, 1944; Garson, *Politics of Sectionalism*, 125–29, 314. FDR's margin of victory in the South was still high (71.4 percent), but it was down considerably from that in 1936 (80.6 percent) and 1940 (78.1 percent). Byrd's Texas electors polled 11.7 percent of the vote; in South Carolina, Byrd won more votes than Dewey. Shannon, "Presidential Politics in the South."

61. *CR* 91/7/9760, Dec. 18, 1945; Albright, "Byrd for Pay-as-You-Go Budget," Washington *Post*, June 10, 1951; Hatch, *Byrds of Virginia*, 476.

62. *RTD*, Jan. 22–31, Feb. 2, March 2, 24, 1945; Blum, *V Was for Victory*, 240, 300; Moore, *Bailey*, 221–24; HFB to W. Stuart Moffett, Jan. 31, 1945, box 189, to C. C. Reed, March 14, 1945, box 190, BP.

63. *RTD*, April 13, 14, 22, 1945; HFB to R. E. Blackwell, April 16, 1945, to Cobb, April 19, 1945, box 185, BP. *The Road to Serfdom* by Friedrich Hayek, a defense of the unregulated free market and an attack on government interference, was popular reading with Byrd and his correspondents. HFB to Daniel Carrison, April 2, 1945.

13. An Unsettled World

1. *CR* 91/6/8190, July 28, 1945; *RTD*, May 2, 7, June 29, 1945; HFB to Richard Byrd, June 30, Nov. 30, 1945, box 426, BP.

2. *RTD*, Sept. 15, 17, 21, Oct. 15, 1946.

3. Ibid., March 13, 1947.

4. Hero, *Southerner and World Affairs*, 5–6; Byrd statement, Oct. 4, 1945, box 402, BP; Elizabeth Gring to HFB, Gring to J. William Fulbright, Jan. 17, 1946, J. William Fulbright Papers, University of Arkansas Library.

5. *CR* 91/9/12163, Dec. 17, 1945; *RTD*, Jan. 11, May 11, 1946; HFB to P. L. Reed, Aug. 1945, box 190, statement, Dec. 17, 1945, box 402, BP.

6. Statements, March 12, April 6, 1947, box 403, BP.

7. Speeches, April 1, 22, 1947, box 367, BP; *CR* 93/3/2952, April 1, 1947, 93/3/3773, April 22, 1947; *RTD*, April 2, 6–8, 1947.

8. *RTD*, April 13, 18, 23, 26, 1947; HFB to Douglas Freeman, March 17, April 22, 1947, box 76, Freeman Papers.

9. Link, *American Epoch*, 709–10.

10. *RTD*, Dec. 26, 1947; speech to National Association of Manufacturers, Dec. 4, 1947, box 367, article for *Dickinsonian*, student newspaper at Dickinson College, article for *Redbook*, Jan. 1948, copies in box 297, HFB to Colgate Darden, March 18, 1948, box 192, BP.

11. Douglas Freeman to HFB, Jan. 31, 1948, box 85, Freeman Papers; *RTD*, March 14, 1948; speech, March 13, 1948, box 368, HFB to Richard Byrd, March 4, 16, 1948, box 426, Byrd voting record, box 349, BP; interview with Harry Byrd, Jr.

12. Interview with Harry Byrd, Jr.; *CR* 91/8/10068, Oct. 26, 1945, 92/8/10671, Aug. 2, 1946; HFB to Alben Barkley, Jan. 10, 1945, Alben Barkley Papers, University of Kentucky Library.

13. Richard Byrd to HFB, Dec. 28, 1946, box 426, HFB to Cary, Feb. 3, 1948, box 185, BP; *RTD*, April 9, 1945, June 5, 1946; HFB to Freeman, Feb. 7, 1948, box 85, Freeman Papers. Byrd was still consulting Freeman on foreign policy issues.

14. HFB to Tuck, Dec. 28, 1945, folder 3341, Tuck Papers.

15. *RTD*, May 5, 10, 25, June 29, Aug. 21, 1945; *CR* 91/9/11532, Dec. 6, 1945; HFB to W. B. Bogart, June 30, 1945, box 185, Truman to Carter Manasco, June 11, 1945, box 402, Truman to HFB, April 25, 1945, scrapbooks, box 53, Byrd statements, May 24, 1945, box 186, BP; HFB to Truman, June 27, 1945, Harry S. Truman Papers, Harry S. Truman Library.

16. Link, *American Epoch*, 673–74.

17. "Senator Byrd Talks about 'Presidents I Have Known,'" *U.S. News and World Report* 53 (Sept. 10, 1962): 84; Griffith, *Crisis of American Labor*, xiii, 15; Lee, *Truman and Taft-Hartley*, 10–20, 36; McCullough, *Truman*, 494.

18. *RTD*, Jan. 11, May 26, 28, 30, 1946; Harry Byrd, "Mutual Responsibility Essential to Labor-Management Peace," *Manufacturers Record*, Feb. 1946, 42, copy in box 296, HFB to Fred Huddlestun, Sept. 5, 1945, box 188, to E. M. Eddy, Feb. 13, 1946, box 186, BP.

19. Hatch, *Byrds of Virginia*, 480.

20. *RTD*, May 10, 11, 15, 16, 19, 22, 23, 24, 1946; *CR* 92/4/4891–95, May 13, 1946, 92/4/5040–44, May 15, 1946, 92/4/5267, May 20, 1946, 92/4/5330–31, May 21, 1946.

21. McClure, *Truman Administration and the Problems of Postwar Labor*, 130; *CR* 92/

5/5687, May 25, 1946; *RTD,* May 26, 30, June 5, 6, 12, Aug. 18, 1946; Byrd statements, box 367, 402, BP.

22. *RTD,* Nov. 22, 23, Dec. 6, 1946; Byrd statements, Nov. 21, Dec. 9, 1946, box 403, speech, Dec. 5, 1946, box 367, BP.

23. *RTD,* Nov. 7, 1946, July 13, 1947. Truman retaliated by calling Fulbright "Senator Halfbright." McCullough, *Truman,* 523.

24. *RTD,* Jan. 7, May 3, 8, 10, 14, 1947; Byrd statement, April 25, 1947, box 403, BP; *Congress and the Nation,* 584–85; Dierenfield, *Keeper of the Rules,* 112–15.

25. Katznelson et al., "Limiting Liberalism," 294, 300; *RTD,* May 5, June 21, 22, 24, 1947; Byrd statement, June 21, 1947, box 403, BP; Link, *American Epoch,* 620–21, 676.

26. *RTD,* Jan. 11, May 5, June 30, 1947, Jan. 13, 1948; statement, Feb. 19, 1947, Fulbright Papers; Senate speech, Feb. 14, 1947, box 367, BP; Ferrell, *Dear Bess,* 548.

27. Senate speech, Jan. 31, 1946, box 366, BP; *RTD,* Feb. 2, 1946.

28. *RTD,* Oct. 30, 31, Dec. 22, 1947, Feb. 15, 1948; McCullough, *Truman,* 590; Hamby, *Beyond the New Deal,* 183; Garson, *Politics of Sectionalism,* 132–47, 172, 194–201, 231, 235; HFB to Archibald Aiken, Feb. 6, 1948, box 187, BP.

29. Speech, Feb. 19, 1948, box 368, BP.

30. *RTD,* Feb. 27, 1948; Crawley, *Bill Tuck,* 140–44; HFB to Tuck, Feb. 26, 1948, box 191, BP; to Tuck, March 4, 1948, folder 3343, Tuck Papers; *CR* 94/2/1730, Feb. 26, 1948.

31. Tuck insisted that he did this on his own after hearing Byrd's Richmond speech. He and Attorney General Staples and Combs worked up the bill which may have been more extreme than Byrd had intended. Latimer interviews with Tuck and Darden; interviews with James Latimer and Paul Saunier.

32. HFB to Combs, Feb. 21, 1948, box 185, to Curry Carter, March 2, 1948, box 186, BP.

33. Interview with Harry Byrd, Jr.

34. James Sweeney, "Golden Silence," 352; Crawley, *Bill Tuck,* 152; HFB to Tuck, Feb. 21, 24, 26, 1948, Tuck to HFB, Feb. 24, 1948, box 191, BP; *RTD,* Feb. 27, 1948; interview with Latimer and Saunier.

35. *RTD,* Feb. 27–29, 1948; Prieur to HFB, March 1, 1948, box 17, Edward L. Breeden, Jr., Papers, UVL; Hutchinson to N. Clarence Smith, March 2, 1948, to James P. Hart, Jr., March 17, 1948, box 10, Hutchinson Papers; John Goldsmith to Francis Miller, Feb. 27, 1948, box 48, Francis Pickens Miller Papers, UVL; Sweeney, "Golden Silence," 354–55.

36. This time Byrd forewarned his son of what was coming. HFB to Harry Byrd, Jr., Feb. 27, 1948, box 428, BP.

37. *RTD,* Feb. 28, March 1, 1948; Switzer to Robertson, March 13, 1948, box 8, to Burr Harrison, March 16, 1948, box 3, Switzer Papers; HFB to Fulbright, March 8, 1948, Fulbright Papers.

38. Sweeney, "Golden Silence," 354–58; Crawley, *Bill Tuck,* 146–50; *RTD,* March 7, 10, 14, 1948; HFB to Tuck, March 18, 1948, folder 3343, Tuck Papers; to Preston Collins, March 22, 1948, Collins to Tuck, March 19, 1948, box 4d, BP.

39. *RTD,* March 6, 9, 14, 1948; HFB to Tuck, March 22, 1948, box 191, to H. G. Kump, May 27, 1948, box 188, to Combs, March 22, 1948, to Horace C. Wilkinson, April 2, 1948, box 4d, to Combs, March 31, 1948, box 185, BP; Crawley, *Bill Tuck,* 154–60; Garson, *Politics of Sectionalism,* 239–60.

40. *RTD,* Feb. 13, 25, 1948; Barr to HFB, June 17, 1947, box 184, Tuck to HFB, March 19, 1948, HFB to Tuck, March 22, 1948, box 191, to Wysor, June 19, 1948, box 195, BP.

41. Switzer to Robertson, June 5, 1948, box 8, Switzer Papers; Robertson to Switzer, June 3, 1948, drawer 110, folder 14, Robertson Papers.

42. Robertson to HFB, May 31, 1949, drawer 110, folder 12, Robertson Papers.

43. Interview with Harry Byrd, Jr.

44. Sweeney, "Golden Silence," 362–63; Crawley, *Bill Tuck*, 160–63; *RTD*, July 3, 4, 6, 1948; Prieur to HFB, July 15, 1948, box 189, BP.

45. *RTD*, July 12–15, 1948; HFB to Combs, July 19, 1948, box 185, BP; Crawley, *Bill Tuck*, 168.

46. *RTD*, July 18, 1948; Ader, "Why the Dixiecrats Failed"; Gore, *Let the Glory Out*, 66.

47. Latimer, *RTD*, July 18, 1948; Tuck to HFB, July 21, 1948, HFB to Tuck, July 24, 1948, folder 3343, Tuck to Tom Burch, July 27, 1948, folder 3340, Preston Collins to Tuck, July 12, 1948, folder 3345, Tuck Papers; HFB to Tuck, July 21, 1948, box 191, Combs to HFB, July 24, Aug. 9, 1948, box 185, BP; Crawley, *Bill Tuck*, 168–72.

48. *RTD*, Aug. 25, Sept. 26, 27, 1948.

49. Hutchinson to Robinette, July 19, 1948, box 10, to George Martin, Aug. 10, 1948, box 11, Hutchinson Papers; *RTD*, Sept. 28, Oct. 19, 1948; Sweeney, "Golden Silence," 366–70; Crawley, *Bill Tuck*, 172–74.

50. *RTD*, Sept. 11, Oct. 9–11, 14, 1948; Combs to Wysor, Sept. 21, 1948, box 7b, Combs Papers; Beagle and Osborne, *Almond*, 50.

51. Thurmond's vote was high in the home counties of Byrd and Tuck, who admitted he voted for Thurmond. Latimer interviews with Tuck and Darden.

52. *RTD*, July 27, 28, Aug. 13, Nov. 8, 9, 1948; Link, *American Epoch*, 676–80; Hutchinson to Henry Fowler, Nov. 4, 1948, Robert Whitehead to J. Howard McGrath, Sept. 28, 1948, box 11, Hutchinson Papers; Henriques, "Organization Challenged," 380.

53. Sweeney, "Golden Silence," 368–71; Garson, *Politics of Sectionalism*, 314; Grant, "1948 Presidential Election in Virginia"; HFB to Tuck, Nov. 17, 18, 1948, folder 3343, Tuck Papers; Crawley, *Bill Tuck*, 174–79.

14. A Changing Virginia

1. Wolfe, "Virginia in World War II," 142–96; Platt, *Virginia in Foreign Affairs*, 111–22.

2. Wolfe, "Virginia in World War II," 22–25; Edwards to HFB, July 9, 1943, box 175, BP.

3. Quoted in Latimer interviews with Darden and Tuck.

4. Crawley, *Bill Tuck*, 41–42; Wilkinson, *Byrd*, 14; HFB to Cary, Nov. 26, 1940, box 157, BP; Muse, "Durability of Byrd"; Muse, Washington *Post*, July 28, 1966. Harry Jr. believed his father was largely responsible for the selections of Pollard, Peery, Darden, and Battle to run for governor. Interview with Harry Byrd, Jr.

5. Crawley, *Bill Tuck*, 43–44; Rochester and Wolfe, "Darden," 295–96; Wolfe, "Virginia in World War II," 38–43; *RTD*, Oct. 13, 16, 18, Nov. 1, 1940, Nov. 9, 1941; interview with Harry Byrd, Jr.; Smith to Combs, Nov. 15, 1940, box 166, BP.

6. Latimer interviews with Darden and Tuck.

7. Crawley, *Bill Tuck*, 43–44; Tuck to William Dillard, Nov. 16, 1940, folder 2830, Tuck Papers; *RTD*, Dec. 15, 17, 22, 1940, Jan. 4, 1941.

8. *RTD*, Aug. 6, Oct. 5, 7, 1941; HFB to S. B. Barham, Oct. 8, 1941, box 172, to W. O. Rogers, Oct. 8, 1941, box 179, to Darden, Aug. 14, 18, 1941, Combs to Darden, Aug. 12, 1941, Darden to HFB, Dec. 27, 1941, Combs to HFB, Oct. 9, 1941, box 173, BP; Rochester and Wolfe, "Darden," 297.

9. Champagne, *Rayburn*, 148; Richard Byrd to HFB, Sept. 19, 1951, box 426, BP.

10. HFB to Freeman, March 20, 1947, box 76, Freeman Papers; interviews with Abbitt and Saunier.

11. HFB to W. S. Battle, Jan. 20, 1942, box 174, BP.

12. *RTD*, March 12, 13, 16, 1942; Rochester and Wolfe, "Darden," 297–303; Wolfe, "Virginia in World War II," 41–54, 102–13; HFB to Darden, Jan. 7, 8, 9, 1942, March 20, April 24, 1942, Darden to HFB, Jan. 12, 1942, box 173.

13. HFB to Combs, March 29, 1945, Combs to HFB, April 26, 1945, box 185, BP.

14. Weisiger, "Combs," 84–90; Combs to HFB, July 26, 1944, box 168, Dec. 11, 1944, box 173, HFB to Combs, Dec. 20, 1944, box 173, BP.

15. Latimer and Stephens quoted in Sweeney, "Byrd and Anti-Byrd," 21.

16. Wysor to HFB, April 20, 1944, HFB to Wysor, April 6, 1944, box 183, BP.

17. Interviews with Harry Byrd, Jr., Godwin, and Abbitt; Latimer interviews with Darden and Tuck; *RTD*, May 5, 1964.

18. Crawley, *Bill Tuck*, 50–65; Sweeney, "Byrd and Anti-Byrd," 30–34; HFB to J. D. Bassett, Feb. 23, 1945, box 185, F. E. Kellam to HFB, Jan. 9, 1945, box 188, G. Alvin Massenburg to HFB, Jan. 19, 1945, box 189, HFB to Stokes, Feb. 13, 1945, box 191, to Wysor, Feb. 21, March 28, 1945, Wysor to HFB, March 30, 1945, box 195, BP; Latimer interviews with Darden and Tuck.

19. Moger, *Virginia*, 354–55; HFB to William Reed, June 30, 1930, box 99, BP; Wysor to Combs, July 11, 1946, box 6b, Hargis to Combs, Jan. 27, 1950, box 8b, Combs Papers.

20. R. O. Norris to HFB, April 28, 1945, HFB to Norris, May 7, 1945, Billy Prieur to HFB, May 7, 1945, box 189, Watkins Abbitt to HFB, May 23, 1945, box 184, BP. Byrd wrote Fred Switzer that he had maintained strict neutrality on the race and told no one how to vote. Leonard Muse believed that "orders went down at the last moment to support Fenwick." HFB to Switzer, Aug. 9, 1945, box 1, Switzer Papers; Muse to Martin Hutchinson, Aug. 18, 1945, box 6, Hutchinson Papers.

21. Martin Hutchinson believed the leadership tried to keep Collins from contesting the results, but when he did, they threw support to him and relied on Judge Gunn, an old friend of Harry Byrd's, to suppress the investigation. Hutchinson to Lloyd Robinette, Oct. 2, 1945, box 7, Hutchinson Papers; Fenwick to A. Laurie Pitts, Jr., Sept. 5, 1945, box 15, Charles R. Fenwick Papers, UVL.

22. *RTD*, Aug. 9, 15, 22, 25, 29, Sept. 23, 30, Oct. 10, 1945, Nov. 24, 1953, Dec. 28, 1954; HFB to George Norris, Sept. 12, 1945, box 189, to Darden, Sept. 5, 1945, to Combs, Sept. 5, 1945, box 185, to Darden, Sept. 18, 1945, box 186, BP; Dabney, *Virginia*, 497, 551.

23. HFB to Darden, Oct. 16, 1945, box 186, to Tuck, Sept. 7, 11, 1945, Jan. 18, 1946, box 191, BP; Crawley, *Bill Tuck*, 74–75; editorial in Manassas *Messenger*, Feb. 15, 1949, box 3, Benjamin Muse Papers, UVL; HFB to Tuck, Dec. 28, 1945, folder 3341, Tuck Papers. Years later, in reference to the reappointment of John Hopkins Hall, a longtime Organization bureaucrat, as head of the Department of Labor and Industry, Tuck was reported to have said, "Mr. Byrd had me elected to office and, if Mr. Byrd tells me to reappoint John Hopkins Hall, Jr., I have no alternative, and I know he is going to tell me to reappoint him." Tuck denied the accusation, but a labor official signed an affidavit swearing the quotation was accurate. *RTD*, Feb. 11–13, 1949.

24. *RTD*, March 15, 1942; HFB to Henry Holt, Dec. 6, 1944, box 182, to Ben Gunter, Dec. 1, 1944, box 176, to Wysor, Sept. 13, 1944, box 183, BP.

25. Breeden to Darden, Dec. 4, 1944, box 9, Breeden Papers; HFB to E. W. Senter, Jan. 18, 1945, box 192, BP.

26. Article in box N8, Dabney papers; Daniels, "Virginia Democracy," 74; Washing-

ton *Post,* June 9, 1957; *RTD,* March 31, 1946; David, Moos, and Goldman, *Presidential Nominating Politics in 1952* 3:10.

27. *RTD,* Dec. 16, 1945, Feb. 20, 21, March 5, 1946, Nov. 9, 1949; Wysor to HFB, May 24, 1945, HFB to Wysor, Oct. 4, 1945, box 195, Wysor to HFB, Sept. 13, 1945, to Prieur, Sept. 14, 1945, HFB to Combs, Feb. 7, 1945, box 185, Wysor to Abbitt, June 29, 1949, box 203, BP; Buni, *Negro in Virginia Politics,* 131–41.

28. *RTD,* Jan. 23, 27, June 19, 1946; HFB to Tuck, Jan. 24, 1946, box 191, to J. H. Bradford, April 12, 1946, box 185, BP.

29. HFB to Smith, Nov. 7, 1945, box 190, BP; Crawley, *Bill Tuck,* 73–74; Wolfe, "Virginia in World War II," 81–84; Friddell, *Darden,* 167.

30. *RTD,* Dec. 9, 1945.

31. *RTD,* Nov. 10, Dec. 6, 1944, Jan. 28, 1946; Crawley, *Bill Tuck,* 82. Union membership in Virginia in 1946 was estimated at approximately 100,000; from 1939 to 1953, it grew from 68,000 to 156,000. Marshall, *Labor in the South,* 299.

32. Crawley, *Bill Tuck,* 94.

33. Ibid., 84–105; Marshall, *Labor in the South,* 246; Walter Scott to Tuck, March 30, 1946, box 191, HFB to Tuck, March 25, 1946, box 191, April 8, 1946, box 181, BP; *RTD,* March 30, 1946.

34. Combs to HFB, April 1, 1946, box 185, BP.

35. *RTD,* April 28, 1946; Dabney to Hutchinson, May 3, 1946, box 7, Hutchinson Papers.

36. HFB to James Garrett, Jan. 29, 1946, box 190, Combs to HFB, March 23, 1946, box 185, HFB to Abbitt, March 27, 1946, box 184, to S. B. Houghton, April 9, 1946, box 190, BP.

37. *RTD,* May 11, 1946; Tuck to HFB, May 15, 1946, box 191, HFB to Goolrick, June 24, 1946, box 187, BP.

38. *RTD,* April 28, June 9, 1946; Sweeney, "Byrd and Anti-Byrd," 46–56; Moss Plunkett to Hutchinson, April 22, 1946, Kemper to Hutchinson, April 30, 1946, Hutchinson to Frank Floyd, June 27, 1946, box 8, Robinette to Hutchinson, May 25, 1946, box 7, Hutchinson Papers.

39. *RTD,* Aug. 3–7, Nov. 6, 1946, Sept. 5, 21, 1947; HFB to Combs, Sept. 15, 1947, box 1b, Combs Papers; Hutchinson to Robinette, Aug. 19, 1946, box 9, Hutchinson Papers; Sweeney, "Byrd and Anti-Byrd," 52–70; Robertson to Switzer, Aug. 1, 1946, box 7, Switzer Papers.

40. *RTD,* May 29, June 6, 1946; Wolfe and Rochester, "Darden," 303; Friddell, *Darden,* 100–101, 150.

41. Dierenfield, *Keeper of the Rules,* 22–33, 48, 108–11; Dierenfield, "Congressman Smith," 170; Albert, *Little Giant,* 227; interviews with Godwin and Abbitt; Frank Wysor to HFB, Aug. 18, 1946, Wysor to Howard Smith, Aug. 18, 1946, box 6b, Combs Papers.

42. Robertson to E. W. Opie, June 28, 1946, drawer 109, folder 26, Robertson to Switzer, June 18, 1946, drawer 109, folder 25, Switzer to HFB, Sept. 9, 1946, drawer 109, folder 27, Robertson Papers; Switzer to Robertson, Aug. 2, 1946, box 7, additional correspondence between Switzer and Robertson, box 7, Switzer Papers; Combs to HFB, Sept. 18, 1946, box 185, BP; *RTD,* Sept. 6, 1946; Dierenfield, *Keeper of the Rules,* 111.

43. *RTD,* Dec. 24, 1944, Dec. 11, 1946; Jan. 7, 1947, Nov. 25, 28, 1948; Crawley, *Bill Tuck,* 181–86; Wilkinson, *Byrd,* 42–44.

44. *RTD,* Jan. 7, 1947, Jan. 15, 1948; HFB to Tuck, Jan. 3, 11, 1947, Tuck to HFB, Jan. 7, 1947, box 191, HFB to Combs, Jan. 21, 1948, box 185, to Wysor, Jan. 4, 1945, Jan. 21,

1948, box 195, BP; HFB to Combs, Sept. 26, 1947, box 1b, Combs Papers; Crawley, *Bill Tuck,* 180–91.

45. Henriques, "Organization Challenged," 372–73; Battle to HFB, Feb. 28, 1947, to Darden, Feb. 28, 1947, box 184, HFB to Combs, Aug. 15, 1947, box 185, Wysor to HFB, June 27, 1947, box 195, BP; Combs to Wysor, June 30, 1947, box 7b, Combs Papers.

46. Combs to Wysor, Sept. 26, 1947, box 7b, to Edwards, Oct. 23, 1947, box 12b, HFB to Fulmer Bright, June 18, 1949, box 1b, Combs Papers; Wilkinson, *Byrd,* 92–95.

47. Henriques, "Organization Challenged," 373–77; Miller, *Man from the Valley,* 173–74; Combs to HFB, May 7, 1947, box 185, Arnold to HFB, July 22, 1948, HFB to Arnold, July 30, 1948, box 184, BP; Combs to Arnold, July 30, 1948, HFB to Combs, Oct. 15, 1948, box 1b, Combs Papers.

48. Combs to Battle, June 11, 15, 1948, box 3b, HFB to Combs, June 12, 1948, to Howard Smith, Nov. 17, 1948, to Battle, Nov. 17, Dec. 9, 1948, Combs to HFB, Sept. 1, 1948, box 1b, Combs to Smith, Nov. 19, 1948, 6b, Combs Papers.

49. HFB to Battle, Sept. 10, 1948, Switzer to HFB, Nov. 24, 1948, Combs to HFB, Dec. 16, 17, 1948, HFB to Combs, Jan. 14, 1949, box 1b, Combs Papers; HFB to Battle, Jan. 14, 1949, box 196, BP.

50. *RTD,* Feb. 11, 1949; Henriques, "Organization Challenged," 379–84.

51. HFB to Kellam, Dec. 29, 1948, to Combs, Jan. 24, 26, 1949, to Edwin Cox, Jan. 26, 1949, box 1b, Combs Papers; HFB to Robert Brock, Feb. 16, 1949, to George Hardy, Feb. 16, 1949, box 200, to Billy Prieur, Feb. 14, 1949, box 201, to Battle, Feb. 15, March 4, April 7, 29, May 10, 25, 1949, box 196, BP; Battle to J. S. Gunn, Feb. 8, 1949, box 29, Miller Papers; *RTD,* Feb. 19, 1949.

52. Henriques, "Organization Challenged," 390–92.

53. Ibid., 394–97; Sweeney, "Byrd and Anti-Byrd," 130–31; *RTD,* June 26, July 10, 11, 17, 18, 20, 1949; Switzer to Burr Harrison, July 19, 1949, box 3, Switzer Papers.

54. Cam B. Perdue, Commissioner of Revenue in Franklin County, to Ben R. Dillon, July 19, 1949, box 33, Miller Papers.

55. *RTD* July 13, 16, 1949; Henriques, "Organization Challenged," 395–96; Sweeney, "Byrd and Anti-Byrd," 135–36; Interviews with Harry Byrd, Jr., and Godwin. Harry Jr. believes this tactic to undercut Edwards is what won the election for Battle since he and Edwards had started the race with fairly even Organization support.

56. Combs to HFB, Jan. 7, 1942, box 173, BP; *RTD,* July 14, 15, 1949; Combs to Hargis, July 28, 1949, box 8b, Combs Papers; Henriques, "Organization Challenged," 398–99; Washington *Post,* June 19, 1957. Combs and Wysor had tried without success to get the Republicans not to hold a primary, hoping this would free Republicans to vote for Battle on primary day. Miller claimed that Wise promised GOP support if Byrd "used his influence to persuade the Virginia delegates to the Republican National Convention to support Robert Taft for the presidency." Jim Latimer has suggested that Wise may have approached Byrd on the subject and was encouraged to proceed. Wise later denied any arrangement. Combs to Wysor, April 14, May 16, 1949, box 9b, Combs Papers; Miller, *Man from the Valley,* 187; interviews with Latimer and Godwin.

57. Henriques, "Organization Challenged," 400–406; HFB to Battle, Aug. 4, 1949, Battle to HFB, Aug. 6, 1949, box 196, HFB to Richard Byrd, Aug. 26, 1949, box 426, BP; Wysor to Combs, Aug. 7, 1949, box 9b, Combs Papers; Sweeney, "Byrd and Anti-Byrd," 145–47; Hutchinson to B. A. Banks, Aug. 3, 1949, box 12, Hutchinson Papers; Miller, *Man from the Valley,* 187.

15. "Too Many Byrds"

1. Anderson, *Outsider in the Senate*, 98; Morgan, *Kerr*, 33; *CR* 84/8/8905, July 12, 1939.

2. White, *Citadel*, 70–76; Wilkinson, *Byrd*, 66–70; McCarthy, *Up 'Til Now*, 53–56; Douglas, *Memoirs*, 198–213; Foley, *New Senate*, 9; see also Matthews, *U.S. Senators and Their World*; Polsby, *Congress and the Presidency*; and Ripley, "Power in the Post-World War II Senate."

3. Manchester, "Byrd Machine."

4. Patterson, *Mr. Republican*, 193, 260, 308, 583; Douglas, *Memoirs*, 203; Strom Thurmond to author; William Proxmire to author; interview with Harry Byrd, Jr.

5. Interviews with Harry Jr. and Dick Byrd, Joe and Teresa Massie, and Harry Byrd III; Hatch, *Byrds of Virginia*, 494; James J. Kilpatrick, "Human Events," Aug. 10, 1957, copy in box 245, BP.

6. Interviews with Byrd's sons.

7. Interviews with Harry Byrd, Jr., Godwin, Latimer, Harrison, and Abbitt; Charles McDowell, Jr., to author, Dec. 7, 1994.

8. Davis, "Fourth Term's Hair Shirt"; see Steven Stowe, *Intimacy and Power*.

9. McDowell, "Weary Report on a Byrd Walk"; Dabney, "Virginia's Man of the Mid-Century."

10. McDowell, "Weary Report on a Byrd Walk"; interviews with Byrd's sons; interview with Senator Russell Long; Hatch, *Byrds of Virginia*, 459, 496, 512; *RTD*, June 21, 1959; Miller, "Giving Them Fits"; HFB to staff, Dec. 23, 1948, box 6, Menefee Papers; HFB to Charlotte Avery, March 6, 1963, box 264, column by W. C. Stouffer in box 157, HFB to Chambers, Dec. 26, 1959, box 243, radio address, "Lee the Man," Jan. 19, 1934, copy in box 359, BP.

11. HFB to Bruce S. Hopping, July 10, 1959, box 248, BP; Hatch, *Byrds of Virginia*, 485; interviews with Byrd's sons; Guy Friddell, *News Leader*, June 11, 1962.

12. Interview with Abbitt; HFB to Joe W. Sandifer, Jr., Oct. 10, 1964, box 301, speeches, Aug. 24, 1939, box 362, Oct. 5, 1963, box 393, BP; see also Sweeney, "Harry Byrd." Sandifer, a Presbyterian minister, had written Byrd for his views on the role of the Christian in politics. The thirteen-page reply, complete with references to the *Bible*, Milton, and Tocqueville, was likely written by one of Byrd's staff, although he certainly concurred in its sentiments. His membership in the Masons also reinforced his religious ideas.

13. Bolling, *Power in the House*, 184.

14. *RTD*, March 15, 16, 20, Oct. 8, 13, 20, 1949; *CR* 95/5/6409, May 18, 1949, 95/11/14121–22, Oct. 7, 1949; Cope, "Frustration of Harry Byrd"; Steinberg, *Man from Missouri*, 339; Harris, "The Senatorial Rejection of Olds"; letters, Truman Papers; HFB to Richard Byrd, Aug. 26, Sept. 28, 1949, box 426, BP.

15. *RTD*, April 22, May 2, 7, 1949; McCoy, *Truman*, 166, 172; *CR* 95/5/5650–54, 5840–49, May 6, 1949; speeches, May 5, 6, 1949, box 368, BP.

16. Truman's private comments to his aides indicated that he was fed up with Byrd; he saw him as little more than a thinly disguised Republican and an obstructionist. Ferrell, *Diary of Ayers*, 244, 290.

17. *RTD*, May 10, 11, 15, 1949; Donovan, *Tumultuous Years*, 126; Franklin Hyde to Truman, May 9, 1949, Truman Papers.

18. Door, "The Man Who Set Virginia One Hundred Years Ahead," 52.

19. Lenchner, "Senate Voting Patterns"; Ross, "Evolution of the Senate"; Rakow,

"Southern Politics in the United States Senate"; Eisele, "Age and Political Change"; Hilty, "Voting Alignments," 1:63, 144; Reedy, *U.S. Senate,* 109.

20. *RTD,* May 17, July 17–22, Sept. 21, 23, 30, Oct. 20, 1949; McCoy, *Truman,* 167, 174, 185, 197–200; *CR* 95/5/6230, May 16, 1949, 95/10/13090–96, Sept. 21, 1949; Lenchner, "Senate Voting Patterns," 72b; Manassas *Messenger,* April 26, 1949.

21. *RTD,* Oct. 13, 1949; speech, Jan. 12, 1950, box 370, Baruch to HFB, Sept. 3, 1950, scrapbooks, box 71, BP. Byrd's article in *American Magazine,* Aug. 1949, was entitled "We're on the Road to Bankruptcy."

22. *NYT Magazine,* Dec. 18, 1949; *Proceedings of the Academy of Political Science* 24 (May 1950): 112–43.

23. *CR* 96/2/2328, Feb. 24, 1950.

24. Ibid., 96/2/2610–22, March 2, 1950.

25. *RTD,* Feb. 25, 27, March 3, 11, 1950; Cope, "Frustration of Byrd"; Humphrey, *Education of a Public Man,* 129–31; Solberg, *Humphrey,* 143–45; Eisele, *Almost to the Presidency,* 90–93.

26. HFB to Collins Denny, March 21, 1950, box 198, BP; Plunkett to Truman, March 6, 1950, box 13, Hutchinson Papers; Bailey and Samuel, *Congress at Work,* 140–41.

27. *RTD,* March 7, 11, 19, 1950; Bailey and Samuel, *Congress at Work,* 141; Switzer to HFB, March 7, 1950, box 1, Switzer Papers.

28. While Hutchinson was not an expert on trust law, he was an able lawyer and a party loyalist. Bailey and Samuel, *Congress at Work,* 140.

29. Henriques, "Byrd Organization Crushes a Liberal Challenge," 9–14; Bailey and Samuel, *Congress at Work,* 137–47; *CR* 96/9/12100–102, Aug. 9, 1950; *RTD,* June 15, 16, 20, Aug. 10, 1950; Freeman to Hutchinson, June 20, 1950, box 13, Hutchinson Papers.

30. RTD, April 3, 1947; Richard Byrd to HFB, Sept. 19, 1950, HFB to Richard Byrd, Sept. 21, 1950, box 426, BP; *CR* 96/11/14887–89, Sept. 15, 1950. Byrd, however, said nothing when Marshall was viciously attacked by McCarthy in June, 1951. Oshinsky, *A Conspiracy So Immense,* 199.

31. *RTD,* Jan. 29, 1950; interview with Harry Byrd, Jr.; HFB to Luther Carson, May 19, 1950, box 198, BP; Schwarz, *Speculator,* 543. Two of Byrd's sons played poker with McCarthy, and Dick remembers one losing session after which Joe jokingly told his father: "You know that west field where you have those apple trees? Well, I own that now." One can only imagine the senator's initial shock at such an announcement. Interview with Dick Byrd.

32. Ferrell, *Truman,* 111–25, Reichard, *Politics as Usual,* 60–62, 71; *CR* 96/7/9533, June 30, 1950, 96/8/11369, July 31, 1950; *RTD,* July 1, Aug. 18, Sept. 29, 1950.

33. *RTD,* Dec. 6, 17, 1950; HFB to Wysor, Dec. 18, 1950, box 228, BP.

34. RTD, Oct. 1, Dec. 17, 1950.

35. *NYT,* April 12, 1951; *RTD,* April 19, 21, May 4, 6, 1951; Robertson to HFB, May 18, 1951, box 204, Byrd statement, April 13, 1951, box 406, BP.

36. *RTD,* Dec. 27, 1949, July 12, 1950, Dec. 7, 1952; *Congress and the Nation,* 389, 1419; HFB to Herbert Hoover, June 19, 1948, May 25, 1950, Jan. 23, 1951, John Taber to HFB, Jan. 23, 1951, Herbert Hoover Papers, Herbert Hoover Presidential Library.

37. *RTD,* Dec. 23, 29, 1950, Jan. 16, Feb. 1, 18, 1951; HFB to Truman, Dec. 22, 1950, Truman Papers; Truman to HFB, Jan. 2, 1951, box 406, BP. Truman, who despite Byrd's charges was a fiscal conservative, actually achieved budget surpluses in fiscal years 1947, 1948, and 1951; Eisenhower did in 1956, 1957, and 1960. *Congress and the Nation,* 388.

38. *RTD*, June 10, 20, 21, July 29, Sept. 12, 19, Oct. 3, 12, 13, 1951; *Pageant Magazine,* Sept. 1951.

39. *RTD*, June 26, July 19, 21, 1951.

40. Latimer, *RTD*, Aug. 13, 1951; ibid., Aug. 13, 14, 20, Oct. 3, 20, 21, Nov. 9, 1951; Robertson to Switzer, Sept. 14, 1951, drawer 111, folder 44, Robertson to Darden, July 10, 1951, drawer 111, folder 43, Robertson Papers; "The South Gets Ready for '52," *Pathfinder* 58 (Sept. 19, 1951): 19; "The South's Plan to Beat Truman," *U.S. News and World Report* 31 (Nov. 30, 1951): 28.

41. *RTD*, Oct. 6, Nov. 2, 1951; Tuck to HFB, Nov. 3, 1951, folder 3696, Tuck Papers.

42. *RTD*, Nov. 9, 11, 28, Dec. 6, 13, 1951; Nixon to HFB, Dec. 17, 1951, scrapbooks, box 74, BP.

43. HFB to Kilpatrick, July 13, 1951, box 8, James J. Kilpatrick Papers, UVL; Andrews to HFB, Oct. 10, 1950, box 196, BP.

44. *RTD*, Feb. 2, 4, 28, 29, March 6, 1952; Fite, *Russell,* 199–200, 273–77.

45. *RTD*, Sept. 29, 1951, March 13, 30, 31, 1952; McCoy, *Truman,* 293–94, 299–300.

16. The Organization Totters

1. *RTD*, March 5, 10, April 3, 4, 11, 1952.

2. Ibid., April 17, 1952; Henriques, "Liberal Challenge," 15–17; Wilson to Hutchinson, June 21, 1950, box 13, Hutchinson Papers.

3. Combs to Wysor, April 7, 1952, HFB to Combs, June 21, 1951, Combs to HFB, Jan. 25, 1952, box 197, HFB to Tuck, Feb. 7, 1952, box 227, to Battle, June 11, 1952, box 196, to William C. Bowen, June 18, 1952, box 204, BP; interview with Albertis Harrison; *RTD,* May 21, 1952. Average attendance for Senate roll calls was 87 percent; Willis Robertson was at 97 percent. RTD, Aug. 3, 1952.

4. Interviews with Byrd's sons, Harry Byrd III, and Joe and Teresa Massie; Hatch, *Byrds of Virginia,* 486. Senator and Mrs. Byrd donated a carillon to the Episcopal church in Berryville in Westy's memory; they used to sit on the verandah at Rosemont in the evenings and listen to its playing.

5. *RTD*, April 2, 9, 10, 18, 22, May 6, June 3, 4, 6, 11, 1952; HFB to John H. Massie, April 18, 1952, box 218, BP; Henriques, "Liberal Challenge," 15–20; Parmet, *Eisenhower and the American Crusades,* 69; *NYT,* July 25, 1952.

6. Henriques, "Liberal Challenge," 18; Wilkinson, *Byrd,* 88; McDowell, *RTD,* May 19, 1952; ibid., May 17–19, 1952.

7. *RTD*, June 4, 7, 13, 15, 17, 19, 26, 1952.

8. Byrd statement, June 21, 1952, box 226, BP; *RTD,* June 22, July 14–17, Aug. 16, 1952; Henriques, "Liberal Challenge," 20–25; Sweeney, "Byrd and Anti-Byrd," 157–85.

9. Henriques, "Liberal Challenge," 14–15, 25–29.

10. *RTD*, July 12, 18, 19, 1952; interview with Abbitt.

11. *RTD*, July 19, 21, 22, 1952.

12. Ibid., July 22, 23, 1952; *NYT,* July 21, 22, 1952.

13. *RTD*, July 22–24, 1952; *NYT,* July 23, 1952; Preston Collins, "The Memoirs and Analysis of Virginia's Participation in the Chicago National Democratic Convention," Aug. 6, 1952, and Byrd memo, box 198, BP.

14. *RTD*, July 24, 1952; *NYT,* July 24, 1952; Collins memoir.

15. *RTD*, July 20, 23, 1952; *NYT*, July 23, 1952; Martin, *Stevenson* 1:591.

16. *RTD*, July 24, 25, 1952; HFB to Battle, Aug. 1, 1952, box 196, BP. A story developed years later that Tuck had been in a "footrace" to the podium with Battle to deliver a Dixiecrat ultimatum to the convention, but the former governor denied any such intention. Crawley, *Bill Tuck*, 210–12.

17. Sweeney, "Revolt in Virginia," 184–88; Greene, *The Crusade*, 149–63, 277; Henriques, "Battle and Virginia Politics," 279–305; *RTD*, July 25, 26, 1952.

18. HFB to Prieur, July 26, 1952, to Jack R. Bryant, July 30, 1952, box 205, BP.

19. Latimer, "Virginia Politics, 1950–1960," 50; Henriques, "Battle and Virginia Politics," 286–96; Hardeman and Bacon, *Rayburn*, 363–66; *NYT*, July 26, 1952.

20. Robertson to E. W. Opie, Aug. 14, 1952, drawer 111, folder 47, Smith to Robertson, Oct. 14, 1952, drawer 111, folder 48, Robertson Papers; HFB to Tuck, Aug. 1, 1952, box 227, BP; *RTD*, July 30, Aug. 1, 2, 7, 10, 24, Sept. 1, 15, 1952.

21. *RTD*, Aug. 23, 29, Sept. 16, 1952; Sweeney, "Revolt in Virginia," 188–90.

22. Interview with Harry Byrd, Jr.; *RTD*, Oct. 13, 15, 18, 1952; HFB to Richard Byrd, Oct. 28, 1952, box 426, BP.

23. *RTD*, Oct. 19, 21, 23, 1952; Whitehead speech, Oct. 27, 1952, box 15, Hutchinson Papers; Barkley quoted in Wilkinson, *Byrd*, 87.

24. *RTD*, Oct. 18, 19, 1952; Miller to HFB, Oct. 15, 1952, box 15, Hutchinson Papers; Sweeney, "Revolt in Virginia," 190–95; Crawley, *Bill Tuck*, 214; Latimer interviews with Tuck and Darden.

25. *RTD*, Nov. 5, 6, 16, 1952; Long to Wysor, Oct. 27, 1952, box 197, BP; Whitehead statement, Nov. 16, 1952, box 1, Hutchinson Papers; Grant, "Eisenhower and the 1952 Republican Invasion of the South"; Sweeney, "Revolt in Virginia," 193–95.

26. *RTD*, Nov. 7, 11, 12, Dec. 11, 30, 1952; HFB to Switzer, Nov. 10, 1952, box 227, BP; Robertson to Frank Robertson, Nov. 7, 1952, drawer 111, folder 49, Robertson Papers. Harry Jr. later admitted the editorial was a mistake and was told so by his father. Interview with Harry Byrd, Jr.

27. HFB to Battle, Jan. 18, 1954, box 229, R. O. Norris to HFB, April 3, 1950, box 203, BP; Henriques, "Battle and Virginia Politics," 140–51. Although many suspected the tax reduction scheme originated with the elder Byrd, it actually came from Harry Jr., with an assist from Allan Donnahoe of the *Times-Dispatch*. He discussed it with his approving father before introducing it. Interview with Harry Byrd, Jr.

28. Wilkinson, *Byrd*, 98–99; Henriques, "Battle and Virginia Politics," 117–34; HFB to Edward Breeden, March 7, 1950, BP; Whitehead speech, Nov. 9, 1953, box 9, Whitehead Papers; Sweeney, "Byrd and Anti-Byrd," 234; *RTD*, Jan. 7, 1953, April 13, 1956, Sept. 1, 1955; Moger, *Virginia*, 366; Darden to David A. Harrison, Jr., Feb. 5, 1954, box N8, Dabney Papers.

29. Wilkinson, *Byrd*, 89–91, 99–100; *RTD*, March 10, 1952; William Spong to author; HFB to Prieur, Sept. 22, 1952, box 203, BP.

30. Henriques, "Battle and Virginia Politics," 160–73, 192–214; Smith, "Boothe," 9–15; HFB to McGinnis, May 24, 1951, to Battle, June 11, 1952, box 196, BP; Latimer, *RTD*, March 19, 1950; ibid., Jan. 17, 1952.

31. Wysor to HFB, July 25, Nov. 2, 1951, to Combs, Oct. 25, 1951, box 228, Sela Davis to HFB, Nov. 7, 1953, Robert Watkins to HFB, Dec. 7, 1953, box 231, BP; Spong to author; Key, *Southern Politics*, 34; Latimer interviews with Tuck and Darden.

32. Prieur to HFB, Nov. 7, 1953, box 231, Combs to Wysor, Dec. 29, 1952, to Byrd,

Nov. 28, 1952, box 197, HFB to Wysor, Jan. 13, 1953, box 240, BP; Beagle and Osborne, *Almond*, 75; Sweeney, "Byrd and Anti-Byrd," 197–203.

33. Dalton to HFB, Oct. 19, 1942, box 173, BP; *RTD*, Sept. 2, 4, 17, 27, Oct. 4, 14, 22, 27, 1953.

34. HFB to Kilpatrick, Oct. 26, Nov. 6, 1953, Kilpatrick to HFB, Oct. 29, Nov. 9, 1953, box 8, Kilpatrick Papers.

35. *RTD*, Oct. 15, 16, 1953, Nov. 4, 1990; interviews with Harrison, Abbitt, and Byrd Jr.; television interview with Harry Byrd, Jr., 1987.

36. *RTD*, Oct. 20, 21, 29, Nov. 5, 1953, Sept. 25, 1977; interview with Harry Byrd, Jr.

37. Heinemann, "Stanley," 337–339; Wilkinson, *Byrd*, 101–5; Fred Switzer to Willis Robertson, Nov. 10, 1953, box 9, Switzer Papers; Tuck to HFB, Nov. 2, 1953, box 231, Wysor to HFB, Nov. 4, 1953, box 240, HFB to Sam Thrasher, Dec. 24, 1953, box 231, BP; *RTD*, Nov. 1, 4, 5, 1953.

38. Anonymous interview.

39. HFB to Tuck, Dec. 2, 1953, box 239, to Smith, Dec. 4, 1953, box 238, to Wysor, Jan. 15, 1954, box 240, to Combs, Dec. 30, 1953, Combs to HFB, Dec. 31, 1953, box 230, BP; HFB to Tuck, Dec. 22, 1953, folder 4907, Harry Byrd, Jr., to Stanley, Jan. 5, 1954, folder 4908, Tuck Papers.

40. *RTD*, Jan. 13, 21, Feb. 16, 24, March 16, 1954; Louise Lacy to Combs, Jan. 21, 1954, box 10b, Combs Papers; HFB to Stanley, Feb. 8, 1954, box 156, Stanley Executive Papers, LV; to Anderson, Dec. 21, 1953, Jan. 7, Feb. 26, 1954, box 232, Anderson to Stanley, Jan. 21, 1954, HFB to Stanley, Feb. 26, 1954, to Lloyd Bird, Feb. 24, 1954, box 231, to Combs, Jan. 22, Feb. 23, 1954, box 230, to Blackburn Moore, Feb. 5, 1954, box 236, BP.

41. *RTD*, Jan. 17, Feb. 11, 20, March 9, 15, 16, 1954, March 4, 1990; Wilkinson, *Byrd*, 106-12; Breeden to R. B. Grinnan, Jr., Feb. 10, 1954, box 28, Breeden Papers; Smith, "Boothe," 18–19. The tax reduction law was repealed in 1956 with little fanfare.

42. Richardson to HFB, March 19, 1954, box 231, HFB to Wysor, March 19, 1954, box 240, BP; interviews with Latimer and Harry Byrd, Jr.; Wilkinson, *Byrd*, 112.

17. Massive Resistance

1. *RTD*, May 18, 1954; Stanley to HFB, May 24, 1954, box 109, Stanley Executive Papers.

2. *Virginian-Pilot*, June 8, 1964; statement, May 17, 1954, box 408, BP; HFB to Stanley, May 27, 1954, box 156, Stanley Executive Papers.

3. HFB to Kilpatrick, May 19, 1954, Kilpatrick to HFB, May 20, 1954, box 8, Kilpatrick Papers; HFB to Moore, May 26, 1954, box 236, BP.

4. *RTD*, May 18, 20, 1954; Howard to Benjamin Muse, April 1, 1954, box 1, Muse Papers.

5. *RTD*, May 20, 1954; Elizabeth Wilson to Stanley, May 27, 1954, Gray to Stanley, May 20, 1954, box 109, Stanley Executive Papers.

6. *RTD*, May 19, 25, 27, 1954; Young to Stanley, May 18, 1954, box 109, Stanley to Gray, May 24, 1954, Stanley Executive Papers.

7. *RTD*, June 11, 26, 1954; Gates, *Massive Resistance*, 30; Combs to HFB, June 14, 1954, HFB to Combs, July 20, 1954, box 230, Frank Wysor to HFB, July 22, 1954, box 240, HFB to Harry Byrd, Jr., July 13, 1954, box 428, BP.

8. Burk, *Eisenhower Administration and Black Civil Rights,* 152–63, 192; Duram, *Moderate among Extremists,* 54–62, 111. Eisenhower told his aide Arthur Larsen that the Brown decision was wrong. Larsen, *Eisenhower,* 124.

9. Armistead Boothe to Stanley, Aug. 7, 1954, Box 229, BP. Blacks were already attending two formerly all-white universities in Virginia, and Catholic schools in Richmond, Roanoke, and Hampton were enrolling their first black students that fall. *RTD,* Sept. 8, 1954; Muse, *Massive Resistance,* 8.

10. The Southside includes most of the area south of the James River, stretching from what was Nansemond County in the east to Patrick County in the west; in 1950 it constituted 18 percent of Virginia's population; it was highly rural; and blacks made up over 40 percent of its population, almost twice their percentage in the state as a whole; in the eastern counties of the area, blacks were over 60 percent of the population. Gates, *Massive Resistance,* 3.

11. Tuck to Howard Smith, June 23, 1954, box 109, Howard Smith Papers, UVL; Tuck to HFB, Sept. 3, 1954, quoted in Crawley, *Bill Tuck,* 220–21. Tuck had replaced Stanley as the congressman from the Fifth District.

12. *Virginian-Pilot,* June 8, 1964.

13. Gray to Watkins Abbitt, July 12, 1954, Watkins M. Abbitt Papers, University of Richmond Library; Gray to HFB, May 29, 1954, Gray to Godwin, May 27, 31, box 1, folder 12, Mills Godwin, Jr., Papers, College of William and Mary Library; *RTD,* June 21, Nov. 2, 1954; Gates, *Massive Resistance,* 31, Muse, *Massive Resistance,* 7.

14. Key, *Southern Politics,* 32; interview with Harry Byrd, Jr.; radio interview, March 7, 1948, box 368, Byrd speech, May 9, 1957, box 380, BP.

15. Crawley, *Bill Tuck,* 226–7; Francis Pickens Miller review of Muse book, Washington *Post,* April 23, 1961; interview with Virginius Dabney.

16. Robertson to HFB, June 28, 1957, Billy Prieur to HFB, Sept. 25, 1957, box 249, Mills Godwin to HFB, Nov. 8, 1957, box 244, BP; John Battle to HFB, Nov. 8, 1958, box 1, John S. Battle Papers, UVL.

17. Wilkinson, *Byrd,* 150–54; Muse, *Massive Resistance,* 26; Bartley, *Rise of Massive Resistance,* 109; Pace, "Chambers Opposes Massive Resistance," 423; Rubin, *Virginia,* 196–97.

18. *RTD,* Aug. 29, 1954; Gates, *Massive Resistance,* 34, 110, 155, 186; Muse, *Massive Resistance,* 163; HFB to Combs, Sept. 27, 1954, box 230, BP.

19. Gates, *Massive Resistance,* 34–41; *RTD,* Oct. 9, Nov. 16, 1954.

20. *RTD,* June 1, Dec. 18, 1955; HFB to Peachy Menefee, Nov. 18, 1955, box 7, Menefee Papers.

21. *RTD,* Nov. 13, 1955; Gates, *Massive Resistance,* 63–65.

22. *RTD,* Oct. 25, Nov. 1, 1955; Byrd statement, Nov. 1, 1955, box 8, Kilpatrick Papers.

23. *RTD,* Nov. 14, 16, Dec. 3, 4, 1955.

24. Corley, "Kilpatrick," 5–26; Gates, *Massive Resistance,* 104–5; Latimer, "Virginia Politics."

25. HFB to Kilpatrick, Dec. 2, 3, 23, 1955, box 8, Kilpatrick Papers.

26. Corley, "Kilpatrick," 28–39; Wilkinson, *Byrd,* 127–29; Hershman, "Rumbling in the Museum," 147–48; Kilpatrick to HFB, Jan. 30, 1956, box 8, Kilpatrick Papers; Ely, *Crisis of Conservative Virginia,* 38–44.

27. Ernest Griffith to HFB, Dec. 21, 1955, box 5d, BP; HFB to Godwin, Dec. 24, 1955, box 1, folder 13, Godwin Papers; HFB to Kilpatrick, Dec. 23, 1955, box 8, Kilpatrick Papers; *RTD,* Dec. 18, 1955.

28. Former governors Darden and Battle, Robert Whitehead, and the State Board of Education argued that the Gray Plan was the surest means of preserving public schools.

29. *RTD*, Dec. 18, 20, 22, 1955, Jan. 10, 11, 17, 18, 1956; Hershman, "Rumbling in the Museum," 116–48; Ely, *Crisis of Conservative Virginia*, 38–39; Heinemann, "Stanley," 343; conversation between Byrd and Stanley, Jan. 10, 1956, box 19, Stanley Executive Papers; Muse, *Massive Resistance*, 17–18; Byrd radio address, Jan. 5, 1956, box 379, BP.

30. Gates, *Massive Resistance*, 100–116; Ely, *Crisis of Conservative Virginia*, 41–42; interview with Godwin.

31. *RTD*, Feb. 15, 26, 1956; interview with Latimer.

32. *RTD*, March 4, July 28, 1956.

33. Several governors had already announced their support for interposition resolutions, and by mid-1957 eight southern legislatures had passed interposition resolutions. Grantham, *Life and Death of the Solid South*, 139.

34. Cohodas, *Thurmond*, 283–84; Badger, "Southern Manifesto," 1–8; Fite, *Russell*, 333–34; Wilhoit, *Politics of Massive Resistance*, 51–55, 78.

35. *RTD*, Aug. 26, 1956.

36. Gates, *Massive Resistance*, 173; Thurmond to author; Fulbright to author; Johnson and Gwertzman, *Fulbright*, 148; Wilhoit, *Politics of Massive Resistance*, 76; J. Forester Taylor to Robert Whitehead, Oct. 14, 1957, box 242, BP; Wilkinson, *Byrd*, 141; Tuck to HFB, March 21, 1956, folder 4938, Tuck Papers.

37. Watt Abbitt to Bill Tuck, May 1, 1956, folder 5460, Tuck to Burr Harrison, May 16, 1956, folder 5460, Tuck Papers; HFB to Claude Beverly, May 2, 1956, 229, BP.

38. Godwin to HFB, June 8, 1956, box 1, folder 14, Godwin Papers; Garland Gray to Smith, June 15, 19, 1956, box 109, Smith Papers; Gray to Tuck, June 15, 1956, folder 5461, Tuck Papers.

39. Smith memo of July 2, 1956 meeting, Smith to HFB, May 4, 1956, box 110, Smith Papers.

40. HFB to Smith, July 3, 1956, box 110, Smith Papers; HFB to Godwin, July 3, 12, 1956, Godwin to HFB, July 9, 1956, box 1, folder 14, Godwin Papers; C. William Cleaton to Tuck, July 6, 1956, folder 5461, Tuck Papers; Gates, *Massive Resistance*, 176.

41. Smith to Stanley, Aug. 21, 22, 1956, box 156, Stanley Executive Papers; Harrison to Smith, Aug. 22, 1956, box 110, Smith Papers; *RTD*, July 7, 24, Aug. 3, 10, 11, 26, 1956.

42. Dr. Edward E. Haddock to author; *RTD*, Aug. 23, 29, 30, Sept. 5, 6, 12, 13, 18, 19, 22, 23, 1956; Hershman, "Rumbling in the Museum," 173–210; Kilpatrick to Donald Richberg, Sept. 3, 1957, Kilpatrick Papers; Ely, *Crisis of Conservative Virginia*, 44–46; Muse, *Massive Resistance*, 30–34.

43. Edward Breeden to Darden, Sept. 26, 1956, box 33, Breeden Papers; Darden quoted in Bemiss, "General Assembly," 13; Neff to Darden, Sept. 22, 1956, box 23, University of Virginia Presidential Papers, UVL.

44. Byrd quoted in Bartley, *Rise of Massive Resistance*, 114; Godwin to HFB, Sept. 26, 1956, box 1, folder 15, Godwin Papers; HFB to Byrnes, Sept. 26, 1956, James Byrnes Papers, Clemson University Library; Byrnes to HFB, Sept. 28, 1956, folder 4938, Tuck Papers; "Virginia: Wrong Turn at the Crossroads," *Time* 68 (Dec. 3, 1956): 19.

45. Ibid.; materials, box 32, Breeden Papers.

46. Bemiss, "General Assembly," 14; Darden to Walter C. Rawls, Aug. 6, 1958, box 24, University of Virginia Presidential Papers; Robertson to Justin Moore, Aug. 1, 1956, drawer 140, folder 17, Robertson to Watkins Abbitt, Jan. 12, 1956, drawer 182, folder 16, Robertson Papers.

47. "Gravest Crisis," *Time* 72 (Sept. 22, 1958): 14; Ely, "Almond," 349–50.

48. Ely, "Almond," 350–52; Wilkinson, *Byrd,* 133–37; Almond interview with Luther Carter, *Virginian-Pilot,* June 8–9, 1964; Remick, "Almond and Byrd," 19–20.

49. Washington *Post,* Jan. 19, 1962; Ely, "Almond," 351; *RTD,* Dec. 12, 1956; Lloyd C. Bird to HFB, Nov. 20, 1956, box 229, HFB to Garnett S. Moore, Dec. 7, 1956, box 248, Prieur to HFB, Dec. 10, 1956, HFB to Gardiner Tyler, Dec. 10, 1956, box 249, Almond to HFB, Dec. 13, 1956, HFB to Almond, Dec. 15, 1956, box 229, to Combs, Dec. 17, 1956, box 230, BP; Switzer to Robertson, Dec. 12, 1956, drawer 114, folder 4, Robertson Papers; Ely, *Crisis of Conservative Virginia,* 54–57.

50. HFB to Dorothy Callenback, Sept. 20, 1957, box 243, BP.

51. Richard Byrd to HFB, Nov. 13, 1955, HFB to Richard Byrd, Jan. 17, 1956, box 426, BP; interviews with Harry Jr. and Dick Byrd and Harry Byrd III.

52. HFB to B. C. Garrett, Jr., Jan. 23, 1957, box 241, BP; HFB to Kilpatrick, March 21, July 26, 1957, box 8, Kilpatrick Papers; *RTD,* March 19, May 10, July 5, 13, 1957; speech, May 9, 1957, box 381, BP; HFB to Dabney, Feb. 27, 1957, box m3, Dabney Papers.

53. Gilmer to HFB, March 12, 1957, HFB to Gilmer, June 28, 1957, Harrison to HFB, June 28, 1957, box 244, Curry Carter to HFB, May 23, 1957, HFB to Lloyd Bird, June 4, 1957, box 242, BP; Kilpatrick to HFB, May 16, 1957, box 8, Kilpatrick Papers.

54. *RTD,* Sept. 1, Oct. 1, 8, 12, 30, 1957; statement, Sept. 25, 1957, box 4d, HFB to W. M. Minter, Nov. 18, 1957, box 248, speech in Halifax, Oct. 30, 1957, box 382, to Earl Fitzpatrick, Sept. 27, 1957, box 244, to H. P. Dunnington, Oct. 28, 1957, box 241, BP.

55. Ely, *Crisis of Conservative Virginia,* 57–63; Almond to HFB, Aug. 6, 1957, box 241, Albertis Harrison to HFB, Oct. 7, 1957, box 244, BP; Bartley, *Rise of Massive Resistance,* 272.

56. Wilkinson, *Byrd,* 138; *RTD,* Nov. 6, 1957.

57. Ibid., Nov. 3, 7, 1957; Ely, "Almond," 352–53; Ely, *Crisis of Conservative Virginia,* 65–67; HFB to D. Tennant Bryan, Nov. 8, 1957, to Joseph Carrigan, Nov. 22, 1957, box 242, BP.

58. Ely, *Crisis of Conservative Virginia,* 61; Beagle and Osborne, *Almond,* 102.

59. Interview with Harry Byrd, Jr.; HFB to Robertson, Feb. 11, 1958, drawer 115, folder 35, Robertson Papers; James Byrnes to HFB, Feb. 13, 1958, Byrnes Papers; newspaper article, box 8, Menefee papers; Muse, *Massive Resistance,* 46; *RTD,* Feb. 13, 1958.

60. Latimer interviews with Tuck and Darden; Crawley, *Bill Tuck,* 244–45; Ely, *Crisis of Conservative Virginia,* 72–73; Battle to Robert Barton, Feb. 20, 1958, box 6, Battle Papers.

61. Washington *Evening Star,* Feb. 26, 1958; HFB to Joseph C. Hutcheson, April 28, 1958, Joseph C. Hutcheson Papers, UVL; Latimer interviews with Tuck and Darden; interviews with Latimer, Harry Byrd, Jr., and Godwin; Dowdey, "Conscience of the Country"; Friddell, *Darden,* 168.

62. HFB to Prieur, July 29, 1958, box 250, Tuck to HFB, Sept. 23, 1958, other materials in box 249, Watkins Abbitt to HFB, Sept. 16, 1958, HFB to Joel Flood, Sept. 22, 1958, box 252, BP; to Godwin, Oct. 20, 1958, box 1, folder 21, Godwin Papers; Ely, *Crisis of Conservative Virginia,* 81.

63. Harrison to HFB, July 16, Aug. 19, 1958, box 244, BP.

64. Muse, *Massive Resistance,* 54; HFB to Abbitt, Oct. 9, 1958, to Prieur, Sept. 25, 1958, box 250, to Almond, Oct. 9, 1958, box 241, BP; Ely, *Crisis of Conservative Virginia,* 192.

65. "Gravest Crisis," *Time* 72 (Sept. 22, 1958): 14; Tuck to HFB, Sept. 26, 1958, box 252, BP.

66. HFB to Prieur, Oct. 3, 1958, box 249, to Kilpatrick, Oct. 18, 1958, box 245, to Hooker, Oct. 21, 1958, box 245, BP.

67. Smith memo, Jan. 27, 1969, box 8731c/1, Smith Papers; interview with Harrison; Tuck to HFB, Oct. 20, 1958, box 252, Harrison to HFB, Sept. 22, 1958 (two letters), box 244, HFB to J. Segar Gravatt, Oct. 20, 1958, box 251, Prieur to HFB, Oct. 10, 1958, box 250, BP; *Virginian-Pilot*, June 9, 1964; Wilkinson, *Byrd*, 141–42; Remick, "Almond and Byrd," 26; Muse, *Massive Resistance*, 85. Harrison and Almond later said they believed the state court would rule against them.

68. Josephine Almond to HFB, Aug. 20, 1958, Almond to HFB, Nov. 12, 1958, box 241, Watkins M. Abbitt to HFB, Oct. 8, 1958, box 249, BP; Ely, *Crisis of Conservative Virginia*, 75–77; Remick "Almond and Byrd," 18, 29–31; Muse, *Massive Resistance*, 99–100; Wilkinson, *Byrd*, 113, 136–37.

69. Dabney, *Across the Years*, 235; *News Leader*, Nov. 15, 1958; *RTD*, Nov. 23, 1958; Bass and De Vries, *Transformation of Southern Politics*, 347.

70. HFB to Almond, Feb. 26, 1959, Almond to HFB, March 13, 1959, box 185, Almond Executive Papers, LV; Samuel Bemiss to Almond, Oct. 16, 1958, box 242, BP; Wilkinson, *Byrd*, 142–45.

71. Ely, *Crisis of Conservative Virginia*, 83–86; *RTD*, Dec. 6, 1958; Remick, "Almond and Byrd," 28; Hershman, "Public School Bonds"; Thompson, "Virginia Education Crisis"; Boushall quoted in Beagle and Osborne, *Almond*, 161.

72. Pleading for his wise counsel, Harrison had warned Byrd of this possibility two weeks before. Harrison to HFB, Jan. 6, 1959, box 244, BP.

73. *RTD*, Jan. 21, 1959; Almond to Tuck, Jan. 15, 1959, Tuck to Almond, Jan. 21, 1959, folder 5077, Tuck Papers; HFB to Almond, Jan. 21, 1959, Almond to HFB, Jan. 22, 1959, box 185, Almond Executive Papers.

74. *Virginian-Pilot*, June 9, 1964; Washington *Post*, Jan. 19–21, 1962; Remick, "Almond and Byrd," 32–34; Beagle and Osborne, *Almond*, 115; Abbitt to author.

75. *Virginian-Pilot*, June 9, 1964; Stephens to Bird, Jan. 24, 1959, Bird to Stephens, Jan. 27, 1959, box 11, Lloyd C. Bird Papers, UVL; Stephens to Godwin, Jan. 24, 1959, box 1, folder 23, Godwin Papers; Remick, "Almond and Byrd," 34; interview with Godwin.

76. McDowell, "Byrd Bore Power without Pretense," *RTD*, Oct. 23, 1966.

77. Ely, *Crisis of Conservative Virginia*, 123–26; interview with Harry Byrd, Jr.; *Virginian-Pilot*, June 9, 1964.

78. Muse, *Massive Resistance*, 131–35; interview with Godwin; Smith memo, Jan. 27, 1969, box 8731c/1, Smith Papers; Ely, *Crisis of Conservative Virginia*, 61; Byrd statement, Jan. 29, 1959, box 411, BP.

79. Materials, box 5d, BP; HFB to Kilpatrick, March 6, 1959, box 6626c–11, Kilpatrick Papers; Harrison to HFB, March 10, April 2, 1959, box 244, BP.

80. Abbott, "Norfolk Business Community"; Tuck to Godwin, Feb. 3, 1959, folder 5468, Tuck Papers; Bartley, *Rise of Massive Resistance*, 115.

81. Ely, *Crisis of Conservative Virginia*, 130–32; Muse, *Massive Resistance*, 160–63; Wilkinson, *Byrd*, 148–49; Bartley, *Rise of Massive Resistance*, 325, 341; Howard Smith to Mosby Perrow, March 5, 1959, box 109, Smith Papers; Kilpatrick to HFB, April 23, 1959, box 6626–11, Kilpatrick Papers; Miller to Almond, April 30, 1959, box 28, Miller Papers.

82. William Spong to author; Remick, "Almond and Byrd," 36; Abbott, "Norfolk Business Community," 116. The governor was shot at on the Capitol grounds on April 12. RTD, April 13, 1959.

83. *Virginian-Pilot*, June 7, 1964.

84. Ely, *Crisis of Conservative Virginia,* 140–42; Muse, *Massive Resistance,* 164–66; Hershman, "Rumbling in the Museum," 375; *RTD,* Aug. 30, 1959.

85. Atlanta *Constitution,* July 20, 1959, copy in box 11, Whitehead Papers.

86. Interview with Harrison.

87. Armistead Boothe to Governor Stanley, Aug. 7, 1954, box 229, BP; Hershman, "Rumbling in the Museum," 3–4, 60, 129, 320. Anthony Badger has argued that many southern moderates, lacking political courage, overestimated racist sentiment and too easily gave up on pursuing a gradualist approach. Badger, "Southern Manifesto," 18–19.

88. See Watkins Abbitt to Garland Gray, July 13, 1954, Abbitt Papers; Bartley, *Rise of Massive Resistance,* 115.

89. Interviews with Godwin and Harrison; Bass and De Vries, *Transformation of Southern Politics,* 347; Spong to author. North Carolina may also have been more effective in preserving segregated schools through its quiet but devious tokenism. See William Chafe, *Civilities and Civil Rights.*

90. Hershman, "Rumbling in the Museum," 250; Wilkinson, *Byrd,* 125–57; interviews with Godwin, Harrison, and Abbitt; Latimer interviews with Tuck and Darden.

91. *Virginian-Pilot,* Aug. 26, 1956, quoted in Pace, "Chambers," 423.

18. "Mr. Republican"

1. HFB to Freeman, Dec. 27, 1952, box 109, Freeman Papers.

2. Eisenhower to HFB, Dec. 17, 1952, box 109, Freeman Papers.

3. *RTD,* Nov. 11, 14, 22, 1952; HFB to Frank Wysor, Nov. 19, 1952, box 228; Humphrey to HFB, March 27, 1956, box 231, BP.

4. *RTD,* Jan. 17, 18, 21–25, 1953; Ambrose, *Eisenhower,* 40–43.

5. *RTD,* Jan. 5, 6, 11, 14, 18, 25, 27, May 24, 1953.

6. Ibid., Jan. 3, Feb. 22, 23, May 16, 1953.

7. Ibid., Jan. 8–10, 1953.

8. Pach and Richardson, *Eisenhower,* 32, 52–55; Sloan, *Eisenhower and the Management of Prosperity,* 11, 14, 17, 35, 73; Saulnier, *Constructive Years,* 1, 16.

9. *RTD,* Feb. 1, March 6, May 6, July 19, 29, 30, Aug. 4, 1953.

10. Ibid., July 30, 31, Aug. 1–3, 1953; HFB to James Allen, Aug. 5, 1953, box 229, BP.

11. Pach and Richardson, *Eisenhower,* 45–46, 85–87; *RTD,* March 6, 7, 11–13, 1953; HFB to Wilson, March 5, 1953, box 407, BP.

12. *RTD,* March 17, 23, 27, April 2, 11, 16, 17, 21, 25, May 9, 24, 1953.

13. Reeves, *McCarthy,* 501; Fried, *Men against McCarthy,* 269; Oshinsky, *Conspiracy So Immense,* 199, 318; *RTD,* July 8, 10–12, Sept. 15, 1953; Byrd statement, July 10, 1953, box 408, BP; Miller, *Lyndon,* 170–71; Dallek, *Lone Star Rising,* 453.

14. *RTD,* July 30, Aug. 3, Dec. 2, 1954; HFB to Harry Byrd, Jr., July 31, 1954, box 428; statement, Aug. 14, 1957, box 382, BP; Fried, *Men against McCarthy,* 310.

15. *RTD,* Jan. 7, 8, March 21, 26, 31, June 5, July 2, 3, 8, 11, 12, 20, 22, Aug. 6, 21, 1954; HFB to R. H. Smith, July 6, 1954, box 238, BP; Sloan, *Eisenhower and the Management of Prosperity,* 138.

16. HFB to Charles Harkrader, Jan. 4, 1954, box 1, Harkrader Papers; *RTD,* Jan. 24, April 2, July 28, 1954, July 1, 1958, March 12, 1959.

17. *RTD,* Jan. 21, Feb. 27, May 8, 22, Aug. 11, Oct. 1, 1954; Pach and Richardson, *Eisenhower,* 55–58. Senator Robertson had a 68 percent pro-Eisenhower rating; Byrd had answered 70 percent of the roll calls, Robertson, 88 percent. Byrd's attendance record on

roll calls was spotty; he usually ranked in the lower half of the senators from 1947 to 1956. Bobby Baker to HFB, Oct. 8, 1956, box 229, BP.

18. *RTD*, April 15, 16, 18, 21, 24, May 5, 7, 1954.

19. Ibid., April 23, 24, May 20, 24, 30, June 19, July 24, 25, 29, Aug. 14, Sept. 10, 1954; Pach and Richardson, *Eisenhower*, 56; Byrd Senate speech, July 22, 1954, box 378, BP.

20. Dallek, *Lone Star Rising*, 436–38, 441; Adams, *Firsthand Report*, 9–10; Griffith, *Ike's Letters to a Friend*, 137; Eisenhower, *Mandate for Change*, 193; newsclippings, BP.

21. Dallek, *Lone Star Rising*, 346, 352–56, 366–71, 422–25, 473–74; Fite, *Russell*, 301–2.

22. Dallek, *Lone Star Rising*, 353; Evans and Novak, *Lyndon Johnson*, 69, 99, 106; interview with Harry Byrd, Jr.; Johnson to HFB, Aug. 3, 1956, box 233, BP.

23. Rose, *Interstate*, xiv, 3–5, 41, 73–78.

24. *RTD*, Jan. 16, 1955; HFB to Hoover, Jan. 29, 1955, Hoover Papers.

25. *RTD*, Jan. 18, 20, 25, Feb. 4, March 19, 1955; Rose, *Interstate*, 79–83.

26. *RTD*, Aug. 30, Dec. 25, 1955, May 20, 23, June 23, 1956; Rose, *Interstate*, 87–92; HFB to Richard Barber, May 17, 1957, box 242, BP; interview with Long.

27. *RTD*, Jan. 17, 18, Feb. 20, March 2, 11, 16, July 23, Dec. 9, 1955.

28. Ibid., Feb. 20, March 24, 29, April 15, 27, May 3, 5, 8, 1955; Dallek, *Lone Star Rising*, 481. Membership in the Organization for Trade Cooperation was defeated. Kaufman, *Trade and Aid*, 126–30.

29. The Lehman amendment failed, 74–13, with Byrd in the company of senators Fulbright, Long, Humphrey, Mansfield, Morse, and Kefauver; John Kennedy was paired with them and Lyndon Johnson paired with the majority. Years later Johnson would ask for a similar "area resolution" to support his use of force in Vietnam. Eisenhower, *Mandate for Change*, 468.

30. *RTD*, Jan. 29, March 28, 1955; *CR* 101/1/1060, Feb. 1, 1955; Pach and Richardson, *Eisenhower*, 98–104; Ambrose, *Eisenhower*, 231–45.

31. HFB to Billy Prieur, Aug. 2, 1955, box 237; Bobby Baker to HFB, Oct. 8, 1956, box 229, BP; *RTD*, Feb. 3, May 11, 15, 1955.

32. Ibid., Jan. 1, 17, July 4, 1956; time capsule letter, July 18, 1956, box 229, HFB to Eisenhower, April 4, 1956, Humphrey to HFB, March 27, 1956, box 231, BP.

33. *RTD*, March 9, 24, April 12, 17, May 19, 26, June 27, July 18, 20, 1956; Dallek, *Lone Star Rising*, 494–96; interview with Long.

34. For an assertion that Eisenhower considered replacing Richard Nixon with Harry Byrd as his running mate in 1956, see Wicker, *One of Us*, 191.

35. HFB to E. H. Ramsey, May 1, 1956, box 233, to E. S. Ashby, July 18, 1956, to Billy Prieur, July 19, Aug. 2, 1956, box 237, BP. For Johnson's views on civil rights at this stage of his career, see Badger, "Southern Manifesto," 13, and Dallek, *Lone Star Rising*, 497.

36. HFB to John F. Kennedy, Aug. 20, 1956, to Joseph Kennedy, March 38, 1956, box 233, to Theodore Green, May 23, 1955, box 231, BP.

37. *RTD*, Aug. 9, 13–18, 24, 1956; HFB to Watkins Abbitt, Aug. 14, 1956, box 229, BP; Martin, *Civil Rights*, 146–52.

38. Virginia's venerable political columnist and historian James Latimer says this was the first time he heard Byrd actually use this phrase to describe what he was going to do. Interview with Latimer.

39. *RTD*, Aug. 26, 1956; Martin, *Civil Rights*, 122; Marshall Beverley to HFB, Aug. 29, 1956, box 198, Smith papers; Muse, *Massive Resistance*, 29, 66, 166.

40. Wilkinson, *Byrd*, 217–20; Whitehead to Abbitt, Aug. 16, 1957, box 12, Whitehead Papers.

41. *RTD*, Aug. 19, Sept. 28, Oct. 10, 20, 1956; Smith to HFB, Oct. 2, 1956, HFB to

Smith, Oct. 4, 1956, box 238; to Tuck, Oct. 9, 1956, Tuck to HFB, Oct. 10, 1956, box 239, BP.

42. *RTD*, Nov. 7, 8, Dec. 2, 1956; HFB to Thelma Stovall, Oct. 17, 1956, James Byrnes to HFB, Sept. 28, 1956, HFB to Byrnes, Oct. 3, 1956, box 237, BP; Grantham, *Death of the Solid South*, 141.

43. Sloan, *Eisenhower and the Management of Prosperity*, 25, 91.

44. *RTD*, Jan. 3, 5, 24, Feb. 2, 3, 10, 13, 14, 27, March 1, 3, 6, 1957; Reichard, *Politics as Usual*, 124–29; Pach and Richardson, *Eisenhower*, 160–64, 190–94; Ambrose, *Eisenhower*, 471–73; Fite, *Russell*, 356.

45. *RTD*, Jan. 13, 16–18, 27, Feb. 6, 1957.

46. Ibid., Jan. 13, 18, 29, Feb. 6, 19, March 5, 16, 1957; Byrd, "Help Us Cut These High Taxes," *Farm Journal*, April 1957; "Senator Byrd takes a Look at Ike's Budget," *U.S. News and World Report* 42 (March 29, 1957): 14, copies in box 299, BP.

47. For Eisenhower's dilemma on the budget, see Sloan, *Eisenhower and the Management of Prosperity*, 98–102; Murphy, "The Budget—and Eisenhower"; Morgan, *Eisenhower versus the Spenders*, 74–98.

48. *RTD*, March 22, 26, 28, April 3, May 9, 1957.

49. Sweeney, "Harry Byrd," 610; Annie Bronson to HFB, June 7, 1944, John Maguire to HFB, June 8, 1944, box 265, BP.

50. *RTD*, March 22, 28, April 1, 4, 22, 29, May 2, 8, 16, 17, 23, June 10, 1957. In reality, the cuts were quite modest and many of them were later restored by emergency appropriations; furthermore, Raymond Saulnier, chairman of the Council of Economic Advisers, believed the budget-cutting exercise in 1957 contributed to the subsequent recession. Saulnier, *Constructive Years*, 104–6; Dallek, *Lone Star Rising*, 515.

51. White quoted in Bartley, *Massive Resistance*, 108; Eisenhower quoted in Pach and Richardson, *Eisenhower*, 169.

52. *RTD*, April 13, May 17, June 17, 19–21, July 13, Aug. 21, Oct. 3, 6, 1957; U.S. Senate, Committee on Finance, *Hearings: Investigation of the Financial Condition of the United States*, 1957–58. The hearings resumed briefly in April 1958.

53. Burk, *Eisenhower and Black Civil Rights*, 204–17; Fite, *Russell*, 336; *RTD*, July 25, 1956, April 9, 13, 1957; speech, April 12, 1957, box 382, BP.

54. Speech, July 16, 1957, box 382, BP; *RTD*, June 9, July 17, 1957.

55. *RTD*, Aug. 2, 8, 23, 30, Sept. 1, 1957; Burk, *Eisenhower and Black Civil Rights*, 219–26; Fite, *Russell*, 336–42; Dallek, *Lone Star Rising*, 518–27; Martin, *Civil Rights*, 162; HFB to Battle, Nov. 14, 23, 1957, box 9, Battle Papers.

56. Reichard, *Politics as Usual*, 146–49; Fite, *Russell*, 372–74.

57. Pfau, *No Sacrifice Too Great*, 225–41; Anderson, *Outsider*, 185–218; Eisenhower, *Waging Peace*, 392–95; Dallek, *Lone Star Rising*, 557–59; Lewis Strauss to HFB, April 18, 1959, HFB to Kilpatrick, May 6, 1959, to Strauss, Dec. 24, 1959, box 260, BP.

58. Byrd voting record, box 349, General Wilton Persons to HFB, Jan. 10, 1959, box 249, BP; *RTD*, Dec. 25, 1958, Feb. 7, Aug. 14, 1959; Pach and Richardson, *Eisenhower*, 212–13, 228; Ambrose, *Eisenhower*, 496–97; Burk, *Eisenhower and Black Civil Rights*, 242.

59. *RTD*, April 28, 29, June 11, 30, 1959.

60. Ibid., Feb. 20, 25, 1960; HFB to Billy Prieur, Feb. 25, 1960, box 249, BP.

61. Fite, *Russell*, 347–48; Dallek, *Lone Star Rising*, 562–64; Dabney, *A Good Man*, 193–94; Burk, *Eisenhower and Black Civil Rights*, 244–46; Sundquist, *Politics and Policy*, 244–50; *RTD*, March 2, 6, 9, 11, April 9, 10, 1960.

62. Sundquist, *Politics and Policy*, 287–307; Anderson, *Outsider*, 262–67; Morgan, *Kerr*, 189–97; Marmor, *Politics of Medicare*, 30–35; *RTD*, Aug. 12, 20, 1960.

63. HFB to Sillers, May 26, 1960, box 243, BP.

64. Sweeney, "Whispers in the Golden Silence," 4–13; Fred Switzer to HFB, April 14, 1960, box 2, Switzer Papers; oral history interview with Lindsay Almond, Feb. 5, 1969, pp. 11–14, Lyndon Johnson Library; *RTD*, April 20, May 23, 1960.

65. Menefee to HFB, July 21, 28, 1960, HFB to Menefee, July 25, 1960, box 9, Menefee Papers; Billy Prieur to HFB, July 21, 1960, box 249, BP; Sweeney, "Whispers in the Golden Silence," 19–20; Dallek, *Lone Star Rising*, 559–81.

66. Mooney, *Politician*, 348–49; HFB to James Byrnes, Aug. 25, 1960, Byrnes Papers.

67. *RTD*, Aug. 19, 22, 26, 1960; Collins Denny, Jr., to Watt Abbitt, with copy to HFB, Sept. 30, 1960, box 241, Garland Gray to HFB, Oct. 7, 1960, Harrison to HFB, Aug. 17, 1960, box 244, BP.

68. Edward Haddock to Gloria Elder, Aug. 9, 1960, box 70, Miller Papers; Sweeney, "Whispers in the Golden Silence," 6, 16–18, 29; Harrison to HFB, Oct. 6, 1960, box 244, BP.

69. *RTD*, Oct. 25, 28, 1960; HFB to Byrnes, Oct. 19, 1960, Byrnes Papers; to Persons, Oct. 28, 1960, box 249, BP.

70. Smith memo, Nov. 10, 1960, 8731A/4, Smith Papers.

71. Sweeney, "Whispers in the Golden Silence," 31–44; *RTD*, Nov. 5, 26, 1960.

72. Of Eisenhower's 160 vetoes, 158 were sustained. Saulnier, *Constructive Years*, 227.

19. "He Gives Us Fits"

1. *CR* 107/1/625–38, Jan. 11, 1961.

2. See speech to Democratic state committee, 1924, box 356, BP.

3. HFB to Clark, Dec. 2, 1960, box 243, BP; *RTD*, Dec. 2, 4, 11, 1960, Jan. 1, 4, 12, 1961. Clark says he discussed this effort with the president-elect, who was searching for ways to advance his legislative agenda through Congress, but he received no encouragement from him. Oral history interview with Joseph S. Clark, Dec. 12, 1965, pp. 83–84, John F. Kennedy Library; Heath, *Decade of Disillusionment*, 63.

4. C. Douglas Dillon to author; Humphrey to HFB, Jan. 10, 1961, box 270, BP; Gore, *Let the Glory Out*, 173; Sorenson, *Kennedy*, 252.

5. *CR* 107/4/4123, 4207, 4192, March 16, 1961, 107/4/4527, March 22, 1961; *RTD*, Feb. 25, March 16, 17, 23, 1961.

6. Washington *Post*, July 23, 1965; Martin, *Stevenson* 2:707; Barton Smith to HFB, Dec. 6, 1963, box 287, BP.

7. HFB to Beverley Byrd, Feb. 7, 1961, box 35, BP; McCarthy, *Up 'Til Now*, 66; *RTD*, May 8, 1961.

8. Morgan, *Kerr*, 213; Carter, *Virginian-Pilot*, Feb. 15, 1964.

9. *CR* 102/4/5523, March 26, 1956, 102/7/9245, May 29, 1956; Fulbright to HFB, Feb. 22, March 13, April 1, May 4, 11, June 22, 1956, HFB to Fulbright, May 8, 1956, Fulbright to Smathers, April 11, May 11, 1956, Smathers to Fulbright, April 16, 1956, Fulbright to Johnson, n.d., Fulbright Papers; *Congress and the Nation*, 420.

10. Dillon to author.

11. Quoted in Fenno, *Congressmen in Committees*, 157.

12. Ripley, *Power in the Senate*, 143, 166; Gore, *Let the Glory Out*, 147; White, *Citadel*, 191; Goodwin, *Little Legislatures*, 60; Fenno, *Congressmen in Committees*, 153–59; Rudder, "Tax Policy," 196, 200; "Swan Song?" *Time* 86 (Nov. 19, 1965): 43; Cater, "Contentious Lords of the Senate"; Associated Press story, June 28, 1959, box 300, BP.

13. Price, *Who Makes the Laws?* 112, 123, 172–83; Fenno, *Congressmen in Committees,* 172–83; "The Gentleman from Virginia," *Time* 79 (Feb. 8, 1962): 23; Cater, "Contentious Lords of the Senate"; Gore, *Let the Glory Out,* 126.

14. Douglas, *In the Fullness of Time,* 427–32; McCarthy, *Up 'Til Now,* 72–75; Anderson, *Outsider,* 139.

15. McCarthy, *Up 'Til Now,* 64–65; Eisele, *Almost to the Presidency,* 167–71.

16. Interview with Senator Long; Committee Clerk to Chairman, Finance Committee, March 28, 1963, box 289, BP.

17. Douglas, *In the Fullness of Time,* 228–29, 235; Gore, *Let the Glory Out,* 103, 159; *CR,* 107/16/21026–28, Sept. 23, 1961; *RTD,* Sept. 24, 1961; speech, Jan. 15, 1962, box 390, BP.

18. *CR* 108/2/1638–40, Feb. 5, 1962; Pearson materials, HFB to Kienel, Jan. 23, 1962, box 276.

19. Bobby Baker, Lyndon Johnson's Senate aide, claimed that Kerr took bribes and traded money for the votes of colleagues. Bobby Baker, *Wheeling and Dealing,* 104–8.

20. Bobby Kennedy thought Kerr "was the only person who could handle Byrd." Schlesinger, *Robert Kennedy,* 390.

21. Morgan, *Kerr,* 37–42, 182; McCarthy, *Up 'Til Now,* 65, 72; Anderson, *Outsider,* 273; interview with Long; Ripley, *Power in the Senate,* 155; Ripley, "Power in the Post-World War II Senate," 465; Parmet, *JFK,* 208–9; David Barnett, Detroit *News,* May 10, 1964, copy in scrapbooks, box 74, BP; Carter, *Virginian-Pilot,* Feb. 15, 1964.

22. *RTD,* June 13, July 20, 28, Aug. 23, Oct. 5, 1961; Giglio, *Presidency of Kennedy,* 102.

23. Heath, *Decade of Disillusionment,* 67–93; *RTD,* Aug. 27, Sept. 22, Oct. 9, 1961; newsclippings, box 265, BP.

24. *RTD,* May 12, 14, 21, 1961; statement, April 28, 1961, box 413, speeches, May 3, 12, 1961, box 389, BP.

25. *RTD,* June 8, 11, 12, Oct. 24, 1961, June 10, 1962. The shelters cost Byrd $6,000 and $7,500 respectively.

26. George Culver to HFB, Aug. 28, 1936, box 132, HFB to W. D. Smith, Sept. 22, 1936, box 142, to Watt Abbitt, Jan. 15, 1952, box 196, to Claude Beverly, May 2, 1956, box 229, to Dr. Paul Magnuson, Dec. 17, 1956, box 238, BP; Dr. Philip Wagley to author; Miller, "Giving Them Fits"; interview with Harry Byrd, Jr.

27. Byrd voting record, box 349, travel itinerary, box 289, HFB to William Rowland, Oct. 20, 1965, box 277, BP; Hatch, *Byrds of Virginia,* 493; Miller, "Giving Them Fits"; *RTD,* June 11, 1961, Jan. 13, 1962.

28. *RTD,* Jan. 12, April 15, 1962.

29. Morgan, *Kerr,* 212, 225–32; Anderson, *Outsider,* 278; Parmet, *JFK,* 209; *RTD,* July 18, 1962.

30. Anderson, *Outsider,* 274; *RTD,* April 1, 3, 1962; Morgan, *Kerr,* 232–33; "Senator Byrd Speaks Up against Kennedy's Tax Plan," *U.S. News and World Report* 52 (May 28, 1962): 98; Gore, *Let the Glory Out,* 157.

31. *RTD,* May 20, 22, July 12, 1962; Douglas, *In the Fullness of Time,* 433–36; *CR* 108/13/18116–20, Aug. 29, 1962.

32. *RTD,* April 15, May 23, June 19, 1962; Miller, "Giving Them Fits"; "The Gentleman from Virginia," *Time* 79 (June 8, 1962): 23, and "Swan Song?" *Time* 86 (Sept. 19, 1965): 43a. Byrd had appeared on the cover of *Time* in 1928 and 1935, but there had not been a lengthy feature story on him in either issue.

33. *RTD,* July 13, Aug. 28, Sept. 7, 18, 1962; *CR* 108/13/17741, 17877, 17893, Aug. 28, 1962; *Congress and the Nation,* 431; *Newsweek* 60 (Oct. 1, 1962): 18; Burner, *Kennedy,* 144; Carter, *Virginian-Pilot,* Feb. 15, 1964.

34. *RTD*, Feb. 7, 11, 21, March 28, Oct. 3, 1962.

35. Memo, Dec. 14, 1962, box 6626c–11, Kilpatrick Papers; Dr. Wagley to author; *RTD*, Jan. 1, 1963.

36. Stein, *Fiscal Revolution*, 330, 375–85; *CR* 108/9/11827, June 27, 1962.

37. Cater, "Contentious Lords of the Senate"; interview with Senator Long; speech, July 13, 1962, box 390, newsclippings, BP; *RTD*, July 9, 10, 1962; Douglas, *In the Fullness of Time*, 453; Kennedy quoted in Bernstein, *Promises Kept*, 152.

38. U.S. Senate, Committee on Finance, *Hearings: Revenue Act of 1963*, (1963), 225; Humphrey to HFB, Oct. 30, 1962, box 270, BP; Heath, *Decade of Disillusionment*, 108; *RTD*, Jan. 18, March 29, 1963.

39. *Time* 81 (Feb. 22, 1963): 23; HFB to James G. Stahlman, Feb. 18, 1963, box 274, to Thomas Boushall, Feb. 21, 1963, box 265, BP; Stein, *Fiscal Revolution*, 451.

40. *Newsweek* 62 (Oct. 14, 1963): 29; *RTD*, Nov. 9, 16, 1963; Robertson to Opie, Sept. 27, 1963, drawer 192, folder 10, Robertson Papers; Heath, *Decade of Disillusionment*, 149; speech, May 3, 1963, box 390, BP.

41. HFB to D. Tennant Bryan, June 17, 1963, box 265, BP; *RTD*, June 11, Aug. 29, Sept. 1, 1963; Heath, *Decade of Disillusionment*, 111–15; Weisbrot, *Freedom Bound*, 69–78; Klarman, "How *Brown* Changed Race Relations," 110–18.

42. *RTD*, Aug. 18, Sept. 21, 25, 1963; speech, Sept. 19, 1963, box 393, HFB to Harold Purcell, Aug. 19, 1963, box 277, to A. Stahman, Sept. 30, 1963, box 274, BP; Heath, *Decade of Disillusionment*, 135–36; Parmet, *JFK*, 316.

43. Carter, *Virginian-Pilot*, Feb. 15, 1964; Charles McManus to HFB, Dec. 5, 1961, box 275, Moley to HFB, Nov. 6, 1963, letters, box 274, Lawrence Spivak to HFB, Sept. 3, 1960, box 260, HFB to Wallace Miller, July 31, 1961, box 275, Byrd, "The Character of Conservatism," Michigan *Times*, March 16, 1962, copy in newsclippings, Byrd, "Thoughts of a Conservative Democrat," *Polemic* 6 (Spring 1961): 18–23, copy in box 300, BP; *RTD*, Aug. 27, 1961; *News Leader*, March 1, 1963.

44. White, "Meet the Honorable Harry (the Rare) Byrd."

45. *CR* 109/3/3447–52, March 4, 1963; *RTD*, March 5, April 3, 1963; Truman to HFB, April 1, 1963; Kansas City *Star*, April 3, 1963, Truman Papers.

46. *RTD*, Nov. 23, 28, 1963; speech, Dec. 11, 1963, box 393, BP.

47. White, *The Professional*, 199; *RTD*, May 6, 1964.

48. Goodwin, *Remembering America*, 261–62; Johnson, *Vantage Point*, 36; Goldman, *Tragedy of Lyndon Johnson*, 48; Heath, *Decade of Disillusionment*, 169; Johnson appointment sheet, Jan. 8, 1964, Lyndon Johnson Papers, Johnson Library; *RTD*, Dec. 6, 1963; *NYT*, Dec. 22, 1963; Dillon to author. Dillon says Byrd made the $100 billion figure the quid pro quo for releasing the bill. Byrd implied this in a letter to Peter A. G. Brown. HFB to Brown, Jan. 10, 1964, box 265, BP.

49. Humphrey, *The Education of a Public Man*, 290–93. Humphrey said Byrd was the only man he ever heard call Johnson by his first name after he became president.

50. Interview with Senator Long; Mann, *Legacy to Power*, 218; White, *The Professional*, 38–39; William McGaffin in Corpus Christi newspaper, July 9, 1964, copy in box 267, BP; *RTD*, May 6, 1964.

51. Goodwin, *Remembering America*, 262–65; Evans and Novak, *Johnson*, 374–75; MacNeil, *Dirksen*, 228.

52. *RTD*, Jan. 24, 27, 31, Feb. 8, 1964; Byrd speech, Jan. 30, 1964, box 393, BP; Humphrey, *Education of a Public Man*, 293; Carter, *Virginian-Pilot*, Feb. 15, 1964; Evans and Novak, *Johnson*, 376; Goldman, *Tragedy of Lyndon Johnson*, 67.

53. *RTD*, Feb. 11, 1964; Fite, *Russell*, 407–8.

54. Whalen, *The Longest Debate*, 124–41; speeches, March 21, April 15, May 20, June 18, 1964, box 393; statement, May 26, 1964, box 415, BP; *RTD*, March 22, April 16, 23, 1964; Ely, *Crisis of Conservative Virginia*, 175.

55. Whalen, *Longest Debate*, 115–18, 168–74, 185, 199–215, 229; Heath, *Decade of Disillusionment*, 175–76; Fite, *Russell*, 409–15; Weisbrot, *Freedom Bound*, 87–89; Graham, *Civil Rights and the Presidency*, 74–86.

56. *RTD*, July 26, 1964; HFB to Frank Burdette, July 23, 1964, box 265, BP.

57. Heath, *Decade of Disillusionment*, 152–53, 170–73.

58. *RTD*, May 23, 24, July 24, Aug. 16, 1964; appointment sheet, May 21, 1964, Johnson Papers.

59. Byrd voting record, box 349, HFB to Sam Thrasher, Feb. 5, 1954, box 239, to Hoffman, June 19, 1964, box 269, BP; Willis Robertson to Stennis, Feb. 12, 1954, drawer 181, folder 20, Robertson Papers; *RTD*, March 8, Aug. 8, 1964.

60. Interviews with Byrd's sons and Harry Byrd III; Hatch, *Byrds of Virginia*, 506–7.

61. *RTD*, Aug. 26, 28, 1964; Harrisonburg *Daily News-Record*, Aug. 27, 1964; Knoxville *Journal*, Aug. 29, 1964, copy in newsclippings, BP; Goldman, *Tragedy of Lyndon Johnson*, 215.

62. *RTD*, Aug. 8, 16, 1964; speech, Aug. 15, 1964, box 394, BP.

20. "His Face against the Future"

1. *RTD*, Nov. 13, 1960; Stephens to HFB, Dec. 9, 1959, Dec. 5, 1960, HFB to Stephens, Dec. 7, 1959, box 260, Gray to HFB, Oct. 7, 1960, box 244, BP.

2. *RTD*, Nov. 20, Dec. 14, 1960; interviews with Harry Byrd, Jr., Godwin, and Harrison; Abbitt to HFB, Dec. 14, 1959, Kilpatrick to HFB, Dec. 14, 1960, box 244, BP; Tuck to Byrd Jr., Nov. 14, 1960, folder 5006, Tuck Papers; Godwin to Abbitt, Dec. 6, 1960, box 1, folder 29, Godwin Papers; Francis Miller to Stephens, Dec. 2, 1960, box 109, Miller Papers.

3. Interviews with Harrison and Godwin; *RTD*, Jan. 15, 17, 24, 1961.

4. *RTD*, March 14, May 17, July 1, 12, 1961; interview with Harrison; HFB to Charles Moses, July 7, 1961, box 268, to Tom Stanley, June 16, 1961, box 287, to Ben Lacy, June 15, 1961, box 270, BP; Virginius Dabney, "Harrison," 365; Wilkinson, *Byrd*, 239.

5. Harrison to HFB, Sept. 9, 1961, HFB to Harrison, Aug. 31, 1961, box 269, BP; Dabney, "Harrison," 365–69; Wilkinson, *Byrd*, 240–50; *RTD*, June 16, 1964; Eisenberg, "Virginia," 55–56; interview with Harrison. The 1960 census revealed that for the first time a majority of Virginians (56%) were living in urban areas. Washington *Post*, July 19, 1965.

6. Interviews with Harrison and Godwin.

7. HFB to Moore, Jan. 18, Feb. 23, 1960, box 248, BP.

8. William C. Battle to HFB, Jan. 14, 1962, box 242, Byrd statement on Almond appointment, box 1d, BP; *RTD*, April 17, 1962, June 29, 1963; Beagle and Osborne, *Almond*, 142–52; Spong to author; Carter, *Virginian-Pilot*, May 26, 1963; interview with Latimer; Ely, *Crisis of Conservative Virginia*, 170.

9. *RTD*, Nov. 21, 1963, Jan. 5, 1964; anonymous interview; Harrison to HFB, Sept. 4, 1963, box 269, Vincent Callahan to HFB, Sept. 3, 1963, box 266, Tuck to HFB, Dec. 17, 1962, box 289, BP; Smith to HFB, March 12, 1963, Burr Harrison to HFB, March 14, 1963, box 59, Smith Papers; Eisenberg, "Virginia," 58; Buni, *Negro in Virginia Politics*, 222–29. In the 1960 presidential election, Virginia ranked forty-sixth in the percentage of per-

sons of voting age casting ballots. In 1966 the Supreme Court ruled the poll tax was unconstitutional in state and local elections as well.

10. HFB to Harrison, Oct. 8, 1962, box 269, Prieur to HFB, Sept. 5, 1963, July 27, 1965, box 277, HFB to Prieur, March 2, 1962, box 265, BP.

11. Wilkinson, *Byrd*, 250–54; Sweeney, "1964 Election," 316–20; *RTD*, July 18–20, 1964; William Chapman, Washington *Post*, July 23, 1965.

12. Lady Bird Johnson, *White House Diary*, 195; interviews with Dick and Helen Byrd and Mills Godwin.

13. *RTD*, Feb. 23, March 15, 1964; interviews with Harry Byrd, Jr., and Abbitt; HFB to John Thorp, Oct. 14, 1964, box 283, BP. Some conjectured at the time that Byrd was planning to step aside after his reelection and allow his son to be appointed to fill out the remainder of his term, a possibility denied by Harry Jr., who, nonetheless, wished later that his father had retired.

14. *RTD*, March 21, June 14, 28, 1964; Atkinson, *The Dynamic Dominion*, 134–38.

15. Campaign materials, boxes 283, 284, HFB to Thomas Walker, Oct. 9, 1964, box 283, BP; Sweeney, "1964 Election," 312–15. May won only 19 percent of the vote; five other independent candidates split the remainder.

16. Henry Valentine to HFB, Oct. 23, 1964, remarks of C. Armonde Paxson, Sept. 24, 1964, box 283, Byrd statement, box 284, BP; Wilkinson, *Byrd*, 255–62; Sweeney, "1964 Election," 324–29, 334–48; Blackford, "Kellam."

17. *News Leader*, Jan. 30, 1964.

18. Interviews with Harry Byrd, Jr., and Godwin; *RTD*, May 5, Oct. 20, 1964; statement, Oct. 21, 1965, Wirtley Lipscomb to HFB, Oct. 19, 1965, box 266, Garland Gray call to Byrd, Oct. 13, 1965, box 267, BP; Wilkinson, *Byrd*, 263–79; Atkinson, *Dynamic Dominion*, 149–56.

19. Moger, *Virginia*, 366; Byrd speech, Aug. 26, 1961, box 389, BP; Chapman, "Byrd's Legacy," Washington *Post*, July 21, 1965. At Byrd's retirement in 1965, Virginia was still near the bottom of the states in appropriations for health and welfare and in the percentage of its college-age students in college.

20. Interview with Harrison; Spong to author; Chapman, "Byrd's Legacy"; Cope, "Frustration of Harry Byrd"; Moger, *Virginia*, 361; Davis, "Fourth Term's Hair Shirt"; Bemiss, "General Assembly," 10.

21. Cope, "Frustration of Harry Byrd"; Moger, "Virginia's Conservative Political Heritage"; Stone quoted in Washington *Post*, Feb. 25, 1973.

22. Heath, *Decade of Disillusionment*, 205, 207.

23. Johnson, *Vantage Point*, 216–17; Goldman, *Tragedy of Lyndon Johnson*, 290–91; Price, *Who Makes the Laws?* 116; Washington *Post*, March 27, 1965; Lawrence O'Brien to Clinton Anderson, Aug. 27, 1965, Johnson Papers; interview with Harry Byrd, Jr.

24. Mike Manatos to Larry O'Brien, Jan. 22, April 14, 1965, White House Central File, box 632, Johnson Papers; Anderson, *Outsider*, 291–96; Heath, *Decade of Disillusionment*, 208–10; *RTD*, June 13, 24, July 10, 1965; statement, July 7, 1965, box 395, BP.

25. Byrd budget, statements, box 415, 1965 voting record, box 353, BP; *RTD*, Sept. 7, 19, 24, 1965.

26. *RTD*, April 3, Aug. 8, 1965; statement, April 2, 1965, box 415, BP; Miller, *Lyndon*, 434; Heath, *Decade of Disillusionment*, 219–21; Weisbrot, *Freedom Bound*, 149–53.

27. David Barnett, Detroit *News*, May 10, 1964, copy in scrapbooks, box 74, BP; *RTD*, May 5, 6, 1964.

28. Schlesinger, *Robert Kennedy*, 712.

29. Interviews with Latimer, Saunier, and Abbitt; Prieur to Menefee, Nov. 1, 1965, box 11, Menefee Papers; Hatch, *Byrds of Virginia*, 513–14; HFB to Harrison, Nov. 6, 1965, box 415, BP; "The Time Has Come," *Newsweek* 66 (Nov. 22, 1965): 40; *RTD*, Nov. 12, 13, 1965. Byrd's retirement letter did not reach Governor Harrison until 10 P. M. on Nov. 10. His retirement was announced publicly on Nov. 11.

30. Newsclippings, BP; *RTD*, Nov. 11, 12, 1965.

31. Barnett, Detroit *News*, May 10, 1964.

32. *RTD*, Nov. 16, 1965; *NYT*, Nov. 14, 1965.

33. Henry Taylor, *RTD*, Nov. 17, 1965; see also Sweeney, "Harry Byrd: Vanished Policies and Enduring Principles."

34. Interview with Beverley Byrd; Wilkinson, *Byrd*, 329–41.

Bibliography

Manuscript Collections

Clemson University Library
  James F. Byrnes

College of William and Mary Library
  Mills E. Godwin, Jr.
  John Garland Pollard
  A. Willis Robertson
  William M. Tuck

Franklin D. Roosevelt Library
  Harry Hopkins
  R. Walton Moore
  Aubrey Williams

Library of Congress
  Clinton Anderson
  Tom Connally
  James A. Farley
  Hal D. Flood
  Douglas Southall Freeman
  Cordell Hull
  Harold L. Ickes
  Robert A. Taft

Library of Virginia
  Edward Griffith Dodson
  Executive Papers of
    J. Lindsay Almond, Jr.
    Harry F. Byrd
    George C. Peery
    John Garland Pollard
    James H. Price
    Thomas B. Stanley
    E. Lee Trinkle

National Archives
  United States Department of Agriculture Records, Records Group 16
  Civilian Conservation Corps Records, Records Group 35
  Federal Emergency Relief Administration Records, Records Group 69

Bibliography

Works Progress Administration Records, Records Group 69
Agricultural Adjustment Administration Records, Records Group 145

Presidential Libraries
  Papers of
    Dwight David Eisenhower
    Herbert Clark Hoover
    Lyndon Baines Johnson
    John Fitzgerald Kennedy
    Franklin Delano Roosevelt
    Harry S. Truman

University of Arkansas Library
  J. William Fulbright

University of Kentucky Library
  Alben Barkley
  Jouett Shouse
  Fred Vinson

University of Richmond Library
  Watkins M. Abbitt

University of Virginia Library
  Frank Bane
  John S. Battle
  Lloyd C. Bird
  Armistead L. Boothe
  Edward L. Breeden, Jr.
  Stuart E. Brown, Jr.
  Harry F. Byrd, Sr.
  Harry F. Byrd, Jr.
  Lewis Preston Collins
  Everett R. Combs
  John Warren Cooke
  Virginius Dabney
  Westmoreland Davis
  Edward Griffith Dodson
  Patrick Henry Drewry
  Charles R. Fenwick
  Roy C. Flannagan
  William A. Garrett
  Carter Glass
  Charles J. Harkrader
  James Hay
  Joseph C. Hutcheson
  Martin A. Hutchinson
  Henry Morrow Hyde

Bibliography

Louis Jaffe
James J. Kilpatrick
Marvin J. Menefee
Francis Pickens Miller
Benjamin Muse
Fred Seibel
C. Bascom Slemp
Howard W. Smith
Louis Spilman
William B. Spong, Jr.
Abram Staples
G. Fred Switzer
Edwin M. Watson
Robert Whitehead
Landon R. Wyatt, Sr.
University of Virginia Presidents' Papers

Virginia Historical Society
J. Lindsay Almond, Jr.
Samuel Merrifield Bemiss
William T. Reed Family
Henry Taylor Wickham
Henry A. Wise Family
Carter Wormeley

Letters to Author

Watkins M. Abbitt, September 13, 1994
Fitzgerald Bemiss, June 1, 1989
Harry F. Byrd, Jr., January 15, 1991
C. Douglas Dillon, July 18, 1989
J. William Fulbright, June 1, 1989
Edward E. Haddock, June 13, 1989
Eugene J. McCarthy, May 26, 1989
Charles McDowell, Jr., December 7, 1994
William Proxmire, July 7, 1989
William Spong, February 7, 1990
John Stennis, July 18, 1989
Strom Thurmond, August 22, 1989
Dr. Philip Wagley, August 20, 1991

Interviews

Watkins M. Abbitt, June 22, 1987
Beverley Bradshaw Byrd, June 7, 1989
Harry Flood Byrd, Jr., June 17, 1987, June 7, 1994

Bibliography

Harry Flood Byrd III, September 2, 1988
Richard Evelyn ("Dick") and Helen Byrd, June 6, 1989
Virginius Dabney, February 4, 1988
Mr. and Mrs. Ralph Dorsey, June 6, 1989
Mills E. Godwin, Jr., August 7, 1987
Albertis S. Harrison, Jr., May 19, 1988
J. Sloan Kuykendall, June 8, 1989
James Latimer, December 13, 1988
Russell Long, August 23, 1989 (telephone)
Joseph and Teresa Massie, June 7, 1989
Paul Saunier, December 13, 1988
Elizabeth Wyeth, May 23, 1989

Newspapers

Bristol *Herald-Courier*
Charlottesville *Daily Progress*
Danville *Register*
Farmville *Herald*
Harrisonburg *Daily News-Record*
Lynchburg *News*
Manassas *Messenger*
New York *Times*
Norfolk *Virginian-Pilot*
Portsmouth *Star*
Richmond *News Leader*
Richmond *Times-Dispatch*
Roanoke *World-News*
Southside Virginia *News* (Petersburg)
Washington *Evening Star*
Washington *Post*
Winchester *Evening Star*

Books

Acts and Joint Resolutions of the General Assembly of the State of Virginia. Richmond.
Adams, Sherman. *Firsthand Report: The Story of the Eisenhower Administration.* New York, 1961.
Albert, Carl. *Little Giant: The Life and Times of Speaker Carl Albert.* Norman, Okla., 1990.
Altmeyer, Arthur J. *The Formative Years of Social Security.* Madison, Wis., 1966.
Ambrose, Stephen E. *Eisenhower: The President.* New York, 1984.
Anderson, Clinton. *Outsider in the Senate.* New York, 1970.
Atkinson, Frank B. *The Dynamic Dominion: Realignment and the Rise of Virginia's Republican Party since 1945.* Fairfax, Va., 1992.
Bailey, Stephen K., and Howard D. Samuel. *Congress at Work.* New York, 1952.

Baker, Bobby. *Wheeling and Dealing.* New York, 1978.

Baker, Richard A. *The United States Senate: A Historical Bibliography.* Washington, D.C., 1977.

Baldwin, Sidney. *Poverty and Politics: The Rise and Decline of the Farm Security Administration.* Chapel Hill, N.C., 1968.

Bartley, Numan V. *The Rise of Massive Resistance: Race and Politics in the South during the 1950's.* Baton Rouge, La., 1969.

Bass, Jack, and Walter De Vries. *The Transformation of Southern Politics.* New York, 1976.

Beagle, Ben, and Ozzie Osbourne. *J. Lindsay Almond: Virginia's Reluctant Rebel.* Roanoke, Va., 1984.

Bemiss, Fitzgerald. *The General Assembly, 1955–1967* (a self-published memoir in possession of author).

Bernstein, Irving. *Promises Kept: John F. Kennedy's New Frontier.* New York, 1991.

Best, Gary Dean. *Herbert Hoover: The Post-presidential Years, 1933–1964.* Stanford, Calif., 1983.

Blum, John Morton. *V Was for Victory: Politics and American Culture during World War II.* New York, 1976.

Bolling, Richard W. *Power in the House: A History of the Leadership of the House of Representatives.* New York, 1968.

Brauer, Carl M. *John F. Kennedy and the Second Reconstruction.* New York, 1977.

Brundage, W. Fitzhugh. *Lynching in the New South: Georgia and Virginia, 1880–1930.* Urbana, Ill., 1993.

Buck, Arthur E. *The Reorganization of State Governments in the United States.* New York, 1938.

Buni, Andrew. *The Negro in Virginia Politics, 1902–1965.* Charlottesville, Va., 1967.

Burk, Robert Fredrick. *The Eisenhower Administration and Black Civil Rights.* Knoxville, Tenn., 1984.

Burner, David. *John F. Kennedy and a New Generation.* Boston, 1988.

Byrnes, James F. *All in One Lifetime.* New York, 1958.

Cappon, Lester. *Virginia Newspapers, 1821–1935.* New York, 1936.

Chafe, William H. *Civilities and Civil Rights: The Struggle for Black Freedom in Greensboro, North Carolina.* New York, 1980.

Champagne, Anthony. *Congressman Sam Rayburn.* New Brunswick, N. J., 1984.

Clark, Joseph S. *Congress: The Sapless Branch.* New York, 1964.

Cohodas, Nadine. *Strom Thurmond and the Politics of Southern Change.* New York, 1993.

Cole, Wayne S. *Charles A. Lindbergh and the Battle against American Intervention in World War II.* New York, 1974.

Collins, Robert M. *The Business Response to Keynes, 1929–1964.* New York, 1981.

Congress and the Nation, 1945–1964. Washington, D.C., 1965.

Congressional Record, 1933–65. Washington, D.C.

Conkin, Paul. *Tomorrow a New World: The New Deal Community Program.* Ithaca, N.Y., 1959.

Crawley, William B., Jr. *Bill Tuck: A Political Life in Harry Byrd's Virginia.* Charlottesville, Va., 1978.

Dabney, Dick. *A Good Man: The Life of Sam J. Ervin.* Boston, 1976.

Dabney, Virginius. *Across the Years: Memories of a Virginian.* New York, 1978.

——. *Dry Messiah: The Life of Bishop Cannon.* New York, 1949.

——. *Virginia: The New Dominion.* Garden City, N.Y., 1971.

Dallek, Robert. *Lone Star Rising: Lyndon Johnson and His Times, 1908–1960.* New York, 1991.

David, Paul T., Malcolm Moos, and Ralph M. Goldman, eds. *Presidential Nominating Politics in 1952.* 3 vols. Baltimore, 1954.

Davis, Kenneth S. *FDR: Into the Storm, 1937–1940.* New York, 1993.

———. *FDR: The New York Years, 1928–1933.* New York, 1979.

DeLauter, Roger U., Jr. *Winchester in the Civil War.* Lynchburg, Va., 1992.

Derthick, Martha. *Policymaking for Social Security.* Washington, D.C., 1979.

Dierenfield, Bruce J. *Keeper of the Rules: Congressman Howard W. Smith of Virginia.* Charlottesville, Va., 1987.

Divine, Robert A. *The Reluctant Belligerent: American Entry into World War II.* New York, 1979.

Donahoe, Bernard F. *Private Plans and Public Dangers: The Story of FDR's Third Nomination.* Notre Dame, Ind., 1965.

Donovan, Robert J. *Tumultuous Years: The Presidency of Harry S. Truman, 1949–1953.* New York, 1982.

Douglas, Paul H. *In the Fullness of Time: The Memoirs of Paul H. Douglas.* New York, 1971.

Dubofsky, Melvyn. *The State and Labor in Modern America.* Chapel Hill, N.C., 1994.

Dulles, Foster Rhea. *Labor in America.* New York, 1949.

Duram, James C. *A Moderate among Extremists: Dwight D. Eisenhower and the School Desegregation Crisis.* Chicago, 1981.

Ebert, Rebecca A., and Teresa Lazazzera. *Frederick County, Virginia: From the Frontier to the Future.* Norfolk, Va., 1988.

Eccles, Marriner. *Beckoning Frontiers.* New York, 1951.

Eisele, Albert. *Almost to the Presidency.* Blue Earth, Minn., 1972.

Eisenberg, Ralph. *Virginia Votes, 1924–1968.* Charlottesville, Va., 1971.

Eisenhower, Dwight D. *Mandate for Change, 1953–1956.* Garden City, N.Y., 1963.

———. *Waging Peace, 1956–1961.* Garden City, N.Y., 1965.

Ely, James. *The Crisis of Conservative Virginia: The Byrd Organization and the Politics of Massive Resistance.* Knoxville, Tenn., 1976.

Evans, Rowland, Jr., and Robert D. Novak. *Lyndon B. Johnson: The Exercise of Power.* New York, 1966.

Farland, Mary Gray, and Beverley Byrd Greenhalgh. *In the Shadow of the Blue Ridge: Clarke County, 1732–1952.* Richmond, 1978

Farley, James A. *Behind the Ballots.* New York, 1938.

———. *Jim Farley's Story.* New York, 1948.

Fenno, Richard F., Jr. *Congressmen in Committees.* Boston, 1973.

Ferrell, Henry C., Jr. *Claude A. Swanson of Virginia: A Political Biography.* Lexington, Ky., 1985.

Ferrell, Robert H. *Harry S. Truman and the Modern American Presidency.* Boston, 1983.

———, ed. *Dear Bess: The Letters from Harry to Bess Truman, 1910–1959.* New York, 1983.

———, ed. *Truman in the White House: The Diary of Eben A. Ayers.* Columbia, Mo., 1991.

Fite, Gilbert C. *Richard B. Russell, Jr.: Senator from Georgia.* Chapel Hill, N.C., 1991.

Foley, Michael. *The New Senate: Liberal Influence on a Conservative Institution, 1959–1972.* New Haven, 1980.

Foster, Gaines M. *Ghosts of the Confederacy.* New York, 1987.

Fraser, Steve, and Gary Gerstle, eds. *The Rise and Fall of the New Deal Order, 1930–1980.* Princeton, N. J., 1989.

Freidel, Frank. *Franklin D. Roosevelt: Launching the New Deal.* Boston, 1973.

——. *Franklin D. Roosevelt: The Triumph.* Boston, 1956.

Friddell, Guy. *Colgate Darden: Conversations with Guy Friddell.* Charlottesville, Va., 1978.

——. *What Is It about Virginia?* Richmond, 1966.

Fried, Richard M. *Men against McCarthy.* New York, 1976.

Garson, Robert A. *The Democratic Party and the Politics of Sectionalism, 1941–1948.* Baton Rouge, La., 1974.

Gates, Robbins L. *The Making of Massive Resistance: Virginia's Politics of Public School Desegregation, 1954–1956.* Chapel Hill, N.C., 1964.

Geddes, Anne. *Trends in Relief Expenditures.* Washington, D.C., 1937.

Giglio, James N. *The Presidency of John F. Kennedy.* Lawrence, Kans., 1991.

Goldman, Eric F. *The Tragedy of Lyndon Johnson.* New York, 1969.

Goodwin, George, Jr. *The Little Legislatures: Committees of Congress.* Amherst, Mass., 1970.

Goodwin, Richard N. *Remembering America: A Voice from the Sixties.* Boston, 1988.

Gore, Albert. *Let the Glory Out: My South and Its Politics.* New York, 1972.

Gottmann, Jean. *Virginia at Mid-Century.* New York, 1955.

Graham, Hugh Davis. *Civil Rights and the Presidency: Race and Gender in American Politics, 1960–1972.* New York, 1992.

Grantham, Dewey. *The Life and Death of the Solid South: A Political History.* Lexington, Ky., 1988.

——. *Southern Progressivism: The Reconciliation of Progress and Tradition.* Knoxville, Tenn., 1983.

Greene, John Robert. *The Crusade: The Presidential Election of 1952.* Lanham, Md., 1985.

Griffith, Barbara S. *The Crisis of American Labor: Operation Dixie and the Defeat of The CIO.* Philadelphia, 1988.

Griffith, Robert. *Ike's Letters to a Friend, 1941–1958.* Lawrence, Kans., 1984.

Hamby, Alonzo L. *Beyond the New Deal: Harry S. Truman and American Liberalism.* New York, 1973.

Hamilton, Virginia Van der Veer. *Lister Hill: Statesman from the South.* Chapel Hill, N.C., 1987.

Harbaugh, William H. *Lawyer's Lawyer: The Life of John W. Davis.* New York, 1973.

Hardeman, D. B., and Donald C. Bacon. *Rayburn: A Biography.* Austin, Tex., 1987.

Hartmann, Susan M. *Truman and the 80th Congress.* Columbia, Mo., 1971.

Hatch, Alden. *The Byrds of Virginia.* New York, 1969.

Heath, Jim. *Decade of Disillusionment: The Kennedy-Johnson Years.* Bloomington, Ind., 1975.

Heinemann, Ronald L. *Depression and New Deal in Virginia: The Enduring Dominion.* Charlottesville, Va., 1983.

Hero, Alfred O., Jr. *The Southerners and World Affairs.* Baton Rouge, La., 1965.

History of the Committee on Finance, United States Senate. Washington, D.C., 1981.

Hogan, Michael J. *The Marshall Plan.* Cambridge, Mass., 1987.

Hoover, Herbert. *Addresses upon the American Road, 1950–1955.* Stanford, Calif., 1955.

Howard, Nathaniel R., ed. *The Basic Papers of George Humphrey as Secretary of the Treasury, 1953–1957.* Cleveland, 1965.

Hoyt, Edwin P. *The Last Explorer: The Adventures of Admiral Byrd.* New York, 1968.

Humphrey, Hubert H. *The Education of a Public Man.* Garden City, N.Y., 1976.

Hutton, James V., Jr. *Local History Articles.* Winchester, Va., 1971.

Ickes, Harold L. *The Secret Diary of Harold L. Ickes.* 3 vols. New York, 1954.

Images of the Past: A Photographic Review of Winchester and Frederick County, Virginia. Winchester, Va., 1980.

Johnson, Haynes, and Bernard M. Gwertzman. *Fulbright: The Dissenter.* Garden City, N.Y., 1968.

Johnson, Lady Bird. *A White House Diary.* New York, 1970.

Johnson, Lyndon Baines. *The Vantage Point.* New York, 1971.

Jolley, Harley E. *The Blue Ridge Parkway.* Knoxville, Tenn., 1969.

Kaufman, Burton I. *Trade and Aid: Eisenhower's Foreign Economic Policy, 1953–1961.* Baltimore, 1982.

Key, V. O., Jr. *Southern Politics in State and Nation.* New York, 1949.

Kimball, Warren F. *The Most Unsordid Act: Lend-Lease, 1939–1941.* Baltimore, 1969.

Kirby, Jack Temple. *Rural Worlds Lost: The American South, 1920–1960.* Baton Rouge, La., 1987.

——. *Westmoreland Davis: Virginia Planter-Politician, 1859–1942.* Charlottesville, Va., 1968.

Larsen, Arthur. *Eisenhower: The President Nobody Knew.* New York, 1968.

Larsen, William. *Montague of Virginia: The Making of a Southern Progressive.* Baton Rouge, La., 1965.

Lee, R. Alton. *Truman and Taft-Hartley.* Lexington, Ky., 1966.

Lekachman, Robert. *The Age of Keynes.* New York, 1966.

Leuchtenburg, William E. *Franklin D. Roosevelt and the New Deal, 1932–1940.* New York, 1963.

Lilienthal, David E. *The Journals of David E. Lilienthal, vol. 1, The TVA Years, 1939–1945.* New York, 1964.

Lindbergh, Charles A. *The Wartime Journals of Charles A. Lindbergh.* New York, 1970.

Link, Arthur S. *American Epoch: A History of the United States since the 1890s.* New York, 1967.

Lipson, Leslie. *The American Governor from Figurehead to Leader.* New York, 1939.

Loevy, Robert. *To End All Segregation: The Politics of the Passage of the Civil Rights Act of 1964.* Lanham, Md., 1990.

McCarthy, Eugene. *Up 'Til Now.* New York, 1987.

McClure, Arthur F. *The Truman Administration and the Problems of Postwar Labor, 1945–1948.* Rutherford, N. J., 1969.

McCoy, Donald R. *The Presidency of Harry S. Truman.* Lawrence, Kans., 1984.

McCullough, David. *Truman.* New York, 1992.

MacNeil, Neil. *Dirksen: Portrait of a Public Man.* New York, 1970.

McWilliams, Tennant S. *The New South Faces the World: Foreign Affairs and the Southern Sense of Self, 1877–1950.* Baton Rouge, La., 1988.

Mann, Robert. *Legacy to Power: Senator Russell Long of Louisiana.* New York, 1992.

Marambaud, Pierre. *William Byrd of Westover, 1674–1744.* Charlottesville, Va., 1971.

Markowitz, Norman D. *The Rise and Fall of the People's Century: Henry A. Wallace and American Liberalism, 1941–1948.* New York, 1973.

Marmor, Theodore R. *The Politics of Medicare.* Chicago, 1970.

Marshall, F. Ray. *Labor in the South.* Cambridge, Mass., 1967.

Martin, John Bartlow. *Adlai Stevenson of Illinois.* 2 vols. Garden City, N.Y., 1976–77.

Martin, John Frederick. *Civil Rights and the Crisis of Liberalism: The Democratic Party, 1945–1976.* Boulder, Colo., 1979.

Matthews, Donald R. *U.S. Senators and Their World.* Chapel Hill, N.C., 1960.

Miller, Francis Pickens. *Man from the Valley: Memoirs of a 20th-Century Virginian.* Chapel Hill, N.C., 1971.

Miller, Merle. *Lyndon: An Oral Biography.* New York, 1980.

Millis, Harry A., and Emily Clark Brown. *From the Wagner Act to Taft-Hartley.* Chicago, 1950.

Moger, Allen. W. *Virginia: Bourbonism to Byrd, 1870–1925.* Charlottesville, Va., 1968.

Mooney, Booth. *The Politician, 1945–1960.* Philadelphia, 1970.

Moore, John Robert. *Senator Josiah William Bailey of North Carolina.* Durham, N.C., 1968.

Morgan, Anne Hodges. *Robert S. Kerr: The Senate Years.* Norman, Okla., 1977.

Morgan, Iwan W. *Eisenhower versus the Spenders: The Eisenhower Administration, the Democrats, and the Budget, 1953–60.* New York, 1990.

Morrison, Joseph L. *Governor O. Max Gardner.* Chapel Hill, N.C., 1971.

Morton, Frederic. *The Story of Winchester in Virginia.* Strasburg, Va., 1925.

Mulder, Ronald A. *The Insurgent Progressives in the United States Senate and the New Deal, 1933–1939.* New York, 1979.

Mullen, Arthur. *Western Democrat.* New York, 1940.

Murray, Robert K. *The 103rd Ballot.* New York, 1976.

Muse, Benjamin. *Virginia's Massive Resistance.* Bloomington, Ind., 1961.

Ogden, Frederic D. *The Poll Tax in the South.* University, Ala., 1958.

Oshinsky, David M. *A Conspiracy So Immense: The World of Joe McCarthy.* New York, 1983.

Pach, Chester J., Jr., and Elmo Richardson. *The Presidency of Dwight D. Eisenhower.* Lawrence, Kans., 1991.

Parmet, Herbert S. *Eisenhower and the American Crusades.* New York, 1972.

——. *Jack: The Struggles of John F. Kennedy.* New York, 1980.

——. *JFK: The Presidency of John F. Kennedy.* New York, 1983.

Patterson, James T. *Congressional Conservatism and the New Deal.* Lexington, Ky., 1967.

——. *Mr. Republican: A Biography of Robert A. Taft.* Boston, 1972.

Pearson, C. C., and J. Edwin Hendricks. *Liquor and Anti-Liquor in Virginia, 1619–1919.* Durham, N.C., 1967.

Pearson, Drew. *Diaries, 1949–1959.* New York, 1974.

Pfau, Richard. *No Sacrifice Too Great: The Life of Lewis L. Strauss.* Charlottesville, Va., 1984.

Platt, Rorin Morse. *Virginia in Foreign Affairs, 1933–1941.* Lanham, Md., 1991.

Pogue, Forrest C. *George C. Marshall: Statesman, 1945–1959.* New York, 1987.

Polenberg, Richard. *Reorganizing Roosevelt's Government.* Cambridge, Mass., 1966.

——. *War and Society: The United States, 1941–1945.* Philadelphia, 1972.

Polsby, Nelson W. *Congress and the Presidency.* Englewood Cliffs, N. J., 1964.

Porter, David L. *Congress and the Waning of the New Deal.* Port Washington, N.Y., 1980.

——. *The Seventy-sixth Congress and World War II, 1939–1940.* Columbia. Mo., 1979.

Pratt, Robert A. *The Color of Their Skin: Education and Race in Richmond, Virginia, 1954–1989.* Charlottesville, Va., 1992.

Preston, Howard Lawrence. *Dirt Roads to Dixie: Accessibility and Modernization in the South, 1885–1935.* Knoxville, Tenn., 1991.

Price, David E. *Who Makes the Laws? Creativity and Power in Senate Committees.* Cambridge, Mass., 1972.

Proceedings of the Thirty-sixth Annual Meeting of the Virginia State Bar Association. 1926.

Pulley, Raymond. *Old Virginia Restored: An Interpretation of the Progressive Impulse, 1870–1930.* Charlottesville, Va., 1968.

Quarles, Garland R. *Some Worthy Lives.* Winchester, Va., 1988.

Reedy, George E. *The U.S. Senate. Paralysis or a Search for Consensus?* New York, 1986.

Reeves, Thomas C. *The Life and Times of Joe McCarthy.* New York, 1982.

Reichard, Gary W. *Politics as Usual: The Age of Truman and Eisenhower.* Arlington Heights, Ill., 1988.

Ripley, Randall B. *Power in the Senate.* New York, 1969.

Rogers, Eugene. *Beyond the Barrier: The Story of Byrd's First Expedition to Antarctica.* Annapolis, Md., 1990.

Roose, Kenneth. *The Economics of Recession and Revival.* New Haven, 1954.

Rose, Mark H. *Interstate: Express Highway Politics, 1939–1989.* Knoxville, Tenn., 1990.

Rosen, Elliot. *Hoover, Roosevelt, and the Brains Trust.* New York, 1977.

Rouse, Park, Jr. *The Great Wagon Road: From Philadelphia to the South.* New York, 1973.

Rubin, Lewis D., Jr. *Virginia: A Bicentennial History.* New York, 1977.

Sabato, Larry. *The Democratic Party Primary in Virginia: Tantamount to Election No Longer.* Charlottesville, Va., 1977.

Saulnier, Raymond J. *Constructive Years. The U.S. Economy under Eisenhower.* Lanham, Md., 1991.

Schlesinger, Arthur M., Jr. *Robert Kennedy and His Times.* 2 vols. Boston, 1978.

Schwarz, Jordan A. *The Speculator: Bernard M. Baruch in Washington, 1917–65.* Chapel Hill, N.C., 1981.

Seale, William. *Virginia's Executive Mansion.* Richmond, 1988.

Singal, Daniel Joseph. *The War Within: From Victorian to Modern Thought in the South, 1919–1945.* Chapel Hill, N.C., 1982.

Sloan, John W. *Eisenhower and the Management of Prosperity.* Lawrence, Kans., 1991.

Smith, Rixey, and Norman Beasley. *Carter Glass: A Biography.* New York, 1939.

Solberg, Carl. *Hubert Humphrey.* New York, 1984.

Sorenson, Theodore. *Kennedy.* New York, 1965.

Stein, Herbert. *The Fiscal Revolution in America.* Chicago, 1969.

Steinberg, Alfred. *The Man from Missouri: The Life and Times of Harry S. Truman.* New York, 1962.

——. *Sam Johnson's Boy: A Close-up of the President from Texas.* New York, 1968.

——. *Sam Rayburn: A Biography.* New York, 1975.

Stern, Mark. *Calculating Visions: Kennedy, Johnson, and Civil Rights.* New Brunswick, N. J., 1992.

Stowe, Stephen. *Intimacy and Power in the Old South: Ritual in the Lives of the Planters.* Baltimore, 1987.

Suggs, Henry Lewis. *P. B. Young, Newspaperman: Race, Politics, and Journalism in the New South, 1910–1962.* Charlottesville, Va., 1988.

Sundquist, James L. *Politics and Policy: The Eisenhower, Kennedy, and Johnson Years.* Washington, D.C., 1968.

Bibliography

Talmadge, Herman, with Mark Winchell. *Talmadge: A Political Legacy, A Politician's Life.* Atlanta, 1987.

Tananbaum, Duane. *The Bricker Amendment Controversy: A Test of Eisenhower's Political Leadership.* Ithaca, N.Y., 1988.

Tinling, Marion, ed. *The Correspondence of the Three William Byrds of Westover, Virginia 1684–1776.* 2 vols. Charlottesville, Va., 1977.

Truman, Margaret. *Harry S. Truman.* New York, 1973.

Tugwell, Rexford, *The Democratic Roosevelt.* Garden City, N.Y., 1957.

Tyler, Lyon Gardiner, ed. *Encyclopedia of Virginia Biography.* 5 vols. New York, 1915.

——, ed. *Men of Mark in Virginia.* 5 vols. Washington, D.C., 1906.

U.S. Senate, Committee on Finance. *Hearings.* Washington, D.C., 1950–63.

Virginia Farm Economics. Department of Agricultural Economics and Rural Sociology, Virginia Polytechnic Institute and State University, 1931–42.

Virginia Farm Statistics. Virginia Department of Agriculture, 1923–49.

Weisbrot, Robert. *Freedom Bound: A History of America's Civil Rights Movement.* New York, 1980.

Whalen, Charles and Barbara. *The Longest Debate: A Legislative History of the 1964 Civil Rights Act.* Cabin John, Md., 1985.

Wheeler, Burton R., with Paul F. Healy. *Yankee From the West.* Garden City, N.Y., 1962.

White, William S. *Citadel: The Story of the U.S. Senate.* New York, 1957.

——. *The Professional: Lyndon B. Johnson.* Boston, 1964.

Wicker, Tom. *One of Us: Richard Nixon and the American Dream.* New York, 1991.

Wilhoit, Frances M. *The Politics of Massive Resistance.* New York, 1973.

Wilkinson, J. Harvie, III. *Harry Byrd and the Changing Face of Virginia Politics, 1945–1966.* Charlottesville, Va., 1968.

Wolfskill, George. *The Revolt of the Conservatives: A History of the American Liberty League.* Boston, 1962.

Younger, Edward, and James T. Moore, eds. *The Governors of Virginia, 1860–1978.* Charlottesville, Va., 1982.

Articles

Abbott, Carl. "The Norfolk Business Community: The Crisis of Massive Resistance." In *Southern Businessmen and Desegregation,* ed. Elizabeth Jacoway and David R. Colburn, pp. 98–119. Baton Rouge, La., 1982.

Ader, Emile B. "Why the Dixiecrats Failed." *Journal of Politics* 15 (Aug. 1953): 356–69.

Albright, Robert. "Byrd, 64, Fights On for Pay-As-You-Go Budget." Washington *Post,* June 10, 1951.

"American Democracy and the Welfare State" (speeches by Harry Byrd and Paul Douglas). *Proceedings of the Academy of Political Science* 24 (May 1950): 112–43.

"Appomattox's Hal Flood." *Virginia and the Virginia County* 5 (Jan. 1951): 23.

Blackford, Frank R. "A Democrat's Democrat: Sidney Severn Kellam." *Virginia Record* 87 (March 1965): 6.

Carter, Luther. Norfolk *Virginian-Pilot,* May 26, 1963, Feb. 15, 1964, June 7–9, 1964.

Cater, Douglas. "The Contentious Lords of the Senate." *Reporter* 27 (Aug. 16, 1962): 27–29.

Chapman, William. Washington *Post,* July 18–24, 1965.

Cobb, James C. "Beyond Planters and Industrialists: A New Perspective on the New South." *Journal of Southern History* 54 (Feb. 1988): 45–68.

Cope, Richard. "The Frustration of Harry Byrd." *Reporter* 3 (Nov. 21, 1950): 21–25.

Crawford, Kenneth. "Extinct Byrd." *Newsweek* 66 (Nov. 29, 1965): 34.

Crawley, William B., Jr. "William Munford Tuck: The Organization's Rustic Rara Avis." In *The Governors of Virginia, 1860–1978,* ed. Edward Younger and James T. Moore, pp. 307–20. Charlottesville, Va., 1982.

Creel, George. "Byrd Song." *Collier's* 100 (Aug. 21, 1937): 21.

Crump, Nancy Carter. "Hopewell during World War I: 'The Toughest Town North of Hell.'" *Virginia Cavalcade* 31 (Summer 1981): 38–47.

Dabney, Virginius. "Albertis S. Harrison, Jr.: Transition Governor." In *The Governors of Virginia, 1860–1978,* ed. Edward Younger and James T. Moore, pp. 361–72. Charlottesville, Va., 1982.

——. "Americans We Like: Governor Byrd of Virginia." *Nation* 126 (June 6, 1928): 632–34.

——. "Virginia's Man of the Mid-Century." *Virginia and the Virginia County* 5 (Jan. 1951): 10.

——. "What We Think of Senator Byrd's Machine." *Saturday Evening Post* 222 (Jan. 7, 1950): 30.

Daniels, Jonathan. "Virginia Democracy." *Nation* 153 (July 26, 1941): 74.

Davenport, Walter. "States Righted." *Colliers* 90 (June 4, 1932): 11.

——. "The Virginia Reel." *Colliers* 84 (Nov. 2, 1929): 12ff.

Davis, Forrest. "The Fourth Term's Hair Shirt." *Saturday Evening Post* 216 (April 8 and 15, 1944): 9.

Davison, Barry. "Byrd: A Machine Totters." *New Republic* 127 (July 21, 1952): 11–13.

Door, Rheta Childe. "The Man Who Set Virginia One Hundred Years Ahead." *McClure's* 60 (Feb. 1928): 52.

Dowdey, Clifford. "The Conscience of the Country." *Virginia Record* 80 (June 1958): 7.

——. "Senator Harry Flood Byrd: Defender of the Faith." *Virginia Record* 78 (Jan. 1956): 24.

Eastern Fruit Grower 20 (Aug. 1956): 6–37. (Box 2, Switzer Papers.)

Egger, Rowland. "Governmental Reorganization and Intergovernmental Relations in Virginia." In *Tax Relations among Governmental Units,* ed. Roy Blough et. al. New York, 1938.

Eisenberg, Ralph. "Virginia: The Emergence of Two-Party Politics." In *The Changing Politics of the South,* ed. William C. Havard, pp. 39–91. Baton Rouge, La., 1972.

Ely, James W., Jr. "J. Lindsay Almond, Jr.: The Politics of School Desegregation." In *The Governors of Virginia, 1860–1978,* ed. Edward Younger and James T. Moore, pp. 349–60. Charlottesville, Va., 1982.

Ferrell, Henry C., Jr. "Claude Augustus Swanson: 'Fully Concur and Cordially Cooperate.'" In *The Governors of Virginia, 1860–1978,* ed. Edward Younger and James T. Moore, pp. 171–82. Charlottesville, Va., 1982.

——. "The Role of Virginia Democratic Party Factionalism in the Rise of Harry Flood Byrd, 1917–1923." In *Essays in Southern Biography,* pp. 146–66. Greenville, N.C., 1965.

"5,000 Acres of Apples." *Service,* a publication of Cities Service, Oct. 1956, 26. (Box 299, BP.)

Folliard, Edward T. "The Byrd Machine." Washington *Post,* June 9–19, 1957.

Fry, Joseph A. "George C. Peery: Byrd Regular and Depression Governor." In *The Governors of Virginia, 1860–1978,* ed. Edward Younger and James T. Moore, pp. 261–76. Charlottesville, Va., 1982.

——. "The Organization in Control: George Campbell Peery, Governor of Virginia, 1934–1938." *Virginia Magazine of History and Biography* 82 (July 1974): 306–30.

——. "Senior Advisor to the Democratic 'Organization': William Thomas Reed and Virginia Politics, 1925–1935," *Virginia Magazine of History and Biography* 85 (Oct. 1977): 445–69.

——, and Brent Tarter. "The Redemption of the Fighting Ninth: The 1922 Congressional Election in the Ninth District of Virginia and the Origins of the Byrd Organization." *South Atlantic Quarterly* 76 (Summer 1978): 352–70.

Garrard, Bill. "The Story of Harry Byrd, Jr." *Virginia and the Virginia County* 6 (Jan. 1952): 16.

"The Gentleman from Virginia." *Time* 79 (June 8, 1962): 23.

Grant, Philip A., Jr. "Eisenhower and the 1952 Republican Invasion of the South: The Case of Virginia." *Presidential Studies Quarterly* 20 (Spring 1990): 285–93.

——. "The 1948 Presidential Election in Virginia: Augury of the Trend towards Republicanism." *Presidential Studies Quarterly* 7 (Summer 1978): 319–28.

"The Gravest Crisis." *Time* 72 (Sept. 22, 1958): 14.

Green, Fitzhugh. "The Mother of Tom, Dick, and Harry." *American Magazine* 105 (Feb. 1928): 19.

Hall, Alvin L. "James Hubert Price: New Dealer in the Old Dominion." In *The Governors of Virginia, 1860–1978,* ed. Edward Younger and James T. Moore, pp. 277–90. Charlottesville, Va., 1982.

——. "Politics and Patronage: Virginia's Senators and the Roosevelt Purges of 1938." *Virginia Magazine of History and Biography* 82 (July 1974): 331–50.

——. "Virginia Back in the Fold: The Gubernatorial Campaign and Election of 1929." *Virginia Magazine of History and Biography* 73 (July 1965): 280–302.

Hamilton, David E. "Herbert Hoover and the Great Drought of 1930." *Journal of American History* 68 (March 1982): 850–75.

Harris, Joseph P. "The Senatorial Rejection of Leland Olds: A Case Study." *American Political Science Review* 45 (Sept. 1951): 674–92.

Hathorn, Guy B. "C. Bascom Slemp: Virginia Republican Boss, 1907–1932." *Journal of Politics* 17 (May 1955): 248–64.

Hawkes, Robert T., Jr. "The Emergence of a Leader: Harry Flood Byrd, Governor of Virginia, 1926–1930." *Virginia Magazine of History and Biography* 82 (July 1974): 259–81.

——. "Harry F. Byrd: Leadership and Reform." In *The Governors of Virginia, 1860–1978,* ed. Edward Younger and James T. Moore, pp. 233–46. Charlottesville, Va., 1982.

Hawley, Ellis W. "The Discovery and Study of a 'Corporate Liberalism.'" *Business History Review* 52 (Autumn 1978): 309–20.

Heinemann, Ronald L. "Harry Byrd for President: The 1932 Campaign." *Virginia Cavalcade* 25 (Summer 1975): 28–37.

——. "Thomas B. Stanley: Reluctant Resister." In *The Governors of Virginia, 1860–1978,* ed. Edward Younger and James T. Moore, pp. 333–48. Charlottesville, Va., 1982.

——. "Virginia in the Twentieth Century: Recent Interpretations." *Virginia Magazine of History and Biography* 94 (April 1986): 131–60.

Henriques, Peter R. "The Byrd Organization Crushes a Liberal Challenge, 1950–1953." *Virginia Magazine of History and Biography* 87 (Jan. 1979): 3–29.

——. "John S. Battle: Last Governor of the Quiet Years." In *The Governors of Virginia, 1860–1978,* ed. Edward Younger and James T. Moore, pp. 321–32. Charlottesville, Va., 1982.

——. "The Organization Challenged: John S. Battle, Francis P. Miller, and Horace Edwards Run for Governor." *Virginia Magazine of History and Biography* 82 (July 1974): 372–406.

Hershman, James H., Jr. "Public School Bonds and Virginia's Massive Resistance." *Journal of Negro Education* 52 (Fall 1983): 398–409.

Hohner, Robert A. "Dry Messiah Revisited: Bishop James Cannon, Jr." In *The South Is Another Land: Essays on the Twentieth-Century South,* ed. Bruce Clayton and John A. Salmond, pp. 151–68. Westport, Conn., 1987.

——. "Prohibition and Virginia Politics: William Hodges Mann versus Henry St. George Tucker, 1909." *Virginia Magazine of History and Biography* 74 (Jan. 1966): 88–107.

Holt, Wythe W., Jr. "The Senator from Virginia and the Democratic Floor Leadership: Thomas S. Martin and Conservatism in the Progressive Era." *Virginia Magazine of History and Biography* 83 (Jan. 1975): 3–21.

Hopewell, John S. "John Garland Pollard: A Progressive in the Byrd Machine." In *The Governors of Virginia, 1860–1978,* ed. Edward Younger and James T. Moore, pp. 247–60. Charlottesville, Va., 1982.

Horan, John F., Jr. "Will Carson and the Virginia Conservation Commission, 1926–1934." *Virginia Magazine of History and Biography* 92 (Oct. 1984): 391–415.

Hunter, Robert F. "Carter Glass, Harry Byrd, and the New Deal, 1932–1936." *Virginia Social Science Journal* 4 (Nov. 1969): 91–103.

——. "Virginia and the New Deal." In *The New Deal,* ed. John Braeman, Robert Bremner, and David Brody, 2:103–36. Columbus, Ohio, 1975.

James, Marquis, interview with Harold Ickes. "The National Domain and the New Deal." *Saturday Evening Post* 205 (Dec. 23, 1933): 10.

Johnson, Gerald W. "Senator Byrd of Virginia." *Life* 17 (Aug. 7, 1944): 80–92.

Katznelson, Ira, Kim Geiger, and Daniel Kryder. "Limiting Liberalism: The Southern Veto in Congress, 1933–1950." *Political Science Quarterly* 108 (Summer 1993): 282–306.

Kaufman, Burton Ira. "Virginia Politics and the Wilson Movement, 1910–1914." *Virginia Magazine of History and Biography* 77 (Jan. 1969): 3–21.

Kilpatrick, James J. Column in "Human Events," Aug. 10, 1957. (Box 245, BP.)

Kirby, Jack Temple. "Westmoreland Davis: Progressive Insurgent." In *The Governors of Virginia, 1860–1978,* ed. Edward Younger and James T. Moore, pp. 209–20. Charlottesville, Va., 1982.

Klarman, Michael J. "How *Brown* Changed Race Relations: The Backlash Thesis." *Journal of American History* 81 (June 1994): 81–118.

Koeniger, A. Cash. "The New Deal and the States: Roosevelt versus the Byrd Organization in Virginia." *Journal of American History* 68 (March 1982): 876–96.

Larsen, William. "Andrew Jackson Montague: Virginia's First Progressive." In *The Governors of Virginia, 1860–1978,* ed. Edward Younger and James T. Moore, pp. 159–70. Charlottesville, Va., 1982.

Latimer, James. "Virginia Politics: The Way It Was." Nine articles in the Richmond *Times-Dispatch,* 1975, based on interviews with Colgate Darden and William Tuck.

McCardle, Carl W. "Lone Crusader for Thrift." *Country Gentleman,* 1943.

McDowell, Charles, Jr. "Byrd Bore Power without Pretense." Richmond *Times-Dispatch,* Oct. 23, 1966.

——. "The Governor Went by Blimp." Richmond *Times-Dispatch,* Sept. 15, 1963.

——. "A Weary Report on a Byrd Walk" Richmond *Times-Dispatch,* June 21, 1959.

Manchester, William. "The Byrd Machine." *Harpers* 205 (Nov. 1952): 80–87.

Marshall, Michael. "Admiral Byrd: A Classic 20th-Century Hero." *University of Virginia Alumni News* 77 (Nov.–Dec. 1988): 18–22.

Miller, Loye. "The Congress: Giving Them Fits." *Time* 80 (Aug. 17, 1962): 11–15.

Moger, Allen W. "Origins of the Democratic Machine in Virginia." *Journal of Southern History* 8 (May 1942): 183–209.

——. "Virginia's Conservative Political Heritage." *South Atlantic Quarterly* 50 (July 1951): 318–29.

Moore, Winifred B., Jr. "The 'Unrewarding Stone': James F. Byrnes and the Burden of Race, 1908–1944." In *The South Is Another Land: Essays on the Twentieth-Century South,* ed. Bruce Clayton and John A. Salmond, pp. 3–27. Westport, Conn., 1987.

Morris, John D. "3,000,000 Apples a Day Keep the Senator Away, in Season." New York *Times,* Nov. 6, 1955.

Murphy, Charles J. V. "The Budget—and Eisenhower." *Fortune* 56 (July 1957): 96.

Muse, Benjamin. "The Durability of Harry Flood Byrd." *Reporter* 17 (Oct. 8, 1957): 26–30.

Newman, C. L. "Virginia's Governor a Master Orchardist." *Progressive Farmer,* March 30, 1927, 8.

Pace, David. "Lenoir Chambers Opposes Massive Resistance: An Editor against Virginia's Democratic Organization, 1955–1959." *Virginia Magazine of History and Biography* 82 (Oct. 1984): 415–29.

Pate, James. "State Supervision of Local Fiscal Officers in Virginia." *American Political Science Review* 25 (Nov. 1931): 1004–8.

Patterson, James T. "A Conservative Coalition Forms in Congress, 1933–1939." *Journal of American History* 52 (March 1966): 757–72.

——. "Eating Humble Pie: A Note on Roosevelt, Congress, and Neutrality Revision in 1939." *Historian* 31 (May 1969): 407–14.

Patterson, Michael S. "The Fall of a Bishop: James Cannon, Jr., versus Carter Glass, 1909–1934." *Journal of Southern History* 39 (Nov. 1973): 493–518.

Polenberg, Richard. "Roosevelt, Carter, and Executive Reorganization: Lessons of the 1930s." *Presidential Studies Quarterly* 11 (Winter 1979): 35–46.

Quarles, Garland. "John Handley and the Handley Bequests to Winchester, Virginia." 1969. (Winchester Public Library.)

Rable, George C. "The South and the Politics of Anti-Lynching Legislation, 1920–1940." *Journal of Southern History* 51 (May 1985): 201–20.

Readnour, Harry Warren. "Fitzhugh Lee: Confederate Cavalryman in the New South." In *The Governors of Virginia, 1860–1978,* ed. Edward Younger and James T. Moore, pp. 111–120. Charlottesville, Va., 1982.

Reed, Robert. "Sporting Venture." *Country Gentleman,* Jan. 1942.

Reeves, Paschal. "Thomas S. Martin: Committee Statesman." *Virginia Magazine of History and Biography* 68 (July 1960): 344–64.

Rhodes, William A. "William Hodges Mann: Last of the Boys in Gray." In *The Governors of Virginia, 1860–1978,* ed. Edward Younger and James T. Moore, pp. 183–94. Charlottesville, Va., 1982.

Ripley, Randall B. "Power in the Post-World War II Senate." *Journal of Politics* 31 (May 1969): 465–92.

Rochester, Stuart I., and Jonathan J. Wolfe. "Colgate W. Darden, Jr.: The Noblest Roman of Them All." In *The Governors of Virginia, 1860–1978*, ed. Edward Younger and James T. Moore, pp. 291–306. Charlottesville, Va., 1982.

Rudder, Catherine E. "Tax Policy: Structure and Choice." In *Making Economic Policy in Congress*, ed. Allen Schick, pp. 196–220. Washington, D.C., 1983.

Sargent, James E. "Clifton A. Woodrum of Virginia: A Southern Progressive in Congress, 1923–1945." *Virginia Magazine of History and Biography* 89 (July 1981): 341–64.

"Senator Byrd Speaks Up against Kennedy's Tax Plan." *U.S. News and World Report* 52 (May 28, 1962): 98.

"Senator Byrd Takes a Look at Ike's Budget." *U.S. News and World Report* 42 (March 29, 1957): 104.

"Senator Byrd Talks about 'Presidents I Have Known.'" *U.S. News and World Report* 53 (Sept. 10, 1962): 84.

Shannon, Jasper. "Presidential Politics in the South." In *The Southern Political Scene, 1938–1948*, ed. Taylor Cole and John H. Hallowell, pp. 464–89. Gainesville, Fla., 1948.

Sherman, Richard B. "'The Last Stand': The Fight for Racial Integrity in Virginia in the 1920's." *Journal of Southern History* 54 (Feb. 1988): 69–92.

——. "The 'Teachings at Hampton Institute': Social Equality, Racial Integrity, and the Virginia Public Assemblage Act of 1926." *Virginia Magazine of History and Biography* 95 (July 1987): 275–300.

Simmons, Dennis E. "Conservation, Cooperation, and Controversy: The Establishment of Shenandoah National Park, 1924–1936." *Virginia Magazine of History and Biography* 89 (Oct. 1981): 387–404.

Sindlar, Allan P. "The Unsordid South: A Challenge to the Democratic Party." In *The Uses of Power: 7 Cases in American Politics*, ed. Alan F. Westin, pp. 229–84. New York, 1962.

Smith, Douglas. "When Reason Collides with Prejudice: Armistead Lloyd Boothe and the Politics of Desegregation in Virginia, 1948–1963." *Virginia Magazine of History and Biography* 102 (Jan. 1994): 5–46.

"The South Gets Ready for '52." *Pathfinder* 58 (Sept. 1951): 19.

"The South's Plan to Beat Truman." *U.S. News and World Report* 31 (Nov. 30, 1951): 28.

Spicer, George W. "From Political Chief to Administrative Chief." In *Essays on the Law and Practice of Governmental Administration*, ed. Charles G. Haines and Marshall E. Dimock, pp. 94–124. Baltimore, 1935.

Strother, Frank. "Youth Takes the Helm in Virginia." *World's Work* 53 (Dec. 1926): 139–48.

"Swan Song?" *Time* 86 (Nov. 19, 1965): 43a.

Sweeney, James R. "The Golden Silence: The Virginia Democratic Party and the Presidential Election of 1948." *Virginia Magazine of History and Biography* 82 (July 1974): 351–71.

——. "Harry Byrd: Vanished Policies and Enduring Principles." *Virginia Quarterly Review* 52 (Autumn 1976): 596–612.

——. "A New Day in the Old Dominion: The 1964 Presidential Election." *Virginia Magazine of History and Biography* 102 (July 1994): 307–48.

——. "Revolt in Virginia: Harry Byrd and the 1952 Presidential Election." *Virginia Magazine of History and Biography* 86 (April 1978): 180–95.

——. "Rum, Romanism, and Virginia Democrats: The Party Leaders and the Campaign of 1928." *Virginia Magazine of History and Biography* 90 (Oct. 1982): 403–31.

——. "Whispers in the Golden Silence: Harry Byrd, Sr., John Kennedy, and Virginia Democrats in the 1960 Presidential Election." *Virginia Magazine of History and Biography* 99 (Jan. 1991): 3–44.

Syrett, John. "Ambiguous Politics: James Price's First Months as Governor of Virginia." *Virginia Magazine of History and Biography* 94 (Oct. 1986): 453–76.

——. "The Politics of Preservation: The Organization Destroys Governor James H. Price's Administration." *Virginia Magazine of History and Biography* 97 (Oct. 1989): 437–62.

Tarter, Brent. "A Flier on the National Scene: Harry F. Byrd's Favorite-Son Presidential Campaign of 1932." *Virginia Magazine of History and Biography* 82 (July 1974): 282–305.

——. "The Making of a University President: John Lloyd Newcomb and the University of Virginia, 1931–1933." *Virginia Magazine of History and Biography* 87 (Oct. 1979): 473–81.

Thompson, Lorin A. "Virginia Education Crisis and Its Economic Aspects." *New South* 14 (Feb. 1959): 3–8.

"Three Famous Byrds from a Fine Old Brood." *Literary Digest* 90 (Aug. 7, 1926): 37–38.

"The Time Has Come." *Newsweek* 66 (Nov. 22, 1965): 40.

Tindall, George B. "Business Progressivism: Southern Politics in the Twenties." *South Atlantic Quarterly* 62 (Winter 1963): 92–106.

Treadway, Sandra Gioia. "Sarah Lee Fain: Norfolk's First Woman Legislator." *Virginia Cavalcade* 30 (Winter 1981): 124–33.

Treon, John A. "The Political Career of Henry De La Warr Flood: A Biographical Sketch, 1865–1921." *Essays in History* (History Club, University of Virginia), 10 (1964–65): 44–64.

Vipperman, Carl J. "The Coattail Campaign: James H. Price and the Election of 1937 in Virginia." *Essays in History* (History Club, University of Virginia), 8 (1962–63): 47–61.

"Virginia: Wrong Turn at the Crossroads." *Time* 68 (Dec. 3, 1956): 19–20.

White, William S. "Meet the Honorable Harry (the Rare) Byrd." *Reader's Digest* 82 (April 1963): 205–12.

Willis, L. Stanley. "E. Lee Trinkle: Prelude to Byrd." In *The Governors of Virginia, 1860–1978*, ed. Edward Younger and James T. Moore, pp. 221–32. Charlottesville, Va., 1982.

——. "'To Lead Virginia Out of the Mud': Financing the Old Dominion's Public Roads, 1922–1924." *Virginia Magazine of History and Biography,* 94 (Oct. 1986): 425–52.

Selected Articles by Harry Byrd
(copies in newsclippings and boxes 293–301, BP)

"Are We Losing Our Freedom?" *American Magazine,* Aug. 1943.

"Bureaucracy and the Farmer." *Scientific American,* Aug. 1934.

"The Business of Growing Apples." *American Fruit Grower Magazine* 46 (March 1926).

Byrd on growing apples. *Virginia Fruit* 18 (Dec. 1930). (Box 93, BP.)

Byrd on the Marshall Plan. *Redbook,* Jan. 1948; *The Dickinsonian* (student newspaper at Dickinson College).

Byrd on philanthropy. *Country Home Magazine,* Dec. 1939.
"The Character of Conservatism." Michigan *Times,* March 16, 1962.
"Comments on the President's Civil Rights Recommendations." *Virginia Club Woman* 20 (April 1948): 10.
"The Cost of Our Government." *Atlantic Monthly,* April 1938.
"Efficiency and Economy in Government the Aim." *Manufacturers Record,* Dec. 1936.
"The Failure of Our National Defense Program." *Reader's Digest* 39 (Nov. 1941): 16–25.
"The Federal Budget Can Be Cut by $4 Billion." *Manufacturers Record* 118 (March 1949): 44.
"The Federal Manpower Muddle." *Manufacturers Record* 3 (Dec. 1942): 25.
"Four Milestones to Totalitarianism." *Forbes* 53 (March 1, 1944): 12–14.
"Government Reorganization." *Country Gentleman* 108 (Oct. 1938): 7.
"The Government's Waste of Manpower." *American Magazine,* April 1945.
"Help Us Cut These High Taxes." *Farm Journal,* April 1957, 35.
"A History of Virginia Highways." *Virginia Record* 78 (Sept. 1956): 9.
"Is Bankruptcy Our Goal?" *Country Gentleman,* Sept. 1949.
"It Must Stop." *True Detective* 39 (Nov. 1942): 50.
"Lumping Debts on Uncle Sam." *Christian Science Monitor,* Oct. 20, 1937.
"Manpower for Our Third Army." *Nation's Business* 30 (Nov. 1942).
"Mutual Responsibility Essential to Labor-Management Peace." *Manufacturers Record* 115 (Feb. 1946): 42.
"Our Duty to Our Fighting Sons." *American War Dads Magazine,* Feb. 1944.
"Piling Federal Deficits on Mounting National Debt." *Investor America* 5 (Feb. 1939): 8.
"Pump Priming a Failure While Deficits Mount." *Manufacturers Record,* June 1938.
"Return to Sound Principles." *Manufacturers Record,* March 1935.
"Saving for Defense." *Banking* 43 (April 1951): 33.
"A Tax Policy for a Prosperous America." *Annals,* Nov. 1949.
"Thoughts of a Conservative Democrat." *Polemic* 6 (Spring 1961): 18–23.
"Uncle Sam's Cash Register." *Commentator,* June 1938.
"U.S. versus the Frankenstein Monster." *Reader's Digest,* July 1943.
"Waste—The Enemy at Home." *Reader's Digest,* Sept. 1942.
"Waste and Its Effects." *Farm Journal,* Oct. 1938.
"Waste Goes On." *American Magazine,* Jan. 1943.
"We're on the Road to Bankruptcy." *American Magazine,* Aug. 1949.
"What Federal Handouts Are Costing You." *American Magazine,* May 1955.
"What We Can Do to End Waste in Government." *Redbook,* Oct. 1946.

Unpublished Studies

Badger, Anthony. "The Southern Manifesto." 1993.
Blanton, S. Walker. "Virginia in the 1920's: An Economic and Social Profile." Ph.D. diss., Univ. of Virginia, 1969.
Cochran, Robert T., Jr. "Virginia's Opposition to the New Deal, 1933–1940." M. A. thesis, Georgetown Univ., 1950.
Corley, Robert G. "James Jackson Kilpatrick: The Evolution of a Southern Conservative, 1955–1965." M. A. thesis, Univ. of Virginia, 1971.
Crawley, William B. "The Governorship of William M. Tuck, 1946–1950: Virginia Poli-

tics in the 'Golden Age' of the Byrd Organization." Ph.D. diss., Univ. of Virginia, 1974.

Curry, Lawrence Hopkins, Jr. "Southern Senators and Their Roll-Call Votes in Congress, 1941–1944." Ph.D. diss., Duke Univ., 1971.

Dierenfield, Bruce J. "Congressman Howard W. Smith: A Political Biography." Ph.D. diss., Univ. of Virginia, 1981.

Dutton, George, "The Cost of Public Education in Virginia from 1870 to 1939." M. A. thesis, Univ. of Virginia, 1941.

Eisele, Frederick Robert. "Age and Political Change: A Cohort Analysis of Voting among Careerists in the U.S. Senate, 1947–1970." Ph.D. diss, New York Univ., 1972.

Foster, Larrie J. "The Negro and the Byrd Political Machine in Virginia, 1926–1952." M. A. thesis, North Carolina College (Durham), 1954.

Fry, Joseph Andrew. "George Campbell Peery: Conservative Son of Old Virginia." M. A. thesis, Univ. of Virginia, 1970.

Goode, Rudyard B. "The Distribution and Disposition of Highway Funds in Virginia." Ph.D. diss., Univ. of Virginia, 1953.

Hall, Alvin L. "James H. Price and Virginia Politics, 1878 to 1943." Ph.D. diss., Univ. of Virginia, 1970.

Hawkes, Robert T., Jr. "The Career of Harry Flood Byrd, Sr., to 1933." Ph.D. diss., Univ. of Virginia, 1975.

Henriques, Peter R. "John S. Battle and Virginia Politics: 1948–1953." Ph.D. diss., Univ. of Virginia, 1971.

Hershman, James Howard, Jr. "A Rumbling in the Museum: The Opponents of Virginia's Massive Resistance." Ph.D. diss., Univ. of Virginia, 1978.

Hilty, James Walter. "Voting Alignments in the United States Senate, 1933–1944." Ph.D. diss., Univ. of Missouri, 1973.

Holsinger, Justus G. "The Process and Development of the Virginia Constitutional Revision of 1928 with Regard to the Reorganization of Administration." M.A. thesis, Univ. of Virginia, 1935.

Hopewell, John. "An Outsider Looking In: John Garland Pollard and Machine Politics in Twentieth Century Virginia." Ph.D. diss., Univ. of Virginia, 1976.

Horn, Herman L. "The Growth and Development of the Democratic Party in Virginia since 1890." Ph.D. diss., Duke Univ., 1950.

Hurlburt, Thomas W. "Significant Trends in Virginia Agriculture between Two World Wars." M.A. thesis, Univ. of Virginia, 1952.

Kaufman, Burton Ira. "Henry De La Warr Flood: A Case Study of Organization Politics in an Era of Reform." Ph.D. diss., Rice Univ., 1966.

Latimer, James. "Virginia Politics, 1950–1960." (Copy in possession of James Latimer.)

Lenchner, Paul. "Senate Voting Patterns and American Politics, 1949–1965." Ph.D. diss., Cornell Univ., 1973.

Margolis, Joel Paul. "The Conservative Coalition in the United States Senate, 1933–1968." Ph.D. diss., Univ. of Wisconsin, 1973.

Massie, Mrs. J. A. "When I Was Very Young." (Copy in possession of Joseph and Teresa Massie.)

Potenziani, David Daniel. "Look to the Past: Richard B. Russell and the Defense of Southern White Supremacy." Ph.D. diss., Univ. of Georgia, 1981.

Rakow, Michael Gerard. "Southern Politics in the United States Senate: 1948–1972." Ph.D. diss., Arizona State Univ., 1973.

Remick, Robert W. "J. Lindsay Almond, Harry F. Byrd, Sr., and the Demise of Massive Resistance, 1956–1959." Senior thesis, Hampden-Sydney College, 1982.

Roebuck, James R., Jr. "Virginia in the Election of 1948." M.A. thesis, Univ. of Virginia, 1969.

Ross, Robert Samuel. "The Evolution of the United States Senate, 1945–1964: A Study of Roll-Call Votes." Ph.D. diss., Univ. of Colorado, 1968.

Simmons, Dennis E. "The Creation of Shenandoah National Park and the Skyline Drive." Ph.D. diss., Univ. of Virginia, 1978.

Sweeney, James R. "Byrd and Anti-Byrd: The Struggle for Political Supremacy in Virginia, 1945–1954." Ph.D. diss., Univ. of Notre Dame, 1973.

Tarter, J. Brent. "Freshman Senator Harry Byrd, 1933–1934." M.A. thesis, Univ. of Virginia, 1972.

Thompson, John Walton, Jr. "Massive Resistance in Virginia." Senior thesis, Princeton Univ., 1961.

Walton, Benjamin F. "An Analysis of Expenditures for Public Schools in Virginia from 1909 to 1939." M.A. thesis, Univ. of Virginia, 1942.

Weisiger, Minor Tompkins. "E. R. Combs: Chief of the Byrd Organization." M.A. thesis, Univ. of Virginia, 1979.

Willis, Leo Stanley. "E. Lee Trinkle and the Virginia Democracy, 1876–1939." Ph.D. diss., Univ. of Virginia, 1968.

Wolfe, Jonathan James. "Virginia in World War II." Ph.D. diss., Univ. of Virginia, 1971.

Miscellaneous

Cartoons of Fred Seibel, University of Virginia Library.

Flood Family History, in possession of Mr. and Mrs. Francis E. Tyler of Eldon.

Latimer, James. Television interviews with Harry Byrd, Jr., and Henry Howell. WCVE, Richmond.

Pamphlets of Shenandoah Apple Blossom Festival. Festival Offices, Winchester, Va.

Radio interview with Charles Bryan on Admiral Richard E. Byrd, PBS, July 29, 1991.

Southern Historical Society Papers 7 (1879): 349–52, 22 (1894): 41–48.

Index

Byrd, Harry Flood (*cont.*)
  positions and votes on (*cont.*)
    254, 360, 366, 371; single appropria-
    tion budget, 255, 301; civil rights legis-
    lation, 255–56, 374–75, 377–78, 397–98,
    402–4, 417; Fair Deal, 287, 293–95; edu-
    cation legislation, 293, 364, 371, 389,
    394, 416; health care legislation, 293,
    371, 378–79, 415–16; military alliances,
    295, 365; Korean War, 299–300; econ-
    omy in government, 301–2, 371–74,
    389; federal debt limit, 357–58, 360,
    366; Hawaiian statehood, 360; Bricker
    amendment, 360; interstate highway
    system, 363–64; nuclear test ban
    treaty, 398; welfare legislation, 404–5,
    416
  presidential campaigns: (1932), 141–54,
    443n, (1944), 234–44; receives votes
    (1956), 370, (1960), 381
  United States senator, 159, 267–68; con-
    flicts of interest, 136–37, 373; appoint-
    ment, 155–58; use of patronage, 156,
    161–62; early support of New Deal,
    160–62, 168, 397; opposition to New
    Deal, 165–83, 205, 238; economic
    views, 200, 202–3; debate with Mar-
    riner Eccles, 200–203; his negativism,
    221, 294; voting with Republicans, 231,
    254–55, 292–95, 314, 357, 360–61, 366,
    376, 390; his independence, 267, 383;
    relations with colleagues, 268, 287–89,
    418; legislative tactics, 287, 385–86,
    391, 393, 402; daily routine, 289–90;
    support from conservatives, 295–96,
    372–73, 398; on socialism, 295–96, 303;
    awards and recognition, 302, 377,
    398–99, 452n; attendance, 307, 366,
    470n; supports "Southern Manifesto,"
    334–36; investigation of Korean War
    ammunition shortages, 358–59; fed-
    eral housing investigation, 361; retire-
    ment, 417, 478n; assessment, 418–19
  committee service: Rules Committee,
    159, 253; Naval Affairs Committee,
    159, 226, 247; Finance Committee, 159;
    chairman of Joint Committee on Re-
    duction of Non-essential Federal Ex-
    penditures, 219–21, 225–27, 230, 253,
    356, 366; Armed Services Committee,
    251, 292, 300, 355, 358, 371, 398; chair-
    man of Finance Committee, 361–63,
    366, 383, 386–89, 391–93, 415–16, 418

Byrd, Harry Flood, Jr. (son), 16, 70, 139,
  150, 160, 244, 260, 282, 284, 307, 314–
  15, 321, 367, 394, 407, 409–10, 413, 420;
  relationship with father, 68, 107, 233–
  34, 351; running newspaper, 107, 176,
  185, 314, 317; wartime service, 233;
  state senate, 257, 317; appointed to
  U.S. Senate, 418
Byrd, Harry Flood III (grandson), 106
Byrd, Helen (daughter-in-law), 108, 136,
  411
Byrd, Jennie Rivers (grandmother), 3
Byrd, Richard Evelyn (great-grandfather),
  2
Byrd, Richard Evelyn (father), 3–7, 9, 25,
  28, 50, 67, 128, 131, 429n, 430n; relationship with wife, 3–4; adviser to
  son, 5, 10, 30, 43, 49, 53, 56; Speaker of
  the House of Delegates, 13; friendship
  with Woodrow Wilson, 14–15
Byrd, Richard Evelyn, Jr. (brother), 5, 6,
  50, 142, 145, 150–51, 153, 155–57, 247,
  267, 315; relationship with brother, 5,
  70, 113–14, 340; flight over North Pole,
  65, 69–70, 432n; competition with
  Lindbergh, 74–75; flight over South
  Pole, 114; Antarctic expeditions, 292,
  340
Byrd, Richard Evelyn (son), 43, 288, 411; relationship with father, 16, 68, 107–8,
  184, 233–34; oversees cannery, 138; wartime service, 233–34
Byrd, Thomas Bolling (brother), 5, 68, 222;
  and apple business, 125, 130–31, 134
Byrd, Thomas Taylor, 2, 8
Byrd, Westwood Beverley (daughter), 233,
  307, 362, 463n; relationship with fa-
  ther, 16, 68, 107–8
Byrd, William I, 2
Byrd, William II, 2
Byrd, William III, 2
Byrd, William (grandfather), 2–3
Byrd Automatic Tax Reduction Law, 317,
  323–24, 464n, 465n
Byrd Machine: *see* Byrd, leader of Organi-
  zation; Organization
Byrd Road Act, 123–24, 439n
Byrnes, James F., 181, 204, 223, 242, 248,
  256, 304–5, 311–12, 314, 338, 381

Campbell amendments (on poll tax),
  273
Cannon, Clarence, 301

Index

Index